SEX DISCRIMINATION IN THE WORKPLACE

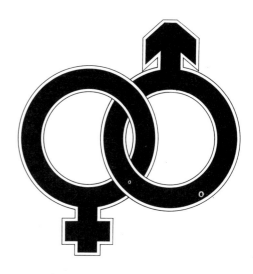

*The Center for
Compliance Information*

EDITOR
Kenneth Lawrence
Center for Compliance Information

LEGAL CONSULTING EDITOR
Katharine A. Klos, Esq.
Member, District of Columbia Bar

AN ASPEN PUBLICATION

Library of Congress Cataloging in Publication Information.

Sex Discrimination in the workplace.

Includes index.

1. Sex discrimination in employment—law and legislation— United States. 2. Sex discrimination against women—law and legislation— United States.
I. Lawrence, Kenneth, 1948-
II. Klos, Katherine A. III. Aspen Systems Corporation.
KF3467.S49   344'.73'014   78-16700
ISBN 0-89443-041-6

Printed in the United States of America

1 2 3 4 5

Table of Contents

Preface

During the next quarter century, declining birth rates, along with rising levels of education and career aspirations of younger women, suggest that the future worklives of the two sexes will more closely resemble each other, both in terms of occupational distribution and time spent in the labor force. Women's employment problems have occurred due to an inability to find or secure jobs commensurate with their abilities and rising expectations. In recent years, both the federal and state governments have enacted numerous laws, orders and regulations intended to reduce and eventually eliminate sex discrimination from employment practices such as hiring, compensation, dissemination of benefits and provision of vocational education and training. The complex, diverse and sometimes conflicting areas of equal employment law present a myriad of problems and pitfalls for those who design personnel policy and implement it on a day to day basis. The mission to avoid employment situations with the potential for allegations of sex discrimination is anything but an easy task. For example, the *Regents of the University of California v. Bakke* case, which is currently before the Supreme Court, suggests that personnel programs instituted specifically for the promotion of equal employment opportunities, could be subject to "reverse discrimination" suits. Equal employment legislation is often enacted in opposition to Supreme Court rulings. The resulting effect is a paradox between legislative and judicial guidelines. For instance, Congressional committees are considering three bills which would override the Supreme Court's ruling in *Gilbert v. General Electric Company,* a landmark decision which offered guidelines to work with in the sensitive area of sex discrimination based on pregnancy.

The Center for Compliance Information serves the growing need of industry for easily-accessible information on vital regulatory compliance issues. For this volume, the Center has systematically compiled information of great value to all professionals involved in personnel policy-making and administration. This wealth of information drawn from both government and private sources has been synthesized in a manner that affords a clear view of problem areas and outlines step by step procedures that can be followed to avoid costly sex discrimination litigation and compliance difficulties.

The volume is divided into logically sequenced, major subject matter sections. The first section presents the federal and state laws, as well as pending legislation, which govern employers' obligations toward such topics as sex-related occupational limitations, affirmative action and equal pay policies. Following this is a section that deals with the special aspects of sex discrimination; such as, policies regarding pregnant workers, reverse discrimination, sexual harassment and discrimination on the basis of sexual orientation. The next two sections carefully explain how to develop personnel procedures that do not sexually discriminate and how to satisfy the procedural requirements that are peculiar to affirmative action programs. Chapter five goes deeply into case law to bring to the surface the prevailing logic of recent court decisions which have addressed sensitive sex discrimination issues. The cases selected for this chapter represent a cross section of sex discrimination issues and court opinions. Each case begins with a legal annotation which fully explains the issues being argued and the court's final ruling. More definitive information is provided in the full text of the court's opinion for each case. The next chapter, which is aptly titled, "Women in the Labor Force," presents categorically, information that is vital for understanding such realities as the new economic role of women, the chief career motivators of today's working women and the unique problems confronting workers with "dual careers." The final two chapters discuss the educational and training status of the contemporary women's workforce and forecast the ways in which the sexual makeup of the American workforce will change through the 1980s. The volume's appendixes contain the full texts of Title VII of the Civil Rights Act of 1964, the Fair Labor Standards Act as amended by the Equal Pay Act of 1963 and Executive Order 11246. These laws form the legal basis for affirmative action, standardized minimum wages and overtime pay policies and other major aspects within the realm of sex discrimination.

In the coming years, progress toward a more sexually equal workforce will likely come as a result of increased litigation activities and stricter enforcement of equal employment laws. The Sex Discrimination In The Workplace volume has been designed to guide personnel decision makers through this evolutionary period in such a way that effective management will prevail, despite the complexities of law and their corresponding compliance problems.

Kenneth Lawrence

1 Federal and state labor laws: the straight and narrow for sex discrimination

Federal labor laws of special interest to women*

Introduction

Extensive legislative activity has marked recent years in areas of special interest to women workers. Minimum wage rates have been raised, and coverage has been greatly expanded. All forms of sex discrimination have been prohibited in most public and private employment. For the first time Federal legislation has begun establishment of comprehensive standards in two fields: occupational safety and health, and private pension and welfare plans for workers.

In barely more than a decade, equal employment opportunity laws have taken a major place in labor legislation. Attacking a wide range of unfair practices and directed against several bases of discrimination (race, color, religion, sex, national origin, age, mental or physical handicap), these laws were not conceived at one time in a single comprehensive package. Initial enactments permitted many exemptions from coverage, differed in strength of enforcement mechanisms, provided differently for persons in public and private employment, and were assigned to different agencies for administration. Amendments broadened the laws and strengthened enforcement, and many laws and regulations were added to meet particular problems.

Increasingly legislators, and the agencies enforcing these laws, are concerned with "systemic" discrimination as well as individual complaints. Where courts have found patterns of employment that result in barriers against women or minorities, whether discrimination was intended or not, new practices have been required. The overlapping of antidiscrimination laws and administrative responsibility has led very recently to better coordination of enforcement efforts among Federal agencies and increased Federal-State cooperation.

Fair Labor Standards Act

The Fair Labor Standards Act (FLSA), generally known as the Federal wage and hour law, has made possible the raising of wage rates for those in the lowest paid occupations and/or industries. It does *not* limit the number of hours that an individual may be employed, but it does require premium pay of 1½ times an employee's regular rate for hours after a specified number—generally 40 a week—the person is "suffered or permitted" to work.

As enacted in 1938, the FLSA established a 25-cent-an-hour minimum wage for covered employment (individuals engaged in interstate commerce or the production of goods for commerce) and provided for a gradual increase to a 40-cent minimum after 7 years. The law has been amended from time to time to increase the minimum rate and to extend coverage to new groups of employees.

*Handbook on Women Workers, U.S. Department of Labor, Women's Bureau.

1974 amendments.   Signed into law by the President on April 8, the 1974 amendments provide for an eventual hourly minimum of $2.30 for all covered workers, but the timetables for various categories to reach that level differ, as follows:

	Rate	*Effective date*
Nonagricultural employees covered prior to February 1, 1967	$2.00	5/1/74
	$2.10	1/1/75
	$2.30	1/1/76
Nonagricultural employees brought under the act in 1967 and later	$1.90	5/1/74
	$2.00	1/1/75
	$2.20	1/1/76
	$2.30	1/1/77
Agricultural employees	$1.60	5/1/74
	$1.80	1/1/75
	$2.00	1/1/76
	$2.20	1/1/77
	$2.30	1/1/78

The FLSA as amended in 1977 provides for a basic minimum wage rate of $2.65 per hour. This minimum wage rate will rise to $2.90 on January 1, 1979, to $3.10 on January 1, 1980, and to $3.35 on January 1, 1981.

All tips received by employees must be retained by them. The employer may consider tips the employee actually received as part of the wages, but credit permitted for such tips cannot exceed 50 percent of the required minimum rate. The tip credit and the cash paid by the employer must equal at least the minimum wage required by the law.

Two large categories brought under the FLSA by the 1974 amendments were all nonsupervisory employees of Federal, State and local governments and private household workers whose compensation constitutes wages for social security purposes (that is, $50 from any employer in a calendar quarter) or who work a total of at least 8 hours a week in one or more households. In the public sector the law had previously applied only to Federal wage board workers, employees of Federal nonappropriated fund activities, and State and local elementary and secondary schools and institutions of higher education, hospitals and residential health care establishments, and local transit operations (covered in 1966) and employees of "preschools" (covered in 1972). The inclusion of private household workers in 1974 represented a major change in the concept of coverage.

The 1974 amendments also extended minimum wage protection to additional agricultural workers, to motion picture theater employees, and to employees of retail or service establishments who handle telegraph messages. The number of protected employees was further increased by phasing out by January 1, 1977, the sales volume test of individual retail or service stores that are part of a chain or a conglomerate.

Types of workers brought under the 40-hour workweek provisions either immediately or in steps included employees of bowling establishments, operating personnel of local transit systems, seafood canning, and processing employees, and hotel and motel employees performing maid or custodial services. Special overtime provisions were established for firefighters and law enforcers employed by public agencies.

Remaining exemptions.   Several types of workers are exempt from both the minimum wage and overtime provisions of the FLSA, while other types are covered as to minimum wage but exempt from overtime requirements.

In terms of numbers affected, the most important exemption from both minimum wage and overtime provisions is that of individuals employed in a professional, executive, or administrative capacity (including persons employed in academic administration or teaching in elementary and secondary schools) or as outside salespersons. Others exempt from both minimum wage and overtime provisions include babysitters employed on a casual basis and persons employed as companions to the aged or infirm; farm workers employed by an employer who did not use more than 500 man-days of farm labor in any calendar quarter of the preceding year; employees of certain seasonal amusement or recreational establishments; and elected State and local officials, their policymaking advisers, and their personal staff. Learners, apprentices, students, and handicapped workers are exempt to the extent that the Secretary of Labor has issued special minimum wage certificates for their employment, as specified. Regulations have been issued by the Secretary of Labor to define the exemption of casual babysitters and companions for the aged or infirm.

Categories exempt from the *overtime* requirements include live-in private household workers, agricultural workers, and certain transportation workers whose industries are subject to regulation under other Federal laws.

Enforcement.   The Wage and Hour Division of the U.S. Department of Labor enforces the FLSA with respect to private and to State and local government employment. Representatives of the Division have the authority to enter places of employment subject to the act and to inspect records, question employees, and investigate conditions and practices as deemed necessary to determine whether violation has occurred or to aid in enforcement. Complaints to the Division's field offices throughout the United States are treated confidentially.

Employers can be required to pay affected employees unpaid back wages or overtime compensation and an additional equal amount as liquidated damages. Unpaid wages may be restored under the supervision of the Secretary of Labor or recovered through court action brought by the Secretary or employees.

It is unlawful to discharge or otherwise discriminate against an employee for filing a complaint or participating in a proceeding under the law. Willful violations of the act may result in criminal prosecution.

Equal Pay Act

The first Federal law against sex discrimination in employment was the Equal Pay Act of 1963, although several States had enacted equal pay laws much earlier and certain wartime Federal regulations had already established the equal pay principle.

The act prohibits employers from paying employees of one sex less than employees of the other sex in the establishment are paid for equal work on jobs that require equal skill, effort, and responsibility and that are performed under similar working conditions.

The law permits differentials based on a seniority system, a merit system, a system measuring earnings by quantity or quality of production, or any other factor other than sex. It prohibits employers from reducing the wage rate of any employee in order to equalize pay between the sexes. It also prohibits labor organizations from causing or attempting to cause employers to violate the provision.

The act became effective June 11, 1964. As an amendment to the Fair Labor Standards Act, it applied to all employees covered by the minimum wage provisions of the FLSA. Since July 1, 1972, when a major breakthrough was made of special concern to women workers, it has covered executive, administrative, and professional employees and outside sales personnel (all of whom are still exempt from the minimum wage and overtime pay requirements of the FLSA).

The Wage and Hour Division of the Department of Labor administers and enforces the equal pay law. In a series of successful cases in Federal courts, including the U.S. Supreme Court, the Department has won both forceful interpretations of the law and large awards of back wages predominantly for women. This record has strengthened the Government's capacity to win compliance without going to court. Over the past 3 years, $16,810,380 in income was restored to 47,553 people under supervision of the Secretary of Labor or through court action brought by him. In addition, the equal pay portions of two major consent decrees won back wages of nearly $7 million each which were not included in the above figures. Employees have also won substantial amounts through private litigation. Even more significant than the back wages are increases in current and future pay rates.

In a landmark decision, a Federal circuit court held that a manufacturer must pay women selector-packers no less than male selector-packer-stackers even though the men were called upon from time to time to perform some 16 additional tasks different from those performed by the women. In concluding that these minor duties were not significant enough to warrant a wage differential between the male and female employees, the court rejected the company's claim that the jobs of men and women have to be identical for them to receive equal pay and asserted that they only have to be "substantially equal." The U.S. Supreme Court denied the company's petition to review the decision. *Shultz* v. *Wheaton Glass Co.*, 421 F. 2d 259, 266; cert. denied, 398 U.S. 905 (1970).

Another court case should also be noted for its delineation of principles central to the enforcement of the Equal Pay Act. In determining that the jobs of nurses' aides and orderlies at a hospital were equal, the Court of Appeals for the Fourth Circuit outlined a number of tests, taken from past court decisions, to be applied to the performance of "extra tasks" which are claimed by employers to make the jobs of men and women unequal. The court stated that higher pay for male employees cannot be considered to be related to extra duties where one or more of the following situations exist: some men receive higher pay without doing the extra work; ; female employees also perform extra duties of equal skill, effort, and responsibility; qualified female employees are not given the opportunity to do the extra work; the supposed extra duties do not in fact exist; the extra tasks consume a minimal amount of time and are of peripheral importance; and third persons who perform the extra tasks as their primary job are paid less than the male employees in question. *Brennan* v. *Prince William Hospital*, 503 F. 2d 282 (1974).

In the first equal pay case reviewed by the U.S. Supreme Court, two circuit courts had disagreed in deciding the issues. Concluding that the company's pay practices ". . . though phrased in terms of a neutral factor other than sex, nevertheless operated to perpetuate the effects of the company's prior illegal practice of paying women less than men for equal work," this historic decision confirmed a number of principles which had previously been stated by lower courts. Specifically, the Court held that shift differences (with the men working at night and the women during the day) did not make the "working conditions" of the men and women "dissimilar" and thus would not justify a larger wage rate for the men (over and above their plantwide night differential); the Court also approved the "substantially equal" (as opposed to "substantially identical") test adopted by the several courts of appeals. In addition, the Court held that Corning did not cure the equal pay violation by integrating the formerly all male and female jobs, and paying the higher rate to the women who transferred to the male or night job and the lower rate to the men who transferred to or were hired for the female or day job. The only way a violation can be remedied under the act, said the Court, is for the lower wages to be raised to the higher. Nor could the company equalize the wages, and then grant an additional increase to the men and women on the night job (as a "red circle" rate), since this rate perpetuated the effects of past discrimination. As a result of this decision, approximately $1 million in back wages was paid. *Corning Glass Works* v. *Brennan*, 417 U.S. 188 (1974).

Title VII of the Civil Rights Act of 1964

A milestone in equal employment opportunity for women was reached with the passage of the Civil Rights Act of 1964. Title VII of that act, effective July 2, 1965, prohibits discrimination based on sex as well as race, color, religion, and national origin in all terms, conditions, or privileges of employment. Provisions of the law are broad enough to encompass new and emerging forms of discrimination.

Title VII is administered by the bipartisan Equal Employment Opportunity Commission (EEOC), whose five members are appointed by the President. Initially powers of the EEOC were limited largely to investigation and conciliation, but in 1972 the act was amended to strengthen enforcement as well as extend coverage.

The act now covers private employers of 15 or more persons, public and private employment agencies, labor unions with 15 or more members, public and private educational institutions, and State and local governments. Not covered are private membership clubs and Indian tribes.

Unlawful practices, if based on *sex*, race, color, religion, or national origin include:

For an employer
to discriminate in hiring or firing, wages and salaries, promotions, or any terms, conditions, or privileges of employment;

For a labor union
to discriminate in membership, classification, or referrals for employment; or to cause or attempt to cause an employer to discriminate;

For an employment agency
to discriminate in classifying or referring for employment;

For any employer, labor union, or joint labor-management committee
to discriminate in training, retraining, or apprenticeship or to print or publish advertisements indicating discriminatory preference or limitation.

Exceptions are permitted when sex is a bona fide occupational qualification reasonably necessary to the normal operation of the business (as in the case of an actor or a wet nurse). Religious institutions may employ persons of a particular religion to further their activities. Also, differentials in compensation may be based on a seniority, merit, or incentive system.

The right to file charge of discrimination is protected by the law. Title VII prohibits an employer from taking, or encouraging others to take, any action against a person for filing a charge of discrimination.

When a complaint is filed in a State or local jurisdiction with an effective fair employment practices law, the agency administering that law must be given an opportunity to resolve the complaint before the EEOC can take action. Periodically the EEOC revises the list of State and local agencies to which it defers.

The EEOC attempts to resolve complaints informally by conciliation and persuasion. If a voluntary agreement is not achieved, EEOC may file suit or the aggrieved persons may file suit on their own within stated time limits. However, if the EEOC finds a probable violation by a governmental agency, it must refer the case to the U.S. Attorney General, who may bring suit.

If prompt judicial action is determined necessary, the EEOC or the Attorney General may seek a court order for relief until a decision is made on the merits of the charge.

Because sex discrimination sometimes takes forms different from race discrimination, the EEOC has issued sex discrimination guidelines. They interpret the bona fide occupational qualification very narrowly—stating, for example, that the refusal to hire an individual cannot be based on assumed employment characteristics of women in general, and that the preferences of customers or existing employees should not be the basis for refusing to hire an individual. They bar hiring based on classification or labeling of "men's jobs" and "women's jobs" or advertising under male and female headings.

The EEOC guidelines declare that State laws that prohibit or limit employment of women (in certain occupations, in jobs requiring the lifting or carrying of specified weights, for more than a specified number of hours, during certain hours of the night, and immediately before and after childbirth) discriminate on the basis of sex, because they do not take into account individual capacities and preferences. Thus, they conflict with and are superseded by title VII. A series of court cases upheld this guideline, and the conflict between State and Federal laws on this point was for the most part resolved in the early 1970's.

Regarding State laws that require minimum wage and premium overtime pay only for women, on the other hand, EEOC deems it an unlawful practice for an employer to refuse to hire women in order to avoid payment of such benefits or not to provide them for men.

Similar provisions apply to other sex-oriented State employment laws, such as those requiring special rest and meal periods or physical facilities for women; if an employer can prove that business necessity precludes providing these benefits to both men and women, he or she must not provide them to members of either sex.

When a law is relatively new, the interpretations of the enforcing agency are frequently challenged in the courts. EEOC has been upheld on many points, and the Supreme Court has said that its administrative interpretations should be given great deference. *Griggs et al.* v. *Duke Power Co.*, 401 U.S. 424 (1971). However, disputed points of EEOC's maternity guideline are under litigation and appeals courts have offered conflicting opinions on the guideline that would harmonize State minimum wage laws for women with title VII by extending the benefits involved to men.

In Arkansas an employer asked the court to declare that the State law requiring overtime pay for women was superseded by title VII. Both district and appeals courts found instead that there was no conflict between the State and Federal laws because the employer could comply with both statutes by paying men and women the overtime rate which the State required for women. *Potlatch Forests, Inc.* v. *Hays et al.*, 318 F. Supp. 1368; aff'd, 465 F. 2d 1081 (1972).

In ruling on a similar California law, another appeals court rejected this reasoning and found the State law in conflict with title VII and unenforceable. The court held that an interpretation which would expand the class of persons to benefit from the State law would take lawmaking power away from the State legislature. *Homemakers, Inc.* v. *Division of Industrial Welfare*, 509 F. 2d 20 (1974).

Each decision will apply within its own circuit, pending resolution of the question by the Supreme Court.

The *Griggs* decision, a race discrimination case that should have wide applicability to sex discrimination, ruled that discrimination need not be intentional to be unlawful. It included the following principle:

Under the [Civil Rights] Act, practices, procedures, . . . neutral on their face, and even neutral in terms of intent, cannot be maintained if they operate to "freeze" the status quo of prior discriminatory employment practices. . . . Congress directed the thrust of the Act to the consequences of employment practices, not simply the motivation.

Federal Contracts

Executive Order 11246, as amended by Executive Order 11375, effective October 14, 1968, to cover sex, sets forth the Federal program to eliminate discrimination by Government contractors. The program stems from the responsibility of the executive branch to establish the terms and conditions on which it will contract with private parties to purchase supplies and services needed for the Government's operations. Since the early 1940's, Presidents have issued Executive orders which use the Government's contracting power to further public policy on fair employement practices for minorities.

Now most Government contracts must incorporate requirements stated in the order, including: "The contractor will take affirmative action to ensure that applicants are employed and that employees are treated during employment without regard to their race, color, religion, sex, or national origin. Such action shall include but not be limited to the following: employment, upgrading, demotion, or transfer; recruitment advertising; layoff or termination; rates of pay or other forms of compensation; and selection for training, including apprenticeship."

The order applies to Federal contractors or subcontractors and contractors who perform work under federally assisted construction contracts exceeding $10,000.

The Secretary of Labor has general enforcement responsibility. The Secretary has delegated to the Office of Federal Contract Compliance responsibility to administer the Government-wide program, to monitor and evaluate the equal employment compliance programs of the contracting agencies, and to develop regulations, orders, and guidelines to implement the Executive order.

Sex discrimination guidelines issued by the OFCC are similar in many respects to those of the EEOC. Provisions concerning maternity benefits and pensions, now under discussion pending revision, would bring these standards more in conformance with EEOC's guidelines.

Under OFCC's Revised Order No. 4, issued December 4, 1971, and most recently amended July 12, 1974, service and supply contractors who have 50 or more employees and a contract of $50,000 or more are required to develop written affirmative action programs. An affirmative action program is described as a set of specific and result-oriented procedures to which a contractor is committed.

In general contractors are required to conduct an in-depth analysis of all levels and job groups of the company work force to see where minorities or women are "underutilized," that is, where there are fewer minorities or women in a particular job group than could reasonably be expected from their availability in the recruitment area. Employers are to eliminate policies which cause this underutilization and to establish numerical goals and timetables for expanding job opportunities for groups previously denied opportunity. Such goals cannot be rigid and inflexible quotas which must be met, but targets reasonably attainable by means of applying every good faith effort to make all aspects of the entire affirmative action program work. The employer must communicate to employees and applicants the existence of the affirmative action program and such elements of the plan as will enable them to know and avail themselves of its benefits.

To assure that the different contracting agencies make the same requirements in evaluating contractors, OFCC established standardized compliance review procedures in Revised Order No. 14, effective May 15, 1974.

Affirmative action under construction contracts involves a different set of procedures because of the temporary nature of the employer-employee relationship in that industry. Area-wide agreements known as "home town" plans are negotiated, or plans are imposed requiring employment of specified numbers of minorities in the building trades. Construction contractors may not discriminate on the basis of sex, but most affirmative action plans do not specify hiring goals for women.

Failure of a contractor to comply with the nondiscrimination pledges of the contract, or with the rules and regulations of the Secretary of Labor, may result in the cancellation, termination, or suspension of the contract in whole or in part, and the contractor may be declared ineligible for further Government contracts.

The growth of affirmative action

The affirmative action obligation of Federal contractors is part of a broader movement toward reexamination of total employment systems. Earlier the phrase "affirmative action" was used with reference to any remedy, such as back pay, to redress the rights of employees. Its purpose is not punitive but to make the employee whole.

Experience in enforcement of equal employment opportunity laws has shown that discrimination cannot be overcome by giving attention only to individual complaints. In recent years courts have recognized that, by nature, discrimination is not directed toward a single individual but is more often a network of deeply embedded practices that place barriers to the full employment of certain groups. Affirmative action has come to be associated with comprehensive plans to identify and remove those barriers.

The examination of a whole employment system was a relatively new idea in the 1960's but by December 1971 the Office of Federal Contract Compliance had sufficient experience with monitoring affirmative action programs for minorities to set forth specific requirements regarding both minorities and women in Revised Order No. 4.

Affirmative action is sometimes required under title VII, but on a somewhat different basis. Unlike the Executive order which makes affirmative action a contractual obligation, title VII does not require such positive programs until after a finding of a pattern of discrimination. Then the Equal Employment Opportunity Commission may set forth specific goals in a conciliation agreement, or Federal courts may order even more rigorous plans to remedy grievances and to offset the continuing effects of past discriminatory practices. The EEOC highly recommends voluntary affirmative action as the most desirable method of assuring fair employment practices and avoiding costly litigation.

A few State and city governments have begun requiring affirmative action of contractors who do business with them.

Age discrimination in employment act

The Age Discrimination in Employment Act of 1967, which became effective June 12, 1968, prohibits discrimination in employment against persons 40 to 65 years old by employers, employment agencies, and labor unions. It is of particular importance to women who reenter the work force after an extended period of full-time family responsibility.

The act now applies to employers of 20 or more persons and labor organizations which have 25 or more members or which refer persons for employment to covered employers, or which represent employees of employers covered by the act. Since May 1, 1974, State and local governments have been covered. Elected officials, their appointees and certain advisers are outside the scope of the act.

It is an unlawful employment practice

- For an *employer* to fail or refuse to hire, or to discharge, or otherwise discriminate against any individual with respect to compensation, terms, conditions, or privileges of employment, or to limit, segregate, or classify in any way which would deprive or tend to deprive an individual of job opportunities, or otherwise adversely affect the person's status as an employee, because of age;

- For an *employment agency* to fail or refuse to refer for employment, or in any other way discriminate, or to classify or refer anyone for employment, on the basis of age;

- For a *labor organization* to exclude or expel from membership, or otherwise discriminate against, or to limit, segregate, or classify its membership, or to classify or fail or refuse to refer for employment, any individual in any way which would deprive or tend to deprive the individual of job opportunity, limit job opportunities, or adversely affect status as an employee or a job applicant, because of age; or to cause or attempt to cause an employer to discriminate.

For certain jobs it may be possible for an employer to establish that age is a bona fide occupational qualification reasonably necessary to the performance of the duties of the job. It is not unlawful to observe the terms of a bona fide seniority system or employee benefit plan such as a retirement, pension, or insurance plan, which is not a subterfuge to evade the purposes of the act (however, such a plan cannot be used as an excuse to refuse to hire an individual).

The Secretary of Labor or any aggrieved person may bring suit under the act. Suits to enforce the act must be brought within 2 years after the violation, or in the case of a willful violation, within 3 years. Before an individual can bring court action, certain prescribed time limits must be met and it is therefore important to contact the nearest office of the Wage and Hour Division promptly.

Handicapped workers

Employers covered by sections of title V of the Rehabilitation Act of 1973, as amended, must take affirmative action to employ and advance in employment qualified handicapped individuals without discrimination based on their physical or mental handicap. Nondiscrimination programs must be carried out for handicapped men and women qualified for training or employment in Federal Government, under Federal contracts and subcontracts in excess of $2,500, and in any program or activity receiving Federal funds. Discrimination is prohibited in hiring or layoff, compensation, seniority, promotion, or training opportunities.

Affirmative action obligations of Federal agencies were announced in January 1974 by the U.S. Civil Service Commission. Regulations covering affirmative action obligations of Federal contractors and subcontractors were issued in June 1974 by the U.S. Department of Labor. Both require outreach and positive recruiting, as well as accommodation to the physical or mental limitation of a handicapped applicant or employee if necessary for compliance.

This nondiscrimination program is unique—it does not set goals or timetables—because accommodation to meet the needs (if any) of a handicapped applicant or employee is individualized to that person's handicap.

Covered Federal contractors and subcontractors that do not comply are subject to sanctions, which range from withholding of partial payment to debarment from further contracting with the Federal Government.

Employees are encouraged to resolve complaints through internal voluntary procedures. However, formal complaints are received by the U.S. Civil Service Commission if the problem is with a Federal agency and by the U.S. Department of Labor if the complaint is against a Federal contractor.

Private pension plans

Many workers are covered by private pension plans. Some of these are established and controlled by the employer, and some are negotiated with unions in collective bargaining agreements. Some are "contributory," where the employee also pays into the fund; and some are "noncontributory," where the employer provides the total input. Plans vary widely in the amount of benefits provided on retirement.

Two areas of pension plans have been of particular concern to women workers. One was the typical exclusion of part-time and part-year workers. The other was the long period of unbroken service usually required in order to achieve "vesting," that is, a nonforfeitable right to retirement benefits. The work pattern of married women of leaving the labor market temporarily because of family responsibilities or changing jobs when their husbands are transferred left a great many women unable to meet plan eligibility and vesting standards, and therefore no pension rights at all, even though at retirement age their total years of work and contributions to pension plans might be only slightly less than those of their male counterparts.

In addition, a great many workers—women and men—who had agreed to employer contributions toward a pension plan as a form of deferred wages realized little or no benefits because, for example, the employer went bankrupt, the company was sold to or merged with another company which refused to continue the plan, or the fund was depleted due to imprudent action by trustees. Almost 10 years of congressional and administration efforts to protect pension plan participants against such personal economic catastrophes resulted in enactment of the Employee Retirement Income Security Act of 1974 (Public Law 93-406, approved September 2, 1974).

This law supplanted the Welfare and Pension Plans Disclosure Act of 1958, which set no eligibility, vesting, funding, or fiduciary standards but did require employers or unions which maintained welfare or pension plans to provide a description and annual reports to participants and to the Secretary of Labor.

The new law, popularly known as the Pension Reform Act, affects up to 35 million workers. It does *not* cover plans for Federal, State, or local government workers; church plans, unless the church or association of churches elects coverage; or plans maintained outside the country primarily for nonresident aliens. It does *not* require companies to set up pension plans or to maintain or raise benefits of existing plans. It does, however, set standards for existing plans whose sponsors decide to continue them and for any new plans that may be established. These standards are in such areas as participation (eligibility), vesting, funding, fiduciary responsibility, and reporting and disclosure. In addition, the Pension Reform Act establishes an insurance program for pension plans and liberalizes provisions for individual pension plans.

Participation and survivor protection.   In general, pension plans must allow any employee who is 25 years old and has had at least a year of service (defined as a minimum of 1,000 hours of employment during a year) to join the plan. A 3-year service requirement can be set if the plan provides for full and immediate vesting. Persons who are within 5 years of retirement may be excluded from the right to join certain kinds of pension plans.

A pension plan which provides benefits in the form of an annuity must provide a participant and his or her spouse with a "joint and survivor annuity," unless the participant declines such protection for the spouse. If the participant is eligible for early retirement and does not retire early, the plan must provide the participant with the opportunity to elect a joint and survivor annuity. The survivor's annuity must be no less than half the joint annuity.

Vesting.   Each pension plan must provide that the employee has a nonforfeitable right at normal retirement age to all his or her contributions to the plan. In addition, each plan must provide as a minimum one of the following three methods of assuring rights to employer contributions on his or her behalf:

(a) *graded vesting,* which gives participants a vested (nonforfeitable) right to 25 percent of accrued benefits after 5 years on the job, with 5-percent increases in vesting for the next 5 years, 10 percent each following year, and 100 percent at the end of 15 years;

(b) *full vesting,* which gives participants total nonforfeitable benefit rights after 10 years of service with the company, but nothing before then;

(c) *the modified "rule of 45,"* which gives participants who have at least 5 years of service 50 percent vesting when age and years of service equal 45, with 10-percent increases in each of the next 5 years, but gives anyone who completes 10 years of service 50 percent vesting and 10 percent more for each additional year of service.

Of particular importance to women is the provision that a break in service cannot cancel vesting time unless the break is longer than the prior service credited toward vesting.

Funding.   Standards are established to assure that contributions to plans are sufficient to pay all pension benefits as they become due and also to cover current operating costs.

Fiduciary responsibility.   Strict standards are established for fiduciaries (persons entrusted with administering plans or managing the assets of employee benefit plan funds) to assure their handling the assets solely in the interest of plan participants. Investments must be diversified so as to minimize the risk of large losses.

Fiduciaries of plans other than profit-sharing plans are prohibited from investing more than 10 percent of a fund's assets in the employer's securities or real estate.

Reporting and disclosure.   Administrators of employee benefit plans are required to furnish each participant and beneficiary summaries of the plan at stated times. Administrators are also required to make detailed annual reports, which must include statements by a qualified public accountant and an enrolled actuary, to the Secretary of Labor.

When vested workers change jobs, reports of their pension rights must be made to the Social Security Administration, which is to send to the individuals a report on their right to vested benefits at retirement time.

Portability.   The law does not require that a worker who changes jobs be able to "carry along" vested benefits. It does, however, provide favorable tax treatment for transfers from one cooperating plan to another.

Portability of pension rights is one of the subjects the Joint Pension Task Force is to study and report back on.

Plan termination insurance.   More than two-thirds of those now enrolled in private pension plans will have their vested pension benefits insured by a new Pension Benefit Guaranty Corporation. If a plan terminates when it is not fully funded and doesn't have enough money to pay the benefits, the Corporation will guarantee at least a portion of the benefits.

Personal plans.   The Pension Reform Act amends the Internal Revenue Code to liberalize provisions for retirement plans of self-employed individuals and shareholder-employees ("Keogh plans"), and provides for a new program of personal retirement plans for workers who are not participating in another pension plan qualified under rules of the Internal Revenue Service.

For self-employed persons who elect to set up individual retirement accounts under the so-called Keogh plan, the law raises the contribution limit from $2,500 to $7,500 (or 15 percent of earned income if less).

The law entitles workers who are not covered by a qualified pension, profit-sharing, or similar plan to set up their own plans by contributing up to the lesser of 15 percent of their compensation or $1,500 to "individual retirement accounts," annuities, or bond programs. Such contributions are excluded from the workers' gross taxable incomes, and earnings on the accounts are tax free. Distribution because of retirement after age 59½ or disability at any age is taxable as ordinary income. A 10 percent excise tax is levied on premature distributions.

Administration and enforcement. Administrative and enforcement responsibilities, other than the termination insurance program, are handled by the Labor Department's Labor-Management Services Administration and Treasury's Internal Revenue Service.

The new law prohibits an employer from discharging workers in order to avoid paying pensions. Failure to comply with standards of the law can be remedied through civil lawsuits by participants and beneficiaries or by the Secretary of Labor, and through tax penalties imposed by the Internal Revenue Service.

Effective date. In general, plans established following the law's enactment must comply with its provisions from the outset. Various timetables are set for existing plans to conform with new standards.

For persons who have retired already, most of the provisions of the new law do not apply. However, if a plan is discontinued without sufficient funds, present retirees under that plan may be protected by the pension insurance program. The Labor Department's Office of Employee Benefits Security will provide information on the status of a plan respecting coverage by the law.

Discrimination. Under another act, title VII of the 1964 Civil Rights Act, an employer may not discriminate between men and women with respect to fringe benefits such as medical, hospital, accident, life insurance, and retirement benefits. Benefits limited to "head of household" or "principal wage earner" are discriminatory.

State and federal labor laws: where lies the clout?*

State labor laws in transition

Introduction to state protective laws for women
Rarely has legislation taken such a marked shift in form and emphasis as the laws applying to women workers. Early in the century special protections for women appeared to be the only means of achieving minimum standards in the workplace, even at the cost of excluding women from some kinds of profitable employment. Later women's increased concern to participate in the full range of job opportunities, and the possibility of improved standards for men and women brought a reevaluation of earlier laws.

*State Labor Laws in Transition, U.S. Department of Labor, Women's Bureau, 1976

This section summarizes employment laws of special interest to women and highlights trends that have become evident in the past years. For example:

- State minimum wage laws increased in number and many States that passed such laws initially for women extended coverage to men. Legislatures and wage boards remained active in increasing minimum rates.

- State equal pay and fair employment practices legislation advanced rapidly after enactment of the Federal Equal Pay Act of 1963 and title VII of the Civil Rights Act of 1964.

- Some of the State "protective" laws, so called because they protected women from long working hours and strenuous or hazardous employment, were declared in direct conflict with Federal laws against sex discrimination because they limited women's opportunity to earn overtime pay or to win skilled jobs and promotions. This conflict was essentially resolved in the late sixties and early seventies by repeals and amendments of State laws, State and Federal administrative rulings, or court decisions. On the other hand, there has been considerable effort to extend to men—through legislation or administrative or judicial decision—other protective laws that conferred benefits only on women.

Laws vary from State to State. Historically State legislatures sometimes took the lead before Congress, sometimes followed Federal initiatives.

Although the focus of this section is on State laws, information is provided on their Federal counterparts to the extent needed to clarify the effect of the State enactments.

Minimum wage

The minimum wage laws are of two basic types: those which contain a minimum in the law itself (statutory rate) and those which empower wage boards to set minimum rates by occupation or industry. Some States combine the two types by enacting a statutory minimum for most employment and providing wage boards to set rates for certain occupations or industries. Only the legislature can change statutory rates, but wage boards may modify rates or issue wage orders for new occupations or industries after complying with specified administrative procedures.

State minimum rates vary widely—from a low of $1 to a high of $2.60 an hour. Some States provide for automatic upward adjustment if the Federal rate is increased.

The Fair Labor Standards Act (FLSA) sets a minimum wage of $2.65/hr for most covered employees. States may set rates higher than the Federal rate; but if a State rate is lower than that set by the FLSA, the Federal rate prevails for all employees who come under its coverage. The FLSA is administered by the U.S. Department of Labor.

There is considerable variation in coverage of State minimum wage laws. Only a few States cover farm employment and private household work (see below). Some exempt such groups as employers with less than a specified number of workers; nonprofit, religious, and charitable institutions; workers in specified occupations; and workers covered by the FLSA. On the other hand, State minimum wage laws often benefit workers in certain local trade and small service establishments not covered by the Federal law.

As of September 1974, State minimum wage laws or orders gave protection to 5,049,000 nonsupervisory employees not covered by the minimum wage provisions of the FLSA. Still 4,774,000 nonsupervisory employees were not assured a minimum wage by either State or Federal law.

Historical record.   The first State minimum wage legislation was a "recommendatory" law in Massachusetts in 1912, which could be enforced by no more than making investigations and publishing names of offenders in the newspapers. Between 1912 and 1923 minimum wage laws were enacted in 14 additional States, the District of Columbia, and Puerto Rico, although two were repealed soon after enactment.

For many years State minimum wage legislation was designed almost exclusively for the protection of women and minors, and did much to raise their extremely low pay in manufacturing and trade and service industries. Most States chose the wage board method of establishing rates during the early years.

Legislative progress was interrupted by a 1923 decision of the U.S. Supreme Court declaring the District of Columbia law unconstitutional on the ground that it deprived liberty of contract in personal employment. *Adkins* v. *Children's Hospital,* 261 U.S. 525.

A struggle ensued. Several State laws were declared unconstitutional by State or Federal courts, and others became inoperative from lack of wage board activity or appropriations. No new minimum wage laws were passed for 10 years.

Then, despite the Supreme Court decision, the depression years of the 1930's brought a revival of interest in minimum wage legislation. States sought new formulations to achieve the minimum wage objective, and these too, were struck down. The issue was not resolved until 1937, when the Supreme Court expressly reversed its *Adkins* decision and upheld the constitutionality of the minimum wage law in the State of Washington. *West Coast Hotel* v. *Parrish,* 300 U.S. 379.

At this point laws that had been held unconstitutional were reexamined. Some of them were declared valid, while others were passed in new form. Several States enacted minimum wage legislation for the first time. Of the 29 jurisdictions that had enacted minimum wage legislation at some time, 22 States, the District of Columbia, and Puerto Rico had minimum wage laws in effect in 1938 when Congress enacted the FLSA (see chart A). The Federal law set a minimum rate for women and men and required premium pay for weekly overtime. Of the early State laws, only the short-lived one in Oklahoma had applied to men as well as women.

During the ensuing decades, many States have passed minimum wage laws for the first time and others extended and strengthened their early enactments. Characteristic modifications have been:

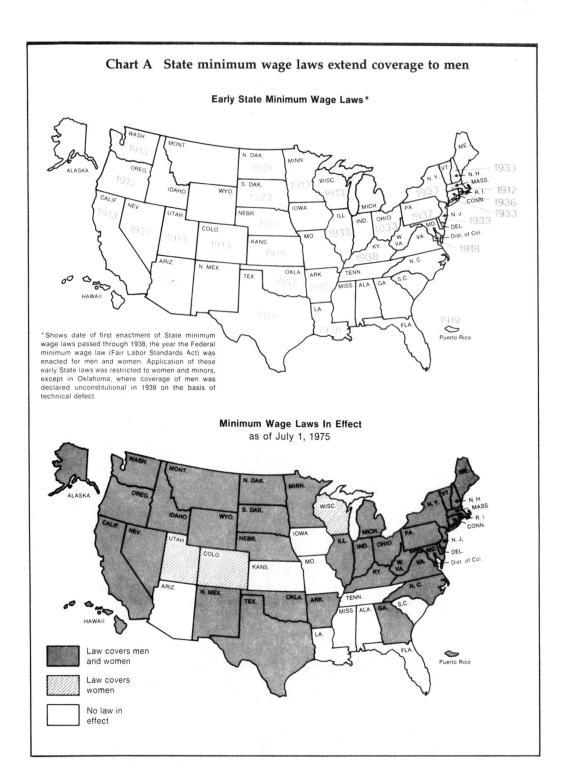

Chart A State minimum wage laws extend coverage to men

Early State Minimum Wage Laws*

*Shows date of first enactment of State minimum wage laws passed through 1938, the year the Federal minimum wage law (Fair Labor Standards Act) was enacted for men and women. Application of these early State laws was restricted to women and minors, except in Oklahoma, where coverage of men was declared unconstitutional in 1939 on the basis of technical defect.

Minimum Wage Laws In Effect
as of July 1, 1975

Law covers men and women

Law covers women

No law in effect

Extension of coverage—
to men;
to additional occupations, for example, private household workers, farm laborers, and employees receiving gratuities; and
to small establishments.

Establishment of a statutory rate in addition to or instead of wage board provisions.

Strengthening of enforcement.

Increase of the statutory rate, sometimes exceeding the Federal rate.

Provision for increasing the State minimum rate whenever the Federal minimum increases, in the same amount and on the same date.

Revision of wage orders.

Addition of premium pay for overtime.

The status of those State minimum wage laws which cover women but not men was altered by the enactment of title VII of the Civil Rights Act of 1964, a Federal law which prohibits discrimination in employment on the basis of race, color, religion, sex, or national origin.

Roster of minimum wage jurisdictions. The jurisdictions with minimum wage laws in effect are:

Alaska	Maryland	Oklahoma
Arkansas	Massachusetts	Oregon
California	Michigan	Pennsylvania
Colorado	Minnesota	Puerto Rico
Connecticut	Montana	Rhode Island
Delaware	Nebraska	South Dakota
District of Columbia	Nevada	Texas
Georgia	New Hampshire	Utah
Hawaii	New Jersey	Vermont
Idaho	New Mexico	Virginia
Illinois	New York	Washington
Indiana	North Carolina	West Virginia
Kentucky	North Dakota	Wisconsin
Maine	Ohio	Wyoming

Kansas and Louisiana have wage board laws, but no minimum rates have been set. Arizona, which had a minimum wage for women and minors, recently repealed coverage of women. Seven States—Alabama, Florida, Iowa, Mississippi, Missouri, South Carolina, and Tennessee—do not have minimum wage laws.

Type of law and employee covered. Nine States, the District of Columbia, and Puerto Rico have laws that set a statutory rate and also provide for wage boards to establish occupation or industry rates. Twenty-six States have statutory rate laws only. Minimum rates set by wage boards are in effect in 5 States.

The following lists show the type of law and employee covered:

a. Statutory rate and wage board law for:

Men and Women

Connecticut	New York	Rhode Island
District of Columbia	Ohio	Vermont
New Hampshire	Oregon	Washington
New Jersey	Puerto Rico	

b. Statutory rate law only for:

Men and Women

Alaska	Maine	North Carolina
Arkansas	Maryland	Ohio
Delaware	Massachusetts	Oklahoma
Georgia	Michigan	Pennsylvania
Hawaii	Minnesota	South Dakota
Idaho	Montana	Texas
Illinois	Nebraska	West Virginia
Indiana	Nevada	Wyoming
Kentucky	New Mexico	

c. Wage board law only for:

Men and Women

California
North Dakota

Women

Colorado
Utah
Wisconsin

Coverage of workers in private households and in farm employment. In recent years workers in private households and in agriculture—workers with little previous coverage—have increasingly come under coverage of State minimum wage laws.

The Federal Fair Labor Standards Amendments of 1974 extended a minimum wage to private household workers starting at $1.90/hr. as of May 1974 and rising to $2.00/hr. as of January 1975, $2.20/hr. as of January 1976, and $2.30 as of January 1977. The minimum wage of agricultural employees, previously covered under the act, was raised from $1.30/hr. to $1.60/hr. as of May 1974, to $1.80/hr. as of January 1975, $2.00/hr. as of January 1976, $2.20/hr. as of January 1977, and $2.30/hr. as of January 1978.

The only States with minimum wage coverage of private household workers in households with one employee are:

California	Montana	Ohio
Maryland	Nevada	South Dakota
Massachusetts	New Jersey	Wisconsin
Minnesota	New York	

In Kentucky, households with at least two private household employees are covered.

Although statutory minimum wage laws in Arkansas, Michigan, Nebraska, and West Virginia do not exempt private household workers, most household workers in these States are not covered because of high numerical exemptions. Wage board laws in Colorado, North Dakota, and Utah do not exempt private household workers, but no wage orders covering them have been issued.

The following jurisdictions have a minimum wage rate applicable to at least some farm employment:

California	Montana	Puerto Rico
Connecticut	Nevada	South Dakota
Hawaii	New Jersey	Texas
Massachusetts	New Mexico	Wisconsin
Michigan	New York	
Minnesota	Ohio	

Premium pay for overtime

Twenty-nine States, the District of Columbia, and Puerto Rico have laws or regulations in effect that provide pay at a premium rate for overtime. These overtime requirements are usually in minimum wage statutes or wage orders, but some are in hours laws.

Most overtime provisions exempt farm employment. Some States specify other exemptions, such as employers covered by or "in compliance with" the Federal overtime standard. However, as in the case of minimum wage, State coverage is sometimes broader than that of the Federal law.

The Federal requirement for most nonfarm workers covered by the minimum wage provisions of the FLSA is 1½ times an employee's regular rate after 40 hours a week.

While New York requires payment of 1½ times the employee's *minimum* hourly rate after a specified number of weekly hours, the other jurisdictions with overtime provisions stipulate 1½ times the *regular* rate after a specified number of daily and/or weekly hours.

The chart on the next page of premium pay requirements in effect shows the type of law and hours after which premium pay is required. Where hours are shown in a range, variations exist based on occupation or industry or on emergency conditions. Because of these variations, the agency administering a law should be consulted for information about specific situations.

One Federal appeals court has ruled that the Arkansas premium pay provision is applicable also to men; however, another appeals court refused to follow that decision with regard to California's overtime requirements in an hours law and wage order applicable to women only, and ruled that they could not be enforced. Rulings by courts or attorneys general in Idaho, Texas, and New Mexico also struck down premium pay requirements in hours laws for women rather than adopting the concept that, under State or Federal antidiscrimination provisions, the benefit should be extended to men. In New Mexico, although women lost their entitlement to overtime pay after 40 hours, they regained it partially through enactment of a requirement for premium pay after 48 hours in the minimum wage law applicable to both men and women.

Equal pay

Thirty-seven States have laws applicable to private employment that prohibit discrimination in rate of pay based on sex (see chart B). An additional 8 States, the District of Columbia, and Puerto Rico do not

	Minimum Wage Law		Hours Law	
	Daily	Weekly	Daily	Weekly
Alaska	8	40		
Arkansas			8	7th consecutive day W
California		40W	8	40/48W
Colorado		40/42W		
Connecticut		40/48		
District of Columbia		40		
Hawaii		40		
Kentucky		40		
Maine		40		
Maryland		40		
Massachusetts		40		
Michigan		46		
Minnesota		48		
Montana		40		
Nevada			8	40
New Hampshire	8			
New Jersey		40		
New Mexico		48		
New York		40/44		
North Carolina				50
North Dakota		48		
Ohio		40		
Oregon		40		
Pennsylvania		40		
Puerto Rico[1]	8	40/44	8	40/48
Rhode Island		40		
Vermont		40		
Washington		40		
West Virginia		46		
Wisconsin			9	48W
Wyoming			8	48W

[1] Time and a half the regular rate after 8 hours daily and 40 hours weekly and double time after 48 hours, except for certain industry wage orders which provide for double time after 8 hours daily and 40 or 44 hours weekly. For women, triple the regular rate after 12 hours daily and 72 hours weekly if not covered by FLSA, or after 60 hours weekly if covered by FLSA.

W=Applicable to women only.

have a separate equal pay law but do prohibit pay discrimination based on sex in their fair employment practices (FEP) or civil rights law. Only 5 States have neither an equal pay law nor an FEP law covering sex discrimination.

The Federal Equal Pay Act was an amendment to the FLSA in 1963. With amendments in 1972 and 1974 it has broad coverage in public and private employment.

Historical Record. Public attention was first sharply focused on equal pay for women during World War I, when large numbers of women were employed in war industries in the same jobs as men, and the National War Labor Board enforced the policy of "no wage discrimination against women on the grounds of sex." In 1919, 2 States—Michigan and Montana—enacted equal pay legislation. For nearly 25 years these were the only States with such laws.

Great progress in the equal pay field was made during World War II, when again large numbers of women entered the labor force, many of them in jobs previously held by men. Government agencies supported the principle of equal pay by establishing policies and regulatory orders.

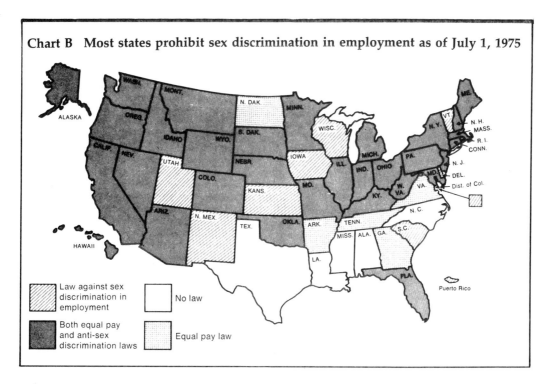

Chart B Most states prohibit sex discrimination in employment as of July 1, 1975

Legend:
- Law against sex discrimination in employment
- Both equal pay and anti-sex discrimination laws
- No law
- Equal pay law

Employers, unions, organizations, and the general public pressed for the removal of wage differentials as a means of furthering the war effort. Ten States passed equal pay laws during the war or the years immediately following.

Twenty-two States had equal pay laws and 2 others included a prohibition of sex discrimination in their FEP acts by 1963, when Congress passed the Federal Equal Pay Act. From this point on, several States enacted equal pay laws, either separately or as part of a minimum wage law, while others moved immediately to the broader FEP type of law.

Equal pay laws are usually enforced by the State labor department or industrial commission; FEP laws, often part of broader human rights laws, are usually administered by a human rights commission.

Roster of equal pay states.   States with equal pay laws applicable to most kinds of private employment:

Alaska	Maine	Ohio
Arizona	Maryland	Oklahoma
Arkansas	Massachusetts	Oregon
California	Michigan	Pennsylvania
Colorado	Minnesota	Rhode Island
Connecticut	Missouri	South Dakota
Florida	Montana	Tennessee
Georgia	Nebraska	Virginia
Hawaii	Nevada	Washington
Idaho	New Hampshire	West Virginia
Illinois	New Jersey	Wyoming
Indiana	New York	
Kentucky	North Dakota	

Fair employment practices

Forty States, the District of Columbia, and Puerto Rico have broad FEP laws (or FEP sections in human rights laws) covering private employment. These vary considerably in coverage, unfair practices specified, and provisions for conciliation or enforcement. From early prohibitions against employment based on race, color, religion, and national origin, the laws have come to include sex, often age, and, in some recent instances, marital status and physical or mental handicap.

Sex discrimination. All the broad State FEP laws include a provision on sex discrimination (see chart C). Prior to enactment of title VII in 1964 only 2 States—Hawaii and Wisconsin—prohibited sex discrimination in employment, although 25 prohibited race discrimination.

Title VII of the Federal Civil Rights Act of 1964 is the major Federal fair employment law. It prohibits discrimination based on race, color, religion, sex, or national origin. It is administered by the Equal Employment Opportunity Commission (EEOC).

A number of cities and counties also have established human rights or fair employment practices commissions. Many of the State and local commissions have enforcement powers similar to those of the EEOC and have adopted in whole or in part certain policy positions of the Federal agency, including the sex discrimination guidelines. The EEOC is required by section 706 of the Federal law to give a State or local office a first opportunity to process a discrimination charge if the agency implements an adequate antidiscrimination law. The agency has 60 days (120 days for an agency that has been operating less than a year) to process a charge before jurisdiction returns to the EEOC. Further, in making its own determinations, the EEOC is to give substantial weight to the final findings and orders of designated "706" agencies.

Chart C   Growth of fair employment legislation and the impact of title VII (through July 1, 1975)

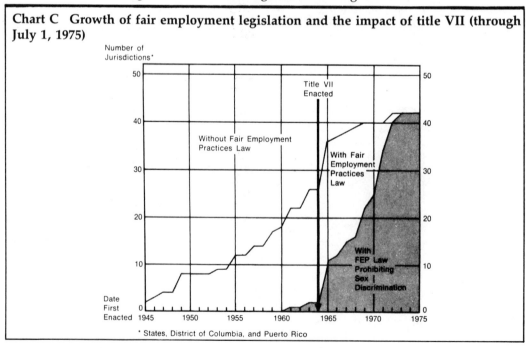

* States, District of Columbia, and Puerto Rico

The major jurisdictions with laws which cover sex discrimination in private employment are indicated below (those to whose enforcement agencies the EEOC defers are shown in caps):

ALASKA	KENTUCKY	OHIO
ARIZONA	MAINE	OKLAHOMA
CALIFORNIA	MARYLAND	OREGON
COLORADO	MASSACHUSETTS	PENNSYLVANIA
CONNECTICUT	MICHIGAN	Puerto Rico
DELAWARE	MINNESOTA	RHODE ISLAND
DISTRICT OF COLUMBIA	MISSOURI	South Carolina
Florida	MONTANA	SOUTH DAKOTA
Hawaii	NEBRASKA	UTAH
IDAHO	NEVADA	Vermont
ILLINOIS	NEW HAMPSHIRE	WASHINGTON
INDIANA	NEW JERSEY	WEST VIRGINIA
IOWA	New Mexico	WISCONSIN
KANSAS	NEW YORK	WYOMING

The EEOC also defers to enforcement agencies of the following:

Baltimore (Md.)	Minneapolis (Minn.)	Seattle (Wash.)
Bloomington (Ind.)	New York (N.Y.)	Springfield (Ohio)
Dade County (Fla.)	Omaha (Nebr.)	Tacoma (Wash.)
East Chicago (Ill.)	Philadelphia, (Pa.)	Virgin Islands
Gary (Ind.)	Rockville (Md.)	

The South Carolina State Human Affairs Commission is limited to using conciliation and persuasion in the private sector but has full enforcement authority against discrimination in public employment. While many of the laws prohibiting sex discrimination in private employment also protect public employees, some State and local jurisdictions use civil service regulations or special orders of a Governor or mayor to do so.

It is interesting to note that even where both Federal and State FEP laws are in effect a local ordinance and human relations commission may be very powerful. In a landmark case the U.S. Supreme Court upheld a city commission's order that a newspaper stop maintaining separate "help wanted" columns designated "Jobs—Male Interest" and "Jobs—Female Interest." The Court denied that the order infringed the First Amendment rights of the newspaper to free expressions of its views. *Pittsburgh Press Co.* v. *Pittsburgh Commission on Human Relations*, 413 U.S. 376 (1973).

Age discrimination. Thirty-four States, the District of Columbia, and Puerto Rico have laws prohibiting age discrimination in private employment. These laws are of particular concern to women because many women enter or reenter the labor market—or shift from part-time employment—after an extended period of major family responsibility. Some age discrimination prohibitions are part of the FEP law and are administered by a human rights commission; others are administered by the commissioner of labor. Age limits for protected persons vary widely.

The Federal Age Discrimination in Employment Act, enacted in 1967 and amended by the Fair Labor Standards Amendments of 1974, prohibits discrimination against persons 40 to 65 years of age in private and public employment by employers of 20 or more, labor organizations, and employment agencies.

The jurisdictions which prohibit age discrimination in private employment are listed below:

Alaska	Kentucky	New York
California	Louisiana	North Dakota
Colorado	Maine	Ohio
Connecticut	Maryland	Oregon
Delaware	Massachusetts	Pennsylvania
District of Columbia	Michigan	Puerto Rico
Georgia	Montana	Rhode Island
Hawaii	Nebraska	South Carolina
Idaho	Nevada	Utah
Illinois	New Hampshire	Washington
Indiana	New Jersey	West Virginia
Iowa	New Mexico	Wisconsin

Title VII, a turning point

The enactment of title VII, the equal employment opportunity section of the Federal Civil Rights Act of 1964, influenced the direction of State legislative activity applicable to women workers.

Early in the century as women first entered the work force in significant numbers, working conditions were very rigorous; wages were very low, and women had neither the organization nor the experience to bargain with strength. State labor legislation in this period emphasized minimum wages, equal pay, and protection against a harsh working environment. "Protective" standards for women only were not enacted on the Federal level. State laws which limited the hours of work or the weight that could be lifted, though supported by many women's groups, posed problems for those women who did not want these restrictions to exclude them from overtime, nightwork, and certain better paying occupations. As the workplace changed with automation, and as women had temporary experience in more skilled jobs during wartime, many persons saw that women's low earnings were not entirely the result of unequal pay for comparable work. More often the problem was that women were permitted entry into only a few traditionally low-paid job categories.

As the civil rights movement gained momentum during the 1960's, significant gains for minorities were accompanied by a renewed interest in equal rights for women. The prohibition of sex discrimination was included in title VII, and the focus of State legislation began to shift away from protective laws for women toward equal employment opportunity.

A sometimes painful transition period found some women in situations where they would have preferred no change in women's labor laws. Other women, however, expected that women's special benefits would be extended to men and restrictions against nightwork, weight-lifing, or the jobs in which women could work would be overthrown.

The agency administering title VII (EEOC) gradually developed a position supporting this expectation in amicus briefs and in formal guidelines. States varied in their response to title VII. Several, including some that enacted FEP laws banning sex discrimination, retained their women's labor laws.

This, however, raised complicated legal issues. Where State and Federal laws are in conflict and the Federal law does not specify that the State standard will prevail, the Federal prevails. The question as to which State laws conflict with Federal law is one that must be decided by the courts, though courts give great deference to Federal agency interpretations. Courts generally have upheld the EEOC position that title VII supersedes State laws restricting women's employment but have differed with each other regarding extension of women's special benefits to men.

While a transition to equal employment opportunity laws and extension or removal of special laws for women workers is not yet complete, most States have passed beyond the period of widespread uncertainty and litigation.

Minimum wage laws give the best example of benefits for women being extended to men. When title VII was enacted 26 years after passage of the Federal FLSA requiring minimum wage and overtime pay without regard to sex, almost half the State minimum wage laws—15 out of 32—applied to women only. As noted earlier, one State repealed coverage of women. However, extensions or new enactments in other jurisdictions have resulted in 39 laws (including those of the District of Columbia and Puerto Rico) that cover both men and women and only 3 that are restricted to women.

There have been comparable gains for men and women in premium pay for overtime since enactment of title VII. In 1964 half of the dozen or so jurisdictions which had premium pay requirements in minimum wage laws or wage orders for one or more occupations or industries covered women only. Many State legislatures have amended or enacted such standards to cover both sexes, and none have repealed them. Now the benefit is provided in 23 States, the District of Columbia, and Puerto Rico for both men and women, and is restricted to women in only 2 States.

When premium pay for women was provided in an hours law, States frequently repealed it and put an overtime provision in a minimum wage law for both sexes. The new law was sometimes more generous than the old but in one or two instances provided a lesser benefit. In 2 States, however, premium pay in an hours law for women was lost through administrative or judicial rulings without legislation to replace it. North Carolina, which had premium pay for men only, amended the law to extend overtime to women. Of the 7 overtime pay provisions in an hours law in 1975, 4 are for women only.

The acceleration of State legislative action extending minimum wage and overtime to both sexes may have been stimulated in part by Federal amendments extending coverage of the minimum wage and overtime provisions of the FLSA in 1966 and 1974, but clearly title VII was a factor.

Maximum hours laws typify the kind of State statute which was repealed or overruled after enactment of title VII. To illustrate the variety and sequence of events, the next section includes a State by State summary of legislative and administrative events on maximum hours since the enactment of title VII. While other types of labor laws for women have not met with as much judicial and legislative attention, their status is clearly altered and can also best be understood in light of title VII guidelines and court decisions. Each State labor department can give information on the extent to which a particular law is in force in that State.

Maximum hours

Today, no State law setting a daily and/or weekly work hours limitation for women only remains unchanged since enactment of title VII.

There is no Federal limitation of general applicability on daily or weekly hours. The FLSA does require most covered workers to be paid 1½ times the regular rate for hours worked beyond 40 a week.

State hours laws for women, which began to be enacted in mid-nineteenth century, regulated not only maximum hours but in some cases days of rest, meal and rest periods, and nightwork also.

After Congress and some of the States required premium pay for overtime, several States relaxed maximum daily and weekly hours provisions for employers complying with overtime pay requirements.

In 1964, 40 States and the District of Columbia had maximum daily or weekly hours laws for women only in one or more occupations or industries. As shown in chart C, changes since enactment of title VII in 1964 have come through one or more of the following actions:

- Legislatures repealed hours laws or changed the mandatory limit to allow voluntary overtime for women or to require premium pay for overtime;

- Courts invalidated State hours laws as conflicting with title VII.

- State attorney general opinions or administrative rulings invalidated hours laws as conflicting with title VII.

Nightwork limitations

The prohibition or regulation of nightwork by adult women remains in only 4 States—California, Kansas, Rhode Island, and Utah—and Puerto Rico. Kansas and Puerto Rico *prohibit* nightwork by adult women in some occupations or industries, whereas California, Rhode Island, and Utah *regulate* it. **There is no comparable Federal law.**

Sex discrimination guidelines issued under title VII of the Civil Rights Act of 1964 state that laws restricting women's employment conflict with and are superseded by title VII.

Nightwork provisions have not been rescinded or repealed in 2 other States—Ohio and Pennsylvania—but a court case and a State attorney general opinion have nullified them. In New Hampshire, the Department of Labor enforces the provision only for those female employees who desire its protection.

Occupational limitations

Only Wyoming still prohibits women from working in mines. **There is no comparable Federal prohibition.**

In Utah the law was amended to remove the absolute prohibition on women working in mines and instead allow the industrial commission to prohibit such work only if it finds it to be detrimental to the women's health and safety. There are women working in Utah mines.

Laws in three other States remain "on the books" but are no longer enforced. In a court case in Ohio, the law was found to be in conflict with title VII of the Civil Rights Act. In Oklahoma, there are no more underground mines. In Pennsylvania, an opinion by the attorney general declared the law to be superseded by the equal rights provision of the State constitution.

Laws and regulations prohibiting employment of women in establishments serving alcoholic beverages and other limitations based on occupation or working conditions are also generally no longer in effect because of conflict with title VII.

Weightlifting limitations

In 1964 about a dozen jurisdictions had some sort of limitation (expressed in pounds, as a percentage of body weight, or simply "excessive") on the weight women workers could be required to lift or carry. Some of the limitations applied only to certain occupations or industries. Now only Puerto Rico has in effect a specific limit—44 pounds—on the weight any woman worker can be required to lift (a limit of 110 pounds is set for men workers). **There is no Federal weightlifting limit.**

A Consolidated Work Order in Oregon prohibits requiring any employee, rather than just women, to lift "excessive weights." In Washington, emergency employment standards effective from May 1 to August 1, 1975, provided that employees recruited for, employed in, or reassigned to jobs involving the lifting, carrying, pushing, or pulling of weights in excess of 20 pounds must be given prior notification of this element of the job and be instructed in proper lifting techniques.

Sex discrimination guidelines issued under title VII of the 1964 Civil Rights Act provide that State laws or administrative regulations which prohibit the employment of women in jobs requiring the lifting or carrying of weights exceeding certain prescribed limits conflict with and are superseded by title VII.

Although not rescinded or repealed, limits on weight lifting by women workers in California, Massachusetts, and Ohio have been nullified by a court case or State attorney general opinion.

It should be noted that, even though courts have overruled arbitrary weight limits for women only, they have not thereby given employers sanction to require tasks beyond a person's strength, but rather require taking account of individual differences.

Limitations on employment before and after childbirth

Only New York and Puerto Rico still have in effect a provision concerning the employment of women before and/or after childbirth. **There is no Federal statute in this area.**

Recap of state maximum hours laws for women only
1964–1975 (as of July 1)

State	Law in 1964	LEGISLATIVE DEVELOPMENTS		Court Case	Attorney General Opinion or Administrative Decision	Law Enforced for 14 or Fewer Employees
		Repeal	Voluntary Overtime (Women)			
ALABAMA						
ALASKA						
ARIZONA	✓	1970				
ARKANSAS	✓				1973	
CALIFORNIA	✓			1971	1971	
COLORADO	✓	1971				
CONNECTICUT	✓	1973			1972	
DELAWARE	✓	1965				
DISTRICT OF COLUMBIA	✓				1970	
FLORIDA						
GEORGIA						
HAWAII						
IDAHO						
ILLINOIS	✓			1970	1970, 1973	✓
INDIANA						
IOWA						
KANSAS	✓				1969	
KENTUCKY	✓	1974		1971	1972	
LOUISIANA	✓			1971		
MAINE	✓				1973	
MARYLAND	✓	1972				
MASSACHUSETTS	✓			1971	1970, 1971	
MICHIGAN	✓	1975			1969	
MINNESOTA	✓	1974			1972	
MISSISSIPPI	✓				1969	
MISSOURI	✓	1972		1971	1971	
MONTANA	✓	1971				
NEBRASKA	✓	1969				
NEVADA	✓	1975				
NEW HAMPSHIRE	✓				1971*	
NEW JERSEY	✓	1971				
NEW MEXICO	✓				1972	
NEW YORK	✓	1970				
NORTH CAROLINA	✓	1973**				
NORTH DAKOTA	✓	1973			1969	
OHIO	✓			1972		✓
OKLAHOMA	✓				1969	
OREGON	✓	1971				
PENNSYLVANIA	✓			1971	1969	
PUERTO RICO						
RHODE ISLAND	✓	1974			1970*	
SOUTH CAROLINA	✓	1972				
SOUTH DAKOTA	✓	1973			1969	
TENNESSEE	✓				1972	
TEXAS	✓		1971		1974***	
UTAH	✓		1973			
VERMONT	✓	1970				
VIRGINIA	✓	1974				
WASHINGTON	✓				1970, 1971	
WEST VIRGINIA	✓					
WISCONSIN	✓				1970	
WYOMING	✓					

*Administrative rulings state that the employer may permit but not require women to work beyond the maximum limitation (voluntary overtime hours).
**However, women are now subject to a maximum hours limitation formerly applying to men only.
***Attorney general ruled voluntary overtime amendment invalid because of conflict with title VII.

Sex discrimination guidelines issued under title VII of the Civil Rights Act of 1964 state that *laws* restricting women's employment conflict with and are superseded by title VII; moreover, *employers* may not discriminate against applicants or employees because of pregnancy.

It was not until the most recent revision of the EEOC sex discrimination guidelines, in April 1972, that the agency specifically listed State limitations on employment of pregnant and immediately postpregnant women as among those found to discriminate on the basis of sex. Even before then, Vermont had repealed its ban on employment 2 weeks before and 4 weeks after childbirth. Connecticut and Massachusetts followed suit in repealing restrictions, and the attorney general of Missouri ruled that employers need no longer comply with the invalid State restriction. Pre- and post-pregnancy employment restrictions in Washington wage orders covering women and minors only in some occupations or industries are no longer enforced, following amendment of female and child labor laws in September 1973 to make them applicable to all persons in employment and eliminate distinctions between the sexes.

The New York law prohibiting employment for 4 weeks after childbirth was amended in 1973 to permit earlier return upon approval of a physician.

The Puerto Rico provision states that pregnant women employed in offices, commercial and industrial establishments, and public utilities are entitled to a rest which includes a period commencing 4 weeks before and ending 4 weeks after childbirth. During that period the women are to be paid one-half of their regular pay, and their jobs must be held for them. To claim these benefits, a woman worker in one of the named establishments must present a medical certification that her state of pregnancy requires the rest. Such certificates are procurable at any public medical facility, without cost. The postnatal rest period may be extended up to 12 additional weeks if a worker suffers a disability attributable to the birth. Discharging a pregnant worker without just cause and refusal to reinstate a worker after childbirth are punishable by fine or award of damages.

Meal periods

Laws or wage orders in effect in 18 States and Puerto Rico require that meal periods—usually unpaid and varying from 20 minutes to 1 hour in duration—be allowed in some or all industries. **There is no comparable Federal law.**

Sex discrimination guidelines issued under title VII of the 1964 Civil Rights Act provide that where meal periods are required for women they shall be provided for men also unless precluded by business necessity, in which case the employer shall not provide them for members of either sex.

In the following jurisdictions meal periods must be allowed both men and women:

Illinois	Nevada	Oregon
Kentucky	New Hampshire	Puerto Rico
Massachusetts	New York	Washington
Nebraska	North Dakota	

In the following States meal period provisions apply to women only:

Arkansas	Kansas	Rhode Island
California	Louisiana	Utah
Colorado	New Mexico	

Wisconsin *recommends* a meal period of at least 30 minutes reasonably close to the usual meal period time or near the middle of a shift.

Although coverage of men in some States came about through extension to them of provisions that previously covered women only, the provisions of other jurisdictions which applied to women only were nullified by a court case or an opinion by a State attorney general or a corporation counsel. Accordingly meal period requirements are no longer generally in effect in the following jurisdictions:

District of Columbia	Ohio
Maine	Pennsylvania

Rest periods

Laws or wage orders in effect in 10 States require 10–15 minute breaks or rest periods during working hours in one or more occupations or industries. **There is no comparable Federal law.**

Sex discrimination guidelines issued under title VII of the 1964 Civil Rights Act provide that where rest periods are required for women they shall be provided for men also unless precluded by business necessity, in which case the employer shall not provide them for members of either sex.

In the following States rest periods must be allowed both men and women:

Kentucky	North Dakota	Washington
Nevada	Oregon	

In the following States rest period provisions apply to women only:

Arkansas	Colorado	Wyoming
California	Utah	

Although coverage of men in 5 States came about through extension to them of provisions that previously covered women only, the rest period provisions of Pennsylvania and Puerto Rico which applied to women only were nullified by an opinion of a State attorney general and a court case.

Seating

A number of jurisdictions—through statutes, minimum wage orders, and other regulations—have established employment standards for women relating to plant facilities such as seats, lunchrooms, dressing rooms, restrooms, and toilet rooms. Only seating provisions are included in the summary. **There are no Federal requirements for seating.**

Sex discrimination guidelines issued under title VII of the 1964 Civil Rights Act provide that where physical facilities are required for women they shall be provided for men also unless precluded by business necessity, in which case the employer shall not provide them for members of either sex.

Laws or regulations in effect in 22 States, the District of Columbia, and Puerto Rico require that seats be provided.

In the following States seats must be provided for both men and women:

Florida   Massachusetts   Oregon

In the following jurisdictions the law requires them only for women:

Alabama	Missouri	Puerto Rico
Arkansas	Montana	Rhode Island
California	New Hampshire	Texas
District of Columbia	New Jersey	Utah
Georgia	New Mexico	West Virginia
Idaho	New York	Wisconsin
Louisiana	Oklahoma	Wyoming

Although coverage of men in Massachusetts and Oregon came about through legislative extension to them of provisions that previously covered women only, the provisions of Maine, Ohio, and Pennsylvania, which applied to women only, were nullified by a court case or an opinion by a State attorney general.

Legislation to prohibit sex discrimination on the basis of pregnancy

On December 7, 1976, the Supreme Court in its *General Electric Company* v. *Gilbert* decision ruled that an employer can exclude pregnancy disability benefits from medical/health insurance programs without violating the 1964 Civil Rights Act. The decision acted as a catalyst causing labor unions and women's rights groups to organize into a united front and to press for legislation to overturn the Supreme Court's edict. Hearings before the Subcommittee on Employment Opportunities on H.R. 5055 and H.R. 6075, legislation to prohibit sex discrimination on the basis of pregnancy, commenced on April 6, 1977. On September 16, 1977, the Senate passed by a 75–11 vote, its version of the same legislation, S. 995. The hearings continue in the House subcommittee with strong testimony being submitted in support of and opposition to the passage of the legislation. Noted supporters include the Carter Administration, numerous federal agencies, labor unions and civil rights groups. Arguing against passage are various business and professional associations, individual firms and private individuals. The high cost of extra benefits and increased employee absenteeism are among the most frequently cited prohibitive rationales.

In addition to the full text of the proposed legislation, selected testimonies presented before the House subcommittee are offered to provide insight into the positive and negative effects that passage of H.R. 5055 and H.R. 6075 would have on industry and the individual worker.

[H.R. 5055, 95th Cong., 1st Sess.]

A bill, to amend title VII of the Civil Rights Act of 1964 to prohibit sex discrimination on basis of pregnancy

Be it enacted by the Senate and House of Representatives of the United States of America in Congress assembled, That title VII of the Civil Rights Act of 1964 is amended as follows:

Section 701 is amended by adding thereto a new subsection (k) as follows:

"(k) The terms 'because of sex' or 'on the basis of sex' include, but are not limited to, because of or on the basis of pregnancy, childbirth, or related medical conditions, and women affected by pregnancy, childbirth, or related medical conditions shall be treated the same for all employment-related purposes, including receipt of benefits under fringe benefit programs, as other persons not so affected but similar in their ability or inability to work, and nothing in section 703(h) of this title shall be interpreted to permit otherwise."

[H.R. 6075, 95th Cong., 1st Sess.]

A bill, to amend title VII of the Civil Rights Act of 1964 to prohibit sex discrimination on the basis of pregnancy

Be it enacted by the Senate and House of Representatives of the United States of America in Congress assembled, That title VII of the Civil Rights Act of 1964 is amended as follows:

SECTION 1. Section 701 is amended by adding thereto a new subsection (k) as follows:

"(k) The terms 'because of sex' or 'on the basis of sex' include, but are not limited to, because of or on the basis of pregnancy, childbirth, or related medical conditions, and women affected by pregnancy, childbirth or related medical conditions shall be treated the same for all employment-related purposes, including receipt of benefits under fringe benefit programs, as other persons not so affected but similar in their ability or inability to work, and nothing in section 703(h) of this title shall be interpreted to permit otherwise."

SECTION 2. The amendment made by this Act shall be effective upon the date of enactment: *Provided,* That an employer who, either directly or through contributions to a fringe benefit fund or insurance program, is providing benefits under a fringe benefit program which is in violation of section 2000e of title 42, United States Code, and the following, as amended by this Act shall not, either directly or by failing to contribute adequately to the fringe benefit fund or insurance program, reduce the benefits or the compensation provided to any employee in order to comply with the provisions of section 2000e of title 42, United States Code, and the following, as amended by this Act.

[S.995, 95th Cong., 1st Sess.]

An act to amend title VII of the Civil Rights Act of 1964 to prohibit sex discrimination on the basis of pregnancy

Be it enacted by the Senate and House of Representatives of the United States of America in Congress assembled,

SECTION 1. That section 701 of the Civil Rights Act of 1964 is amended by adding at the end thereof the following new subsection:

"(k) The terms 'because of sex' or 'on the basis of sex' include, but are not limited to, because of or on the basis of pregnancy, childbirth, or related medical conditions; and women affected by pregnancy, childbirth, or related medical conditions shall be treated the same for all employment-related purposes, including receipt of benefits under fringe benefit programs, as other persons not so affected but similar in their ability or inability to work, and nothing in section 703(h) of this title shall be interpreted to permit otherwise."

SECTION 2. (a) Except as provided in subsection (b) the amendment made by this Act shall be effective on the date of enactment.

(b) The provisions of the amendment made by section 1 of this Act shall not apply to any fringe benefit program or fund, or insurance program which is in effect on the date of enactment of this Act, until July 1, 1978, or one hundred and eighty days after enactment of this Act whichever is the greater time period.

SECTION 3. Until the expiration of a period of one year from the date of enactment of this Act or, if there is an applicable collective-bargaining agreement in effect on the date of enactment of this Act, until the termination of that agreement, no person who, on the date of enactment of this Act is providing either by direct payment or by making contributions to a fringe benefit fund or insurance program, benefits in violation with this Act shall, in order to come into compliance with this Act, reduce the benefits or the compensation provided any employee on the date of enactment of this Act, either directly or by failing to provide sufficient contributions to a fringe benefit fund or insurance program: *Provided*, That where the costs of such benefits on the date of enactment of this Act are apportioned between employers and employees, the payments or contributions required to comply with this Act may be made by employers and employees in the same proportion: *And provided further*, That nothing in this section shall prevent the readjustment of benefits or compensation for reasons unrelated to compliance with this Act.

Passed the Senate September 16 (legislative day, September 15), 1977.

Attest: J. S. KIMMITT,
Secretary

Testimony of Laurence Gold, Special Counsel, AFL-CIO, before the subcommittee on employment opportunities of the House Education and Labor Committee

AFL-CIO's interest.   The AFL-CIO supports the principle of equality of opportunity in the workplace, and has worked hard to assure that employers eliminate practices which discriminate against minorities and women. To further that goal, the AFL-CIO devoted its efforts to passage of Title VII of the Civil Rights Act of 1964.

To complement our legislative program the AFL-CIO and its affiliates have sought to further the important goal of employment equality for women through collective bargaining agreements that contain the best possible benefits—including income support coverage—for all workers, including pregnant workers. In those negotiations, we have found that some employers *would* extend coverage to pregnancy-related disabilities, but that others would do no more in this area than was required by law. Accordingly, such unions as the International Union of Electrical, Radio and Machine Workers, AFL-CIO, and the Communications Workers of America AFL-CIO determined to work through the courts to make clear to employers that Title VII did impose a legal requirement to treat pregnant women fairly. Those unions were in the forefront of the litigation to help secure better benefits for women, and in particular for pregnant women. The AFL-CIO, too, joined in that litigation by filing briefs *amicus curiae* in the Supreme Court in support of the position of its affiliates.

After the decision in *Gilbert* v. *General Electric,* it became clear to the AFL-CIO that legislation was needed, and needed promptly, if the goal of fair treatment for pregnant workers was to be realized. Therefore, the Federation joined with a broad-based coalition of organizations and individuals to help secure legislation clarifying that Title VII was in fact always intended to provide the protection to pregnant women for which AFL-CIO and many others had been working.

Why the legislation is important.   Ultimate equality for working women entails far more than simply eliminating "women's jobs" and "men's jobs." It means assuring that women are treated as having the same long-term interest in staying on the job as men, and in assuring that they have the same opportunity as men to keep a job. Much of the disparate treatment of women in employment has come from unfounded assumptions about their lack of interest in continuing careers because at some time they are likely to become pregnant and to have children. In fact, discrimination against women in employment revolves in large part around the pregnancy question. Failing to pass legislation to overrule the Supreme Court's decision in *Gilbert* v. *General Electric* will permit such discrimination to continue.

Practices regarding pregnancy which have adversely affected women workers.   Employers in the United States have in some instances sought to exclude women generally from employment on the ground that women may become pregnant, and that the pregnancy could make continuance on the job difficult. See, e.g. *Cheatwood* v. *South Central Bell Telephone Co.*, 303 F. Supp. 754 (M.D. Ala. 1969). Women applying for jobs have customarily been, and still are, questioned about their marital status, and their intentions in regard to childbearing and use of birth control. Still other employers have in effect fired women at some specified stage in a pregnancy, permitting them to reapply for jobs later as new employees with attendant loss of seniority privileges and pension rights.

Of course, mandatory separation where loss of seniority is involved has ramifications beyond a temporary loss of pay. Women dependent upon their income but intending to have children may be constrained to accept less desirable jobs which do not provide for mandatory pregnancy leave. Further, if seniority is lost, a woman's entire career could be affected: there may be no job to return to when she has recovered or, if she does return to her old position, she will have a slower advancement to higher positions, because other employees hired later will have priority.

Another discriminatory employer practice affecting pregnant women is the exclusion from the provision for a certain number of absences with pay for days lost due to sickness, prohibiting use of accumulated sick leave for absences due to pregnancy, childbirth, or recovery therefrom. The obvious result of such a policy, is to cause the women affected to lose payment of wages or a portion thereof even though they return to work promptly upon recovery, and even though the effect of permitting use of accumulated sick leave on the employer is precisely what it would have been if any other disability had occurred.

The overall effect of the special disadvantages imposed on pregnant women, and women workers because they might become pregnant, is to relegate women in general, and pregnant women particularly, to a second-class status with regard to career advancement and continuity of employment and wages.

These disadvantages are particularly serious because 70% of the 35 million women who work do so out of economic necessity—they are divorced, widowed, single, or married to men who earn less than $7,000 per year and who therefore must depend on two salaries to make ends meet. Many of these women are likely to be working when they are pregnant. We know that because the number of women with preschool children who are in the workforce has steadily risen, until currently almost 40% of mothers with children under 6 work. So for financial or other reasons, women are not as much regarding child-bearing and child-rearing as cause for substantial breaks in their career, and are more than ever likely to need adequate income protection for the short time during which they are medically disabled from working.

Disability benefits as an example of disadvantageous treatment of pregnant workers. The refusal of employers to cover pregnancy-related disabilities the same as other medical disabilities was the problem that precipitated the *Gilbert* case. That refusal of equal treatment is an excellent example of the irrationality of discrimination against pregnant workers, and the crippling effect of such discrimination on women workers. Employers state that both sick leave and disability insurance have certain business purposes. General Electric noted in its 1957 Annual Report that the overall purpose of benefit plans is "to attract top-quality people at all levels and encourage them to make their careers with the company."

Disability insurance is intended a) to remove the fear of loss of income when it is most needed; b) to encourage employees to receive medical attention as soon as possible, thus minimizing the severity of disabilities and assuring maximum productivity; c) to foster morale and loyalty to the company; d) to provide for maximum use by supervisors of trained employees by creating a disincentive to forcing an employee able to work to stay home.

Clearly, all of these purposes apply with full force to women who are medically unable to work because of pregnancy. First, the need for assured income is if anything greater during childbirth related disabilities than during other periods an employee cannot work for physical reasons. The possibility of lost time due to physical disability is not a vague fear but certainty during the period immediately before labor begins. And, the need for assured income during the period immediately following childbirth is heightened by the need to support the new infant, and by the added cost of child-care when the woman does return to work. To assure herself of needed income, a woman intending to bear children could well choose an otherwise undesirable job providing income maintenance during pregnancy-related disabilities over a position affording better career prospects.

Second, a woman who is not covered by a disability program for the period of childbirth and recovery therefrom is likely to return to work before she is fully able to assume her former responsibilities. As a result, her performance may be impaired, with a loss of productivity which could hamper her future advancement.

Third, the exclusion of pregnancy-related disabilities is certain to make an affected woman, and indeed all women with plans to bear children, feel that they are less-valued employees, and that the employer has little regard for their careers. As a result, the desire for advancement may be impaired, and the link to the company as a long-term employer lessened. The argument that the fact that many women who take pregnancy leave without pay fail to return to work justifies disparate treatment of pregnancy-related disabilities is entirely circular. That is to say, if an employer excludes such women from a program designed to promote employees' loyalty to the company, it is little wonder that they do not display that loyalty.

Finally, when the company has no responsibility for sustaining the income of a woman disabled by physiological aspects of childbirth, supervisors are encouraged to insist that she stay home, rather than accommodating the job to her condition. For example, an employer faced with the prospect of paying prolonged disability benefits to a man whose heart condition makes his stressful job impossible for him would, rationally, attempt to find a less-stressful but nonetheless productive job he can perform. If it has no such liability with regard to pregnancy-related disabilities, then in those situations in which pregnancy or complications thereof render the woman unable to perform her original job at peek efficiency, the impetus will be to put her on leave rather than retain her in another capacity. Indeed, an employer who does not provide income maintenance for pregnancy-related disabilities would be much more likely to mandate arbitrary pregnancy separation policies, since such policies would then be cost-free to the employer.

Passage of H.R. 5055 is vitally important to end practices which seriously and adversely affect pregnant women workers just described, and to reverse the Supreme Court's ruling about pregnancy-related disability benefits in the *Gilbert* case.

Why the cost argument against H.R. 5055 is unsound. The argument most often raised by employers against prohibiting pregnancy-related discrimination is that the cost of equal treatment is too high. To answer that argument, at this point we wish to focus on the costs of providing the same income maintenance coverage for pregnancy-related disabilities as is provided for all other disabilities. First, we will examine the high figures that have been suggested to show why they are just plain unrealistic, and then we will try, on the basis of the best data available to us, to estimate what the actual additional cost of coverage would be if this legislation passes.

The unrealistic estimates.   A very high cost estimate for H.R. 5055 has been floated around in an effort to kill the bill. It is G.E.'s estimate, introduced at the trial in the *Gilbert* case, of the cost for providing all U.S. employees covered for short term disability with maternity coverage on the same basis as coverage for any other disability. G.E. as the defendant in that case suggested that the increase in total benefits per year over those now provided would be $1.6 billion. To reach that figure, G.E. calculates the cost of providing pregnancy-related disability coverage to women workers with pregnancy-related disabilities, then deducts the cost "benefits currently provided" for pregnancy related disabilities.

Although G.E.'s approach is right, the figures it uses are based on several greatly misleading assumptions. First, G.E. calculates that it would cost about $1.845 billion to provide complete coverage for pregnancy-related disabilities for an average coverage of 30 weeks. However, uncontroverted testimony in the *Gilbert* case showed that more than 90% of women would be disabled an average of only 6 weeks. So the G.E. figures on cost throughout the United States have to be divided by 5. (Also, some plans exclude payments for the first 8 days of disability. In such cases, women would only get *paid* for 5 weeks.) Even if *no* other adjustments were made in the G.E. statistics, taking one-fifth of the 30 weeks cost and deducting the current costs figure puts H.R. 5055's cost at $145 million. This is a far cry from G.E.'s $1.6 billion claim.

Second, G.E. in arriving at its claim deducts $225 million for benefits now provided. But fourteen jurisdictions (13 states and the District of Columbia), which accounted for almost 40% of the births in the United States in 1975, now require employers to provide some kind of disability-benefits coverage for pregnancy under their own *state* laws. And, not all employers in those jurisdictions were, at the time G.E. made its estimate, providing such coverage. Therefore, the cost of the coverage which must be provided independent of any change in Title VII, whether or not it is being provided at this very minute, must be substantially increased. When the costs effect of these state laws is taken into account, the cost of H.R. 5055 is further reduced.

Finally, the G.E. cost figures do not in any way take into account the extent to which eliminating pregnancy discrimination saves the employer money—by encouraging good, experienced workers to stay on the job, thereby increasing productivity and reducing costs of retraining, and reducing the likelihood that workers will use unemployment compensation. Nor does it take into account the saving to other citizens, because such benefits reduce the likelihood that workers with pregnancy-related disabilities will need to resort to unemployment compensation or welfare benefits.

Each of the miscalculations made by G.E. provides a guide for looking at the other inflated cost figures for H.R. 5055 stated by those opposed to H.R. 5055. If correct assumptions or facts about the basic factors—the duration of benefits, the amount to be paid, the number of employees already covered or lawfully required to be covered by such plans—are not used, the resulting gross "cost" figures will not be accurate.

The recurrence of industry over-estimates on cost of providing pregnancy-related disabilities coverage is apparent from statistics provided by the Society of Actuaries. Their tables show that for plans for the years 1972 through 1974, (the most recent for which figures are available), the amounts actually paid by companies of less than 1,000 employees were from 38% to 40% of the amounts that the actuaries estimated would be paid. The wrong estimates were attributed to declining birthrates; those same declining birthrates will continue to affect the cost of providing disability benefits for pregnancy-related disabilities. These figures provide some guidance to what credence should be given to some of the high cost figures used as scare-tactics by employers and insurance companies.

What are the actual costs.   Accurately projecting the actual increase in costs to employers of amending Title VII by H.R. 5055 is slightly more difficult.

One should first examine the estimates of increased cost per employee of extended coverage other than industry figures presently available. One study which has been done shows that annual costs of covering pregnancy-related disabilities under disability benefits plans may average $15 per employee using April, 1974, data. Another shows that on the basis of 1971–72 data, expense would total about $20 per employee. Still another study shows that if costs are related to female employees only; the "unit cost" (cost per employee) would be about $41 using 1971–72 data. Finally, yet another study shows that annual costs would average approximately $40 to $50 per female employee for a paid leave of 14–16 weeks. As we have pointed out, that is about twice the average leave present experience indicates would be compensable. Therefore, the cost per employee of the coverage which would be required is not great at all, and when compared to the cost to the employer of turnover, and the great hardship and inequity to women by not providing it, it seems even smaller.

Another way to look at the cost data is to ascertain how much passage of H.R. 5055 would increase overall hourly wage costs. Those figures show that the increase would be miniscule between $.004 and $.01 to the hourly rate of employees in an affected company, or an increase to the wage bill of between 1/10 and 2/10 of one percent.

A final method of approach is to calculate the cost impact of H.R. 5055 on disability plans from the best available data and on the basis of the most reasonable assumptions suggested by that data. The cost figure we arrive at is about $1.50 per American worker or roughly $130 million in total cost. And this cost estimate does not take into account even the most obvious monetary benefits to the employer—reduction in turn-over, and reduction in tax-supported unemployment compensation and welfare costs. Certainly, the critical public goal of equal treatment for women, and the elimination of the loss of talent caused by discrimination, is worth far more than these relatively small amounts.

In 1975, 1,918,214 babies were born outside the fourteen jurisdictions which already require pregnancy-related disability coverage discussed previously. We can assume that about 40% of those are born to women working during pregnancy. (That assumption in turn rests on the reasonable premise that a disproportionate number of those pregnant workers don't work in the 14 jurisdictions already requiring coverage.) Thus, in 1975 there were approximately 767,285 women potentially to be covered by pregnancy-related disability benefits plans (assuming one baby per mother). Of this number we can assume that approximately 63%, or 460,371, work for employers having some form of income maintenance during temporary disabilities. Again this is assuming that there is not a disproportion of women covered by such plans in the 14 already-covered jurisdictions. Of those, approximately 40% would have maternity coverage for an average maximum of six weeks. That leaves 276,273 women giving birth in 1975 who worked for employers having disability plans which did not cover pregnancy. Assuming the average short term disability benefit for women in 1975 was about $78 per week, providing disability benefits for pregnancy-related disabilities for the full average period of six weeks would cost American industry roughly $130 million in increased costs.

Finally, we have been advised that a bill has been drafted which incorporates the language of H.R. 5055 and adds a further provision which states that employers who are now discriminating in regard to pregnancy-related disabilities will not be able, if this bill is enacted, to decrease, or cause to be decreased, the benefits or compensation provided to their employees generally in order to come into compliance. I wish to take this occasion to state the AFL-CIO's support for such a perfecting amendment. The principle embodied in the amendment is incorporated in the Equal Pay Act and is the one the courts have generally followed in Title VII cases. It is evident that legislation designed to correct discrimination cannot achieve its objective if an employer who has been discriminating responds by decreasing benefits or compensation. The proper rule is that such an employer must correct his wrong and put all his employees in an equal position by raising the discriminatees to the position of his other employees. While the amendment simply states existing law explicitly, in light of the statements of some of those opposed to H.R. 5055 that the result of the bill will be to lower the benefits and compensation of workers not presently being discriminated against, we believe it is sound to spell out the intent of the legislation.

*Statement of the National Association of Manufacturers on H.R. 6075
submitted to the Subcommittee on Employment Opportunities of the
House Committee on Education and Labor*

As a representative of more than 13,000 employers of all sizes, the National Association of Manufacturers is deeply concerned with equal employment opportunity.

We have closely studied provisions of H.R. 6075 which amends Title VII of the Civil Rights Act in order to clarify the Act's provisions as they relate to pregnancy. The NAM recognizes the important contributions which women make through their work and we continue to support and encourage equal treatment of women in all phases of employment. We feel that discrimination against any employee, whether on the basis of sex, race, religion or national origin, is ultimately detrimental to business operations.

We do not wish to argue the issue of discrimination, however, for as we see it, the question of whether or not to treat pregnancy as any other disability is not necessarily a women's issue. The true decision that must be made is how far society chooses to go in subsidizing parenthood. We do not pretend that all pregnancies are planned or that pregnancy is entirely voluntary. We have, however, moved into an era when a couple has considerable control over becoming parents. Within this climate, it is appropriate to ask how much of the economic responsibility for parenthood will be assumed by those men and women who choose to have children and how much of the responsibility will be assumed by society—either directly through taxation or indirectly through requirements placed on employers.

It is time, in dealing with social legislation, to begin setting some priorities, because it is becoming more and more apparent that we cannot do all things. In the broadest sense of the term, our resources are limited and we must begin to think in terms of where we are going and how we want to use our resources.

The issue of cost may not be a legitimate factor when balanced off against equitable treatment. However—and this has been illustrated year after year in extended debate on national health insurance—cost certainly must be considered in making important social decisions. The cost for rearing a family of four is estimated to be around $250,000 from cradle through college. The extent to which society can assume this cost is virtually unlimited. Congress *could* require that employers pay all of a family's medical expenses; Congress *could* require that employers provide disability benefits for pregnancy; Congress *could* require that employers provide paid leave to both mothers and fathers for child rearing; Congress *could* require employers to finance day-care centers; and Congress *could* require employers to subsidize a child's college or vocational education. But all members of Congress certainly must ask themselves if their constituents are prepared to pay the cost for any of these requirements.

The NAM believes that H.R. 6075, in its sweeping language and broad implications, goes too far in requiring employers to assume the economic responsibilities of parenthood. And no one should be so naive to think that employers will bear the cost alone. All of their employees (either directly or indirectly), and ultimately the consumer will share the burden.

The scope of H.R. 6075. This bill was introduced as a reaction to the Supreme Court's decision in *General Electric Company* v. *Gilbert*. The emotionality surrounding this case has obscured a practical consideration of the merits of this legislation. We would point out that the Gilbert case involved one company with one plan and that the central issue was coverage of pregnancy under a weekly accident and sickness benefit plan.

Enactment of H.R. 6075 would affect all employers, many of whom already provide coverage for pregnancy. Furthermore, it would impact not just disability plans, but all employer-sponsored benefit plans. Consideration of this bill should be taken out of the context of the Gilbert case and it sould be evaluated separately. We believe that Congress is taking a much too simplistic view of a very complex issue. In the past, we have seen other "employee protection" legislation passed. But the true impact and burdens of such legislation on business operations has been enormous. We would hope that before this happens again, serious consideration will be given both to the true need for H.R. 6075 and to the practical implications of the bill as it is currently written.

Need for the legislation? There is a pervasive, erroneous notion that employers arbitrarily choose what they will and will not cover in employee benefit plans. The truth is that, in providing benefits, employers generally respond to employees' needs—articulated either through collective bargaining or directly from employees. Union-free employers frequently conduct employee benefit surveys to compile reliable statistics on how employees wish the benefit dollars to be spent. This same observation can be made on employer personnel policies, i.e. they generally adhere to the needs of the employees.

In its testimony before this Subcommittee last April, the Campaign to End Discrimination Against Pregnant Workers stated as justification for this legislation the following:

"Employers routinely fire pregnant workers, refuse to hire them, strip them of seniority rights, and deny them sick leave and medical benefits given other workers."

This statement simply is not true today and could not be verified statistically. It is a very rare medical plan that totally excludes any coverage for pregnancy-related treatment; approximately 40 percent of disability plans in effect today provide some coverage for pregnancy; and seniority rights are usually protected through a company's leave of absence policy.

The AFL-CIO told the Subcommittee on Employment Opportunities that:

"Much of the disparate treatment of women in employment has come from unfounded assumptions about their lack of interest in continuing careers because at some time they are likely to become pregnant and have children."

The truth is that women who bear children have not consistently indicated such an interest in a continuing career. The best data available shows that 40 to 50 percent of women taking pregnancy leave do not return to work. When a woman takes time off to have a child, there is inevitably some break in her career. But the length of that interruption has traditionally been determined to a large degree by the woman herself.

With the changing nature of the workforce and continuing problems with inflation, it becomes apparent that more women will seek coverage for pregnancy-related expenses. But the details of this coverage can much better be determined jointly by employees and employers than through legislation such as H.R. 6075, which in its presently written form will be extremely expensive to society.

Practical implications of H.R. 6075: Section 1.   As we interpret the language of Section 1 of H.R. 6075, the bill would not only require that employers cover pregnancy under disability plans (as was the issue in the *Gilbert* case), but that pregnancy will be covered in such plans like any other disability. Furthermore, Section 1 is susceptible to the interpretation that pregnancy must be covered under employer-sponsored medical plans and that this coverage must be equal to that for any other medical condition.

The NAM wonders if Congress really intends such sweeping legislation. If the intent of the legislation is to insure that coverage for pregnancy, childbirth, and other medical conditions be included in fringe benefit plans, then the language should be changed; because what we have now in Section 1 would do more than that. Of course, the total impact of Section 1 on benefit plans would come to light only after the employer is given the responsibility for compliance—after the massive interpretive regulations which this bill would require are promulgated—but we can already point to problems.

Disability plans: The duration of benefit payments under disability plans varies all over the board. Some plans only pay for a maximum of a few weeks; others pay as much as 52 weeks. Within the administration of these plans, the benefit period for disabilities also varies considerably: it may be two weeks for pneumonia and it may be six months for a heart attack. The benefit period is determined largely by the attending physician who certifies disability and also, to some extent, by the plan's experience with an illness, i.e. the standard duration of incapacitation. Under such plans, disabilities must be treated individually. In other words, what is adequate time off for one disability may be quite inadequate for another type of disability. Therefore, adequate time off for pregnancy would not necessarily be comparable to that for a broken toe or major surgery.

Whereas all other benefit periods are related only to the ability of the employee to work, pregnancy is different. The actual disability period for the woman must be separated from the subsequent needs of the child. As the Act is currently written, pregnancy disability could realistically be expected to begin with morning sickness and continue through childbirth until a physician certifies the woman as able to work. Since doctors are inclined to listen to the patient's view on ability to work, he may have difficulty separating her well-being from her desire to stay with the child.

In its testimony, The Campaign to End Discrimination Against Pregnant Workers stated that:

" . . . all pregnant women have some period of disability, beginning in the normal pregnancy with labor itself and continuing through the normal recuperation period of 3 to 8 weeks after childbirth."

It is very unlikely, however, that under Section 1 as it is currently written such a limitation could be applied to the disability period. If a plan pays benefits to a maximum of 52 weeks and a doctor certifies the woman's disability for that length of time, then under Section 1 employers would be required to pay benefits for a full year.

Also under Section 1, the term "related medical conditions" is undefined. Would post-partum depression be included? And if so, what would happen to a plan that excludes payment of mental and emotional disorders? Would the plan then have to cover all types of depression? This possibility raises the spectre of a significant portion of employees—both men and women—drawing extended benefits for emotional problems. And the potential for abuse in this area is horrendous.

Finally, there is the probability that, without some reasonable limitation on duration of benefits, an employer's disability plan could become a type of extended severance pay plan. Since 40 to 50 percent of the women who take pregnancy leave do not return to work, it can be anticipated that close to half of the disability payments will constitute severance pay. Such a situation would result in a special termination benefit for a single class of employee (pregnant women) which is denied other employees.

Medical plans: The language of Section 1 appears to require that medical plans provide the same coverage for maternity expenses as it does for other types of illness or injury. This requirement shows a serious lack of understanding of group medical plans. Furthermore, it promises to exacerbate the problems employers are having with health care cost escalation—a situation which is reaching crisis stage.

It is a relatively rare medical plan that covers all types of disorders and all types of services on the same basis. A plan may, for example, require a cost-sharing from the employee of 20 percent for purely physical disorders but require a 50 percent cost-sharing for mental disorders. A plan may cover certain procedures if peformed in a hospital while excluding those procedures if performed in a doctor's office.

The very divergent nature of medical plan coverages makes the requirements of Section 1 virtually impossible. The first problem employers will have with Section 1 is figuring out how to alter their medical plans so that all coverages are equal. For example, will a plan which uses a surgical schedule be in violation of the Act if obstetrical procedures are reimbursed at a different rate from an appendectomy? Suppose a plan pays hospital benefits for all other disabilities up to a maximum of 180 days but limits the number of days for a normal pregnancy to 20 days? Will the plan be required to cover hospital stays for a normal pregnancy up to 180 days? These kinds of requirements would result in serious over-coverage in medical plans and would require needless increases in premiums.

Furthermore, as we interpret Section 2, if a medical plan provides more liberal benefits for pregnancy than for other disabilities, then all benefits must be brought up to equal those for maternity. For example, if a plan provides first dollar coverage for doctor visits related to pregnancy but requires a $50 deductible for doctor visits related to other treatment, it appears that Section 2 would require that the deductible be totally eliminated. Another example: A plan might cover hospital charges for a normal pregnancy at 80% up to a maximum of $600, then after a $100 deductible pays the excess expenses at 100%. But this same plan might pay hospital expenses for other disabilities at 80% up to a maximum of $2,000 and then pay 100% of the excess. In this instance, the plan would have to be completely redesigned to bring all other reimbursements in line with the more liberal pregnancy schedule. These examples are not unrealistic and the changes which would be required fly in the face of employers' efforts to rationally contain escalating health care costs through plan design.

We can also point to another problem. Some medical plans require that maternity benefits be paid only if conception occurred after the effective date of the plan. In order to equalize treatment of pregnancy, a plan could require that all disabilities be subject to a "pre-existing conditions" provision. However, it appears that Section 2 would prohibit such an action, since this provision could have the effect of reducing benefits for other disabilities. The only thing an employer could do would be to eliminate the requirements for pregnancy, thus picking up a medical liability which was in effect before the employee came under his plan.

Effective date: A final general note—this bill provides no lead-in time for employers to amend their plans. Should this bill be enacted, some reasonable period must be provided for employers to set up the coverage the bill mandates. As a purely practical matter it is necessary not only to plan fiscally for the added coverage, but also to redesign plans and re-negotiate with insurance carriers, where necessary. The practical reality that these changes could not be accomplished overnight must be considered.

Practical implications of H.R. 6075: Section 2. The practical problems resultant from Section 1 pale by comparison with those of Section 2. Indeed, if the function of H.R. 6075 is to eliminate differential treatment resulting from pregnancy, Section 2 is superfluous at best: the Act's purpose is fully achieved by the first section. More accurately, Section 2 appears to have been appended as a continuous penalty to those employers foolish enough to have offered benefit plans in the past. It says in effect that employers who yesterday excluded pregnancy from fringe benefit plans—although such treatment was fully permissible at the time—must compensate by not only adding on these new benefits but also continuing them indefinitely into the future—this despite the fact that the employer was never obliged to provide any benefits to begin with and would not be so obliged now had he not offered benefits at all. Indeed it serves as competitive punishment to those who have afforded their employees fringe benefits vis a vis those who have provided none at all.

Section 1 gives us the problem of determining the level at which benefits must be provided. Section 2 creates a further problem: that of the duration for which such benefit plans must continue. It is questionable whether the wording of Section 2 would allow even an employer whose plan has been brought into compliance ever to reduce benefits across the board. Would demonstration of imminent bankruptcy constitute acceptable grounds for benefit reduction? It is not clear. Assuming the sufficiency of dire consequences, would anything less suffice? We question seriously whether an employer could even modify a benefit package upward if such modification were to substantially reduce or eliminate one kind of benefit. We fear Section 2 will bind an employer to present benefits (plus, of course, pregnancy coverage) as a permanent minimum. Further assuming at some point an employer might be allowed to free himself from this obligation, at what date might he do so? A year later? Two? Ten? Finally, apart from the employer who seeks to change his benefit plan at some future time, what of the employer who can neither pass on nor absorb these added costs to begin with? Advocates of the bill lend assurances: the legislative language lends none.

The employer's contribution to the funding of these added benefits must, according to Section 2, be "adequate." It is possible that contribution adequacy will require that even under contributory plans *no* added costs for pregnancy coverage be borne by the employee. (The illogic of such a situation goes as follows: if an employee is paying say 20% or $200 for benefits, he/she should not have to pay anything more for coverage that through hindsight should have been included initially—this, despite the fact that had the coverage been included previously the employee would have been paying 20% of the cost of pregnancy coverage as well). Thus the employer will be made to bear more than the 80% he anticipated, presumably ever after. Of course employers who, for the first time, adopt plans in the future, are free to set an 80/20 employer/employee contribution ratio—or whatever ratio they choose. Indeed the premiums of these employers need not reflect the added costs of pregnancy at all. The employers are completely free to set their contribution ratio at whatever level would yield the dollar amount which they would have paid without the inclusion of pregnancy. Seventy percent, sixty, whatever—the total cost of pregnancy can thus be borne by the employee.

Section 2 injures not only the employer, but the employee as well. It is a clear infringement of the protections provided under the Taft Hartley Act—interference with the employee's right to bargain collectively over the terms of their contracts. Beyond those employees covered by Taft Hartley, Section 2 denies all employees the right to determine whether this is in fact a benefit they want. As discussed earlier, we believe this is a benefit more appropriately the subject of negotiation than legislation.

In sum, Section 2 may create the situation under which plans currently in effect must be amended to provide current coverages plus pregnancy coverage indefinitely into the future. Existing benefits will become a permanent minimum, and no additional employee contribution for the newly mandated coverage may be demanded. Whether the employees want such coverage is irrelevant.

By singling out one classification of employers, Section 2 offers an arbitrary, inequitable and manifestly illogical approach to a complex situation. While supporters of the bill argue existing precedent for prohibiting any reduction of benefits, the pregnancy benefit situation is clearly distinguishable. First, the very inclusion of pregnancy benefits itself precludes any continuing effects of its ever having been excluded, and second, unlike the subject of statutory precedent, there is no legal or practical requirement that benefits be provided at all.

As an elementary rule of contracts one may void an agreement entered into in reasonable reliance upon a material misstatement of fact. We maintain that by analogy the employer who would not have provided any benefits had the ultimate costs been known, should in all fairness be allowed to discontinue his plan.

Equity and fairplay call for it. It is arbitrary and capricious discrimination against employers providing benefits in favor of employers who don't.

Conclusion.   To summarize our position, the NAM believes that H.R. 6075 is social legislation that goes too far in requiring employers, and ultimately society, to assume the financial responsibilities of parenthood. The language of Section 1 as it relates to the coverage of pregnancy, childbirth, and related medical conditions under fringe benefit plans is much too broad and would allow employers virtually no leeway in setting realistic limitations to such coverages. We find the requirements of Section 2 to be blatantly unfair.

This bill is a simplistic approach to a complex problem affecting all of society. We urge that Congress not move with unstudied haste on this bill. The implications are enormous and we recommend that they be fully explored before this bill is put to any vote.

2 Special aspects of sex discrimination in employment

Reverse discrimination: Bakke and beyond

Review of the Bakke Issue

On the surface, *Bakke* v. *Regents of University of California,* a case currently before the U.S. Supreme Court, involves an individual white male's attempt to prove that the University of California at Davis' medical school admission policy discriminated against him because of his race. However, because the medical school's Special Admissions Program reserves a certain number of openings for "disadvantaged applicants," a classification which has excluded whites, the Court's decision whether to allow or disallow the preferential treatment which lies at the heart of the program, may have far reaching effects on affirmative action, with its race and sex based hiring and promotion goals and timetables.

In 1973 and again in 1974, the Respondent, Allen Bakke, applied for admission to the medical school at the University of California at Davis. His application was one of 2600 received for the 1973 entering class. Competition that was keen due to there only being 100 openings for the class became even more so in that the Special Admissions Program reserved 16 of those openings for educationally and economically disadvantaged students.

After being turned down both years, Bakke filed a complaint against the University. In his quest for mandatory, injunctive and declaratory relief, Bakke alleged that he should be admitted to the medical school on the grounds that he was qualified for admission and had been turned down only due to his being white. His complaint further alleged that the special program accepted only minority applicants and that it allowed certain minority applicants to enter the school who were not as qualified as nonminorities who were denied admission.

The University filed a cross complaint seeking declaratory relief to the effect that its Special Admission Program was valid. It claimed that an applicant's status as a minority member was only one consideration; that the program promoted a greater diversity in the student body and the medical profession in general and extended medical educational opportunities to the educationally and economically disadvantaged.

Although the trial court found that the program did discriminate against Bakke, it did not direct the University to admit him to the medical school. Both Bakke and the University appealed the decision and the request was granted. The University's regular admissions criteria were discussed before the California Supreme Court. In accordance with the regular program, five criteria are taken into account before an applicant is granted or denied an admissions interview. The criteria include the applicant's scores on the Medical College Admission Test, undergraduate grade point average, work experience, extracurricular activities and letters of recommendation. Point scores are attached to each of these criteria and applicants with enough points are granted interviews. Points are given to the interview itself and combined into a total point score for each applicant. Out of a possible 500 points in 1973, Allen Bakke scored 468. In 1974 he managed 549 out of a possible 600. Bakke's grade point average of 3.51 and MCAT verbal, quantitative, science and general information scores of 96, 94, 97 and 72 respectively were partially responsible for his total points accrued. Minority students accepted under the special program had grade point averages as low as 2.11 in 1973 and 2.21 in 1974. Under the regular admissions program, applicants with grade point averages less than 2.5 were not even granted interviews.

In light of this and other evidence presented, the California Supreme Court found that the University's special program was not in itself unconstitutional except that its standards were applied in a racially discriminatory manner. Therefore, the Court required that the University adopt and apply standards which would afford educationally and economically disadvantaged applicants of all races an equal opportunity for admission to the medical school through the special admission program.

Appeals efforts have brought the case to the U.S. Supreme Court. *Amicus curiae* (friend of the court) briefs have been filed, in record numbers, in support of and opposition to both parties. Beyond simple support and opposition, the briefs offer enlightened points of view concerning the possible ramifications the Supreme Court's decision will have on medical school admissions policies and entrance into any institution supported by public funds, future "reverse discrimination" cases, fine points of constitutional law and so on. The *amicus curiae* brief filed by the Equal Employment Advisory Council is one that looks to the impending decision as one which could seriously affect the future affirmative action responsibilities required of the private employer. The brief calls to the attention of the Supreme Court the predicament that the private employer often finds himself in; that is, implementing an affirmative action plan is prerequisite for securing government contracts, but doing so may hold him liable for similar "reverse discrimination" suits.

Brief *amicus curiae* of the Equal Employment Advisory Council

Interest of the amicus curiae

This brief *amicus curiae* of the Equal Employment Advisory Council (EEAC) is submitted pursuant to the written consent of all parties. EEAC is a voluntary, non-profit association, organized as a corporation under the laws of the District of Columbia. Its membership includes a broad spectrum of employers from throughout the United States, including both individual employers and trade and industry associations. The principal goal of EEAC is to represent and promote the common interest of employers and the general public in the development and implementation of sound government policies, procedures and requirements pertaining to nondiscriminatory employment practices.

Substantially all of EEAC's members, or their constituents, are subject to the provisions of Title VII of the Civil Rights Act of 1964, as amended (42 U.S.C. §§ 2000e *et seq.*). In addition, those EEAC members, or their constituents, who are federal contractors are required to comply with Executive Order 11246 (amended by Executive Order 11375) and supporting regulations, which, in part, contain extensive affirmative action requirements. As such, the members of EEAC have a direct interest in the issues presented for the Court's consideration in this case, which involve the legality of the Petitioner's preferential admissions policy under which minority applicants were admitted as students to the Petitioner's Medical School to the exclusion of allegedly better qualified nonminority applicants.

Preliminary statement

The importance of this case to private employment affirmative action plans

This case, arising in the context of a university's minority preference admissions program, can be expected to have far-reaching consequences for employers who have entered into affirmative action plans (AAPs) either voluntarily, or under compulsion from federal agencies or courts. This is the first case in which this Court has decided to address directly the constitutional validity of any type of affirmative action plan under which the administering entity, be it a university or employer, has made a decision to allocate limited educational or employment opportunities *solely on the basis of race* in order to rectify an underrepresentation of minorities in a student body or workforce.

Lacking directly applicable Supreme Court precedent, affirmative action programs in private sector employment are now governed by a confusing mixture of often inconsistent federal and state court decisions, government regulations and collective bargaining agreements. Lower court decisions and agency policy determinations dealing with employment discrimination often are based upon Supreme Court decisions in other subject areas, even though the standards for determining whether discrimination has occurred may differ under the Constitution or applicable statutory scheme. It is reasonable, therefore, to expect that the courts, federal agencies, employers and unions will look to the decision in this case for guidance in attempting to determine the extent to which this Court will permit affirmative action in employment.

The Court's ruling here could do much to resolve a dilemma now facing employers. Presently, employers who fail to adopt AAPs to increase the numbers of minorities and women in their workforces risk loss of their federal contracts, exposure to Title VII class actions and agency complaints, and widespread publicity of alleged discrimination. On the other hand, employers who do adopt affirmative action programs which give job preferences to minorities and/or women may be found to have committed "reverse discrimination" against nonminority or male employees, who can be expected to demand monetary or other relief. Employers are thereby placed in the ironic and unfair position of facing liability to nonminorities and males because of good faith attempts to comply with requirements found in statutes, executive orders or other government directives intended to pevent discrimination.

This dilemma is compounded by a significant split in court opinion over the permissibility of preferential treatment of minorities or women absent a showing of discrimination by the particular employer involved. Also unclear is whether such a showing may be based upon statistical evidence alone, or whether, and in what circumstances, additional corroborating evidence may be required.

We recognize that the Constitutional and legal arguments for and against affirmative action will be thoroughly briefed to the Court by the parties and numerous other *amici curiae* in this case. EEAC does not take a position on that issue. We merely urge that, whatever conclusion the Court reaches, full consideration be given to the implications of this case for private employment affirmative action programs. To that end, we offer in this brief, for the Court's reference, an explication of the specific legal and practical contexts in which employment AAPs presently exist. It is hoped that, by framing its opinion herein with a full awareness of these implications, the Court may provide some answers to the quandary facing employers.

Several principles which the Court should clarify to provide needed guidance in this area are set forth in the third section of this brief. In particular, we urge the Court to annunciate in its decision in this case a rule that, as a general matter, a defendant in a "reverse discrimination" suit will not be held liable to nonminority or male claimants if:

a. its affirmative action plan was adopted in a good faith attempt to comply with the requirements of Title VII, Executive Order 11246, a consent decree or other court or agency requirements, and

b. its actions in implementing the plan were reasonably related to these good faith objectives.

Furthermore, even if affirmative action pursuant to a good faith AAP is found to be illegal "reverse discrimination," we urge the Court to make it clear that any remedies should be *prospective* only and limited to injunctions against further implementation of the program. Preferential treatment undertaken at the behest of the government, against the background of unsettled and inconclusive legal precedents, and without any intention of victimizing a portion of society, should not subject employers to monetary liability. Any award of backpay in such circumstances should be explicitly forbidden, for it would penalize compliance with federal regulations.

Adoption of these clarifying principles would be consistent with prior holdings of the Court that potential defendants who must act in the fact of unsettled legal principles will not be "charged with predicting the future course of constitutional law." *Pierson* v. *Ray*, 386 U.S. 547, 557 (1967).

Argument

I. Current court decisions and federal agency regulations effectively compel employers to adopt affirmative action plans which give preferential treatment to minorities and women

A major portion of the employer community in the United States, including more than 300,000 federal contractors, have adopted and are currently implementing affirmative action plans designed to increase the numbers of women and minorities in their employ.

In general, AAPs are premised upon statistics showing that various job groups in the employer's workforce do not reflect a proportionate utilization of minorities or women potentially available from the appropriate surrounding labor market area. Although such "underutilization" may not necessarily subject the employer to liability under antidiscrimination statutes, federal government agencies such as the Equal Employment Opportunity Commission (EEOC) and the Office of Federal Contract Compliance Programs (OFCCP) nonetheless often rely upon such underrepresentation statistics as a basis for requiring employers to adopt numerical employment or promotional criteria such as "goals" and "timetables," and to make "good faith efforts" (41 C.F.R. § 60–60.9, Part B, XII(B)(2)) to meet these criteria for utilization of members of an "affected class."

In addition, in a number of cases in which employer discrimination under Title VII of the Civil Rights Act of 1964 (Title VII) has been proven, courts have ordered the imposition of remedial quotas under which statistical imbalances must be rectified by hiring or promoting fixed ratios of minorities or women. Still other employers, in order to comply with Title VII and to diminish their potential liability to minorities and women, voluntarily have adopted AAPs to increase their utilization of women and minorities, either independently or through collective bargaining agreements with their employees' union representatives.

As case history indicates, the concept of affirmative action embodies a requirement that special consideration be given to such characteristics as race, sex or national origin. When race- or sex-based employment criteria are used, however, other persons not benefitted by the AAP may question whether such preferential treatment of minorities or women is legally permissible, especially when the program appears to have an adverse impact on their employment opportunities in a universe of finite employment opportunities.

It is important to bear in mind, however, that even if such preferential treatment of minorities and women impacts adversely on nonminorities or males, it is extremely unlikely that this result was invidiously intended by the entity enacting the plan. It is more likely that the AAP was adopted as a good faith response to compelling pressures to eliminate traditional exclusionary discrimination against minorities and women. It is the position of the *Amicus*, EEAC, that the employer's good faith reasons for enacting an affirmative action plan must be given great weight when determining the extent of the employer's liability, if any, in "reverse discrimination" suits.

A. Regulations enforcing executive order 11246 require contractors to develop and implement AAPs to remedy any statistical underrepresentation of minorities or women regardless of its cause.

1. Mere statistical underutilization requires the implementation of goals and timetables.   Presidential Executive Order 11246 (30 Fed. Reg. 12319 (1965)), as amended by Executive Order 11375 (32 Fed. Reg. 14302 (1967)) (the Order or E.O. 11246), requires that all nonexempt government contracts and subcontracts include an equal opportunity clause pursuant to which the contractor or subcontractor undertakes not to discriminate on the basis of race, color, religion, sex or national origin and also to take affirmative action to ensure that applicants and employees are treated "without regard" to these factors (Sec. 202(1)).

The directives of the Order are implemented by rules and regulations issued by the Secretary of Labor, which require (with limited exceptions) that *every* federal supply and service contractor or subcontractor develop a written affirmative action program. Each AAP must include statistical workforce and utilization analyses. If the employer's utilization of women or any minority group representing more than 2% of the area population is "deficient," the contractor must develop an affirmative action program which must include "specific and result-oriented procedures" (such as goals and timetables) to overcome the underutilization in any particular job group. 41 C.F.R. §§ 60–2.10, –2.12. *See generally Legal Aid Society of Alameda County* v. *Brennan*, 381 F. Supp. 125, 8 FEP Cases 178 (N.D. Cal. 1974).

"Underutilization" is defined as "having fewer minorities or women in a particular job group than would reasonably be expected by their availability." 41 C.F.R. § 60–2.11 (b). "Availability" is determined by consideration of "at least all" of eight factors—including data on minority and female population and unemployment, available skills and training facilities (41 C.F.R. § 60–2.11)—with respect to every grouping of jobs in every establishment of the employer. Every individual job title must be so scrutinized, with those which are similar in terms of wage rates, content and career opportunity grouped for such study.

Once underutilization is identified in *any* job group at a particular contractor's facility, the responsible compliance agency requires that goals and timetables be established to correct the deficiency by the contractor applying "every good faith effort." (41 C.F.R. § 60-2.12(B)). According to OFCCP, a *goal* is stated as a percentage of the total employees in the job group. Ultimate goals must be equal to the availability percentage or estimate. The *timetable* is developed so that the ultimate goal can be reached within the minimum feasible time. Unless it appears that the *ultimate* goal can be achieved within twelve months, the contractors must also establish *interim* or *annual* goals. These are described as "annual rates of hiring and/or promoting minorities and women until the ultimate goal is reached.

The Labor Department's Office of Federal Contract Compliance Programs (OFCCP) is responsible for monitoring the contractors' performance under E.O. 11246. While it retains general supervisory authority, OFCCP has delegated the day-to-day responsibility for enforcing the program to several compliance agencies in other Executive Departments, such as the Departments of Defense and Commerce.

The statistical imbalances that trigger these affirmative action requirements *need not be connected to any showing of past or present discrimination.* Thus, shortly after the promulgation of OFCCP Order No. 4, Laurence H. Silberman, the Former Under Secretary of Labor, testified that:

One of the things interesting about the [OFCCP's] affirmative action concept, it is not antidiscrimination. It goes beyond that . . .

We and the compliance agencies put pressure on contractors to come up with commitments *even though those contractors are not guilty of any discrimination,* but because we think they are required under the Executive order to go beyond, to provide affirmative action.

Since they are not guilty of discrimination, it is not exactly the kind of situation where you can go to an enforcement posture, but rather you say to that contractor, you have to make an extra effort beyond what the civil rights laws are in this country and go beyond that in order to get a Government contract. *Hearings on S. 2515, etc., Before the Subcommittee on Labor of the Senate Committee on Labor and Public Welfare,* 92nd Cong., 1st Sess. 77 (1971) (hereinafter cited as *Hearings*) (emphasis added).

Accordingly, even employers who may be justified in asserting that a statistical imbalance is *not* the product of discrimination are nevertheless required to adopt an AAP or face the sanction proceedings described below.

The legality of these requirements has never been definitively established. Several courts have approved Labor Department affirmative action "Home Town" plans expressly addressed to remedying proven egregious and long-standing exclusion of minorities by various construction unions. None of these cases, however, directly sanctions the adoption of an AAP by an employer whose statistical imbalance is not established as the product of past discrimination through a full and fair administrative hearing procedure. Moreover, several recent Title VII decisions have invalidated AAPs which were not premised on past discrimination by the particular employer involved, but rather were enacted to comply with government-required affirmative action.

2. Severe sanctions for non-compliance with OFCCP demands effectively compel contractors to engage in preferential employment practices. Sanction proceedings can be brought against a contractor for such discrepancies as failing to adopt an AAP at each of its establishments, substantially deviating from an AAP, or "failing to develop or implement an AAP which complies with the OFCCP's regulations." *See* 41 C.F.R. §§ 60-1.26(a), 60-2.2(b). Thus, an allegation by a compliance officer that there is an underutilization of minorities or women in any job group may result in enforcement (i.e., sanction) proceedings against the contractor. *See* 41 C.F.R. § 60-1.26(a), amended in 42 Fed. Reg. 3460 (1977). If the agency determines to proceed to its own enforcement hearing procedures (set forth in 41 C.F.R. § 60-30, 42 Fed. Reg. 3462, *et seq.*), the contractor faces cancellation or termination of all federal contracts (or any part thereof); withholding progress payments on a contract; or, debarment from future contracts.

Other severe sanctions may be, and have been, applied to contractors even *before* any agency hearing on the alleged violation. Under 41 C.F.R. § 60-2.2(b), amended in 42 Fed. Reg. 3460, when it comes to the "attention" of the individual "contracting officer" that such underutilization exists, he "*shall* declare the contractor/bidder nonresponsible . . ." (emphasis added). Interested compliance agencies are notified of this "nonresponsibility," and are then required to withhold further contract awards from the alleged offending contractor.

Such contract passover may occur when underutilization is alleged with respect to only one job group within a particular facility, even though the contractor may otherwise be in complete compliance with the Order. Protection from such *"de facto"* debarment without a hearing appears to be within the "sole discretion" of the Director, OFCCP. *See* 41 C.F.R. § 60-2.2(b), as amended 41 Fed. Reg. 3462.

Because these sanctions for non-compliance are so severe and the opportunities to challenge OFCCP and compliance agency policies so restricted, compliance with the agency's affirmative action requirements is generally the only practical course available to employers whose business is directly or indirectly dependent to any substantial degree on government contracts.

B. Inconsistent judicial use of statistical evidence impels many employers to adopt AAPs to avoid potential findings of discrimination under federal statutes. Additionally, compelling impetus to develop and implement effective affirmative action programs results from court decisions under Title VII basing *prima facie* findings of employment discrimination upon statistical evidence. Even for those employers who have never engaged in any discriminatory practices, the prospect of having to assume the burden to *prove* that statistical disparities in their utilization of minorities and women were *not* produced by discrimination is enough to cause most employers to take aggressive steps to eliminate such disparities as quickly as possible.

The lower courts have divided over the proper role that statistics play in determining Title VII liability. A number of appellate court decisions have found *prima facie* cases of illegal disparate treatment established *solely* by statistical evidence. Other decisions, however, caution that the reliance upon unexamined statistics, unsupported by additional corroborating evidence of discrimination, often presents serious analytical difficulties. Accordingly, these courts have expressed a reluctance to base a finding of discrimination on statistics alone, without looking into whether the disparity might have a nondiscriminatory cause.

The Court noted in *T.I.M.E.-D.C.* v. *U.S., supra,* 14 FEP Cases at 1520-21 that:

statistics [alleged to demonstrate a *prima facie* showing of Title VII liability] are not irrefutable; they come in infinite variety and, like any other kind of evidence, they may be rebutted. In short, their usefulness depends on all of the surrounding circumstances.

While this language suggests a balanced approach, it clearly implies that employers whose workforce statistics do not reflect full utilization of minorities and women will continue to face the potentially difficult burden of proving a negative—i.e., that the statistical disparities did not result from discriminatory causes. It is evident, therefore, that employers must continue to evaluate their employment practices from a statistical perspective and cannot rest assured that they will not be held in noncompliance with Title VII unless their work complements mirror the racial and sexual composition of the surrounding population.

Faced with these court decisions as they attempt to assess their potential Title VII liability, many employers understandably conclude that the only safe course is to attempt to hire and promote minorities and women at rates that would satisfy the most stringent of court-established standards by, in effect, factoring race and sex considerations into their selection criteria. Indeed, in many instances, preferential hiring policies may be the only effective method to achieve statistical parity within a foreseeable time span.

II. Existing court decisions raise doubts about the validity of OFCCP's preferential treatment requirements, but do not provide sufficient guidance to enable employers to determine the permissible limits of affirmative action

In attempting to discern the extent to which preferential treatment of women and minorities may be used to correct statistical imbalances in their workforces, employers are now confronted with differing agency and court interpretations of the governing laws and policies.

As previously established, the OFCCP requires the implementation of goals and timetables to correct any statistical imbalance, *irrespective of the cause of such imbalance* and before any hearing has been held to determine whether the imbalance has been created by illegally discriminatory factors. This approach seems to contrast with two developing lines of judicial authority. First, unlike the OFCCP, the federal courts generally have exhibited extreme caution in approving, even as remedies, employment schemes that involve preferential treatment of minorities and/or women who cannot demonstrate that they are the individual victims of discrimination. Secondly, several recent district court decisions have held that employment practices favoring minorities or women constituted illegal discrimination against whites or males under Title VII. These cases have caused great concern among employers. At present, however, the state of the law is such that employers cannot determine with any degree of assurance what kinds of affirmative action the law permits or what the government may validly require. The impact of these two lines of cases on employment affirmative action is discussed below.

A. Judicial decisions discussing the propriety of preferential treatment to remedy proven discrimination.

Employers seeking guidance in determining the extent to which private preferential treatment is permissible have searched logically for analogous principles in federal court decisions in which preferential remedies have been awarded to remedy proven race or sex discrimination. In actual practice, however, the direction provided by such cases is lessened by the lack of consistency in the lower courts' pronouncements concerning the legality and extent of such remedies under the federal antidiscrimination laws.

Perhaps the most broadly-stated judicial approval of racially-based employment decisions appears in *German v. Kipp, supra,* 14 FEP Cases 1197, 1204-1205 (W.D. Mo. 1977), where the court permitted preferential promotions, even while acknowledging the absence of employer discrimination or identifiable victims thereof. And *see U.S. v. Elevator Constructors, Local 5,* 538 F.2d 1012, 13 FEP Cases 81, 88 (3d Cir. 1976), and cases cited therein; and *EEOC v. AT&T,* 14 FEP Cases 1210 (3d Cir. 1977).

Most other appellate decisions, however, have expressed reluctance in granting quota relief, even where past discrimination has been proved. Indeed, the Third Circuit itself remarked in disapproving a quota remedy in a case where sex discrimination violative of Title VII had been found:

Quotas are an extreme form of relief and, while this Court has declined to disapprove their use in narrow and carefully limited situations [citations omitted], certainly that remedy has not been greeted with enthusiasm. *Ostapowicz v.*

Johnson Bronze Co., 541 F.2d 394, 13 FEP Cases 517, 523 (3d Cir. 1976), *cert. denied,* 14 FEP Cases 266, *reh. denied,* 97 S. Ct. 1187 (1971).

The Fourth Circuit has urged similar restraint, again in a case where statutory violations had been proved:

> [T]he necessity for preferential treatment should be carefully scrutinized and . . . such relief should be required only when there is a *compelling need for it. Patterson* v. *American Tobacco Co.*, 535 F.2d 257, 274, 12 FEP Cases 314, 327 (4th Cir. 1976), *cert. denied,* 429 U.S. 920 (emphasis added).

See also Harper v. *Kloster,* 486 F.2d 1134, 6 FEP Cases 880 (4th Cir. 1873).

Additionally, a number of decisions indicate that the preferential relief may go no further than to eliminate the identifiable lingering effects of previous discriminatory practices by the particular employer. *Boston Chapter, NAACP, Inc.* v. *Beecher,* 504 F.2d 1017, 8 FEP Cases 855 (1st Cir. 1974), *cert. denied,* 421 U.S. 910; *Western Addition Community Organization* v. *Alioto,* 514 F.2d 542, 10 FEP Cases 527 (9th Cir. 1975), *cert. denied,* 423 U.S. 994; *Morrow* v. *Crisler, supra,* 491 F.2d 1053, 7 FEP Cases 586 (5th Cir. 1974), *cert. denied,* 419 U.S. 895, 8 FEP Cases 1007.

These cases indicate that even in the context of proven race discrimination, temporary, carefully circumscribed resort to racial criteria should be made only when "the Chancellor determines that it represents the *only* rational, non-arbitrary means of eradicating past evils." *NAACP* v. *Allen,* 493 F.2d 614, 7 FEP Cases 873 (5th Cir. 1974) (emphasis added).

The Second Circuit has shown particular reluctance to impose preferential treatment of minorities. In *Bridgeport Guardians, Inc.* v. *Members of the Bridgeport Civil Service Commission,* 482 F.2d 1333, 5 FEP Cases 1344, 1349-50 (2d Cir. 1973) that court approved temporary racial hiring quotas for the city's police department, but disapproved promotion quotas because "[t]he impact of the quota upon [incumbent whites] would be harsh and can only exacerbate rather than diminish racial tensions." Moreover, the hiring quota was approved "somewhat gingerly" even though the city had persisted in using an archaic employment test, failed to seek minority recruits, and the quota was well below the minority population of the city and, presumably, did not suggest the concept of parity hiring. The court, indeed, found that "the most crucial consideration . . . is that this is *not a private employer* and *not simply an exercise in providing minorities with equal opportunity employment.*" 5 FEP Cases at 1350 (emphasis added).

In *Kirkland* v. *New York State Department of Correctional Services,* 520 F.2d 420, 427, 11 FEP Cases 38 (2d Cir. 1975), *rehearing en banc denied,* 531 F.2d 5, 11 FEP Cases 1253 (2d Cir. 1975), *cert. denied,* 429 U.S. 823 (1976), the court criticized racial quotas as "repugnant to the basic concepts of a democratic society" and observed that the Second Circuit had approved quotas only where there was a clear-cut pattern of long-continued and egregious racial discrimination and the absence of a showing of "identifiable reverse discrimination." 520 F.2d at 427, 11 FEP Cases at 43. The *Bridgeport Guardians* distinction between hiring quotas and promotion quotas was echoed in *Kirkland,* and repeated in *Chance* v. *Board of Examiners,* 534 F.2d 993, 11 FEP Cases 1450 (2d Cir. 1976), *mod. on other grounds,* 534 F.2d 1007, 13 FEP Cases 150 (2d Cir. 1976), *cert. denied,* 45 U.S.L.W. 3803 (May 14, 1977).

Finally, in *EEOC* v. *Local 638*, 532 F.2d 821, 12 FEP Cases 755 (2d Cir. 1976) the court interpreted its own *Kirkland* decision as having promulgated *twofold requirements* for the imposition of temporary quotas of all kinds: *a clear cut pattern of long-continued and egregious racial discrimination, and the dispersal of the effects of "reverse discrimination" among a group of non-minority persons who are not "identifiable."*

In sum, the lower courts, while not entirely consistent in their approaches to quotas and other preferential remedies in cases of employment discrimination, generally have been much more reluctant to require such remedies than the OFCCP. It is not clear at present whether these judicial discussions of the propriety of quotas to remedy proven, egregious discrimination are applicable at all to contractors who are ordered by the OFCCP to enact AAPs premised only on statistical underutilization. But certainly the courts' evident misgivings about the legitimacy of preferential treatment, even in the former context, create further cause for anxiety on the part of employers faced with agency pressures to bring their practices into compliance with the government's affirmative action requirements.

B. The "reverse discrimination" decisions.   The full extent of the dilemma confronting employers can be understood only by considering the agency requirements and court decisions discussed above in juxtaposition with the growing line of precedents holding employers' affirmative action efforts resulted in illegal "reverse discrimination" against nonminority or male employees or applicants. Several federal district courts recently have invalidated AAPs which were adopted voluntarily and were *not* premised upon a showing of past discrimination by the particular employer. For example, in *Anderson* v. *San Francisco School District,* the court permanently enjoined the school board from carrying out a voluntarily-adopted, five-year quota for the assignment, appointment, and promotion of minority school administrators. In a similar case involving a municipal government, the City of Berkeley was enjoined from discriminating against white applicants by its voluntary implementation of an AAP designed to correct an "underutilization" of minorities. The city's plan was adopted in recognition of a "history of discriminatory employment practices throughout all segments of American society" without specifically acknowledging any such discrimination on the part of the city itself. The court stressed that "while quotas merely to attain racial balance are forbidden, quotas to correct past discriminatory practices are not." 12 FEP Cases at 939.

A similar result occurred in *Weber* v. *Kaiser Aluminum & Chem. Corp.,* in which Kaiser and the United Steelworkers Union enacted an agreement establishing goals and timetables to achieve a desired minority ratio in their apprenticeship programs. As openings occurred, one minority was required to enter for every nonminority. There was no showing that Kaiser had ever discriminated against blacks. Rather, the agreement was motivated by a desire to comply with OFCCP utilization requirements and to avoid litigation by minorities over their lack of workforce representation. In setting aside the agreement as violative of Title VII, the court indicated that courts, and not private parties, should grant affirmative relief and then only when it was necessary to eliminate the effects of past discrimination.

Likewise, the Title VII reverse discrimination decision in *Cramer* v. *Virginia Commonwealth University*, 415 F. Supp. 673, 12 FEP Cases 1397 (E.D. Va. 1976), *appeal pending* (4th Cir. No. 76-1937), vividly demonstrates both the quandary facing employers who attempt to comply with federal AAP requirements, and the need for clarification of their position by this Court. The court invalidated a voluntary AAP establishing hiring policies favoring women under which the university sought to recruit women for its faculty "in order to compensate for alleged past deficiencies in minority hiring, and *to attempt to bring the school's employee hiring practices into accord with prevailing federal guidelines.*" *Id.*, 415 F. Supp. at 675, 12 FEP Cases at 1398. (emphasis added). Those guidelines were found to include E.O. 11246, and directives pursuant thereto issued by the Department of Health, Education and Welfare. The university's reliance on federal agency requirements, however, was rejected as a defense by the court, which then criticized the federal government for "requiring employers to engage in widespread, pervasive and invidious sex discrimination through the implementation of the pervading affirmative action programs . . .", and for ". . . perpetuating the very social injustices which it so enthusiastically and properly seeks to remedy." See 415 F. Supp. at 680, 12 FEP Cases at 1402.

In light of these decisions finding reverse discrimination, the legality of employment decisions which grant preferential treatment based upon race or sex is now open to serious question, particularly in the absence of a court finding that such treatment is necessary to remedy specific, proven acts of past discrimination. Thus, given the present agency policies requiring an AAP when *any* statistical imbalance exists, federal contractors are regularly placed in the exceedingly vulnerable position of having to choose between (a) loss of contracts and other severe sanctions; or (b) adoption of an AAP which may not withstand scrutiny against a claim of illegal reverse discrimination, and also which might go beyond that which a court would order if it were to determine an appropriate remedy under Title VII.

III. The court should formulate principles that provide guidance for employers who must reconcile affirmative action requirements with potential reverse discrimination liability

The *Amicus*, EEAC, submits that the dilemma of employers described above is intolerable and cries out for a resolution which only this Court can now provide. Accordingly, EEAC respectfully urges the Court to articulate in its decision in this case certain clarifying principles that will furnish guidance to help resolve the present quandary.

First, the previous discussion has demonstrated that, as a general rule, the courts impose goals or quotas only as remedies of last resort where there is a history of flagrant, long-standing discrimination on the part of an employer. In contrast, the OFCCP and other agencies routinely require goals that often have the effect of preferential quotas, even when statistical imbalances have not been connected with proven illegal discrimination. It is EEAC's position that preferential treatment should not be *required* to remedy underutilization of women or minorities in a student body or workforce until *after* full and fair hearing procedures establish that the imbalance was the result of illegal discriminatory causes. The existence of illegal discrimination should be the first, not the last, area of federal agency inquiry where preferential treatment is sought. Requiring government agencies to apply legal principles which parallel those established by the courts in Title VII cases would do much to eliminate the present confusion over this issue.

Second, further clarification is required by this Court to identify for the lower courts the limits of permissible preferential treatment of minorities and women. In this regard, the *Amicus* urges this Court to endorse the position that has been adopted by the Second Circuit in its opinions in *Kirkland* v. *New York State Department of Correctional Services* and *EEOC* v. *Local 638.* These cases conclude that preferential remedies, even to remedy egregious proven past discrimination, can pass constitutional and statutory scrutiny only when they operate in the absence of identifiable "reverse discriminatees." Thus, the Second Circuit has indicated that it would approve hiring goals and quotas only where the negative impact on innocent nonminorities or males will be diffused among an unidentifiable group of unknown potential applicants. On the other hand, that court has questioned quota remedies involving promotions and training, since in such cases, the "reverse discrimination" victims will be readily identifiable.

Third, if the Court should affirm the court below and find that the University's AAP illegally discriminated against Plaintiff Bakke, it should be with the clear indication that the Court will not "charg[e]" potential reverse discrimination defendants "with predicting the future course of constitutional law." Fundamental principles of fairness require that until this Court delineates the permissible limits of affirmative action, the entity which enacts an AAP should not be held liable to nonminority or male employees if the plan was adopted:

a. in a good faith attempt to comply with the requirements of Title VII, Executive Order 11246, a consent decree or other court or agency requirements, and
b. its actions in implementing the plan were reasonably related to these good faith objectives.

Fourth, remedies available to a "reverse discriminatee" should be *prospective* only and limited to injunctions against further implementation of the affirmative action program. This Court should indicate that back pay or other monetary relief would unfairly penalize employers, universities, or others who have attempted in good faith to comply with what they perceived the law required as to their utilization of minorities and women.

This Court has indicated that the award of back pay is discretionary, and equitable considerations may render it inappropriate in particular cases. *See Albemarle Paper Co.* v. *Moody, supra,* 422 U.S. 405. The issues in question here readily meet the standards set forth in *Albemarle.* Much more is involved here than the "mere absence of bad faith" (422 U.S. at 422, 10 FEP Cases at 1189) on the part of a particular employer. At question is employer liability for affirmative good faith attempts to comply with what this Court has identified in other cases as the "primary" objective of Title VII—the removal of barriers to minorities "that have operated in the past *to favor* an identifiable group of *white* employees over other employees." *See Griggs* v. *Duke Power Co., supra,* 401 U.S. at

429-30, 3 FEP Cases at 177 (emphasis added) cited with approval in *Albemarle Paper Co.* v. *Moody, supra,* 422 U.S. at 417, 10 FEP Cases at 1187.

Additionally, the Fifth Circuit has suggested that where discrimination is "government imposed" by the OFCCP, a back pay order would work a "substantial injustice" and should be carefully scrutinized by the district court. *See Stevenson* v. *International Paper Co.,* 516 F.2d 1013, 10 FEP Cases 1386, 1395 (5th Cir. 1975).

Similarly, virtually all courts considering the issue have found back pay to be an inappropriate remedy where employers' good faith reliance upon a state protective statute ultimately was found to constitute unlawful Title VII discrimination. These cases reveal several factors analogous to the affirmative action context. They consistently emphasize the "dilemma" facing employers who did not have the benefit of a definitive judicial or even quasi-judicial determination as to the validity of their course of action. They also point out that "[p]rior to a judicial determination, such as evidenced in this opinion an *employer can hardly be faulted* for following the explicit provisions of applicable state law." (Emphasis added). Such equitable relief from monetary damage liability is *prospective* in application, would be limited in nature, and need not be extended to AAPs adopted *after* this Court ultimately determines the extent to which race- or sex-conscious employment decisions are constitutionally or otherwise permissible.

Until such determination is made, employers will be left in the untenable position of having to choose between lawsuits—suits filed by state or federal agencies, minorities or women for failure to establish a result- or goal-oriented affirmative action program, or suits filed by nonminorities or males for actions taken pursuant to such programs if they are adopted. Federal contractors and subcontractors face a similar problem. Approval of an AAP by a compliance agency carries no guarantee of immunity from claims of reverse discrimination, yet failure to be awarded such approval can lead to severe penalties, including debarment from future government contracts, cancellation of existing agreements, and the possibility of additional lawsuits. Until the present situation is resolved, employers will continue to face the real prospect of defending themselves in court regardless of the employment practices they adopt.

Conclusion

In recognition of the facts and arguments presented to the Court by the *Amicus,* EEAC, it is respectfully submitted that the administration of the federal antidiscrimination statutes and executive programs would benefit greatly if this Court were to adopt the guidelines suggested by the *Amicus.* Such guidance from this Court would do much to eliminate the present confusion surrounding employers' obligations to undertake affirmative action to remedy instances of underutilization of minorities and women.

Policies for pregnant workers: a source of discrimination*

Maternity standards

Social and economic developments in recent decades have caused pressure for reconsideration of traditional treatment of pregnant workers. For example, there was a dramatic shift in expert medical opinion with regard to continued normal activity of women in the later stage of pregnancy. And with the growing dependence of families on dual paychecks and the determination of many couples to restrict the number of children, there was increased reluctance on the part of women workers to accept long-term retirement from the labor force as soon as their first child was expected.

Controversy on this issue continues in labor-management negotiations, legislative debates, and the courts. Meanwhile there have been significant changes in laws and practices, as well as attention on occupational environments newly suspected of being hazardous for workers and their unborn children.

Over the last few years, there has been a definite shift away from penalizing women workers who become pregnant, and toward protecting the job rights of such women and giving them the option of deciding when to leave the job temporarily.

Changes in state laws banning pregnant workers and/or denying them benefits

Restrictions on employment of pregnant and postpregnant workers. One of the ways pregnant women workers have been penalized was forcing them off the job at a certain point before the anticipated date of childbirth and/or forbidding return to work for a specified period following termination of pregnancy. As of January 1, 1969, six States had prohibitions against the employment of pregnant and immediately postpregnant women; Puerto Rico also had provisions in this area. Today, only the Puerto Rico provisions remain intact and they are not restrictive.

In 1970, even before such restrictions were formally listed as one of the types of "protective" labor laws that were discriminatory and contrary to title VII of the Federal Civil Rights Act, Vermont took action and repealed its ban on employment 2 weeks before and 4 weeks after childbirth.

Connecticut repealed its 4-weeks-before-and-4-weeks-after ban in 1972, and Massachusetts followed suit in 1974 (in the latter case the ban had not been enforced for some time pursuant to a State attorney general decision).

In 1973 New York amended its law prohibiting employment 4 weeks after childbirth to permit earlier return upon approval of a physician. Also in 1973 the attorney general of Missouri ruled that the State

*Handbook on Women Workers, U.S. Department of Labor, Women's Bureau.

law which made it illegal to employ a woman within 3 weeks before or 3 weeks after childbirth was invalid as being in conflict with the ban on sex discrimination under Federal law, and that employers need no longer comply with the State restriction.

In Washington State, where prohibitions against employment of women 4 months before and 4 or 6 weeks after childbirth (with some variation permitted upon an employer's request and with a doctor's certificate) were set forth in minimum wage orders for some occupations or industries that covered women and minors only, the legislature amended the female and child labor laws in September 1973 to apply to all "persons" in employment and eliminate distinctions between the sexes. Enforcement of the prohibitions has ceased.

The Puerto Rico provisions state that pregnant women employed in offices, commercial and industrial establishments, and public utilities are entitled to a rest which includes a period commencing 4 weeks before and ending 4 weeks after childbirth. During that period the women are to be paid one-half of their regular pay, and their jobs must be held for them. To claim these benefits, a woman worker in one of the named establishments must present a medical certification that her state of pregnancy requires the rest. Such certificates are procurable at any public medical facility, without cost. The postnatal rest period may be extended up to 12 additional weeks if a worker suffers a disability attributable to the birth. Discharging a pregnant worker without just cause and refusal to reinstate a worker after childbirth are punishable by fine or award of damages.

Temporary Disability Insurance. Only five States and Puerto Rico have temporary disability insurance laws to provide income when people are unable to work because of disabilities not related to accident or illness from the job.

The Hawaii statute, which denied benefits during pregnancy except when complications resulted in total disability, was amended in May 1973 to grant benefits to any individual in current employment who suffers disability resulting from pregnancy or termination of pregnancy. In California a court decision in May 1973 ruled that the State's restriction of benefits for disability caused by or in connection with pregnancy to a period beginning with the 29th day after termination of pregnancy was unconstitutional. The legislature then changed its law, to limit benefit payments to claimants disabled because of abnormal and involuntary complications of pregnancy certified to by a doctor.

New Jersey, which originally excluded disabilities related to pregnancy, amended its law several years ago to provide that pregnancy may be deemed a sickness during the 4 weeks immediately preceding the expected birth and the 4 weeks immediately following termination of pregnancy (the period during which unemployment benefits may not be paid).

In both New York and Puerto Rico benefits are payable only for disability which occurs after a woman has worked in covered employment for at least 2 consecutive weeks following the termination of pregnancy. Rhode Island provides a lump sum payment up to $250 upon childbirth.

Unemployment compensation.   Pregnant workers have commonly been subject to special disqualification provisions in State unemployment compensation laws. These provisions were in addition to the usual penalties for "voluntary quits" and the universal disqualification of any claimant who is not able to and available for work. For the most part the penalty set for a pregnant worker who has been laid off was the same as if she had quit voluntarily. Thus, a woman who is caught in a plant shutdown in say, the first month of pregnancy might be denied benefits not only for the 8 months before childbirth but also thereafter until she has found another job and worked a stated period before being laid off again. During much of that time her former coworkers might be drawing benefits to which, absent the special disqualification, she would be entitled except in the few weeks of actual inability to work.

As of April 1968, 37 States and the District of Columbia had special disqualifications for pregnancy in their unemployment compensation laws. By the end of June 1975, court decisions, statutory changes, and attorney general decisions had reduced the count of such jurisdictions to 19—Alabama, Arkansas, Colorado, Delaware, District of Columbia, Indiana, Kansas, Maryland, Minnesota, Montana, Nevada, New Jersey, Ohio, Oregon, Rhode Island, Tennessee, Texas, Utah, and West Virginia.

In several of the jurisdictions that still have some kind of special disqualification because of pregnancy, the provision is considerably less repressive than formerly. For example, the Maryland disqualification, which used to be a flat 4 months before and 2 months after childbirth, is now only for any time the claimant is physically unable to work. And in Oregon pregnancy is mentioned as one of the disabilities which may cause claimants to be presumed unable to work until the administrator determines otherwise—in contrast to the former flat disqualification from the week of leaving until 6 weeks after childbirth. Indiana's law, while still disqualifying women who leave work voluntarily because of pregnancy, no longer deems all pregnant claimants unavailable for work.

Federal guidelines

Three Federal agencies have issued or proposed issuing guidelines on treatment of pregnant employees or applicants for employment. In addition, the Citizens' Advisory Council on the Status of Women (a group appointed by the President) adopted the following statement of principle on job-related maternity benefits on October 29, 1970:

Childbirth and complications of pregnancy are, for all job-related purposes, temporary disabilities and should be treated as such under any health insurance, temporary disability insurance, or sick leave plan of an employer, union, or fraternal society. Any policies or practices of an employer or union, written or unwritten, applied to instances of temporary disability other than pregnancy should be applied to incapacity due to pregnancy or childbirth, including policies or practices relating to leave of absence, restoration or recall to duty, and seniority.

No additional or different benefits or restrictions should be applied to disability because of pregnancy or childbirth, and no pregnant woman employee should be in a better position in relation to job-related practices or benefits than an employee similarly situated suffering from other disability.

Equal employment opportunity commission. Sex discrimination guidelines under title VII, first issued in December 1965, have been revised several times as policy positions on various points firmed. The current guidelines, issued April 5, 1972, EEOC's first to deal with childbirth, are as follows (Title 29, Chapter XIV, Part 1604 of the Code of Federal Regulations):

§ 1604.10 Employment policies relating to pregnancy and childbirth.

(a) A written or unwritten employment policy or practice which excludes from employment applicants or employees because of pregnancy is in prima facie violation of title VII.

(b) Disabilities caused or contributed to by pregnancy, miscarriage, abortion, childbirth, and recovery therefrom are, for all job-related purposes, temporary disabilities and should be treated as such under any health or temporary disability insurance or sick leave plan available in connection with employment. Written and unwritten employment policies and practices involving matters such as the commencement and duration of leave, the availability of extensions, the accrual of seniority and other benefits and privileges, reinstatement, and payment under any health or temporary disability insurance or sick leave plan, formal or informal, shall be applied to disability due to pregnancy or childbirth on the same terms and conditions as they are applied to other temporary disabilities.

(c) Where the termination of an employee who is temporarily disabled is caused by an employment policy under which insufficient or no leave is available, such a termination violates the Act if it has a disparate impact on employees of one sex and is not justified by business necessity.

Office of Federal Contract Compliance, U.S. Department of Labor. Guidelines on sex discrimination by Federal contractors, effective June 9, 1970, include the following (Title 41, Chapter 60, Part 60-20 of the Code of Federal Regulations):

§ 60-20.3 Job Policies and Practices

(g) Women shall not be penalized in their conditions of employment because they require time away from work on account of childbearing. When, under the employer's leave policy the female employee would qualify for leave, then childbearing must be considered by the employer to be a justification for leave of absence for female employees for a reasonable period of time. For example, if the female employee meets the equally applied minimum length of service requirements for leave time, she must be granted a reasonable leave on account of childbearing. The conditions applicable to her leave (other than the length thereof) and to her return to employment shall be in accordance with the employer's leave policy.

If the employer has no leave policy, childbearing must be considered by the employer to be a justification for a leave of absence for a reasonable period of time. Following childbirth, and upon signifying her intent to return within a reasonable time, such female employee shall be reinstated to her original job or to a position of like status and pay, without loss of service credits.

On December 27, 1973, the OFCC published proposed revisions of its guidelines that would make the childbirth sections like those of the EEOC, except that the first paragraph would read "Women shall not be rejected for employment, suspended from employment, or required to take leave involuntarily solely on account of the condition of pregnancy," and the words "Medically verifiable" would be used to open the second paragraph.

Department of Health, Education, and Welfare. On October 1, 1972, the Office for Civil Rights of the Department of Health, Education, and Welfare issued additional guidelines under Executive Order 11246, to show the applicability of the Executive order to higher education. These guidelines address not only policies relating to pregnancy and childbirth but also personal leave for child care; as follows:

Leave Policies

A university contractor must not discriminate against employees in its leave policies including *paid* and *unpaid* leave for educational or professional purposes, sick leave, annual leave, temporary disability, and leave for purposes of personal necessity. (emphasis supplied)

Employment Policies Relating to Pregnancy and Childbirth

B. *Mandatory period of leave:* Any policy requiring a mandatory leave of absence violates the Executive Order unless it is based on individual medical or job characteristics. In such cases the employer must clearly demonstrate an overriding need based on medical safety or "business necessity," i.e., that the successful performance of the position or job in question requires the leave. For example, service in a radiation laboratory may constitute a demonstrable hazard to the expectant mother or her child. A mandatory period of leave should not, however, be stipulated by the university; the length of leave, whether mandatory or voluntary, should be based on a bona fide medical need related to pregnancy or childbirth.

E. *Child care leave:* If employees are generally granted leave for personal reasons, such as for a year or more, leave for purposes relating to child care should be considered grounds for such leave, and should be available to men and women on an equal basis. A faculty member should not be required to have such leave counted toward the completion of a term as a probationary member, unless personal leave for other reasons is so considered. Nor should such leave time be subtracted from a stated term of appointment, or serve as a basis for nonrenewal of a contract.

The June 1975 regulations for carrying out the provisions of title IX of the Education Amendments of 1972 include the following (Title 45, Subtitle A, Part 86 of the Code of Federal Regulations):

§ 86.57 Marital or Parental Status.

(b) *Pregnancy.* A recipient shall not discriminate against or exclude from employment any employee or applicant for employment on the basis of pregnancy, childbirth, false pregnancy, termination of pregnancy, or recovery therefrom.

(c) *Pregnancy as a temporary disability.* A recipient shall treat pregnancy, childbirth, false pregnancy, termination of pregnancy, and recovery therefrom and any temporary disability resulting therefrom as any other temporary disability for all job related purposes, including commencement, duration and extensions of leave, payment of disability income, accrual of seniority and any other benefit or service, and reinstatement, and under any fringe benefit offered to employees by virtue of employment.

(d) *Pregnancy leave.* In the case of a recipient which does not maintain a leave policy for its employees, or in the case of an employee with insufficient leave or accrued employment time to qualify for leave under such a policy, a recipient shall treat pregnancy, childbirth, false pregnancy, termination of pregnancy and recovery therefrom as a justification for a leave of absence without pay for a reasonable period of time, at the conclusion of which the employee shall be reinstated to the status which she held when the leave began or to a comparable position, without decrease in rate of compensation or loss of promotional opportunities, or any other right or privilege of employment.

Policy positions of state fair employment practices agencies

Several of the agencies that administer State human rights/civil rights/ fair employment practices laws have issued formal statements of their policy position on sex discrimination, and most of these statements address the matter of childbirth leave.

Possibly the most striking example of changing attitudes toward pregnant workers is the fact that in *Washington* —a State which, as noted above, for years prohibited women's employment before and after childbirth —the Human Relations Commission has promulgated the following as a part of the State administrative code:

Pregnancy is an expectable incident in the life of a woman. Many women of childbearing age depend on their jobs for economic support. Practices such as terminating pregnant women, refusing to grant leave or accrued sick pay for disabilities relating to pregnancy, or refusing to hire women for responsible jobs because they may become pregnant, impair the opportunity of women to obtain employment and to advance in employment on the same basis as men. Such practices discriminate against women because of their sex.

The Commission declares that refusal to hire a pregnant woman must be justified and offers as an acceptable reason a training program that cannot accommodate absence of a new employee within the next 2 months because of childbirth. If an employee takes a leave of absence only for the actual period of disability relating to pregnancy or childbirth, the employer must reinstate her or give her a similar job of at least the same pay. Refusal to do so must be justified. Benefits or privileges available for other temporary disabilities must be available also for disabilities resulting from pregnancy or childbirth.

The Civil Rights Commission of *Michigan* formally adopted the entire sex discrimination guidelines issued under title VII of the Federal Civil Rights Act as policy to be followed under the State law. Other States that pattern childbirth leave policies after the EEOC's are *Colorado, Iowa, Kansas, Maryland,* and *Wisconsin.*

There is considerable variation among the other States with respect to childbirth leave policies. For example, the *Illinois* Fair Employment Practices Commission states that refusal of an employer to grant reasonable leaves to female employees during pregnancy, childbirth and convalescence constitutes discrimination contrary to State law. "[E]ven if an employer grants maternity leaves, a uniform rule which requires every woman to stop work upon reaching a certain month of pregnancy is too rigid . . . [T]he point at which a pregnant woman should commence her leave . . . should be based upon a medical evaluation of the individual in relation to her job, which evaluation should include the opinion of the employee's attending physician."

Regulations adopted by the *Massachusetts* Commission Against Discrimination under authority of the State fair employment practices law and a special maternity statute require employers in general to treat childbirth disability as other temporary disabilities are treated. However, regardless of marital status, females who meet the probationary period and notice requirements are entitled to an 8-week maternity leave and reinstatement without loss of employment benefits.

Minnesota Department of Human Rights sex discrimination guidelines require employers to grant up to 6 months maternity leave of absence whether or not leave of absence is granted for illness. Upon signifying her intent to return within the leave period, a female employee is entitled to reinstatement without loss of seniority. All maternity leave benefits apply to both married and unmarried employees.

In a series of statements in answer to some civil rights questions frequently posed by employers in connection with preemployment inquiries, the *New Jersey* Division of Civil Rights states that pregnant women employees are entitled to maternity leave where leaves are permitted for illness, military service, study, or any other reason. Employers may limit the length of maternity leaves to that which is granted for other disabilities. "To the extent possible, the woman should get her same job back or at least an equal job without loss of seniority."

A statement issued by the *New York* Division of Human Rights incorporates the basic portions of EEOC's childbirth policy, but also includes the following:

It is an unlawful discriminatory practice for an employer to establish an arbitrary point in pregnancy for commencement of maternity leave or to establish an arbitrary minimum period of time for duration of such leave. The employee must be permitted to continue working as long as she is physically able to perform the duties of her position and must be permitted to return to work as soon after confinement as she is physically able to resume performance of her duties.

Guidelines issued by the *Oregon* Bureau of Labor in June 1971 generally follow those of OFCC in requiring employers to grant maternity leave for a "reasonable period of time." The stated prime objective in considering the validity of maternity leave practices is to insure to working women continuity of employment without loss of benefits. And "Factors demonstrably necessary to job performance, health, safety, and the employer's reasonable need for orderly operation of business should be considered from the perspective of that prime objective." Furthermore:

Because there are factors of infinite variety which might affect a reasonable policy, it is not possible to establish any arbitrary standards for when a maternity leave should begin or end. Under normal circumstances the employee cannot be required to cease work prior to the day she desires unless demonstrable evidence of factors adversely affecting health can be shown.

In *Pennsylvania* sex discrimination guidelines last amended in December 1971 generally follow the OFCC wording about childbirth leave. They also, however, state:

The conditions applicable to childbirth leave and to return to employment may be in accordance with the employer's regular leave policy, provided that the female employee shall be entitled to receive any accumulated sick, disability, and vacation benefits accrued by her at the time of the leave. She shall not be required to leave at the expiration of an arbitrary time period during pregnancy and may continue to work as long as she is capable of performing the duties of her job.

In *Washington,* in addition to comprehensive guidelines on maternity quoted above in part, the Human Rights Commission has adopted preemployment inquiry guidelines that declare that all questions as to pregnancy and medical history concerning pregnancy and related matters are unfair practices.

State laws requiring maternity leave

At least three States have gone beyond "guidelines" and have enacted laws protecting job rights of pregnant workers.

Massachusetts amended its general laws in 1972 to provide that employers, as defined in the State fair employment practices act, must give reemployment rights without loss of service credits and benefits to female employees who meet length of service and notice requirements and who have been absent for no more than 8 weeks for the purpose of giving birth (Ch. 790, Acts 1972, approved July 19, 1972). The law gives the employer discretion on whether the maternity leave is to be with or without pay. Moreover, the employer need not provide for the cost of any benefits, plans, or programs during the period of maternity leave unless the employer so provides for all employees on leave of absence. If other persons of equal seniority have been laid off because of economic conditions or other changes in operating conditions, the employer is not required to restore a returning employee to her original position or a similar one; however, she must be given preferential consideration for another position to which she was entitled as of the date of her leave. Refusal to reinstate female employees following a maternity leave as specified or otherwise failing to comply is deemed unlawful under the fair employment practices law.

In *Connecticut* the Fair Employment Practices Act was amended effective October 1, 1973 (P.A. 73-647, L. 1973, approved June 20, 1973), to state:

§ 31-126. Unfair employment practices. It shall be an unfair employment practice . . . (g) for an employer, by himself or his agent, (i) to terminate a woman's employment because of her pregnancy or (ii) to refuse to grant to said employee a reasonable leave of absence for disability resulting from such pregnancy or (iii) to deny to said employee, who is disabled as a result of pregnancy, any compensation to which she is entitled as a result of the accumulation of disability or leave benefits accrued pursuant to plans maintained by said employer. Upon signifying her intent to return, such employee shall be reinstated to her original job or to an equivalent position with equivalent pay and accumulated seniority, retirement, fringe benefits and other service credits unless, in the case of a private employer, the employer's circumstances have so changed as to make it impossible or unreasonable to do so.

In *Montana* a law applicable to public and private employers and effective July 1, 1975 (Ch. 320, Laws 1975, approved April 8, 1975), reads in part:

(1) It shall be unlawful for an employer or his agent, (a) to terminate a woman's employment because of her pregnancy, or (b) to refuse to grant to the employee a reasonable leave of absence for such pregnancy, or (c) to deny to the employee, who is disabled as a result of pregnancy, any compensation to which she is entitled as a result of the accumulation of disability or leave benefits accrued pursuant to plans maintained by her employer; provided that the employer may require disability as a result of pregnancy to be verified by medical certification

that the employee is not able to perform her employment duties, or (d) to retaliate against any employee who files a complaint with the commissioner under the provisions of this act, or (e) to require that an employee take a mandatory maternity leave for an unreasonable length of time.

Reinstatement provisions in this law are very similar to those in Connecticut's.

Litigation

A number of court cases have been generated in recent years on the matter of rights of workers during pregnancy and immediately thereafter. The issue has been considered by several State human rights agencies, as well as by State and Federal courts at various levels. Many court suits were brought by teachers, with the assistance of the DuShane Emergency Fund of the National Education Association. Other employee organizations and women's groups have also supported litigation.

In January 1974 the U.S. Supreme Court ruled that requiring public school teachers to leave work 4 or 5 months in advance of childbirth violates the due process clause of the 14th Amendment because it unduly penalizes a female teacher for deciding to bear a child. *Cleveland Board of Education* v. *LaFleur, Cohen* v. *Chesterfield County School Board,* 414 U.S. 632 (1974). The Court held a restriction on return to the classroom until the beginning of the next regular semester after the child was 3 months old also to be a denial of due process.

The Court rejected the school boards' argument that the requirements were based on concern for the teacher and her unborn child and on the need for maintaining continuity of classroom instruction. In a footnote, however, it left open the possibility that it might allow a termination of employment "at some firm date during the last few weeks of pregnancy."

Another footnote explained that the teachers involved in the cases (in which appellate courts had reached conflicting conclusions) were placed on maternity leave before title VII of the 1964 Federal Civil Rights Act was extended to State agencies and educational institutions and before sex discrimination guidelines issued under the law were amended to provide that "a mandatory leave or termination policy for pregnant women presumptively violated title VII." However, "while the statutory amendments and the administrative regulations are of course inapplicable to the cases now before us, they will affect like suits in the future." The Court went on to note maternity policies for employees of the Federal Government and Federal contractors and then stated: "We of course express no opinion as to the validity of any of these regulations."

Another case on which the Supreme Court ruled recently involved California's denial of State temporary disability insurance benefits to workers who undergo normal pregnancy. The Court found in June 1974 that the exclusion does not amount to invidious discrimination under the equal protection clause of the 14th Amendment. *Geduldig* v. *Aiello,* 417 U.S. 484 (1974). Specifically, it found that "The State has a legitimate interest in maintaining the self-supporting nature of its insurance program," and that:

There is no evidence in the record that the selection of the risks insured by the program worked to discriminate against any definable group or class in terms of the aggregate risk protection derived by that group or class from the program. There is no risk from which men are protected and women are not. Likewise, there is no risk from which women are protected and men are not.

The Court implied in the decision that it did not view the discrimination as "suspect" and therefore did not see pregnancy as a sex classification. It did not, however, rule directly on the question.

Although title VII was not an issue in the California case, the Equal Employment Opportunity Commission filed an *amicus* brief supporting its position that pregnancy disabilities should be treated as any other temporary disability for employment-related purposes. Parts of the brief were quoted by Justice Brennan in a dissenting opinion, joined in by Justices Douglas and Marshall. Justice Brennan called the majority view an "apparent retreat" from the Court's standard of judicial scrutiny when a legislative classification has turned on "male" or "female." In his view:

by singling out for less favorable treatment a gender-linked disability peculiar to women, the State has created a double standard for disability compensation: a limitation is imposed upon the disabilities for which women workers may recover, while men receive full compensation for all disabilities suffered, including those which affect only or primarily their sex, such as prostatectomies, circumcision, hemophilia and gout. In effect, one set of rules is applied to females and another to males. Such dissimilar treatment of men and women, on the basis of physical characteristics inextricably linked to one sex, inevitably constitutes sex discrimination.

This statement is disputed, however, by Footnote 20 of the majority opinion, which reads:

The dissenting opinion to the contrary, this case is thus a far cry from cases like *Reed* v. *Reed*, 404 U.S. 71, and *Frontiero* v. *Richardson*, 411 U.S. 677, involving discrimination based upon gender as such. The California insurance program does not exclude anyone from benefit eligibility because of gender but merely removes one physical condition—pregnancy—from the list of compensable disabilities. While it is true that only women can become pregnant, it does not follow that every legislative classification concerning pregnancy is a sex-biased classification like those considered in *Reed, supra* and *Frontiero, supra*. Normal pregnancy is an objectively identifiable physical condition with unique characteristics. Absent a showing that distinctions involving pregnancy are mere pretexts designed to effect an invidious discrimination against the members of one sex or the other, lawmakers are constitutionally free to include or exclude pregnancy from the coverage of legislation such as this on any reasonable basis, just as with respect to any other physical condition.

The lack of identity between the excluded disability and gender as such under this insurance program becomes clear upon the most cursory analysis. The program divides potential recipients into two groups—pregnant women and nonpregnant persons. While the first group is exclusively female, the second includes members of both sexes. The fiscal and actuarial benefits of the program thus accrue to members of both sexes.

A summary compiled in August 1974 showed that in general Federal courts had tended to disapprove arbitrary quit dates for pregnant workers challenged on constitutional due process or equal protection grounds. State court decisions applying state and local FEP laws to maternity leave policies also have generally favored the rights of pregnant workers.

Although the issue of pregnant women *staying on the job* seems to be fairly well settled, the issue of *benefits* is another matter. Where conciliation attempts following adoption of the pregnancy disability benefits guidelines under title VII have not been successful, the EEOC has begun to use its new authority to file suit against employers who refuse to comply. Meanwhile, several decisions by lower courts in cases brought earlier by or in behalf of individual workers who had been denied pregnancy disability benefits reached the appellate level. Among these were *Wetzel* v. *Liberty Mutual Insurance Co.*, 372 F.Supp. 1146 (W.D. Pa. 1974), *Gilbert* v. *General Electric Co.*, 375 F.Supp. 367 (E.D. Va. 1974), *Farkas* v. *South Western City School District* (8 FEP 288), and *Communications Workers of America* v. *American Telephone and Telegraph Co., Long Lines Department* (S.D. N.Y. 1974).

The first three of these appealed decisions—all rendered prior to the Supreme Court decision in *Aiello*—held that an employer's exclusion of pregnancy from its disability benefit program was a discriminatory practice based on sex and thus violated title VII. In the other case, the district court judge was not persuaded by the argument of plaintiff employee groups and the EEOC that the *Aiello* decision resulted from deference given to State legislation on social welfare policy and that such deference was not warranted employers to title VII. However, rather than dismissing the complaints outright, he certified a question to the appeals court with a right to replead.

By the end of June 1975, several circuit courts—including one with jurisdiction over *Wetzel*—had upheld the guidelines, but employers continued to resist. The Supreme Court agreed to review the question during its 1975–76 term.

The appeals ruling in *Wetzel* drew a sharp distinction between the constitutional analysis required in *Aiello* and the statutory interpretation involved in the case under consideration. In addition, it rejected an analogy of the self-supporting State program that excluded only *normal* pregnancy and delivery disabilities to the company plan that excluded *all* pregnancy-related disabilities—pointing out that the employer's income protection plan would not cover a disability suffered by a pregnant woman but would have covered the disability had the woman not been pregnant.

The court examined the legislative history of the act and determined that the company's counsel had not shown any evidence that would indicate the guidelines are inconsistent with any congressional intent. With respect to the argument that the 1972 guidelines were inconsistent with EEOC's earlier policy position on pregnant workers, the court declared that the administering agency "has issued the guidelines to keep pace with changes in society's attitudes." Moreover: "The evolutionary process is a necessary function of our legal system—a system that must remain flexible and adaptable to ever-changing concepts of our society . . . . We feel that the legislative purpose of the Act is furthered by the EEOC guidelines and that the guidelines are consistent with the plain meaning of the statute."

As to the employer's contention that exclusion of pregnancy was justified because pregnancy is voluntary and illnesses are not, the court stated that voluntariness is no basis to justify disparate treatment of pregnancy. It pointed out that disabilities that could result from knowingly undertaking potentially harmful activities such as drinking intoxicating beverages, smoking, skiing, etc., were all covered under the income protection plan. The court further declared that pregnancy itself may not be voluntary.

On the illness question, the court pointed out that employer disability insurance plans are offered to alleviate the economic burdens caused by the loss of income and the incurrence of medical expenses that arise from the pregnancy. A woman disabled by pregnancy has much in common with a person disabled by a temporary illness—income loss because of absence from work and medical and hospitalization expenses (the latter even more likely for the pregnant woman than for a person with a temporary illness).

In addition to ruling that the exclusion of pregnancy benefits from the income protection plan which included other kinds of temporary disabilities was a violation of title VII, the court reached the same conclusion with respect to the company's requirement that employees return from a maternity leave of absence within a certain time period or lose their jobs.

Sexual harassment

Discrimination defined by the courts

Title VII requires the employer to maintain working conditions that are free of sexist intimidation and harassment. This duty extends to management's taking positive action where necessary to redress or eliminate employee or supervisory misconduct along these lines. For example, where a female employee is promoted or transferred to a formerly all male department, a sexually tense situation might arise in that department. Extra support may be necessary on the part of supervisory personnel to insure that the change of employment conditions does not prejudice the employee in her new position or force her to resign.

If a female employee becomes the object of sexually derogatory, oral and written remarks, jokes or gestures, and the situation is brought to the attention of the employee's supervisor, failure to act on the matter would be judged as management's condoning of the conduct. The EEOC is sensitive to the complaints of women alleging such instances of harassment, and stands ready to take harassment and intimidation issues to court to secure relief for the alleged victim.

Perhaps the extreme application of the sexual harassment concept is the predicating of an employee's career success on a willingness to submit to the sexual demands of that employee's supervisor. Case history dictates that women who have been victimized by such conduct have been successful in suits against their employers. Firms taken to court over such matters often try to show that the incident in question was an isolated one, one that was not sanctioned by management or one that took place unbeknownst to management. Regardless of the propriety of management's argument, the courts often equate an individual supervisor's actions with company policy or at least conduct condoned by management. The best defense a company can use in preventing such across the board equations is to have a written policy that spells out the fact that management will not tolerate a supervisor's use of his position to secure the sexual cooperation of his subordinates. Records showing disciplinary action taken against such conduct are also helpful in showing that management stands ready to uphold the rights and dignity of its employees. Where management can be shown to be unsympathetic or indifferent to acting on an employee's allegations that sexual harassment has occurred, the victim's success in court becomes an almost sure thing. Arguments to the effect that sexual harassment is not in itself, sex discrimination, have not been successful. The courts have ruled that making sexual submission a prerequisite to career success is placing an employment barrier before an employee that would not exist were the employee a member of the opposite sex. Based upon this logic, sexual harassment is often construed as sex discrimination within the meaning of title VII. In order to develop a thorough understanding of how the courts have responded to sexual harassment allegations, see the three cases featured in Chapter V that deal with this unique form of sex discrimination.

Discrimination on the basis of sexual orientation

Limited legal protection

Homosexuality, transsexuality and bisexuality are usually regarded as unconventional sexual orientations. Individuals with these sexual orientations are not protected from employment discrimination by title VII. However, the courts have from time to time ruled in favor of homosexuals alleging that they were either denied employment or discharged unlawfully. The grounds were that such practices deprive the individual of liberty and property under the Fourteenth Amendment to the Constitution. Three cases involving alleged sex discrimination due to the plaintiffs' unconventional sexual orientation can be found in Chapter V.

Due to unfavorable public opinion, possible adverse reactions in the workforce, personal preference and other reasons, many employers apparently would not knowingly hire a confirmed or suspected homosexual. This being the case, the homosexual job applicant may have to conceal his sexual preference in order to secure employment. Once hired, the hidden homosexual (or individual having another unconventional sexual orientation) often works in fear of being discovered. Discovery often triggers harassment from co-workers and supervisors and may force the employee to quit or result in his being fired.

On the issue of discharging the homosexual employee, it has not been held as unlawful to do so where it can be proved that there exists an observable and reasonable relationship between the employee's sexual orientation and his substandard job performance. Additionally, proof that a homosexual has committed or will commit criminal acts may serve as a defense for his dismissal.

Although homosexuals are not considered a protected class within the meaning of title VII, there are a number of groups that offer aid and counsel to homosexuals wishing to fight various forms of discrimination through court action. Such groups stand ready to defend the homosexual whose dismissal was based solely on the employer's personal standards that regard unconventional sexual orientation as immoral, indecent, disgraceful or harmful. In protecting the company from legal reprisal, the employer should weigh the actual impact the homosexual's continued employment would have on the company against such criteria as:

- the type of position the person holds or may hold with the company;
- the type of position the employee may be promoted to, with respect to responsibility and/or security sensitivity;
- the nature and seriousness of the conduct;
- circumstances surrounding the conduct;
- recency of the conduct;
- the age of the employee at the time of the conduct; and
- the absence or presence of efforts toward rehabilitation.

3 Developing personnel procedures that are not sexually discriminatory

What recruiting procedures should be followed to achieve compliance?

In order to comply with anti-discrimination laws it is essential for the company to develop written nondiscriminatory procedures by which the selection of employees may be done in ways that will not screen out female candidates. Federal officials often investigate a company's recruiting policy as the first step in a follow-up to a discrimination charge.

The law does not require companies to hire a specific number of employees from both sexes. However, if an investigation uncovers a substantial imbalance between male and female employees, the chances of avoiding legal troubles will be much better if the company has a written recruitment policy that has taken discriminatory practices into account and has seen to it that those who administer the policy do so effectively.

The Equal Employment Opportunity Act of 1972 (EEO Act), which amended the Civil Rights Act of 1964 requires companies to make and keep records by which it can be determined whether a discriminatory employment practice existed. With the presence of government regulations and the threat of possible discrimination suits, a company must protect itself by keeping careful records of every interaction between itself and a job applicant.

General recruiting considerations

Title VII requires all company recruiting activities to be designed so as not to exclude females. Companies that have substantially unisex work forces should be particularly aware of their fair recruiting responsibilities. There are three basic requirements that account for fair recruiting:

- that recruiting be done in a manner that gives realistic notification of job vacancies to females, and that females are given an opportunity to apply for those vacancies (such action on your part should be fully documented);
- that hiring qualifications do not unfairly exclude female applicants; and
- that women's applications be fairly and promptly processed.

Certain recruiting methods have come under close governmental scrutiny as evidence of unfair employment practices. Beyond a point-blank policy of hiring "males only," there are less obvious means of achieving the same effect. Recruiting exclusively in men's schools, employing only through agencies that traditionally refer male job candidates and limiting the residential area from which employees are hired are all considered unlawful practices.

In order to avoid many of the pitfalls that can lead to unfair recruiting, such recruiting procedures should be standardized, objective and centrally reviewed. Allowing individual department heads to publicize vacancies and recruit for their specific needs constitutes unstandardized and subjective procedures which are often seen as arbitrary and discriminatory by the courts.

Methods commonly utilized to increase recruitment of women are:

- use of female recruiters;

- participation in "job fairs" and similar efforts sponsored by women's groups;

- soliciting referrals from NOW, welfare rights organizations, Women's Equity Action League, Professional Women's Careers, black women's sororities, service groups and from local community organizations and leaders;

- actively recruiting at high schools and colleges with substantial female enrollments;

- formal briefing sessions on company premises with, and plant tours for women's organizations;

- special employment programs for women, including summer jobs for underprivileged students and the like;

- recruiting brochures that picture work situations which include female employees on the job.

Job descriptions

Generally job descriptions are composed of the task to be performed, physical and environmental demands, communication skills needed, location of the position within the organizational structure, and any special requirements needed before or after appointment such as licenses, certification or training. Often job descriptions leave out the most important ingredient—general knowledge and skills required for performing the usual duties of the job.

Under Title VII where your job requirements contribute to a disparate effect on females, management must be prepared to show how such requirements are directly related to the successful performance of the job. An aggrieved employee or job applicant needs only to demonstrate the disparate effect resulting from the requirement, she does not need to prove a discriminatory intent on the part of the company.

The company must exercise caution when translating the job description into requirements set forth for applicants. This involves the determination of the degree of importance that will be placed on an applicant's skills, interests, experience, education, personality and physical characteristics for the performance of the job's duties. This is a fairly easy task when the job requires a high degree of a specialized skill, but when the job could be mastered by virtually anyone receiving a bit of training, you must be sure that you are not placing too high a standard for an applicant to achieve in order to qualify.

Employment advertising

It is unlawful for a company to advertise a job opening in a manner indicating any preference, limitation, specification or discrimination based on sex, except where the restrictive criterion is a bona fide occupational qualification.

Any sort of personnel activities undertaken by representatives of the company that discourage women from applying for jobs can make the company subject to civil suit. For this reason no employee, from the parking lot guard to a receptionist, should be permitted to give "friendly advice" to the effect that a would-be applicant need not apply.

Once management is satisfied that none of its employees is giving negative word of mouth advertising, the personnel manager should take a close look into what the company's job advertisements actually say. It might unintentionally be eliminating female job applicants by the way job vacancies are advertised. While statements that appear in want ads such as "June graduates, recent college grads, girls or boys" obviously exclude individuals whose ages are between 40 and 65 "deliveryman, waiter, and pressman" carry sex bias, even though you would be just as satisfied with women who might take the job that was available.

Biased job advertising can be eliminated by following the following procedures:

- Place classified ads only under "Help Wanted" or "Help Wanted, Male-Female" listings. Be sure that the content of ads does not give preference to a particular sex.

- Advertise in media directed towards women.

- Include the phrase "Equal Opportunity Employer, M/F" in all job advertisements.

- Emphasize interest in recruiting both sexes for jobs that have been traditionally stereotyped as "male" or "female."

The following list shows how traditional stereotypical job titles can be written in a non-sexist fashion:

Cranemen	Crane Operators
Forgemen and hammermen	Forge and hammer operators
Clergymen	Clergy
Public relations men	Public relations specialists
Credit men	Credit and collections managers
Newsboys	Newspaper vendors
Office boys	Office helpers
Pressmen	Printing press operators
Seamstresses	Dressmakers
Boatmen and canalmen	Boat operators
Fishermen and oystermen	Fishers, hunters and trappers
Longshoremen	Longshore workers
Laundresses	Launderers

If you are a government contractor and are required to develop an affirmative action program, Executive Order 11246 sets forth certain requirements that must be followed with respect to job advertising, they are:

1. State that all qualified applicants will receive consideration for employment without regard to race, color, religion, sex or national origin;

2. Use display or other advertising which includes an appropriate insignia prescribed by the Director of the Office of Federal Contract Compliance;

3. A single advertisement which is grouped with other ads must clearly state that all employers in the group assure qualified applicants equal employment opportunity;

4. Use the phrase "An Equal Opportunity Employer."

Placing job orders with employment agencies

Title VII and the Federal Age Discrimination in Employment Act makes it unlawful for a company to attempt to place a discriminatory job order specifying race, color, sex, religion, national origin or age. In fact the EEOC has ruled that an employment agency that fills a job order knowing that the requested restrictions are not bona fide occupational qualifications will share the legal responsibilities with the hiring company.

Employment applications, applicant registration and questions permitted

Some companies do not make a practice of accepting job applications at all. It might be false logic to assume that by hiring only when there are vacancies that the company is giving everyone an equal opportunity for all job openings. To comply with fair employment practice laws it is advisable to accept employment applications, especially from females, even at times when there are no vacancies. This is particularly important if the workforce is made up predominantly of males. If applicants are tipped off about a job opening only by word of mouth, more likely than not only male friends of employees will get the word.

If the company does accept applications it is unlawful to turn a female applicant away due to an absence of a vacancy, or to falsely claim that you do not maintain a waiting list. With respect to waiting lists, it is in the best interest of companies striving to attain legal compliance to refer to applicants registered on the list in a way that would not exclude female applicants. "First come—first served" has become for many a maxim of basic justice, but it does not always hold true. If a company maintained a policy of closing waiting list registration to female applicants and only after a period of time took away the restriction, considering applicants solely by their position on the list would contribute to the continuation of a sexually segregated work force.

Although the design of job applications varies from business to business, most contain elements that help identify potential past, present, and future problems concerning the applicant without discriminating against the applicant. The following questions pertain to those elements commonly used in applicant screening:

- Has the applicant changed jobs frequently in the past few years?

- Does his employment history show a lack of continuity? This can be determined by checking the dates indicating when the applicant was enrolled as a student and the previous period of employment.

- What was the applicant's previous salary? This is a good indicator of how much responsibility the applicant held in past jobs, as job titles are often misleading.

- Ask the applicant to list references. If the list does not include former or present supervisor, ask why. Some references can be verified by telephone, others may be asked to respond to written questions such as: Would you rehire the applicant?

- For questions arising over the applicant's educational background, official transcripts may be obtained from any or all institutions the applicant claims to have attended.

- Other information may be solicited, such as the primary language which the applicant reads, writes, and speaks; which social, political and other organizations the applicant belongs to or participates in; and the names of persons to be notified in case of an emergency.

An interviewer may ask pre-employment questions about an applicant's children or plans for children or marriage, providing whatever questions are asked are directed routinely toward applicants of both sexes. It is unlawful if a man's answer leads to a different consequence from what a woman's answer does. For example, questions such as; "Do you plan to get married? Do you have or intend to have children? Do you plan to turn your children over to a day care program?" could be construed by a woman who was unsuccessful in obtaining a job as screens to employment opportunities.

Dual sets of application forms.   The practice of using dual application forms, that is one form for males and another for females, is illegal. Applications should not contain questions concerning an applicant's race, religion, national origin, age, child care arrangements or other such inquiries. If you need to have new forms printed, a draft must be sent to the EEOC for review and approval.

Unlawful employee referrals

It is unlawful for companies having substantially all-male work forces to hire primarily from a word-of-mouth referral system. Where such systems account for only a small portion of the company's hiring, the larger part stemming from state employment commissions, private agencies, equal opportunity employment advertising or walk-ins, that part done by word-of-mouth is not illegal.

It is a common practice to require applicants to state the names of relatives and close friends who are or have been employed by the company. There is nothing illegal about this practice in itself; however if your work force is predominantly white male, and a large percentage of them had close friends or relatives working for the company at the time of their applications, the friends and relatives procedure becomes legally suspect as a form of discrimination. This applies to summer hiring as well. Hiring only college students or sons of employees for summer help is considered an unlawful employment practice.

Front door walk-ins

If a company has a virtually all male labor force, therefore having in the community a reputation of not hiring women, there is a strong likelihood that females would avoid seeking employment there. In such a case, the flow of front door walk-ins would be limited to male applicants, thus perpetuating a sexually segregated work force, thus violating Title VII.

Conducting job interviews

If a company relies on casual or unscored interview methods and its applicant rejection rate is higher for females than for males, the firm could be called upon to present evidence as to the validity of its interviewing procedures. Refusing to even interview a female candidate is an unlawful employment practice.

Interviews are perhaps the most valuable means for obtaining details regarding prior background that often do not come through on application forms or resumés. Most companies hope that through an interview they will be able to evaluate personal traits and attitudes that often indicate future job success. Once an interviewer has received a candidate's application, the interviewer may ask the candidate such questions as:

- What specific type of position do you feel you are qualified for?

- What special preparations have you made in qualifying for the job?

- Can you relate experiences you have had that are relevant to the job you are applying for?

- Have you ever been fired from a job? If so, for what reasons?

- What are your reasons for wanting this particular job?

The interviewer should cautiously weigh the candidate's responses and be particularly mindful of cynical or demeaning statements about previous employers, negative statements about your company's products or service or those connected with the candidate's present employer.

The interviewer should avoid saying anything that might be construed as an infringement of a job candidate's constitutional rights. Even innocent assertions like, "You stand a good chance, but we've only hired men for this position in the past," seem to imply sex bias in the company's hiring policy.

Even if it would be possible to reach a final determination about an applicant at the close of the interview, it is still advisable to tell the applicant that higher management will have to be consulted before a decision can be made. When a final decision is reached, the applicant should be promptly notified.

What hiring and job assignment procedures should be followed to achieve compliance?

The government policy concerning equal employment opportunity with respect to sex extends to virtually every aspect of the employer-employee relationship. Title VII extends a ban on discrimination regarding compensation, terms, conditions or privileges of employment. Government contractors responsible to Executive Order 11246 are required to develop affirmative action programs to provide equal employment opportunity in employment, upgrading, demotion or transfer; recruitment or recruitment advertising; layoff or termination; rates of compensation; and training and apprenticeship selection.

If, by virtue of a candidate's application or interview, there is reason to doubt the qualifications of that candidate, it is best to not offer the job to that candidate. Leaving a position vacant until the right person comes along is better than hiring the wrong person, as finding grounds for dismissal could be substantially more difficult. When the decision is made to hire an applicant, it is advantageous to organize a report containing a list of all applicants that were considered for the job. Indicate by each name a comment or two about them that led to the decision, also make positive comments about their qualifications, where applicable. In lieu of a formal report, this information may be transcribed onto each application form before filing. If called on to explain why a certain candidate did not make the grade, these records will provide all the necessary information.

In the case where a candidate was chosen over a female, the best defense for the decision would be an indication that the passed-over candidate did not possess certain skills that have been held as "a must" for all past applicants. If the required skills are job related and personnel has been consistent in its demands for all applicants, and has documented action taken on all applications, the company would be reasonably safe should an unsuccessful candidate attempt to prove that a discriminatory employment practice prevented her from being hired.

It would be difficult for a court to rule against a company that could document the facts that it:

- placed job posters at predominantly women's schools;
- actively recruited in women's schools and colleges;
- included the phrase "Equal Opportunity Employer, M/F" in job advertisements;
- hired through state employment services;
- participated in community-oriented affirmative action programs;
- has hired a percentage of females over a given period of time proportional to their percentage in the community;
- has promoted a proportional number of female workers to males;
- has not denied jobs to qualified female applicants.

Many states prohibit or limit the use of lie detectors in employment situations. Companies wishing to use such devices as a means for screening job applicants or promotion candidates must check with state authorities first. Like any form of testing, the use of lie detectors must not be done as an effort to deny employment or promotion opportunities to females.

General hiring and job assignment considerations
Companies that engage in affirmative recruiting efforts that substantially increase the flow of female applicants could still fall short of compliance if, because of such high standards few are actually hired. Companies

must be prepared to demonstrate that hiring standards do not automatically screen out female applicants based on their speech, dress or work habits, unless those standards are job related.

The common denominator to compliance with respect to hiring is that everyone should be given an equal chance for employment. A company understandably would be reluctant to hire a woman if the entire work force was male. Such a hire would necessitate the provision of separate restrooms and possible other facilities. However, unless the installation of dual facilities would burden the company with an unreasonable expense the law will not sanction a lack of facilities as an excuse for closing off employment opportunity for women.

Job assignments must be treated with the same "open to all" attitude that is required for general hiring. Women, for instance, must not be closed out of positions that require heavy lifting, nor should men be forced to do heavy labor exclusively, with no opportunity for obtaining an inside office job that affords more access to advancement. The length of rest periods, coffee breaks and lunch breaks must be the same for both sexes. If certain shifts have no rest periods and have shorter lunch breaks but accordingly pay more, women must not be excluded from them due to an effort to provide more rest time for female employees.

How to reject unsuitable applicants.   Observing certain precautions will help minimize the number of complaints filed against a company. Complaints, whether justified or not can be expensive in time, money and lost good will. Naturally costs are even higher when the complaining party is victorious in court. Personnel practices are made vulnerable by the relative ease of filing a complaint. All that is required is a telephone call to the right compliance agency by anyone who was turned down for a job. Aggrieved applicants do not even need an attorney to get an investigation started. It is often the front door walk-in or over-the-phone inquiry that causes the most problems. If personnel's response to such an inquiry is: "Sorry—we have no vacancies;" and word gets back to the person that someone had been hired for a job after all, the company could expect trouble.

Unqualified applicants can be rejected regardless of their status as females. Because such rejections are delicate personnel matters, it is advantageous to prepare a non-discriminatory strategy that can be applied to all interviewees. Applicant rejection criteria may be developed from the following examples:

1. Know ahead of time the type of person you are seeking, and put the criteria in writing. In addition to the skills required for the job description include the desired aptitudes, abilities, background and experience, education and interests, and personality and character traits clearly necessary for the job.

2. Prepare a written list of "knock out" questions such as: "Do you have a chauffer's license, or could you get one?" . . . . "Would you object to relocating if necessary?" . . . . "Would you or your spouse object to your being away from home a few days each month?" Answers to these and questions like them will readily screen out many who are obviously unsuitable.

3. Try to get obviously unsuitable candidates to turn down the job. This can be done by emphasizing all of the negative aspects of the job such as heavy labor, late night hours, extensive travel, and whatever.

4. Allow the applicant who persists to complete an application form. Make it clear to the applicant that all applications will have to be reviewed in order to determine which applicant is the most qualified.

5. Once you have made your selection send a letter of rejection to all unsuccessful applicants, as oral rejections are subject to misunderstanding. Word your letter to the effect that: "The qualifications of the person finally selected more exactly fit our needs at the present time."

6. Be prepared to demonstrate how the successful candidate actually was more qualified. Your applicant rejection file should not only include all of the application forms, but a record of all telephone contacts and copies of letters sent to and received from applicants.

Marital status, parental status, illegitimacy

A company's policy of not hiring married women is a violation of Title VII if the company does not also prohibit the hire of married men. The key to offering equal employment opportunity, with respect to a particular applicant's marital or parental status, is based on the consideration that whatever is done for one sex, must be done for the other. Accordingly, the EEOC has ruled that a company cannot refuse employment opportunity solely because of a woman's pregnancy or because she is an unwed mother. This stand is based upon the reasoning that a man does not have to worry about hiding pregnancy and that unless he admits it, there is no way to prove that he is an unwed father.

It is common for a woman to be turned down for a job because she has pre-school age children at home. The customary assumption is that she will have certain maternal duties that might often keep her away from her work. If the same restrictions are not placed on fathers of pre-school age children, refusing to hire a woman due to conflicts that might arise from being a parent to young children is against the law.

Some firms have rules that forbid or restrict the employment of married women. Rules such as a company's refusal to hire wives of employees, requiring employees who marry other employees to resign within 30 days of the marriage, or denying severance pay to a woman who was terminated because of marriage are discriminatory. However, both the EEOC and the courts have found in favor of companies with rules that prohibit husbands and wives from working in the same departments. Usually such rules allow the married couple to decide which of them should resign, and if they cannot or refuse to, the one having less seniority may be legally terminated by company management.

Sexual designations and orientations

Classifying a job as "male" or "female" or maintaining separate lines of progression or seniority lists based on sex is unlawful where the separate designations would adversely affect an employee and unless the reasons for the separation were based on bona fide occupational qualifications, [42 C.F.R. § 1604.3].

In order to comply with this regulation a company must not arbitrarily classify jobs in ways that:

- would exclude females from jobs labeled "male" or from a position in a "male" line of progression, and vice versa,

- would result in prohibiting men scheduled for layoff from displacing less senior females on a "female" seniority list, and vice versa, and

- would serve to exclude members of either sex from jobs normally held by members of the opposite sex, because of a job's "light" or "heavy" designation.

Appearance and grooming

Grooming and appearance rules violate Title VII if they discriminate against any individual with regard to his employment status or pay, or if such rules segregate or classify employees in ways that deprive them of employment opportunities because of their race, color, religion, sex or national origin, [Section 703(a), 42 U.S.C. § 200e-2(a)].

Rules that limit the length of a male employee's hair are among those most frequently attacked as discriminatory. Management's position is further complicated by the legal community's inability to agree on the issue. The EEOC and several lower courts have held that hair length requirements that apply to men are unlawful where no like limitations are imposed on women. Other courts have taken the opposite position on similar matters. Since one is usually on firm ground when standards are based solely on bona fide occupational qualifications, it is probably in the company's best interest to keep such criteria in mind when establishing hair-length standards. Where safety or health is clearly involved, the EEOC has no argument with standards requiring employees to wear short hair, or use hair nets.

Prejudice displayed by supervisors and other employees

The methods used in investigating charges of alleged discrimination must be objective, expedient and consistent with management's treatment of similar cases in the past. If it can be established that employees who are members of the majority group have not been given special rights or preferential consideration, it is likely that the matter would be concluded without the intervention of a compliance agency. An inconsistent, or less than thorough follow through on the part of management, is a breeding ground for compliance difficulties.

Title VII holds management responsible for making every reasonable effort to control various discriminatory activities that often occur in the workforce. For instance, if it is brought to management's attention that one of the company's supervisors is so prejudiced against women that a practice of not assigning any women to his department becomes necessary, the company would likely be found not in compliance with Title VII in that it would have restricted the conditions of employment for female employees.

Prejudice, both mild and flagrant is often directed at particular employees by their fellow workers. Although telling "off color" jokes in the presence of female employees may have been offered allegedly "in fun," if a female employee is offended by that type of humor and brings the matter to management's attention, the company must investigate and take action to control such activities. Otherwise, failure to take action might be construed as condoning the practice.

Exceptions for bona fide occupational qualifications

A company may legally deny employment to an individual on the basis of sex, where such denial results from a bona fide occupational qualification. This means that the restrictions placed on certain jobs are reasonably necessary to the normal operation of business.

Business necessity. If a company is charged with an alleged discrimination based on a person's sex, the practice will be found lawful despite the disparate effect it has on women if it can be proved that the practice was based on a business necessity. In considering such cases the courts weigh the strength of the business need against the adverse impact on the affected class.

Company testing or educational requirements are often targets for discrimination charges. In such instances company management is required to establish the relationship between the requirement and job performance. In justifying educational requirements, the company will need to demonstrate how the practice carries out the purpose claimed, and that there are no acceptable alternatives which would equally or better accomplish the business purpose that would have a lesser impact on women.

The courts do not consider business necessity to be equated with business convenience. Discrimination is not defensible as a business necessity because of management's desires to conform to traditional practices, avoid union pressure, or to appease customers.

Safety and efficiency considerations. If the safe and efficient operation of a business requires hiring one sex exclusively for certain jobs, the resulting discrimination on the basis of sex may not be held unlawful. The best defense against charges of discrimination would be to determine the acceptable performance standards required for a job and to leave sex out of the question. For instance, if it is likely that the weight lifting capabilities of women would not permit them to perform the duties of a particular job, it is probably a better idea to make the job available to anyone of either sex, provided they can lift the amount of weight necessary.

This same strategy holds true for almost all deficiencies one might associate with members of a particular sex in general. If experience dictates that women are better suited for assembling intricate electrical components, rather than close the job off to men, the same goal can be accomplished by giving male applicants a trial and evaluating their performance.

State protective legislation. Many states have enacted laws or set forth administrative regulations with respect to the employment of women. Such laws prohibit or limit the employment of women in certain occupations such as jobs requiring the lifting or carrying of weights exceeding prescribed limits or jobs requiring work during certain hours of the night or for more than a specified number of hours per day or per week, or for certain periods of time before and after childbirth. This type of law has been categorized as state protective legislation for women. Both the EEOC and the courts have taken the position that these state protective laws for women will not be considered a defense to an otherwise established unlawful employment practice or as a basis for the application of the bona fide occupational qualification stipulation for employment.

What benefit, compensation and terms of employment policies should be developed in order to achieve compliance?

As far as legal compliance is concerned it is not unlawful for a company to develop different standards of compensation or terms or conditions of employment, in accordance with a bona fide seniority or merit system, or a system that measures earnings by the quantity or quality of production, or to employees who work in different locations, as long as the differences are not attributable to an intention to discriminate because of sex.

General benefits, compensation and terms of employment considerations
The benefits derived from a company profit-sharing or retirement plan, or the payment of death benefits must be disbursed equitably without regard to sex.

A profit-sharing plan that permits male employees to receive shares only after reaching age 50 is discriminatory if female employees are able to receive shares at any time they leave their jobs, regardless of age.

A retirement plan is unlawful under Title VII if it:

- requires female employees to work to higher age levels in order to receive benefits than are required of male employees;

- provides females lower benefits than males;

- allows females to retire with full benefits at a particular age, but allows only partial benefits to males who retire at the same age;

- requires a certain number of years service for one group in order to be eligible for retirement, but places no such requirement on other groups;

- requires higher contribution rates for one group than for others.

A death benefit policy is discriminatory under Title VII if it does not compensate surviving spouses of deceased female employees, while extending such benefits to surviving wives of deceased male employees.

Fringe benefits
Although the costs of providing fringe benefits such as health and life insurance, sick leave and vacations may be greater for one sex than for the other, such cost differentials are not considered a defense against discrimination charges that stem from benefit inequities. However, under Executive Order 11246, if your company's contribution to benefit

plans is equal for male and female employees, or if resulting benefits are equal, the company would be considered to be in compliance.

This formula—what is done for one must be done for all—can be applied to all aspects of fringe benefits. Companies cannot give preference when providing fringe benefits to those who are the "heads of the household" or "the principal wage earner." This being the case, a health insurance program is discriminatory if it:

- covers male employees' wives but not female employees' husbands;

- allows male employees to purchase additional coverage for their wives but denies such options to female employees;

- excludes pregnancy benefits;

- differentiates between male and female employees with respect to the amount of benefits;

- in the case where two employees marry each other, does not allow the female to continue her individual benefits, but rather automatically places her under her husband's policy.

A company may lawfully provide varying benefits such as vacations and sick leave under a bona fide plan when such benefits are standardized according to a formula involving age and length of service requirements.

Maternity benefits

Following the Supreme Court decision in [*General Electric Co.* v. *Gilbert*, 429 U.S. 125 (1976)] a company may lawfully exclude from its nonoccupational sickness and accident benefit plan disabilities due to pregnancy, miscarriage, abortion, childbirth and recovery. However, if a company offers maternity coverage to spouses of employees, it is unlawful to deny such coverage to employees themselves.

Pregnancy leave

Title VII prohibits the denial of employment to a woman because she is pregnant. According to EEOC guidelines, maternity leave is to be dealt with as either sick leave or other types of leave. If a woman is sick or physically incapacitated by pregnancy or childbirth, the necessary leave must be treated as sick leave, and such leave is subject to the same eligibility requirements that affect leave for non-maternity reasons. That is, if a woman would be entitled to take up to two weeks of leave to recuperate from the flu, she must not be required to work for a period of one year for the company before being eligible to take two weeks for maternity purposes. Eligibility for such leave may not be denied to unmarried females.

Management cannot set an arbitrary mandatory date at which women must begin maternity leave. The factors that apply to her return-to-work date are the same as those that determine when she would return from any other leave: physical condition, amount of leave accumulated, the job and so on.

If the new mother wishes to take additional leave in order to spend more time at home with her baby, and this time off is not prescribed by her physician, the company must treat that leave like any other non-sick leave. Depending upon the organization, such additional leave might be classified as vacation with or without pay, or whatever is generally permissible.

If a company has no leave plan and is inclined to discharge a female employee because of her need to leave work due to pregnancy, the practice would be considered unlawful if it has a disparate effect on one sex and is not justified by business necessity. EEOC policy requires that a leave of absence be granted for pregnancy whether or not it is granted for illness.

Treating female employees who return from maternity leaves of absence as new hires is a violation of Title VII. For instance, it is unlawful to require such employees to forfeit their seniority status due to the necessary leave. When it comes time to reinstate a female employee who is returning to work following a maternity leave of absence, treating her the same as you would other disabled employees is probably the best policy. If a company has held jobs open for employees who were absent while recuperating from a skiing accident or automobile injury, the EEOC would consider closing an absent-while-pregnant woman's job as an unlawful employment practice. A company wishing to avoid the need to automatically rehire women returning from leaves of absence can do so by developing a policy to evaluate all applications, allowing itself the option of filling vacancies with the most qualified persons. To implement such a policy, the company must, in order to protect itself, monitor its rehire statistics. In so doing the firm can avert charges that more men were rehired than women.

Equal pay policies

The Fair Labor Standards Act (FLSA) as amended by the Equal Pay Act sets minimum wage, overtime pay and equal pay standards for every employee engaged in interstate commerce, or in the production of goods for interstate commerce. These regulations are enforced by the Department of Labor's Wage and Hour Division. If a company's employees come under FLSA coverage, it is unlawful for that company to discriminate on the basis of sex with regard to pay when equal work is performed on jobs by employees of both sexes, where such jobs require equal skills, effort and responsibility, and where such jobs are performed under similar working conditions. Failure to comply with the provisions of the FLSA might subject the company to a discrimination suit that could result in having to restore aggrieved employees with back pay.

A company may lawfully vary the amount of payment when such differentials are based on seniority or merit systems, systems that base pay on the quantity or quality of production or other systems provided the differential is not based on sex.

Male-female jobs.   Unless job limitations according to sex are based on bona fide occupational qualifications, the practice of restricting certain job opportunities to one sex exclusively is unlawful. The following criteria are unlawful but are in common use as factors serving to close jobs to one sex:

- an assumption that the turnover rate among women is higher than among men;

- a notion that women are less capable than men of aggressive salesmanship;

- a notion that men are less capable than women for work requiring dexterity;

- a lack of restroom and/or locker facilities for both sexes;

- the preference of co-workers, management, clients or customers for one sex, except where necessary for authenticity.

If any jobs in a company are designated males-only or females-only, management must be prepared to prove to a compliance investigator that the sex separation does not discriminate against one sex with regard to pay. When a male leaves a position and is replaced by a female, it would be contrary to the FLSA to pay the female at a lower rate than her predecessor. Therefore, if certain circumstances justify a difference in pay, it would be advantageous to have the circumstances well documented. For instance, if a male employee was required to first engineer an entire production system and later manage it, and the replacement female had to assume only the management duties, a decision to pay her less than her predecessor would be justified.

Overtime. If male and female employees perform equal work during regular hours, and some continue working into an overtime period, the company may lawfully pay a higher wage for the overtime hours, provided the same pay scale is applied to both sexes [29 C.F.R. 1800.116(a)].

Vacation or holiday pay. Vacation or holiday pay is treated as wages by the FLSA. If in order to be entitled for such compensation one sex is required to work more hours than the other, the pay differential is prohibited.

Employee benefit plans. You may contribute varying amounts to employee insurance plans or similar benefits, provided the resulting benefits are the same for both sexes.

Commission. The establishment of different rates of commission is not unlawful as long as the differential is not based on sex.

How to avoid violations. In order to stay in compliance with respect to employees' pay, examine company compensation policies to be sure that the company is:

- paying women the same wages for the same work as men;

- giving women the same opportunities for promotions as men;

- preparing women for promotion through training as thoroughly as men.

The following strategies are not legally acceptable means for equalizing pay for employees:

- enacting pay cuts to the higher paid employees;
- firing or disciplining employees or discriminating against them for taking grievances to the Wage-Hour Division;
- discharging female employees so as to avoid paying them equal wages.

Wage differentials that are in compliance
Wage differentials that are the results of merit or seniority systems, incentive or other plans are legally permissible provided they are not discriminatory or part of systems responsible for past discrimination.

Red circle rates. It is a common practice to temporarily assign employees to jobs other than their regular classifications. It is legally permissible to continue to pay such employees at their usual rates, regardless of the fact that others performing the same duties are paid higher or lower rates. This practice is known as red circling, and can be done only on a temporary basis. After one month, the temporary nature of red circle assignments could draw attention as a discriminatory pay practice.

Temporary reassignment. Whenever an employee's temporary assignment becomes permanent, that employee's rate of pay must be adjusted according to the rates paid to employees who work regularly at the same assignment if they are paid more. Otherwise the aggrieved employee might have grounds to enter suit against the company and attempt to collect back pay damages.

Equal work standards
With respect to equal pay for equal work, the concept of equal work does not mean identical work. Actually, the test is whether jobs require equal skill, effort, and responsibility, and whether they are performed under similar working conditions. Job titles and classifications are not to be used as pay determinants; job requirements and performance are.

Skills. Equal skill includes such factors as experience, training, education and ability. As a pay determinant, only those skills that are required for job performance should be considered; skills above and beyond do not enter into the pay picture.

Effort. Equal effort is the measurement of physical or mental exertion required for the performance of a job. Effort can be considered equal, even though it is exerted in different ways. If two employees operate similar machinery, the only difference being that one occasionally has to lift boxes, the effort as far as pay is concerned would be equal. Only if the lifting effort occupied a considerable portion of the work cycle would you have to consider adjusting that employee's pay.

Responsibility. The question of responsibility as a pay determinant involves the degree of accountability an employee is faced with in the performance of job duties in relation to the importance of the job. Employees who assume higher degrees of responsibility can justifiably be paid at a higher rate than others. For instance, an employee who can be called on to fill in during a supervisor's absence could be entitled to a higher wage than the employees who could not be delegated such responsibility. Also considered as responsibility factors are the degree to which work is supervised, and the degree to which teamwork and public contact is required.

Similar working conditions. Where an employee must face hazards, disagreeable conditions or the need for personal expenditure to a degree higher than other employees, such conditions may be used as determinants in adjusting the rate of pay. Otherwise, the fact that employees perform jobs in different parts of the plant generally will not establish a difference in working conditions as far as pay is concerned.

Segregated facilities and activities
Title VII requires that company facilities and company supported activities be open to employees without regard to sex. Accordingly, the following practices are considered unlawful:

- maintaining or supporting of sexually segregated employee social clubs; and,

- conducting sexually segregated social functions such as Christmas parties or picnics.

In order to comply with Title VII and avoid charges of sex discrimination, you must provide restroom and shower facilities for women that are equal to those provided for your male employees. Only by proving the installation of such facilities would bring forth an undue hardship will a company be exempted from this duty. With regard to social functions, it is not unlawful to hold a golf outing or stag party for men only, as long as a similar suitable activity is held for your female employees.

Testing procedures that do/do not comply
According to EEOC definition, tests are any paper-and-pencil or performance measure that is used as a basis for making employment decisions. Also included are all formal, scored, quantified or standardized techniques of assessing employment suitability.

Testing is widely utilized as a method for screening job applicants and for determining employee promotion qualifications in that they:

- predict by measuring aptitudes required for skills-learning which applicants would/would not likely perform job duties successfully;

- evaluate achieved competence to perform specific tasks by measuring occupational knowledge, skills and abilities;

- provide an objective basis for comparing applicants apart from personal appearance, interviewer bias or past friendship.

Since the results of the tests may significantly affect a decision to hire a job applicant or approve an employee's promotion, and because the grading and interpretation are entirely under company control, the law requires that all elements of testing discrimination due to sex be eliminated.

Because Title VII prohibits discrimination in all employment practices, all aspects of the tests administered must be job related. If the tests or any parts of them adversely affect the performance of females, the ability to prove job relatedness is doubly important. Mechanical ability tests have traditionally screened out a disproportionate number of females. The EEOC examines such tests very carefully, as well as their job relatedness.

Selection procedures, use of standardized tests, and validation
In recent years the Equal Employment Opportunity Coordinating Council (EEOCC), which is comprised of the Department of Labor, EEOC, Justice Department, Civil Service Commission and the Civil Rights Commission, has tried to draft uniform selection guidelines for compliance. All agencies concurred on the resulting guidelines with the exception of the EEOC. Until uniformity is achieved, industry will have to comply with both sets. For the most part the new guidelines are nothing more than the EEOC standards with certain points expanded. Compliance with both sets would put your company ahead of the basic requirements, and companies that meet the requirements established in only one set of guidelines would be on reasonably safe ground should a court appearance be necessary.

The principle underlying both sets of selection procedure guidelines is that such procedures that have an adverse impact on women are considered against the law. The two sets of guidelines differ in their definitions of adverse impact. The EEOC's guidelines do not define the term. The EEOCC's guidelines apply what is known as a 4/5th's rule. This rule states that a selection rate is adverse if it is less than 80 percent of the group with the highest selection rate. According to the new guideline's "bottom line" approach, compliance agencies will examine the total success of a company's equal employment record before attacking a single selection procedure.

Because the law makes it necessary for management to prove the validity of whatever tests are used, many firms have opted to discontinue the practice of testing. The reason for the general reluctance to test is not actually based on the requirement to validate, but on the method of validation prescribed by the EEOC.

There are three methods by which tests can be validated: content, construct and criterion-related. Content validity, such as a typing test, uses a sample of the work that is to be performed as the test. Construct validity tests measure a skill that is typically necessary for successful job performance. These two testing methods are the most popular in that they are economically administerable, are not time consuming, and are reasonably accurate in predicting a candidate's likelihood for success.

However, under EEOC guidelines, content and construct validity are only permissible when the preferred method, criterion-related, is not feasible.

Criterion-related validity may be accomplished in one of two ways. The predictive validation method requires testing all applicants; however, the selection of employees is done without regard to their test scores. After a period of time has passed, the job performance of the employees is evaluated and compared with their individual test scores. The ratio that exists between the employees' job performance and their degree of success attained on the test, establishes the validity of that test.

Concurrent validation is the other criterion-related type. This procedure is carried out by taking a representative sample of current employees and rating each employee's job performance. Following this, the employees are tested, and the resulting scores are compared to their job ratings. The ratio established between job rating and test score determines the validity of the test. This validity depends greatly on how objective the supervisors are in analyzing specific performance criteria in order to rate individual employees, and whether the sample of employees used in the test was a truly representative sample of the workforce, including employees from both sexes.

Industry has long argued that criterion-related validity produces excellent tests; however, the point of testing is to improve the overall quality of the workforce by hiring employees with high performance potentials. Contrary to the EEOC guidelines, the new guidelines adopted by the EEOCC grant companies the option of using whichever type of test validation that best suits their needs.

Assuming a standardized test to be valid simply because it is in popular use, or its author and publisher is widely respected, may lead to compliance trouble.

Tests such as the Purdue Mechanical Ability Test have been ruled as discriminatory against females, and the Humm-Wadsworth Test's temperament profiles have also been found invalid. Prior to purchasing a standardized test, read through the accompanying information packet to see if there is a compliance statement. If you have questions about a test's compliance conformity, contact your local EEOC office for information.

Relating tests to job assignments

Because a test in itself is neither valid nor invalid, the only way that you can prove the job-relatedness of a test is to conduct a validity study. Because the skills required for a particular job vary from one company to another, management must not depend on validity studies that were performed by others. However, in the case of a multiunit organization, if there is virtually no difference from facility to facility in the requirements for a certain job, there would be no need to run separate validity studies.

When performing a validation study on a test, be sure that the attributes selected for examination are directly related to successful job performance. If a job requires a working knowledge of general mathematics only, testing for proficiency in algebra is not necessary and may serve to invalidate the test.

In cases where the economic and human risks involved in hiring an unqualified applicant are greater than the risks involved in rejecting a qualified one, the law sides with management in a decision to make the screening tests more rigorous than usual. For example, management would have reasons to justify requiring more than a pilot's license alone of candidates for the position of corporation pilot.

Absence of validation in testing

Although you should never rely on the general reputation of a test in lieu of conducting your own validation study, if conducting such a study is technically impossible, you are permitted by law to rely on validation studies conducted by other organizations, provided there are no major differences in the jobs and skills criteria [29 C.F.R. § 1607.7]. You may find such studies in test manuals and in professional literature.

What promotion and transfer criteria are considered in compliance?

The EEOC and the federal courts more and more are looking upon supervisory performance ratings as tests needing validation. Because these ratings are heavily weighted in decisions surrounding an employee's being considered for promotion and transfer, you must build precautions into your performance-appraisal system to ensure valid and reliable ratings that are free from discriminatory bias.

Whenever the application of performance-appraisal data has an adverse impact on women, there is a strong possibility of a Title VII violation. The EEOC requires supervisory ratings to be related to observable, objective standards of work performance, and that they be made in accordance with uniform, carefully specified procedures.

General promotion and transfer considerations

Although a failure to post notices of job openings is not in itself illegal, both the OFCC and the EEOC will, when acting on a related discrimination complaint, ask management to demonstrate that the failure-to-post procedure is nondiscriminatory.

It is generally required that posting be done in a way that is appropriate to the organization. This may be accomplished by advertising job openings in an internal plant newsletter, or by posting notices along main avenues in the various departments. Since it is required that employees have direct access to the information, a reliance on word of mouth advertising is not sufficient.

Failure to notify employees of promotion opportunities and required qualifications may result in a Title VII violation. Court ordered posting procedures usually require notices to contain a specific job description for each vacancy, the rate of pay, and information regarding the qualifications for the job and where to file applications.

The compliance agencies in their attempts to facilitate the upgrading and promotion of women may be looking at posting with a certain degree of tunnel vision. One of industry's strongest objections to posting is that it takes too long to fill a vacancy. The length of delay depends upon how long the notice must remain posted, how many bids are received and the selection criteria involved. It is further argued that a company that yields to public and union pressure and adopts a completely open, company-wide posting policy, would be inviting a number of problems. This type of system often requires a large administrative staff to conduct interviews and administer tests, or encourages supervisors to try to get around the system in order to speed things up. Thus, new morale problems are raised. A company can build a good case for why it does not wish to post job vacancies by combining with the preceding management difficulties the following elements, some of which serve to backfire on the cause of equal advancement opportunity:

- considering the increased number of bids, management is often forced to seek a selection criterion that is easy to evaluate, such as seniority, this tendency could screen out the very people who have been the victims of past sex discrimination;

- because more people become aware of their consideration and competition, arguments will likely arise among employees who are dissatisfied over management's selection;

- in predominantly male work forces, it is mathematically likely that most bids will come from male employees, the result being that female candidates may lose out to more qualified males;

- such a system may encourage spur-of-the-moment decisions about the employee's career.

If a company does post job openings, its efforts to encourage female and minority employees to apply for positions, particularly where there is underutilization, would constitute a good faith act on behalf of management. Such actions as these should be documented for future use.

Selection of employees for promotion

Because the compliance agencies have taken a watchdog stance with respect to advancement opportunities for female employees, the acid test for whatever system you utilize is how well it will stand up in court. If a female employee charges the company with discrimination because she was not promoted, management will have to demonstrate that some male employees with qualifications equal to hers were passed over as well. The reason for denying promotion opportunities to female employees must be based on the fact that the unsuccessful candidates did not measure up to standards as well as did the person finally selected. Because the courts look favorably on management's good faith attempts to accommodate the aggrieved employee, the method of selection could very likely provide the necessary evidence.

Automatic consideration.   This procedure is one that selects the next qualified employee in line as a simple means for filling vacancies. Although such systems minimize the investment of administrative time, they are in limited use for a number of reasons. In the first place the system is generally unappealing to employees because once they have entered a specific line of progression, their chances for changing departments or having rapid access to advancement are remote. Secondly, the EEOC does not consider closed selection systems to be indicative of a company's good faith efforts toward promoting female employees. It could be concluded that in order for such a system to meet the various compliance requirements, there would have to be a good percentage of female employees dispersed throughout the company's organizational structure.

Company discretion. Under this system the personnel manager or department supervisor has the sole authority to select the worker to be promoted. This system is in very limited use due to the fact that management's selections are frequently challenged by union grievance procedures; and because of the system's indifference to employees' carrer objectives, the compliance agencies do not often sanction such practices.

Employee requests. In spite of the many disadvantages to open posting, the EEOC still holds such systems in high regard with respect to selection fairness. By utilizing a selection system based on employee requests, you may be able to realize most of the advantages of posting but fewer disadvantages. A company can implement such a system by performing the following steps:

- publish a list of all jobs in the company and their corresponding requirements;
- counsel employees to realistically assess their abilities;
- allow each employee to submit job bids to a bid box or the personnel office (these are requests to be considered for a particular job/jobs whenever a vacancy arises);
- limit the number of bids that may be submitted by each employee, but make it known that employees do not have to submit the maximum number of bids;
- inform employees that their bids will remain active until they themselves rescind them, and that they may upon rescinding one, bid on another job;
- establish a definite cut off period for consideration of requests (such as one week before a vacancy occurs);
- establish a backup procedure so that all personnel understand what steps will be taken in the event that no qualified requests are received.

Instituting an employee request system will bring about the customary administrative difficulties that accompany any procedural change. For example, one could expect to be deluged with requests the first week the system is operational, and the purchase of additional files may be necessary to accommodate the paperwork. However, the request system will be less complicated to administer than the posting procedure, and will take far less time. As soon as a vacancy arises, supervisors will have on hand a ready supply of requests from which to choose. Another advantage is that employees will be less inclined to jump at the first promotion chance that comes along. Given a copy of the company organizational chart, employees will be able to see exactly where the routes for advancement lie with respect to available jobs, and will have a good idea as to whether or not they are qualified to enter a particular line of progression.

Although the employee request system is not a panacea, it does satisfy the majority of the objectives of management, employees individually, the union and the compliance agencies.

The use of seniority in selection for promotion

Bona fide seniority systems that account for preference in promotion, transfer, overtime, work and vacation schedules do not violate Title VII, provided that such systems are nondiscriminatory and do not by their neutral conduct perpetuate past sex discrimination.

Prior to the enactment of the Civil Rights Act of 1964, females as a group were not protected against discriminatory employment practices. For compliance purposes it is a misconception to believe that women's seniority accrual began in 1965. Such practices are often treated as examples of "residual" or "hangover" discrimination.

According to the law, when a company has discriminated in the past and when its present policies renew discriminatory effects, those personnel policies must be changed unless it can be proved that they are based on legitimate, nondiscriminatory business necessities. In order to qualify for the business necessity exemption a company would have to prove that the methods in question are essential to the safety and efficiency of its operation. The test that compliance agencies will apply to alleged business necessities is whether safety and efficiency can be served by a reasonable alternative that has a less discriminatory effect.

Seniority practices that are apparently neutral are often scrutinized as possible sources of discrimination. Consider the situation where a company has established dual lines of progression, one for skilled workers, the other for those who are unskilled. The practice itself is permissible under Title VII; however, if a condition for advancement in a formerly all male progression is the seniority that has been accrued in that line, the practice serves to exclude female employees in the line and is therefore considered discriminatory. You must be certain that female employees at one job level are not stonewalled due to the next job in line's requirement of heavy lifting or other undesirable conditions. The key to compliance is to allow individuals from both sexes to enter into all lines of progression. Restricting any group to lines leading only to labor positions, and reserving skilled lines that lead to more interesting and higher paying jobs for other groups exclusively will lead to compliance troubles.

Discriminatory bias in job transfers

If a company's departmental structure was organized in a way that resulted in exclusion of women from having access to certain departments, it would be unlawful to restrict departmental transfer, even if such restrictions are provisions of a collective bargaining agreement.

Lateral transfer rules.   Whatever the motive: higher pay, a more desirable shift, or a change from a labor to an office-type job, no employee should be denied an opportunity for making a lateral transfer, provided the employee is qualified to assume the duties of the position applied for. Because some transfers, such as moving from production into a clerical job, may mean that the one-time hourly wage earner would become a full-time salaried employee, there will be a number of changes that the employee may not anticipate. Taking time to counsel the prospective transferee is the sort of good faith activity that could help a company avoid charges of unfair employment practices. Although becoming a salaried employee may mean the employee is entitled to certain benefits such as hospitalization and profit-sharing, it may also mean the end of overtime pay opportunities. By first making the opportunity available, and then explaining the advantages and disadvantages accompanying either decision, management will have taken sufficient steps with regards to compliance in this area.

Educational requirements for lateral transfers. If certain levels of education are required for entrance into a department or a particular job classification, the company must be certain that the requirements are job related, and not arbitrary means for screening out disadvantaged employees. The EEOC has found the requirement of a high school or college education, for instance, to be invalid for many positions.

Seniority and wage carryover. Requiring a female employee to forfeit prior service seniority as a condition for qualifying for a lateral transfer is considered discriminatory. Similarly, requiring a newly transferred employee to revert back to an entry-level pay scale is not permissible when such a practice serves as a means by which female employees are discouraged from making lateral transfers.

What training procedures should be followed in order to achieve compliance?

According to Title VII it is unlawful to deny a person admission into a training or apprenticeship program because of that person's sex. This duty extends to include the publication of advertising or printing of notices relating to such training or retraining programs. That is, unless there is a bona fide occupational qualification involved, training advertisements may not indicate a preference with regard to sex.

Companies wishing to obtain an exemption to the "open-to-all" requirement may do so by filing a written request supported by a statement of reasons with the Secretary of Labor [29 C.F.R. § 30.19].

General training considerations

Whether an apprenticeship committee is a union function or a joint labor-management responsibility, the committee may not require qualifications for membership or entrance into the program that do not reasonably relate to the skills required on the job. If there is a sex or racial imbalance with respect to skilled positions, and the cause for the imbalance can be traced to the training program, management will have to prove the discriminatory policies are based on legitimate business necessities, and that there is no reasonable alternative that could accomplish employment goals with a less discriminatory effect. The following conditions related to training programs are examples of noncompliance:

- applying higher or more stringent admission standards to females;

- giving false, misleading or incomplete information to females about procedures for membership application, referral, or apprenticeship training;

- limiting the number of journeymen and apprentices, thereby fostering underutilization.

Denying training opportunities on the basis of sex

Due to government pressure there is a trend among unions to recruit women into their membership and various training programs. Unions finding themselves to be short of compliance may attempt to shift the blame onto management. By making it known, perhaps through a written statement, that management fully intends to operate an equal opportunity training program, a company might be able to shortstop union efforts to escape the burden, and avoid having to make related concessions with the union at the bargaining table.

It is a common practice to consider new hires as trainees or probationary workers, with the thought that if the new hire does not work out after a period of time, the employee will be discharged. It is very important from a compliance standpoint to avoid such casual, unwritten training policies. In order to avoid possible charges of discrimination stemming from such a discharged employee, management would be well advised to follow these steps:

- inform the employee at the outset of the trainee status;

- put all provisions of the training program in writing;

- be certain the employee understands the length of the training period, and the nature of formal instruction to be received;

- designate the employee's date of placement into the permanent workforce as part of the training sequence, rather than a response to a manpower need.

What layoff procedures should be followed to achieve compliance?

The standards for determining when a person shall be laid off or recalled must be the same for all employees, not applied differently for males and females. Any company rules that call for automatic discharge must be examined closely to be sure that the rules do not impact more severely on female employees.

If it becomes necessary to reduce the workforce, companies required to follow an affirmative action plan are often caught in a conflict between the layoff provisions of the affirmative action plan, and those that are required under a collective bargaining agreement. Employers who have gone to the courts for help have gotten a variety of opinions. Some courts have held the conciliation agreement between a company and the EEOC to be more binding than a collective bargaining agreement. In such cases where layoffs are necessary, the reduction in force must be carried out in a way that does not result in decreasing the female percentage in the workforce.

Other courts have handed down opposing opinions, stating that the provisions of a collective bargaining agreement must be adhered to, regardless if such action is in conflict with a company's affirmative action plan. Once the matter is settled by a Supreme Court decision, industry will have concrete guidelines to follow with respect to layoff procedures. Until such time, if layoffs become necessary the company should note how the courts in its jurisdiction have ruled on the issue and plan a course of action consistent with those rulings.

Layoffs under discriminatory application of seniority rules

In certain instances where a female employee has proven her being laid off resulted from the fact that she was unable to acquire enough seniority in a once males-only job, the EEOC has ruled the practice unlawful.

On the other hand, seniority rights were won only after years of labor disputes and legal development. Seniority protection against layoffs is probably the most important seniority right of them all. Section 703(h) of Title VII states that a seniority system is acceptable provided the differences between sex groups are not the results of an "intention" to discriminate. If female employees acquired less seniority than males because of a company's intentionally discriminatory hiring practices, resulting layoffs based on its seniority system would be just as vulnerable in court as any other employment practices.

Effect of layoffs on affirmative action plans

A company that is required to adhere to an affirmative action plan has the duty to achieve equal employment through intensified recruitment of women. In the event the company is forced to make workforce cutbacks, it is probable that females will be the most adversely affected. If there are no reasonable alternatives to laying off members of the protected classes, management may wish as a demonstration of good faith, to provide counseling on unemployment benefits; realistic appraisal of their being called back to work, and where necessary, advice on other job possibilities.

It is required, as a feature of an affirmative action plan, to monitor layoffs. To do this records must be kept on employees who have been laid off: indicating the number of employees, their names, effective date, number of males and females in each job classification, reason for layoff and recall rights.

Bumping

When plant-wide layoffs are necessary, the question as to whether one employee has the right to "bump" another depends on the plant seniority of the two employees, rather than the seniority acquired by each individually at the lower level job.

Rehiring after layoff

If an employee or group of employees proved to the EEOC that their being laid off was the result of some form of discrimination, the agency would likely require the company to provide one of the following recall remedies:

- the immediate recall of aggrieved employees to their former jobs, or recall to the next vacancy in those jobs;

- appropriate back pay, seniority and fringe benefits from the time of layoff until the recall date;

- eliminate the factors that caused the layoff and could be responsible for future layoffs;

- if the discrimination resulted from a policy, a new nondiscriminatory policy must be developed to replace it;

- if the discrimination resulted from a deviation from normal company policy, monitoring methods must be instituted in order to avoid a repeat error;

- if the discrimination resulted from a provision set forth in a collective bargaining agreement, that agreement must be modified in order to prevent similar discrimination from occurring in the future.

What termination procedures should be followed to achieve compliance?

From a compliance standpoint, it is necessary that employee dismissals be based on unsatisfactory performance. Therefore it is important to document each instance when management counseled the employee about performance quality. If an employee was given three explicit warnings but nothing was put into writing, that employee could later claim that the warnings never took place. Management's warning an employee is the same thing as a demand for improvement. Therefore, if the employee does make an effort to improve, that effort should be documented as well. If discharging an employee due to his unsatisfactory performance results in a court action, the company's case will be more convincing if it reflects occasions where the appropriate supervisor praised and encouraged the employee in addition to necessary instances of admonition. To protect against charges brought forth from a discharged employee, gather copies of the following documents into one file:

- the employee's official personnel file;

- a chronology of conferences and correspondence indicating appropriate dates, brief summaries of the orders of discussion, and other pertinent comments;

- a list of the employee's problem areas, including a documentation of each for explanation;

- company policies and procedures pertinent to the case.

General termination considerations

If an employee who was discharged due to substandard performance charges his firm with discrimination, the company may defeat the charges by producing a production log as evidence. Such a log would indicate the quality and quantity of production accomplished each day by each employee. Demonstrating the fact that other women workers on the job were able to perform satisfactorily is the best line of defense.

Similarly, it is not unusual for a female trainee who was dismissed during or immediately following the program administered by a male supervisor, to claim that dismissal was a result of discrimination. To disprove such a charge management needs only to show that other female trainees made the grade, and are working successfully on the job. This is one advantage to including a healthy sampling of females in the training program.

Discharging female employees for reasons other than unsatisfactory performance may lead to compliance difficulties. For instance, frequently an employee will be dismissed because of an inability to get along with co-workers. If the employee is a female, management will have to investigate the situation to see if the problem was simply an unresolvable personality conflict, or one resulting from discrimination. If the employee in question was not the subject of any harassment; rather the problem was basically the employee's inability to work with others, sex notwithstanding, discharging the employee would not constitute discrimination.

Discharge for pregnancy and non-rehire after pregnancy leave

Discharging a female employee because of her substandard performance is legal, provided management can document conferences that were held regarding her performance and future with the company. Discharging a woman simply because she is pregnant is not legally permissible. The matter becomes arguable if it is believed that, due to the extent of her condition, her continuing to work would probably jeopardize her health or the health of her baby. However, a supervisor's concern for her health may not be a defense for dismissing her. Rather, a decision to dismiss the pregnant woman can be defended on the grounds that because of the extent of her condition, she is no longer able to safely and efficiently perform the duties of her job. Attempts to work out an alternative to dismissal, such as leave of absense, leave without pay or vacation is often a sufficient counter to discrimination charges.

Companies that have no written pregnancy leave policies are most often the ones subject to pregnancy-related discrimination charges. In the absence of a written policy, difficulties that arise in these situations may be avoided by treating a woman who is forced to leave her job temporarily the same way that other employees are treated who need to leave temporarily for nonmaternity reasons.

Dismissals for breaches of discipline

There is nothing in the law that prevents management from discharging a female employee for breaking valid company rules such as those prohibiting tardiness. If such a discharged employee files a discrimination charge with the EEOC, the company will be better prepared to defend itself if it can be shown that management had conducted a reasonable, fair and routine investigation of the matter. It is essential to become aware of all circumstances involved before taking a discharge action. Be certain before discharging a female employee that there were no discriminatory overtones surrounding the incident. Finally, when carrying out disciplinary action or prescribing discharge, make sure that the actions are accomplished in a completely nondiscriminatory fashion.

4 Affirmative action: background, requirements and strategies

Developing and implementing a workable affirmative action program

Laws and orders that provide legal basis for affirmative action

Affirmative action is not a requirement of one equal employment opportunity law or order, but several. Each equal employment opportunity law protects one or more minority class or sex. Not all minority classifications have to do with race or ethnic background, some are based on physical handicap or the fact that an individual is a veteran of the Vietnam Era. Compliance in the area of equal employment opportunity is a changing scene. As new laws and orders are passed, extending protection against discrimination to still more groups, employers will need to include those groups in their affirmative action programs. The following equal employment opportunity laws and orders require affirmative action from all businesses subject to them:

- Title VII of the Civil Rights Act of 1964, as amended in 1972 by the Equal Opportunity Act (prohibits discrimination because of sex, race, color, religion, or national origin, in any term, condition or privilege of employment);

- Executive Order 11246, as amended by Executive Order 11375 (requires written affirmative action programs from all businesses with federal government contracts of $50,000 or more who employ 50 or more employees);

- The Equal Pay Act of 1963 and the Fair Labor Standards Act of 1972 (requires employers to provide equal pay for men and women performing similar work);

- The Age Discrimination in Employment Act (prohibits employment discrimination against persons between the ages of 40 and 65 years);

- Title VI of the Civil Rights Act of 1964 (prohibits discrimination based on race, color or national origin in all programs or activities which receive federal financial aid);

- State and local laws (many state and local governments prohibit employment discrimination and require affirmative action on behalf of businesses located in their respective jurisdictions);

- The National Labor Relations Act (prohibits discrimination on the basis of race, religion or national origin and establishes the requirement to refrain from entering into agreements with unions that practice discrimination);

- The Rehabilitation Act of 1973 (prohibits discrimination against handicapped persons who are employed by or seek employment with businesses holding government contracts);

- The Vietnam Era Veterans Readjustment Assistance Act of 1974 (prohibits discrimination against disabled veterans and veterans of the Vietnam Era and applies to businesses covered by Executive Order 11246);

- Other equal employment opportunity laws (employment discrimination is prohibited by the Civil Rights Acts of 1866 and 1870 and the Equal Protection Clause of the 14th Amendments to the Constitution).

Agencies responsible for affirmative action enforcement

Two agencies, the EEOC and the OFCC are authorized by Title VII and Executive Order 11246 to enforce the affirmative action requirement. The difference in how the EEOC and OFCC imposes the duty to take affirmative action does not lie in what is required, but rather, when does the duty apply. Under Title VII, the duty to take affirmative action is only imposed upon a business that was proven in court to have discriminated in violation of Title VII. In such cases, the court orders the company to undertake affirmative action to remedy the discriminatory consequences of past discrimination and safeguard against its recurrence.

According to Executive Order 11246, the OFCC requires companies holding contracts with the federal government to make a self-determination as to the need for affirmative action. If company management discovers the fact that it employs a disproportionate number of females to males or minority group members to non-minorities, that company must adopt a written affirmative action plan to remedy the discriminatory situation in order to maintain its status as a government contractor, and to be considered for future government contracts.

Court ordered affirmative action plans

According to Title VII § 706(5)(g), if a company is charged with intentionally engaging in an unlawful employment practice and the court finds a violation of Title VII, the court can order the company to cease the discriminatory practice, and order such affirmative action as:

- reinstatement or hiring of employees,

- disbursement of back pay, or

- provide any other relief the court deems as equitable and appropriate.

There is no set, court imposed program of affirmative action that is prescribed for all companies. Each court ordered program is tailored to meet the needs of the individual case. The following is a presentation in brief, featuring the highlights of various court ordered affirmative action programs.

In order to curtail a discriminatory "pattern and practice" by a labor union, the Second Circuit Court upheld the District Court's decision in *United States v. Lathers, Local 46*, 471 F.2d 408 (1973), to require the immediate issuance of 100 work permits to minority applicants. The union contested the ruling on the grounds that it violated Title VII § 703(j). However, the Second Circuit Court pointed out the fact that while Title VII prohibits quotas that are imposed for the purpose of attaining racial or sex balance, quotas imposed to correct past discriminatory practices are permissible.

Once the courts have found discrimination, that is, a Title VII violation, not only will it be ordered that the "affected class" (those who have suffered or continue to suffer the effects of past discrimination) be given access to employment, but members of the affected class must be restored to their "rightful economic status." Therefore, the remedy to disburse back pay may be awarded to an entire affected class for a period of up to two years prior to the date on which the discrimination charge was filed.

Following federal court action, an agreement was established between the American Telephone and Telegraph Company and the EEOC, part of which required the company to make a one-time payment of approximately $15-million to thousands of employees charged to have suffered from discriminatory employment practices. Additionally, the company had to pay $50-million in yearly installments for promotion and wage adjustments to female and minority employees.

This agreement was the product of two years of litigation. Although AT&T officials maintained the company was committed to and carrying out an affirmative action program, the court imposed the following remedial measures in addition to the company's existing program:

- setting specific hiring and promotion targets, especially those that would increase female and minority utilization in all job levels. (The EEOC and OFCC were given the job of regularly reviewing these goals and the company's progress toward compliance.)

- establishing goals for hiring men for previously all-female jobs,

- making women and minority employees eligible for craft or management positions, based upon their qualifications and seniority,

- paying promoted employees on the basis of seniority, and

- establishing programs to aid the promotion of all female college graduate employees hired since 1965 who desire a higher level position.

The substance of a court ordered affirmative action plan is not determined by the court itself. Rather, the details are worked out by the EEOC and OFCC, and where appropriate, the particular government agency with which the company in question holds contracts.

The EEOC is authorized to initiate proceedings to compel compliance for any company that fails to comply with a court ordered affirmative action program [Title VII § 706(i)].

Can a court ordered affirmative action program be appealed? The proceedings instituted against a company for noncompliance with a court order can result in fines over and above the remedies prescribed in the court order. If a company is subject to, what in management's opinion is an unjust settlement, rather than ignore the court order, the firm would be well advised to appeal the decision of the court. Companies in this situation have the right to appeal a court ordered affirmative action program [28 U.S.C. § 1291 and 1292].

How can an affirmative action program benefit the company?

In addition to those who are required to, many companies have found it to their advantage to develop their own affirmative action programs on a voluntary basis. Whether required or not, the following have been cited as advantages gained through the development and implementation of an affirmative action program:

- developing and implementing an affirmative action program will help the company comply with the law,

- monitoring the company's progress in meeting its own affirmative action goals will help reduce the likelihood of aggrieved employees filing discrimination charges with the compliance agencies,

- relying upon an affirmative action program as evidence, will strengthen the company's case, in the event it is ever charged with unlawful discrimination,

- operating under an affirmative action program may help the company secure government contracts, if and when the firm decides to bid for them, and

- following the recruiting, hiring, and promotion strategies that accompany an affirmative action program may help increase the firm's available labor market, thus enabling it to hire a greater number of quality applicants, in addition to keeping valued employees on the job.

Guidelines for developing an affirmative action program

Before devising a plan to aid in compliance efforts, it is important to know the kinds of practices that are considered discriminatory by the compliance agencies. Basically, the agencies categorize discrimination as either overt or systemic. Overt discrimination is the type when one individual has been discriminated against because of sex, race, color, religion, national origin or handicap. Systemic discrimination is more widespread and often carries severe penalties. Personnel practices that over the years have led to different treatment of male and female, or majority and minority employees come under this classification. Company recruiting programs, testing procedures, rates of pay and other conditions of employment are the areas where systemic discrimination most frequently occurs. The fact that systemic discrimination impacts on affected classes rather than individuals alone, accounts for why ensuing penalties are so high.

Adhering to the following guidelines will enable management to identify possible sources of overt and systemic discrimination and take action to counter the situations responsible.

- Demonstrate genuine commitment to the program by allocating sufficient resources to do an effective job. For instance, if affirmative action requires an accelerated recruiting program in order to attract female applicants the additional costs of the program will need to be figured into the budget.

- Provide incentives to gain the support of supervisors and managers. Perhaps special training or general orientation to affirmative action would be beneficial. Supervisory performance should be monitored through an ongoing evaluation process that is geared to measuring their commitment to the program.

- Survey the present workforce by department and job classification. Where there are areas of underutilization or over concentration of minority individuals or employees of one sex, establish goals and timetables by which progress toward offsetting the imbalance can be measured.

- Introduce the management person in charge of the affirmative action program and all equal employment matters. Be sure that whoever is delegated the task of managing the program is given sufficient authority to carry out policies effectively.

- Wherever possible, promote women and minority employees to jobs on the supervisory level. They will serve as models for fellow employees to emulate. Be certain that those who are integrated into these higher level positions are qualified, otherwise the move may be seen as tokenism by certain other employees.

- Following an overall personnel procedures analysis, modify any condition that may be construed as systemic discrimination. The analysis should concentrate on all pre-employment procedures, the upward mobility system, wage and salary structure, fringe benefits, annual leave, layoff and recall policies, termination, and so on. Review all union contract provisions that affect these procedures.

- Get the company involved in supporting any community action program aimed at improving conditions such as housing, transportation and education, which affect employability.

- Periodically evaluate the affirmative action program. When employees complain of discriminatory treatment, give each case careful consideration. This sort of troubleshooting is instrumental for keeping the program effective.

- Institute special programs to train and avail employment to economically and educationally disadvantaged individuals.

No affirmative action program is going to be a panacea for all of the equal employment difficulties a company may face. The preceding guidelines are offered as fundamental steps for achieving compliance and improving the workforce. Remember, developing the program is only part of the job; adhering to and improving it is the other.

Issue a written equal employment opportunity policy with commitment to affirmative action

Companies that are required to develop affirmative action programs must prepare in writing, the details of their particular program [41 C.F.R. § 60-1.40(a)]. If an employer voluntarily elects to develop a program, it is advisable to put it into writing as well. The company's chief executive must take the initial step by preparing a concise statement of equal employment policy. This statement is usually accompanied by an open letter from the chief executive in which he reaffirms his commitment to affirmative action. A statement of equal employment policy should:

- State that the company will not at any time discriminate against anyone because of his sex, race, color, religion, national origin, age, physical handicap or status as a Vietnam Era veteran of the armed forces in the recruitment, hiring, training and promotion of persons in all job classifications.

- affirm top management's attitude toward the policy,

- indicate that personnel actions such as compensation, benefits, training, transfers, layoffs, tuition assistance, etc., will be administered without discrimination,

- note that the policy is issued in accordance with the Civil Rights Act of 1964 and/or Executive Order 11246,

- make it known that the policy requires affirmative action on the part of management,

- indicate the company official who is responsible for equal employment matters,

- establish reporting and auditing procedures, and

- explain the chief executive's plans to evaluate the system and modify it as necessary.

Exhibit 1 is a typical example of a company's statement of equal employment policy.

In order to underscore the importance management places on the company's affirmative action program, it is essential that the chief executive issues a firm statement of personal commitment, legal obligations and the necessity for equal employment opportunity as a business concern. This statement is usually drafted in the form of an open letter to all employees and accompanies the company's equal employment policy statement. Exhibit 2 is an example of such a letter.

Facility manager's statement of reaffirmation.   In addition to the chief executive's letter of reaffirmation, a supporting statement signed by the manager of each facility is necessary. The manager's statement should indicate:

- the manager's attitude toward the company's equal employment opportunity policy and affirmative action program,

- which individual or individuals in the facility is responsible for administering the program,

- procedures that will be used for monitoring and reporting.

Exhibit 1

Smithways Products Corporation Equal Employment Policy

Smithways Products Corporation, through responsible managers, shall recruit, hire, upgrade, train and promote in all job titles without regard to sex, race, color, religion, national origin, age, handicap, or the fact that an individual is a disabled veteran or a veteran of the Vietnam Era, except where sex and age are essential bona fide occupational requirements, or where handicap is a bona fide occupational disqualification.

Managers shall insure that all other personnel actions such as compensation, benefits, layoffs, returns from layoffs, Corporation-sponsored training, educational tuition assistance, social and recreational programs, shall be administered without regard to sex, race, color, religion, national origin, age, handicap, or the fact that an individual is a disabled veteran or a veteran of the Vietnam Era, except where sex and age are essential bona fide occupational requirements, or where handicap is a bona fide occupational disqualification.

Managers shall base employment decisions on the principles of Equal Employment Opportunity and with the intent to further the Corporation's commitment.

Managers shall take affirmative action to insure that females, minority group individuals, veterans of the Vietnam Era and qualified handicapped persons and disabled veterans are introduced into the workforce and that these employees are encouraged to aspire for promotion and are considered as promotional opportunities arise.

The basic thrust of the manager's statement is his reaffirmation of the company's equal employment opportunity policies which stipulate that recruiting, hiring, and promotions will be made without regard to sex, race, color, religion, national origin, handicap or a person's status as a disabled veteran or veteran of the Vietnam Era. The message will further establish the fact that decisions on employment will be made so as to further the principles of equal employment opportunity, and that promotion decisions will be made in accordance with these principles in the same sense that general personnel practices and social and recreational programs will be.

Copies of the chief executive's and manager's reaffirmations, as well as the Equal Employment Policy must be conspicuously posted so that employees may be informed of their content. Posting is generally done at the following locations:

- reception room,
- general office,
- department bulletin boards,
- locker rooms.

Exhibit 2

TO: ALL EMPLOYEES
FROM: Peter J. Barnes, President

Accompanying this letter is a copy of Smithways Products Corporation's Equal Employment Opportunity Policy designed to strengthen and reaffirm our commitment to employ and utilize people in all job titles in accordance with their abilities. The Corporation's position is unmistakably clear with respect to Equal Employment Opportunity for females, minorities, veterans of the Vietnam Era, and qualified handicapped persons and disabled veterans.

Smithways Products Corporation has a commitment at all organizational levels to provide equal hiring, training, compensation, promotion, transfer, layoff and recall benefits to all individuals, including qualified disabled veterans and veterans of the Vietnam Era, without regard to sex, race, religion, color, national origin, age or handicap, except where sex and age are essential bona fide occupational requirements or where handicap is a bona fide occupational disqualification. The Corporation is committed to these policies not only because of our status as a Federal Government contractor, but also because of our firm conviction that adherence to these principles will contribute significantly to the success of the Corporation.

All managers and supervisory personnel are specifically charged with assuring, through enlightened leadership, the continued and positive support by all employees of these policies, and with taking positive steps to comply with the Equal Employment Opportunity, Handicapped and Veterans Policies, both as to spirit and intent. Those employees who have authority to promote and hire have a special responsibility to assure the success of our commitment and their effectiveness in this area will constitute an integral part of their performance evaluation.

Each of us must also be alert to avoid remarks or utterances that could be interpreted as sexual, racial, religious or ethnic insults. Our fellow employees are entitled to be treated with respect. Each of us is too vital to the success and growth of our business to risk any misunderstanding in this regard. We can neither condone nor tolerate disrespect for personal dignity.

Sincerely,

Peter J. Barnes

Peter J. Barnes

Assign responsibility for implementing the program
In order for affirmative action to meet compliance requirements, and succeed in achieving equal employment goals, it is essential to assign the management responsibilities to an individual in a top management position. Only persons in the upper strata of the business are likely going to possess the degree of authority required in gaining the cooperation of department heads and other supervisors, on whose support, the success of the program rests.

In general, the major responsibilities that accompany affirmative action program management are training, auditing, reporting and serving as a liaison. More specifically, the responsibilities include:

- identifying problems and establishing goals and objectives,
- helping managers and supervisors solve problems related to equal employment opportunity,
- acting as liaison between the company and the compliance agencies and various community organizations,
- serving as an information source on equal employment opportunity matters for managers and supervisors,
- insuring facilities such as locker rooms and rest rooms are comparable for both sexes,
- designing and implementing systems for reporting and auditing,
- checking periodically for proper poster display,
- performing periodic audits on training and hiring programs, and promotion patterns,
- reviewing employee qualifications to assure female and minority employees have access to promotions and transfer,
- encouraging female and minority employee participation in company-sponsored training, educational, social and recreational programs, and
- reminding supervisors that they will be periodically evaluated in their commitments to the equal employment opportunity policy.

Complete a utilization analysis of the workforce

Government contractors who come under the jurisdiction of the OFCC are required to perform an analysis of all major job classifications at each facility. This analysis must include an explanation if it is determined that females or minorities are being underutilized at the time the analysis is performed [41 C.F.R. § 60-2.11(a)]. Underutilization is an employment condition where there are fewer females or minorities in a particular job classification than would be reasonably expected by their availability in the local labor market. Underutilization often indicates some form of discrimination is being practiced. A workforce analysis may show areas of concentration of females or minorities in certain job classifications. Heavy concentrations of such employees in the lower classifications is also considered an indicator for possible discrimination.

The statistical segment of a workforce analysis is actually done in two parts. One part involves strictly in-house statistics, that is, a determination as to where women and minorities are located within the job strata in the company. The other side of the statistics requirement involves investigation into the availability of women and minority group individuals in the local labor market.

The in-house analysis requires the identification of the number and percentage of female and minority employees currently employed in each division, office and major job classification. Although the EEO-1 form is similar in the kind of information sought, the survey for affirmative action purposes requires more detailed information with respect to job and pay levels.

In order to document efforts in identifying areas of underutilization and concentration, many firms use forms such as the one in Exhibit 3.

Many companies find statistics relevant to the local labor area are more difficult to obtain. There are certain variables that make female and minority "availability" statistics educated approximations. The variables include:

- the nature of the business,

- the location of the business and its proximity to communities with high minority group populations, and

- the accuracy of statistics relevant to the number of females and minority group individuals who are unemployed.

Statistics regarding a geographical area's population and how it is broken down into majority and minority percentages, and its unemployment situation with respect to the percentage of females and minorities who are unemployed may be obtained by contacting:

- the directors of research and statistics at your state and local industrial relations, labor, and employment securities offices.

- state, county and municipal offices of the census, and

- Census Bureau
  U.S. Department of Commerce
  Washington, DC 20233.

Companies who have faced litigation over a charge of discrimination usually have had to demonstrate the validity of their employment statistics. Be certain to document correspondence that you may carry on with any of the preceding authorities for the purpose of gathering statistics relevant to your local labor market.

Identify problem areas by organization units and job groups
A comprehensive utilization analysis of the work force and relevant labor and recruiting areas may well bring to light cases of underutilization of females and minorities. By job classification, underutilization occurs most frequently as follows:

- for women and minority males—Officials and Managers, Professionals, Technicians and Skilled Craftworkers;

- for women—Sales workers (except for over-the-counter sales) and Semi-skilled Craftworkers; and

- for minorities—Sales workers, Office and Clerical.

Beyond establishing goals for eliminating any cases of underutilization, affirmative action requires management to troubleshoot all person-

Exhibit 3

Survey of Current Employment

JOB CATEGORIES	Wage/Salary or Grade	TOTAL EMPLOYEES			MINORITY GROUP EMPLOYEES							
		Total Employees	Total Male	Total Female	MALE				FEMALE			
					B	H	A	AI	B	H	A	AI
SALES WORKERS Total /5/												
Market Coordinator	14-21	1	1									
Field Sales	12-18	4	3	1		1				1		
OFFICE & CLERICAL Total /7/												
Exec. Secretary	7-10	1		1					1			
Warehouseman	7-10	1	1									
Dept. Secretary	7-9	3		3					1			
Research Clerk	7-9	2	1	1								
CRAFTSMEN (SKILLED) Total /4/												
Layout Technician	8-14	2	1	1								
Pasters	7-9	2		2					1			
LABORERS (UNSKILLED) Total /2/												
Cleaners	6-9	2	2									
SERVICE WORKERS Total /11/												
Field Representatives	10-14	3	2	1	1							
Acquisitions Specialist	10-14	8	4	4	1					1		

Exhibit 3
(Side Two)

Survey of Current Employment

JOB CATEGORIES	Wage/Salary or Grade	TOTAL EMPLOYEES			MINORITY GROUP EMPLOYEES							
					MALE				FEMALE			
		Total Employees	Total Male	Total Female	B	H	A	AI	B	H	A	AI
OFFICIALS AND MANAGERS Total /4/												
V.P.'s and Directors	30-39	1	1	0								
Mgr. Editor	21-29	1	1	0								
Mkt. Mgr.	21-29	1	1	0								
Graphics Mgr.	14-21	1	1	0								
PROFESSIONALS Total /5/												
Artists	12-21	2	1	1	1						1	
Writers	12-21	3	1	2						1		
OPERATIVES (SEMI-SKILLED) Total /3/												
Compositor	8-15	2		2					1			
Cataloger/Analyst	8-15	1	1									
Total Employees		41	22	19	3	1	0	0	4	3	1	0

nel practices and take corrective action if any of the following conditions are detected:

- lateral and/or vertical movement of female or minority employees occurs at a lesser rate than that of nonminority or male employees,
- the selection process screens out a significantly higher percentage of females or minorities than males or nonminorities,
- application and other preemployment forms are not in legal compliance,
- job descriptions are not synchronized in relation to actual functions and duties,
- there have been no techniques developed or formalized for evaluating the equal employment opportunity program,
- the unavailability of suitable housing limits recruitment efforts and employment of qualified minority individuals,
- the unavailability of transportation (public and private) to your plant inhibits minority employment,
- labor unions, employment agencies and subcontractors connected with your business are not aware of or following through on their equal employment responsibilities,
- purchase orders do not contain an equal employment opportunity clause,
- equal employment opportunity posters are not on display,
- the company's equal employment opportunity policy does not have the support of managers, supervisors and employees,
- training programs show an underrepresentation of female and minority participants,
- tests and other selection techniques are not validated by methods required for legal compliance,
- test forms are not validated by location, work performance and inclusion of females and minorities in sample,
- the rate of referral for males and nonminorities is significantly higher than for females and minorities,
- female and minority employees are excluded from or are not encouraged to participate in company-sponsored activities or programs,
- segregation is found to exist in some departments, and
- the seniority system lends itself to discrimination, such as where a disparity by sex or minority group status exists between length of service and types of job held.

Carefully document any employment situation suspected as a potential source of discrimination. Because the effectiveness of the program is measured by its ability to correct underutilization and other problems, improvements, especially the slight ones, only become apparent when management makes an objective and accurate summation of the equal employment situation as it exists prior to affirmative action.

Exhibit 4 is exerpted from a manager's memorandum in which he recorded his determinations derived from his investigations into areas responsible for underutilization. This particular exerpt focuses on problems that were identified by a job group analysis.

Establish goals and time schedules for compliance

Following the workforce analysis, any problems with respect to discrimination that exist in various departments or job groups will become apparent. If there is a concentration of minorities or females in the lower echelon job groups, or if such employees constitute a very low percentage of the workforce, or the number of females and minorities hired is disproportionately small by comparison to the number of females and minorities who are unemployed in the hiring area, management must establish specific written goals and timetables for the purpose of

Exhibit 4

MEMORANDUM
TO: DEPARTMENT SUPERVISORS   SUBJECT: Job Group Analysis
FROM: B. J. RIDDLE, MANAGER   DATE: 9/9--

We recognize the underutilization of females generally throughout many of the craft job groups. Despite consistent efforts to identify and encourage females to bid on available jobs, our experience has been that females fail to bid on these positions or do not consider such positions as "women's work." There has been a noted absence of minorities in our Manager/General Supervisor and Professional job groups. Recruitment efforts have been undertaken from the Corporate level on a nation-wide basis and also on the local level at the neighboring colleges and universities. One reason for this absence is that there have been few openings within the last few years within this job group and also that there are large numbers of professionals available within the Company structure. In the Manager/General Supervisor job group this absence is accounted for by the fact that these positions require considerable experience and exposure to Company practices and procedures and also to the fact that there have been a number of plant closings and consolidations.

There are no minorities in the Secretarial job group possibly as a result of the location of the facility although there is a labor pool of minorities in the nearby metropolitan area. We have been unsuccessful in encouraging minority candidates to commute to this facility for employment.

In the Operative group, females have traditionally not selected jobs within this job group. It has been our experience that rather than accept a position in this group, females have elected to either go on lay-off or have obtained a note from their doctor advising that they are not capable of performing these jobs.

---

eliminating the disparity in the workforce. These goals must be kept separately for females and minority individuals.

If a company holds contracts with the federal government and has a substantial disparity in the utilization of one minority group or men or women of a particular minority group, the OFCC may require management to establish separate goals and timetables for that minority group. This requirement may be extended to include separate goals and timetables by sex to be maintained for certain job classifications and organizational units.

The long range goal should be the projected ratio of female and minority employees in a given job classification to their representation in the relevant labor force. For in-house purposes, a five-year plan that is revised annually is preferred by many firms. However, for external purposes, such as preparing reports for the various compliance agencies, a one-year plan is sufficient. It is important to remember that the goals established are not rigid. Think of them as targets that are "reasonably attainable" by the application of good faith efforts [Revised Order 4 § 60-2.30].

Many employers who are interested in implementing affirmative action on a voluntary basis are hesitant about setting goals. The skepticism arises largely from equating goals with quotas, and quotas are suspect for causing reverse discrimination. It should be remembered a quota is a figure that must be met. For compliance purposes, a company is responsible for the effort put forth in achieving its goals. If a goal cannot be met, the law requires first that the company reassess the goal from the standpoint of attainability. If the goal could be attained, the company must reconsider the effort that was put into meeting the goal. Following these steps, either the goal itself or the amount of effort exerted will need to be modified. Perhaps a company missed its goal established for hiring women. When considering the amount of effort that was put into increasing the number of women hired, if modifying selection procedures was the only action taken, that company could step up its efforts by expanding the geographical area in which job advertisements and basic recruiting is done. Such efforts do not jeopardize male candidates, rather they increase exposure to a larger number of would-be employees. After this is accomplished, employee selection based on individual qualifications will ensure quality employees without risking compliance difficulties or charges of discrimination.

Documentation is necessary with respect to goals and timetables. It is advisable to maintain separate goals for females and minorities. Records should be kept on file indicating which goals were met and which were not. For those goals that were not met, indicate the reasons why and what action is planned for correcting the problems.

It is necessary to get departmental or divisional supervisors involved in the goal-setting process, in that their support is essential for meeting affirmative action goals. Also, goals that are based on the suggestions of supervisors are likely going to be more realistic than ones established without their input.

Top management often gets departmental and divisional supervisors involved by sending a memorandum to such supervisors explaining the purpose for affirmative action goals, and the criteria on which they must be based. Exhibit 5 is an example of such a memorandum.

Exhibit 5

MEMORANDUM
TO: DEPARTMENTAL SUPERVISORS   SUBJECT: AFFIRMATIVE
                                                  ACTION GOALS

FROM: T. C. Dalton, Vice President   DATE: 9/2/--

Each department will establish goals and timetables to rectify underutilization of women and minorities. This is the basic thrust of Roundtree Corporation's Affirmative Action Program. Goals which are established should be significant, measurable and attainable given the commitment of each organizational unit and its good faith efforts. The internal workforce utilization analysis and the analysis of the relevant external labor area provide the basic data on which goals and timetables are formulated. In combination with Roundtree's Equal Employment Opportunity Policy, Affirmative Action goals and timetables will be established. The following are the parameters for goal and timetable determination:

- goals and timetables will be determined for women and minorities separately,

- in establishing timetables to meet goals, you must consider the anticipated expansion for your department, and contraction and turnover of your workforce,

- specific goals and timetables for women and minorities are to be established for each category of employment (e.g., office, factory, apprenticeship, college, professional, etc.), and for each promotional category (e.g., hourly to exempt, office, factory, professional, etc.),

- the nature of the goals and timetables you establish should be based on;

  a) the degree of underutilization within the specific job group,

  b) the scope of the relevant work area recruited from,

  c) the availability of qualified or qualifiable women and minorities in the relevant work area,

  d) the number of job openings available (as determined by turnover, expansion, etc.),

  e) the commitment of your department to correct underutilization of women and minorities, and

  f) the Affirmative Action Program and Equal Employment Policy of Roundtree Corporation.

Develop and monitor personnel procedures to achieve affirmative action goals

The elimination of discriminatory barriers is approached through affirmative action in three phases:

- taking immediate action to "equalize" wage and benefit structures that formerly discriminated on the basis of an individual's sex or minority group membership,

- projecting on an annual basis, the actual numbers of females and minorities you intend to employ at each job level, until

- realizing the long range equal employment goals established for the company, such that at the conclusion of the multi-year program, the company has hired and promoted a sufficient number of individuals from each sex and minority group that was originally identified as being underutilized, so that workforce statistics are in accord with the statistics showing the availability of such groups in the firm's hiring area.

In order to achieve short and long range affirmative action goals, management must analyze and modify, where appropriate, the following personnel procedures:

- recruiting,

- selection,

- promotion,

- wage and salary structure,

- benefits and conditions of employment,

- layoff, recall, discharge, demotion, and disciplinary action, and

- revision of union contracts.

Recruiting. A recruiting preference to "front door walk-ins" and word-of-mouth referrals is often a major cause for perpetuating a non-minority, all male workforce. Basically, eliminating these two sources of applicants is a prerequisite for meeting affirmative action goals. All equal employment opportunity recruiting efforts should be documented. Many companies have found it beneficial to utilize an applicant flow record that reflects each applicant's name, sex, race, referral source, date of application, and position applied for. For the purpose of monitoring the progress made toward achieving goals departmentally, it is also advantageous to include such information as the disposition of the application, the date of hire and level of entry pay, and which department hired the applicant, on the form. Exhibit 6 is an example of the applicant flow record.

A quarterly review of the applicant flow record will show the numbers of females and minority individuals hired within that time period. Analyzing this data from the standpoint of job classifications enables a firm to determine whether certain levels remain out of reach for particular groups of applicants.

Exhibit 6

Bryant Materials Company
Applicant Flow Record

(Organization Unit) __Main Office__

(Location) __Smithton, Oregon__

(Time Period) __1/5 - 3/5/--__

Person Preparing Report __Marshal Beasley__

DATE	NAME	RACE	SEX	POSITION APPLYING FOR	REFERRAL SOURCE	FED CATEGORY OF JOB	DISPOSITION	Complete only if here				
								JOB TITLE	DATE OF HIRE	RATE OF PAY	ORG. UNIT WHO HIRED	
1/8	Jose Mieza	H	M	Keypunch	Advrtsmt	OC	2	Op-1	1/9	9.5	Bkpng.	
1/11	Martha Billings	W	F	Office	Walk in	OC	1					
1/14	Deborah Brown	B	F	Artist	Advrtsmt	P	2	Pr-1	2-1	11	Grphs.	

1. Interviewed, no offer
2. Interviewed, offer extended, & hired
3. Interviewed, offer extended, but rejected

The applicant flow record documents the results of the recruiting program. The elements that make up the program can be geared to facilitate affirmative action efforts. The following conditions may be considered fundamental in developing a recruiting program that is designed to reduce and eliminate underutilization:

- provide training to all persons involved with interviewing job candidates,

- use females and minorities, wherever possible, in interviewing, participating in "career nights," appearing on promotional posters and other facets of recruiting,

- stress in job advertisements the firm's commitment as an equal opportunity employer to hire qualified persons from both sexes and without regard to one's minority group membership,

- communicate the affirmative action policy to all employment agencies, appropriate government agencies (such as the Veterans Administration), high schools, colleges and universities, and local career development centers.

Selection Procedures. Court history indicates that company selection procedures are primary sources of employment discrimination. In order to achieve affirmative action goals, all tests, background inquiries and interviewer rating systems must be conducted according to the company's equal employment policy. By taking the following actions, you can eliminate the majority of those selection procedures that foster underutilization:

- be sure that no tests that are required for employment have an adverse effect on females or minorities and have such tests professionally validated as effective, significant predictors of effective job performance,

- avoid over-the-phone prescreening that could serve to discourage female or minority applicants, or cause interviewers to form premature, negative opinions about applicants' qualifications or suitability,

- limit pre-employment questions and questions on job applications to those that are clearly job-related, avoiding, where possible, questions related to an applicant's sex, race, religion, national origin, education, arrest and conviction record, credit rating, marital status, physical health, etc.,

- conduct a job analysis to determine which tasks are actually required and how often they are required for a particular position, focusing on those skills and traits that are necessary to do the job, and

- analyze job descriptions, and eliminate any functions that could be construed as "window dressing" that serves to discourage or disqualify female or minority applicants.

Promotion, transfer, job progression, training and seniority proce-
dures. Examine the present system, both the formal and informal type. Who makes decisions related to job assignment, promotion and transfer; and on what are those decisions based? If it appears that any group is being kept away from the avenues of promotion, those barriers must be removed. Management can eliminate the barriers and thus facilitate the achievement of affirmative action goals by taking the following remedial actions:

- require that all selection procedures that determine promotability are professionally validated and do not adversely affect females and minorities,

- require that all promotion, transfer and access to training considerations be based on an employee's ability and work record,

- require supervisors to include a specified percentage of females and minorities among those promoted, the percentage being in accord with established affirmative action goals,

- develop a formal employee evaluation program that is based on measurable, objective factors,

- develop a remedial action file (if there is serious underutilization at certain job levels) that contains records of female and minority employees who are qualified for promotions, and refer to the file first when promoting employees, and

- develop a career counseling program to encourage females and minorities in "dead-end" jobs to take on additional responsibility and participate in training programs, in order that they might become eligible for promotion.

As is the case for all procedures developed for affirmative action, a firm should document the results of its affirmative promotion program. Many companies utilize forms such as the one in Exhibit 7 for this purpose. A quarterly review of such records will provide an opportunity to monitor the progress being made in promoting female and minority employees.

Many companies have found that one of the best ways to transform "dead-ended" employees into promotable ones is to provide an affirmative training program. Training can be disseminated through various means, such as:

- an in-house program, utilizing supervisors and other employees as instructors,

- an in-house program offered in cooperation with a local adult education system or manpower program,

- an out-of-house program offered at various business or technical schools, and manpower training centers, or

- a formal apprenticeship program conducted by a joint labor-management training committee or in-house staff.

Exhibit 7

Bryant Materials Company
Promotion and Transfer Record

Organizational Unit ___ Main Office
Location ___ Smithton, Oregon
Time Period ___ 1/5 - 3/5
Person Preparing Data ___ Marshal Beasley

←— complete only if promoted or transferred —→

DATE	NAME	RACE	SEX	PRESENT POSITION & S.G.	PRESENT PAY	PRESENT ORG. UNIT	PRESENT EEO-1 CATEGORY	DISPO-SITION	NEW POSITION & S.G.	NEW ORG. UNIT	NEW DEPT. NAME & NO.	NEW EEO-1 CAT.	EEO-1 STATUS CHANGE (yes-no)	AMT. SALARY CHANGE (+or-)	NEW SALARY	TRANSFER =T PROMOTION =P
1/9	Alan Ray	W	M	Elec. B	9.5	Asmbly	C	3								
2/7	B. Jones	B	M	Wldr. A	6.9	Shop	C	1	Wldr. B	Same	Same	C	Yes	+1.5	8.4	=P
2/9	M. Smith	B	F	Sec. A	7.9	Offc	OC	3								

1 = Interviewed
2 = Not interviewed
3 = Interviewed, but no change

A simple form such as the example in Exhibit 8 can be used as a record of employees who have entered or completed a training program. Quarterly reviews of such a record will indicate the number of female and minority employees who have become promotable due to their having successfully completed necessary training. If a review shows a lack of participation on the part of such employees, management will need to take action to make female and minority training a priority for department supervisors.

Wage and salary structure. Several costly back pay awards have been made where the courts have found wage discrimination, mostly on the basis of sex. Therefore, it is advisable to examine the company's wage and salary structure, and make appropriate adjustments to facilitate achievement of affirmative action goals.

Reviewing the wage and salary structure begins with comparing job descriptions and actual functions of jobs held by men and women of all minority and nonminority groups, length of service and other factors affecting pay rates. This must be done to comply with the Equal Pay Act's requirement that equal pay be awarded for equal (substantially similar) work. Specifically, equal pay, in terms of base pay, overtime opportunity, bonuses, commissions, etc., must be granted for jobs requiring equal skill, responsibility and effort.

Benefits and conditions of employment. Affirmative action requires that no minority group or sex should be excluded from company employment benefits. Review all company benefit programs such as insurance (life and hospitalization), retirement, pension, profit-sharing, and leave to ensure that benefits are equally available without discrimination. As in pay discrimination, a large percentage of benefit program disparities occur in the availability of benefits being different for male and female employees. The key to avoiding such disparities is to be sure that:

- benefits for husbands and families of female employees are the same as those for wives and families of male employees,

- benefits available to wives of male employees are also available to female employees, and that

- no benefits are awarded on the basis of an employee's being the "head of the household" or similar condition.

Layoff, recall, discharge, demotion and disciplinary action. Affirmative action requires that standards used for deciding when an employee shall be terminated, demoted or disciplined, laid off or recalled must be the same for all employees. In order to avoid possible charges of discrimination with respect to such standards, it is advisable to put them into writing.

Exit interviews should be conducted with all employees who wish to terminate employment. If an employee resigns due to an inability to secure advanced training or a promotion, management may be able to gain insight into certain personnel procedures that are discriminatory.

Exhibit 8

Bryant Materials Company
Training Activity Record

Organizational Unit Main Office
Location Smithton, Oregon
Time Period 1/5 – 3/5
Person Preparing Data Marshal Beasley

TYPE OF TRAINING	NAME OF PARTICIPANT	RACE	SEX	DURATION OF TRAINING	DATE COMPLETED	JOB BEFORE TRAINING	PAY BEFORE TRAINING	JOB AFTER TRAINING (If same, so indicate)	PAY AFTER TRAINING (If same, so indicate)
On/Job	J. Arlo	H	M	6 mos.	2/9	Stkrm	6.2	Machnst A	7.5
Apprntc	A. Olson	B	M	2 Yrs.	2/19	Prnt Asst	6.8	Printer A	8.0
Com Col	P. West	W	F	2 Smstrs	3/1	Sales	9.0	Mkt. Coodntr	10.2

Where this is the case, it might be possible to correct the conditions responsible for at least part of the underutilization problem without risking compliance difficulties.

Keep a record of all terminations such as the example in Exhibit 9. The record should indicate the employee's name, race/ethnic designation, sex, job category, and the date and reason for leaving the company.

Similar records may be developed for layoffs and demotions. This is particularly important where employment contraction impacts heavily on female and minority employees. Because layoffs could adversely affect a company's affirmative action program, alternatives to layoff should be explored and implemented if possible. Some companies have implemented such alternatives as:

- transferring newly hired female and minority employees to jobs not affected by layoff,

- modifying work schedules in order to continue employment for affected employees, or by

- designating female and minority employees as "critical talent," thus protecting them from layoff.

Where alternatives to layoff are not practical or possible, try to give the affected employees a realistic appraisal of their recall status, offer counseling on unemployment benefits, and if possible, advise them of job possibilities with other firms.

Revision of union contracts. Affirmative action requires that all union contracts must be reviewed, and revised if necessary, to prevent their containing any discriminatory employment practices. Every collective bargaining agreement must include a non-discrimination clause. For compliance purposes, "threat of suit or strike," is not considered a valid reason for not taking affirmative action against barriers in the contract.

If reviewing a union contract identifies barriers such as discriminatory membership, seniority or referral practices, the union, upon management's recommendation, is legally responsible for revising such contract provisions. Should the union refuse to do so, management can make the changes itself without violating the good faith bargaining provisions of the National Labor Relations Act.

Auditing affirmative action progress. The task of evaluating progress toward achieving affirmative action goals is the responsibility of the management official in charge of the program. The bulk of the data necessary for performing a regular internal audit may be extracted from the company's survey of current employment, selection process, promotion, and termination and layoff records. These records, which have been outlined previously in this chapter, must be maintained by the manager or supervisor in charge of each division or department. A quarterly narrative report, based on an analysis of these data should be provided by such supervisors to the company official in charge of affirmative action. From these reports, that official is able to evaluate the progress, and identify components of the program that need improve-

Exhibit 9

Bryant Materials Company
Termination Record

Organizational Unit ___Main Office___

Location ___Smithton, Oregon___

Time Period ___1/5 – 3/5___

Person Preparing Date ___Marshal Beasley___

DATE	NAME	RACE	SEX	DATE OF INITIAL HIRE	POSITION AT TIME OF TERMINATION	DATE OF TERMINATION	EEO-1 CATEGORY DESIGNATION	ORG. UNIT SEPARATED FROM	DEPT. & NO. TERM- INATED FROM	REASON FOR TERM- INATION
1/9	J. Barlow	B	F	7/2/--	Secretary	1/19/--	OC	#1 Office	Same	Moving
2/10	L. Smith	W	M	3/10/--	Machinist	3/1/--	C	Shop 5	Shop 1	Other Job
2/14	B. Lewis	W	F	2/26/--	Bkkpr.	3/9/--	OC	#5 Office	Same	Other Job

ment. Quarterly narrative reports should contain the following information:

- the affirmative action objective for that department,
- an account of progress made toward affirmative action goals during that quarter,
- a notation as to whether the progress is on schedule with the department's timetable,
- an explanation of special problems that have been encountered and serve to deter progress, and
- a statement concerning proposed affirmative action for the coming quarter.

OFCC regulations require government contractors to prepare and make available the following reports:

- survey of current employment by race, national origin, sex, job classification, salary or wage level,
- analysis of internal and external workforce availability by sex, race and national origin,
- identification of areas of underutilization and concentration, and establishment of hiring and promotion goals and timetables,
- records on applicant flow, procedures of the selection process; hires, placements, promotions, requests for transfers, transfers and training program participation by sex, race and national origin,
- sources of referrals and hires, by sex, race and national origin,
- resignations, layoffs and dismissals by sex, race and national origin, and
- the progress of company departments or divisions toward goals.

Government contractors are also required to develop an affirmative action file. This file must include applications of all females and minority persons who are neither accepted nor rejected, but who are nonetheless qualified for a position with the contractor.

How to publicize an affirmative action program externally
Despite an internal commitment to affirmative action, it is unlikely that a sufficient number of female and minority applicants are going to be made aware of the employment opportunities that are available. From the standpoint of reaching those individuals that the firm needs to hire, an external publicity program can be considered a necessity.

Annual letter sent to regularly used recruitment sources.   An analysis of company affirmative action reports will indicate special employment needs that should be met during the forthcoming year. The personnel department must communicate these needs to all recruiting sources that are used on a regular basis. Sources such as various advertising media, public and private employment agencies and educational institutions all must be informed of the firm's employment needs. Of equal importance is the communicating of a directive to the effect that the company cannot legally conduct business with any source of referrals which discriminates against minorities or on the basis of sex. In fact, employment agencies are specifically covered by Title VII, and are subject to legal action if they do not comply.

Exhibit 10 is an example of such a letter. It is advisable to attach a copy of the company's Equal Employment Opportunity Policy to the letter.

Similarly, whenever it is decided to subscribe to the services of a new recruiting source, be sure to send a personal letter, such as the one in Exhibit 10, and a copy of the company's Equal Employment Opportunity Policy, along with specific employment needs, to the new agency or office.

Letters to advertising media.   Inform all media through which the company advertises job openings that as an equal employment opportunity employer:

Exhibit 10

Mr. James Smith
Director: Smith Employment Agency
Greenville, Ohio

Dear Mr. Smith

Almac Corporation and its subsidiaries are concerned that they fulfill their roles as equal opportunity employers. We request your vigorous support in our affirmative action effort as it relates to providing employment opportunity for minority groups and women. We do not discriminate against any employee or applicant for employment because of sex, race, color, age, handicap, or the fact that an individual is a disabled veteran or veteran of the Vietnam Era.

Utilization of any agency is predicated upon their full compliance with our Equal Employment Opportunity Policy. We request that qualified women and minorities be referred to us for any job opening listed with your agency. We further request that qualified males be referred for traditionally "female" jobs.

Please acknowledge your support of our commitment by signing a copy of this letter and returning it to us. Thank you.

Sincerely,

Gerald A. Westing

Gerald A. Westing,
Comptroller

- all advertisements must include an Equal Opportunity Employer Male/Female statement,

- job advertisements cannot appear in sex-segregated columns, and

- no illustrated advertisements can picture women or minority individuals working at stereotypical jobs.

Letters to Subcontractors, vendors and suppliers.   Government contractors are required by Executive Order 11246 to notify all subcontractors, vendors and suppliers with whom contracts are let, of the company's duties as an equal opportunity employer. Exhibit 11 is an example of such a letter. Executive Order 11246 also requires that all purchase orders, contracts, leases, etc., include an Equal Opportunity clause, with revocation clauses for noncompliance.

Exhibit 11 (Side 2) is a copy of the attachment sent to the subcontractor. The example illustrates how the form would appear after it had been completed and returned to the government contractor.

Exhibit 11
(Side 1)

```
Mr. John H. Wiley
President:  Andeda Transfer, Incorporated
Hartsburg, Indiana

Dear Mr. Wiley:

    As your firm is well aware, Almac Corporation and its wholly
owned subsidiaries are equal opportunity employers.

    Pursuant to Executive Order 11246 as amended, you are advised
that under the provisions of government contracting and in ac-
cordance with the Executive Orders, contractors and subcontractors
are obliged to take affirmative action to provide equal employment
opportunity without regard to sex, race, creed, color, national
origin or age.

    We expect to see our commitment to equal opportunity employment
reflected in the sexual and racial composition of your firm's
workforce and urge a vigorous affirmative action program to over-
come underutilization.

    The attached form will need to be completed and returned to us
at your earliest convenience.  Thank you.

                              Sincerely,

                              Gerald A. Westing

                              Gerald A. Westing
                              Comptroller
```

Exhibit 11
(Side 2)

Supplier Name __Andeda Transfer Company__   Telephone _000-0009_

Street Address _7922 Lester Road_   City _Hartsburg_   State _IN_

Zip Code __00000__   Number of Employees __35__

This Firm Is:

    __X__ Independently Owned and Operated.

    _____ An Affiliate)   Parent Company _____
           or   )
    _____ A Subsidiary) OF   Address _____
           or   )
    _____ A Division   )

__X__ Small Business   _____ Large Business

	Seller Has	Seller Has Not
Held contracts or subcontracts subject to the Equal Opportunity Clause of Executive Order 11246.		X
Filed the Equal Employment Opportunity Information Report EEO-1 for the period ending March 31 prior.	X	
File Equal Employment Opportunity Information Report EEO-1 When required.	X	
Developed a written Affirmative Action Program.	X	

Seller's Equal Employment Opportunity Program has _____ Has not __X__ been subject to a Government Equal Opportunity Compliance Review.
If so, when _____ .

Seller acknowledges receipt of the notice to prospective subcontractors of requirement for certification of nonsegregated facilities and certifies _____ does not certify __X__ compliance with that requirement.

Signature __John H. Wiley__   Title _President_

Date ____3/5/--____

           PLEASE RETURN FORM TO: The Comptroller
                               Almac Corp.

5 Case studies involving significant court action taken on sex discrimination issues

Introduction to case studies

Understanding the implications of judicial decisions resulting from suits brought under provisions of the Constitution and various civil rights statutes is essential to management's efforts to develop effective equal employment programs that are consistent with the law. The cases featured in this chapter represent a cross section of civil rights court actions dealing with sex discrimination and personnel administration. Each case is prefaced with an "Analysis of the Issue" to identify the key aspects of alleged sex discrimination addressed in the full text treatment of the case. Readers seeking definitive statements of the court decisions can go beyond the analysis section and rely on the decisions themselves.

Williams v. Saxbe

[413 F. Supp. 654 (D.D.C. 1976)]

Sex discrimination in employment—sexual advances

Analysis of the issue

The plaintiff, formerly employed by the U.S. Department of Justice, Community Relations Service, claimed that she was terminated in retaliation for her refusal to submit to the sexual advances of her supervisor. On the grounds that submission to the advances was an artificial barrier placed before female employees, the plaintiff stated a claim of sex discrimination under Title VII. The defendant argued that the plaintiff was denied employment due to unwillingness to furnish sexual considerations demanded by her supervisor, not because she was a woman; and that as such, the action was not one that was prohibited by the statute. The defendant further argued that the issue involved an isolated personal incident that should not be of concern to the court. On the former argument, the court ruled that because submission to the supervisor's sexual advances was an arbitrary barrier placed by this superior before female employees exclusively, the conduct violated Title VII. Countering the "isolated incident" argument, the court stated that if it was the policy or practice of the employee's supervisor to require sexual submission by female employees, it was likewise the policy or practice of the agency itself, thus qualifying the action as one prohibited by Title VII.

Full text of opinion

CHARLES R. RICHEY, District Judge:—Plaintiff, Diane R. Williams, brings this action to recover damages and for other relief as a result of defendants' alleged violations of the provisions of Title VII of the Civil Rights Act of 1964, as amended by the Equal Employment Opportunity Act of 1972, 42 U.S.C. § 2000e et seq., and other acts of Congress; specifically, plaintiff alleges that she has been denied equal employment opportunities in the Department of Justice because of her sex. Plaintiff was a female employee of the Community Relations Services ("CRS") of the Department of Justice from approximately January 4, 1972 to September 22, 1972, at which time her employment with the CRS was terminated. Defendants are the Attorney General of the United States and the Director of the CRS of the Department of Justice.

This action is before the Court at this time for review of the administrative record. Pending before the Court are defendants' motion to dismiss, defendants' renewed motion for summary judgment, and plaintiff's motion for judgment. While plaintiff originally sought a trial de novo, plaintiff has since stipulated to have the Court render a final decision on the agency record.

This Court perceives there being two issues presented for resolution. This first issue is whether the retaliatory actions of a male supervisor, taken because a female employee declined his sexual advances, constitutes sex discrimination within the definitional parameters of Title VII of the Civil Rights Act of 1964. The second issue is twofold: how should the administrative record be reviewed, and what result should be reached based on the record.

In order to properly address the first issue, the factual and procedural background of this action must be considered.

On January 4, 1972, plaintiff began her employment with the CRS as a public information specialist ("PRO"), Grade GS-7, under a temporary appointment not to exceed one month. Within a short time after her employment commenced, the Civil Service Commission reviewed plaintiff's status and converted her appointment to a career conditional, Grade GS-8, effective January 23, 1972, subject to a one-year probationary period, retroactive from January 4, 1972. During plaintiff's employment, her immediate supervisor was a Mr. Harvey Brinson. On September 11, 1972, Mr. Brinson advised the plaintiff of his intention to terminate her and, by notice dated September 21, 1972, her termination was made effective on September 22, 1972. In the interim, September 13 to be exact, plaintiff filed a formal complaint alleging sex discrimination.

Plaintiff's discrimination complaint alleged, in essence, that she had had a good working relationship with Mr. Brinson up until she refused a sexual advance made by Mr. Brinson in June. She asserted that thereafter Mr. Brinson engaged in a continuing pattern and practice of harassment and humiliation of her, including but not limited to, unwarranted reprimands, refusal to inform her of matters for the performance of her responsibilities, refusal to consider her proposals and recommendations, and refusal to recognize her as a competent professional in her field. On the other hand, the alleged basis for terminating plaintiff was her poor work performance during this same period.

After an investigation of plaintiff's allegations was conducted, plaintiff received notice from an Equal Employment Opportunity officer that a finding of no discrimination was proposed and that she had various options to pursue, including an administrative hearing. Plaintiff elected to have the hearing, which was held in May and June of 1973. On September 11, 1973, the Complaints Examiner issued his recommended decision, which was a finding of no discrimination based on sex. This recommendation was adopted by the Complaint Adjudication Officer on December 21, 1973, apparently because in the agency's view the evidence did not establish "any causal relationship" between her rejection of Mr. Brinson and his subsequent treatment of her and her ultimate termination. Plaintiff then filed the instant action.

Upon its initial review of the record, this Court determined that the record revealed proof suggestive of discrimination on the basis of sex. The Court also found that at the agency level the government made no attempt to show an absence of discrimination, but rather, the onus appeared to have been placed on the plaintiff to affirmatively prove sex discrimination. The Court therefore remanded the case to the agency for additional administrative hearings wherein the government would have the burden to affirmatively establish the absence of discrimination by the clear weight of the evidence, citing Hackley v. Johnson, 360 F.Supp. 1247 (D.D.C. 1973).

On remand, the second Hearing Examiner found that the agency had not met its burden. Additionally, the Examiner concluded that plaintiff "was discriminated against because of sex in the acts of her immediate supervisor in intimidating, harassing, threatening and eventually terminating her." Hearing Examiner's decision of February 21, 1975. The Examiner based his decision on a finding that "Mr. Brinson was of a disposition to and did make personal advances towards [the plaintiff] and that these advances were rejected by [the plaintiff]," and that at that time, May 1972, he could not conclude that Mr. Brinson was "truly experiencing work performance and/or conduct difficulties with [the plaintiff]." In concluding his analysis, the Examiner stated:

A review of the proposed termination notice and of Mr. Brinson's testimony concerning the merits of the reasons for complainant's termination shows that such reasons were not serious deficiencies in work performance and/or conduct. It appears that many of the reasons were based on incidents in which good supervision would have been preventative, and that good supervision was not forthcoming because of the situation which Mr. Brinson had created by his attempts at fostering a personal relationship with complainant and the subsequent rejection.

Because all of the incidents occurred or were noted within a time period of June to August 1972, it is difficult to accept the premise that complainant, who had been a relatively good employee during the first six months of her employment, would have so many deficiencies noted in such a short time period. The alleged enumerated deficiencies occurring simultaneously with a rejection of personal advances based on sex, lends itself to an inference of sex discrimination. In my opinion, the agency has not sufficiently produced evidence consistent with its burden to affirmatively establish the absence of sex discrimination by the clear weight of the evidence in this case.

The Examiner therefore recommended that the plaintiff be reinstated with back pay.

The Complaint Adjudication Officer, who was the same officer that reviewed the first Complaints Examiner's recommendation as well, rejected the recommendation of the second Hearing Examiner in an opinion dated March 12, 1975. After expressing some consternation over the fact that the Court did not specifically identify what evidence was suggestive of discrimination, the Complaint Adjudication Officer reviewed the Examiner's recommendation, and found that he could not "conclude that [the plaintiff's] termination resulted from sex discrimination within the meaning of the Department's equal employment opportunity regulations." Complaint Adjudication Officer's decision of March 12, 1975.

It is obvious to this Court, and apparently to the parties, that it was the opinion of the Complaint Adjudication Officer, and thus the agency, that the conduct complained of in this case does not come within the definitional parameters of sex discrimination. Defendants have reasserted this opinion, claiming that the complaint therefore does not state a cause of action and should be dismissed.

As noted above, the motion to dismiss presents the issue of whether the retaliatory actions of a male supervisor, taken because a female employee declined his sexual advances, constitutes sex discrimination within the definitional parameters of Title VII of the Civil Rights Act of 1964, as amended. This Court finds that it does. Defendants, however, make a cogent and almost persuasive argument to the contrary.

The defendants' argument is bottomed on locating the "primary variable" in the alleged class, which must be the gender of the class member to come within the protection of Title VII of the Civil Rights Act. Defendants reason that:

"Examination of . . . cases where sex discrimination has been found reveals that the particular stereotype involved may well have caused the creation of the class. However, the impetus for creation of the class must be distinguished from the primary variable which describes the class. The impetus for creation of the class may well be a sexual stereotype, i.e. women are weak, or women are not business-minded, but the class itself cannot be described, the boundaries cannot be set in terms of stereotypes. Rather, the class is described, by a variable which distinguishes its members from people outside the class. In previous sex discrimination cases, this primary variable was gender and, therefore, the applicability of the Act was triggered. Thus, conceptually, sexual stereotypes are irrelevant to the actual determination of whether an impermissible class exists. For example, if an employer enforced a policy that only women could be "roustabouts," an impermissible classification would arise, a classification described by the primary variable, gender, and the Act would be triggered despite the absence of a sexual stereotype. Therefore, in the instant case, even assuming that a sexual stereotype was at the root of Brinson's alleged imposition of a sexual condition, such a factor is irrelevant to the description of the alleged class. Accordingly, since the primary variable in the claimed class is willingness *vel non* to furnish sexual consideration, rather than gender, the sex discrimination proscriptions of the Act are not invoked. Plaintiff was allegedly denied employment enhancement not because she was a woman but rather because she decided not to furnish the sexual consideration claimed to have been demanded. Therefore, plaintiff is in no different class from other employees, regardless of their gender or sexual orientation, who are made subject to such carnal demands." Defendants' Brief in Support of the Motion to Dismiss.

While defendants' argument is appealing, it obfuscates the fact, that, taking the facts of the plaintiff's complaint as true, the conduct of the plaintiff's supervisor created an artificial barrier to employment which was placed before one gender and not the other, despite the fact that both genders were similarly situated. It is the opinion of this Court that plaintiff has therefore made out a cause of action under 42 U.S.C. § 2000e-16(a). The reason for this Court's opinion is that it rejects the defendants' narrow view of the prohibition of the statute, which is the result of what this Court perceives as an erroneous analysis of the concept of sex discrimination as found in Title VII, to which the Court now turns.

The fact that "Congress intended to strike at the entire spectrum of disparate treatment of men and women resulting from sex stereotypes," Sprogis v. United Air Lines, Inc., 444 F.2d 1194, 1198, 623 (7th Cir. 1971), does not mean that only a "sex stereotype" can give rise to sex discrimination within Title VII. The statute prohibits "*any* discrimination based on . . . sex. . . . " Subsection 717(a) of the Equal Employment Opportunity Act of 1972, 42 U.S.C. § 2000e-16(a). [Emphasis added]. On its face, the statute clearly does not limit discrimination to sex stereotypes. And while there is language in the legislative history of the amendment that indicates that Congress did want to eliminate impediments to employment erected by sex stereotypes, these expressions do not provide a basis for limiting the scope of the statute, particularly since there is ample evidence that Congress' intent was not to limit the scope and effect of Title VII, but rather, to have it broadly construed. Furthermore, the plain meaning of the term "sex discrimination" as used in the statute encompasses discrimination between genders whether the discrimination is the result of a well-recognized sex stereotype or for any other reason. It is important in this regard to note that Title VII is applicable to men as well as to women.

There therefore can be no question that the statutory prohibition of § 2000e-16(a) reaches *all* discrimination affecting employment which is based on gender. While the defendants would appear to agree that it is not essential that a "sex stereotype" be the cause of the disparate treatment, it is their view that a policy or practice is not sex discrimination within the meaning of § 2000e-16(a) unless the class is described by what they call the primary variable, i.e. gender. Defendants' analysis goes one step further. They contend that § 2000e-16(a) sex discrimination may only be found when the policy or practice is applicable to only one of the genders because of the characteristics that are peculiar to one of the genders. When applied to this case, defendants' analysis has produced the argument that since the criteria of "willingness to furnish sexual consideration" could be applied to both men and women, then the class cannot be said to be defined *primarily* by gender and therefore there can be no § 2000e-16(a) sex discrimination.

Defendants' argument must be rejected because a finding of sex discrimination under § 2000e-16(a) does not require that the discriminatory policy or practice depend upon a characteristic peculiar to one of the genders. That a rule, regulation, practice, or policy is applied on the basis of gender is alone sufficient for a finding of sex discrimination. Phillips v. Martin Marietta Corp., 400 U.S. 542 (1971); Sprogis v. United Air Lines, Inc., supra. In Martin Marietta, the Supreme Court, while vacating the decision of the Fifth Circuit, accepted the Fifth Circuit's finding that there was discrimination even though it was not based upon a characteristic peculiar to one gender. The Fifth Circuit had held that a policy which allowed the hiring of men who had pre-school children for certain positions, but not allowing the hiring of women with pre-school children for the same position, was sex discrimination in violation of Title VII, 411 F.2d 1 (1969). The court of appeals rejected the argument that sex discrimination could only be found if the policy depended solely upon gender. Rather, the court stated:

We are of the opinion that the words of the statute are the best source from which to derive the proper construction. The statute proscribes discrimination based on an individual's race, color, religion, sex, or national origin. A per se violation of the Act can only be discrimination based solely on one of the categories i.e., in the case of sex; women vis-a-vis men. When another criterion of employment is added to one of the classifications listed in the Act, there is no longer apparent discrimination based solely on race, color, religion, sex or national origin. It becomes the function of the courts to study the conditioning of employment on one of the elements outlined in the statute coupled with the additional requirement, and to determine if any individual or group is being denied work due to his race, color, religion, sex or national origin. Id. at 3–4.

The Supreme Court did not reject this analysis, but rather, vacated the lower court's decision because the practice could have been permissible if there was evidence to show that it was a "bona fide occupational qualification" under § 703(e) of the Act. 400 U.S. at 544.

The Sprogis case concerned a "no-marriage" rule which provided that stewardesses had to be unmarried when hired and remain unmarried under penalty of discharge. 444 F.2d at 1196, 1196 n.2. The no-marriage rule could have been applied to men as well as women, since both are capable of marriage. The criteria of marriage can also not be said to be a characteristic peculiar to one of the genders. Nevertheless, the court held that the rule resulted in sex discrimination in violation of Title VII. Id. at 1198. The court found it sufficient that the rule was applied to women and not to men, despite the fact that they were similarly situated.

The requirement of willingness to provide sexual consideration in this case is no different from the "pre-school age children" and "no-marriage" rules of Martin Marietta and Sprogis. As here, none of those rules turned upon a characteristic peculiar to one of the genders. It was and is sufficient to allege a violation of Title VII to claim that the rule creating an artificial barrier to employment has been applied to one gender and not to the other. Therefore, this Court finds that plaintiff has stated a violation of Title VII's prohibition against "any discrimination based on . . . sex. . . . "

The recent case of Geduldig v. Aiello, 417 U.S. 484 (1974) does not require that the defendant's interpretation or, rather, limitation of § 2000e-16(a) sex discrimination be accepted. The Geduldig analysis has been found to be inapplicable to Title VII cases. See Lombard, *Sex: A Classification in Search of Strict Scrutiny,* 21 Wayne L. Rev. 1355, 1366, 1366 n.47-52 (1975); see also Communication Workers of America v. A.T. & T. Co., C.A. No. 461 (2d Cir. March 26, 1975). This is understandable since Geduldig concerned the question of whether the refusal to extend insurance protection to pregnancy as a covered disability under a state insurance program resulted in an invidious discrimination in violation of the Constitutional standard as opposed to the statutory standard of Title VII.

Nor do the so-called "hair cases" cited by the defendant, Dodge v. Giant Food, Inc., 488 F.2d 1333 (D.C. Cir. 1973); Fagan v. National Cash Register Co., 481 F.2d 1115 (D.C. Cir. 1973); Boyce v. Safeway Stores, Inc., 351 F.Supp. 402 (D.D.C. 1972); require that this Court adopt the analysis asserted by the defendant. In one of those cases, the regulation or policy was found applicable to both men and women, 481 F.2d at 1124 n. 20; 351 F.Supp. at 403. Further, the courts in all of these cases found that any disparate treatment in the regulation or policy involved was permissible under the exception found in § 703(e) of the Act. E.g., 481 F.2d at 1125. But this finding should not be confused with the threshhold analysis of whether sex discrimination is extant. Disparate treatment was assumed in two of those cases. What they were then concerned with was whether the disparate treatment was permissible under the exception to the Act. See also Weeks v. Southern Bell Tel. & Tel. Co., 406 F.2d 228 (5th Cir. 1969). The only case of any distinction, Dodge, refused to find sex discrimination because the Court concluded that: "Title VII never was intended to encompass sexual classifications having only an insigificant effect on employment opportunities." 488 F.2d at 1337. Assuming Title VII permits a weighing of the effect of a particular policy or regulation, this Court could not find the instant policy or practice to have an insigificant effect.

Nor does this Court agree that it should adopt the agency's interpretation merely because it is entitled to be given extra consideration. Since this Court has found that the agency's interpretation does not comport with the scope and purpose of the statute, this court may reject the agency's decision. Volkswagenwerk Aktiiengesellschaft v. Federal Maritime Commission, 390 U.S. 261, 272 (1968).

Finally, defendants argue that plaintiff has not made out a case of sex discrimination under the Act because, the instant case was not the result of a policy or a regulation of the office, but rather, was an isolated incident which should not be the concern of the courts and was not the concern of Congress in enacting Title VII. But this argument is merely based upon defendants' view of the facts, coupled with a fear that the courts will become embroiled in sorting out the social life of the employees of the numerous federal agencies. First, whether this case presents a policy or practice of imposing a condition of sexual submission on the female employees of the CRS or whether this was a nonemployment related personal encounter requires a factual determination. It is sufficient for purposes of the motion to dismiss that the plaintiff has alleged it was the former in this case. For, if this was a policy or practice of plaintiff's supervisor, then it was the agency's policy or practice, which is prohibited by Title VII. Secondly, the decision of the Court that plaintiff has stated a cause of action under Title VII will not have the feared result defendants urge. What the statute is concerned with is not interpersonal disputes between employees. Rather, the instant case reveals the statutory prohibition on the alleged discriminatory imposition of a condition of employment by the supervisor of an office of an agency.

This Court concludes that plaintiff has stated a cause of action under 42 U.S.C. § 2000e-16(a). The Court next turns to the motions for summary judgment and the administrative record.

As stated above, after the complaint was filed in this case the Court determined that plaintiff had presented proof suggestive of sex discrimination. The Court remanded the case because the agency had placed the burden of proof on the plaintiff rather than bearing the burden to affirmatively establish the absence of discrimination. On remand, the Hearing Examiner found that there was a causal connection between plaintiff's supervisor's conduct and plaintiff's termination and that the defendant had failed to meet its burden. The Complaint Adjudication Officer reversed this decision on the ground that, in his opinion, the conduct complained of did not come within the meaning of sex discrimination. Plaintiff has moved for judgment on the merits, asking this Court to reject the decision of the Complaint Adjudication Officer and instate the decision of the Hearing Examiner, or alternatively to declare that the plaintiff was terminated without cause, and award her appropriate relief. The defendant has filed a renewed motion for summary judgment asserting that the record demonstrated that plaintiff was terminated for good cause and that there was no causal connection between her supervisor's advances, and her termination from the agency.

Reveiw of the administrative decision of the agency in this case is complicated by the fact that the Complaint Adjudication Officer's decision, which is the final decision of the agency, was defective on two grounds. First, that the decision rejected the Hearing Examiner's decision in the belief that the administrative complaint had not set forth a cause of action under Title VII. Since this Court has found otherwise, it rejects the contrary decision of the Complaint Adjudication Officer. Second, the Complaint Adjudication Officer rejected the decision of the Hearing Examiner because he thought the Examiner failed to consider the testimony of Ms. Ruth Spencer that was adduced at the supplementary hearings. He predominantly relied upon this testimony to conclude that the termination of plaintiff's employment was based on a "clash between two apparently strong-willed persons neither of whom would submit to the other" and was therefore not based on sex discrimination. Unfortunately, he does not reveal under what standard this conclusion was reached, nor does his decision indicate whether he viewed the plaintiff or the defendant having the burden of proof. In this Court's opinion, the decision of the Complaint Adjudication Officer is therefore wholly unsatisfactory to the point of being practically incapable of review.

Under these circumstances, this Court would normally remand the case to the administrative agency so that the Complaint Adjudication Officer could properly review the decision of the hearing examiner. See Davis, *Administrative Law Treatise* § 16.05 at 323 (1972). However, this Court has previously remanded this case to the administrative agency under directions to apply the proper standards and believes that it would be unjust as well as contrary to the intent of Title VII to remand the case again. The Court has therefore completely reviewed the record, as supplemented, to determine whether the Hearing Examiner's decision that the government had failed to affirmatively establish the absence of discrimination by the clear weight of the evidence was based on substantial evidence and was rational.

This Court finds that the conclusion of the Hearing Examiner was both supported by ample evidence in the record and was a reasonable interpretation of that evidence. Plaintiff had alleged that subsequent to her rejection of her supervisor's advances as well as her supervisor's rejection of her request for a promotion, her supervisor began a program of harassment and criticism designed to have her employment terminated. The inference drawn was that since she had refused to submit to the sexual condition of her supervisor, he had retaliated by creating a basis for her discharge from the agency. The connection between the advances of her supervisor, which advances were not disputed, and the subsequent criticism by the supervisor of her work, was supported by the timing of the incident: the commencement of his criticisms of her alleged employment deficiencies when there had been no prior proof of criticism. This connection was sought to be broken by the defendant by an attempt to show that the alleged employment deficiencies of the plaintiff were true and were therefore the real reason for her discharge, and not merely a pretext. Much of the record was spent by both sides attempting to prove or disprove the allegations concerning plaintiff's work performance. The result of all of this evidence was inconclusive. The only thing that could be concluded was that plaintiff and her supervisor were experiencing some work problems and that during this time both parties were openly critical of each other.

In reviewing the evidence from the point of view of the plaintiff, the Court finds that the record made produced little more than a prima facie case. In fact, at one point it appears that the plaintiff was unclear whether she viewed her supervisor's conduct as retaliation for her refusal to submit to his advances or retaliation for her attempt to advance her employment status. Nevertheless, there was evidence to support her allegation that the advances did occur and that the retaliation was a result of her refusal to comply with this condition. There was also evidence that other persons had been similarly subjected to this condition, all of whom were women.

A careful examination of the record shows that there was substantial evidence upon which the hearing officer could reasonably conclude that the Government did not affirmatively prove the absence of discrimination by the clear weight of the evidence. As stated above, the evidence concerning plaintiff's work performance was inconclusive at best, and hardly established by the clear weight that the allegations were not a pretext. While the defendant attempted to show that the advances were unrelated to the subsequent action of plaintiff's supervisor, none of the evidence directly established this contention. Ms. Ruth Spencer's testimony, on which the Complaint Adjudication Officer relied, was not only hearsay, but also, her testimony consisted almost entirely of what she thought plaintiff believed was the problem in the office. This can hardly be said to establish as fact that the supervisor's advances were not a condition of employment imposed upon the plaintiff, but rather a nonemployment related interpersonal encounter.

Having found that the Hearing Examiner's decision was based upon substantial evidence and was a reasonable interpretation of the evidence, the Court will deny defendants' renewed motion for summary judgment. And while the Court will grant plaintiff's motion for judgment on the basis of the administrative record, the Court can do no more than issue a declaration that the defendants violated 42 U.S.C. § 2000e-16(a), since the parties have not addressed what specific relief is appropriate and lawful under the circumstances. The Court will therefore issue an order disposing of the motions and requiring the parties to submit memoranda on the question of remedies.

Upon consideration of defendants' motion to dismiss the complaint, defendants' renewed motion for summary judgment, and plaintiff's motion for judgment, and in accordance with the Memorandum Opinion of the Court of even date herewith, it is, by the Court, this 20th day of April, 1976.

ORDERED, that defendants' motion to dismiss the complaint be, and the same hereby, is denied; and it is

FURTHER ORDERED, that defendants' renewed motion for summary judgment be, and the same hereby is, denied; and it is

FURTHER ORDERED, that plaintiff's motion for judgment be, and the same hereby is, granted; and it is

FURTHER ORDERED, that within five (5) days of the date of this Order the plaintiff shall file with the Clerk of this Court and serve opposing counsel with a memorandum concerning what specific relief is appropriate and lawful in this case, and the defendant shall file a responsive memorandum thereto within five (5) days from receipt of plaintiff's memorandum.

Tomkins v. Public Service Electric & Gas Co.
[_____ F.2d _____ (3rd Cir. 1977)]

Sex discrimination— submission to sexual advances as condition of employment

Analysis of the issue

The plaintiff claimed that she was a victim of sex discrimination as defined by Title VII, on the grounds that her supervisor advised her that her continued success and advancement with the company depended upon her agreeing to have sexual relations with him. She also asserted that the supervisor stated that no one at the company would help her if she filed a complaint over the matter. The supervisor's statement eventually proved true. The plaintiff's desire to leave the company due to the incident was changed by a promise of a transfer to another department where she would maintain her position and not work under the supervisor in question. After a long wait the transfer did materialize, but it was in fact a demotion. In addition, her supervisors engaged in activities of harassment such as giving the plaintiff false and adverse employment evaluations and disciplinary layoffs. The physical and emotional distress suffered by the plaintiff because of these activities resulted in her frequently being absent from work. Her high rate of absenteeism was responsible for her termination. The court agreed that the plaintiff's rights under Title VII had been violated. This conclusion was based on the facts that the requirement to submit to sexual demands was a condition of employment that would not have been placed before a male employee, and that the employer, after having learned of the incident, did not undertake any remedial action.

Full text of opinion

ALDISERT, Circuit Judge:—The question presented is whether appellant Adrienne Tomkins, in alleging that her continued employment with appellee Public Service Electric and Gas Co. [PSE&G] was conditioned upon her submitting to the sexual advances of a male supervisor, stated a cause of action under Title VII of the Civil Rights Act of 1964, as amended, 42 U.S.C. § 2000e et seq. The district court determined that appellant did not state a claim under Title VII, and dismissed her complaint. 422 F.Suppl. 553, (D.N.J. 1976). Taking the allegations of Tomkins' complaint as true, see Walker, Inc. v. Food Machinery, 382 U.S. 172, 174–75 (1965); Conley V. Gibson, 355 U.S. 41, 45–46, (1957), we find that a cognizable claim of sex discrimination was made and, accordingly, we reverse the dismissal of the complaint and remand the case to the district court for further proceedings.

Taken as true, the facts set out in appellant's complaint demonstrate that Adrienne Tomkins was hired by PSE&G in April 1971, and progressed to positions of increasing responsibility from that time until

August 1973, when she began working in a secretarial position under the direction of a named supervisor. On October 30, 1973, the supervisor told Tomkins that she should have lunch with him in a nearby restaurant, in order to discuss his upcoming evaluation of her work, as well as a possible job promotion. At lunch, he made advances toward her, indicating his desire to have sexual relations with her and stating that this would be necessary if they were to have a satisfactory working relationship. When Tomkins attempted to leave the restaurant, the supervisor responded first by threats of recrimination against Tomkins in her employment, then by threats of physical force, and ultimately by physically restraining Tomkins. During the incident, he told her that no one at PSE&G would help her should she lodge a complaint against him.

Tomkins' complaint alleges that PSE&G and certain of its agents knew or should have known that such incidents would occur, and that they nevertheless "placed [Tomkins] in a position where she would be subjected to the aforesaid conduct of [the supervisor] and failed to take adequate supervisory measures to prevent such incidents from occurring." It further alleged that on the day following the lunch, Tomkins expressed her intention to leave PSE&G as a result of the incident. She agreed to continue work only after being promised a transfer to a comparable position elsewhere in the company. A comparable position did not become available, however, and Tomkins was instead placed in an inferior position in another department. There, she was subjected to false and adverse employment evaluations, disciplinary layoffs, and threats of demotion by various PSE&G employees. Tomkins maintains that as a result of the supervisor's conduct and the continued pattern of harassment by PSE&G personnel, she suffered physical and emotional distress, resulting in absenteeism and loss of income.

In January 1975, PSE&G fired Tomkins. Following her dismissal, she filed an employment discrimination complaint with the Equal Employment Opportunity Commission, which ultimately issued a Notice of Right to Sue. After Tomkins filed suit in district court, PSE&G moved to dismiss the complaint on various grounds, including failure to state a claim upon which relief may be granted. In addressing the motion, the district court bifurcated the issues raised in the complaint. The court denied the company's motion to dismiss Tomkins' claim of company retaliation against her for complaining about her supervisor's conduct. However, the company's motion to dismiss Tomkins' claim against PSE&G for his actions was granted for failure to state a claim. The latter judgment was determined final by the district court under Rule 54(b), Fed. R. Civ. P., and this appeal followed.

Section 703(a)(1) of Title VII, 43 U.S.C. § 2000e-2(a)(1), provides that "it shall be an unlawful employment practice for an employer . . . to discharge any individual . . . or otherwise to discriminate against any individual with respect to . . . terms, conditions, or privileges of employment because of such individual's . . . sex. . . . " In order to state a claim under this provision, then, it is necessary that Tomkins establish both that the acts complained of constituted a condition of employment, and that this condition was imposed by the employer on the basis of sex.

Tomkins claims that the sexual demands of her supervisor imposed a sex-based "term or condition" on her employment. She alleges that her promotion and favorable job evaluation were made conditional upon her granting sexual favors, and that she suffered adverse job consequences as a result of this incident. In granting appellees' motion to dismiss, however, the district court characterized the supervisor's acts as "abuse of authority . . . for personal purposes." 422 F.Supp. at 556. The court thus overlooked the major thrust of Tomkins' complaint, i.e., that her employer, either knowingly or constructively, made acquiescence in her supervisor's sexual demands a necessary prerequisite to the continuation of, or advancement in, her job.

The facts as alleged by appellant clearly demonstrate an incident with employment ramifications, one within the intended coverage of Title VII. The context within which the sexual advances occurred is itself strong evidence of a job-related condition: Tomkins was asked to lunch by her supervisor for the express purpose of discussing his upcoming evaluation of her work and possible recommendation of her for a promotion. But one need not infer the added condition from the setting alone. It is expressly alleged that the supervisor stated to Tomkins that her continued success and advancement at PSE&G were dependent upon her agreeing to his sexual demands. The demand thus amounted to a condition of employment, an additional duty or burden Tomkins was required by her supervisor to meet as a prerequisite to her continued employment.

The issue whether the additional condition was imposed because of Tomkins' gender, as required by Section 703(a)(1), gave rise to various hypotheticals in the briefs and oral argument presented to this court. For example, appellees urge that the supervisor could "just as easily" have sought to satisfy his sexual urges with a male, and thus his actions were not directed only toward the female sex.

Similar to the argument that his acts were merely personal rather than constituting an additional condition of employment, such hypotheticals are irrelevant in the posture in which the appeal reaches this court. It is to the face of the complaint that we must look. And the complaint clearly alleges that Tomkins was discriminated against, "on the basis of her sex", by virtue of her supervisor's actions and PSE&G's acquiescence in those actions. Specifically, Tomkins averred that PSE&G knew or should have known the facts complained of. Reading the complaint in the light most favorable to Tomkins, the essence of her claim is that her status as a female was the motivating factor in the supervisor's conditioning her continued employment on compliance with his sexual demands.

Cases dealing with the issue presented in this appeal are scarce, and our research has produced no controlling precedent. Reference to certain of the cases is helpful, however, for a discernible pattern emerges from the decisions.

The District of Columbia Circuit was presented with similar facts in Barnes v. Costle, No. 74-2026 (D.C. Cir. July 27, 1977), a Title VII action in which appellant alleged that her job was abolished in retaliation for her refusal to engage in sexual relations with her male supervisor. Plaintiff claimed that in the course of her employment, the supervisor made a number of sexual advances and conditioned any enhancement of her job status on her acquiescing to his sexual demands. Noting appellant's assertion that "she became the target of her supervisor's sexual desires because she was a woman, and was asked to bow to his demands as the price for holding her job," Slip Opinion at 15, the Court of Appeals determined that the alleged facts constituted a violation of Title VII, and therefore reversed the district court's grant of summary judgment in favor of defendant.

The Fourth Circuit, in Garber v. Saxon Business Products, No. 76-1610 (4th Cir. Feb. 14, 1977) (per curiam), reversed a district court's grant of a dismissal on similar facts. In the court's view, plaintiff's complaint that she had been terminated for refusing her male superior's sexual demands "allege[d] an employer policy or acquiescence in a practice of compelling female employees to submit to the sexual advances of their male superiors in violation of Title VII." A similar result was reached in Williams v. Saxbe, 413 F.Supp. 654, (D.D.C. 1976) (appeal pending), where it was determined that retaliatory actions of a male supervisor, taken because a female employee declined his sexual advances, constitute an "artificial barrier to employment which was placed before one gender and not the other," 413 F.Supp. at 657, and thus sex discrimination violative of Title VII.

Faced with claims that at first appear similar, two district courts reached different results. In Corne v. Bausch and Lomb, Inc., 390 F.Supp. 161, (D. Ariz. 1975), rev'd & remanded on other grounds, advances by a male employee to female fellow employees did not constitute actionable sex discrimination under Title VII. Corne is distinguishable from the facts before us because plaintiff Corne did not allege that acquiescence in the sexual advances was required as a condition of her employment. Appellant Tomkins, by contrast, clearly alleged such an employment nexus. Also distinguishable from the current appeal is Miller v. Bank of America, 418 F. Suppl. 122, (N.D. Cal. 1973) (appeal pending). Plaintiff Miller alleged that her male supervisor promised her job advancement in return for engaging in sexual relations with him, and subsequently dismissed her when she refused to do so. Not only was it undisputed that defendant bank discouraged such employee misconduct, but plaintiff had failed to avail herself of a bank complaint procedure designed to resolve precisely this sort of complaint. The Miller court drew a clear distinction between those facts and a situation where an employer is implicated in a complaint of improper sexual advances:

[T]here may be situations in which a sex discrimination action can be maintained for an employer's action, or tacit approval, of a personnel policy requiring sex favors as a condition of employment.

418 F.Supp. at 236. Although these cases are not dispositive of this appeal, they disclose a pattern of how sexual advances in the employment context do or do not constitute a Title VII violation. The courts have distinguished between complaints alleging sexual advances of an individual or personal nature and those alleging direct employment consequences flowing from the advances, finding Title VII violations in the latter category. This distinction recognizes two elements necessary to find a violation of Title VII: first, that a term or condition of employment has been imposed and second, that it has been imposed by the em-

ployer, either directly or vicariously, in a sexually discriminatory fashion. Applying these requirements to the present complaint, we conclude that Title VII is violated when a supervisor, with the actual or constructive knowledge of the employer, makes sexual advances or demands toward a subordinate employee and conditions that employee's job status—evaluation, continued employment, promotion, or other aspects of career development—on a favorable response to those advances or demands, and the employer does not take prompt and appropriate remedial action after acquiring such knowledge.

We do not agree with the district court that finding a Title VII violation on these facts will result in an unmanageable number of suits and a difficulty in differentiating between spurious and meritorious claims. The congressional mandate that the federal courts provide relief is strong; it must not be thwarted by concern for judicial economy. More significant, however, this decision in no way relieves the plaintiff of the burden of proving the facts alleged to establish the required elements of a Title VII violation. Although any theory of liability may be used in vexatious or bad faith suits, we are confident that traditional judicial mechanisms will separate the valid from the invalid complaints.

The judgment of the district court will be reversed and the cause remanded for further proceedings.

Miller v. Bank of America
[418 F.Supp. 233 (N.D. Cal. 1976)]

Sexual advances not seen as Title VII violation

Analysis of the issue

The plaintiff, a former employee of the Bank of America, claimed to have
been a victim of sex discrimination within the meaning of Title VII. She
alleged that her supervisor promised her a better job provided she coop-
erated with his sexual demands. The plaintiff further asserted that her
eventual discharge resulted from her refusal to cooperate. The court
took into account the facts that the defendant operated under a policy of
disciplining and/or discharging employees found guilty of such misconduct; and that the plaintiff did not contact the bank's Employer Relations
Department about the matter. The Employer Relations Department is
equipped to handle employee complaints such as the one at issue, and
would have instituted a full investigation into the matter. Considering
the extent to which the defendant protects its employees from the sort of
abuse the plaintiff alleged to have suffered, the court concluded that the
incident would rightly be classified as an isolated and unauthorized sex
misconduct of one employee to another. Since the plaintiff could not
show evidence that would support a claim to the effect that the misconduct was a policy or practice of the employer, the court ruled that Title
VII had not been violated.

Full text of opinion

SPENCER WILLIAMS, District Judge:—This matter is before the Court
on defendant's motion for summary judgment, duly noticed, argued
and submitted.

Plaintiff, a black woman, was an NCR operator for defendant Bank.
She claims that her operations supervisor, a white male, promised her a
better job if she would be sexually "cooperative", and caused her dismissal when she refused.

Plaintiff failed to avail herself of the services of Bank's Employer
Relations Department that was established to investigate employee
complaints, including complaints of sexual impropriety and sexual advances. Instead, she filed a written charge with the EEOC and, upon
receiving her right-to-sue letter, filed the instant action.

Jurisdiction is invoked pursuant to 42 U.S.C.A. § 1981 and 42
U.S.C.A. § 2000e *et seq.* Plaintiff seeks injunctive relief, reinstatement,
back pay and attorney's fees for alleged sex discrimination in violation of
Title VII of the Civil Rights Act of 1964.

It is undisputed that Bank has a policy of discouraging sexual advances of the sort here alleged and of affirmatively disciplining employees found guilty of such conduct.

Section 2000e-2(a) provides that "it shall be an unlawful employment practice for an employer (1) to . . . discharge . . . any individual . . . because of such individual's . . . sex. . . . "

The issue before the Court is whether Title VII was intended to hold an employer liable for what is essentially the isolated and unauthorized sex misconduct of one employee to another.

Little can be gleaned from the legislative history of the specific prohibition against sex discrimination. It was never the subject of Legislative Committee hearings but was added to the 1964 Civil Rights Act by amendment offered during debate in the House. And the debate on the amendment was devoted primarily to its possible adverse impact on the balance of Title VII. The Congressional Record fails to reveal any specific discussions as to the amendment's intended scope or impact. In addition, the great bulk of reported cases, unlike the instant case, concern established company policies that have been found either to violate, or not to violate, the prohibition against sex discrimination.

The parties have been able to present, and the Court has been able to find, but two reported cases which address the question of employer liability for unauthorized isolated sex-related acts by one employee against another.

In *Corne v. Bausch & Lomb, Inc.*, 390 F.Supp. 161 (D.Ariz.1975), the court found that unwelcome verbal and physical sex advances by a male supervisor to two female employees, which compelled them to terminate their employment, created no rights to relief under Title VII. In granting defendant's motion to dismiss, the court stated:

"Nothing in the complaint alleges nor can it be construed that the conduct complained of was company directed policy which deprived women of employment opportunities. A reasonably intelligent reading of the statute demonstrates it can only mean that an unlawful employment practice must be discrimination on the part of the employer, Bausch and Lomb. Further, there is nothing in the Act which could reasonably be construed to have it apply to 'verbal and physical sexual advances' by another employee, even though he be in a supervisory capacity where such complained of acts or conduct had no relationship to the nature of the employment." 390 F.Supp. at 163.

In *Williams v. Saxbe*, 413 F.Supp. 654 (D.D.C.1976), the court, in denying defendant's motion to dismiss, held that retaliatory actions, taken because a female employee declined her supervisor's sexual advances, constitute sex discrimination within Title VII. However, in so ruling, the court stated:

" . . . whether this case presents a policy or practice of imposing a condition of sexual submission on the female employees . . . or whether this was a non-employment related personal encounter requires a factual determination. It is sufficient for purposes of the motion to dismiss that the plaintiff has alleged it was the former in this case."

And following the above quote, the court noted:

"Paragraph 21 of the Complaint alleges that the supervisor's conduct was a policy or practice imposed on the plaintiff and other women similarly situated. This is an essential allegation for presenting a cause of action. *Plaintiff's theory has never been that this was merely an isolated personal incident.*" (Emphasis added.)

In the instant case, the two affidavits of L. G. Zugnoni, Bank Vice-President, categorically allege that it is the policy of the Bank to prevent and prohibit moral misconduct, including sexual advances, and to suspend and/or dismiss and/or reprimand in some other manner employees who have made sexual advances to their co-employees, subordinate employees or superior employees.

No affidavits filed by plaintiff controvert these factual allegations. In her affidavit, plaintiff alleges that:

"Mr. Taufer (her supervisor) fired me because I . . . rejected his sexual advances", and that
"I believe that Defendant Bank has and had a policy or practice of permitting males in a supervisory position, specifically Mr. Taufer, to put . . . female employees in subsidiary roles demeaning to their dignity, and a role which . . . female employees had to play in order to remain employed with defendant. . . . "

Furthermore, plaintiff cannot validly claim Bank's tacit approval of Taufer's conduct since, as noted above, she failed to bring the matter to Bank's attention by filing a complaint with Bank's Employer Relations Department and allowing it to conduct an appropriate investigation.

Obviously, as in *Williams v. Saxbe, supra,* there may be situations in which a sex discrimination action can be maintained for an employer's active, or tacit approval, of a personnel policy requiring sex favors as a condition of employment. But as stated in *Corne,* 390 F.Supp. at page 163,

"It would be ludicrous to hold that the sort of activity involved here was contemplated by the Act. . . . [A]n outgrowth of [such a holding] would be a potential federal lawsuit every time any employer made amorous or sexually oriented advances toward another."

In addition, it would not be difficult to foresee a federal challenge based on alleged sex motivated considerations of the complainant's superior in every case of a lost promotion, transfer, demotion or dismissal. And who is to say what degree of sexual cooperation would found a Title VII claim? It is conceivable, under plaintiff's theory, that flirtations of the smallest order would give rise to liability. The attraction of males to females and females to males is a natural sex phenomenon and it is probable that this attraction plays at least a subtle part in most personnel decisions. Such being the case, it would seem wise for the Courts to refrain from delving into these matters short of specific factual allegations describing an employer policy which in its application imposes or permits a consistent, as distinguished from isolated, sex-based discrimination on a definable employee group.

Since plaintiff has failed to demonstrate that there remain any genuine issues of material fact herein defendant's motion for summary judgment is granted.

IT IS HEREBY ORDERED, ADJUDGED AND DECREED that judgment be entered in favor of the defendant and against the plaintiff.

Jacobs v. Martin Sweets Co.
[550 F.2d 364 (6th Cir. 1977)]

Discharging an employee who is pregnant and unmarried violates Title VII

Analysis of the issue

In this appeals case, the plaintiff, a former employee of the Martin Sweets Company, alleged that she was discharged because she had become pregnant and was unmarried. The plaintiff was hired as an executive secretary to the senior vice president on December 9, 1970. From that date until May of 1972, the plaintiff received highly positive performance evaluations and accordingly was afforded salary increases. However, following this period, the employee's good standing was tainted by tardiness and periods of absenteeism. On the occasion when her supervisor learned of the employee's pregnancy, he called her into his office and privately informed her that neither he nor the president could tolerate or approve of her situation, and therefore she was being given two weeks notice prior to the termination of her employment with the company. During her final two weeks, the plaintiff was without prior notice and against her will, demoted to a clerical position in the purchasing department. The move, which did not include a cut in salary, was explained as one made necessary by a shortage of personnel in that department. Evidence to the contrary caused the court to think otherwise. The court learned in testimony that the company policy toward pregnancy was that employees were permitted to work through the sixth month of pregnancy. This rule, however, was not enforced; in common practice employees were allowed to work up until the time where continued work would present a danger to the pregnant employee's health. Evidence was conclusive that the plaintiff was not extended this privilege. The defendant argued that in order for the plaintiff to prove that a Title VII violation existed, she would have to show that she was treated differently than she would have been were she a male, expectant parent. The defendant's point being that it must be shown that among similarly situated men and women, there had been disparate treatment. In response, the court said that one could not equate the condition of pregnancy with being an expectant parent, thus disallowing the "similarly situated" logic. Furthermore, distinguishing wed from unwed pregnancy would effectively exclude all pregnancies from Title VII protection, which would be contrary to the intent of the law. In concluding that the employer's actions violated Title VII, the court upheld the district court's ruling, which awarded the plaintiff $3500 to cover attorney's fees, and increased that amount by $1000 to defray costs incurred in pursuing the appeal.

Full text of opinion

MILLER, Judge:—This action, involving alleged sex discrimination in employment because of unwed pregnancy, was brought by Rose M.

Jacobs ("Jacobs") against The Martin Sweets Company, Inc., Louisville, Ky. ("Sweets Co." or "Company"), under the provisions of Title VII of the Civil Rights Act of 1964 ("Act"), Pub. L. No. 88–352, 78 Stat. 253, 42 U.S.C. § 2000e et seq. Sweets Co. appeals from that portion of the district court's amended judgment awarding back wages to Jacobs in the sum of $7,500 pursuant to 42 U.S.C. § 2000e-5(g). Jacobs appeals from that portion of the amended judgment dismissing the class action allegations of her complaint with prejudice. She also asks that the district court's award of attorney's fee be reversed, with certain directions for recomputation. We affirm those portions of the amended judgment pertaining to back wages and the class action issue; the portion pertaining to attorney's fee is modified to the extent that the fee awarded is to be increased by the sum of $1,000 for services rendered on this appeal.

Jacobs began her employment with the Sweets Co. on December 9, 1970, as executive secretary to James Hanna, the Senior Vice President. She received an increase in salary to $600 per month on April 1, 1971, an outstanding annual performance evaluation in February of 1972, and a second increase in salary to $633 per month in May of 1972; however, during 1972 she was warned by Hanna on several occasions about her tardiness and absenteeism. During her employment with the Company she was unmarried.

Jacobs' testimony was that on September 8, 1972, Hanna called her into his office, shut the doors, and said he had heard from other employees that she was pregnant, which she confirmed; that he declared he could not tolerate it, Martin Sweets, the President, would never approve of it, and he was giving her two weeks' notice, with her last day to be September 22; and that Hanna stated "there would be no problem whatsoever with getting me a more than good recommendation if I needed it." Following this meeting, Jacobs contacted the District Office of the Equal Employment Opportunity Commision (EEOC), where she spoke with the Department Director, Robert Jeffries, who advised that it would be illegal for the Company to fire her due to her pregnancy and suggested that she get the matter in writing if at all possible. On September 12 she presented two documents to Hanna: (1) a request that he write a letter of recommendation, with the letter indicating it was not due to her work but to her pregnancy that she was being let go; and (2) a notice to her, for Hanna's signature, stating that the Company was required to terminate her employment due to her being pregnant and not married "in order to avoid embarrassment to the company and to yourself," and that the Company intended to issue her a letter of recommendation. She said that Hanna refused to sign and that, while leaving his office, she heard him place a telephone call and ask for the Company's attorney.

Jacobs further testified that on the morning of September 14, S. J. Popson, one of Sweets Co.'s vice presidents, came into her office and told her that Hanna had directed him the night before to supervise her immediate transfer to the Purchasing Department and that she was to clean out her desk, get all her things together, turn in her keys, and not return to the office except under supervision; that this was the first she had heard about a change in her assignment, Hanna having said nothing to her about it. She stated that Popson told her that her pregnancy had been mentioned to him by Hanna; that he did not tell her the transfer was temporary; and that later that day, after her typewriter, office equipment, and other personal things had been moved to the Purchasing Department, she filed a charge against the Company with the EEOC. She also stated that the Purchasing Agent told her that Hanna had called him, also the night before, about the transfer and had said it was to try to get her to quit. Jacobs further stated that her job in the Purchasing Department was "just a clerical position"; that, notwithstanding several attempts on her part, Hanna refused to see her until September 28, when she told him that she had filed suit with the EEOC and would not be returning to the Company; and that she came in on September 25, picked up her paycheck of September 22, and worked in the Purchasing Department, but that the main reason was to try to see Hanna about staying on with the Company in her former position.

Additional testimony of Jacobs was that she received a notice from Hanna, dated September 18, advising, *inter alia*, that "under current company policy any employee who becomes pregnant shall be allowed to work as her physical condition permits and as long as the work will not jeopardize her health"; that she also received a copy of a notice, dated September 18, to the Purchasing Agent from Hanna, subject: "Temporary Transfer of Rose Jacobs," reciting that due to the senior officer of the Company being on an extended trip and the need for only one executive secretary, it was more feasible to use the senior executive secretary and to transfer Jacobs to the Purchasing Department "to fulfill the overload requirements," with no change in hours and no reduction in salary.

S. J. Popson testified that Hanna had telephoned him the evening of September 13 and told him that he was to supervise Jacobs' transfer from Hanna's office to the Purchasing Department; that he was not to leave Jacobs alone in the office; that he should get her key to the office after her things were moved out, lock the office, and not allow her to return; that Hanna's instructions were carried out the next morning; and that he did not recollect whether Hanna told him to tell Jacobs that the transfer was temporary. The record also shows the following on direct examination of Popson by Jacobs' lawyer:

Q. Did Mr. Hanna discuss Miss Jacobs' pregnancy with you that evening in that conversation?
A. In that conversation? All I can say is I can't imagine that it wasn't discussed. I wouldn't take the conversation [sic] and do the job without asking why. And I'm sure that we did go into the ramifications. But as far as the details of what was discussed, I really couldn't remember specifics.

Robert Jeffries, Department Director of the District Office of the EEOC during the period involved, stated that he took a telephone call on or about September 12 from a lawyer for Sweets Co., inquiring about the law pertaining to pregnancy; that the lawyer "asked me to fully explain the laws where the pregnant party was married or unmarried"; and that the conversation pertained to the Company and Jacobs, who had previously talked to him about the Company and her being pregnant and unmarried.

The Company's attorney, Marvin Hirn, testified that his assistant telephoned the District Office of the EEOC in September of 1972; that the call was precipitated by Hanna's call to him on September 12, during which "we entered into a discussion of the company's pregnancy policy"; and that, based on the information his assistant received from the EEOC, he advised Hanna that Jacobs should be permitted to work as long as she was able.

Hanna insisted, *inter alia*, that he did not tell Jacobs that she was fired or would be fired because she was pregnant and unmarried. He stated that Jacobs' "temporary" transfer to the Purchasing Department was to help with the overload and because he did not trust her after she had tendered to him what he labeled a "false statement" for him to sign; that, prior to Martin Sweets' departure for an extended overseas trip on August 31, Sweets told him to utilize Sweets' secretary during his absence; that highly sensitive negotiations involving the Company had been going on, of which only Sweets, Hanna, and Sweets' secretary were to have knowledge; that he had previously considered using Jacobs for additional help in the Purchasing Department during Sweets' absence; and that, although the Company's Policies and Procedures Manual provided for termination of employment of pregnant employees at the end of six months of pregnancy, this had never been enforced, the Company allowed such employees to work as long as they were able, consistent with their health, and jobs were held open for employees on pregnancy leave. He agreed that it was a common occurrence in the Purchasing Department that the work load increased during the last six months of the year.

The district court's determination that, because she was pregnant and unmarried, Jacobs was given two weeks' notice of termination of her employment on September 8, 1972, and was transferred, without consultation and against her wishes, from her job as executive secretary to the Senior Vice President of the Company to a clerical position in the Purchasing Department on September 14, is supported by substantial evidence and is not clearly erroneous. *Smith v. South Central Bell Telephone Co.*, 518 F.2d 68 (CA 6 1975). The district court's further determination that these actions constituted a termination and/or constructive termination of Jacobs' employment is also supported by substantial evidence, including the reasonable inferences to be drawn therefrom *See NLRB v. Tennessee Packers, Inc., Frosty Morn Division*, 339 F.2d 203 (CA 6 1964). Although there is conflicting testimony in the record, the district court had the benefit of hearing some of the key witnesses and observing their demeanor.

That Sweets Co. intended the two weeks' notice of termination given Jacobs on September 8 to be carried out is shown by Crawford's testimony that Hanna told him that Jacobs' computer check would be voided and that he should give her a typewritten check adjusted to what should be paid through September 22, in accordance with the practice when employees left the Company. The naked fact that Jacobs came in and worked on September 25 for the purpose of trying to see Hanna does not overcome the fact that her employment had been earlier terminated and/or constructively terminated. Sweets Co. contends that

Jacobs' transfer to the Purchasing Department was "temporary." However, Hanna himself testified that he didn't think he orally told Jacobs it was temporary, so it was not until she received a copy of the notice of September 18 to the Purchasing Agent (a document that could be considered self-serving) that the transfer was labeled "temporary." It is further contended that Jacobs voluntarily quit, but there are two answers to this: (1) "It cannot be said that a man voluntarily quits the employment of the master after he had been notified that his services are no longer desired." *Stark Distillery Co. v. Friedman,* 150 Ky. 820, 823, 150 S.W. 981, 983 (1912); and (2) Although Jacobs received a copy of the notice from Hanna to the Purchasing Agent that there would be no change in her hours and salary, the fact remains that the transfer from her position as executive secretary to clerical duties in the Purchasing Department was a demotion which, at the time of the transfer on September 14, had the appearance of being permanent. Taking into account the reason for such a demotion—that she was pregnant and unmarried, the conditions involving the transfer could properly be considered intolerable and her "quitting" involuntary. *See NLRB v. Tennessee Packers, Inc., Frosty Morn Division, supra.*

The dispositive question is whether the district court erred in concluding, as a matter of law, that the termination and/or constructive termination of Jacobs' employment constituted a violation of section 703 of the Act, 42 U.S.C. § 2000e-2(a), which provides:

It shall be an unlawful employment practice for an employer—

(1) to fail or refuse to hire or to discharge any individual, or otherwise to discriminate against any individual with respect to his compensation, terms, conditions, or privileges of employment, because of such individual's race, color, religion, sex, or national origin; or

(2) to limit, segregate, or classify his employees in any way which would deprive or tend to deprive any individual of employment opportunities or otherwise adversely affect his status as an employee, because of such individual's race, color, religion, sex, or national origin.

Sweets Co. argues that "Jacobs has never shown that had she been a male expectant parent, she would have been treated any differently by the Sweets Company." The sophistry of this argument is that it equates pregnancy with the condition of "expectant parent" in a male. Pregnancy is a condition unique to women, so that termination of employment because of pregnancy has a disparate and invidious impact upon the female gender. The point of the argument is that there must be men and women similarly situated who are treated in a disparate manner. The point is not well taken, for it would effectively exclude pregnancy from protection in *all* Title VII cases. The Supreme Court has stated that maternity leave rules directly affect "one of the basic civil rights of man." *Cleveland Board of Education v. LaFleur,* 414 U.S. 632, 640, 94 S.Ct. 791, 796, 39 L.Ed.2d 52, 60 (1974). To exclude such a basic civil right from protection against invidious employment termination would be contrary to the policy to which Title VII is directed, namely: that race, religion, nationality, and sex are irrelevant factors in employment opportunity. *Griggs v. Duke Power Co.,* 401 U.S. 424, 436, 91 S.Ct 849, 856, 28 L.Ed.2d 158, 167 (1971); *Holthaus v. Compton & Sons, Inc.,* 541 F.2d 651 (CA 8 1975).

Sweets Co. next argues that Jacobs has not shown that she would have received different treatment had her premarital sexual activity not resulted in pregnancy and that the EEOC's guideline applicable to pregnancy is unconstitutional because it is "an attempt to control the moral policies of a private company with respect to the premarital sexual behavior of individuals of both sexes." However, the district court found that Jacobs' employment was terminated because she was pregnant and unmarried—not because of her premarital sexual activity. Apart from the EEOC's guideline, which, in the absence of a showing that it conflicts with the letter or spirit of the Act (not shown here), is entitled at least to some weight, the district court's finding establishes a prima facie case of discrimination. *See McDonnell Douglas Corp. v. Green*, 411 U.S. 792, 93 S.Ct. 1817, 36 L.Ed.2d 668 (1973). Sweets Co's argument that the "unmarried" portion of the finding renders Jacobs' pregnancy different for purposes of Title VII is supported only by its citation to *Wardlaw v. Austin School District* (not officially reported), the facts of which are substantially different. The argument impliedly suggests that this court permit "artificial, arbitrary, and unnecessary barriers to employment" (condemned in *Griggs v. Duke Power Co., supra* at 431, 91 S.Ct. at 853, 28 L.Ed.2d at 164) in the case of unwed pregnancy, while declaring such barriers unlawful in the case of wed pregnancy. However, there is no evidence that such a classification has any rational relationship to the normal operation of Sweets Co.'s business. *Phillips v. Martin Marietta Corp.*, 400 U.S. 542, 544, 91 S.Ct. 496, 497–98, 27 L.Ed.2d 613, 615–16 (1971). *See Griggs v. Duke Power Co., supra* at 431, 91 S.Ct. at 853, 28 L.Ed.2d at 164.

In view of the foregoing, we hold that the district court committed no error in concluding, as a matter of law, that the termination and/or constructive termination of Jacob's employment constituted a violation of section 703 of the Act, 42 U.S.C. § 2000e-2(a).

The district court found that Jacobs' employment discrimination claim was entirely separate from her attack on Sweets Co.'s policy with respect to medical payments expense and sick pay during pregnancy; that there was no evidence that Jacobs suffered any actual or threatened loss or was likely to suffer any loss as a result of that policy; that Jacobs was not employed by Sweets Co. at any time during which it would have been appropriate and timely for her to demand payment under or challenge the validity of that policy; and that Jacobs did not make any actual claims for pregnancy-related expenses that were denied by the Company. These findings are supported by substantial evidence and are not clearly erroneous. *Smith v. South Central Bell Telephone Co., supra.*

The decisive issue is whether the district court erred in determining that Jacobs lacked both the requisite standing under Article III of the Constitution and class action status under Fed.R.Civ.P. 23(a), so that she was not a proper party to maintain a class action attacking the Company's pregnancy/sick pay/medical expense policy.

Jacobs argues that her claim of unlawful termination of employment because of pregnancy involves all present or future employees adversely affected by all the Company's pregnancy policies. However, we agree with the district court that she has not satisfied "the threshold requirement imposed by Art. III of the Constitution that those who seek to invoke the power of federal courts must allege an actual case or controversy." *O'Shea v. Littleton*, 414 U.S. 488, 493 94 S.Ct. 669, 675, 38 L.Ed.2d 674, 682 (1974). We note that Jacobs' complaint alleges that her employment was unlawfully terminated because of her sex (when she would have been approximately six-weeks pregnant). However, she has not alleged, much less shown, "specific, concrete facts" demonstrating that the Company's policy regarding medical payments expense and sick pay during pregnancy was applied to her. *Warth v. Seldin*, 422 U.S. 490, 508, 95 S.Ct. 2197, 2210, 45 L.Ed.2d 343, 360 (1975). As found by the district court, she did not make any actual claims for pregnancy-related expenses that were denied by the Company.

With respect to Jacobs' status under Fed. R.Civ.P. 23(a), she cites *Tipler v. E. I. duPont deNemours & Co.*, 443 F.2d 125, 130 (CA 6 1971), and *Wetzel v. Liberty Mutual Insurance Co.*, 508 F.2d 239, 247 (CA 3), *cert. denied*, 421 U.S. 1011, 95 S.Ct. 2415, 44 L.Ed.2d 679 (1975), both of which held that a complainant who is no longer employed may still be an adequate representative of a class of employees. However, unlike the complainants in those cases, Jacobs has not shown that she belongs to the class she seeks to represent. *See Linda R. S. v. Richard D.*, 410 U.S. 614, 617 n.4, 93 S.Ct. 1146, 1148 n.4, 35 L.Ed.2d 536, 540 n.4 (1973). Jacobs says it is "difficult to understand how the interests of the class are protected by allowing the unlawful practices to continue until some other employee has the temerity [sic] to challenge the Sweets Company policies," but this ignores the requirement of Fed.R.Civ.P. 23(a)(3) that Jacobs' claim be "typical" of the claims of the class. The district court correctly determined that Jacobs lacked class action status under Fed.R.Civ.P. 23(a).

Jacobs contends that the district court abused its discretion in making an award of $3,500 for attorney's fee and asks that this portion of the court's amended judgment be reversed with directions that a fee be awarded for services in the district court and on appeal based on hours times hourly rate times other relevant factors, principally the contingent nature of the representation. She points out that the affidavit accompanying her motion for award of fee shows that her counsel had devoted 129.3 hours on the case; that an award of $3,500 would amount to only $27 per hour.

Section 706(k) of the Act, 42 U.S.C. § 2000e–5(k), provides that: "In any action or proceeding under this subchapter the court, in its discretion, may allow the prevailing party . . . a reasonable attorney's fee as part of the costs. . . . " Although this court has interpreted the statute to require the award of a fee that would approximate the customary fee in the community for similar work, it is clear that more than a simple division of an award by the number of hours devoted to the case is needed to support a conclusion that the district court abused its discretion. *Singer v. Mahoning County Board of Mental Retardation*, 519 F.2d 748 (CA 6 1975). On the record before us, we are not persuaded that the district court abused its discretion. However, it is evident that Jacobs' counsel has expended considerable professional time and effort on this appeal, so that the fee allowed below should be increased to reflect such services.

Those portions of the amended judgment pertaining to back wages and the class action issue are affirmed. That portion pertaining to attorney's fee is modified to the extent that the fee awarded below is increased by $1,000 for services rendered on this appeal.

Affirmed and modified.

Allen v. Lovejoy
[553 F.2d 522 (6th Cir. 1977)]

Name change upon marriage requirement as sex discrimination

Analysis of the issue

An employer that suspends a newly married female employee for refusing to comply with a rule requiring her to change her name on personnel forms to that of her husband violates Title VII, where no such rule applies to male employees. This ruling reverses an earlier U.S. District Court decision where it was concluded that although the rule did discriminate against women, it was not the type of sex discrimination Title VII was meant to proscribe. The plaintiff was unmarried when she was hired as a clerk for Shelby County, Tennessee. After her marriage, it was requested that she sign a form authorizing the personnel office to change her name on various forms from her maiden to her married name. The plaintiff's supervisor explained that compliance with the name change rule was mandatory. When verbal notice was ineffective in bringing about the authorization, the supervisor sent the plaintiff a written order requiring her to comply with the rule. The plaintiff's refusal to comply with the written order resulted in her suspension without pay. Several months later, when the county adopted a policy requiring employees' personnel forms to bear the same name that appeared on their social security cards, the plaintiff was reinstated to her former position. Although the policy change adopted by the county is in keeping with Title VII requirements, treatment afforded the plaintiff under the previous policy was considered discriminatory on the basis of sex. The amount of back pay to which the plaintiff is entitled has not been determined by the court.

Full text of opinion

LIVELY, Circuit Judge:—This is an appeal from summary judgment in favor of Shelby County, Tennessee and several county employees in an action charging that plaintiff was suspended from her employment in the county health department in violation of her constitutional right to be free of discrimination on account her sex. A declaratory judgment, preliminary and permanent injunctions and damages were sought pursuant to 42 U.S.C. §§ 1983, 1985 and 1988. Injunctive relief and back pay were also requested under Title VII of the Civil Rights Act of 1964, 42 U.S.C. § 2000e *et seq.* Interrogatories were filed and answered and depositions of the plaintiff and defendant Lovejoy were taken prior to a hearing on the motion of the defendants for summary judgment.

The plaintiff was unmarried when she was employed as a statistical clerk for family planning by the Health Department of Shelby County. Her employment records reflected her maiden name, Anna Marie Hill. After her marriage in December 1973 plaintiff was requested by a personnel clerk to sign prescribed forms authorizing the change of her name on personnel forms of her employer to Allen, the surname of her husband. Plaintiff refused this request and was then advised by two of her immediate supervisors that she was required to comply with the "name change policy" of the County. She then made an appointment with defendant Lovejoy, the director of the department, and was told that compliance was mandatory.

Plaintiff was suspended without pay on March 22, 1974 following her refusal to obey a written order from Dr. Lovejoy to effect the name change on the personnel records. She was reinstated to her previous position on August 16, 1974 following implementation by the Health Department of a new policy adopted by the Shelby County Board of Commissioners on June 20, 1974. Under the new policy the personnel records of county employees carry the name shown on each employee's social security card.

Though the court found that the name change policy of the defendants did discriminate against women, it concluded that "[c]ompelling a married woman to use her husband's last name on personnel forms does not constitute the type of sex discrimination Title VII was meant to proscribe." The court equated the name change policy with rules concerning hair length, separate restrooms and height and weight requirements, which have been upheld.

The plaintiff has appealed the dismissal of her claims under Title VII and § 1983. She has made no issue on appeal of the dismissal of her claims under §§ 1985 and 1988. In addition to the County itself and Lovejoy, the appellees are the three members of the Shelby County Board of Commissioners (the governing body of the County) and the director of personnel of the Health Department.

We conclude the district court erred in holding that the discrimination practiced by the defendants is not the kind which Title VII proscribes. 42 U.S.C. § 2000e–2(a)(1) provides—

§ 2000e–2. Unlawful employment practices—Employer practices
(a) It shall be an unlawful employment practice for an employer—

> (1) to fail or refuse to hire or to discharge any individual, or otherwise to discriminate against any individual with respect to his compensation, terms, conditions, or privileges of employment, because of such individual's race, color, religion, sex, or national origin[.]

Speaking of Title VII, the Supreme Court wrote in *Griggs v. Duke Power Co.*, 401 U.S. 424, 431, 91 S.Ct. 849, 853, 28 L.Ed.2d 158 (1971), "What is required by Congress is the removal of artificial, arbitrary, and unnecessary barriers to employment when the barriers operate invidiously to discriminate on the basis of racial or other impermissible classification." A rule which applies only to women, with no counterpart applicable to men, may not be the basis for depriving a female employee who is otherwise qualified of her right to continued employment.

Our cases dealing with grooming standards and height and weight requirements do not require a different result. In *Barker v. Taft Broadcasting Co.*, 549 F.2d 400 (6th Cir., 1977), we dealt with a grooming code for *both* men and women employees which prescribed different restrictions on the hair styles of each sex and found no discrimination on the basis of sex "within the traditional meaning of that term." *Id.* at 401. The *Barker* holding is in harmony with such decisions as that of the Fifth Circuit in *Causey v. Ford Motor Company*, 516 F.2d 416 (1975), which denied a claim of discrimination based on the maintenance of separate restrooms for men and women. As long as workers of each sex are provided adequate facilities there is no discrimination. The district court cited *Smith v. Troyan*, 520 F.2d 492 (6th Cir. 1975), *cert. denied*, 426 U.S. 934, 96 S.Ct. 2646, 49 L.Ed.2d 385 (1976), which was not a Title VII case. There the court applied a "rational relationship" test to find that minimum height requirements for police officers were constitutionally permissible while minimum weight requirements were not. These requirements had been attacked by the plaintiff on equal protection grounds.

This court's recent decision in *Whitlow v. Hodges*, 539 F.2d 582 (6th Cir.), *cert. denied*, 429 U.S. 1029, 97 S.Ct. 654, 50 L.Ed.2d 632 (1976), is inapposite. That case did not involve employment or the requirements of Title VII, but was concerned with a Kentucky regulation which requires a married woman to use her husband's surname in applying for a driver's license. The outcome of *Hodges* was determined by the Supreme Court's summary affirmance of a three-judge district court's holding that an identical Alabama regulation did not offend the equal protection clause of the Fourteenth Amendment. *See Forbush v. Wallace*, 341 F.Supp. 217 (M.D.Ala.1971), *aff'd*, 405 U.S. 970, 92 S.Ct. 1197, 31 L.Ed.2d 246 (1972). In the present case we are dealing with a specific congressional enactment designed to eliminate discrimination in employment. When such discrimination is found to exist, it is not necessary to prove a constitutional violation. Those discriminated against are entitled to relief unless it is precluded by some other provision of the Act.

We conclude that the district court erred in granting summary judgment to all of the defendants. Upon remand the district court will determine the amount of back pay to which the plaintiff is entitled, noting that she testified that she made no effort to find other employment during the period of her suspension. Entitlement to back pay is qualified by 42 U.S.C. § 2000e–5(g) which provides: "Interim earnings or amounts earnable with reasonable diligence by the person or persons discriminated against shall operate to reduce the back pay otherwise allowable."

Though the plaintiff named individual county officers and employees as well as Shelby County as defendants in this action, it is clear that Shelby County is the only proper defendant with respect to the Title VII claim. Shelby County was the plaintiff's employer and was the "respondent named in the charge" filed with the Equal Employment Opportunity Commission. *See* 42 U.S.C. § 2000e–5(f)(1). The "respondent" is defined as the employer charged with violation of the Act, § 2000e– 5(b), and is described as the one against whom affirmative relief, including back pay, may be adjudged. § 2000e–5(g). The County is not immune from a money judgment for back pay by reason of the Eleventh Amendment. The Supreme Court recently held that Congress authorized federal courts to award money judgments against states in the 1972 amendments to Title VII. *Fitzpatrick v. Bitzer*, 427 U.S. 445, 96 S.Ct. 2666, 49 L.Ed.2d 614 (1976). *A fortiori*, there is no immunity for political subdivisions of the states. *See Incarcerated Men of Allen County Jail v. Fair*, 507 F.2d 281 (6th Cir. 1974).

In view of our conclusions with respect to the Title VII claim, it is not necessary to consider the § 1983 claim. The demand for a declaratory judgment and injunctive relief was clearly rendered moot by the reinstatement of plaintiff pursuant to the new official policy of the County with respect to employees' names on personnel records. There is no reason to believe the County will return to its "old ways." *United States v. W. T. Grant Co.*, 345 U.S. 629, 632, 73 S.Ct. 894, 97 L.Ed. 1303 (1953). Thus the only relief possible under the § 1983 claim would be a money judgment for damages. There was no serious effort to establish bad faith or malice on the part of any of the defendants which would justify punitive damages; therefore any award under § 1983 would be limited to compensatory damages. Since the plaintiff will be "made whole" by the back pay award, any § 1983 damages would be cumulative.

The judgment of the district court is reversed insofar as it dismissed the complaint against Shelby County, Tennessee, and is affirmed in its dismissal of the complaint as to the remaining defendants. (The judgment omitted the name of the defendant Ramsay through oversight. An order should be entered dismissing as to this defendant). The case is remanded for further proceedings to determine the back pay award to which the plaintiff is entitled.

CELEBREZZE, Judge, dissenting.

I would affirm for the reasons set forth in Judge Bailey Brown's opinion, and this Court's decision in *Whitlow v. Hodges*, 539 F.2d 582 (6th Cir. 1976), *cert. denied*, 429 U.S. 1029, 97 S.Ct. 654, 50 L.Ed.2d 632 (1976).

Voyles v. Davies Medical Center
[403 F. Supp. 456 (N.D. Cal. 1975)]

Discharge due to employee's intent to undergo sex-conversion surgery is not unlawful discrimination

Analysis of the issue

The plaintiff, a former employee of the Davies Medical Center, claimed that her being discharged due to her expressed intentions to undergo sex-conversion surgery, was an act of sex discrimination within the meaning of Title VII. The defendant asserted that its decision to discharge the plaintiff was based on a supposition that having an employee on the staff prior to and after such surgery, would likely have an adverse effect on patients and co-workers. Furthermore, the defendant moved to have the action dismissed on the ground that Title VII does not extend protection from employment discrimination to transsexuals. The court understood Title VII's ban on sex discrimination to be one that prohibited conduct which, if the victim had been a member of the opposite sex, would not have occurred. The term "opposite sex" cannot embrace transsexuals, homosexuals or bisexuals. Seeing nothing in the legislative history of Title VII that would indicate a congressional intent to include transsexuals into the fold of protected classes, the court dismissed the action.

Full text of opinion

SPENCER WILLIAMS, District Judge:—Plaintiff brings this action seeking injunctive as well as monetary relief under 42 U.S.C. § 2000e *et seq.* for alleged violations of her civil rights caused by defendant terminating plaintiff from its employ.

Prior to January 1975 plaintiff was employed by defendant as a hemodialysis technician. During the last week in January plaintiff informed defendant's director of personnel that she, plaintiff, intended to undergo sex conversion surgery. Shortly thereafter plaintiff was discharged by defendant for the conceded reason that she intended to change sex and that such a change might have a potentially adverse effect on both the patients receiving treatment at the dialysis unit and on plaintiff's co-workers caring for those patients.

Defendant moves to dismiss the action upon the ground that the complaint fails to state a claim upon which relief can be granted. Title 42 U.S.C. § 2000e-2(a)(1) provides in relevant part:

It shall be an unlawful employment practice for an employer—

(1) to fail or refuse to hire or to discharge any individual, or otherwise to discriminate against any individual . . . because of such individual's . . . sex. . . .

Plaintiff contends that her claims of discrimination based on her transsexualism fall within the purview of this section. It is this Court's opinion, however, that employment discrimination based on one's transsexualism is not, nor was intended by the Congress to be, proscribed by Title VII of the Civil Rights Act of 1964, of which 42 U.S.C. § 2000e-2(a)(1) is part.

Section 2000e-2(a)(1) speaks of discrimination on the basis of one's "sex." No mention is made of change of sex or of sexual preference. The legislative history of as well as the case law interpreting Title VII nowhere indicate that "sex" discrimination was meant to embrace "transsexual" discrimination, or any permutation or combination thereof. Indeed, neither party has cited, nor does research disclose, a single case which holds squarely that Title VII provides redress for claims of the sort raised here.

Furthermore, even the most cursory examination of the legislative history surrounding passage of Title VII reveals that Congress' paramount, if not sole, purpose in banning employment practices predicated upon an individual's sex was to prohibit conduct which, had the victim been a member of the opposite sex, would not have otherwise occurred. Situations involving transsexuals, homosexuals or bisexuals were simply not considered, and from this void the Court is not permitted to fashion its own judicial interdictions.

Recognizing this apparent oversight, various members of the House of Representatives have, on three separate occasions during this year alone, introduced as of yet unenacted legislation which would amend § 2000e-2(a) to include "affectional or sexual preference" as additional basis upon which employers are precluded from discharging their employees. HR 166, 94th Cong., 1st Sess. (1975); HR 2667, 94th Cong., 1st Sess. (1975); HR 5452, 94th Cong., 1st Sess. (1975) (HR 5452 was referred to the House Committee on the Judiciary on March 25, 1975, and subsequently referred to the Subcommittee on Civil and Constitutional Rights on March 31, 1975, where its disposition is still pending). Thus, it becomes clear that in enacting Title VII, Congress had no intention of proscribing discrimination based on an individual's transsexualism, and only recently has it attempted to include conduct within the reach of Title VII which is even remotely applicable to the complained-of activity here.

Accordingly, IT IS HEREBY ORDERED, ADJUDGED AND DECREED that pursuant to the Court's Order Granting Defendant's Motion to Dismiss in the above-entitled action, judgment be entered in favor of defendant and against plaintiff.

Grossman v. Board of Education
[_____ F. Supp. _____ (D.N.J. 1975)]

Employee's discharge due to sex reassignment is not prohibited by Title VII

Analysis of the issue
The plaintiff was employed as an elementary schoolteacher for six years prior to being discharged for having undergone a sex reassignment operation. Paula, formerly Paul, M. Grossman claimed that the discharge constituted sex discrimination within the meaning of Title VII. The defendant, the Bernards Township Board of Education, asserted that the reason for the plaintiff's discharge was that her continued employment as a classroom teacher would likely inflict psychological harm upon the students of Bernards Township, not because of the plaintiff's status as a woman. The court could not find anything in the legislative history of Title VII that would substantiate the inclusion of transsexuals into the group of protected classes, and therefore, dismissed the case.

Full text of opinion
GEORGE H. BARLOW, District Judge:—This is an action instituted by the plaintiff, Paula Grossman, alleging that she has been wrongfully discharged from her position as a teacher by the defendant, Bernards Township Board of Education. Plaintiff's dismissal occurred following a sex reassignment operation performed on March 5th, 1971, by virtue of which plaintiff assumed certain sexual characteristics of the female gender. Such dismissal, it is asserted, constitutes unlawful discrimination on the basis of sex. Jurisdiction is alleged pursuant to the provisions of 29 U.S.C. § 151, et. seq., 28 U.S.C. § 1343, and 42 U.S.C. § 2000e, et seq. The matter is before the Court at this time on the motion of the defendant to dismiss the action pursuant to FED. R. CIV. P. 8(a), 12(b)(1); and 12(b)(6), or, in the alternative, for summary judgment. FED. R. CIV. P. 56(c). Plaintiff has responded by filing a motion for partial summary judgment on that portion of her complaint arising under Title VII of the Civil Rights Act of 1964, as amended by the Equal Employment Opportunity Act of 1972, 42 U.S.C. § 2000e, et seq.

Plaintiff was first employed, as Paul Grossman by the Bernards Township Board of Education in 1957. During the six-year period prior to her discharge, she worked as a music teacher with elementary school students, primarily in grades four, five and six. Plaintiff was suspended by the school board on August 19th, 1971, pursuant to the provisions of N.J.S.A. 18A:6–10.

N.J.S.A. 18A:6–10 provides:
"No person shall be dismissed or reduced in compensation,

(a) if he is or shall be under tenure of office, position or employment during good behavior and efficiency in the public school system of the state, or

(b) if he is or shall be under tenure of office, position or employment during good behavior and efficiency as a supervisor, teacher or in any other teaching capacity in the Marie H. Katzenbach school for the deaf, or in any other educational institution conducted under the supervision of the commissioner;

except for inefficiency, incapacity, unbecoming conduct, or other just cause, and then only after a hearing held pursuant to this subarticle, by the commissioner, or a person appointed by him to act in his behalf, after a written charge or charges, of the cause or causes of complaint, shall have been preferred against such person, signed by the person or persons making the same, who may or may not be a member of members of a board of education, and filed and proceeded upon as in this subarticle provided.

Nothing in this section shall prevent the reduction of the number of any such persons holding such offices, positions or employments under the condition and with the effect provided by law."

Certain charges against the plaintiff were thereafter certified to the Commissioner of Education, and hearings were held on December 8th, 9th, 10th, 17th, 27th and 28th, 1971. On April 10th, 1972, the Commissioner of Education sustained the plaintiff's suspension, and found that just cause was present to require her dismissal. Of the five separate charges presented to the Commissioner for his consideration, plaintiff's suspension was affirmed, and her dismissal grounded, only upon Charge Three, which, as amended by the Commissioner, provides:

"Paul Monroe Grossman knowingly and voluntarily underwent a sex-reassignment from male to female. By doing so, he underwent a fundamental and complete change in his role and identification to society, thereby rendering himself incapable to teach children in Bernards Township because of the potential her (Grossman's) presence in the classroom presents for psychological harm to the students of Bernards Township. Therefore, Paula a/k/a Paul Monroe Grossman should be dismissed from the system by reason of just cause due to incapacity."

The New Jersey State Board of Education unanimously affirmed the Commissioner's determination in favor of dismissal on February 7th, 1973. (See Exhibit C.) Thereafter, review of these administrative decisions was sought in the Appellate Division of the Superior Court of New Jersey, wherein plaintiff's dismissal was once again affirmed. In Re Tenure Hearing of Grossman, 127 N.J. Super. 13, 316 A.2d 39. (App. Div. 1974). Plaintiff's petition for certification was denied by the New Jersey Supreme Court on May 29th, 1974. In Re Tenure Hearing of Grossman, 65 N.J. 292, 321 A.2d 253 (1974). On September 24th, 1974, the Equal Employment Opportunity Commission (EEOC), responding to a charge of sex discrimination filed on August 11th, 1972, found no reasonable cause to believe that Bernards Township had discriminated against the plaintiff on the basis of sex. This action followed.

Plaintiff seeks to invoke the jurisdiction of this Court under the provisions of the Natonal Labor Relations Act, as amended by the Labor Management Relations Act of 1947, 29 U.S.C. § 151, et seq. The precise nature of plaintiff's labor claim, whether in the form of an unfair labor practice or otherwise, is not set forth in the pleadings. This is of no moment, however, as the Court is satisfied that the defendant is not an "employer" within the meaning of the Act, and is, accordingly, exempt from its coverage. In this regard, 29 U.S.C. § 152(2) provides, in pertinent part:

"The term 'employer' includes any person acting as an agent of an employer, directly or indirectly, but shall not include the United States or any wholly owned government corporation, or any Federal Reserve Bank, or any State or political subdivision thereof. . . . "

Public school boards, such as this defendant, fall within the scope of that exemption granted to states and their political subdivisions. Police Department of Chicago v. Mosley, 408 U.S. 92, 102 n. 9 (1972); Children's Village, Inc., 197 NLRB No. 135. As such, plaintiff's complaint could not properly state a cause of action under the National Labor Relations Act, and that part of the complaint which seeks relief hereunder must be dismissed. FED. R. CIV. P. 12(b)(6).

Alternatively, the plaintiff alleges a cause of action arising under various provisions of the civil rights statutes, with subject matter jurisdiction vested in the district court pursuant to 28 U.S.C. § 1343. In the first instance, plaintiff claims a deprivation of those rights guaranteed by 42 U.S.C. § 1981:

"All persons within the jurisdiction of the United States shall have the same right in every State and Territory to make and enforce contracts, to sue, be parties, give evidence, and to the full and equal benefit of all laws and proceedings for the security of persons and property *as is enjoyed by white citizens,* and shall be subject to like punishment, pains, penalties, taxes, licenses, and exactions of every kind, and to no other." (Emphasis added.)

Even a cursory examination of § 1981 and related cases indicates that its purpose was to afford protection from discrimination based on race, not sex. Rackin v. University of Pennsylvania, 386 F.Supp. 992. 1008–09 (E.D.Pa. 1974); League of Academic Women v. Regents of the University of California, 343 F.Supp. 636, 638–40 (N.D. Cal. 1972). No allegation of racial discrimination appears anywhere in the plaintiff's pleading, and, accordingly, the complaint fails to state any cause of action arising under 42 U.S.C. § 1981.

Nor does the complaint state a claim within the purview of 42 U.S.C. § 1983 or 42 U.S.C. § 1985. Each of these statutes establishes liability only on the part of "persons" who, acting individually or in concert, may have subjected the plaintiff to a deprivation of those rights, privileges or immunities guaranteed by the United States Constitution. Plaintiff, proceeding through counsel, has named the Bernards Township Board of Education as the sole party defendant. The school board is not, however, a "person" within the meaning of 42 U.S.C. § 1983 or 42 U.S.C. § 1985. Weathers v. West Yuma County School District R-J-1, 387 F.Supp. 552, 555-56 (D. Colo. 1974); King v. Caesar Rodney School District, 380 F.Supp. 1112, 1114 n. 1 (D. Del. 1974); Potts v. Wright, 357 F.Supp. 215 (E.D. Pa. 1973).

Plaintiff's assertion of a claim arising under 42 U.S.C. § 1988 is also without merit. This statute creates no independent substantive federal cause of action, but were merely "intended to complement the various acts which do create federal causes of action for the violation of federal civil rights". Moor v. County of Alameda, 411 U.S. 693, 702 (1973). As such, § 1988 does not enjoy the stature of an "Act of Congress providing for the protection of civil rights", and, therefore, cannot provide the district court with jurisdiction under 28 U.S.C. § 1343(4). The plaintiff also having failed to state a claim under §§ 1981, 1983, or 1985, federal jurisdiction is not available under any of the subsections of 28 U.S.C. § 1343.

As a final alternative, the plaintiff alleges that the defendant's conduct constituted an unlawful employment practice in violation of Title VII of the Civil Rights Act of 1964, as amended by the Equal Employment Opportunity Act of 1972, 42 U.S.C. § 2000e, et seq. In this regard, 42 U.S.C. § 2000e-2(a)(1) provides:

"(a) It shall be an unlawful employment practice for an employer—

(1) to fail or refuse to hire or to discharge any individual, or otherwise to discriminate against any individual with respect to his compensation, terms, conditions, or privileges of employment, because of such individual's race, color, religion, sex, or national origin."

The defendant vigorously denies the allegation of sex discrimination, arguing that such could not have occurred because the plaintiff, despite the medical and surgical procedures performed, remains a member of the male gender. The Court finds it unnecessary and, indeed, has no desire, to engage in the resolution of a dispute as to the plaintiff's present sex. Rather, we assume for the purpose of this action that the plaintiff is a member of the female gender. In such an instance, despite the plaintiff's conclusory allegations of sex discrimination, it is nevertheless apparent on the basis of the facts alleged by the plaintiff that she was discharged by the defendant school board *not* because of her status as a female, but rather because of her *change* in sex from the male to the female gender. No facts are alleged to indicate, for example, that plaintiff's employment was terminated because of any stereotypical concepts about the ability of females to perform certain tasks, Pond v. Braniff Airways, Inc., 500 F.2d 161, 166 (5th Cir. 1974), nor because of any condition common only to woman. Wetzel v. Liberty Mutual Ins. Co., 511 F.2d 199, (3rd Cir. 175) (pregnancy).

There is, unfortunately, a scarcity of legislative history relating to the inclusion of "sex" as a prohibited source of employment discrimination in Title VII of the Civil Rights Act of 1964. House Report No. 914, 88th Cong., 2d Sess. (1964), which accompanied the Act, makes no reference to the elimination of employment discrimination based on sex, limiting its language to matters of race, color, religion, and national origin. U.S. Code Cong. & Adm. News 1964, p. 2391, 2401. Indeed, it would appear that the Act was amended to include the category of "sex" in its final form without any prior legislative hearings or debate directed to that amendment. Wetzel v. Liberty Mutual Ins. Co., supra. 511 F.2d 199, 204 (3rd Cir. 1975); *Developments in the Law—Employment Discrimination and Title VII of the Civil Rights Act of 1964*, 84 Harv. L. Rev. 1109, 1167 (1971). In the absence of any legislative history indicating a congressional intent to include transsexuals within the language of Title VII, the Court is reluctant to ascribe any import to the term "sex" other than its plain meaning. Accordingly, the Court is satisfied that the facts as alleged fail to state a claim of unlawful job discrimination based on sex. While the final determination of the EEOC is in no manner binding on this Court, Tuma v. American Can Co., 373 F.Supp. 218, 229 n. 15 (D.N.J. 1974), we note that the Commission also concluded that the defendant's conduct did not constitute discrimination on the basis of sex.

No other jurisdictional basis has been asserted by counsel for the plaintiff, and any consideration of the defendant's alternative motions or the plaintiff's partial summary judgment motion is unnecessary in light of the above determinations. Accordingly, the motions of the defendant to dismiss the complaint because of its failure to state a claim upon which relief might be granted, FED. R. CIV. P. 12(b)(6), and due to the lack of subject matter jurisdiction, FED. R. CIV. P. 12(b)(1), are granted, without costs. An appropriate order will be submitted by counsel for the prevailing party.

Powell v. Read's, Inc.
[436 F. Supp. 369 (D. Md. 1977)]

Transsexuals are not protected against employment discrimination by Title VII

Analysis of the issue

The plaintiff alleged that her being fired after working for one day as a waitress constituted discrimination against transsexuals. She asserted that such discrimination was prohibited by Title VII. In attempting to establish grounds for her allegation, the plaintiff, Sharon M. Powell, told the court that a customer who knew her as Michael D. Powell, her male identity, informed the defendant that the plaintiff was engaged in a trial period of living as a woman. Such trial periods are prerequisite for individuals contemplating sex change operations. It was this knowledge, according to the plaintiff, that caused her employer to fire her. Denying the plaintiff's assertion, the defendant claimed that he fired the plaintiff only because the woman the plaintiff was hired to replace, returned to work. The defendant also claimed that even if the plaintiff could prove her allegations true, she would not be entitled to any sort of relief because Title VII protection was not extended to cover transsexuals. With the court in agreement, the case was dismissed.

Full text of opinion

JOSEPH H. YOUNG, District Judge:—Sharon M. Powell, a/k/a Michael D. Powell, born a male and still legally a male, a transsexual presently engaged in a trial venture of living as a woman as a prerequisite to having a sex change operation, claims unlawful sex-based discrimination in employment under Title VII of the Civil Rights Act of 1964, as amended, 42 U.S.C. § 2000e-2. Read's Inc., has moved to dismiss the complaint alleging that the acts alleged, even if proven, fall outside the prohibitions of Title VII.

As Sharon M. Powell, plaintiff applied for a job with defendant as a waitress at its store in Salisbury Mall, Salisbury, Maryland. On September 10, 1976, the first day of employment, plaintiff was fired. The alleged ground of dismissal was the return to employment of the woman plaintiff had been hired to replace. However, plaintiff suggests the real ground was the supervisor's discovery that plaintiff was a man, through the report of a customer who had known plaintiff as a man. Plaintiff asks the Court to declare that employment discrimination directed toward transsexuals violates rights under 42 U.S.C. § 2000e, *et seq.* Defendant argues that discrimination against transsexuals is not a violation of Title VII, and, therefore, that plaintiff has failed to state a claim upon which relief can be granted.

The few decisions in this area clearly support defendant's position. In *Voyles v. Ralph K. Davies Medical Center*, 403 F.Supp. 456 (N.D.Cal. 1975), the plaintiff was admittedly discharged from a job as a hemodialysis technician because she intended to undergo sex conversion surgery. In granting the defendant's motion for summary judgment, the Court held that Title VII does not reach situations involving transsexuals, homosexuals or bisexuals and noted the various Congressional efforts to introduce legislation reaching this area as an additional indicator that such individuals are not presently covered by law.

In *Grossman v. Bernards Township Board of Education*, 11 E.P.D. ¶ 686, CCH Employment Practices Decisions (D.N.J.1975) the plaintiff was discharged from his job as a teacher following a sex change operation. The court dismissed the complaint, finding that Title VII focuses on discrimination because of the *status* of sex or because of sexual stereotyping, rather than on discrimination due to a *change* in sex.

In *Smith v. Liberty Mutual Insurance Company*, 395 F.Supp. 1098 (N.D. Georgia 1975), a male was not hired for a job due to his effeminate behavior. Summary judgment was granted for the employer, with the court holding that discrimination for "affectional or sexual preference" is not discrimination within the meaning of Title VII.

As plaintiff indicates in ¶ 10 of the Complaint, the Equal Employment Opportunity Commission (hereinafter EEOC) also holds that discrimination against transsexuals is not protected by existing law. While the EEOC's conclusion is not binding on the Court, it is one more indication that those who have considered the matter do not find § 2000e *et seq.* susceptible to an interpretation which would embrace transsexuals.

A reading of the statute to cover plaintiff's grievance would be impermissibly contrived and inconsistent with the plain meaning of the words. The court in *Grossman, supra,* noted that the prohibitions against sex discrimination were added to the Civil Rights Act of 1964 at a late stage in the legislative process and lack a background of debate or legislative history, stating:

> In the absence of any legislative history indicating a congressional intent to include transsexuals within the language of Title VII the Court is reluctant to ascribe any import to the term 'sex' other than its plain meaning.

11 E.P.D. at 6884–85. Accordingly, it follows that the Complaint in the instant case does not state a cause of action under the Civil Rights Act of 1964, and this Court has no jurisdiction over the claim.

Plaintiff seeks to distinguish this case from those cited by pointing out various differences in the fact patterns, but the attempted distinctions are insignificant. The gravamen of the Complaint is discrimination against a transsexual and that is precisely what is not reached by Title VII.

The plaintiff's memorandum opposing dismissal appears to suggest a different basis of discrimination than that alleged in the Complaint. Whereas the Complaint seeks relief from discrimination against transsexuals, the memorandum suggests that Read's hires only women for food serving positions and that plaintiff was discharged for being a male, not for being a transsexual. But this is not the basis upon which plaintiff seeks relief.

Accordingly, it is this 30th day of August, 1977 by the United States District Court for the District of Maryland, ORDERED:

That defendant's motion to dismiss the Complaint, pursuant to Rule 12(b)(1) and 12(b)(6), Federal Rules of Civil Procedure be, and the same is, hereby GRANTED.

Smith v. Troyan
[520 F.2d 492 (6th Cir. 1975)]

Sex discrimination in height, weight and testing requirements

Analysis of the issue

The plaintiff in this case instituted a class action under 42 U.S.C. 1983 charging that the City of East Cleveland's use of minimum height and proportionate weight requirements in hiring its police officers discriminated against women and was therefore in violation of the Constitution. She further charged that the City's use of the Army General Classification Test (AGCT) discriminated against her on the basis of race and sex. The Court of Appeals believed that although height may be gender-related, a classification based on height need not be treated as an explicit gender classification, since it affects both men and women. Even if the classification were gender-related, it could be sustained under the Equal Protection clause if "it bears a rational relationship to a legitimate State objective." On this reasoning, the Appeals Court reversed a lower court ruling and sustained the defendant's height requirement, but could find no rational support for the weight requirement. The reason for this being the fact that neither physical strength nor psychological advantage are solely determined by weight. The court also reversed the District Court's findings of racial disparity in the general qualification test, since it was only part of an overall hiring process. Racial disparity in a subtest does not invalidate the entire test or hiring process.

Full text of opinion

JOHN W. PECK, Circuit Judge—Plaintiff-appellee, a five-foot, five-inch, 136-pound black woman, filed in district court a class action against certain "city defendants" and certain "federal defendants" charging that the city's use of minimum height and "proportionate" weight requirements in hiring its police officers unconstitutionally discriminated against her on the basis of sex and that the city's similar use of the Army General Classification Text (AGCT) unconstitutionally discriminated against her on the basis of race and sex.

The district court found that the height and weight requirements discriminated against women, that the AGCT discriminated against blacks, and that, as a matter of state law, a veteran's preference had been applied improperly. The court, however, found insufficient evidence that the AGCT discriminated against women. 363 F.Supp. 1131 (N.D. Ohio 1973).

Defendants have appealed from the district court's findings of unconstitutional discrimination as to the height and weight requirements and as to the AGCT. Plaintiff has cross-appealed from the district court's refusals to find that the AGCT unconstitutionally discriminates against women and to award attorney's fees.

East Cleveland Administrative Code § 123.07(d) requires police applicants to "be at least five feet, eight inches in height. . . . " The district court found no "rational support" for and invalidated the requirement. A detailed, in-depth discussion probing the height requirement's relationship, or lack therof, to physical strength, physical fitness, physical agility, ability to view crowds, ability to drive cars, arm reach, ability to absorb blows, and psychological advantage, however, preceded the court's finding.

On appeal, defendants claim that the height requirement, though disqualifying disproportionately more women than men, is a non-gender-based classification and, consequently, constitutionally permissible through the relaxed standard of equal protection review. Even if the height requirement were considered a gender classification, defendants claim it would be constitutionally permissible.

Few reported opinions have directly assessed the constitutionality of height requirements. See Callis, Minimum Height and Weight Requirements as a Form of Sex Discrimination, 25 Labor L.J. 736 (1974). *Hardy v. Stumpf,* 37 Cal.App.3rd 958, 112 Cal.Rptr. 739 (1st Dist. 1974), invalidating a five-foot, seven-inch requirement for Oakland police officers, relied heavily on the instant district court's reasoning and on the "suspect" character of the height classification. Other height requirements for various occupations have been invalidated on the basis of state statutes. See, e.g., *New York State Div. of Human Rights v. New York City Dep't of Parks & Recreation,* 38 A.D.2d 25, 326 N.Y.S.2d 640 (1971) (municipal lifeguard), *New York State Div. of Human Rights v. New York-Pennsylvania Professional Baseball League,* 36 A.D.2d 364, 320 N.Y.S.2d 788, aff'd, 29 N.Y.2d 921, 329 N.Y.S.2d 99, 279 N.E.2d 856 (1972) (baseball umpire), and *Moore v. City of Des Moines Police Dep't,* 2 CCH Empl.Prac.Guide ¶5181 (CP No. 881, Iowa Civil Rights Comm'n, filed July 11, 1973) (police). See also *In Re Shirley Long,* U.S. Civil Serv. Comm'n Bd. of Appeals & Review (Nov. 13, 1972). Of four courts which have refused to invalidate police height requirements, only one sustained the height requirement in light of evidence of the sexually disparate impact of the height requirement. Compare *Hail v. White,* 8 CCH Empl.Prac.Dec. ¶ 9637 (N.D.Cal.1973) (sustaining height requirement against Title VII claim), with *Castro v. Beecher,* 459 F.2d 725, 734 (1st Cir. 1972), *Arnold v. Ballard,* 390 F.Supp. 723, 738 (N.D.Ohio 1975), and *Mulligan v. Wilson,* 110 N.J.Super. 167, 264 A.2d 745 (1970). Still other courts have found it unnecessary to decide the legality of certain height requirements. See, e.g., *Pond v. Braniff Airlines, Inc.,* 500 F.2d 161, 162 (5th Cir. 1974); *Lum v. New York City Civil Serv. Comm'n,* 9 CCH Empl. Prac. Dec. ¶ 9947 (S.D.N.Y.1975).

The Supreme Court and this court, however, have recently dealt often with gender or gender-related classifications. *Geduldig v. Aiello,* 417 U.S. 484, 94 S.Ct. 2485, 41 L.Ed.2d 256 (1974), recognized that for constitutional purposes a classification even with an impact exclusively on one gender need not necessarily be treated as if an explicit gender classification.

"While it is true that only women can become pregnant, it does not follow that every legislative classification concerning pregnancy is a sex-based classification. . . . Absent a showing that distinctions involving pregnancy are mere pretexts designed to effect an invidious discrimination against the members of one sex or the other, lawmakers are constitutionally free to include or exclude pregnancy from the coverage of legislation such as this on any reasonable basis. . . .

"The lack of identity between the excluded disability and gender as such under this insurance program becomes clear upon the most cursory analysis. The program divides potential recipients into two groups—pregnant women and nonpregnant persons. While the first group is exclusively female, the second includes members of both sexes." 417 U.S. at 496–97 n. 20, 94 S.Ct. at 2492.

See Comment, *Geduldig v. Aiello*, Pregnancy Classifications and the Definition of Sex Discrimination, 75 Colum.L.Rev. 441, 443–48 (1975) [hereinafter Pregnancy Classifications]. Height requirements create even less exclusively gender-related classes. While one of the two *Geduldig* classes was exclusively of one gender, neither of the East Cleveland classes is exclusively of one gender. The class of persons too short to be eligible consists approximately of 95 per cent of the women and 45 per cent of the men between the eligible ages; the class of persons tall enough to be eligible consists approximately of five per cent of the women and 55 per cent of the men.

Like the Supreme Court in *Geduldig,* lower federal courts have sustained state action disproportionately, or exclusively, affecting one gender. See, e. g., *Reynolds v. McNichols*, 488 F.2d 1378, 1383 (10th Cir. 1973) (city "hold and treat" ordinance for prostitutes); *Bond v. Virginia Polytechnic Institute & State University*, 381 F.Supp. 1023 (W.D.Va.1974) (university student health plan's failure to provide for gynecological examinations and pap tests).

Even if the height requirement is viewed as gender discrimination, see *Satty v. Nashville Gas Co.*, 384 F.Supp. 765, 771 n. 1 (M.D. Tenn. 1973), aff'd 522 F.2d 850 (6th Cir. 1975), it must be sustained if it "bears a rational relationship to a [legitimate] state objective." *Reed v. Reed*, 404 U.S. 71, 76, 92 S.Ct. 251, 254, 30 L.Ed.2d 225 (1971). The Supreme Court, and this court, have recently upheld even explicit gender classifications. See, e. g., *Schlesinger v. Ballard*, 419 U.S. 498, 95 S.Ct. 572, 42 L.Ed.2d 610 (1975); *Kahn v. Shevin,* 416 U.S. 351, 94 S.Ct. 1734, 40 L.Ed.2d 189 (1974); *Robinson v. Board of Regents*, 475 F.2d 707 (6th Cir. 1973), *cert. denied,* 416 U.S. 982, 94 S.Ct. 2382, 40 L.Ed.2d 758 (1974). More importantly perhaps, the classifications the Supreme Court has found unconstitutional have been explicit gender classifications, where the members of the resulting classes have, by definition, only their gender in common. See, e. g., *Stanton v. Stanton*, 421 U.S. 7, 95 S.Ct. 1373, 43 L.Ed.2d 688 (1975); *Weinberger v. Wiesenfeld*, 420 U.S. 636, 95 S.Ct. 1225, 43 L.Ed.2d 514 (1975); *Taylor v. Louisiana*, 419 U.S. 522, 95 S.Ct. 692, 42 L.Ed.2d 690 (1975); *Frontiero v. Richardson*, 411 U.S. 677, 93 S.Ct. 1764, 36 L.Ed.2d 383 (1973); *Stanley v. Illinois*, 405 U.S. 645, 92 S.Ct. 1208, 31 L.Ed.2d 551 (1972); *Reed v. Reed*, 404 U.S. 71, 92 S.Ct. 251, 30 L.Ed.2d 225 (1971). Like *Geduldig,* however, the members of the classes in *Cleveland Bd. of Educ. v. LaFleur*, 414 U.S. 632, 94 S.Ct. 791, 39 L.Ed.2d 52 (1974), *aff'g* 465 F.2d 1184 (6th Cir. 1972), had more (their pregnancies or lack thereof) in common than their genders, but the Supreme Court, instead of equal protection analysis, relied upon the "fundamental" choice to have a child to invalidate mandatory pre- and post-partum leaves. See 94 S.Ct. at 802 (Powell, J., concurring in result); Pregnancy

Classifications, *supra*, at 454–55. The Court, however, found "no rational relationship" between the mandated leaves and "the valid state interest of preserving continuity of [educational] instruction." 94 S.Ct. at 798.

We think the district court erred in finding no "rational support" for the height requirement. If East Cleveland's height requirement lacks "rational support," so do height requirements elsewhere. Plaintiff's own exhibits demonstrate that forty-seven of forty-nine state highway patrols and police forces and twenty-nine of twenty-nine municipal police departments surveyed have, or at least then had, height requirements (ranging from five feet, six inches to six feet). See Note, Height Standards in Police Employment & the Question of Sex Discrimination: the Availability of Two Defenses for a Neutral Employment Policy Found Discriminatory Under Title VII, 47 So.Calif.L.Rev. 585, 586–9 (1974) [hereinafter Height Standards]. That certain government entities, including the Wisconsin highway patrol, the Pennsylvania state police (2 CCH Empl. Prac Guide ¶ 5177 [1973]) and the Law Enforcement Assistance Administration (33 Fed.Reg. 6415 [March 9, 1973]), no longer utilize or favor height requirements cannot rebut the nearly universal use of height requirements in hiring police. Such widespread use, of course, does not compel a finding of constitutionality, but "is plainly worth considering" in determining the "rationality" and constitutionality of height requirements. *Manning v. Rose,* 507 F.2d 889, 892 (6th Cir. 1974), quoting *Leland v. Oregon,* 343 U.S. 790, 798, 72 S.Ct. 1002, 96 L.Ed. 1302 (1952).

Moreover, at least three East Cleveland Police officials testified uncontradictedly and adamantly to the need for the height requirement. The chief of detectives, with twenty-six years' police experience, testified to the psychological advantage of a taller officer; a shift commander, with over seventeen years' experience, testified to the advantage of height in effecting arrests and emergency aid; and, the police chief testified similarly. Though plaintiff's expert witnesses discounted the importance of height and though the district court accepted that discounting, 363 F.Supp. at 1140–4, noteworthily, no expert had police experience.

The district court also discounted certain "functions claimed to be related to height and weight [because those functions] actually took only a small portion of the average patrolman's time and . . . [because] traffic-related matters accounted for more than three-quarters of the patrolman's working time." That an occupational function consumes a *de minimis* proportion of one's workday, however, does not necessarily diminish the need for selecting one who can best perform that function. A lifeguard may well spend all but fifteen minutes of an entire summer observing swimmers and keeping the beach free of litter, but in those fifteen minutes swimming ability to rescue a drowning swimmer becomes vitally crucial.

Even if plaintiff's experts were correct, and even if modern police practices discount the importance of height, there would still be "rational support" for the height requirement. The equal protection clause requires nothing greater than "rational support." As Mr. Justice Stewart has written,

"[The Fourteenth Amendment no longer gives courts] power to strike down state laws 'because they may be unwise, improvident, or out of harmony with a particular school of thought.' That era long ago passed into history." *Dandridge v. Williams*, 397 U.S. 471, 484–85, 90 S.Ct. 1153, 1161, 25 L.Ed.2d 491 (1970) (citations omitted).

East Cleveland Administrative Code § 123.07(c) authorizes the Director of Health to establish physical standards for police applicants. In their appellate brief, defendants admit that "[a]s a matter of custom, East Cleveland has followed certain weight 'guidelines' or 'ranges' to judge the fitness of an applicant." See 363 F.Supp. at 1136 n. 3. The 150-pound minimum weight requirement disqualifies approximately 80% of the women, but only 26% of the men, meeting the height requirement.

Despite a thorough review of the record, we can find no rational support for the weight requirement. Defendants' brief asserts that the weight requirement was designed "to judge the fitness of an applicant." But plaintiff's expert witness uncontradictedly testified that weight, in itself, is, at best, a poor predictor of fitness; he testified that body composition—the relationship between muscle and body fat—is much better, and that body composition can be determined quite simply. Moreover, the weight requirement is neither rationally related to physical strength nor to psychological advantage. East Cleveland utilizes other tests to determine strength, and plaintiff's expert denied a correlation between strength and weight. Most of the police officials' testimony concerning psychological advantage was confined to height, and in any event a police officer's clothing would make it difficult for the potential police assaulter to differentiate closely concerning a police officer's weight. The assaulter could hardly tell whether a full clothed police officer weighs 145, or 155, pounds, even assuming that if he could such knowledge would be relevant in his decision as to whether to assault an officer or not.

Defendants claim that the district court erred in invalidating the AGCT for its racially disparate impact because the "total examination process" has no such impact. Defendants claim that the difference between the 33% of black applicants and the 29% of black police hires (seven of twenty-four from 1969–73) is insufficient to require defendants to justify the AGCT as job-related. Even if defendants had the burden of justifying the AGCT, they argue that the use of the test would be permissible as being job-related.

Without reaching the question of the AGCT's job-relatedness, or lack thereof, we hold that plaintiff has failed to demonstrate prima facie that the test is unlawfully discriminatory. Though general ability, or intelligence, tests have often been invalidated for their racially disproportionate impacts, see, e. g., *Boston Chapter, NAACP, Inc. v. Beecher*, 504 F.2d 1017 (1st Cir. 1974), *Bridgeport Guardians, Inc. v. Bridgeport Civil Serv. Comm'n*, 482 F.2d 1333 (2d Cir. 1973), *Walston v. County School Bd.*, 492 F.2d 919 (4th Cir. 1974), *Baker v. Columbus Municipal Separate School Dist.*, 462 F.2d 1112 (5th Cir. 1972), *Carter v. Gallagher*, 452 F.2d 315 (8th Cir. 1971), *cert. denied*, 406 U.S. 950, 92 S.Ct. 2045, 32 L.Ed.2d 338 (1972), *Davis v. Washington*, 512 F.2d 956 (D.C.Cir.1975), the disproportionate impacts have been in the hiring, rather than in the test results in and of themselves. See, e. g., *Davis, supra*, at 961 n. 32 (blacks 72% of applicants taking test, but only 55% of new police officers); *Vulcan Society v. Civil Serv. Comm'n*, 490 F.2d 387, 392 (2d Cir. 1973) (blacks and Hispanics 11.5% of applicants, but less than 5% of those with more than "a marginal chance" of appointment); *Arnold v. Ballard*, 9 CCH Empl.Prac.Dec. ¶ 9921 (N.D.Ohio 1975) (blacks more than 13% of applicants, but less than 4% of appointed officers); *Kirkland v. New York State Dep't of Correctional Services*, 374 F.Supp. 1361 (S.D.N.Y.1974) (blacks and Hispanics 8.1% of those taking test, but only 1.3% of those "likely to be" promoted); *Commonwealth v. O'Neill*, 348 F.Supp. 1084, 1087–89 (E.D.Pa.1972), *modified*, 473 F.2d 1029 (3rd Cir. 1973) (blacks approximately 35% of applicants, but only 27.5%, 25.3%, 15.3%, 11.2% and 7.7% of new police hires from 1966–70).

The Second Circuit has observed that,

"[w]here the plaintiffs have established that the disparity between the *hiring* of Whites and minorities is of sufficient magnitude, then there is a heavy burden on the defendant to establish that the examination creating the discrimination bears a demonstrable relationship to successful performance of the jobs for which they were used. . . . " *Bridgeport Guardians, supra,* 482 F.2d at 1337.

Similarly, *Kirkland, supra,* rejected defendants' attempt to fragment the examination process to show no racially disparate impact.

"Any . . . approach [other than scrutinizing the overall examination procedure] conflicts with the dictates of common sense. Achieving at least a passing score on the examination in its entirety determines eligibility for appointment, regardless of performance on individual sub-tests. Accordingly, plaintiffs' case stands or falls on comparative pass rates alone." 374 F.Supp. at 1370.

That blacks fare less well than whites on the AGCT, a "subtest" in the process of hiring East Cleveland police officers, is insufficient in itself to require defendants to justify the AGCT as being job-related. Carried to its logical extreme, such a criterion would require the elimination of individual questions marked by poorer performance by a racial group, on the ground that such a question was a "subtest" of the "subtest."

Plaintiff cross-appeals that the district court erred in refusing to find that she had established prima facie that the AGCT unconstitutionally discriminates against women. We hold that the district court properly refused to find prima facie discrimination because of the only two women who have taken the AGCT in applying for the East Cleveland police one fared better than the national norm, one lower; and because testing and psychological data, though perhaps forecasting that women will fare less well on the AGCT than men, is far from being "uncontroverted testimony" that women will fare less well. *Boston Chapter, NAACP v. Beecher,* 504 F.2d 1017, 1021 (1st Cir.), *aff'g* 371 F.Supp. 507 (D.Mass.1974); *Bridgeport Guardians, Inc. v. Bridgeport Civil Serv. Comm'n,* 482 F.2d 1333, 1338–39 (2d Cir. 1973); *Castro v. Beecher,* 459 F.2d 725, 734 (1st Cir. 1972); *Officers for Justice v. Civil Serv. Comm'n,* 371 F.Supp. 1328 1333–34 (N.D.Cal.1973). Rather than being "uncontroverted" that women will fare less well, defendants' expert testified that black women will fare better than black men on "test[s] of aptitude, intellectual aptitude."

Especially considering our view of the merits, we find no abuse of discretion in the district court's denial of attorney's fees.

Reversed in part; affirmed in part.

Boyd v. Ozark Airlines

[419 F.Supp. 1061 (E.D.Mo. 1976)] *aff'd* _____ F.2d
_____ (8th Cir. 1977)

Minimum height requirements as sex discrimination

Analysis of the issue

The plaintiff, Rose Mary Boyd, alleged that Ozark Airline's minimum height requirement for pilots discriminated against women. The airline, which did not employ any women among its 380 pilots, required pilots to be a minimum of five feet-seven inches tall. The plaintiff, who otherwise was qualified as a commercial pilot applicant, was able to prove statistically that the five feet-seven inch requirement excluded approximately 25.8 percent of the males and 93 percent of the females in the 18–34 years of age group. When no consideration is given to age, the requirement would exclude 11.24 percent of the males and 74.19 percent of the females actively flying. It was clear to the court that the requirement did have a disparate effect on women; however, the defendant was able to prove through expert testimony, the fact that a minimum height requirement was necessary to ensure the safe operation of the aircraft. The defendant asserted the design of the cockpits for the two types of aircraft flown by Ozark required that in order for a pilot to have free and unfettered use of all instruments and still have the ability to meet the design eye reference point, (to be afforded an undistorted view) the pilot needed to be five feet-eight inches tall. After hearing other airlines testify to the propriety of their own height requirements and taking the military requirement of five feet-four inches into account, the defendant conceded that a person five feet-five inches tall could safely fly the aircraft. Because the court found merit in the imposition of a minimum height requirement as a bona fide occupational qualification, the court ordered the defendant to adopt the five feet-five inch minimum. The court also required the defendant to pay $2500 to the plaintiff for attorney's fees.

Full text of opinion

JOHN F. NANGLE, District Judge:—Plaintiff Rose Mary Boyd brought this action pursuant to Title VII of the Civil Rights Act of 1964, 42 U.S.C. § 2000e et seq., 28 U.S.C. §§ 2201 and 2202, claiming discrimination on the basis of sex.

The case was tried before the Court without a jury. The Court having considered the pleadings, the testimony of the witnesses, the documents in evidence, the stipulations of the parties, and being otherwise fully advised in the premises, hereby makes the following findings of fact and conclusions of law as required by Rule 52, Federal Rules of Civil Procedure:

Plaintiff Rose Mary Roth Boyd is a female resident of the state of Missouri and was during all times relevant herein a citizen of the United States. Plaintiff represents a class composed of all future female applicants who meet the reasonable qualifications of serving as an airline pilot with defendant airlines.

Defendant Ozark Air Lines, Inc. (hereinafter "Ozark") is a Delaware corporation doing business in the state of Missouri. Ozark is engaged in the intra- and inter-state transportation of passengers and cargo. Defendant is an employer within the meaning of 42 U.S.C. § 2000e(b).

Defendant presently employs approximately 380 pilots, all male. It has never employed a female pilot. Defendant has established certain minimum criteria which applicants must meet in order to be considered for employment. These criteria consist of

(a) Age: 20–30 years old;

(b) Minimum flight experience (correlated to age);

(c) Professional permits and certificates;

(d) Education: high school graduate with college preferred;

(e) Satisfactory completion of defendant's examination;

(f) Height: 5'7" to 6'2".

Plaintiff challenges herein only the requirement relating to height. This criterion has been in effect since at least May of 1960.

Plaintiff is presently employed as Chief Flight Instructor at St. Charles Flying Service. She has worked there approximately four years. Plaintiff met all of defendant's pre-employment criteria, with the exception of height. Plaintiff is slightly shorter than 5'2" tall. Plaintiff has never flown either the DC-9 nor the FH227, the two types of aircraft flown by defendant airlines.

Plaintiff first filed an application with defendant airlines in the early spring of 1973. At this time, plaintiff was married to an Ozark pilot and the evidence tended to show that her then-husband brought the application home to her, without bringing the list of pre-employment criteria along with it. This application was reviewed by Peter Scherwin, defendant's Director of Flight Operations, with plaintiff. Sherwin advised plaintiff to attain an additional rating and to increase flight time. The evidence established that Sherwin encouraged plaintiff to seek a position as a pilot. There is no evidence which indicates that Sherwin had looked at that part of the application which indicated plaintiff's height, nor that he realized that plaintiff was only 5'2" tall.

In August of 1973, plaintiff updated the information on her application to indicate that she had obtained an additional rating and had increased her flight time.

In the fall of 1973, Sherwin advised plaintiff that she did not meet defendant's minimum height requirement. At the same time, however, he indicated that it might be possible to waive this requirement and mentioned the names of those persons at defendant airlines who would have the authority to waive this requirement. The evidence clearly established that Sherwin did all he could to encourage plaintiff to seek the position as a pilot.

Plaintiff wrote a letter to Charles Mounts, Vice-President of Industrial Relations at defendant airlines, explaining why she, as a woman, wished to become an airline pilot.

Plaintiff was given an interview and tested, on March 26, 1974. The tests were written tests. On April 22, 1976, plaintiff was advised by a form letter that while she satisfied defendant's criteria, she had not been selected for inclusion in the next training group. No reasons were given although defendant has continually maintained that the reason for the rejection was plaintiff's height.

Defendant's decision to deny plaintiff a place in the training class was not, in whole or in part, based on plaintiff's sex. The sole reason that plaintiff was denied a position was because plaintiff failed to meet defendant's minimum height requirement.

Statistics presented by plaintiff establish that for the age group encompassing 18 to 34 years, a 5'7" height requirement excludes approximately 25.8% of the males and approximately 93% of the females. Among active fliers, without a distinction made for age, the height requirement eliminates 11.24% of the males and 74.19% of the females. Thus, the evidence established that defendant's height requirement had a disparate impact upon women.

It was conceded by virtually every witness herein that a pilot must have free and unfettered operation of the controls in the aircraft. The cockpits of the airplanes involved herein are designed around a design eye reference point. When a pilot is seated so that his eyes are in that reference point, he has the ability to see over the glare shield of the plane and still be able to view and reach all the instruments inside the cockpit. Should a pilot sit below the design eye reference point, the change in the angle of vision can cause a distorted view of the land below, thus causing landing difficulties.

When plaintiff was seated in the cockpit of the FH227, she was unable to fully rotate the wheel once she had located herself in the design eye reference point. The testimony of her own witness was that the wheel "bound with her thigh, making it inoperable". In the DC-9, when plaintiff was seated in the design eye reference point, the clearance between the wheel and her thigh was four centimeters, or approximately 1.57 inches. Credible evidence established that because of the vibrations of the airplane in flight, a clearance of 1.57 inches was insufficient to assure free and unfettered use of the controls of the plane. The evidence clearly established that plaintiff at a height of 5'2" would be unable to fly the DC-9 and FH227 used by Ozark.

Various other commercial airlines maintain minimum height requirements. Testimony indicated that Delta Airlines has a minimum of 5'8" and both American Airlines and Continental Airlines require their pilots to be 5'6" tall. The United States military presently maintains a minimum height requirement for pilots of 5'4". Defendant has conceded that it considers 5'5" to be the minimum required to safely fly an airplane.

Testimony presented established that a person's height does not necessarily determine the way that height is distributed. Certain people may have long bodies and short legs while others might have the reverse proportions. The only adequate method of determining whether an applicant is of the proper body proportions to be able to reach all the controls in the cockpit at the design eye reference point is to place the applicant in a simulated cockpit. The only available simulator, however, is in Pittsburgh and the costs of obtaining one here in St. Louis, or transporting applicants to Pittsburgh would be prohibitive.

This Court has jurisdiction over the subject matter and the parties in accordance with 42 U.S.C. § 2000e-5(f).

Plaintiff has asserted that she was denied a position as a pilot because of her sex. The Court has concluded that plaintiff's sex was not a factor in defendant's decision but instead, that the decision was based on the fact that plaintiff did not meet the minimum height requirements. The statistical evidence adduced, however, establishes that defendant's minimum height requirement has a disparate impact upon women among its 380 pilots, establishes a prima facie case of discrimination. Rogers v. International Paper Company, 510 F.2d 1340 (8th Cir. 1975), vacated on other grounds, 423 U.S. 809 (1975); Gilmore v. Kansas City Terminal Railway Company, 509 F.2d 48 (8th Cir. 1975). Accordingly, the burden shifts to defendant to establish that this height requirement is both job-related and a business necessity. See Albemarle Paper Company v. Moody, 422 U.S. 405 (1975); Holthaus v. Compton & Sons, Inc., 514 F.2d 651 (8th Cir. 1975).

To establish that a practice is a business necessity, which operates as a defense to a charge of sex discrimination, defendant must show that the requirement fosters safety and efficiency and is *"essential* to that goal". United States v. N.L. Industries, Inc., 479 F.2d 354 (8th Cir. 1973) (emphasis in original).

> [T]he business purpose must be sufficiently compelling to override any . . . [sexual] impact; the challenged practice must effectively carry out the business purpose it is alleged to serve; and there must be available no acceptable alternative policies or practices which would better accomplish the business purpose advanced or accomplish it equally well with a lesser differential . . . [sexual] impact. Robinson v. Lorillard Corporation, 444 F.2d 791, 798, (4th Cir. 1971), cert. dismissed, 404 U.S. 1006, 1007.

Defendant has amply met its burden of establishing that a height requirement is a business necessity. The evidence showed that pilots must have free and unfettered use of all instruments within the cockpit and still have the ability to meet the design eye reference point. In view of the cockpit design, over which defendant has little control, a height requirement must be established. The cockpit can only accommodate a range of heights. Defendant has chosen to draw the line at 5'7". The evidence established, however, that a requirement of 5'5" which would lessen the disparate impact upon women, would be sufficient to insure the requisite mobility and vision. Accordingly, the Court will order defendant to lower its height requirement to 5'5".

Plaintiff argues that the necessity of imposing a height requirement must be validated empirically. See C.F.R. § 1607.1 et seq. In Spurlock v. United Airlines, Inc., 475 F.2d 216, 219 (10th Cir. 1972), the court stated:

> When a job requires a small amount of skill and training and the consequences of hiring an unqualified applicant are insignificant, the courts should examine

closely any pre-employment standard or criteria which discriminate against minorities. In such a case, the employer should have a heavy burden to demonstrate to the court's satisfaction that his employment criteria are job-related. On the other hand, when the job clearly requires a high degree of skill and the economic and human risks involved in hiring an unqualified applicant are great, the employer bears a correspondingly lighter burden to show that his employment criteria are job-related. Cf. 29 C.F.R. § 1607.5(c)(2)(iii). The job of airline flight officer is clearly such a job. United's flight officers pilot aircraft worth as much as $20 million and transport as many as 300 passengers per flight. The risks involved in hiring an unqualified applicant are staggering. The public interest clearly lies in having the most highly qualified persons available to pilot airliners. The courts, therefore, should proceed with great caution before requiring an employer to lower his preemployment standards for such a job.

The Court agrees with this reasoning. A height requirement is unquestionably job-related. The evidence on this point, as recited above, is overwhelming. Empirical data is not required, Spurlock, supra, as there is adequate expert testimony on this point.

Plaintiff asks the Court to take judicial notice of Civil Air Regulation 4b.353(c), 19 Fed. Reg. 4464 (1954), now codified in 14 C.F.R. § 25.777(c) (1976), which provides:

The controls must be located and arranged, with respect to the pilots' seats, so that there is full and unrestricted movement of each control without interference from the cockpit structure or the clothing of the minimum flight crew . . . when any member of this flight crew, from 5'2" to 6'0" in height, is seated with the seat belt fastened.

This provision, however, is not correlated with the requirement that the pilots, when seated in the cockpit, have the requisite visibility. See 14 C.F.R. § 25.773 which does not impose a height range. While defendant's airplanes of necessity must meet the requirements of § 25.777, the airplanes must also be constructed so as to afford the maximum visibility required. Whether plaintiff was able to reach the controls while seated in the airplanes was not disputed herein; what was disputed was her ability to reach the controls upon attaining the proper visibility. The regulation is silent on this point.

Plaintiff, in her post-trial brief, has submitted a series of charts, derived from exhibits which were refused at trial. These charts supposedly list deficiencies in qualifications possessed by defendant's pilots, and a comparison of women's application with those of incumbent pilots hired thereafter. The Court must conclude that these charts are inadmissible herein. See Rule 1006, Federal Rules of Evidence.

The Court has concluded that the imposition of a height requirement is both job-related and a business necessity. The Court has further concluded, however, that defendant's height requirement is unnecessarily high and to that extent, is violative of Title VII, 42 U.S.C. § 2000e et seq. The Court will order that defendant lower its minimum height requirement to 5'5".

Plaintiff has asked for attorney's fees in the amount of $10,450.00 plus costs herein. As plaintiff has prevailed in part herein, the Court will award attorney's fees. After careful consideration of the record herein, the Court is of the opinion that attorney's fees in the amount of $2,500.00 are reasonable and will be awarded. It is the Court's further conclusion that each party shall bear its own costs.

Pursuant to the memorandum filed this date,

IT IS HEREBY ORDERED, ADJUDGED, and DECREED that defendant Ozark Air Lines, Inc. shall have judgment against plaintiff Rose Mary Boyd on her individual claim.

IT IS FURTHER ORDERED, ADJUDGED, and DECREED that defendant Ozark Air Lines, Inc. be and is enjoined from imposing a minimum height requirement in excess of 5'5" for the position of airline pilot.

IT IS FURTHER ORDERED, ADJUDGED, and DECREED that defendant Ozark Air Lines, Inc. shall pay attorney's fees to plaintiff in the amount of $2,500.00 and that each party shall bear its own costs herein.

Fountain v. Safeway Stores, Inc., et al.
[_____ F. Supp. _____ (N.D. Cal. 1975)]

Dress code standards not violative of Title VII

Analysis of the issue
The plaintiff, a former employee of Safeway Stores, Incorporated, claimed that his discharge which resulted from his refusal to wear a necktie on the job, constituted sex discrimination within the meaning of Title VII. The plaintiff further asserted that his union's refusal to process his grievance was a breach of its duty of fair representation. The court heard the plaintiff's argument that the employer's dress code's rule that male employees must wear neckties, requires male employees to comply with standards that differ from standards applicable to female employees. The court held that the employer's imposition of a dress code was justified, in light of its legitimate interest in the personal appearance of its employees. The issue therefore gravitated to whether the necktie requirement imposed unreasonable burden upon male employees. Because the plaintiff could not prove that the requirement placed any more of a burden on men than the standards that applied to female employees burdened them, the court held that the imposition of dress code standards did not discriminate on the basis of sex. On the issue of the union's alleged breach of fair representation, the plaintiff's suit could only proceed if he could prove that the union's refusal to process his grievance was arbitrary and unreasonable. The plaintiff alleged that when he relayed his complaint to the union, the union only told him that he had a "bad case." In view of the facts presented, the court ruled that the union's action was not motivated by hostility, was not arbitrary or unreasonable, and therefore found in favor of the defendant union.

Full text of opinion
STANLEY A. WEIGEL, District Judge:—Defendant Safeway Stores, Inc., fired plaintiff from his job as a grocery clerk in San Pablo, California, for refusing to wear a necktie as required by Safeway's dress code. Plaintiff contends the firing constituted discrimination on the basis of sex in violation of Title VII of the Civil Rights Act of 1964, 42 U.S.C. § 2000e et seq. Plaintiff also alleges that his discharge was in breach of a collective bargaining agreement which (1) prohibits discrimination on the basis of sex and (2) requires the employer to provide the employee with any necessary "special constume or unusual clothing not part of his existing wardrobe." Plaintiff also sues Retail Clerks Union Local 1179, alleging that the Union breached its duty of fair representation to plaintiff by refusing to process his grievance relating to his discharge. Plaintiff seeks reinstatement with back pay. The "uniform" claim is brought as a class action on behalf of all male clerks of Safeway. It seeks declaratory and injunctive relief as well as damages in the amount of the sum of the cost of two ties for each class member no longer working for Safeway.

Both Safeway and the Union move to dismiss for failure to state a claim or for summary judgment. The material facts are not in dispute.

The role of the Court is limited to interpreting section 703 of the Civil Rights Act of 1964, 42 U.S.C. § 2000e-2, which provides:

(a) It shall be an unlawful employment practice for an employer—

    (1) to fail or refuse to hire or to discharge any individual, or otherwise to discriminate against any individual with respect to his compensation, terms, conditions, or privileges of employment, because of such individual's . . . sex. . . .

Safeway requires its employees of both sexes to conform to regulations governing personal appearance. Plaintiff does not contend that the dress code sets standards for male employees which, when considered as a whole, in the light of contemporary styles of dress, are more stringent than the standards set for female employees. Cf. EEOC Dec. No. 70-920, June 22, 1970.

Requiring male employees to adhere to different standards of dress than female employees is not unlawful unless it is shown that the standards place an unreasonable burden on one sex as compared with the other. There has been no such showing in this case. Safeway has a legitimate interest in the appearance of its employees while they are at work and dealing with Safeway customers. Plaintiff's claim of sex discrimination must be rejected.

Suit against defendants based upon an alleged breach of the collective bargaining agreement cannot proceed unless there is an unresolved material issue of fact relating to the Union's breach of its duty of fair representation. Vaca v. Sipes, 386 U.S. 171 (1967). This duty is breached only if it is shown that the Union's refusal to process plaintiff's grievance was arbitrary, unreasonable, or in bad faith.

The affidavit submitted by the Retail Clerks Union in support of its motion for summary judgment is to the effect that plaintiff's grievance was without merit and that the Union refused to process it for that reason. On the facts in this case, the Union's action was neither arbitrary nor unreasonable.

As to any bad faith on the Union's part, it is unclear whether plaintiff has even placed the Union's motive in issue. His complaint seems to go only to the merits of the Union's interpretation of the collective bargaining agreement. In his opposition to the Union's motion, plaintiff does speak of the Union's motive as being a potential issue in this litigation. However, since plaintiff has not disclosed any reason to question the Union's motive, he is not entitled to have his pleadings construed liberally in his favor. International Longshoremen's Union v. Kuntz, 334 F.2d 165 (9th Cir. 1964).

Even construing the complaint as alleging bad faith on the Union's part, summary judgment is still appropriate because plaintiff has presented no specific facts in support of such a conclusory allegation. See Lusk v. Eastern Products Corp. 427 F.2d 705 (4th Cir. 1970). Plaintiff relies entirely on his complaint, which states only that the Union told him he had a "bad case". Plaintiff has offered no affidavits to indicate that the Union was motivated by hostility toward him or failed to consider his grievance. He has made no effort to inform this Court of any reasons, if they exist, why he might be presently unable to present by affidavit facts essential to justify his position. In these circumstances, summary judgment is appropriate.

Accordingly, IT IS HEREBY ORDERED that summary judgment be and hereby is entered in favor of the defendants, Safeway Stores, Inc., and Retail Clerks Union Local 1179, AFL-CIO, and against the plaintiff, Clifton Fountain, on all claims for relief.

This action came on for trial (hearing) before the Court, Honorable STANLEY A. WEIGEL, United States District Judge, presiding, and the issues having been duly tried (heard) and a decision having been duly rendered,

It is Ordered and Adjudged

That Summary Judgment is granted in favor of defendants Safeway Stores, Inc., and Retail Clerks Union Local 1179, AFL-CIO and against the plaintiff, Clifton Fountain, on all claims for relief.

Plaintiff's Motion to Alter and Vacate Judgment came on regularly for hearing before the undersigned on April 10, 1975 at 2:15 p.m. Plaintiff was represented by Kipperman, Shawn & Keker, and defendant Safeway Stores, Incorporated was represented by Littler, Mendelson & Fastiff and Retail Clerks Union Local 1179, AFL-CIO, was represented by Thorton C. Bunch, Jr. The Court having considered the Motion, the memoranda in support thereof and in opposition thereto, the record in the case, and being duly advised in the premises, hereby orders that said Motion to Alter and Vacate Judgment should be and is hereby DENIED.

Willingham v. Macon Telegraph Publishing Company
[507 F.2d 1084 (5th Cir. 1975)]

Sex discrimination not found in grooming requirements

Analysis of the issue

The Plaintiff brought this individual action under Title VII. The defendant, as a newspaper establishment in a community, felt it had a legitimate interest to maintain favorable relations with the residents of the community with whom it conducts business. In that interest, the defendant established a grooming code requiring male and female employees who came in contact with the public to be neatly dressed and groomed in accordance with standards generally accepted in the business community. The defendant interpreted its regulations to exclude employment of men with long hair. The plaintiff was denied employment for this reason and alleges that the grooming code, as interpreted, is sex discrimination in that if he were a female with the same length of hair, he would have been able to secure a job with the newspaper. The type of discrimination at issue in this case involves what the court terms "sex plus." The defendant is not refusing to hire males in general but only males with one seemingly neutral characteristic: long hair. The EEOC supported the plaintiff's position that grooming codes that distinguish between sexes are violations of section 703 of Title VII. This court, however, did not accept the EEOC's position, distinguishing between "sex plus" discrimination involving a fundamental characteristic of one sex and characteristics, as with long hair, that have an insignificant effect on job opportunities. Unlike the female's fundamental right to have children, the right to wear long hair does not involve any fundamental characteristic of males. Grooming regulations do not significantly bar employment opportunities; rather, they are more closely related to the efficient operation of a business. On those grounds, the court held that Title VII had not been violated.

Full text of opinion

SIMPSON, Circuit Judge:—Alan Willingham, plaintiff-appellant, applied for employment with defendant-appellee Macon Telegraph Publishing Co., Macon, Georgia (Macon Telegraph) as a display or copy layout artist on July 28, 1970. Macon Telegraph refused to hire Willingham. The suit below alleged that the sole basis for refusal to hire was objection to the length of his hair. On July 30, 1970, he filed a complaint with the Equal Employment Opportunity Commission (E.E.O.C.), asserting discrimination by Macon in its hiring policy based on sex, and therefore in violation of Sec. 703(a), Civil Rights Act of 1964, Title 42, U.S.C., § 2000e–2(a).

The E.E.O.C. investigated the alleged discrimination and eventually advised Willingham that there was reasonable cause to believe that Macon Telegraph had violated the cited portion of the Civil Rights Act of 1964, and that he was entitled to file suit. On December, 17, 1971, Willingham filed suit, alleging *inter alia* that Macon Telegraph's hiring policy unlawfully discriminated on the basis of sex. On April 17, 1972, the district court granted summary judgment in favor of defendant Macon Telegraph, finding no unlawful discrimination. Willingham v. Macon Telegraph Publishing Co., M.D.Ga.1972, 352 F.Supp. 1018. Upon Willingham's appeal from the district court decision a panel of this circuit reversed, finding the presence of a prima facie case of sexual discrimination and directing remand for an evidentiary hearing Willingham v. Macon Telegraph Publishing Co., 5 Cir. 1973, 482 F.2d 535 (Simpson, Circuit Judge, dissenting). Upon en banc consideration we vacate the remand order of the original panel and affirm the district court.

The factual background of this case is set forth in the district court opinion and in the majority and dissenting opinion of the original panel. There is no substantial dispute between the parties as to the facts the more important of which we repeat here for convenience. Willingham was 22 years of age when he applied for work with Macon Telegraph in late July, 1970. Shortly before, during the Fourth of July holidays, an "International Pop Festival" was held at Byron, Georgia, a village about 15 miles from Macon. This event, attended by hundreds of thousands of young people, is described in footnote 3 to the dissenting opinion, 482 F.2d at 539:

The record shows that Macon community disapproval of long-haired males had been recently exacerbated by an "International Pop Festival" on July 3, 4, 5, 1970, at Byron, Georgia, a small community 15 miles from Macon. The crowds attracted to Byron were variously estimated at between 400,000 and 500,000 people. Bearded and long-haired youths and scantily dressed young women flooded the countryside. Use of drugs and marijuana was open. Complete nudity by both sexes, although not common was frequently observed. Of course the managing officials of the Macon Telegraph Publishing Company were peculiarly aware of community indignation over excesses during the Byron Pop Festival because of the wide publicity in its own daily newspaper. The appellee was entitled to consider that the business community of Macon, including its own advertisers, was particularly sour on youthful long-haired males at the time of Willingham's application of July 28, 1970. It was a fair inference on the part of company officials that advertisers would share an attitude not significantly different from that of the community in general.

In short, Macon Telegraph's management believed that the entire business community it served—and depended upon for business success—associated long hair on men with the counter-culture types who gained extensive unfavorable national and local exposure at the time of the festival. Therefore the newpaper's employee grooming code, which required employees (male and female) who came into contact with the public to be neatly dressed and groomed in accordance with the standards customarily accepted in the business community, was interpreted to exclude the employing of men (but not women) with long hair. Willingham's longer than acceptable shoulder length hair was thus the grooming code violation upon which Macon Telegraph based its denial of employment.

Willingham's complaint to the E.E.O.C. and his federal suit were both grounded upon Sec. 703 of the Civil Rights Act of 1964, Title 42, U.S.C. § 2000e–2, which provides, in pertinent part, that:

(a) It shall be an unlawful employment practice for an employer—(1) to fail or refuse to hire or to discharge any individual, or otherwise to discriminate against any individual with respect to his compensation, terms, conditions, or privileges of employment, because of such individual's . . . sex . . . ; or (2) to limit, segregate, or classify his employees in any way which would deprive or tend to deprive any individual of employment opportunities or otherwise adversely affect his status as an employee, because of such individual's . . . sex. . . .

Willingham's argument is that Macon Telegraph discriminates amongst employees based upon their sex, in that female employees can wear their hair any length they choose, while males must limit theirs to the length deemed acceptable by Macon Telegraph. He asserts therefore that he was denied employment because of his sex: were he a girl with identical length hair and comparable job qualifications, he (she) would have been employed. A majority of the original panel which heard the case agreed, and remanded the case to the district court for a finding of whether or not the discrimination might not be lawful under the "bona fide occupational qualification" (B.F.O.Q.) statutory exception to Sec. 703. Since we agree with the district court that Macon Telegraph's dress and grooming policy does not unlawfully discriminate on the basis of sex, the applicability of the B.F.O.Q. exception will not be considered in this opinion.

The unlawfulness vel non of employer practices with respect to the hiring and treatment of employees in the private sector, as contemplated by Sec. 703 and applied to the facts of this case, can be determined by way of a three step analysis: (1) has there been some form of discrimination, i. e., different treatment of similarly situated individuals; (2) was the discrimination based on sex; and (3) if there has been sexual discrimination, is it within the purview of the bona fide occupational qualification (BFOQ) exception and thus lawful? We conclude that the undisputed discrimination practiced by Macon Telegraph is based not upon sex, but rather upon grooming standards, and thus outside the proscription of Sec. 703. This determination pretermits any discussion of whether, if sexual discrimination were involved, it would be within the BFOQ exception.

Although our judicial inquiry necessarily focuses upon the proper statutory construction to be accorded Sec. 703, it is helpful first to define narrowly the precise issue to be considered. For two reasons, we have no question here of whether or not due process or equal protection standards need be applied. Firstly, there is no state action present giving rise to a constitutional question, and secondly, no claim of deprivation of a constitutional right is advanced. Cf. Karr v. Schmidt, 5 Cir. 1972, 460 F.2d 609 (en banc) with Lansdale v. Tyler Junior College, 5 Cir. 1972, 470 F.2d 659 (en banc) (grooming regulations within the public school systems and institutions of higher learning). Similarly, we are not concerned with discrimination based upon sex alone. That situation obtains when an employer refuses to hire, promote, or raise the wages of an individual solely because of sex, as, for instance, if Macon Telegraph had refused to hire any women for the job of copy layout artist because of their sex.

Willingham relies on a more subtle form of discrimination, one which courts and commentators have often characterized as "sex plus". In general, this involves the classification of employees on the basis of sex *plus* one other ostensibly neutral characteristic. The practical effect of interpreting Sec. 703 to include this type of discrimination is to impose an equal protection gloss upon the statute, i. e. similarly situated individuals of either sex cannot be discriminated against vis à vis members of their own sex unless the same distinction is made with respect to those of the opposite sex. Such an interpretation may be necessary in order to counter some rather imaginative efforts by employers to circumvent Sec. 703.

Inclusion of "sex plus" discrimination within the proscription of Sec. 703 has legitimate legislative and judicial underpinning. An amendment which would have added the word "solely" to the bill, modifying "sex", was defeated on the floor in the House of Representatives. 110 Cong.Rec. 2728 (1964). Presumably, Congress foresaw the debilitating effect such a limitation might have upon the sex discrimination amendment. Further, the Supreme Court, in Phillips v. Martin Marietta Corp., 1971, 400 U.S. 542, 91 S.Ct. 496, 27 L.Ed.2d 613, found expressly that "sex plus" discrimination violates the Civil Rights Act. The employer in *Phillips* refused to accept job applications from women with pre-school age children, but had no such policy with respect to male applicants. The defendant argued that it was not discriminating between men and women, but only amongst women, and then only with respect to a neutral fact—pre-school age children. In a short per curiam decision, the Supreme Court held that if the legislative purpose of giving persons of like qualifications equal employment opportunity irrespective of sex were to be effected, employers could not have one hiring policy for men and another for women. Thus "sex plus" discrimination against being a woman *plus* having pre-school age children, was under the facts of that case just as unlawful as would have been discrimination based solely upon sex.

In this analytical context, then, the single issue in this case is precisely drawn: Does a particular grooming regulation applicable to men only constitute "sex plus" discrimination within the meaning of Sec. 703, as construed by the Supreme Court? Willingham and numerous amici curiae have advanced several arguments supporting an affirmative answer to the question. We proceed to consider these arguments.

The primary premise of Willingham's position is that "sex plus" must be read to intend to include "sex plus any sexual stereotype" and thus, since short hair is stereotypically male, requiring it of all male applicants violates Sec. 703. While the Supreme Court did not explicate the breadth of its rationale in *Phillips*, it seems likely that Mr. Justice Marshall at least might agree with Willingham. In his special concurrence he noted that any hiring distinction based upon stereotyped characterizations of the sexes violates the Act, and went on to say that such discrimination could never be a BFOQ exception, an issue expressly left open in the majority's per curiam opinion. Phillips v. Martin Marietta Corp., supra, 400 U.S. at 545, 91 S.Ct. at 498, 27 L.Ed.2d at 616.

Willingham finds further comfort in Sprogis v. United Air Lines, Inc., 7 Cir. 1971, 444 F.2d 1194. Plaintiff there was a female stewardess who challenged an airline rule that stewardesses were not allowed to marry, but with no such provision for male stewards or other employees. The *Sprogis* court found the rule to be an unlawful form of "sex plus" discrimination, relying in part on *Phillips*. In reference to "sex plus" the court noted that "[i]n forbidding employers to discriminate against individuals because of their sex, Congress intended to strike at the entire spectrum of disparate treatment of men and women *resulting from sex stereotypes.*" Sprogis v. United Air Lines, Inc., supra, 444 F.2d at 1198 (emphasis supplied). Treating the emphasized language in its broadest sense, it is possible that the court felt that all sexual stereotypes violate Sec. 703. Several district courts apparently agree with this construction, at least insofar as personal dress and appearance codes are concerned. See Aros v. McDonnell Douglas Corp., C.D.Cal.1972, 348 F.Supp. 661 (dress and grooming code constitutes sexual discrimination when applied differently to males and females); Donohue v. Shoe Corp. of America, C.D.Cal.1972, 337 F.Supp. 1357 (rule requiring short hair on men, but not on women, is prima facie violation of Sec. 703); Roberts v. General Mills, Inc., N.D.Ohio 1971, 337 F.Supp. 1055 (rule allowing female employees to wear hairnets, but requiring men to wear hats—and therefore keep their hair short—violates Sec. 703).

Finally, the E.E.O.C. by administrative decision, regulation, and on amicus brief here, fully supports Willingham's position. In its administrative decisions, the Commission has uniformly held that dress and grooming codes that distinguish between sexes are within Sec. 703, and can only be justified if proven to be a BFOQ. The Commission's regulations go a step further, assuming (we infer) that such codes are sexually discriminatory and asserting that "[t]he refusal to hire an individual based on stereotyped (sic) characterizations of the sexes" does not warrant the application of the BFOQ exception. Title 29 C.F.R. § 1604.2(a)(1)(ii) (1973). We are mindful also that "[t]he administrative interpretation of the Act by the enforcing agency is entitled to great deference," Griggs v. Duke Power Co., 1971, 401 U.S. 424, 434–435, 91 S.Ct. 849, 854–855, 28 L.Ed.2d 158, 165.

The beginning (and often the ending) point of statutory interpretation is an exploration of the legislative history of the Act in question. We must decide, if we can there find any basis for decision, whether Congress intended to include *all* sexual distinctions in its prohibition of discrimination (based solely on sex or on "sex plus"), or whether a line can legitimately be drawn beyond which employer conduct is no longer within reach of the statute.

We discover, as have other courts earlier considering the problem before us, that the meager legislative history regarding the addition of "sex" in Sec. 703(a) provides slim guidance for divining Congressional intent. The amendment adding "sex" was passed one day before the House of Representatives approved Title VII of the Civil Rights Act and nothing of import emerged from the limited floor discussion. Diaz v. Pan American World Airways, 5 Cir. 1971, 442 F.2d 385, 386. Ironically, the amendment was introduced by Representative Howard Smith of Virginia, who had opposed the Civil Rights Act, and was accused by some of wishing to sabotage its passage by his proposal of the "sex" amendment. Note, Employer Dress and Appearance Codes and Title VII of the Civil Rights Act of 1964, 46 So.Cal.L. Rev. 965, 968; Note, Developments in the Law-Employment Discrimination and Title VII of the Civil Rights Act of 1964, 84 Harv.L.Rev. 1109, 1167 (1971). And while it is argued that a lack of change in this section in the 1972 amendments to the Act evidences Congressional agreement with the position of the E.E.O.C., it may be argued with equal force that the law was insufficiently developed at the time the amendments were considered to support any change. We find the legislative history inconclusive at best and draw but one conclusion, and that by way of negative inference. Without more extensive consideration, Congress in all probability did not intend for its proscription of sexual discrimination to have significant and sweeping implications. We should not therefore extend the coverage of the Act to situations of questionable application without some stronger Congressional mandate.

We perceive the intent of Congress to have been the guarantee of equal job opportunity for males and females. Providing such opportunity is where the emphasis rightly lies. This is to say that the Act should reach any device or policy of an employer which serves to deny acquisition and retention of a job or promotion in a job to an individual *because* the individual is either male or female. The language of the Supreme Court in *Griggs* regarding racial discrimination applies with equal (but not greater) force to sexual discrimination: "The objective of Congress in the enactment of Title VII is plain from the language of the statute. It was to achieve equality of employment opportunities and remove barriers that have operated in the past to favor an identifiable group of white employees over other employees." Griggs v. Duke Power Co., supra, 401 U.S. at 429–430, 91 S.Ct. at 853, 28 L.Ed.2d at 163. We expressed this thought in *Diaz:* "[I]t is reasonable to assume, from a reading of the statute itself, that one of Congress' main goals was to provide equal access to the job market for both men and women." Diaz v. Pan American World Airways, supra, 442 F.2d at 386. Indeed, the Supreme Court made the same point in *Phillips* by saying that "Section 703(a) of the Civil Rights Act of 1964 requires that persons of like qualifications be given employment opportunities irrespective of their sex." Phillips v. Martin Marietta Corp. supra, 400 U.S. at 544, 91 S.Ct. at 497–498, 27 L.Ed.2d at 615.

Juxtaposing our view of the Congressional purpose with the statutory interpretations advanced by the parties to this action elucidates our reasons for adopting the more narrow construction. Equal employment *opportunity* may be secured only when employers are barred from discriminating against employees on the basis of immutable characteristics, such as race and national origin. Similarly, an employer cannot have one hiring policy for men and another for women *if* the distinction is based on some fundamental right. But a hiring policy that distinguishes on some other ground, such as grooming codes or length of hair, is related more closely to the employer's choice of how to run his business than to equality of employment opportunity. In *Phillips,* supra, the Supreme Court condemned a hiring distinction based on having pre-school age children, an existing condition not subject to change. In Sprogis v. United Air Lines, supra, the Seventh Circuit reached a similar result with respect to marital status. We have no difficulty with the result reached in those cases; but nevertheless perceive that a line must be drawn between distinctions grounded on such fundamental rights as the right to have children or to marry and those interfering with the manner in which an employer exercises his judgment as to the way to operate a business. Hair length is not immutable and in the situation of employer vis à vis employee enjoys no constitutional protection. If the employee objects to the grooming code he has the right to reject it by looking elsewhere for employment, or alternatively he may choose to subordinate his preference by accepting the code along with the job.

We agree with the District of Columbia Circuit's treatment of the problem. Dodge v. Giant Food, Inc., D.C.Cir. 1973, 488 F.2d 1333, following that court's earlier decision in Fagan v. National Cash Register Co., 1973, 157 U.S.App.D.C. 15, 481 F.2d 1115. In *Fagan,* the plaintiff employee was discharged for refusal to comply with a company grooming rule because of his long hair, and sued under Sec. 703(a). Dismissal of his suit was affirmed, on the ground that hair length is not constitutionally or statutorily protected, and hence its regulation as to men but not women designed to further the employer's legitimate business interest, is not sexual discrimination. Fagan v. National Cash Register Co., supra, 481 F.2d at 1125. Enlarging upon this principle, the court held in *Dodge* that hair length regulations "are classifications by sex . . . which do not represent any attempt by the employer to prevent the employment of a particular sex, and which do not pose distinct employment disadvantages for one sex. Neither sex is elevated by these regulations to an appreciably higher occupational level than the other. We conclude that Title VII never was intended to encompass sexual classifications having only an insignificant effect on employment opportunities." Dodge v. Giant Food, Inc., supra, 488 F.2d at 1337.

We adopt the view, therefore, that distinctions in employment practices between men and women on the basis of something other than immutable or protected characteristics do not inhibit employment *opportunity* in violation of Sec. 703(a). Congress sought only to give all persons equal access to the job market, not to limit an employer's right to exercise his informed judgment as to how best to run his shop.

We are in accord also with the alternative ground mentioned in both the District of Columbia Circuit cases and relied upon by Judge Bootle in his memorandum decision in *Willingham:* "From all that appears, equal job opportunities are available to both sexes. It does not appear that defendant fails to impose grooming standards for female employees; thus in this respect each sex is treated equally." Willingham v. Macon Telegraph Publishing Co., supra, 352 F.Supp. at 1020. See also Dodge v. Giant Food Co., supra, 488 F.2d at 1336, Fagan v. National Cash Register Co., supra, 481 F.2d at 1124 n. 20; Boyce v. Safeway Stores, D.D.C.1972, 351 F.Supp. 402, 404. This frame of analysis removes Willingham's complaint completely from the Sec. 703(a) "sex plus" category, because both sexes are being screened with respect to a neutral fact, i.e., grooming in accordance with generally accepted community standards of dress and appearance. Since Macon Telegraph applies this criterion to male and female applicants, the equal protection gloss has no applicability.

We are as persuaded by the arguments of Macon Telegraph and its *amici* supporters as we are unpersuaded by those of Willingham. Support for the latter lies in the concurring opinion of Mr. Justice Marshall in *Phillips,* supra. With deference, his views appear to be his alone. The fact that he separately concurred without being joined by any other justice is a fair indication that he speaks there only for himself. And while *Griggs* teaches that agency interpretation is due "great deference", we, as did the District of Columbia Circuit in *Fagan,* note the equally significant qualifying explanatory statement: "Since the Act and its legislative history support the Commission's construction, *this affords good reason* to treat the guidelines as expressing the will of Congress." (Emphasis added). Fagan v. National Cash Register Co., supra, 481 F.2d at 1125, quoting Griggs v. Duke Power Co., supra, 401 U.S. at 434, 91 S.Ct. at 855, 28 L.Ed.2d at 165–166. The language of the statute as to the issue before us is anything but clear. Indeed, judicial construction was required simply to reach the abstract principle of "sex plus"; and the legislative history supports, if anything, the wisdom of narrow construction. Finally, we are in accord with the result reached in Sprogis v. United Air Lines, supra, and with much of its dicta, particularly that regarding stereotypes, but only insofar as it is intended to embrace distinctions touching immutable characteristics or protected rights.

Nothing that we say should be construed as disparagement of what many feel to be a highly laudable goal—maximizing individual freedom by eliminating sexual stereotypes. We hold simply that such an objective may not be read into the Civil Rights Act of 1964 without further Congressional action. Private employers are prohibited from using different hiring policies for men and women only when the distinctions used relate to immutable characteristics or legally protected rights. While of course not impervious to judical scrutiny, even those distinctions do not violate Sec. 703(a) if they are applied to both sexes.

Affirmed.

WISDOM, Circuit Judge, joined by TUTTLE, GOLDBERG and GODBOLD, Circuit Judges, dissenting.

I dissent for the reasons stated in the original opinion of the panel. Willingham v. Macon Telegraph Publishing Co., 5 Cir. 1973, 482 F.2d 535.

King v. New Hampshire Department of Resources and Economics Development

[420 F.Supp. 1317 (D.N.H. 1976), *aff'd* _____ F.2d _____ (1st Cir. 1977)]

Sex discrimination—failure to hire

Analysis of the issue

This sex discrimination claim filed under Title VII involved a young woman who applied unsuccessfully for two consecutive years for summer employment as an officer with the Hampton Beach, New Hampshire Meter Patrol. She argued that the all-male nature of the meter patrol's officers roster was kept intact by virtue of the patrol chief's policy and practice of rehiring all returning summer employees and filling vacancies with male applicants, generally those employed at the same school where the chief taught. The defendant was able to provide evidence to support the non-discriminatory nature of his decision to hire a more qualified male applicant for the second summer in question. However, the court concluded that questions asked in the plaintiff's initial interview with the chief were asked for the purpose of disqualifying her because of her sex. Specifically, the plaintiff was asked whether she had any experience using a sledge hammer, and whether she thought she was capable of participating in stakeouts or making unassisted arrests. The court could see no connection between such abilities and the ability to perform the duties entailed in issuing parking citations and collecting money from state-owned parking meters. It was decided that the chief displayed a discriminatory attitude and failed to give the applicant fair consideration. The unlawful rejection occurred in the summer of 1975. Even though the plaintiff was lawfully rejected in 1976, the court awarded her with back pay damages covering both years, on the grounds that if she were hired in 1975, she would have been rehired for 1976, given the chief's policy of automatic rehire.

Full text of opinion

BOWNES, District Judge:—The plaintiff, Mary Pat King, is a twenty-four year old woman who is a permanent resident of Hampton, New Hampshire, residing at Acorn Street.

The defendant Hampton Beach Meter Patrol is a subsidiary agency of the Division of Parks of the Department of Resources and Economic Development of the State of New Hampshire.

Plaintiff alleges that defendant's refusal to employ her as an officer of the Hampton Beach Meter Patrol (Meter Patrol) was a result of discrimination based on her sex in violation of 42 U.S.C. § 2000e *et seq.*

Defendant denies that it discriminated against plaintiff and contends that "[d]efendant's refusal to hire plaintiff was solely on account of her lack of fitness for the position, as evidenced by an unfavorable and unreliable work record elsewhere." It also states that "[c]ompeting applicants possessed superior references and work experience."

Jurisdiction is pursuant to 28 U.S.C. § 1343(4), 28 U.S.C. § 2201, and 42 U.S.C. § 2000e–5(f)(1)(A).

There are five steps which must be accomplished before a plaintiff may bring a civil action pursuant to 42 U.S.C. § 2000e. They have been set forth succinctly in *Kaplowitz v. University of Chicago*, 387 F.Supp. 42, 48 (N.D.Ill.1974):

In order to better understand defendant's arguments it is useful to set forth briefly the statutory scheme encompassed by 42 U.S.C. § 2000e *et seq.* Any individual claiming to have been the victim of an unlawful employment practice may file a charge with the Equal Employment Opportunity Commission, which commission was created under the statute to handle these charges. 42 U.S.C. §§ 2000e–4 and 2000e–5(a). The EEOC investigates the charge and makes a determination as to whether there is probable cause to believe the charge is true. If there is not, the charge is dismissed; if there is, the Commission attempts to resolve the problem through informal methods of conference, conciliation, and persuasion. 42 U.S.C. § 2000e–5(b). If conciliation efforts fail the EEOC notifies the aggrieved party, and a civil action may be commenced by either the EEOC itself or the charging party. 42 U.S.C. § 2000e–5(f).

Even if the EEOC dismisses the charge, a complaining party may still file a civil action under § 2000e–5(f). However, bringing a charge before the EEOC is a jurisdictional prerequisite to the filing of a suit for Title VII violations under this section. *Bowe v. Colgate-Palmolive Co.*, 416 F.2d 711, 719 (7th Cir. 1969).

In addition, plaintiff must follow the procedures delineated in 42 U.S.C. § 2000e–5(c):

(c) *State or local proceedings.* In the case of an alleged unlawful employment practice occuring in a State, or political subdivision of a State, which has a State or local law prohibiting the unlawful employment practice alleged and establishing or authorizing a State or local authority to grant or seek relief from such practice or to institute criminal proceedings with respect thereto upon receiving notice thereof, no charge may be filed under subsection (a)[(b)] by the person aggrieved before the expiration of sixty days after proceedings have been commenced under the State or local law, unless such proceedings have been earlier terminated, provided that such sixty-day period shall be extended to one hundred and twenty days during the first year after the effective date of such State or local law. If any requirement for the commencement of such proceedings is imposed by a State or local authority other than a requirement of the filing of a written and signed statement of the facts upon which the proceeding is based, the proceeding shall be deemed to have been commenced for the purposes of this subsection at the time such statement is sent by registered mail to the appropriate State or local authority.

Plaintiff has complied with each of these procedures.

Because plaintiff alleges continuing discrimination, her initial compliance with the various procedural requirements will serve as a jurisdictional basis for this court to consider her allegations involving all three years.

A charge of discrimination is *not* filed as a preliminary to a lawsuit. On the contrary, the purpose of a charge of discrimination is to trigger the investigatory and conciliatory procedures of the EEOC. Once a charge has been filed, the Commission carries out its investigatory function and attempts to obtain voluntary compliance with the law. Only if the EEOC *fails* to achieve voluntary compliance will the matter ever become the subject of court action. Thus it is obvious that the civil action is much more intimately related to the EEOC investigation than to the words of the charge which originally triggered the investigation. Within this statutory scheme, it is only logical to limit the permissible scope of the civil action to the scope of the EEOC investigation which can reasonably be expected to grow out of the charge of discrimination. *Sanchez v. Standard Brands, Inc.,* 431 F.2d 455, 466 (5th Cir. 1970).

In the instant case, the Equal Employment Opportunity Commission (EEOC) has investigated and has been given the opportunity to conciliate. The purpose of the EEOC filing requirements has been met. This court does not find any essential difference between prior and subsequent acts in terms of whether they can be alleged in a judicial complaint so long as the allegations in the complaint could reasonably be expected to grow out of the EEOC charge or the EEOC investigation. *Sanchez, supra,* 431 F.2d 455; *Ortega v. Construction General Lab. U. No. 390,* 396 F.Supp. 976 (D.Conn.1975). Title VII

contemplates that no *issue* will be the subject of a civil action until the EEOC has first had the opportunity to attempt to obtain voluntary compliance. *Sanchez, supra,* 431 F.2d at 467. (Emphasis added.)

The act alleged is clearly within the scope of both the complaint and the EEOC investigation. *Accord, Guay v. Public Service Company,* Civ. No. 76–61, Interim Order (D.N.H. 7/26/76).

In each of the past three summers, 1974, 1975, and 1976, plaintiff has applied for employment to James C. Connor, Chief of the Hampton Beach Meter Patrol, and, in each of these years, she was turned down after personal interviews with Connor.

Connor selects personnel without guidelines and with little supervision from the Division of Parks in Concord. During his tenure as Chief, which goes back to 1965, there have been two women hired for the Meter Patrol, but they have been clerks or secretaries, not Meter Patrol officers. He offered a position of Meter Patrol officer to a woman in 1975, but she was unable to accept. Other women have spoken with Connor about employment, but no other woman has filed an application for the position.

There are five full-time Meter Patrol officers and five part-time officers. Their principal duty is to patrol the meters in Hampton Beach, which extend from the Hampton River on the south along the Boulevard to North Beach with two breaks in the rows of meters and many "leased-out" areas which would otherwise be metered. Patrol is performed either on foot or on motorcycle.

The daily duties of a Meter Patrol officer include patrolling the meters, ticketing violators, and dealing with people whose cars are towed. In addition, Meter Patrol officers might become responsible for unjamming meters, helping out with health problems, and supervising accident scenes until the police arrive.

Meter Patrol officers are in charge of taking fine boxes to the banks, and they have access to all money collected as fines on any given day.

The officers carry no weapons or handcuffs; the Town of Hampton is responsible for general police work. Officers do make use of heavy tools, but this constitutes less than 1% of the job. Connor concluded that there is no reason why a woman could not perform the duties of a Meter Patrol officer.

Plaintiff's job application shows that she made application for a job with the Meter Patrol of Hampton Beach on March 19, 1974. It gives her name, sex, age, social security number, and an address in West Somerville, Massachusetts, where plaintiff was a student at Tufts University. It also gives her marital status, weight (108 pounds), and other detailed information. Also included is a Massachusetts telephone number. The application shows that plaintiff was willing to accept full or part-time employment.

The second page gives a history of schools attended and dates concluding with plaintiff's attendance at Tufts University from 1970 through 1974 and her then anticipated Bachelor of Arts in Child Study. The application also reveals that plaintiff has a driver's license and teaching certification. There are spaces provided, but not filled in, for an employment record.

On the back of the application in a space for additional information are two names, Mrs. Hollingsworth and Mrs. Debbie Pugatch. These names are in different ink and were, according to the testimony, supplied at the interview. After Mrs. Pugatch's name is an address and explanation "(teacher/student-taught with)." Three additional references are given: Sgt. John Nickerson, Victor Demarco [sic], and Dr. Segmour Friedland. The application is signed "Mary Pat King."

Stapled to the application is a piece of paper with additional information: "Kings Supermarket, Orange, N.J., 1968; Hollingsworth Hotel, 1972, waitress; Lincoln House, 1972; waitress Jerry's Restaurant." Connor testified that this note is in his handwriting, that he had recently affixed the note to the application, and that he believed, but was not sure, that the note was from his initial interview with plaintiff in 1974.

After filing a job application in the spring of 1974, plaintiff had an interview with Connor. The interview lasted twenty minutes and there was no discussion, only some mention, of her experience as a student-teacher. There was no discussion of her work experience as a waitress or her extracurricular experience as a one-to-one tutor with emotionally-disturbed boys at the Hobb's School.

Much of the support for plaintiff's allegation that she is the victim of sex discrimination comes from the discussion which allegedly took place at this interview. She was asked if she had ever used a sledge hammer, and she replied: "No, but I would be willing to learn to use one." Connor than told her that Meter Patrol officers were sometimes required to use one to help the State maintenance crew in servicing meters. Connor told plaintiff that she might sometimes need to become involved in making arrests and stakeouts, and he asked how she would "run someone in." She replied that, if she needed help, she would seek it from the Town of Hampton Police.

Plaintiff was asked "a whole list of qualifications from a sheet." These included experience in construction, in stress situations, and in communications, as well as others. She felt "encouraged" before the interview but during the interview she felt "defensive."

Plaintiff had arranged to call Connor regarding her application. When she called, Connor said there were no vacancies because of returning members from previous years, but that she was "first or second on his list." She never received any other notification of the rejection or acceptance of her application.

Connor remembers that plaintiff was not quite sure how to present herself as a job applicant in the 1974 interview. He did not recall discussing plaintiff's ability to use a sledge hammer. Connor then identified a memorandum from himself to Mr. Carpenter in the Division of Parks, Exhibit 19, in which he said:

One misquote was about the sledge hammer. All applicants are asked among other things about construction experience. Because of her 108 lb. weight I asked if she had ever tried to use one. We use a 20 lb. driving device and a 16 lb. sledge hammer.

The memo refreshed Connor's recollection. He remembered asking her if she could use a sledge hammer because he questioned whether she could safely wield the hammer.

Connor did remember asking plaintiff how she would handle an arrest. He asked plaintiff about construction experience because of her size, not her sex, and he has asked others about construction experience.

Connor did not consider experience at waitressing or sales clerking to be much of an asset to the Meter Patrol. Neither provide sufficient opportunity to interact with other people, particularly under stress situations.

Connor knew that plaintiff had worked at Jerry's Restaurant and at Lincoln House from her 1974 interview and had been given the name of plaintiff's teaching supervisor at Tufts, Mrs. Pugatch, and the names of two personal references, Mr. DeMarco and Dr. Friedland.

Plaintiff had testified that she left her employment at Lincoln House because she had been asked out by the manager, Mr. Dougherty, had turned him down, and had subsequently been baited and given a sufficiently hard time to prevent her from adequately performing her duties as a waitress.

Connor testified that he had attempted to reach Mrs. Pugatch, but had been unable. He did speak with Dougherty from the Lincoln House, who said that plaintiff had quit due to teasing. This revealed to Connor that plaintiff might not be able to work under stress. Connor, a teacher at Pentucket Regional School during the school year, relied heavily on Dougherty who had been a student of his and who is a "respected" member of the Hampton community. Connor was unable to reach Mona, the supervisor at Jerry's Restaurant, or Dr. Friedland. Connor did speak with DeMarco, who said she was a nice girl and that he should have a woman on the Patrol. At one point, Connor, who seemed confused about when he spoke with whom, spoke with the owner of Jerry's Restaurant, who did not remember plaintiff.

Connor did hire one person for Meter Patrol in 1974, William J. Martin, a copy of whose application is Plaintiff's Exhibit 14. Martin was a thirty year old teacher at Pentucket Regional School, the same school at which Connor is a teacher. Martin is a 1966 graduate of Northeastern University with a Bachelor of Science in Education. He had taken additional courses in counseling at Massachusetts State College at Salem and had been teaching at the Pentucket Regional School for over seven years. Martin was still a member of the Meter Patrol during the summer of 1976. It is defendant's contention that Martin was a better candidate for Meter Patrol than King and that is the reason why she was not hired to fill the only vacancy that year.

In February or March of 1975, plaintiff called Connor at home to ask if she were still first or second on his list. He affirmed her position on his list, but said that he did not know whether there were any job openings.

Plaintiff did not file a new application, but sent the following letter instead:

P.O. Box 9
Hampton, N.H.
March 21, 1975

Dear Mr. Connor,

Above is my new address. Last summer, I worked as a salesperson at J. and J.'s Sportswear at Hampton Beach. In the fall, I worked in the country store of Applecrest Orchards.

I have taken another French course and have had additional practical experience in Canada. I feel that this will be a tremendous asset to me on the Meter Patrol, also a very good knowledge of the area.

Thank you very much.
Sincerely,
Mary Pat King

Plaintiff claims that she tried to reach Connor by telephone several times on April 9th and 10th, finally reaching him in the evening of the 10th. He seemed angry with her. She was told that all his men were coming back and that he knew of no openings.

On May 1st, plaintiff received a postcard which asked her to arrange an interview with Connor. The interview was held on May 3rd at the Meter Patrol office. Plaintiff was asked for job references from the current date all the way back to her job at Kings, a part-time high school job. She was not asked to explain any negative references. She was not asked for information concerning her employment at Applecrest Gift Shop or J. and J.'s Sportswear. Connor did give her the Meter Patrol phone number, which she did not write down correctly.

Connor made notes at the 1975 interview. There are additional undated notes which Connor believes to be from 1975.

He claims to have been aware of plaintiff's additional work experience from her letter and from his notes. He also noted that she spoke French, which had been polished during a recent trip to Canada.

Connor had no reason to change his opinion of plaintiff after the 1975 interview. He did check her work reference at Applecrest and got a very positive response, but nothing specific enough to be applicable to her application to the Meter Patrol. Connor did not reach Mr. Attaya of J. and J.'s Sportswear. He was sure it would be a favorable reference, since she had been invited back to the job, and he was sure it would be difficult to reach Attaya because of the seasonal basis of Hampton Beach business. He did not believe that Attaya would add much to his knowledge of plaintiff's qualifications because of the close supervision given to store clerks as opposed to Meter Patrol officers.

Alan Mason, a teacher at Pentucket Regional School for seven or eight years, and Connor's assistant in 1975 and 1976, was also present at the interview. He testified and confirmed most of Connor's testimony concerning that year and 1976. Mason testified concerning other areas still to be discussed. His testimony has been considered, but, for the sake of brevity, will not be discussed further as it mostly reiterates testimony by Connor.

On May 10th, plaintiff was notified by letter that she was not hired.

On July 23, 1975 plaintiff again met with Connor. This meeting, called at Connor's request, seems to have been only for the purposes of discussing plaintiff's previous application and denial. Plaintiff recalled no discussion concerning unfavorable references from previous jobs or any defects in the application itself. Connor testified that the meeting was not an official interview. Plaintiff had originally thought she was to have a job interview. In fact, she did fill out a new application. The new application, besides the information contained in the first application, provides a relatively complete job history. It gives an address of Box 9, Hampton, New Hampshire, and a telephone number at J. and J.'s Sportswear and new personal references.

In late July of 1975, Connor was notified that the Legislature had appropriated funds for an additional Meter Patrol officer. Connor contacted plaintiff for a new interview. The two could not arrange a mutually convenient time, and they agreed to let the last official interview serve.

Connor contacted plaintiff's superior at Jerry's Restaurant. She told him, according to Connor, that plaintiff had not been prompt and sometimes did not show up due to personal problems and had been terminated for these reasons. Connor also called Kings, where plaintiff had worked while attending high school. Kings confirmed that plaintiff had worked there and left because of school vacation. Mrs. Hollingsworth of Hollingsworth Inn, could not recall plaintiff, but her accountant did confirm that plaintiff had worked there.

Brian Liberty, a twenty year old resident of Portsmouth, New Hampshire, applied for this position in 1975. Liberty, who had completed his sophomore year at Plymouth State College, provided references from previous employment, which included responsibilities for loading trucks, making deliveries, bagging groceries, and cleaning a grocery store. Connor was impressed with Liberty's references and his general manner and appearance. Liberty was hired.

Frank Linnane also applied and was employed as a Meter Patrol officer in 1975. Linnane, who was forty-nine years old at the time of his initial application, is a high school graduate. Linnane is an Army Veteran who had been employed by the United States Post Office at Hampton for the previous sixteen years. Prior to that, he spent twelve years working for a lumber corporation. Linnane supplied no references on the written application.

Richard Ladd applied for the Meter Patrol position in 1975 and was hired. Ladd, a forty-seven year old science teacher with a master's degree in education and teaching certification, also applied and was hired as a Meter Patrol officer. Ladd is an Army Veteran who has taught at the same high school for twenty-two years. He had been employed for the preceding ten summers as director of recreation for the Town of Hampton and had spent one summer as a police and meter patrol person for the Hampton Police.

In the spring of 1976, plaintiff reapplied for Meter Patrol, was reinterviewed, and was turned down again. Her application reveals no information which has not already been discussed.

In the fall of 1975, Connor learned that plaintiff had worked at Hampton National Bank. He had seen plaintiff in the bank and inquired concerning her employment because he was afraid, if the bank had employed her, that he might not have considered all of her qualifications. Mrs. Sandbold, the Branch Manager, told Connor that plaintiff had been slow at her work, that her supervisor had warned her that her work had not been adequate, and that plaintiff had come in and quit the next day. Connor learned that there had been some emotional outburst and that plaintiff had quit without notice.

Plaintiff had never mentioned her work at the bank in the 1976 job interview or her application.

Connor called Dr. Richard Hamilton, Superintendent of Schools, because plaintiff had indicated that she was a substitute teacher during the previous school year. Hamilton informed him that plaintiff had worked a total of five days.

Connor did hire an employee for Meter Patrol in 1976. The person he hired had been his assistant for seven years.

Connor also testified that he offered a job to a woman in 1975, but that the woman could not accept the job for personal reasons. The same woman applied in 1976, but Connor's previous assistant was deemed more qualified and filled the only job vacancy.

Mr. Attaya, the manager of J. & J.'s Sportswear, testified on behalf of plaintiff. His testimony reveals that she has been a superior employee at J. & J.'s Sportswear.

John Cole, plaintiff's current supervisor at Pawtuckaway State Park in Raymond, testified to plaintiff's performance of her current duties as a toll collector. He stated that she performed her job well and showed initiative in some of the assignments he had given her which were not strictly a part of her job as toll collector.

Mr. William Carpenter, Supervisor for Park Operations for the Division of Parks, also testified concerning the job specifications and qualifications for a toll collector at a State park and for a Meter Patrol officer at Hampton Beach.

Although Cole testified that plaintiff performed her job well, it appears that the job of toll collector is not equivalent to the job of Meter Patrol officer, since it does not require the same degree of trustworthiness or the ability to perform without supervision.

In *McDonnell Douglas Corp. v. Green*, 411 U.S. 792, 802–803, 93 S.Ct. 1817, 1824, 36 L.Ed.2d 668 (1973), the Supreme Court delineated the test for a prima facie case of discrimination in violation of 42 U.S.C. § 2000e.

The complainant in a Title VII trial must carry the initial burden under the statute of establishing a prima facie case of racial discrimination. This may be done by showing (i) that he belongs to a racial minority; (ii) that he applied and was qualified for a job for which the employer was seeking applicants; (iii) that, despite his qualifications, he was rejected; and (iv) that, after his rejection, the position remained open and the employer continued to seek applicants from persons of complainant's qualifications. In the instant case, we agree with the Court of Appeals that respondent proved a prima facie case. [8 Cir.] 463 F.2d 337, 353. Petitioner sought mechanics, respondent's trade, and continued to do so after respondent's rejection. Petitioner, moreover, does not dispute respondent's qualifications and acknowledges that his past work performance in petitioner's employ was "satisfactory."

The burden then must shift to the employer to articulate some legitimate, nondiscriminatory reason for the employee's rejection. We need not attempt in the instant case to detail every matter which fairly could be recognized as a reasonable basis for a refusal to hire.

In this case, plaintiff belongs to a protected class, which satisfies the first requirement. There is no dispute that plaintiff applied for the job of Meter Patrol officer. The job of Meter Patrol officer is not particularly different from the job performed by the myriad of meter maids who can be seen performing their jobs daily. This court takes judicial notice that no special education or skill is needed to perform the job of meter maid or Meter Patrol officer, and I find that plaintiff was qualified for the job for which she applied. Plaintiff was rejected despite her qualifications.

The fourth part of the *McDonnell* test was designed for a situation in which discrimination is alleged in the course of defendant's receiving seriatim applications. In the instant case, defendant selected employees from a pool of applicants. Therefore, I need not apply the fourth part of the *McDonnell* test.

I rule that, in a case where employees are selected from a pool of applicants, and the first three parts of the *McDonnell* test have been proven, and where a prima facie case of discriminatory animus has been shown, it may be fairly presumed that the employer has failed to adequately consider the plaintiff's application. Therefore, when these elements have been established by the plaintiff

[t]he burden then must shift to the employer to articulate some legitimate, nondiscriminatory reason for the employee's rejection. *McDonnell, supra*, 411 U.S. at 802, 93 S.Ct. at 1824

This holding is supported in *Gillin v. Federal Paper Board Company, Inc.*, 479 F.2d 97 (2d Cir. 1973). In *Gillin*, the plaintiff claimed that her employer's refusal to promote her constituted discrimination based solely on sex. The defendant admitted that she had not been considered for the job for which she applied, and that this failure to consider her application was based solely on sex.

While the ultimate prize was won by the male who had superior qualifications, this in our view does not purge Federal of its prior discriminatory act of refusing to consider her at all not *solely* because of lack of qualification but because she was a woman. While Gillin did not have all of the qualifications for the position, she fell clearly within the group entitled to initial consideration especially in a company which purported to have a policy of promoting from within. Having had some familiarity with and experience in most if not all the facets of the position, the refusal of Varsho to consider her because she was a woman, is clearly a mischief which the statute was designed to prevent. We hold therefore that the court below was in error in not considering this point and in assuming that Sweezey's superior qualifications presumably cured the previous act of discrimination. In sum we find no wrong in hiring Sweezey instead of Gillin but we hold that Federal did transgress by failing to consider Gillin not simply because she was not qualified but also because she was a woman.

When Connor asked plaintiff if she could use a sledge hammer, he was displaying a discriminatory animus. His questions relating to the construction industry, which bears little or no relationship to the job of Meter Patrol officer, only serve to reinforce this court's view that Connor did not give plaintiff's application fair consideration, if he did, indeed, give it any consideration at all. Plaintiff has met her burden of showing a discriminatory animus on the part of Connor.

Were this not sufficient, Connor's admission that he told plaintiff she was first or second on the list adds considerably to plaintiff's proof. There was no cause for Connor to deliberately mislead plaintiff and hold out false hopes.

Defendant's claim that the job was given to an applicant with superior qualifications does not, by itself, relieve it of the necessity of showing that it did, indeed, give the plaintiff fair consideration. The alleged fact that defendant hired a superior applicant may well be some evidence of the defendant's good faith consideration of plaintiff; however, the defendant here did not give the plaintiff fair consideration. The Court in *Pond v. Braniff Airways, Incorporated*, 500 F.2d 161, 165–166 (5th Cir. 1974) stated:

Of course it is true, as urged by Braniff, that where an employer can demonstrate no discrimination in the selection or advancement of employees, but rather that the employer in the best of faith merely weighed each person's talents then choosing the man over the woman (or woman over the man), no case is made out under Title VII. But the inquiry does not necessarily stop here. Courts must be extremely careful to determine that the reasons given for selecting a male applicant over a female applicant are not simply a ruse disguising true discrimination. Courts must further carefully scrutinize the employer's explanations for its conduct once the aggrieved employee has proved a prima facie case of discrimination. . . . The line that must be drawn is a fine one—because interpreting an employer's motives on the basis of its actions is at times hazardous, especially when there exists potentially valid and seemingly plausible business explanations as to such actions which in fact mask a true intent to discriminate.

A crucial fact in this case is Connor's predisposition to hire fellow teachers, especially those from his own school. Availability for a summer job and experience with teenagers may be a part of the job, but plaintiff was available, and experience of this sort is hardly an essential element in what is one of the labor force's entry level jobs. In this case, the fact that plaintiff hired a teacher from Pentucket Regional School in 1974 for a job without written specifications only adds to plaintiff's contention that she was not given fair consideration. The fact that this discrimination is not protected by Title VII does not in any way detract from plaintiff's case.

In order to establish an "unlawful employment practice" or "unlawful discrimination" on the basis of sex within the intent and meaning of the "Law against discrimination," . . . it is not necessary that the sex discrimination be the sole reason for the employment practice under attack. If discrimination on the basis of sex played at least a part and was a causal factor in the failure of complainant to be given the job . . . , discrimination in violation of the statute has been established." *Harvard v. Bushberg Brothers, Inc.*, 137 N.J.Super. 537, 350 A.2d 65, 67 (1975). (Citations omitted.)

Defendant cites as controlling *Parham v. Southwestern Bell Telephone Company*, 433 F.2d 421 (8th Cir. 1970). In that case, the plaintiff alleged discrimination individually and as representative of a class. The plaintiff had been interviewed and tentatively offered a position with the defendant company. During the investigation of his past employment history, the defendant discovered that the plaintiff had an extremely poor employment record, and, as a result, withdrew its tentative job offer. That Court, in finding no individual discrimination, found that the plaintiff was rejected because of his qualifications. The Court found a good faith effort on the part of the defendant.

Here, I find no such good faith. I find that the defendant exhibited a discriminatory animus toward plaintiff and that his articulated reasons served merely as a cover for the discrimination which occurred at the consideration stage.

Therefore, I find that, in 1974 and 1975, defendant discriminated against plaintiff on the basis of her sex. I further find that, in 1976, defendant met his burden of articulating legitimate reasons for not hiring plaintiff. In 1976, plaintiff's veracity and trustworthiness were challenged by her failure to disclose her less than favorable employment experience at the local bank, giving defendant legitimate grounds for rejecting her application.

Plaintiff complied with the filing requirements of 42 U.S.C. § 2000e and received the requisite statutory notice of right to sue by letter dated June 4, 1976, from J. Stanley Pottinger, Assistant United States Attorney General.

For three successive summers, the summers of 1974, 1975, and 1976, plaintiff applied to Connor for a summer job as a member of the Hampton Beach Meter Patrol.

She was refused employment after personal interviews in all three years.

The Meter Patrol is a uniformed force employing approximately ten individuals during the summer months. They are not equipped with weapons or handcuffs.

The Hampton Beach Meter Patrol is responsible for maintaining over 1,500 State-owned parking meters and controlling vehicular parking at Hampton Beach.

Meter Patrol employees are responsible for checking parking meters for overtime violations, writing and processing violations and dealing with the public with respect thereto, arranging for towing of illegally-parked vehicles, and repairing damaged parking meters.

The essential duties of the Meter Patrol are: foot patrol of State-owned parking areas, ticketing vehicles for the purpose of enforcing parking laws, collection of coins from meters, and record-keeping in relation to these functions. Meter Patrol officers are not subject to close supervision in any of their activities; therefore, the position requires a relatively high degree of reliability and responsibility. The job also includes dealing with people of high school and college age.

There are not now, nor have there ever been, any female officers of the Meter Patrol.

James Connor, as Chief of the Meter Patrol, is primarily responsible for the hiring of personnel.

The State of New Hampshire does not maintain, and Connor does not apply, rigid eligibility criteria for employee selection.

Employees are selected by Connor on the basis of his evaluations of them, which are formulated from information provided in the applications, interviews and his conversations with the references supplied by the applicants.

Connor has made it a practice to rehire the previous year's employees automatically, and to interview new candidates when a new position becomes available or when a vacancy occurs.

One vacancy for a position as Meter Patrol person existed for the summer of 1974.

In March, 1974, plaintiff filed a written application for a job as Meter Patrol officer with Connor.

Plaintiff was interviewed by Connor in the spring of 1974.

Plaintiff graduated from Tufts University, Medford, Massachusetts, receiving her B.A. degree in child study in June of 1974.

Plaintiff's work experience, at the time of her interview with Connor in 1974, included, in broad outline, the following: one semester of supervised student-teaching at the Elliot Pearson School in Medford, Massachusetts, in 1974; waitressing full-time at the Hollingsworth Motor Inn, Hampton Beach, New Hampshire, for about four weeks in the summer of 1973; waitressing full-time at the Lincoln House Restaurant, Hampton Beach, New Hampshire, for about seven weeks each in the summers of 1971 and 1972; waitressing full-time at Jerry's Restaurant for about three weeks in the summer of 1971; and working part-time as a grocery check-out clerk at Kings Supermarket, Orange, New Jersey, in 1970.

At the time of plaintiff's 1974 interview with Connor, plaintiff, having resided in Hampton for a number of summers with her family prior to becoming a permanent resident of the Town in June, 1974, was familiar with the Hampton Beach area and acquainted with some personnel of the Town of Hampton police force.

When plaintiff was interviewed by Connor in the spring of 1974, she was qualified for a position as Meter Patrol officer.

In 1974 and 1975, there were no written specifications for the job as Meter Patrol person.

In 1974, during his interview with plaintiff, Connor asked plaintiff whether she could wield a sledge hammer, and he indicated that the ability to do so was a qualification for the job as Meter Patrol officer.

The ability to use heavy tools was not a qualification for employment as a Meter Patrol officer in 1974 or 1975.

In 1974, during his interview with plaintiff, Connor asked whether plaintiff would be able to "run someone in" if this became necessary.

The ability to make an unassisted arrest was not a qualification for employment as a Meter Patrol officer in 1974 or 1975.

Connor's inquiries of plaintiff during her 1974 interview expressed discrimination based upon sex, without any *bona fide* basis for such discrimination.

Connor received a response from a former employer of plaintiff's to the effect that she had been unable to get along with people. Connor did not pursue the other employment references.

In May, 1974, William John Martin filed a written application for a job as Meter Patrol officer with Connor and was hired.

Martin's job credentials were superior to plaintiff's in the spring of 1974.

In 1974, Connor discriminated against plaintiff by failing to give her application fair consideration.

Martin's job qualifications were superior, and Connor would have hired Martin even had plaintiff been a man.

On March 21, 1975, plaintiff reapplied, by letter, for a position as Meter Patrol officer and furnished the names of her employers since the summer of 1974.

Two vacancies for a position as Meter Patrol officer existed in May, 1975.

On May 3, 1975, plaintiff was interviewed a second time by Connor for a position as Meter Patrol officer.

At the time of her May 3rd interview with Connor, plaintiff had additional work experience as a sales clerk at J. and J.'s Sportswear Co., Hampton Beach, New Hampshire, for about ten weeks in the summer of 1974; as sales clerk at Applecrest Orchards, Hampton Falls, New Hampshire, for about eight weeks in the fall of 1974.

At the time of the May, 1975, interview, plaintiff was qualified for the job of Meter Patrol officer.

At the time of the May 3, 1975, interview, plaintiff had been offered reemployment by J. and J.'s Sportswear Co. for the summer of 1975.

Plaintiff's employer, J. and J.'s Sportswear Co., was satisfied with plaintiff's work in the summer of 1974, and would have given a good reference, if contacted in May, 1975.

Connor did not contact J. and J.'s Sportswear Co.

In May of 1975, Connor checked one reference supplied by plaintiff and received a very positive response.

Plaintiff was not hired after the May 3, 1975, interview.

In May, 1975, Brian J. Liberty filed a written application with Connor for a job as Meter Patrol officer and was hired on May 10, 1975.

In May, 1975, Richard Jackman Ladd filed a written application with Connor for a job as Meter Patrol officer and was hired on May 10, 1975.

Brian J. Liberty's job credentials were not superior to plaintiff's in May, 1975.

Richard Jackman Ladd's job credentials were superior to plaintiff's in May, 1975.

Connor refused to hire plaintiff in May, 1975, due to her sex.

Plaintiff swore out her discrimination complaint with the New Hampshire Commission for Human Rights on May 1, 1975, prior to her May 3rd interview. It was filed subsequently. In it, she complained of alleged discrimination by Connor in both 1974 and 1975.

Plaintiff was invited to another interview in July of 1975, as a result of the creation of a new position.

There were two other persons interviewed for the new job, one a female and one a male.

At the time, Connor rechecked an employment reference, Jerry's Restaurant, and was told that plaintiff had been fired from the job due to unreliability. Connor attempted to contact two personal references, but was unsuccessful in making contact.

The male candidate was offered and accepted the position.

In July, 1975, Connor's failure to hire plaintiff was not based upon her sex.

Plaintiff filed a new application in 1976 and was interviewed.

There was a vacancy in the Meter Patrol for the summer of 1976.

Plaintiff's 1976 application contained one employment reference not contained in her previous applications. She stated that she was a substitute teacher in the Hampton School District, and that the position was "continuing."

Plaintiff did not reveal, on her 1976 application form, that she had been employed during September and October of 1975 by the Hampton National Bank.

On the day of plaintiff's 1976 interview, Connor knew that she had worked at the Seabrook Branch of the Hampton National Bank during September and October of 1975, and that she had quit the job.

During the 1976 interview, Connor asked plaintiff whether she had obtained employment other than that listed on her application, and her response was, "No."

Plaintiff was not hired in 1976. Connor hired a former Meter Patrol employee for the available position.

In 1976 Connor's failure to hire plaintiff was not based upon her sex.

Plaintiff is not awarded any damages for the year 1974, since I have found that, even if she had not been discriminated against, she would not have been hired for that year.

Connor's discrimination against the plaintiff did result in her not being hired in 1975, and she is to be awarded damages for that year: the amount she would have earned working on the Meter Patrol less the amount actually earned.

She is also entitled to damages on the same basis for the year 1976. Connor testified that he automatically rehired returning officers of the Meter Patrol. If plaintiff had been hired in 1975, she would have been rehired in 1976.

COMPUTATION OF DAMAGES
1975

Amount earnable: Hampton Beach Meter Patrol	$3.52 per hour
	×40 hours
	$140.80 per week
	×10 weeks
	$1,408.00
Amount earned: J. and J.'s Sportswear Co.	828.18
Back Pay Damages	$579.82

Amount earnable: Hampton Beach Meter Patrol	$1,408.00
Amount earned: Pawtuckaway State Park	1,155.52
Back Pay Damages	$252.48
Total Back Pay Damages— 1975 and 1976	$832.30

42 U.S.C. § 2000e-5(k) provides:

In any action or proceeding under this subchapter the court, in its discretion, may allow the prevailing party, other than the Commission or the United States, a reasonable attorney's fee as part of the costs, and the Commission and the United States be liable for costs the same as a private person.

Judgment for the plaintiff in the amount of $832.30 plus attorneys' fees in the amount of $1,500.

SO ORDERED.

Bowe v. Colgate-Palmolive Co.
[416 F.2d 711 (7th Cir. 1969)]

Dual seniority systems and weight-lifting requirements

Analysis of the issue

Present and former Colgate-Palmolive employees instituted this action alleging violations of the 1964 Civil Rights Act. The plaintiffs claimed that they were discriminated against by a system of job classification which deprived them access to certain jobs and that they were subject to discriminatory layoffs under a segregated plant seniority system based on sex. The company used a dual seniority system which separated men from women and classified jobs as light and heavy types. Women were restricted to light jobs, classifying all jobs for which lifting weights of 35 pounds and over as heavy ones. In the initial trial, the court held that defendants acted reasonably in imposing the 35-pound restriction on female employees and refused to hear the claims of certain plaintiffs who had not filed charges with the EEOC. The Appeals Court held that seniority systems permitting men to bid for jobs plantwide, but restricting women to light jobs violated the Civil Rights Act. It also concluded that although the company was entitled to set a minimum lifting requirement, the requirement should be imposed on all employees. Each employee should be afforded the opportunity to demonstrate his or her ability to perform more strenuous jobs. The Court also held that Title VII does not require each and every plaintiff to file an action with EEOC in order to be entitled to relief. If the action is a class action, all members of the class similarly situated might be entitled to relief even if no charges were filed with the EEOC. Therefore, those plaintiffs who had not filed charges with the EEOC were entitled to recover back pay.

Full text of opinion

KERNER, Circuit Judge:—Plaintiffs are present and/or former female employees of defendant Colgate-Palmolive Company (Colgate) who were represented, for collective bargaining purposes, by defendant International Chemical Workers Union, Local No. 15 (Union) at Colgate's Jeffersonville, Indiana, plant. Plaintiffs sued Colgate and the Union under Title VII of the Civil Rights Act of 1964, 42 U.S.C. § 2000e et seq. charging that they were intentionally discriminated against by a system of job classification which deprived them of various opportunities in the plant and that they were subjected to discriminatory layoffs under a segregated plant seniority system based on the employees' sex.

Prior to trial, the court below required plaintiffs to elect whether they would proceed in this action or whether they would seek remedy under the collective bargaining agreement through arbitration. The court also refused to consider the claims of certain plaintiffs who had not filed charges with the Equal Employment Opportunity Commission

(EEOC) and had not received notice of the right to sue from the EEOC, having determined that this action could not be maintained as a class action for purposes of applying a back pay remedy for the layoffs. After trial by the court without a jury, a memorandum opinion was filed which found for the Union in full, and for Colgate on all issues on the merits except as to certain layoffs under the segregated seniority lists in November, 1965. The crux of the lower court's opinion on the merits is its holding that Colgate acted reasonably in imposing a 35-pound weight-lifting limit on jobs which were open to females, thus foreclosing them from competing for jobs requiring lifting of more than 35 pounds. The facts are carefully set out in Bowe v. Colgate-Palmolive Co., 272 F.Supp. 332, esp. 340–360 (S.D. Ind. 1967). Except for portions of the partial relief granted below, we reverse.

The first major issue for our consideration is whether the trial court acted properly in requiring plaintiffs to elect whether they would pursue their statutory remedy in this action or seek arbitration of grievances under the collective bargaining contract. Thus, the court required an election of remedies prior to any decision on the merits in either of the available fora.

The situation facing the trial court was one in which there exists concurrent jurisdiction under the statutory scheme and under the grievance and arbitration process for the resolution of claims against an employer and a union. The analogy to labor disputes involving concurrent jurisdiction of the N.L.R.B. and the arbitration process is not merely compelling, we hold it conclusive.

While we recognize that there is a burden placed on the defendant who must defend in two different fora, we also note that there may be crucial differences between the two processes and the remedy afforded by each. Also, as with unfair labor practice cases, in a case involving an alleged breach of a contract brought before an arbitrator, the arbitrator may consider himself bound to apply the contract and not give the types of remedy which are available under the statute. Conversely, an action in court may not be able to delve into all the ramifications of the contract nor afford some types of relief available through arbitration, *e.g.*, back pay prior to the date of the statute. United Steelworkers of America, A.F.L.-C.I.O. v. American Int'l Aluminum Corp., 334 F.2d 147 (5th Cir. 1964).

Moreover, in an action brought under Title VII, the charging party and suing plaintiff acts as a private attorney general who "takes on the mantle of the sovereign." Jenkins v. United Gas Corp., 400 F.2d 28, 32 (5th Cir. 1968). See also Oatis v. Crown Zellerbach Corp., 398 F.2d 496 (5th Cir. 1968). When, as frequently happens, the alleged discrimination has been practiced on the plaintiff because he or she is a member of a class which is allegedly discriminated against, the trial court bears a special responsibility in the public interest to resolve the dispute by determining the facts regardless of the position of the individual plaintiff. *Jenkins, supra* at 33, n. 10 of 400 F.2d. This is only fair to the defendant as it avoids forcing him to defend a multiplicity of actions.

Accordingly, we hold that it was error not to permit the plaintiffs to utilize dual or parallel prosecution both in court and through arbitration so long as election of remedy was made after adjudication so as to preclude duplicate relief which would result in an unjust enrichment or windfall to the plaintiffs. American Int'l Aluminum, *supra* at 152 of 334 F.2d. *Cf.* N.L.R.B. v. Geo. E. Light Boat Storage, Inc., 373 F.2d 762, 767–768 (5th Cir. 1967).

Colgate uses an unusual system of plant-wide seniority due to the uncertainty from week to week as to which jobs in the plant will operate. Each week, every employee completes a job preference sheet for the following week with job assignments being made on the basis of seniority. The seniority system is bifurcated into separate eligibility lists for men and women. While men may bid for jobs plant wide, women are restricted to jobs which do not require lifting more than 35 pounds. The history and mechanics of this unusual system are fully set out at 272 F. Supp. 340–347. The Union also bears responsibility for this system since it continued to abide by it as enshrined in the contract in force on the effective date of Title VII and since it preserved some parts of the system in its 1966 contract with Colgate. However, as shown below, there is no liability on the part of the Union due to the failure of any of the plaintiffs to comply with the jurisdictional requisites for filing a suit against the Union.

The trial court carefully analyzed the various facts relating to the weight-lifting restriction and concluded that Colgate had acted reasonably and in the interest of the safety of its female employees in imposing the 35-pound restriction. 272 F. Supp. at 353–357, and 363–366. While this was a carefully reasoned and conscientious approach, we hold it error as it is based on a misconception of the requirements of Title VII's anti-discrimination provisions.

The trial court relied on 42 U.S.C. § 2000e-2(e) which permits discrimination in hiring by sex where sex "is a bona fide occupational qualification reasonably necessary to the normal operation of that particular business or enterprise" and § 2000e-3(b) which similarly permits discrimination in job advertisements where sex "is a bona fide occupational qualification for employment." The court also relied on § 2000e-7 which states that the Act shall not be deemed to relieve those covered under it from any liability imposed by state law, except where such law would require the doing of "any act which would be an unlawful employment practice under this subchapter." Thus, the court succumbed to the erroneous argument that state laws setting weight-lifting restrictions on women were not affected by Title VII. While we agree with the court's noting of the EEOC's statement that it cannot be assumed that Congress intended to strike down all such state legislation, we also observe that that statement was presented to the court out of its proper context. The EEOC guideline on sex as a "bona fide occupation qualification" (BFOQ) reads, in pertinent part, 29 C.F.R. §§ 1604.1 and 1604.2 (1968):

§ 1604.1 Sex as a bona fide occupational qualification.

(a) The Commission believes that the bona fide occupational qualification exception as to sex should be interpreted narrowly. Labels—"Men's jobs" and "Women's jobs"—tend to deny employment opportunities unnecessarily to one sex or the other.

* * * * * *

(3) Most States have enacted laws or administrative regulations with respect to the employment of women. These laws fall into two general categories:

(i) Laws that require that certain benefits be provided for female employees, such as minimum wages, premium pay for overtime, rest periods or physical facilities;

(ii) Laws that prohibit the employment of women in certain hazardous occupations, in jobs requiring the lifting of heavy weights, during certain hours of the night, or for more than a specified number of hours per day or per week.

(b) The Commission believes that some state laws and regulations with respect to the employment of women, although originally for valid protective reasons, have ceased to be relevant to our technology or to the expanding role of the woman worker in our economy. We shall continue to study the problems posed by these laws and regulations in particular factual contexts, and to cooperate with other appropriate agencies in achieving a regulatory system more responsive to the demands of equal opportunity in employment.

(c) The Commission does not believe that Congress intended to disturb such laws and regulations which are intended to, and have the effect of, protecting women against exploitation and hazard. Accordingly, the Commission will consider limitations or prohibitions imposed by such state laws or regulations as a basis for application of the bona fide occupational qualification exception. However, in cases where the clear effect of a law in current circumstances is not to protect women but to subject them to discrimination, the law will not be considered a justification for discrimination. So, for example, restrictions on lifting weights will not be deemed in conflict with Title VII except where the limit is set at an unreasonably low level which could not endanger women.

An employer, accordingly, will not be considered to be engaged in an unlawful employment practice when he refuses to employ a woman in a job in which women are legally prohibited from being employed or which involve duties which women may not legally be permitted to perform because of hazards reasonably to be apprehended from such employment.

* * * * * *

§ 1604.2 Separate lines of progression and seniority systems.

(a) It is an unlawful employment practice to classify a job as "male" or "female" or to maintain separate lines of progression or separate seniority lists based on sex where this would adversely affect any employee unless sex is a bona fide occupational qualification for that job. Accordingly, employment practices are unlawful which arbitrarily classify jobs so that:

(1) A female is prohibited from applying for a job labeled "male," or for a job in a "male" line of progression; and vice versa.

(2) A male scheduled for layoff is prohibited from displacing a less senior female on a "female" seniority list; and vice versa.

(b) A seniority system or line of progression which distinguishes between "light" and "heavy" jobs constitutes an unlawful employment practice if it operates as a disguised form of classification by sex, or creates unreasonable obstacles to the advancement by members of either sex into jobs which members of that sex would reasonably be expected to perform.

By way of further interpretation of its guidelines, especially § 1604.1(a) (3)(c) relating to weight-lifting limits, the EEOC has, in three separate cases, indicated that this guideline is not to be read as an approval of general weight-limits by sex in any state or even in a particular industry, but that consideration must be given on a highly individualized basis. It views such broad limitation as violative of its prohibition against the use of broad class stereotypes including those in which sex is the stereotyping factor. In Case Nos. CH 7-3-183, et al., August 31, 1967, the EEOC voided a 35-pound weight limit imposed by one employer on all women employees holding that "individuals [must] be considered on the basis of individual capacities and not on the basis of any characteristics generally attributed to the group." In Case Nos. AU 68-10-209E, et al., July 24, 1968, the EEOC held that an agreement between an employer and union limiting females to jobs involving lifting weights of less than 55 pounds was based on a generic classification which was arbitrary and discriminatory and based on a "stereotyped characterization of the sexes," rather than consideration of individual capacities as to physical strength and particular job requirements. Finally, in Case Nos. CL-68-11-326E, et al., Sept. 26, 1968, fn. 1 (a case involving another major Indiana employer), the EEOC expressly stated its disagreement with the particular decision below.

If anything is certain in this controversial area, it is that there is no general agreement as to what is a maximum permissible weight which can be safely lifted by women in the course of their employment. The states which have limits vary considerably. Most of the state limits were enacted many years ago and most, if not all, would be considered clearly unreasonable in light of the average physical development, strength and stamina of most modern American women who participate in the industrial work force. Almost all state limits are below the 33 to 44.1 pounds recommended by an investigatory committee of the International Labor Organization (I.L.O.) in March, 1964. Even those limits were rejected by the I.L.O. and the provision finally adopted in I.L.O. Convention No. 127 (June 28, 1967) simply states that no worker should transport loads "which, by reason of its weight is likely to jeopardize his health or safety" and that the maximum weight of loads for women "shall be substantially less than that permitted for adult male workers." At the same time, Recommendation 127 was adopted stating that the maximum load for an adult male should be 55 kg. or 121 pounds. While there was no agreement as to a maximum load for women, the I.L.O. experts individually suggested limits ranging from 60.5 to 76.9 pounds, virtually twice the limit agreed to by the court below.

We agree with the Secretary of Labor insofar as he stated that it is best to consider individual qualifications and conditions, such as the physical capability and physiological makeup of an individual, climatic conditions, and the manner in which the weight is to be lifted. See also, Cheatwood v. South Central Bell Telephone & Telegraph Co., 304 F. Supp. 107 (M.D.Ala., 1969). There is a significant difference in job requirements which must be considered just as carefully as the physiological capabilities of individual employees. Thus, there are probably very few plant workers (male or female) who could not lift a 38-pound case with a handle and move it 10 feet once during a shift. If, however, the case had to be moved further, or more frequently, or lifted to a shoulder-height shelf, the degree of exertion is increased and the number of those capable of performing it is diminished.

Accordingly, we hold that Colgate may, if it so desires, retain its 35-pound weight-lifting limit as a general guideline for all of its employees, male and female. However, it must notify all of its workers that each of them who desires to do so will be afforded a reasonable opportunity to demonstrate his or her ability to perform more strenuous jobs on a regular basis. Each employee who is able to so demonstrate must be permitted to bid on and fill any position to which his or her seniority may entitle him or her. On remand, the court shall study the problem together with the parties and devise and adopt a system which will afford this opportunity to each employee desiring it.

Colgate has raised some procedural issues which it urges would preclude recovery by at least some of the plaintiffs. The first issue related to the time sequence involved in filing suit and various formalities regarding the EEOC charge. Subsequently, this Court decided this issue in another Title VII case, Choate v. Caterpillar Tractor Co., 402 F.2d 357 (7th Cir. 1968). We accept Colgate's concession that *Choate* disposes of this issue adversely to Colgate and lays it to rest in this case.

Colgate also argued that there was a failure of necessary joinder in the actions below as none of its male employees were made parties to the action. The issue is frivolous. The Union was made a party and its duty was to represent the male employees as well as the female employees. There is nothing in the law which precluded the Union from recognizing the injustice done to a substantial minority of its members and from moving to correct it. This is an internal union matter which had to be resolved within the Union and did not require intervention by the employer. See Humphrey v. Moore, 375 U.S. 335, 84 S.Ct. 363, 11 L.Ed.2d 370 (1964).

Colgate also argued that the trial court was correct in deciding not to issue a preliminary injunction against it to compel discontinuance of the discriminatory practices. We believe that this was error, in part. Had the court correctly perceived the meaning of BFOQ, it would have issued an injunction. However, it could not issue one against the discriminatory layoffs as the determination of this issue was dependent on the type of careful proofs adduced at trial and therefore not appropriate for preliminary injunctive relief under the peculiar facts of this case.

It is a jurisdictional prerequisite to the filing of a suit under Title VII that a charge be filed with the EEOC against the party sought to be sued. 42 U.S.C. § 2000e-5(e). This provision serves two important purposes. First, it notifies the charged party of the asserted violation. Secondly, it brings the charged party before the EEOC and permits effectuation of the Act's primary goal, the securing of voluntary compliance with the law. While we believe that the Union was not entirely blameless in permitting discrimination to exist and could have worked harder to eliminate the residual and continuing effects of the blatant prior discrimination, it is undisputed that at no time was the Union ever charged before the EEOC as a party in violation of Title VII. Accordingly, the Union cannot be held liable for any of the damages resulting from the discrimination and the trial court's determination in favor of the Union is affirmed.

Having determined that the court below erred in holding the weight-limit to be a BFOQ, the decision that the November layoffs were discriminatory is now more strongly supported. For the reasons stated below, and in this opinion as to the BFOQ, that part of the trial court's decision is affirmed.

However, the court committed error in determining that only those plaintiffs who filed a charge with the EEOC were permitted to recover back pay. It should have permitted recovery by the intervening plaintiffs and required the posting of a notice allowing any other similarly situated employee to apply to the court for appropriate relief.

A suit for violation of Title VII is necessarily a class action as the evil sought to be ended is discrimination on the basis of a class characteristic, *i.e.*, race, sex, religion or national origin. In our view, it is undistinguishable on this point from actions under Title II relating to discrimination in public accommodations. In Newman v. Piggie Park Enterprises, Inc.,

390 U.S. 400, 401-402, 88 S.Ct. 964, 19 L.Ed.2d 1263 (1968), the court held that since vindication of the public interest is dependent upon private suits, the suits are private in form only and a plaintiff who obtains an injunction does so "as a 'private attorney general', vindicating a policy that Congress considered of the highest priority." Oatis v. Crown Zellerbach Corp., 398 F.2d 496, 499 (5th Cir. 1968), and Jenkins v. United Gas Corporation, 400 F.2d 28, 35 (5th Cir. 1968), hold similarly as to Title VII actions regarding racial discrimination. We agree with the Fifth Circuit and perceive no reason under the law or the cases why the same should not be true of Title VII actions against sex discrimination. See also Quarles v. Philip Morris, Inc., 271 F.Supp. 842 (D.Va. 1967).

We are also unable to perceive any justification for treating such a suit as a class action for injunctive purposes, but not treat it so for purposes of other relief. The clear purpose of Title VII is to bring an end to the proscribed discriminatory practices and to make whole, in a pecuniary fashion, those who have suffered by it. To permit only injunctive relief in the class action would frustrate the implementation of the strong Congressional purpose expressed in the Civil Rights Act of 1964. To require that each employee file a charge with the EEOC and then join in the suit would have a deleterious effect on the purposes of the Act and impose an unnecessary hurdle to recovery for the wrong inflicted. We agree with the holding in Oatis, supra at 498, that:

It would be wasteful, if not vain, for numerous employees, all with the same grievance, to have to process many identical complaints with the EEOC. The better approach would appear to be that once an aggrieved person raises a particular issue with the EEOC which he has standing to raise, he may bring an action for himself and the class of persons similarly situation.

To the extent that any dicta in Hall v. Werthan Bag Corp., 251 F.Supp. 184 (M.D.Tenn. 1966), holds contra, we reject it.

Colgate argues that the language of 42 U.S.C. § 2000e-5(e) requires that each person seeking recovery must first file a charge with the EEOC and then formally join in or institute suit for recovery. This is not required in order to serve the policy behind that section. The purpose of the section (as observed above in discussing the Union) is to provide for notice to the charged party and to bring to bear the voluntary compliance and conciliation functions of the EEOC. Also, as noted by this court in Choate v. Caterpillar Tractor Corp., 402 F.2d 357 (7th Cir. 1968), and in Cox v. United States Gypsum Co., 409 F.2d 289, 291 (7th Cir. 1969), another important function of filing the charge is to permit the EEOC to determine whether the charge is adequate. Finally, the charge determines the scope of the alleged violation and thereby serves to narrow the issues for prompt adjudication and decision. Cf. Edwards v. North Amer. Rockwell Corp., 291 F.Supp. 199 (C.D.Calif. 1968).

It is apparent that each of these purposes is served when any charge is filed and a proper suit follows which fairly asserts grievances common to the class to be afforded relief in the court. There can be no claim of surprise in such a situation. Also, as held in Miller v. Int'l Paper Co., 408 F.2d 283, 285 (5th Cir. 1969): no procedural purpose could be served by requiring scores of substantially identical grievances to be processed through EEOC when a single charge would be sufficient to effectuate both the letter and spirit of Title VII. Wherefore we reverse the decision below on this point and hold that this suit may properly be treated as a class action under Title VII as to all forms of relief to which any and all members of the class may be entitled by virtue of Colgate's discriminating practices.

42 U.S.C. § 2000e-5(g) requires that if the court finds an intentional unlawful employment practice, it may enjoin the practice "and order such affirmative action as may be appropriate." This grant of authority should be broadly read and applied so as to effectively terminate the practice and make its victims whole. This was not done here. As held in *Jenkins, supra* at 33-35 of 400 F.2d, the District Court when applying Title VII should, after a finding of an unlawful employment practice which is plant-wide in nature, actively make the court available to all those members of the injured class who may be entitled to relief. *Cf.* Fibreboard Paper Prods. Corp., 138 N.L.R.B. 500, 554-56 (1962), *enforced,* 379 U.S. 203, 85 S.Ct. 398, 13 L.Ed.2d 233 (1964). The full remedial powers of the court must be brought to bear and all appropriate relief given.

In the instant case, this requires that all those who were discriminatorially laid off be compensated at the highest rate of pay for such jobs as they would have bid on/and qualified for if a non-discriminatory seniority scheme would have been in existence. This relief should be made available to all who were so damaged whether or not they filed charges and whether or not they joined in the suit. The court shall, on remand, also enter such appropriate injunctive orders as may be required to completely eliminate the discriminatory system and any residual effect.

We have considered the few remaining lesser points and find no determinative issues among them. On the issue of proof of damage, we affirm the lower court's determination that sufficient proof was adduced to support the relief. The deduction of unemployment compensation was proper, being a valid exercise of the trial judge's discretion pursuant to 42 U.S.C. § 2000e-5(g).

The case is remanded to the District Court for the Southern District of Indiana for further proceedings in conformity with this opinion.

Affirmed in part, reversed in part, modified and remanded.

Manhart v. City of Los Angeles
[553 F.2d 581 (9th Cir. 1976), *cert. granted,* _____ U.S. _____ (1977) (No. 76–1810)]

Requirement to make women contribute larger amounts to a retirement plan than men violates Title VII

Analysis of the issue

The plaintiff in this action claimed that the employer's retirement plan which required female employees to contribute 15 percent from their wages more than their male counterparts, violated Title VII. The district court heard the defendant's argument that the reason women were required to make larger contributions to the plan was the fact that women, on the average, live longer than men, and therefore draw more in benefits from the plan after retiring. The court did not agree with this reasoning stating that the simple fact that women as a group may outlive men as a group does not necessarily mean that an individual woman will live longer. The retirement plan that requires women as individuals to contribute more to the plan because of their sex, does in fact discriminate against women on the basis of sex. The court also dismissed the application of the bona fide occupational qualification exception to Title VII on the grounds that the Department of Water and Power could operate normally and provide the city of Los Angeles with the same amount of water and power even if required to charge its male and female employees the same amount in contributions to the retirement plan. Finally, the court deemed the sexually disparate contribution schedule as violative of the Equal Pay Act. The Equal Pay Act permits wage differentials only when the differential is based on criteria other than sex; and legislative history of the Equal Pay Act indicates that coverage extends to pension plans and other actuarily based employee programs. Ruling for the plaintiff, the court ordered the defendant to refund the amount of overcharge to affected employees and to refrain from operating a pension plan that requires female employees to make larger contributions than males.

Full text of opinion

DUNIWAY, Circuit Judge:—The question presented in this case is whether a retirement plan which requires women employees to contribute from their wages 15% more than similarly situated male employees because of the longer average life expectancy of women violates the Civil Rights Act of 1964, Title VII, as amended by the Equal Employment Opportunity Act of 1972, 42 U.S.C. § 2000e-2. The district court held that the plan violated Title VII, enjoined the employer from charging the higher contribution rate against women, and awarded a refund of all excess contributions made on or after April 5, 1972. *Manhart v. City of Los Angeles, Department of Water and Power,* C.D.Cal., 1975, 387 F.Supp. 980.

This is a class action brought by women employees and retirees of the City of Los Angeles, Department of Water and Power [hereinafter "Department"]. The defendants are the Department, the members of the Board of Commissioners of the Department, the members of the Board of Administration of the Department's Employees' Retirement, Disability, and Death Benefit Insurance Plan, the Department's chief accounting officer, and the Department's general manager.

All employees of the Department are required to participate in the established retirement plan which is funded and managed solely within the Department. Each employee must make a monthly contribution to the retirement plan, and the Department matches that contribution 110%. These funds are deposited with the city treasurer but are kept separate and apart from all other monies of the city. The chief accounting employee of the Department is the only person authorized to withdraw money from the retirement account.

The aspect of this program which gives rise to this case is that women employees are required to contribute approximately 15% more than men employees who are identically situated. The Department's justification is that because women get the same monthly benefits upon retiring and because, on the average, they live approximately five years longer, they must, as a group, contribute more.

In June of 1973, the International Brotherhood of Electrical Workers, Local #18, representing the named plaintiffs, filed a charge with the Equal Employment Opportunity Commission [EEOC] alleging that the higher contribution requirement for women was sex discrimination in violation of the Civil Rights Acts of 1871 and 1964. The United States Department of Justice issued a Notice of Right to Sue letter in September of 1973, and this action was filed during that same month.

In their second amended complaint, filed on July 18, 1974, the plaintiffs stated four separate claims for relief, each of which, however, was based upon the same set of facts. The first claim was based upon Title VII, the second upon the Civil Rights Act of 1871, 42 U.S.C. § 1983, the third upon the Fourteenth Amendment to the Constitution, and the fourth, a pendent claim, upon Article 1, §§ 1 and 21, of the Constitution of California.

The plaintiffs' first amended complaint had also asserted claims resting on the same four theories, but had not set them up as separate claims. On March 26, 1974, the court granted in part and denied in part the defendants' motion to dismiss. It granted the motion of the Department, the two boards, and their members in their capacities as members, to dismiss the claim that was based upon 42 U.S.C. § 1983, on the ground that the Department and the Board are not "persons" within the meaning of that section. It denied the motion of the Board members in their individual capacities to dismiss the § 1983 claim, holding that they are "persons," and that they are not immune from suit under § 1983. It granted the motion of all defendants to dismiss the § 1983 claim insofar as any of it accrued more than three years before the action was filed on September 26, 1973. It denied the motion to dismiss the Title VII claim, except that it granted the motion as to any claim arising before March 24, 1972. It dismissed the claim under the California Constitution. It did not rule on the claim under the Fourteenth Amendment. And it allowed 20 days for the filing of a second amended complaint. After the second amended complaint was filed, no motion was made by any of the defendants to strike or otherwise dispose of those of the allegations that were inconsistent with the court's order of March 26, 1974.

On June 20, 1975, the court granted the plaintiffs' motion for summary judgment, holding that the plan violated Title VII. On the same day it entered a judgment, declaring that the plan, insofar as it requires larger contributions from female employees than from their male counterparts, violates Title VII, and specifically § 703(a)(1) (42 U.S.C. § 2000e-2(a)). The judgment also enjoins requiring larger contributions from females and orders that the Department refund the excess contributions collected on and after April 5, 1972, plus interest at 7%, and that defendants pay counsel for plaintiffs' reasonable attorneys' fees. The judgment says nothing about the claims based on § 1983, the Fourteenth Amendment or the California Constitution.

On July 7, 1975, the defendants appealed from the judgment. This appeal is our No. 75-2729. On July 11, 1975, the plaintiffs appealed from "that portion of the judgment . . . which denies relief to the plaintiffs based on the causes of action and defendants dismissed by the Court in its Order Granting and Denying in Part Defendants' Motion to Dismiss, entered on or about March 26, 1974." This appeal is our No. 75-2807. On July 17, the district judge denied a motion by the defendants for a stay of the judgment. They appealed on July 30, 1975. This is our No. 75-2905. We later entered an order staying the judgment pending appeal, insofar as it requires the refund of contributions.

After oral argument before us, and in response to an inquiry from the bench, counsel for plaintiffs stipulated, and we ordered, that the plaintiffs "have heretofore abandoned all claims under 42 U.S.C. § 1983 against individual officials in their individual capacities."

The judgment of June 20, 1975, embodies an injunction against requiring larger contributions from women than from men, and requiring restitution of excess contributions previously paid. As an injunction, it is appealable under 28 U.S.C. § 1292(a)(1). It is not appealable as a final judgment under 28 U.S.C. § 1291. It does not dispose of any claim except the claim under Title VII. It runs only against the defendants, the Department, the two Boards, and their members as such, but not the defendant members individually. It says nothing about the claims or defendants dismissed in the district court's order of March 26, 1974. There is no "express determination that there is no just reason for delay" nor "express direction for the entry of judgment." (F.R.Civ.P. 54(b)).

We have no jurisdiction of this appeal. The judgment does not do what the notice of appeal says that it does. The order of March 26, 1974, was interlocutory. It did not purport to determine any issue finally. It permitted amendment of the complaint, and the amendment restated, separately, all of the claims asserted but commingled in the original complaint. The plaintiffs were entitled to amend as they did, and the defendants, to protect their record, should have called to the attention of the court the fact that the amended complaint did not fully comply with the court's order of March 26, 1974. The court was not required to reconsider that order but the defendants should have at least suggested that it embody in its subsequent judgment the decision that it made in its

March 26, 1974, order, thus disposing of the plaintiffs' claims. The claims remain pending because the judgment does not dispose of them.

It is no answer to say that the plaintiffs have voluntarily abandoned their claims under 42 U.S.C. § 1983 against the individual defendants. That abandonment binds the plaintiffs, but it does not affect their claims against the Department and its Boards and their members and employees in their official capacities under § 1983. Those claims are still pending in the district court and are not properly before us.

Because we have granted a stay, and because we are now affirming the judgment this appeal is moot.

The basis of the defendants' appeal is that, while requiring women to make larger contributions discriminates against women, there is a sound basis for the requirement, making it a discrimination based on longevity, not sex, and therefore not the kind of invidious discrimination that Title VII was intended to abolish. We disagree.

It is undisputed that the overriding purpose of Title VII is to require employers to treat each employee (or prospective employee) as an individual, and to make job related decisions about each employee on the basis of relevant individual characteristics, so that the employee's membership in a racial, ethnic, religious, or sexual group is irrelevant to the decisions. *See Griggs v. Duke Power Co.,* 1971, 401 U.S. 424, 436, 91 S.Ct. 849, 28 L.Ed.2d 158. To require every individual woman to contribute 15% more into the retirement fund than her male counterpart must contribute because women "on the average" live longer than men is just the kind of abstract generalization, applied to individual women because of their being women, which Title VII was designed to abolish. Not all women live longer than all men, yet each individual woman is required to contribute more, not because she as an individual will live longer, but because the members of her sexual group, on the average, live longer.

The Department argues, however, that Congress did not intend Title VII to prohibit drawing sexual distinctions when there is a statistically valid basis for doing so and when it is impossible to determine ahead of time when the individual employee is going to die. Thus it is argued that, because it is undisputed that women on the average do live longer, and because it is not possible to predict which women will actually live longer, Title VII ought to permit a higher contribution requirement for all women.

The problem raised by this case is unique. There have been two basic policies which have guided the courts in prior Title VII litigation: (1) the policy against attributing general group characteristics to each individual member of the group, the major thrust of the statute, and (2) the policy allowing relevant employment factors to be considered in differentiating among individuals. *See* Bernstein & Williams, *Title VII and the Problem of Sex Classifications in Pension Programs,* 74 Col.L.Rev. 1203, 1219 (1974). Heretofore, these two policies have not conflicted because in cases where general group characteristics were attributed to the individual employee, the relevant employment characteristics were capable of being individually measured. *Id.* at 1220. For example, in *Rosenfeld v. So. Pacific Co.,* 9 Cir., 1971, 444 F.2d 1219, we held that refusing to hire women for positions which entailed long hours and heavy physical effort violated Title VII because it entailed attributing the generally weaker physique of women to all women. An important basis of our decision was the fact that each individual woman applicant could actually be tested to see whether the relevant characteristic of strength was or was not in fact lacking.

This same consideration has been present in cases finding illegal: (1) the refusal to allow women to work overtime because of a belief that women as a group cannot work the long hours that men can, *Schaeffer v. San Diego Yellow Cabs, Inc.*, 9 Cir., 1972, 462 F.2d 1002; (2) the forced retirement of all women at an earlier age than men because of a belief that, on the average, men were capable of adequate performance longer than women, *Rosen v. Public Service Electric and Gas Co.*, 3 Cir., 1973, 477 F.2d 90; *Bartmess v. Drewrys U.S.A., Inc.*, 7 Cir., 1971, 444 F.2d 1186; (3) the termination of women employees who married because of a belief that, on the average, women could not work effectively and keep an adequate home life, *Sprogis v. United Air Lines, Inc.*, 7 Cir., 1971, 444 F.2d 1194; (4) the refusal to hire men as flight attendants because men, on the average, are said to be emotionally unsuited for that type of work, *Diaz v. Pan Am. World Airways, Inc.*, 5 Cir., 1971, 442 F.2d 385; (5) the refusal to hire women as telephone switchmen because of a belief that, on the average, women are incapable of working the long hours and doing the heavy lifting involved, *Weeks v. Southern Bell Telephone & Telegraph Co.*, 5 Cir., 1969, 408 F.2d 228; (6) requiring pregnant women to take mandatory leave after six months of pregnancy because, on the average, pregnant women are supposed to be incapable of working adequately after that point, *Berg v. Richmond Unified School Dist.*, 9 Cir., 1975, 528 F.2d 1208; (7) the refusal to hire women with preschool children because of a belief that family responsibilities would interfere with their job performance, *Phillips v. Martin Marietta Corp.*, 1971, 400 U.S. 542, 90 S.Ct. 496, 27 L.Ed.2d 613.

In the present case a relevant characteristic in determining how large an individual's retirement contribution should be is an informed prediction as to how long the person will live. But this characteristic, unlike those in the prior cases, is impossible to determine on an individual basis at the time when the contribution must be made. Thus, the policy of allowing relevant factors to be considered can be met only by allowing the group longevity statistics to be attributed to the individual members of the group. Yet this is exactly what the thrust of Title VII prohibits. We are therefore faced with the unique case in which the policy against per se discrimination directly conflicts with the policy of allowing relevant factors to be considered.

To support its argument that the actuarial distinctions are permitted under Title VII, the Department points to both the "bona fide occupational qualification exception" in 42 U.S.C. § 2000e-2(e) and the Bennett Amendment to Title VII, 42 U.S.C. § 2000e-2(h). Reconciliation of the conflicting policies noted above would be easy if Congress had specifically covered the kind of actuarial distinction that is before us in one of the exceptions which the Department cites. Both, however, are very general and have no language relating to actuarially determined discrimination, much less to pension plans.

Title 42 U.S.C. § 2000e-2(e) states that an employer may discriminate on the basis of religion, sex, or national origin "where religion, sex, or national origin is a bona fide occupational qualification reasonably necessary to the normal operation of that particular business or enterprise." EEOC, which is charged with administering and enforcing Title VII and whose interpretations of that statute are entitled to great deference, *Griggs v. Duke Power Co., supra,* 401 U.S. at 433-34, 91 S.Ct. 849; *Hutchison v. Lake Oswego School Dist. #7,* 9 Cir., 1975, 519 F.2d 961, 965, has issued guidelines directing that the BFOQ exception "be interpreted narrowly." 29 C.F.R. § 1604.2(a). In one of the few cases ruling on this exception, the Fifth Circuit has said:

the use of the word "necessary" in [§ 2000e-2(e)] requires that we apply a business *necessity* test, not a business *convenience* test. That is to say, discrimination based on sex is valid only when the *essence* of the business operation would be undermined . . . .
Diaz v. Pan Am. World Airways, Inc., supra, 442 F.2d at 388 [italics in original].

See also Weeks v. Southern Bell Telephone & Telegraph Co., supra, 408 F.2d at 232.

Discriminating against women in setting the amount of retirement contributions in no way affects the ability of the Department to provide water and power to the citizens of Los Angeles. Even if it could be said that the relevant business function here involved is that of providing employees with a stable and secure pension program there is no showing that sexual discrimination is necessary to protect the essence of that function. Actuarial distinctions arguably enhance the ability of the employer and the pension administrators to predict costs and benefits more accurately, but it cannot be said that providing a financially sound pension plan requires an actuarial classification based wholly on sex. This is especially true when distinctions based on many other longevity factors (*e.g.,* smoking and drinking habits, normality of weight, prior medical history, family longevity history) are not used in determining contribution levels. Thus, we find that the BFOQ exception does not permit the sexual classification challenged in this case.

In its original proposed form, 42 U.S.C. § 2000e-2(h) stated that discrimination among employees was permitted if based on a bona fide seniority or merit system, a system rewarding quantity or quality of production, different work locations, or professionally developed ability tests. Because the inclusion of "sex" as one of the categories of discrimination made illegal by Title VII was done by last minute amendment, received almost no attention, and produced no legislative history, *see* 110 Cong.Rec. 2720 (Rep. Green's remarks, Feb. 10, 1964); Bernstein & Williams, *supra,* 74 Col.L.Rev. at 1216-17, Senator Bennett became concerned that the Act might inadvertently conflict with the Equal Pay Act of 1963, which had received careful attention the year before. Therefore, he proposed, and Congress approved, an amendment to § 2000e-2(h), which reads:

It shall not be an unlawful employment practice under this subchapter for any employer to differentiate upon the basis of sex in determining the amount of the wages or compensation paid or to be paid to employees of such employer if such differentiation is authorized by the provisions of section 206(d) of Title 29 [the Equal Pay Act].

Title 29 U.S.C. § 206(d)(1), which was thus incorporated into the Civil Rights Act of 1964 by the Bennett Amendment, says that it shall be unlawful to discriminate on the basis of sex in paying wages:

except where such payment is made pursuant to (i) a seniority system; (ii) a merit system; (iii) a system which measures earnings by quantity or quality of production; or (iv) a differential based on any other factor other than sex.

It is exception iv which the Department says permits the kind of actuarially based discrimination that is in question here. However, it does not seem reasonable to us to say that an actuarial distinction based entirely on sex is "based on any other factor other than sex." Sex is exactly what it is based on.

Additionally, the legislative history of the Equal Pay Act indicates that the general language of § 206(d)(1) was not intended to exempt pension plans, or any actuarially based employee program, from its coverage. The House Committee on Education and Labor, which reported out the Equal Pay Act, commented on the exceptions as follows:

> Three specific exceptions and one broad general exception are also listed. It is the intent of this committee that any discrimination based upon any of these exceptions shall be exempted from the operation of this statute. As it is impossible to list each and every exception, the broad general exclusion has been also included. Thus, among other things, shift differentials, restrictions on or differences based on time of day worked, hours of work, lifting or moving heavy objects, differences based on experience, training, or ability would also be excluded. It also recognizes certain special circumstances, such as "red circle rates." This term is borrowed from War Labor Board parlance and describes certain unusual, higher than normal wage rates which are maintained for many valid reasons. For instance, it is not uncommon for an employer who must reduce help in a skilled job to transfer employees to other less demanding jobs but to continue to pay them a premium rate in order to have them available when they are again needed for their former jobs.
>
> House Report #309 to accompany H.R. 6060, May 20, 1963, Committee on Labor and Education, reprinted in 1963 *U.S. Code Cong. & Admin. News* pp. 687, 689 (88th Cong., 1st sess.).

This is the only legislative history coming from the House concerning the exceptions upon which the Department relies. It seems clear that, at least in the House, exception iv was seen only as a catch-all category which would permit distinctions similar to those based on seniority, merit, or production but which do not literally fall into any of those categories, and not a disguised grant of legitimacy for pension plan discrimination based on sex.

The report of the Senate Committee on Labor and Public Welfare indicates that, unlike the House committee, the Senate committee did specifically consider how pension and insurance plans would fit into the scheme of the Equal Pay Act. It commented:

> Furthermore, questions can legitimately be raised as to the accuracy of defining such costs as pension and welfare payments as related to sex. It has been pointed out that the higher susceptibility of men to disabling injury can result in a greater cost to the employer, and that these figures as to health and welfare costs can only be applied plant-wide. It may be that it is more expensive to hire women in one department but it is more expensive to hire men in another, and overall cost figures may demonstrate conclusively that the employer has made a sound decision to hire women and pay them on an equal basis.
>
> It is the intention of the committee that where it can be shown that, on the basis of all of the elements of the employment costs of both men and women, an employer will be economically penalized by the elimination of a wage differential, the Secretary can permit an exception similar to those he can permit for a bona fide seniority system or other exception mentioned above.

Senate Report #176 to accompany S. 1409, May 13, 1963, Committee on Labor and Public Welfare, at p. 4 (88th Cong., 1st sess.).

This seems to indicate that the Senate had a broader view of exception iv than did the House in that, when an employer can demonstrate that he incurs significant costs because of employing a particular sex, exception iv would allow the Secretary of Labor, through the Wage-Hour Administrator, to grant an exception from the provisions of the Act.

However, in this case there is nothing in the record to show, and the Department does not claim, that it requires higher contributions from women because it would be economically penalized if it did not; it requires the higher contributions only because it believes that the pension fund itself will thereby be better funded and easier to administer. Thus, whatever the Senate committee had in mind about the Equal Pay Act, it would not, when grafted onto the provisions of Title VII, be the kind of broad exception to the rule against per se discrimination which the Department needs to justify the contribution rate differential here involved. Neither the clear language of the statute, § 206(d)(1), nor the legislative history supports the Department's position.

Nonetheless, the Department points to a dialogue between Senator Humphrey, the floor manager of the 1964 Civil Rights Act, and Senator Randolph, which occurred during the floor debate on the 1964 Act (not the Equal Pay Act) and Title VII.

SEN. RANDOLPH: Mr. President, I wish to ask of the Senator from Minnesota [Mr. Humphrey] who is the effective manager of the pending bill, a clarifying question on the provisions of Title VII. I have in mind that the social security system, in certain respects, treats men and women differently. For example, widows' benefits are paid automatically; but a widower qualifies only if he is disabled or if he was actually supported by his deceased wife. Also, the wife of a retired employee entitled to social security receives an additional old age benefit; but the husband of such an employee does not. These differences in treatment as I recall, are of long standing. Am I correct, I ask the Senator from Minnesota, in assuming that similar differences of treatment in industrial benefit plans, including earlier retirement options for women, may continue in operation under this bill, if it becomes law?

SEN. HUMPHREY: Yes. That point was made unmistakably clear earlier today by the adoption of the Bennett amendment; so there can be no doubt about it.

110 Cong. Rec. 13663-64, June 12, 1964.

Although this does seem to give support to the Department's position, we do not find it to be persuasive legislative history. The discussion occurred hours after passage of the Bennett Amendment and cannot be said to be part of the legislative history of that amendment. The Department claims that although the statement was made after the Bennett Amendment was adopted, it was still made before the Senate voted on the entire Civil Rights Act. Thus, it claims that Senator Randolph and others who may have wanted to preserve such distinctions were misled into not offering a further amendment for that purpose. This argument might have some merit were it not for the fact that the same Congress (the 88th) passed both the Civil Rights Act and the Equal Pay Act, and it seems unlikely that Senator Humphrey's erroneous interpretation of the latter misled many, if any, senators. It certainly misled no members of the House. So far as appears, members of the House never heard of it.

We note, too, that every case that has considered whether sex-based early retirement options violate Title VII has held that they do, although it does not appear that the colloquy between Senators Randolph and Humphrey was called to the attention of the courts. *See Chastang v. Flynn and Emrich Co.*, 4 Cir., 1976, 541 F.2d 1040 (1976); *Rosen v. Public Service Electric & Gas Co.*, *supra*; *Bartmess v. Drewrys U.S.A., Inc.*, *supra*; *Fitzpatrick v. Bitzer*, D.Conn., 1974, 390 F.Supp. 278, 287-88, *aff'd*, 2 Cir., 1975, 519 F.2d 559, *rev'd on other grounds*, 1976, 427 U.S. 445, 96 S.Ct. 2666, 49 L.Ed.2d 614. *See also Peters v. Missouri Pacific R. Co.*, 5 Cir., 1973, 483 F.2d 490, 492, n. 3.

As we have noted, Senator Humphrey's remark reflects an erroneous interpretation of the Equal Pay Act. Because all that the Bennett Amendment did was to incorporate the exemptions of the Equal Pay Act into Title VII, it is questionable whether the Senator's statement, made during the debates on the incorporating statute, would be significant when it erroneously interprets the incorporated statute.

The Department cites as additional authority interpretations of the Equal Pay Act by the Administrator of the Wage and Hour Division of the Department of Labor. As the official charged with enforcing and interpreting the Equal Pay Act, his interpretations of that Act are entitled to great deference. *Udall v. Talman*, 1965, 380 U.S. 1, 85 S.Ct. 792, 13 L.Ed.2d 616. However, the interpretation relied on by the Department, appearing at 29 C.F.R. § 800.116(d), merely states that in providing benefit plans for employees through outside insurers an employer does not violate the Equal Pay Act if either the amount contributed by the employer for each employee is the same and resulting benefits are different or if the amount of the benefit is the same while the employer contributions differ. While this reflects the Wage-Hour Administrator's general thinking, it does not deal directly with our case of an employer requiring greater pension plan contributions from women employees when the plan is funded and administered by the employer and its employees.

We note, too, that to the extent that the Wage-Hour Administrator's interpretation does deal with the present case, his interpretation conflicts with that of EEOC, which administers Title VII and whose interpretations of Title VII must be given great deference. Therefore, the EEOC interpretations of the Bennett Amendment are worthy of more deference than are those of the Wage-Hour Administrator relating to the Equal Pay Act. The EEOC regulation, 29 C.F.R. § 1604.9(e & f), makes it a violation of Title VII where a benefit plan provides unequal benefits to employees even if employer contributions are equal. However, like the Wage-Hour Administrator's, these regulations do not squarely cover the present case. Thus, the Department's reliance on administrative interpretation is misplaced.

Our opinion of the effect of Title VII in this case is reinforced by the fact that following the passage of Title VII Congress did expressly exempt actuarially based pension and retirement funds from the provisions of the Age Discrimination Act of 1967, 29 U.S.C. § 623(f)(2). In fact, during deliberations on the 1964 Civil Rights Act, Senator Smathers moved to add "age" as one of the types of discrimination made illegal by Title VII, but the amendment was defeated in part because of a concern that inclusion of "age" as a Title VII protected category might have "tremendous implications" on industrial group insurance and pensions.

Equal Employment Opportunity Commission, Legislative History of Titles VII and IX of Civil Rights Act of 1964, at 3174 (1968). This tends to indicate that Congress did foresee that actuarially based plans would fall under the provisions of Title VII, and that it felt that age discrimination, but not sex discrimination, on such a basis was proper. Thus, by not adding "age" to Title VII in 1964 and not making a pension plan exception to its terms for "sex," and by later prohibiting age discrimination in a separate bill which does make a pension plan exception to its terms for age, Congress gave a strong indication that it did intend to place sex discrimination in pension and retirement plans, even when based on actuarially sound tables, within the type of discrimination forbidden by Title VII.

We emphasize that our holding rests on the clear policy behind Title VII of requiring that each employee be treated as an individual. Setting retirement contribution rates solely on the basis of sex is a failure to treat each employee as an individual; it treats each employee only as a member of one sex. We do not pass judgment on the legality of a plan which determines contribution rates based on a significant number of actuarially determined characteristics, one of which is sex. Our holding is limited to the proposition that when sex is singled out as the only, or as a predominant, factor, the employee is being treated in the manner which Title VII forbids.

One district court case has dealt with a situation very similar to ours. In *Henderson v. Oregon*, D.Or., 1975, 405 F.Supp. 1271, the court relied heavily on the lower court decision in the present case in holding a scheme similar to that involved here illegal under Title VII.

Our holding agrees with the only administrative ruling dealing with the exact question before us, one made by the EEOC. EEOC Dec. #75-146, Jan. 13, 1975, 2 *CCH Employment Practices* 4190, ¶ 6447. Relying in part on its earlier interpretation, noted *supra*, the Commission held:

An inescapable corollary to this principle is that an employer may not require a higher contribution from members of one sex where benefits to members of both sexes are the same.

[This] is based upon the fundamental Title VII precept that generalizations relating to sex, race, religion, and national original cannot be permitted to influence the terms and conditions of an *individual's* employment, even where the generalizations are statistically valid.

The Department finally argues that even if the higher contribution required of women violates Title VII, it would be unfair to refund to the plaintiffs the amounts that they contributed in excess of the amounts that similarly situated male employees contributed. The Department says that it was acting in good faith in that it believed that state law requiring that retirement plans be run on a "sound actuarial basis" (Cal.Gov't Code § 45342) mandated the use of sex-based actuarial tables, and that paying these contributions back to the women employees would leave the retirement plan underfunded.

The rule that we have adopted relating to monetary awards for past violations of Title VII is stated in *Schaeffer v. San Diego Yellow Cabs, Inc.*, 9 Cir., 1972, 462 F.2d 1002.

In the case of damages of this nature, a court must balance the various equities between the parties and decide upon a result which is consistent with the purposes of the Equal Employment Opportunities Act, and the fundamental concepts of fairness. *Id.* at 1006.

The defendant in *Schaeffer* argued that in denying women overtime work it had relied in good faith on a state statute requiring that women not work more than eight hours a day, and that therefore it was unfair to make it pay damages for an unwitting violation. We rejected that defense with the following comment:

> Rather than drawing any hard and fast rule concerning the defense of good faith reliance on a state statute, we believe that in each case the merits of the plaintiff's claim and the public policy behind it must be balanced against the hardship on a good faith employer. *Id.* at 1007.

Applying this test to the case at bar, we find that the district court did not abuse its discretion in awarding plaintiffs a refund of their excess contributions.

In the first place, the state statute requiring that such plans be administered on a sound actuarial basis by no means requires that the Department use sex-based, and only sex-based, distinctions. In *Schaeffer*, where we found a back pay award proper, the statute prohibiting women from working more than eight hours a day placed a much greater compulsion on the employer to refuse women overtime work than the statute in the present case placed on the Department to require higher retirement contributions.

Second, *Schaeffer* was a case where back pay was awarded to women for work that they did not perform but which they had sought. The plaintiffs did not earn the award; they were merely denied the opportunity to earn it. This case involves *restitution*, a situation where the plaintiffs actually earned the amount in question, but then had it taken from them in violation of Title VII. It is one of the primary purposes of Title VII to "make persons whole for injuries suffered on account of unlawful employment discrimination." *Albemarle Paper Co. v. Moody*, 1975, 422 U.S. 405, 418, 95 S.Ct. 2362, 2372, 45 L.Ed.2d 280. In light of this purpose we find plaintiffs' claim to recover money rightfully theirs to be very compelling.

In contrast to the plaintiffs' compelling claim, we find the Department's "good faith" defense to be less than compelling. The Supreme Court has recently commented on this "good faith" defense as follows:

> But, under Title VII, the mere absence of bad faith simply opens the door to equity; it does not depress the scales in the employer's favor. If backpay were awardable only upon a showing of bad faith, the remedy would become a punishment for moral turpitude, rather than a compensation for workers' injuries. This would read the "make whole" purpose right out of Title VII, for a worker's injury is no less real simply because his employer did not inflict it in "bad faith." *Albemarle Paper Co. v. Moody, supra*, 422 U.S. at 422, 95 S.Ct. at 2374.

The impact of returning the excess contributions to the plaintiffs in this case is far from oppressive. The amount involved is only 15% of the contributions made by a minority of the Department's employees for the 33-month period from April 5, 1972, to December 31, 1974. This might leave the plan somewhat under-funded, but a number of solutions to that problem are readily available. Benefits could be lowered. Current contributions from all employees could be increased. The Department could raise its matching percentage on current contributions, or it could make a lump sum payment into the fund to offset the reimbursements. However, whatever the adjustments that would have to be made, we do not find that the burden on the pension plan or the Department is sufficient to offset the compelling claim of the plaintiffs to recover the money which they were wrongfully required to contribute. *See also Rosen v. Public Service Electric and Gas Co., supra,* 477 F.2d at 95-96.

In No. 75-2729, the judgment is affirmed.

In No. 75-2807, the appeal is dismissed.

In No. 75-2905, the appeal is dismissed as moot. The stay heretofore granted by this court will expire when the mandate issues.

On petition for rehearing

Appellants petition for a rehearing and suggest a rehearing *in banc.* Their principal reliance is upon the decision of the Supreme Court in *General Electric Co. v. Gilbert,* 1976, 429 U.S. 125, 97 S.Ct. 401, 50 L.Ed.2d 343, which was decided on December 7, 1976, just two weeks after our decision was filed on November 23, 1976. We conclude that the *General Electric* case does not require a change in our judgment, for several reasons.

First, in that case, as in *Geduldig v. Aiello,* 1974, 417 U.S. 484, 94 S.Ct. 2485, 41 L.Ed.2d 256, upon which the Court primarily relied, the facts were different from the facts in the case at bar. In each of those cases, a program of disability insurance was involved, and in each pregnancy was excluded as a disability. The Court held that the exclusion was not a discrimination based upon gender as such. It pointed out that the exclusion of pregnancy as a disability "divides potential recipients [of benefits] into two groups—pregnant women and non-pregnant persons. While the first group is exclusively female, the second includes members of both sexes." *General Electric, supra,* 429 U.S. at 135, 97 S.Ct. at 407, quoting from *Geduldig, supra,* 417 U.S. at 496-97, n. 20, 94 S.Ct. 2485. Thus, said the Court, the exclusion of pregnancy "was not in itself discrimination based on sex," 429 U.S. 125, at 135, 97 S.Ct. 401, at 407.

The same cannot be said of the pension plan of the Department in the case at bar. A greater amount is deducted from the wages of every woman employee than from the wages of every man employee whose rate of pay is the same. How can it possibly be said that this discrimination is not based on sex? It is based upon a presumed characteristic of women as a whole, longevity, and it disregards every other factor that is known to affect longevity. The higher contribution is required specifically and only from women as distinguished from men. To say that the difference is not based on sex is to play with words.

In addition, as the Court pointed out in *General Electric,* under the disability programs in that case and in *Geduldig,* "The 'package' going to relevant identifiable groups . . . —male and female employees—covers exactly the same categories of risk, and is facially nondiscriminatory in the sense that '[t]here is no risk from which men are protected and women are not. Likewise, there is no risk from which women are protected and men are not.' *Geduldig,* 417 U.S. at 496-97, 94 S.Ct. at 2492" *General Electric,* 429 U.S. 125, p. 138, 97 S.Ct. 401, p. 409. "[G]ender-based discrimination does not result simply because an employer's disability benefits plan is less than all inclusive." *Id.* at 138, 97 S.Ct. at 409 (footnote omitted).

The pension plan in the case at bar is different. The monthly benefit is the same for men and for women, but the cost to women is higher than the cost to men, and this is solely because they are women. Thus the plan is facially discriminatory because, while the plan is all inclusive as to retirement benefits, it is discriminatory, on the basis of sex alone, as to costs to the employees.

Finally the Court's opinion in *General Electric* requires that we reconsider our analysis of the legislative history of the Bennett Amendment. However, upon that reconsideration, we conclude that a different result is not required in this case. Appellants stress the Court's reliance, in *General Electric,* upon the colloquy between Senators Humphrey and Randolph, discussed in *General Electric* at 429 U.S. 125, at 144, 97 S.Ct. 401 at 412, and in our opinion at 589-590. We did not find it to be persuasive legislative history; the Supreme Court did find it persuasive. We are, of course, bound by that conclusion, but we do not think that it follows that the judgment in this case is erroneous.

In *General Electric,* the Court relied also, and, we think, more heavily, on rulings of the Wage and Hour Administrator construing the Equal Pay Act, and on the fact that EEOC rulings were inconsistent with each other as well as with the rulings of the Administrator (429 U.S. 125, at 142-145, 97 S.Ct. 401 at 411-412). In our case, there are no such inconsistencies.

In his brief as amicus curiae in this case, the Secretary of Labor points out that he (or the Administrator acting for him) "has never approved a practice of requiring women employees to make contributions to a pension plan which are larger than those required of similarly situated men employees." The rulings of the Secretary on which the Department relies do not deal with a requirement that female employees must make greater contributions to the plan than male employees, a requirement which diminishes the current available or "take home" wages of women, as compared to those of men.

In his June 18, 1964 opinion letter, the Administrator disapproved of a wage differential between men and women based upon alleged higher costs of employing women, a part of those costs being for pensions. In an Interpretive Bulletin issued February 11, 1966 (3 F.R. 2657, 29 C.F.R. § 800.151), the Administrator said:

A wage differential based on claimed differences between the average cost of employing the employer's women workers as a group and the average cost of employing the men workers as a group does not qualify as a differential based on any "factor other than sex," and would result in a violation of the equal pay provisions, if the equal pay standard otherwise applies. To group employees solely on the basis of sex for purposes of comparison of costs necessarily rests on the assumption that the sex factor alone may justify the wage differential—an assumption plainly contrary to the terms and purposes of the Equal Pay Act. Wage differentials so based would serve only to perpetuate and promote the very discrimination at which the Act is directed, because in any grouping by sex of the employees to which the cost data relates, the group cost experience is necessarily assessed against an individual of one sex without regard to whether it costs an employer more or less to employ such individual than a particular individual of the opposite sex under similar working conditions in jobs requiring equal skill, effort, and responsibility.

There are no rulings of the Secretary or Administrator inconsistent with this. The one which the Department. cites, issued September 9, 1965, and amended May 6, 1966, 30 F.R. 11504 and 31 F.R. 6770, 29 C.F.R. § 800.116(d) deals with employer contributions, not compulsory employee contributions which are here involved, and which, under 29 C.F.R. § 800.151 cannot be unequal.

No ruling of EEOC conflicts with 29 C.F.R. § 800.151. Nor has EEOC taken inconsistent positions in relation to the problem before us. Its position is stated in 29 C.F.R. § 1604.9, issued April 5, 1972, 37 F.R. 6836, and in EEOC Dec. #75-146 of Jan. 13, 1975, 2 *CCH Employment Practices* 4190, ¶ 6447, both discussed in our opinion. We know of no prior inconsistent rulings. Thus this case is quite unlike *General Electric,* where there was conflict between EEOC rulings and between rulings of EEOC and those of the Secretary of Labor. Here, the administrative rulings, as they relate to the problem before us, are consistent and support the result that we have reached.

The petition for a rehearing is denied. The suggestion of a rehearing *in banc* has been transmitted to all judges of the court, and no judge has requested a vote on the suggestion. Rule 35(b) F.R.App.P. The suggestion of a rehearing *in banc* is rejected.

KILKENNY, Circuit Judge, dissenting:

I share the views of the majority on the jurisdictional issues, but have serious reservations with respect to the manner in which the majority disposes of the appellants' claims in No. 75-2729. In my opinion, they should have been allowed to prove their case.

I am convinced that the legal principles enunciated in *General Electric Co. v. Gilbert,* 429 U.S. 125, 97 S.Ct. 401, 50 L.Ed.2d 343 (1976), are here controlling and that the district court erred in granting a summary judgment against the appellants. At a minimum, the court should have conducted a trial on the issue of whether the appellants' retirement plan was justified on the basis of recognized actuarial tables showing the difference in longevity between males and females. As it now stands, the lower court here made the same mistake as the district court in *General Electric* in its refusal to consider any cost differential defense. As stated by the Supreme Court:

"The District Court was wrong in assuming, as it did, 375 F.Supp., at 383, that Title VII's ban on employment discrimination necessarily means that 'greater economic benefit[s]' must be required to be paid to one sex or the other because of their differing roles in 'the scheme of human existence.' " *General Electric* at 139, 97 S.Ct. at 410, n. 17.

The uncontroverted affidavits in the record before the district court and now before us show clearly that women live substantially longer than men and that the higher female contribution [approximately 15% more than male employees] is fully justified on an actuarial basis. These affidavits further show that this plan, like all annuity plans, is based upon the life expectancy of its beneficiaries, and that mortality tables in use throughout the western commercial world separate male mortality rates from female mortality rates. Moreover, one affiant states that the plan before us was adopted as a result of his 1972 study of the mortality rates of the appellants' employees. The plan follows the "1951 Group Annuity Mortality Table" published in the *Transactions of the Society of Actuaries.*

Consistent with all available studies and plans, this particular plan uses separate mortality tables for men and women and was used to determine the total monies that had to be set aside for the lifetime retirement allowances of employees. Many other relevant facts are set forth in these affidavits, including the undisputed statement that no tables have as yet been developed which measure life expectancy on a *unisex* basis, as required by the majority. Furthermore, these affidavits attest to the fact that unisex mortality tables, if developed, could lead to a result which adversely affects the financial integrity of annuity or pension plans such as here before us.

Against this background, the majority purports to distinguish *General Electric*. From the general finding in *General Electric* that the exclusion of pregnancy was not in itself discrimination based upon sex, it is apparent to me that the Supreme Court has rejected the broad doctrines espoused by the majority. Moreover, neither *Craig v. Boren*, 429 U.S. 190, 97 S.CT. 451, 50 L.Ed.2d 397 (1976), nor *Califano v. Goldfarb*, —— U.S. ——, 97 S.Ct. 1021, 51 L.Ed.2d 270 (1977), detract from what is said in *General Electric*. To summarily conclude, like the majority, that "[t]o say that the difference [here] is not based on sex is to play with words . . . ." is simply an inadequate response to the issues presented. I am of the impression that the majority, rather than the appellants, is playing with words. The appellants' claim deserves more consideration than this conclusory statement.

The majority similarly glosses over the language in *General Electric* regarding the *effect* of the exclusion of pregnancy. The Court recognized that a proper showing of "gender-based effects" may be sufficient to establish a *prima facie* case under Title VII, but it was not there present, and it is not here present. This is made manifest by a comparison of the circumstances here present with those of *General Electric*. As stated in *General Electric*:

". . . As in *Geduldig, supra,* [417 U.S. 484, 94 S.Ct. 2485, 41 L.Ed.2d 256 (1974)] *we start from the indisputable baseline that '[t]he fiscal and actuarial benefits of the program . . . accrue to members of both sexes,'* 417 U.S., at 497 n. 20, [94 S.Ct. at 2492]. We need not disturb the findings of the District Court to note that there is neither a finding, nor was there any evidence which would support a finding, that the financial benefits of the Plan *'worked to discriminate against any definable group or class in terms of the aggregate risk protection derived by that group or class from the program,' id.,* at 496 [, 94 S.Ct., at 2492]. The Plan, in effect (and for all that appears), is nothing more than an insurance package, which covers some risks, but excludes others, see *id.,* at 494, 496-497, [94 S.Ct. at 2491-2492]. The 'package' going to relevant identifiable groups we are presently concerned with— General Electric's male and female employees—covers exactly the same categories of risk, *and is facially nondiscriminatory in the sense that '[t]here is no risk from which men are protected and women are not. Likewise, there is no risk from which women are protected and men are not.' Geduldig,* 417 U.S., at 496-497, [94 S.Ct., at 2492]. *As there is no proof that the package is in fact worth more to men than to women, it is impossible to find any gender-based discriminatory effect in this scheme simply because women disabled as a result of pregnancy do not receive benefits; that is to say, gender-based discrimination does not result simply because an employer's disability benefits plan is less than all inclusive.* For all that appears, pregnancy-related disabilities constitute an *additional* risk, unique to women, and the failure to compensate them for this risk does not destroy the presumed parity of the benefits, accruing to men and women alike, which results from the facially evenhanded *inclusion* of risks. To hold otherwise would endanger the common-sense notion that an employer who has no disability benefits program at all does not violate Title VII even though the 'underinclusion' of risks impacts, as a result of pregnancy-related disabilities, more heavily upon one gender than upon the other. Just as there is no facial gender-based discrimination in that case, so, too, there is none here." *General Electric* at 138-140, 97 S.Ct. at 409-410. [Emphasis Added.] [Footnotes Omitted.]

Similarly, it is obvious here that the fiscal and actuarial benefits of the plan accrue to the members of both sexes. As in *General Electric*, the plan is facially nondiscriminatory to the extent that there is no risk for which one sex is covered and the other is not. Because of the additional contribution made by both the employer and the women employees, the aggregate risk protection for men and women is identical. As a consequence of objectively identifiable characteristics [reflected in actuarial statistics], this plan impacts more heavily upon women than men. [But women live longer than men and ultimately recover as much if not more.] This was also the case in *General Electric* and the Court there refused to find a Title VII violation. Its reasoning is made abundantly clear in Footnote 17, which reads:

"Absent proof of different values, the cost to 'insure' against the risks is, in essence, nothing more than extra compensation to the employees, in the form of fringe benefits. If the employer were to remove the insurance fringe benefits and, instead, increase wages by an amount equal to the cost of the 'insurance,' there would clearly be no gender-based discrimination, even though a female employee who wished to purchase disability insurance that covered all risks would have to pay more than would a male employee who purchased identical disability insurance, due to the fact that her insurance had to cover the 'extra' disabilities due to pregnancy. While respondents seem to acknowledge that the failure to provide any benefit plan at all would not constitute sex-based discrimination in violation of Title VII, see note 18, *infra,* they illogically also suggest that the present scheme does violate Title VII because

'A female must spend her own money to buy a personal disability policy covering pregnancy disability if she wants to be fully insured against a period of disability without income, whereas a male without extra expenditure is fully insured by GE against every period of disability.' Supplemental Brief for Martha Gilbert *et al.* on Reargument, at 11. Yet, in both cases—the instant case and the case where there is no disability coverage at all—the ultimate result is that a woman who wished to be fully insured would have to pay an incremental amount over her male counterpart due solely to the possibility of pregnancy-related disabilities. Title VII's proscription on discrimination does not require, in either case, the employer to pay that incremental amount. . . ." *General Electric* at 139, 97 S.Ct. at 409-410.

In one respect, at least, the present facts are more compelling than those of *General Electric* because the employer here was actually paying more for each female employee than for each male employee. The just quoted language would have allowed the employer/appellants to pay the same amount for each, in which case each female employee would have received less insurance protection than each male employee. If no insurance at all was provided under the plan, each female employee, if she purchased outside insurance, would have to pay more than her male counterpart for the same amount of insurance. In either case, after *General Electric* it is illogical to argue that a Title VII violation would result.

Throughout its opinion, the majority substantially exaggerates the strength of its position. It suggests that the Supreme Court was more concerned with inconsistent administrative interpretations than it was with our original and erroneous view of the legislative history. To support its position, the majority finds that there are no such inconsistencies in the case before us. I disagree.

The Wage and Hour Administrator of the Department of Labor has promulgated a number of regulations. After *General Electric,* I question the vitality of the one quoted by the majority; one [29 CFR § 800.116(d)] noted by the Supreme Court in *General Electric* is more in point. This regulation states

"If employer contributions to a plan providing insurance or similar benefits to employees are equal for both men and women, no wage differential prohibited by the equal pay provisions will result from such payments, even though the benefits which accrue to the employees in question are greater for one sex than the other. The mere fact that the employer may make unequal contributions for employees of opposite sexes in such a situation will not, however, be considered to indicate that the employer's payments are in violation of section 6(d), if the resulting benefits are equal for such employees." [Emphasis Added.]

The majority's tortured views on the obvious breadth of *General Electric* become apparent in its writing around and failure to accept the Supreme Court's application of this regulation. This regulation, as I read it, contemplates the actuarial equivalent of the scheme before us. If employer contributions are equal for men and women, there is no statutory violation even though the resulting benefits are not equal as between men and women. The majority fails to appreciate the significance of this. In the context of pension plans, this rule makes sense only if it is read to impliedly authorize the funding of employee pension plans upon the basis of separate mortality tables. This regulatory justification for a plan with equal contributions and unequal benefits cannot be ignored in the variation before us.

In 1965, the EEOC promulgated regulations under which it agreed to follow the relevant interpretations of the Wage and Hour Division. 29 CFR § 1604.7(b) provided:

"Accordingly, the Commission will make applicable to equal pay complaints filed under Title VII the relevant interpretations of the Administrator, Wage and Hour Division, Department of Labor. These interpretations are found in 29 Code of Federal Regulations, Part 800.119–800.163. *Relevant opinions of the Administrator interpreting 'the equal pay for the equal work standard' will also be adopted by the Commission."* 30 F.R. 14928. [Emphasis Added.]

This regulation was maintained until the EEOC repealed it in 1972, 37 F.R. 6836. Now, 29 CFR § 1604.8 discusses the applicability of defenses raised under the Equal Pay Act [administered by the Wage and Hour Division] and states that the EEOC will no longer be bound by the interpretations of the Department of Labor, Wage and Hour Division. Moreover, the EEOC in 1972 for the first time revised its regulations to add 29 CFR § 1604.9(f), which provides that:

"It shall be an unlawful employment practice for an employer to have a pension or retirement plan which establishes different optional or compulsory retirement ages based on sex, *or which differentiates in benefits on the basis of sex. . . ."* [Emphasis Added.]

The majority entirely overlooks the fact that this is inconsistent with prior pronouncements of the EEOC and with the other administrative agencies, including the Department of Labor. Under these circumstances, the most recent EEOC interpretation is entitled to little if any weight. *See General Electric* 429 U.S. at 139-143, 97 S.Ct. at 410-411 where the Court refused to find a Title VII violation even though the employer's plan conflicted with the EEOC regulation. *See also Espinoza v. Farah Mfg. Co.*, 414 U.S. 86, 92-6, 94 S.Ct. 334, 38 L.Ed.2d 287 (1973). It is also significant that this most recent EEOC interpretation is in conflict with the legislative history of the Bennett Amendment.

One must sympathize with the plight of the appellants—a plan drawn up to comply with the regulations of the Wage and Hour Division will inevitably conflict with the recent regulations of the EEOC. This typifies the type of "no win" situation alluded to by the Supreme Court in *General Electric* [429 U.S. at 140, 97 S.Ct. at 410, n. 18], and reinforces my conclusion that the discrimination, if any, fostered by this plan is of a type which did not concern Congress when enacting Title VII. Moreover, the majority does not come to grips with the very serious ramifications of its decision. *Unless and until* unisex tables are developed, an employer, to comply with the EEOC regulations on equal benefits, may not charge any additional amounts to his female employees. In thus forcing the employer himself to cover the added amount necessary to assure equal benefits, this makes the employment of females economically unattractive, a result clearly at odds with the thrust of Title VII.

I would grant the petition for rehearing, set aside the judgment of the lower court and remand for a trial on the issue of whether the distinctions under the plan are mere pretexts designed to effect an invidious discrimination against the members of the female sex.

Final Action Taken By The Supreme Court, ____U.S. ____(1978)
(No. 76-1810)
On April 25, 1978 the Supreme Court upheld, for the most part, the rulings of the U.S. District Court and Ninth U.S. Circuit Court of Appeals, finding that the requirement of larger pension contributions by female employees violated Section 703(a)(1) of Title VII. Justice John Paul Stevens, writing for the majority stated "The differential was discriminatory in its 'treatment of a person in a manner which but for the person's sex would be different.' . . . Even though it is true that women as a class outlive men, that generalization cannot justify disqualifying an individual to whom it does not apply." However, the Supreme Court did not hold with the lower courts' rulings granting retroactive refunds of the extra payments made into the pension fund, the High Court believing the pension plan to be one that was established in good faith and that repayment in this class action would have a "devastating" effect financially on the employer. The Supreme Court vacated the appeals court decision, 553 F.2d 581, and remanded the case for a final settlement that is consistent with the High Court's ruling.

General Electric v. Gilbert
[429 U.S. 125 (1976)]

Sex discrimination on the basis of pregnancy

Analysis of the Issue

The plaintiffs, employees of the defendant, claim that their employee benefit plan which excludes disability benefits for pregnancy, a disability only possible among women, results in a less comprehensive program of employee compensation for females than for males, and therefore violates Title VII. The Supreme Court, in reversing an earlier Court of Appeals decision, reasoned that refusing pregnancy pay is not inconsistent with the law because the refusal is not based on sex but on a condition that is "significantly different from the typical covered disease or disability." Justice Rehnquist asserted for the majority that pregnancy is not a disease, but rather is often a "voluntarily undertaken and desired condition." In response to the less comprehensive plan argument, Rehnquist stated that "gender based discrimination does not result simply because an employee disability plan is less than all inclusive." This position was furthered by the Court's assertion that the plan did not protect men from any risk from which women were not protected.

Full text of opinion

Mr. Justice REHNQUIST delivered the opinion of the Court:—
Petitioner, General Electric Company, provides for all of its employees a disability plan which pays weekly nonoccupational sickness and accident benefits. Excluded from the plan's coverage, however, are disabilities arising from pregnancy. Respondents, on behalf of a class of women employees, brought this action seeking, *inter alia*, a declaration that this exclusion constitutes sex discrimination in violation of Title VII of the Civil Rights Act of 1964, as amended, 42 U.S.C. § 2000e. The District Court for the Eastern District of Virginia, following a trial on the merits, held that the exclusion of such pregnancy-related disability benefits from General Electric's employee disability plan violated Title VII, 375 F.Supp. 367. The Court of Appeals affirmed, 519 F.2d 661 and we granted certiorari, 423 U.S. 882. We now reverse.

As part of its total compensation package, General Electric provides nonoccupational sickness and accident benefits to all employees under its Weekly Sickness and Accident Insurance Plan (the "Plan") in an amount equal to 60% of an employee's normal straight time weekly earnings. These payments are paid to employees who become totally disabled as a result of a nonoccupational sickness or accident. Benefit payments normally start with the eighth day of an employee's total disability (although if an employee is earlier confined to a hospital as a bed patient, benefit payments will start immediately), and continue up to a maximum of 26 weeks for any one continuous period of disability or successive periods of disability due to the same or related causes.

The individual named respondents are present or former hourly paid production employees at General Electric's plant in Salem, Va. Each of these employees was pregnant during 1971 or 1972, while employed by General Electric, and each presented a claim to the company for disability benefits under the Plan to cover the period while absent from work as a result of the pregnancy. These claims were routinely denied on the ground that the Plan did not provide disability benefit payments for any absence due to pregnancy. Respondents thereafter filed individual charges with the EEOC alleging that the refusal of General Electric to pay disability benefits under the Plan for time lost due to pregnancy and childbirth discriminated against her because of sex. Upon waiting the requisite number of days, the instant action was commenced in the District Court. The complaint asserted a violation of Title VII. Damages were sought as well as an injunction directing General Electric to include pregnancy disabilities within the Plan on the same terms and conditions as other nonoccupational disabilities.

Following trial, the District Court made findings of fact, conclusions of law, and entered an order in which it determined that General Electric, by excluding pregnancy disabilities from the coverage of the Plan, had engaged in sex discrimination in violation of § 703(a)(1) of Title VII, 42 U.S.C. § 2000e-2(a)(1). The District Court found that normal pregnancy, while not necessarily either a "disease" or an "accident," was disabling for a period of six to eight weeks, that approximately "ten per cent of pregnancies are terminated by miscarriage, which is disabling," and that approximately 10% of pregnancies are complicated by diseases which may lead to additional disability. The District Court noted the evidence introduced during the trial, a good deal of it stipulated, concerning the relative cost to General Electric of providing benefits under the Plan to male and female employees, all of which indicated that, with pregnancy-related disabilities excluded, the cost of the Plan to General Electric per female employee was at least as high, if not substantially higher, than the cost per male employee.

The District Court found that the inclusion of pregnancy-related disabilities within the scope of the Plan would "increase G.E.'s [disability benefits plan] costs by an amount which, though large, is at this time undeterminable." 375 F.Supp., at 378. The District Court declined to find that the present actuarial value of the coverage was equal as between men and women, but went on to decide that even had it found economic equivalence, such a finding would not in any case have justified the exclusion of pregnancy-related disabilities from an otherwise comprehensive nonoccupational sickness and accident disability plan. Regardless of whether the cost of including such benefits might make the Plan more costly for women than for men, the District Court determined that "[i]f Title VII intends to sexually equalize employment opportunity, there must be this one exception to the cost differential defense." 375 F.Supp. at 383.

The ultimate conclusion of the District Court was that petitioner had discriminated on the basis of sex in the operation of its disability program in violation of Title VII, 375 F.Supp., at 385-386. An order was entered enjoining petitioner from continuing to exclude pregnancy-related disabilities from the coverage of the Plan, and providing for the future award of monetary relief to individual members of the class affected. Petitioner appealed to the Court of Appeals for the Fourth Circuit, and that court by a divided vote affirmed the judgment of the District Court.

Between the date on which the District Court's judgment was rendered and the time this case was decided by the Court of Appeals, we decided Geduldig v. Aiello, 417 U.S. 484 (1974), where we rejected a claim that a very similar disability program established under California law violated the Equal Protection Clause of the Fourteenth Amendment because that plan's exclusion of pregnancy disabilities represented sex discrimination. The majority of the Court of Appeals felt that Geduldig was not controlling because it arose under the Equal Protection Clause of the Fourteenth Amendment, and not under Title VII, 519 F.2d, at 666-667. The dissenting opinion disagreed with the majority as to the impact of Geduldig, 519 F.2d, at 668-669. We granted certiorari to consider this important issue in the construction of Title VII.

Section 703(a)(1) provides in relevant part that it shall be an unlawful employment practice for an employer

". . . to discriminate against any individual with respect to his compensation, terms, conditions, or privileges of employment, because of such individual's race, color, religion, sex, or national origin," 42 U.S.C. § 2000e-2.

While there is no necessary inference that Congress, in choosing this language, intended to incorporate into Title VII the concepts of discrimination which have evolved from court decisions construing the Equal Protection Clause of the Fourteenth Amendment, the similarities between the congressional language and some of those decisions surely indicates that the latter are a useful starting point in interpreting the former. Particularly in the case of defining the term "discrimination," which Congress has nowhere in Title VII defined, those cases afford an existing body of law analyzing and discussing that term in a legal context not wholly dissimilar from the concerns which Congress manifested in enacting Title VII. We think, therefore, that our decision in Geduldig v. Aiello, supra, dealing with a strikingly similar disability plan, is quite relevant in determining whether or not the pregnancy exclusion did discriminate on the basis of sex. In Geduldig, the disability insurance system was funded entirely from contributions deducted from the wages of participating employees, at a rate of 1% of the employee's salary up to an annual maximum of $85. In other relevant respects, the operation of the program was similar to General Electric's disability benefits plan, see 417 U.S., at 487-489.

We rejected appellee's Equal Protection challenge to this statutory scheme. We first noted that:

"We cannot agree that the exclusion of this disability from coverage amounts to invidious discrimination under the Equal Protection Clause. California does not discriminate with respect to the persons or groups which are eligible for disability insurance protection under the program. The classification challenged in this case related to the asserted under-inclusiveness of the set of risks that the State has selected to insure." 417 U.S., at 494.

This point was emphasized again, when later in the opinion we noted that

"this case is thus a far cry from cases like Reed v. Reed, 404 U.S. 71 (1971), and Frontiero v. Richardson, 411 U.S. 677 (1973), involving discrimination based upon gender as such. The California insurance program does not exclude anyone from benefit eligibility because of gender but merely removes one physical condition—pregnancy—from the list of compensable disabilities. While it is true that only women can become pregnant, it does not follow that every legislative classification concerning pregnancy is a sex-based classification like those considered in Reed, supra, and Frontiero, supra. Normal pregnancy is an objectively identifiable physical condition with unique characteristics. Absent a showing that distinctions involving pregnancy are mere pretexts designed to effect an invidious discrimination against the members of one sex or the other, lawmakers are constitutionally free to include or exclude pregnancy from the coverage of legislation such as this on any reasonable basis, just as with respect to any other physical condition.

"The lack of identity between the excluded disability and gender as such under this insurance program becomes clear upon the most cursory analysis. The program divides potential recipients into two groups—pregnant women and nonpregnant persons. While the first group is exclusively female, the second includes members of both sexes." 417 U.S., at 496-497, n. 20.

The quoted language from Geduldig leaves no doubt that our reason for rejecting appellee's equal protection claim in that case was that the exclusion of pregnancy from coverage under California's disability benefits plan was not in itself discrimination based on sex.

We recognized in Geduldig, of course, that the fact that there was not sex-based discrimination as such was not the end of the analysis, should it be shown "that distinctions involving pregnancy are mere pretexts designed to effect an invidious discrimination against the members of one sex or the other," 417 U.S., at 496-497, n. 20. But we noted that no semblance of such a showing had been made:

"There is no evidence in the record that the selection of the risks insured by the program worked to discriminate against any definable group or class in terms of the aggregate risk protection derived by that group or class from the program. There is no risk from which men are protected and women are not. Likewise, there is no risk from which women are protected and men are not." 417 U.S., at 496-497.

Since gender-based discrimination had not been shown to exist either by the terms of the plan or by its effect, there was no need to reach the question of what sort of standard would govern our review had there been such a showing. See Frontiero v. Richardson, 411 U.S. 677 (1973); Reed v. Reed, 404 U.S. 71 (1971).

The Court of Appeals was therefore wrong in concluding that the reasoning of Geduldig was not applicable to an action under Title VII. Since it is a finding of sex-based discrimination that must trigger, in a case such as this, the finding of an unlawful employment practice under § 703(a)(1), 42 U.S.C. § 2000e-2(a)(1), Geduldig is precisely in point in its holding that an exclusion of pregnancy from a disability benefits plan providing general coverage is not a gender-based discrimination at all.

There is no more showing in this case than there was in Geduldig that the exclusion of pregnancy benefits is a mere "pretext designed to effect an invidious discrimination against the members of one sex or the other." The Court of Appeals expressed the view that the decision in Geduldig had actually turned on whether or not a conceded discrimination was "invidious" but we think that in so doing it misread the quoted language from our opinion. As we noted in that opinion, a distinction which on its face is not sex related might nonetheless violate the Equal Protection Clause if it were in fact a subterfuge to accomplish a forbidden discrimination. But we have here no question of excluding a disease or disability comparable in all other respects to covered diseases or disabilities and yet confined to the members of one race or sex. Pregnancy is of course confined to women, but it is in other ways significantly different from the typical covered disease or disability. The District Court found that it is not a "disease" at all, and is often a voluntarily undertaken and desired condition, 375 F.Supp., at 375, 377. We do not therefore infer that the exclusion of pregnancy disability benefits from petitioner's plan is a simple pretext for discriminating against women. The contrary arguments adopted by the lower courts and expounded by our dissenting brethren were largely rejected in Geduldig.

The instant suit was grounded on Title VII rather than the Equal Protection Clause, and our cases recognize that a prima facie violation of Title VII can be established in some circumstances upon proof that the *effect* of an otherwise facially neutral plan or classification is to discriminate against members of one class or another. See Washington v. Davis, 426 U.S. 229, 96 S.Ct. 2040, 2051, (1976). For example, in the context of a challenge, under the provisions of § 703(a)(2), to a facially neutral employment test, this Court held that a prima facie case of discrimination would be established if, even absent proof of intent, the consequences of the test were "invidiously to discriminate on the basis of racial or other impermissible classification," Griggs v. Duke Power Co., 401 U.S. 424, 431 (1971). Even assuming that it is not necessary in this case to prove intent to establish a prima facie violation of § 703(a)(1), but cf. McDonnell Douglas Corp. v. Green, 411 U.S. 792, 802-806 (1973), the respondents have not made the requisite showing of gender-based effects.

As in Geduldig, supra, respondents have not attempted to meet the burden of demonstrating a gender-based discriminatory effect resulting from the exclusion of pregnancy-related disabilities from coverage. Whatever the ultimate probative value of the evidence introduced before the District Court on this subject in the instant case, at the very least it tended to illustrate that the selection of risks covered by the Plan did not operate, in fact, to discriminate against women. As in Geduldig, supra, we start from the indisputable baseline that "[t]he fiscal and actuarial benefits of the program . . . accrue to members of both sexes." 417 U.S., at 497 n.20. We need not disturb the findings of the District Court to note that there is neither a finding, nor was there any evidence which would support a finding, that the financial benefits of the Plan "worked to discriminate against any definable group or class in terms of the aggregate risk protection derived by that group or class from the program," id., at 496. The Plan, in effect (and for all that appears), is nothing more than an insurance package, which covers some risks, but excludes others, see id., at 494, 496-497. The "package" going to relevant identifiable groups we are presently concerned with—General Electric's male and female employees—covers exactly the same categories of risk, and is facially nondiscriminatory in the sense that "[t]here is no risk from which men are protected and women are not. Likewise, there is no risk from which women are protected and men are not." Geduldig, 417 U.S., at 496-497. As there is no proof that the package is in fact worth more to men than to women, it is impossible to find any gender-based discriminatory effect in this scheme simply because women disabled as a result of pregnancy do not receive benefits; that is to say, gender-based discrimination does not result simply because an employer's disability benefits plan is less than all inclusive. For all that appears, pregnancy-related disabilities constitute an *additional* risk, unique to women, and the failure to compensate them for this risk does not destroy the presumed parity of the benefits, accruing to men and women alike, which results from the facially evenhanded *inclusion* of risks. To hold otherwise would endanger the common-sense notion that an employer who has no disability benefits program at all does not violate Title VII even though the "underinclusion" of risks impacts, as a result of pregnancy-related disabilities, more heavily upon one gender than upon the other. Just as there is no facial gender-based discrimination in that case, so, too, there is none here.

We are told, however, that this analysis of the congressional purpose underlying Title VII is inconsistent with the guidelines of the EEOC, which, it is asserted, are entitled to "great deference" in the construction of the Act, Griggs, supra, 401 U.S., at 433-434; Phillips v. Martin Marietta Corp., 400 U.S. 542, 545, (1971) (Marshall, J., concurring). The guideline upon which respondents rely most heavily was promulgated in 1972, and states in pertinent part:

"Disabilities caused or contributed to by pregnancy, miscarriage, abortion, childbirth, and recovery therefrom are, for all job-related purposes, temporary disabilities and should be treated as such under any health or temporary disability insurance or sick leave plan available in connection with employment. . . . [Benefits] shall be applied to disability due to pregnancy or childbirth on the same terms and conditions as they are applied to other temporary disabilities." 29 CFR § 1604.10(b).

In evaluating this contention it should first be noted that Congress, in enacting Title VII, did not confer upon the EEOC authority to promulgate rules or regulations pursuant to that Title. Albemarle Paper Co. v. Moody, 422 U.S. 405, 431 (1975). This does not mean that EEOC guidelines are not entitled to consideration in determining legislative intent, see Albemarle, supra; Griggs v. Duke Power Co., 401 U.S., at 433-434; Espinoza v. Farah Mfg. Co., 414 U.S. 86, 94 (1973). But it does mean that courts properly may accord less weight to such guidelines than to administrative regulations which Congress has declared shall have the force of law, see Standard Oil Co. v. Johnson, 316 U.S. 481, 484 (1942), or to regulations which under the enabling statute may themselves supply the basis for imposition of liability, see, e.g., § 23(a), Securities Act of 1934, 15 U.S.C. § 78w(a). The most comprehensive statement of the role of interpretative rulings such as the EEOC guidelines is found in Skidmore v. Swift & Co., 323 U.S. 134, 140, 4 WH Cases 866 (1944), where the Court said:

"We consider that the rulings, interpretations and opinions of the Administrator under this Act, while not controlling upon the courts by reason of their authority, do constitute a body of experience and informed judgment to which courts and litigants may properly resort for guidance. The weight of such a judgment in a particular case will depend upon the thoroughness evident in its consideration, the validity of its reasoning, its consistency with earlier and later pronouncements, and all those factors which give it power to persuade, if lacking power to control."

The EEOC guideline in question does not fare well under these standards. It is not a contemporaneous interpretation of Title VII, since it was first promulgated eight years after the enactment of that Title. More importantly, the 1972 guideline flatly contradicts the position which the agency had enunciated at an earlier date, closer to the enactment of the governing statute. An opinion letter by the General Counsel of EEOC, dated October 17, 1966, states:

"You have requested our opinion whether the above exclusion of pregnancy and childbirth as a disability under the longterm salary continuation plan would be in violation of Title VII of the Civil Rights Act of 1964.

"In a recent opinion letter regarding pregnancy, we have stated, 'The Commission policy in this area does not seek to compare an employer's treatment of illness or injury with his treatment of maternity since maternity is a temporary disability unique to the female sex and more or less to be anticipated during the working life of most women employees. Therefore, it is our opinion that according to the facts stated above, a company's group insurance program which covers hospital and medical expenses for the delivery of employees' children, but excludes from its long-term salary continuation program those disabilities which result from pregnancy and childbirth would not be in violation of Title VII."

A few weeks later, in an opinion letter expressly issued pursuant to 29 CFR § 1601.30, the EEOC's position was that "an insurance or other benefit plan may simply exclude maternity as a covered risk, and such an exclusion would not in our view be discriminatory," G. E. Exhibit No. 12.

We have declined to follow administrative guidelines in the past where they conflicted with earlier pronouncements of the agency. United Housing Foundation, Inc. v. Forman, 421 U.S. 837, 858-859, n. 25 (1975); Espinoza v. Farah Mfg. Co., supra, 414 U.S., at 92-96. In short, while we do not wholly discount the weight to be given the 1972 guideline, it does not receive high marks when judged by the standards enunciated in Skidmore, supra.

There are also persuasive indications that the more recent EEOC guideline sharply conflicts with other indicia of the proper interpretation of the sex-discrimination provisions of Title VII. The legislative history of Title VII's prohibition of sex discrimination is notable primarily for its brevity. Even so, however, Congress paid especial attention to the provisions of the Equal Pay Act, 29 U.S.C. § 206(d), when it amended § 703(h) of Title VII by adding the following sentence:

"It shall not be an unlawful employment practice under this subchapter for any employer to differentiate upon the basis of sex in determining the amount of the wages or compensation paid or to be paid to employees of such employer if such differentiation is authorized by the provisions of section 206(d) of Title 29." 42 U.S.C. § 2000e-2(h).

This sentence was proposed as the Bennett Amendment to the Senate Bill, 110 Cong. Rec. 13647 (1964), and Senator Humphrey, the floor manager of the bill, stated that the purpose of the amendment was to make it "unmistakably clear" that "differences of treatment in industrial benefit plans, including earlier retirement options for women, may continue in operation under this bill if it becomes law." 110 Cong. Rec. 13663-13664 (1964). Because of this amendment, interpretations of section 6(d) of the Equal Pay Act are applicable to Title VII as well, and an interpretive regulation promulgated by the Wage and Hour Administrator under the Equal Pay Act explicitly states:

"If employer contributions to a plan providing insurance or similar benefits to employees are equal for both men and women, no wage differential prohibited by the equal pay provisions will result from such payments, even though the benefits which accrue to the employees in question are greater for one sex than for the other. The mere fact that the employer may make unequal contributions for employees of opposite sexes in such a situation will not, however, be considered to indicate that the employer's payments are in violation of section 6(d), if the resulting benefits are equal for such employees." 29 CFR § 800.116(d) (1975).

Thus even if we were to depend for our construction of the critical language of Title VII solely on the basis of "deference" to interpretative regulations by the appropriate administrative agencies, we would find ourselves pointed in diametrically opposite directions by the conflicting regulations of the EEOC, on the one hand, and the Wage and Hour Administrator, on the other. Petitioner's exclusion of benefits for pregnancy disability would be declared an unlawful employment practice under § 703(a)(1), but would be declared not to be an unlawful employment practice under § 703(h).

We are not reduced to such total abdication in construing the statute. The EEOC guideline of 1972, conflicting as it does with earlier pronouncements of that agency, and containing no suggestion that some new source of legislative history had been discovered in the intervening eight years, stand virtually alone. Contrary to it are the consistent interpretation of the Wage and Hour Administrator, and the quoted language of Senator Humphrey, the floor manager of Title VII in the Senate. They support what seems to us to be the "plain meaning" of the language used by Congress when it enacted § 703(a)(1).

The concept of "discrimination," of course, was well known at the time of the enactment of Title VII, having been associated with the Fourteenth Amendment for nearly a century, and carrying with it a long history of judicial construction. When Congress makes it unlawful for an employer to "discriminate . . . on the basis of . . . sex . . .", without further explanation of its meaning, we should not readily infer that it meant something different than what the concept of discrimination has traditionally meant, cf. Morton v. Mancari, 417 U.S. 535, 549 (1974); Ozawa v. United States, supra, 260 U.S. 178, 193 (1922). There is surely no reason for any such inference here, see Gemsco v. Walling, 324 U.S. 244, 260 (1945).

We therefore agree with petitioner that its disability benefits plan does not violate Title VII because of its failure to cover pregnancy-related disabilities. The judgment of the Court of Appeals is *Reversed.*

Concurring opinions

Mr. Justice STEWART, concurring:—I join the opinion of the Court holding that General Electric's exclusion of benefits for disability during pregnancy is not a *per se* violation of § 703(a)(1) of Title VII, and that the respondents have failed to prove a discriminatory effect. Unlike my Brother Blackmun, I do not understand the opinion to question either Griggs v. Duke Power Co., 401 U.S. 424 specifically, or the significance generally of proving a discriminatory effect in a Title VII case.

Mr. Justice BLACKMUN, concurring in part. I join the judgment of the Court and concur in its opinion insofar as it holds (a) that General Electric's exclusion of disability due to pregnancy is not, *per se*, a violation of § 703(a)(1) of Title VII; (b) that the plaintiffs in this case therefore had at least the burden of proving discriminatory effect; and (c) that they failed in that proof. I do not join any inference or suggestion in the Court's opinion—if any such inference or suggestion is there—that effect may never be a controlling factor in a Title VII case, or that Griggs v. Duke Power Co., 401 U.S. 424 (1971), is no longer good law.

Dissenting opinions

Mr. Justice BRENNAN, with whom Mr. Justice MARSHALL concurs, dissenting:—The Court holds today that without violating Title VII of the Civil Rights Act, 42 U.S.C. § 2000e, a private employer may adopt a disability that compensates employees for all temporary disabilities except one affecting exclusively women, pregnancy. I respectfully dissent. Today's holding not only repudiates the applicable administrative guideline promulgated by the agency charged by Congress with implementation of the Act, but also rejects the unanimous conclusion of all six Courts of Appeals that have addressed this question. See Communication Workers of America v. AT&T Co., 513 F.2d 1024, (CA2 1975), petition for cert. pending No. 74-1601; Wetzel v. Liberty Mutual Ins. Co., 511 F.2d 199, (CA3 1975), vacated on juris. grounds, 424 U.S. 737 (1976); Gilbert v. General Electric Co., 519 F.2d 661 (CA 4), cert. granted, 423 U.S. 822 (1975); Tyler v. Vickery, 517 F.2d 1089, 1097-1099 (CA5 1975); Satty v. Nashville Gas Co., 522 F.2d 850 (CA6 1975), petition for cert. pending, No. 75-536; Hutchison v. Lake Oswego School Dist., 519 F.2d 961 (CA9 1975), petition for cert. pending, No. 75-1049.

This case is unusual in that it presents a question the resolution of which at first glance turns largely upon the conceptual framework chosen to identify and describe the operational features of the challenged disability program. By directing their focus upon the risks excluded from the otherwise comprehensive program, and upon the purported justifications for such exclusions, the Equal Employment Opportunity Commission, the women plaintiffs, and the lower courts reason that the pregnancy exclusion constitutes a prima facie violation of Title VII. This violation is triggered, they argue, because the omission of pregnancy from the program has the intent and effect of providing that "only women [are subjected] to a substantial risk of total loss of income because of temporary medical disability." Brief of EEOC, at 12.

The Court's framework is diametrically different. It views General Electric's plan as representing a gender-free assignment of risks in accordance with normal actuarial techniques. From this perspective the lone exclusion of pregnancy is not a violation of Title VII insofar as all other disabilities are mutually covered for both sexes. This reasoning relies primarily upon the descriptive statement borrowed from Geduldig v. Aiello, 417 U.S. 484, 496-497, 8 FEP Cases 97, 102 (1974): "There is no risk from which men are protected and women are not. Likewise, there is no risk from which women are protected and men are not." Ante, at 12, 13 FEP Cases, at 1663. According to the Court, this assertedly neutral sorting process precludes the pregnancy omission from constituting a violation of Title VII.

Presumably, it is not self-evident that either conceptual framework is more appropriate than the other, which can only mean that further inquiry is necessary to select the more accurate and realistic analytical approach. At the outset, the soundness of the Court's underlying assumption that the plan is the untainted product of a gender-neutral risk-assignment process can be examined against the historical backdrop of General Electric's employment practices and the existence or nonexistence of gender-free policies governing the inclusion of compensable risks. Secondly, the resulting pattern of risks insured by General Electric can then be evaluated in terms of the broad social objectives promoted by TitleVII. I believe that the first inquiry compels the conclusion that the Court's assumption that General Electric engaged in a gender-neutral risk-assignment process is purely fanciful. The second demonstrates that the EEOC's interpretation that the exclusion of pregnancy from a disability insurance plan is incompatible with the overall objectives of Title VII has been unjustifiably rejected.

Geduldig v. Aiello, supra, purports to be the starting point for the Court's analysis. There a state-operated disability insurance system containing a pregnancy exclusion was held not to violate the Equal Protection Clause. Although it quotes primarily from one footnote of that opinion at some length, ante, at 8-9, the Court finally does not grapple with Geduldig on its own terms.

Considered most favorably to the Court's view, Geduldig established the proposition that a pregnancy classification standing alone cannot be said to fall into the category of classifications that rest explicitly on "gender as such," 417 U.S., at 496 n.20. Beyond that, Geduldig offers little analysis helpful to decision of this case. Surely it offends common sense to suggest, ante, at 10, that a classification revolving around pregnancy is not, at the minimum, strongly "sex related." See, e.g., Cleveland Board of Education v. LaFleur, 414 U.S. 632, 652 (1974) (Powell, J., concurring). Indeed, even in the insurance context where neutral actuarial principles were found to have provided a legitimate and independent input into the decisionmaking process, Geduldig's outcome was qualified by the explicit reservation of a case where it could be demonstrated that a pregnancy-centered differentiation is used as a "mere pretext . . . designed to effect an invidious discrimination against the members of one sex. . . ." 417 U.S., at 496-497, n.20.

Thus, Geduldig itself obliges the Court to determine whether the exclusion of a sex-linked disability from the universe of compensable disabilities was actually the product of neutral, persuasive actuarial considerations, or rather stemmed from a policy that purposefully downgraded women's role in the labor force. In Geduldig, that inquiry coupled with the normal presumption favoring legislative action satisfied the Court that the pregnancy exclusion in fact was prompted by

California's legitimate fiscal concerns, and therefore that California did not deny equal protection in effectuating reforms "one step at a time." 417 U.S., at 495. But the record in this case makes such deference impossible here. Instead, in reaching its conclusion that a showing of purposeful discrimination has not been made, ante, at 10, the Court simply disregards a history of General Electric practices that have served to undercut the employment opportunities of women who become pregnant while employed. Moreover, the Court studiously ignores the undisturbed conclusion of the District Court that General Electric's "discriminatory attitude" toward women was "a motivating factor in its policy," 375 F.Supp. 367, 383 (ED Va. 1974), and that the pregnancy exclusion was neither "neutral on its face" nor "in its intent." Id., at 382.

Plainly then, the Court's appraisal of General Electric's policy as a neutral process of sorting risks and "not a gender-based discrimination at all," ante, at 10, cannot easily be squared with the historical record in this case. The Court, therefore, proceeds to a discussion of purported neutral criteria that suffice to explain the lone exclusion of pregnancy from the program. The Court argues that pregnancy is not "comparable" to other disabilities since it is a "voluntary" condition rather than a "disease." Ibid. The fallacy of this argument is that even if "nonvoluntariness" and "disease" are to be construed as the operational criteria for inclusion of a disability in General Electric's program, application of these criteria is inconsistent with the Court's gender-neutral interpretation of the company's policy.

For example, the characterization of pregnancy as "voluntary" is not a persuasive factor, for as the Court of Appeals correctly noted, "other than for childbirth disability, [General Electric] has never construed its plan as eliminating *all* so-called 'voluntary' disabilities," including sport injuries, attempted suicides, venereal disease, disabilities incurred in the commission of a crime or during a fight, and elective cosmetic surgery. 519 F.2d, at 665. Similarly, the label "disease" rather than "disability" cannot be deemed determinative since General Electric's pregnancy disqualification also excludes the 10% of pregnancies that end in debilitating miscarriages, 375 F.Supp., at 377, the 10% of cases where pregnancies are complicated by "diseases" in the intuitive sense of the word, ibid., and cases where women recovering from childbirth are stricken by severe diseases unrelated to pregnancy.

Moreover, even the Court's principal argument for the plan's supposed gender neutrality cannot withstand analysis. The central analytical framework relied upon to demonstrate the absence of discrimination is the principle described in Geduldig: "There is no risk from which men are protected and women are not, . . . [and] no risk from which women are protected and men are not." 417 U.S., at 496-497, cited ante, at 12. In fostering the impression that it is faced with a mere underinclusive assignment of risks in a gender-neutral fashion—that is, all other disabilities are insured irrespective of gender—the Court's analysis proves to be simplistic and misleading. For although all mutually contractible risks are covered irrespective of gender, but see n. 4 supra, the plan also insures risks such as prostatectomies, vasectomies, and circumcisions that are specific to the reproductive system of men and for which there exist no female counterparts covered by the plan. Again, pregnancy affords the only disability, sex-specific or otherwise, that is excluded from coverage. Accordingly, the District Court appropriately remarked: "[T]he concern of defendants in reference to pregnancy risks, coupled with the apparent lack of concern regarding the balancing of other statistically sex-linked disabilities, buttresses the Court's conclusion that the discriminatory attitude characterized elsewhere in the Court's finding was in fact a motivating factor in its policy." 375 F.Supp., at 383.

If decision of this case, therefore, turns upon acceptance of the Court's view of General Electric's disability plan as a sex-neutral assignment of risks, or plaintiffs' perception of the plan as a sex-conscious process expressive of the secondary status of women in the company's labor force, the history of General Electric's employment practices and the absence of definable gender-neutral sorting criteria under the plan warrants rejection of the Court's view in deference to the plaintiffs'. Indeed the fact that the Court's frame of reference lends itself to such intentional, sex-laden decisionmaking makes clear the wisdom and propriety of EEOC's contrary approach to employment disability programs.

Of course, the demonstration of purposeful discrimination is not the only ground for recovery under Title VII. Notwithstanding unexplained and inexplicable implications to the contrary in the majority opinion, this Court, see Washington v. Davis, 426 U.S. 229, 44 LW 4789, 4791-4792 (1976); Albemarle Paper Co. v. Moody, 422 U.S. 405, 422 (1975); McDonnell Douglas Corp. v. Green, 411 U.S. 792, 802 (1973); Griggs v. Duke Power Co., 401 U.S. 424, 432 (1971), and every Court of Appeals now have firmly settled that a prima facie violation of Title VII, whether under § 703(a)(1) or § 703(a)(2), also is established by demonstrating that a facially-neutral classification has the *effect* of discriminating against members of a defined class.

General Electric's disability program has three divisible sets of effects. First, the plan covers all disabilities that mutually inflict both sexes. But see n.4 supra. Second, the plan insures against all disabilities that are male-specific or have a predominant impact on males. Finally, all female-specific and -impacted disabilities are covered, except for the most prevalent, pregnancy. The Court focuses on the first factor—the equal inclusion of mutual risks—and therefore understandably can identify no discriminatory effect arising from the plan. In contrast, EEOC and plaintiffs rely upon the unequal exclusion manifested in effects two and three to pinpoint an adverse impact on women. However one defines the profile of risks protected by General Electric, the determinative question must be whether the social policies and aims to be furthered by Title VII and filtered through the phrase "to discriminate" contained in § 703(a)(1) fairly forbid an ultimate pattern of coverage that insures all risks except a commonplace one that is applicable to women but not to men.

As a matter of law and policy, this is a paradigm example of the type of complex economic and social inquiry that Congress wisely left to resolution by the EEOC pursuant to its Title VII mandate. See H. R. Rep. No. 92-238, 92d Cong., 2d Sess., U.S. Cong. & Admin. News, at 2144 (1972). And, accordingly, prior Title VII decisions have consistently acknowledged the unique persuasiveness of EEOC interpretations in this area. These prior decisions, rather than providing merely that

Commission guidelines are "entitled to consideration," as the Court allows, ante, at 15, hold that EEOC's interpretations should receive "great deference." Albemarle Paper Co. v. Moody, supra, 422 U.S., at 431; Griggs v. Duke Power Co., supra, 401 U.S., at 433-434; Phillips v. Martin Marietta Corp., 400 U.S. 542, 545 (1971) (Marshall, J., concurring). Nonetheless, the Court today abandons this standard in order squarely to repudiate the 1972 Commission guideline providing that "[d]isabilities caused or contributed to by pregnancy . . . are for all job-related purposes, temporary disabilities . . . [under] any health or temporary disability insurance or sick leave plan. . . ." 29 CFR § 1604.10(b). This rejection is attributed to two interrelated events: a seven-year delay between Title VII's enactment and the promulgation of the Commission's guideline, and interim letters by EEOC's General Counsel expressing the view that pregnancy is not necessarily includable as a compensable disability. Neither event supports the Court's refusal to accord "great deference" to EEOC's interpretation.

It is true, as noted, ante, at 17, that only brief mention of sex discrimination appears in the early legislative history of Title VII. It should not be surprising, therefore, that the EEOC, charged with a fresh and uncharted mandate, candidly acknowledged that further study was required before the contours of sex discrimination as proscribed by Congress could be defined. See 30 Fed. Reg. 14927 (1965). Although proceeding cautiously, the Commission from the outset acknowledged the relationship between sex discrimination and pregnancy, announcing that "policies would have to be devised which afforded female employees reasonable job protection during periods of pregnancy." EEOC First Annual Report to Congress, fiscal year 1965-1966, at 40. During the succeeding seven years, EEOC worked to develop a coherent policy toward pregnancy-oriented employment practices both through the pursuit of its normal adjudicatory functions and by engaging in comprehensive studies with such organizations as the President's Citizen Advisory Council on the Status of Women. See, e.g., Address of Jacqueline G. Gutwilling, Chairwoman, Citizens' Advisory Council, cited in IV App., at 1161. These investigations on the role of pregnancy in the labor market coupled with the Commission's "review . . . [of] its case decisions on maternity preparatory to issuing formal guidelines," ibid., culminated in the 1972 guideline, the agency's first formalized, systematic statement on "employment policies relating to pregnancy and childbirth."

Therefore, while some seven years had elapsed prior to the issuance of the 1972 guideline, and earlier opinion letters had refused to impose liability on employers during this period of deliberation, no one can or does deny that the final EEOC determination followed thorough and well-informed consideration. Indeed, realistically viewed, this extended evaluation of an admittedly complex problem and an unwillingness to impose additional, potentially premature costs on employers during the decisionmaking stages ought to be perceived as a practice to be commended. It is bitter irony that the care that preceded promulgation of the 1972 guideline is today condemned by the Court as tardy indecisiveness, its unwillingness irresponsibly to challenge employers' practices during the formative period is labelled as evidence of inconsistency, and this indecisiveness and inconsistency are bootstrapped into reasons for denying the Commission's interpretation its due deference.

For me, the 1972 regulation represents a particularly conscientious and reasonable product of EEOC deliberations and, therefore, merits our "great deference." Certainly, I can find no basis for concluding that the regulation is out of step with congressional intent. See Espinoza v. Farah Mfg. Co., 414 U.S. 86, 94 (1973). On the contrary, prior to 1972, Congress enacted just such a pregnancy-inclusive rule to govern the distribution of benefits for "sickness" under the Railroad Unemployment Insurance Act, 45 U.S.C. § 351(K)(2). Furthermore, shortly following the announcement of the EEOC's rule, Congress approved and the President signed an essentially identical promulgation by the Department of Health, Education, and Welfare under Title IX of the Education Amendments of 1972, 20 U.S.C. (Supp. II) § 1681(a). See 45 CFR § 86.57(c). Moreover, federal workers subject to the jurisdiction of the Civil Service Commission now are eligible for maternity and pregnancy coverage under their sick leave program. See Federal Personnel Manual, c. 630, subch. 13, § 13-2 (April 30, 1975).

These policy formulations are reasonable responses to the uniform testimony of governmental investigations which show that pregnancy exclusions built into disability programs both financially burden women workers and act to break down the continuity of the employment relationship, thereby exacerbating women's comparatively transient role in the labor force. See, e.g., U.S. Dept. of Commerce, Consumer Income (Series P-60, No. 93, July 1974); Women's Bureau, U.S. Dept. of Labor, Underutilization of Women Workers (rev, ed. 1971). In dictating pregnancy coverage under Title VII, EEOC's guideline merely settled upon a solution now accepted by every other Western industrial country. Dept. of Health, Education, and Welfare, Social Security Programs Throughout the World, 1971, at ix, xviii, xix. I find it difficult to comprehend that such a construction can be anything but a "sufficiently reasonable" one to be "accepted by the reviewing courts." Train v. Natural Resources Defense Council, 421 U.S. 60, 75 (1975).

The Court's belief that the concept of discrimination cannot reach disability policies effecting "an *additional* risk, unique to women. . . ." ante, at 13, is plainly out of step with the decision three Terms ago in Lau v. Nichols, 414 U.S. 563 (1974), interpreting another provision of the Civil Rights Act. There a unanimous Court recognized that discrimination is a social phenomenon encased in a social context and, therefore, unavoidably takes its meaning from the desired end-products of the relevant legislative enactment, end-products that may demand due consideration to the uniqueness of "disadvantaged" individuals. A realistic understanding of conditions found in today's labor environment warrants taking pregnancy into account in fashioning disability policies. Unlike the hypothetical situations conjectured by the Court, ante, at 13-14 and n. 17, contemporary disability programs are not creatures of a social or cultural vacuum devoid of stereotypes and signals concerning the pregnant woman employee. Indeed, no one seriously contends that General Electric or other companies actually conceptualized or developed their comprehensive insurance programs disability-by-disability in a strictly sex-neutral fashion. Instead, the company has devised a policy that, but for pregnancy, offers protection for all risks, even those that are "unique to" men or heavily male dominated. In light of this social experience, the history of General Electric's employment practices, the otherwise all-inclusive design of its disability program, and the burdened role of the contemporary working woman, the EEOC's construction of sex discrimination under § 703(a)(1) is fully consonant with the ultimate objective of Title VII, "to assure equality of employment opportunities and to eliminate those discriminatory practices and devices which have fostered [sexually] stratified job environments to the disadvantage of [women]." McDonnell Douglas Corp. v. Green, supra, 411 U.S., at 800.

I would affirm the judgment of the Court of Appeals.

Mr. Justice STEVENS, dissenting.

The word "discriminate" does not appear in the Equal Protection Clause. Since the plaintiffs' burden of proving a prima facie violation of that constitutional provision is significantly heavier than the burden of proving a prima facie violation of a statutory prohibition against discrimination, the constitutional holding in Geduldig v. Aiello, 417 U.S. 484 (1974), does not control the question of statutory interpretation presented by this case. And, of course, when it enacted Title VII of the Civil Rights Act of 1964, Congress could not possibly have relied on language which this Court was to use a decade later in the Geduldig opinion. We are, therefore, presented with a fresh, and rather simple, question of statutory construction: Does a contract between a company and its employees which treats the risk of absenteeism caused by pregnancy differently from any other kind of absence discriminate against certain individuals because of their sex?

An affirmative answer to that question would not necessarily lead to a conclusion of illegality, because a statutory affirmative defense might justify the disparate treatment of pregnant women in certain situations. In this case, however, the company has not established any such justification. On the other hand, a negative answer to the threshold question would not necessarily defeat plaintiffs' claim because facially neutral criteria may be illegal if they have a discriminatory effect. An analysis of the effect of a company's rules relating to absenteeism would be appropriate if those rules referred only to neutral criteria, such as whether an absence was voluntary or involuntary, or perhaps particularly costly. This case, however, does not involve rules of that kind.

Rather, the rule at issue places the risk of absence caused by pregnancy in a class by itself. By definition, such a rule discriminates on account of sex; for it is the capacity to become pregnant which primarily deferentiates the female from the male. The analysis is the same whether the rule relates to hiring, promotion, the acceptability of an excuse for absence, or an exclusion from a disability insurance plan. Accordingly, without reaching the questions of motive, administrative expertise, and policy, which Mr. Justice Brennan so persuasively exposes, or the question of effect to which Mr. Justice Stewart and Mr. Justice Blackmun refer, I conclude that the language of the statute plainly requires the result which the courts of appeals have reached unanimously.

Geduldig v. Aiello
[417 U.S. 484 (1974)]

Sex discrimination due to pregnancy in a disability benefits program

Analysis of the issue

California's disability insurance system pays benefits to persons in private employment because of a disability not covered by workmen's compensation. The system is funded entirely from contributions deducted from wages, and participation in the program is mandatory unless employees are protected by a voluntary private plan approved by the State. This action was brought by four women, who otherwise would have qualified for benefits but for an exclusion in the statute of disabilities attributable to pregnancies. A State court decision, which occurred after this action was initiated, construed the statute's exclusion as applying only to normal pregnancies. Since three of the women suffered abnormal complications as a result of pregnancy, their cases contained no controversy. In this case the plaintiff claims that the California disability insurance program discriminates against women in violation of the 14th Amendment by not paying benefits for disabilities arising from normal pregnancies. In a 6-3 majority opinion, the Supreme Court held that this classification did not violate the Equal Protection Clause. The decision was based on the grounds that for social welfare programs, as long as the classification is rationally supportable, the Court would not overturn the State's judgment. On the basis of managing costs, the Court believed the State had a legitimate interest in maintaining a self-supporting program. Furthermore, the Court pointed out that the classification was not based upon gender, but rather on a dichotomy between pregnant women and nonpregnant persons. The Court required that an actual intent to discriminate against pregnant women be shown before such a classification is labelled sex discrimination under the Constitution, Title VII and the EEOC Guidelines not being discussed in the majority opinion.

Full text of opinion

Mr. Justice STEWART delivered the opinion of the Court:—For almost 30 years California has administered a disability insurance system that pays benefits to persons in private employment who are temporarily unable to work because of disability not covered by workmen's compensation. The appellees brought this action to challenge the constitutionality of a provision of the California program that, in defining "disability," excludes from coverage certain disabilities resulting from pregnancy. Because the appellees sought to enjoin the enforcement on this state statute, a three-judge court was convened pursuant to 28 U.S.C. §§ 2281 and 2284. On the appellees' motion for summary judgment, the District Court, by a divided vote, held that this provision of the disability insurance program violates the Equal Protection Clause of the Fourteenth Amendment, and therefore enjoined its continued enforcement. 359 F.Supp. 792. The District Court denied a motion to stay its judgment pending appeal. The appellant thereupon filed a similar motion in this Court, which we granted. Hansen v. Aiello, 414 U.S. 897, 94 S.Ct. 208, 38 L.Ed.2d 142. We subsequently noted probable jurisdiction of the appeal. 414 U.S. 1110, 94 S.Ct. 838, 38 L.Ed.2d 736.

California's disability insurance system is funded entirely from contributions deducted from the wages of participating employees. Participation in the program is mandatory unless the employees are protected by a voluntary private plan approved by the State. Each employee is required to contribute one percent of his salary, up to an annual maximum of $85. These contributions are placed in the Unemployment Compensation Disability Fund, which is established and administered as a special trust fund within the state treasury. It is from this Disability Fund that benefits under the program are paid.

An individual is eligible for disability benefits if, during a one-year base period prior to his disability, he has contributed one percent of a minimum income of $300 to the Disability Fund. In the event he suffers a compensable disability, the individual can receive a "weekly benefit amount" of between $25 and $105, depending on the amount he earned during the highest quarter of the base period. Benefits are not paid until the eighth day of disability, unless the employee is hospitalized, in which case benefits commence on the first day of hospitalization. In addition to the "weekly benefit amount," a hospitalized employee is entitled to receive "additional benefits" of $12 per day of hospitalization. "Weekly benefit amounts" for any one disability are payable for 26 weeks so long as the total amount paid does not exceed one-half of the wages received during the base period. "Additional benefits" for any one disability are paid for a maximum of 20 days.

In return for his one-percent contribution to the Disability Fund, the individual employee is insured against the risk of disability stemming from a substantial number of "mental or physical illness[es] and mental or physical injur[ies]." Cal.Unemp.Ins.Code § 2626. It is not every disabling condition, however, that triggers the obligation to pay benefits under the program. As already noted, for example, any disability of less than eight days' duration is not compensable, except when the employee is hospitalized. Conversely, no benefits are payable for any single disability beyond 26 weeks. Further, disability is not compensable if it results from the individual's court commitment as a dipsomaniac, drug addict, or sexual psychopath. Finally, § 2626 of the Unemployment Insurance Code excludes from coverage certain disabilities that are attributable to pregnancy. It is this provision that is at issue in the present case.

Appellant is the Director of the California Department of Human Resources Development. He is responsible for the administration of the State's disability insurance program. Appellees are four women who have paid sufficient amounts into the Disability Fund to be eligible for benefits under the program. Each of the appellees became pregnant and suffered employment disability as a result of her pregnancy. With respect to three of the appellees, Carolyn Aiello, Augustina Armendariz, and Elizabeth Johnson, the disabilities were attributable to abnormal complications encountered during their pregnancies. The fourth, Jacqueline Jaramillo, experienced a normal pregnancy, which was the sole cause of her disability.

At all times relevant to this case, § 2626 of the Unemployment Insurance Code Provided:

" 'Disability' or 'disabled' includes both mental or physical illness and mental or physical injury. An individual shall be deemed disabled in any day in which, because of his physical or mental condition, he is unable to perform his regular or customary work. *In no case shall the term 'disability' or 'disabled' include any injury or illness caused by or arising in connection with pregnancy up to the termination of such pregnancy and for a period of 28 days thereafter.*" (Emphasis added.)

Appellant construed and applied the final sentence of this statute to preclude the payment of benefits for any disability resulting from pregnancy. As a result, the appellees were ruled ineligible for disability benefits by reason of this provision, and they sued to enjoin its enforcement. The District Court, finding "that the exclusion of pregnancy-related disabilities is not based upon a classification having a rational and substantial relationship to a legitimate state purpose," held that the exclusion was unconstitutional under the Equal Protection Clause. 359 F.Supp., at 801.

Shortly before the District Court's decision in this case, the California Court of Appeal, in a suit brought by a woman who suffered an ectopic pregnancy, held that § 2626 does not bar the payment of benefits on account of disability that results from medical complications arising during pregnancy. Rentzer v. California Unemployment Insurance Appeals Board, 32 Cal.App.3d 604, 108 Cal.Rptr. 336 (1973). The state court construed the statute to preclude only the payment of benefits for disability accompanying normal pregnancy. The appellant acquiesced in this construction and issued administrative guidelines that exclude only the payment of "maternity benefits"—*i.e.*, hospitalization and disability benefits for normal delivery and recuperation.

Although *Rentzer* was decided some 10 days before the District Court's decision in this case, there was apparently no opportunity to call the court's attention to it. The appellant, therefore, asked the court to reconsider its decision in light of the construction that the California Court of Appeal had given to § 2626 in the *Rentzer* case. By a divided vote, the court denied the motion for reconsideration. Although a more definitive ruling would surely have been preferable, we interpret the District Court's denial of the appellant's motion as a determination that its decision was not affected by the limiting construction given to § 2626 in *Rentzer*.

Because of the *Rentzer* decision and the revised administrative guidelines that resulted from it, the appellees Aiello, Armendariz, and Johnson, whose disabilities were attributable to causes other than normal pregnancy and delivery, became entitled to benefits under the disability insurance program, and their claims have since been paid. With respect to appellee Jaramillo, however, whose disability stemmed solely from normal pregnancy and childbirth, § 2626 continues to bar the payment of any benefits. It is evident that only Jaramillo continues to have a live controversy with the appellant as to the validity of § 2626. The claims of the other appellees have been mooted by the change that *Rentzer* worked in the construction and application of that provision. Thus, the issue before the Court on this appeal is whether the California disability insurance program invidiously discriminates against Jaramillo and others similarly situated by not paying insurance benefits for disability that accompanies normal pregnancy and childbirth.

It is clear that California intended to establish this benefit system as an insurance program that was to function essentially in accordance with insurance concepts. Since the program was instituted in 1946, it has been totally self-supporting, never drawing on general state revenues to finance disability or hospital benefits. The Disability Fund is wholly supported by the one percent of wages annually contributed by participating employees. At oral argument, counsel for the appellant informed us that in recent years between 90% and 103% of the revenue to the Disability Fund has been paid out in disability and hospital benefits. This history strongly suggests that the one-percent contribution rate, in addition to being easily computable, bears a close and substantial relationship to the level of benefits payable and to the disability risks insured under the program.

Over the years California has demonstrated a strong commitment not to increase the contribution rate above the one-percent level. The State has sought to provide the broadest possible disability protection that would be affordable by all employees, including those with very low incomes. Because any larger percentage or any flat dollar-amount rate of contribution would impose an increasingly regressive levy bearing most heavily upon those with the lowest incomes, the State has resisted any attempt to change the required contribution from the one-percent level. The program is thus structured, in terms of the level of benefits and the risks insured, to maintain the solvency of the Disability Fund at a one-percent annual level of contribution.

In ordering the State to pay benefits for disability accompanying normal pregnancy and delivery, the District Court acknowledged the State's contention "that coverage of these disabilities is so extraordinarily expensive that it would be impossible to maintain a program supported by employee contributions if these disabilities are included." 359 F.Supp., at 798. There is considerable disagreement between the parties with respect to how great the increased costs would actually be, but they would clearly be substantial. For purposes of analysis the District Court accepted the State's estimate, which was in excess of $100 million annually, and stated: "[I]t is clear that including these disabilities would not destroy the program. The increased costs could be accommodated quite easily by making reasonable changes in the contribution rate, the maximum benefits allowable, and the other variables affecting the solvency of the program." *Ibid.*

Each of these "variables"—the benefit level deemed appropriate to compensate employee disability, the risks selected to be insured under the program, and the contribution rate chosen to maintain the solvency of the program and at the same time to permit low-income employees to participate with minimal personal sacrifice—represents a policy determination by the State. The essential issue in this case is whether the Equal Protection Clause requires such policies to be sacrificed or compromised in order to finance the payment of benefits to those whose disability is attributable to normal pregnancy and delivery.

We cannot agree that the exclusion of this disability from coverage amounts to invidious discrimination under the Equal Protection Clause. California does not discriminate with respect to the persons or groups which are eligible for disability insurance protection under the program. The classification challenged in this case relates to the asserted underinclusiveness of the set of risks that the State has selected to insure. Although California has created a program to insure most risks of employment disability, it has not chosen to insure all such risks, and this decision is reflected in the level of annual contributions exacted from participating employees. This Court has held that, consistently with the Equal Protection Clause, a State "may take one step at a time, addressing itself to the phase of the problem which seems most acute to the legislative mind. . . . The legislature may select one phase of one field and apply a remedy there, neglecting the others. . . ." Williamson v. Lee Optical Co., 348 U.S. 483, 489, 75 S.Ct. 461, 465, 99 L.Ed. 563 (1955); Jefferson v. Hackney, 406 U.S. 535, 92 S.Ct. 1724, 32 L.Ed.2d 285 (1972). Particularly with respect to social welfare programs, so long as the line drawn by the State is rationally supportable, the courts will not interpose their judgment as to the appropriate stopping point. "[T]he Equal Protection Clause does not require that a State must choose between attacking every aspect of a problem or not attacking the problem at all." Dandridge v. Williams, 397 U.S. 471, 486-487, 90 S.Ct. 1153, 1162, 25 L.Ed.2d 491 (1970).

The District Court suggested that moderate alterations in what it regarded as "variables" of the disability insurance program could be made to accommodate the substantial expense required to include normal pregnancy within the program's protection. The same can be said, however, with respect to the other expensive class of disabilities that are excluded from coverage—short-term disabilities. If the Equal Protection Clause were thought to compel disability payments for normal pregnancy, it is hard to perceive why it would not also compel payments for short-term disabilities suffered by participating employees.

It is evident that a totally comprehensive program would be substantially more costly than the present program and would inevitably require state subsidy, a higher rate of employee contribution, a lower scale of benefits for those suffering insured disabilities, or some combination of these measures. There is nothing in the Constitution, however, that requires the State to subordinate or compromise its legitimate interests solely to create a more comprehensive social insurance program than it already has.

The State has a legitimate interest in maintaining the self-supporting nature of its insurance program. Similarly, it has an interest in distributing the available resources in such a way as to keep benefit payments at an adequate level for disabilities that are covered, rather than to cover all disabilities inadequately. Finally, California has a legitimate concern in maintaining the contribution rate at a level that will not unduly burden participating employees, particularly low-income employees who may be most in need of the disability insurance.

These policies provide an objective and wholly noninvidious basis for the State's decision not to create a more comprehensive insurance program than it has. There is no evidence in the record that the selection of the risks insured by the program worked to discriminate against any definable group or class in terms of the aggregate risk protection derived by that group or class from the program. There is no risk from which men are protected and women are not. Likewise, there is no risk from which women are protected and men are not.

The appellee simply contends that, although she has received insurance protection equivalent to that provided all other participating employees, she has suffered discrimination because she encountered a risk that was outside the program's protection. For the reasons we have stated, we hold that this contention is not a valid one under the Equal Protection Clause of the Fourteenth Amendment.

The stay heretofore issued by the Court is vacated, and the judgment of the District Court is reversed.

Reversed.

Mr. Justice BRENNAN, with whom Mr. Justice DOUGLAS and Mr. Justice MARSHALL join, dissenting:—Relying upon Dandridge v. Williams, 397 U.S. 471, 90 S.Ct. 1153, 25 L.Ed.2d 491 (1970), and Jefferson v. Hackney, 406 U.S. 535, 92 S.Ct. 1724, 32 L.Ed.2d 285 (1972), the Court today rejects appellees' equal protection claim and upholds the exclusion of normal-pregnancy-related disabilities from coverage under California's disability insurance program on the ground that the legislative classification rationally promotes the State's legitimate cost-saving interests in "maintaining the self-supporting nature of its insurance program[,] . . . distributing the available resources in such a way as to keep benefit payments at an adequate level for disabilities that are covered, . . . [and] maintaining the contribution rate at a level that will not unduly burden participating employees . . . ." Ante, at 249. Because I believe that Reed v. Reed, 404 U.S. 71, 92 S.Ct. 251, 30 L.Ed.2d 225 (1971), and Frontiero v. Richardson, 411 U.S. 677, 93 S.Ct. 1764, 36 L.Ed.2d 583 (1973), mandate a stricter standard of scrutiny which the State's classification fails to satisfy, I respectfully dissent.

California's disability insurance program was enacted to supplement the State's unemployment insurance and workmen's compensation programs by providing benefits to wage earners to cushion the economic effects of income loss and medical expenses resulting from sickness or injury. The legislature's intent in enacting the program was expressed clearly in § 2601 of the Unemployment Insurance Code:

"The purpose of this part is to compensate in part for the wage loss sustained by individuals unemployed because of sickness or injury and to reduce to a minimum the suffering caused by unemployment resulting therefrom. This part shall be construed liberally in aid of its declared purpose to mitigate the evils and burdens which fall on the unemployed and disabled worker and his family."

To achieve the Act's broad humanitarian goals, the legislature fashioned a pooled-risk disability fund covering all employees at the same rate of contribution, regardless of individual risk. The only requirement that must be satisfied before an employee becomes eligible to receive disability benefits is that the employee must have contributed one percent of a minimum income of $300 during a one-year base period. Cal.Unemp.Ins.Code § 2652. The "basic benefits," varying from $25 to $119 per week, depending upon the employee's base-period earnings, begin on the eighth day of disability or on the first day of hospitalization. §§ 2655, 2627(b), 2802. Benefits are payable for a maximum of 26 weeks, but may not exceed one-half of the employee's total base-period earnings. § 2653. Finally, compensation is paid for virtually all disabling conditions without regard to cost, voluntariness, uniqueness, predictability, or "normalcy" of the disability. Thus, for example, workers are compensated for costly disabilities such as heart attacks, voluntary disabilities such as cosmetic surgery or sterilization, disabilities unique to sex or race such as prostatectomies or sickle-cell anemia, pre-existing conditions inevitably resulting in disability such as degenerative arthritis or cataracts, and "normal" disabilities such as removal of irritating wisdom teeth or other orthodontia.

Despite the Code's broad goals and scope of coverage, compensation is denied for disabilities suffered in connection with a "normal" pregnancy—disabilities suffered only by women. Cal.Unemp.Ins.Code §§ 2626, 2626.2 (Supp. 1974). Disabilities caused by pregnancy, however, like other physically disabling conditions covered by the Code, require medical care, often include hospitalization, anesthesia and surgical procedures, and may involve genuine risk to life. Moreover, the economic effects caused by pregnancy-related disabilities are functionally indistinguishable from the effects caused by any other disability: wages are lost due to a physical inability to work, and medical expenses are incurred for the delivery of the child and for postpartum care. In my view, by singling out for less favorable treatment a gender-linked disability peculiar to women, the State has created a double standard for disability compensation: a limitation is imposed upon the disabilities for which women workers may recover, while men receive full compensation for all disabilities suffered, including those that affect only or primarily their sex, such as prostatectomies, circumcision, hemophilia, and gout. In effect, one set of rules is applied to females and another to males. Such dissimilar treatment of men and women, on the basis of physical characteristics inextricably linked to one sex, inevitably constitutes sex discrimination.

The same conclusion has been reached by the Equal Employment Opportunity Commission, the federal agency charged with enforcement of Title VII of the Civil Rights Act of 1964, as amended by the Equal Employment Opportunity Act of 1972, 42 U.S.C. § 2000e et seq. (1970 ed., Supp. II), which prohibits employment discrimination on the basis of sex. In guidelines issued pursuant to Title VII and designed to prohibit the disparate treatment of pregnancy disabilities in the employment context, the EEOC has declared:

"Disabilities caused or contributed to by pregnancy, miscarriage, abortion, childbirth, and recovery therefrom are, for all job-related purposes, temporary disabilities and should be treated as such under any health or temporary disability insurance or sick leave plan available in connection with employment. Written and unwritten employment policies and practices involving matters such as the commencement and duration of leave, the availability of extensions, the accrual of seniority and other benefits and privileges, reinstatement, and payment under any health or temporary disability insurance or sick leave plan, formal or informal, shall be applied to disability due to pregnancy or childbirth on the same terms and conditions as they are applied to other temporary disabilities." 29 CFR § 1604.10(b).

In the past, when a legislative classification has turned on gender, the Court has justifiably applied a standard of judicial scrutiny more strict than that generally accorded economic or social welfare programs. Compare Reed v. Reed, 404 U.S. 71, 92 S.Ct. 251, 30 L.Ed.2d 225 (1971), and Frontiero v. Richardson, 411 U.S. 677, 93 S.Ct. 1764, 36 L.Ed.2d 583 (1973), with Dandridge v. Williams, 397 U.S. 471, 90 S.Ct. 1153, 25 L.Ed.2d 491 (1970), and Jefferson v. Hackney, 406 U.S. 535, 92 S.Ct. 1724, 32 L.Ed.2d 285 (1972). Yet, by its decision today, the Court appears willing to abandon that higher standard of review without satisfactorily explaining what differentiates the gender-based classification employed in this case from those found unconstitutional in *Reed* and *Frontiero*. The Court's decision threatens to return men and women to a time when "traditional" equal protection analysis sustained legislative classifications that treated differently members of a particular sex solely because of their sex. See. *e.g.,* Muller v. Oregon, 208 U.S. 412, 28 S.Ct. 324, 52 L.Ed. 551 (1908); Goesaert v. Cleary, 335 U.S. 464, 69 S.Ct. 198, 93 L.Ed. 163 (1948); Hoyt v. Florida, 368 U.S. 57, 82 S.Ct. 159, 7 L.Ed.2d 118 (1961).

I cannot join the Court's apparent retreat. I continue to adhere to my view that "classifications based upon sex, like classifications based upon race, alienage, or national origin, are inherently suspect, and must therefore be subjected to strict judicial scrutiny." Frontiero v. Richardson, *supra,* 411 U.S., at 688, 93 S.Ct. at 1771. When, as in this case, the State employs a legislative classification that distinguishes between beneficiaries solely by reference to gender-linked disability risks, "[t]he Court is not . . . free to sustain the statute on the ground that it rationally promotes legitimate governmental interests; rather, such suspect classifications can be sustained only when the State bears the burden of demonstrating that the challenged legislation serves overriding or compelling interests that cannot be achieved either by a more carefully tailored legislative classification or by the use of feasible, less drastic means." Kahn v. Shevin, 416 U.S. 351, 357-358, 94 S.Ct. 1734, 1738, 40 L.Ed.2d 189 (1974) (Brennan, J., dissenting).

The State has clearly failed to meet that burden in the present case. The essence of the State's justification for excluding disabilities caused by a normal pregnancy from its disability compensation scheme is that covering such disabilities would be too costly. To be sure, as presently funded, inclusion of normal pregnancies "would be substantially more costly than the present program." Ante, at 2491. The present level of benefits for insured disabilities could not be maintained without increasing the employee contribution rate, raising or lifting the yearly contribution ceiling, or securing state subsidies. But whatever role such monetary considerations may play in traditional equal protection analysis, the State's interest in preserving the fiscal integrity of its disability insurance program simply cannot render the State's use of a suspect classification constitutional. For a while "a State has a valid interest in preserving the fiscal integrity of its programs[,] . . . a State may not accomplish such a purpose by invidious distinctions between classes of its citizens.

. . . The saving of welfare costs cannot justify an otherwise invidious classification." Shapiro v. Thompson, 394 U.S. 618, 633, 89 S.Ct. 1322, 1330, 22 L.Ed.2d 600 (1969). Thus, when a statutory classification is subject to strict judicial scrutiny, the State "must do more than show that denying [benefits to the excluded class] saves money." Memorial Hospital v. Maricopa County, 415 U.S. 250, 263, 94 S.Ct. 1076, 1085, 39 L.Ed.2d 306 (1974). See also Graham v. Richardson, 403 U.S. 365, 374-375, 91 S.Ct. 1848, 1853-1854, 29 L.Ed.2d 534 (1971).

Moreover, California's legitimate interest in fiscal integrity could easily have been achieved through a variety of less drastic, sexually neutral means. As the District Court observed:

"Even using [the State's] estimate of the cost of expanding the program to include pregnancy-related disabilities, however, it is clear that including these disabilities would not destroy the program. The increased costs could be accommodated quite easily by making reasonable changes in the contribution rate, the maximum benefits allowable, and the other variables affecting the solvency of the program. For example, the entire cost increase estimated by defendant could be met by requiring workers to contribute an additional amount of approximately .364 percent of their salary and increasing the maximum annual contribution to about $119." 359 F.Supp. 792, 798.

I would therefore affirm the judgment of the District Court.

Zichy et al. v. City of Philadelphia
[329 F. Supp. 338 (E.D. Pa. 1975)]

Disability insurance program—exclusion of pregnancy benefits

Analysis of the issue

The plaintiff, an employee of the city of Philadelphia, instituted this class action suit on behalf of all women employed and formerly employed by the city from 1966 on. She claimed that the City's policy of denying its female employees the use of sick leave for maternity-related disabilities is sexually discriminatory under Title VII and 42 U.S.C. 1983. The Court held that the city violated Title VII by maintaining a policy which allowed the use of sick leave for disabilities incurred as a result of complications accompanying abnormal pregnancies, but did not permit the use of sick leave for disabilities incurred during normal pregnancies. The city contended that its policy allows the use of sick leave only for illness and injury, rather than general disability, and that normal pregnancy cannot be considered an illness or an injury. The Court held in favor of the plaintiff, basing its determination on the facts that the EEOC guidelines on pregnancy do not permit distinction between normal and abnormal pregnancy and childbirth; work disability stemming from pregnancy or childbirth deserves equal treatment as other temporary disabilities; and, that as a matter of practice, the city extended sick leave permission for physical disability generally, rather than for disability from injury or illness exclusively, disability from normal pregnancy and childbirth being the only exception. The Court granted declaratory and injunctive relief to restrain the city from denying the use of sick leave for maternity-related disabilities but delayed the award of damages for back pay until further hearings could be held.

Full text of opinion

NEWCOMER, District Judge:—We have before us cross motions for summary judgment in the instant case. For the reasons set forth below, we grant plaintiffs' motion for judgment to the extent of a declaration that the denial by defendant of the use of sick leave for maternity-related disabilities is illegal, and to the extent of an injunction against continued enforcement of the policy. By the same token, we deny defendant's motion to the extent it seeks judgment contrary to that which we have determined plaintiffs merit.

Plaintiffs originally brought this action challenging the above described policy of the City of Philadelphia as unconstitutional under the Equal Protection and Due Process Clauses of the Fourteenth Amendment and under the Civil Rights Act of 1871, 42 U.S.C. § 1983.

Plaintiff Zichy subsequently filed a charge against the defendant city under Title VII of the Civil Rights Act of 1964, as amended, 42 U.S.C. § 2000e et seq., with the Equal Employment Opportunity Commission within the time limit prescribed by the statute. After Ms. Zichy received from the Commission a "Notice of Right to Sue" on February 22, 1974, plaintiffs amended the complaint in the action before this Court to add Title VII as an additional ground for relief.

In toto, plaintiffs request: declaratory and injunctive relief against the defendant's policy on the use of sick leave for maternity-related disabilities, damages for back pay, loss of benefits and promotions, humiliation and harassment plaintiffs have suffered, and any other relief this Court may determine.

Jurisdiction of this action is under 28 U.S.C. § 1343(1)-(4), 28 U.S.C. §§ 2201 and 2202, and 42 U.S.C. § 2000e-5(f). We have previously certified the class of plaintiffs for this action under F.R.Civ.P. 23(b)(2) to consist of:

". . . all female persons currently and formerly employed by the City of Philadelphia from September 14, 1966, who, during the course of their employment, have been, are being, or will be caused to take non-paying maternity leave rather than being permitted to use accumulated sick leave for temporary disabilities caused or contributed to by pregnancy, childbirth, and the recovery therefrom, and those female employees who were caused to resign and accept positions with loss of seniority and benefits upon returning to work after recovering from said disability."

As of 1973, defendant employed 32,000 persons, of whom a large percentage are women.

Plaintiffs also raised in their complaint a question as to the denial of unpaid maternity leaves of absence from 1966 until September, 1973. Plaintiffs contend these denials were made on a sex discriminatory basis, but defendant denies this charge and the facts which plaintiffs allege in support of it. Since such dispute exists on the facts of this claim, plaintiffs do not seek summary judgment on it in the motion now before us, but instead request summary judgment only on the claim dealing with the sick leave and maternity disability question.

In addition, plaintiffs seek in the current motion only a grant of summary judgment as to liability, with a reservation for later decision of the issue of relief. This is, plaintiffs at this time request only a declaration of the illegality of defendant's policy concerning sick leave and an injunction against continued enforcement of the policy. As we said at the outset of this opinion, because we believe bifurcation of liability and relief is the proper manner of deciding this case, we limit our decision today in accordance with plaintiffs' request.

Neither party disputes the facts relating to defendant's policy in the use of sick leave for maternity related disabilities.

The City of Philadelphia is a municipal corporation organized under the laws of the Commonwealth of Pennsylvania, employs more than fifteen (15) persons, and has had since January 1, 1954, a sick leave plan for its employees. Under that plan, all permanent, Civil Service employees who work full time or part time in excess of twenty (20) hours a week earn sick leave as a form of compensation merely by coming to work every day. Such leave is earned at the rate of one and two-thirds (1⅔) days per month, with a maximum permissible accumulation of 200 days.

When taking sick leave, a city employee continues to earn his or her normal salary and to accrue seniority, does not lose the privilege of taking promotional examinations for the time out, has the time out credited for service and will receive the same raises as other employees in his or her classification who were not on sick leave. In addition, the employee continues to accumulate sick leave while on leave, will suffer no adverse effect on promotions, will resume the same position held prior to the commencement of such sick leave upon return, and will have no change in anniversary date of employment, pension plan, vacation time, and other fringe benefits as a result of using the sick leave.

Section 21 of the Civil Service Regulations controls the granting and use of sick leave. Section 21.011 reads:

"21.011. Authorized Sick Leave—includes, with the approval of the appointing authority, the absence from duty with pay of an employee because of his illness or non-service-connected injury, his appointments with doctors or other recognized practitioners in the treatment of such illness or injury to the extent of time required to complete such appointments, or his exposure to contagious disease."

As a matter of practice, sick leave is granted for such diverse reasons as an alcoholic "hangover", elective surgery, lung cancer or emphysema, or broken legs from skiing. While such conditions can occur as readily in both men and women, sick leave is also granted for conditions which are unique to either sex. A man, for example, may use sick leave for a prostatectomy. Similarly, a woman may use sick leave for an abortion or miscarriage.

Women are not, however, entitled under present practice to use sick leave for absence resulting from pregnancy or birth-related delivery, at least to the extent such pregnancy and delivery occur in "normal" fashion, that is, without complications. The city instead governs absence because of maternity and child birth under Civil Service Regulation 22.12, which reads:

"22.12 MATERNITY LEAVE. In accordance with Section 22.02 of these Regulations, a permanent employee shall be granted a maternity leave without pay. The employee shall retain her same position, if such leave does not exceed six (6) months duration."

In accordance with this policy, the city has not granted paid sick leave to those employees who take a leave of absence because of pregnancy and have a child delivered without any complications during the pregnancy or the birth.

We have noted to this point a distinction in the city's policy towards "normal" pregnancy and birth as opposed to pregnancy and birth with "complications". Such distinction merits some elaboration. While the regulations under which the city governs sick leave and maternity leave contain no express distinction between normal and complicated pregnancies and birth, the city contends, with supporting affidavit which plaintiffs do not challenge, that it does make such a distinction in practice. The city asserts that while it does not grant sick leave for normal pregnancy and birth, it does allow female employees to use accumulated sick leave for any complications that develop during the pregnancy. It is not necessary that such complication develop prior to the employee's beginning her leave of absence for maternity reasons. If complications develop during a maternity leave of absence, the employee may apply to have such period of time charged against sick leave until the employee recovers from the complications or exhausts her accumulated sick leave, whichever occurs first.

As set forth in the above discussion, however, those women with normal, uncomplicated pregnancies and deliveries may not use sick leave to cover their maternity-related absence from work. These women must instead take the unpaid maternity leaves described above.

For such women, the consequences of having to take maternity leave rather than using sick leave are significant. Besides receiving no pay for the period of absence, the employee on maternity leave loses the benefits, mentioned above, which she enjoys in the use of sick leave. During maternity leave, the employee accumulates neither seniority, sick leave, nor vacation time, her time required for annual increment and anniversary date is deferred for the period of the maternity leave, and the annual rate of pay for her pension purposes is lowered for that particular year by the period of leave.

Plaintiff Kathleen Zichy has been an employee of the City of Philadelphia since February 20, 1967 as a management trainee in the Examination Division of the Personnel Department of the city. On approximately April 26, 1972, she requested of defendant permission to use sick leave accrued during her employment for purposes of recovery from childbirth and for any period of disability occurring during her pregnancy. By letter of May 5, 1972, Foster Roser, personnel director of the city, denied her request. As of September 1, 1972, Ms. Zichy had earned approximately sixty-four and seven sixteenths (64 7/16) sick leave days. She subsequently became disabled from pregnancy and left work on November 16, 1972.

Plaintiff Jane Schofer, who became an employee of the city on July 28, 1969, began unpaid maternity leave on February 14, 1972. On August 29, 1972, her husband wrote to Mr. Herman Greenberg, personnel director of the Free Library, where Ms. Schofer worked, requesting that sick leave benefits accumulated during his wife's, Jane Schofer's, employment be paid to his wife for the time she was absent from work in preparing for and recovery from childbirth. By letter of September 5, 1972, Mr. Greenberg advised Mr. Schofer that the Civil Service Regulations did not permit the use of sick leave for maternity purposes. As of February 14, 1972, when she began her maternity leave, Ms. Schofer was entitled to thirty-three (33) days of sick leave.

As the above recitation of facts indicates, the pregnancy leave of Plaintiff Zichy occurred after March 24, 1972, the date on which municipal corporations were included under Title VII of the Civil Rights Act of 1964, 42 U.S.C. § 2000e et seq. The maternity leave of Plaintiff Schofer occurred prior to March 24, 1972.

The question before us is whether the city's policy of denying to its female employees the use of sick leave for maternity-related disabilities constitutes discrimination by sex in violation of Title VII. We conclude that it does.

While we find the authority cited by plaintiffs persuasive we rest our conclusion squarely upon the recent decision by our Court of Appeals in Wetzel v. Liberty Mutual Insurance Company, 511F.2d 199 (3rd

Cir., 1975). In *Wetzel*, decided after submission of briefs in our case, the Court of Appeals affirmed a district court's decision by summary judgment that Liberty Mutual violated Title VII by not including disability from pregnancy among the disabilities covered by the company's employee income protection plan. Under the company's plan, which was a fringe benefit funded partially by employee contributions, an employee out of work because of an illness requiring the care of a doctor received a percentage of his salary for the duration of his leave. The plan did not, however, cover any leaves or temporary absences for disabilities due to or related to pregnancy, and the company consequently paid no benefits under the plan for such pregnancy-related disabilities.

In holding that this policy constituted discrimination by sex in violation of Title VII, the *Wetzel* Court held, first of all, that contrary to defendant's assertion, the Supreme Court's decision in Geduldig v. Aiello, 417 U.S. 484, 94 S.Ct. 2485, 41 L.Ed.2d 256 (1974), did not compel the Court of Appeals to hold in defendant's favor on the Title VII question. As in this case, the defendant in *Wetzel*, in arguing that its income protection policy did not constitute sex discrimination in violation of Title VII, had relied virtually entirely upon *Geduldig*.

As the *Wetzel* Court accurately pointed out, however, the *Geduldig* decision, while dealing with alleged sex discrimination, involved the issue only of whether such discrimination violated the Equal Protection Clause of the Fourteenth Amendment, and did not involve, discuss, or resolve the issue of whether such discrimination violated Title VII. For this reason alone, the *Wetzel* Court said, reliance on *Geduldig* to resolve a Title VII issue was misplaced. *Wetzel*, 511 F.2d at p. 203.

Wetzel further distinguished *Geduldig*, involving a California state disability insurance program which did not cover disabilities relating to normal pregnancy, from the facts of its case. For one thing, *Wetzel* noted, the sources of funding the disability programs respectively in its case and *Geduldig* were different, and for another, the Liberty Mutual plan excluded disabilties resulting from all pregnancies while the program in *Geduldig* excluded only disabilities from "normal" pregnancies. *Wetzel*, 511 F.2d at p. 203.

In the instant case, the facts of the city's sick leave program are not precisely the same as the *Wetzel* facts, and consequently perhaps not as distinguishable from the facts of *Geduldig*. In the instant case, for example, the funds for sick leave benefits come presumably from the same source as all employee salaries, namely, general tax revenues. In addition, as noted in our statement of facts and similar to *Geduldig's* facts, the city's sick leave policy in this case in practice excludes only disabilities and absence from work resulting from normal pregnancies, while disabilities resulting from pregnancies with complications are covered.

We do not, however, think these factual differences from the case in *Wetzel* dictate a change in our conclusion that, under *Wetzel*, the Court's *Geduldig* decision does not control our decision in this case. As noted above, *Wetzel* held *Geduldig* inapplicable to the Title VII issue the *Wetzel* Court faced because *Geduldig*, argued and decided on Fourteenth Amendment grounds alone, simply did not deal with Title VII.

In light of this holding, the subsequent distinction by *Wetzel* of the facts of its case from those of *Geduldig* was unnecessary to the *Wetzel* Court's decision that *Geduldig* did not dispose of the *Wetzel* Title VII issue. Accordingly, the similarity or distinction of the facts of the employment program in question here from those in question in either *Wetzel* or *Geduldig* will not render *Geduldig* more or less applicable to the Title VII issue in the instant case. If, under *Wetzel*, Geduldig did not dispose of the *Wetzel* Title VII issue because *Geduldig* did not deal with Title VII, then *Geduldig* does not control the disposition of a Title VII issue in any case, whatever the facts of the employment program such latter case involves.

After holding Geduldig inapplicable to the Title VII issue then before the Court of Appeals, the *Wetzel* Court then proceeded with a statutory analysis of whether the income protection program in question violated Title VII.

First, the Court said, Title VII was enacted for the broad purpose of eliminating disparate or discriminatory treatment in employment, in the sense of artificial or arbitrary impediments, based on race, color, religion, sex, or national origin. Wetzel, 511 F.2d at p. 204.

Second, the Court said, while the prohibition against discrimination on the basis of sex may originally have been offered in a less-than-serious manner, the failure of Congress to amend Title VII in subsequent years indicated that Congress intended the Act's broad purpose to prohibit discrimination to be applied as readily to discrimination on the basis of sex as to discrimination on the other expressly prohibited bases. *Wetzel,* 511 F.2d at p. 204.

Third, the Court said, to effectuate the goals of Title VII, Congress created the EEOC, and gave it the power to issue regulations or guidelines that would indicate the discriminatory practices the Act proscribed. These guidelines, said the Court, are the agency's interpretation of the statute, and consequently are to be given great deference except where application of the guideline would be inconsistent with an obvious congressional intent not to reach the employment practice in question.

The *Wetzel* Court then noted that certain of these guidelines issued by the EEOC prohibited an employer from discriminating, because of pregnancy, with respect to employment policies and fringe benefits. The guidelines to which the Court referred provided:

" § 1604.9 Fringe benefits

"(a) 'Fringe benefits', as used herein, includes medical, hospital, accident, life insurance and retirement benefits; profit sharing and bonus plans; leave; and other terms, conditions, and privileges of employment.

"(b) It shall be an unlawful employment practice for an employer to discriminate between men and women with regard to fringe benefits.

* * * * * *

"1604.10 Employment policies relating to pregnancy and childbirth.

* * * * * *

"(b) Disabilities caused or contributed to by pregnancy, miscarriage, abortion, childbirth, and recovery therefrom are, for all job-related purposes, temporary disabilities and should be treated as such under any health or temporary disability insurance or sick leave plan available in connection with employment. Written and unwritten employment policies and practices involving matters such as the commencement and duration of leave, and availability of extensions, the accrual of seniority and other benefits and privileges, reinstatement, and payment under any health or temporary disability insurance or sick leave plan, formal or informal, shall be applied to disability due to pregnancy or childbirth on the same terms and conditions as they are applied to other temporary disabilities."

The Court found without merit the defendant's argument that the Court should not defer to these guidelines because they were inconsistent with the EEOC's earlier position and were inconsistent with the policy and understanding of Title VII. In the Court's view, the EEOC was entitled to adjust its guidelines to the changing concepts of our society, and that Congress recognized that this would be the case. Viewing the above-outlined guidelines as consistent with Title VII's plain meaning, the Court held these guidelines entitled to deference. *Wetzel*, 511 F.2d at pp. 205-206.

The Court then said that under these guidelines, and specifically under 29 C.F.R. § 1604.10(b), "it is discriminatory to treat pregnancy differently from other temporary disabilities." *Wetzel*, 511 F.2d at p. 205. Applying this principle to the facts of the case before it, the Court concluded that Liberty Mutual's income protection plan, which expressly excluded all pregnancy disabilities while at the same time covering all other disabilities except those voluntarily inflicted, discriminated against women in violation of the EEOC guidelines and Title VII. *Wetzel*, 511 F.2d at p. 206.

In reaching this conclusion, the Court expressly rejected the argument that Liberty Mutual could justifiably exclude pregnancy disabilities because pregnancy is voluntary, while illnesses are not. As the Court said:

"Voluntariness is no basis to justify disparate treatment of pregnancy. There are a great many activities that people participate in that involve a recognized risk. Most people undertake these activities with full knowledge of the potential harm. Drinking intoxicating beverages, smoking, skiing, handball and tennis are all types of activities in which one could sustain harm.

According to Liberty Mutual's policy, all disabilities that could result from the above activities are covered under the income protection plan. Even if we were to accept appellant's argument of voluntariness, we find that some voluntary disabilities are covered while voluntary disability that is preculiar to women is not so covered. Either way we find no support for appellant's argument. Moreover, pregnancy itself may not be voluntary. Religious convictions and methods of contraception may play a part in determining the voluntary nature of a pregnancy. There is no 100% sure method of contraception, short of surgery, and for health reasons many women cannot use the pill. This court will not accept "voluntariness" as a reasonable basis for excluding pregnancy from appellant's income protection plan." *Wetzel*, 511 F.2d at p. 206.

The Court similarly rejected Liberty Mutual's argument that it could exclude pregnancy disability from its plan because pregnancy is not a sickness. As the Court said:

"We believe that pregnancy should be treated as any other temporary disability. Employers offer disability insurance plans to their employees to alleviate the economic burdens caused by the loss of income and the incurrence of medical expenses that arise from the inability to work. A woman, disabled by pregnancy, has much in common with a person disabled by a temporary illness. They both suffer a loss of income because of absence from work; they both incur medical expenses; and the pregnant women will probably have hospitalization expenses while the other person may have none, choosing to convalesce at home.

Thus, pregnancy is no different than any other temporary disability under an income protection plan offered to help employees through the financially difficult times caused by illness.

Under Liberty Mutual's plan nearly all disabilities are covered. We believe that an income protection plan that covers so many temporary disabilities but excludes pregnancy because it is not a sickness discriminates against women and cannot stand." *Wetzel,* 511 F.2d at p. 206.

The Court also rejected Liberty Mutual's argument that its plan did not violate Title VII because of the company's legitimate interest in maintaining the financial integrity of the plan. As the Court said, Liberty Mutual had offered no statistical evidence that the increased cost for pregnancy benefits would be "devastating", and that under EEOC guidelines, ". . . cost is no defense under Title VII to this particular issue. 29 C.F.R. § 1604.9(e)."

Finally, the Court rejected Liberty's argument that the plan's exclusion of pregnancy disabilities could stand because such exclusion policy was neutral on its face. Even if neutral on its face, the Court said, such policy treats a protected class of persons in a disparate manner, and "(t)his is precisely what Title VII intends to strike down." *Wetzel,* 511 F.2d at p. 206, citing Griggs v. Duke Power Co., 401 U.S. 424, 91 S.Ct. 849, 28 L.Ed.2d 158 (1971).

We have dealt with *Wetzel* at such length because we believe its holding and rationale fall squarely on point with the case now before us. Defendant in this case rests its argument that its sick leave policy does not violate Title VII almost entirely in *Geduldig.* As set forth above, *Wetzel* expressly held that *Geduldig* does not govern disposition of a sex discrimination issue under Title VII, and such holding in *Wetzel* disposes of defendant's *Geduldig* argument here.

To the *Wetzel* Court's well reasoned treatment of *Geduldig's* nonapplicability to Title VII cases, we would add only that apart from the fact that *Geduldig* was not a Title VII case, its statement that exclusion of pregnancy disabilities does not constitute sex discrimination which violates the Fourteenth Amendment cannot be taken also to hold that such exclusion also does not violate Title VII, simply because the standards for establishing discrimination by sex are respectively different under the Fourteenth Amendment and Title VII. The principal difference between the two standards is that under the Fourteenth Amendment, sex discrimination becomes illegal only if intended, while under Title VII proof of intent is unnecessary and discriminatory impact alone establishes liability. The *Geduldig* majority, in fact, relied expressly on the absence of discriminatory intent in holding that the exclusion of pregnancy disabilities from the California income protection plan did not establish sex discrimination in violation of the Fourteenth Amendment of *Geduldig,* 417 U.S. at 496, 94 S.Ct. at 2492, 41 L.Ed.2d at 264, nt. 20.

Wetzel similarly disposes of defendant's argument that § 1604.10(b) of the EEOC guidelines, quoted above, does not establish that exclusion of disabilities resulting from normal pregnancy, as opposed to disabilities resulting from complicated pregnancy, is discriminatory. The income protection plan at issue in *Wetzel* excluded disabilities from all pregnancies, normal or complicated, and the Court, in holding that § 1604.10(b) made it a violation of Title VII to treat pregnancy disabilities differently than other disabilities, at no point distinguished between normal and complicated pregnancies.

Nor do we think that § 1604.10(b) suggests or permits such a distinction. § 1604.10(b) speaks of "Disabilities caused or contributed to by pregnancy . . . childbirth, and recovery therefrom . . ." and says nothing about a distinction between normal and complicated pregnancy and childbirth. We think the only issue under § 1604.10(b) is whether the disability is caused by the pregnancy or childbirth. This regulation shows no evidence that the EEOC intended that courts in applying it should attempt the further and potentially unadministerable task of determining whether the pregnancy or childbirth causing the work disability was normal rather than complicated.

Furthermore, in so interpreting § 1604.10(b), we do not, contrary to defendant's argument, equate "pregnancy" with "disability". Pregnancy need not at all stages disable a woman from work, and only when pregnancy or childbirth does so disable her does § 1604.10(b) become applicable to the employer's treatment of her. Plaintiffs here themselves emphasize that they seek relief only for the denial of sick leave for the time that pregnancy or childbirth disables the woman from working, and not for the time that the woman, while pregnant, could nonetheless work but elects not to in order, for example, to prepare for childbirth.

Similarly, we believe *Wetzel* adequately disposes of defendant's suggestion here that its sick leave policy does not discriminate because such policy allows sick leave only for illness or injury, rather than general disability, and normal pregnancy does not constitute illness or injury. Whether or not pregnancy or childbirth constitute "illness", the *Wetzel* Court expressly said that considering the effects and purposes of an employer's income protection plan, work disability because of pregnancy or childbirth deserves the same treatment as other temporary disabilities. While *Wetzel* dealt with an income protection plan, we believe the same reasoning applies readily to a sick leave plan. Such plans are instituted to alleviate the hardship which would otherwise befall an employee temporarily physically disabled from working. The employee disabled from pregnancy or childbirth has just as much need for such protection as the employee disabled because of strictly defined illness or injury. Denial of sick leave to the employee disabled because of pregnancy or childbirth thus constitutes different treatment of that employee's needs than those of the employee otherwise disabled, but without rational basis for such distinction.

Indeed, we would note that an employee stands to lose far more by not having use of a sick leave plan like that involved here than from an income protection plan like that involved in *Wetzel*. Whereas the income protection plan preserves only a portion of the employee's pay, the absent employee under the city's sick leave plan here continues not only to receive his full salary, but also to accrue future sick leave as well as time for pension, vacation, promotional, and anniversary date purposes, and other fringe benefits. If the "illness/non-illness" rationale cannot justify the difference in treatment involved in the income protection plan in *Wetzel*, even less can it justify the substantially greater difference in treatment which the sick leave plan here in issue involves.

Perhaps more basically, however, defendant's "illness" argument fails for the simple reason that defendant does not administer its sick leave program to cover only disability from illness or injury. While defendant's sick leave policy, at least under the language of the governing Civil Service Regulation 21.011, would allow use of sick leave for absence from work because of illness or injury, in practice defendant allows use of sick leave for absence from work for reasons other than illness or injury, such as elective surgery or alcoholic hangovers. In practice, therefore, defendant extends sick leave for physical disability generally, rather than only for physical disability from illness or injury, with the only exception to this policy being disability from normal pregnancy and childbirth. In such light, we find that much more reason to conclude that defendant's different treatment of maternity-related disabilities rests on no justifiable basis.

Finally, the fact that the employer here is a city has no bearing on the above discussion. Title VII applies to municipal corporations as readily as to private employers, so long as the municipal corporation employs fifteen or more employees in each working day of twenty or more calendar weeks in the current or preceding calendar year, which criteria defendant meets in this case. See 42 U.S.C. § 2000e(a) and (b), as amended 1972.

Accordingly, we conclude that defendant's policy of denying the use of sick leave for maternity-related disabilities violates Title VII's prohibition against sexual discrimination in employment. For the purposes of our present order, we need not decide the issue of damages or the related issue of whether Title VII compels the defendant to remedy any continuing effects of its denial of sick leave for maternity-related disability in the past and up to the date of this order. We will consider these issues only after the presentation of further evidence and oral argument.

In light of our decision on Title VII grounds, we need not reach the issue of whether defendant's sick leave policy also violates the Fourteenth Amendment.

Satty v. Nashville Gas Co.

[384 F.Supp. 765 (M.D. Tenn. 1974), 522 F.2d 850 (6th Cir. 1975), *cert. granted*, ____ U.S. ____ (1978) (No. 75-536)]

Employer's benefit policies concerning pregnancy-related disabilities: What violates/does not violate Title VII?

Analysis of the issue

The plaintiff in this proceeding alleged that by virtue of being pregnant, she became the victim of her employer's benefits, leave, pay and seniority policies which discriminated on the basis of sex. She asserted that her employer's group insurance plan which only covered 50 percent of maternity fees was discriminatory. The court however, ruled that because female employees were given the same insurance benefits that wives of male employees were provided, the program did not violate Title VII. However, the court did find that the employer's requirement that pregnant employees take maternity leave, instead of sick leave, did violate Title VII. This conclusion was based on the fact that accompanying the mandatory maternity leave came the loss of seniority for job-bidding purposes. Also taken into consideration was the fact that employees suffering other non-work-related disabilities were entitled to use sick leave, an option which allows the employee to keep his job-bidding seniority intact, in addition to being entitled to collect pay during the disability period. While the plaintiff was on maternity leave, her position in the accounting department was phased out. Upon returning to work, the plaintiff was required to take a temporary position until a permanent one became available. This practice was carried out in accordance with the defendant's written personnel policies. The defendant, upon reinstating an employee who was absent on leave, would, according to policy, credit the employee with seniority previously accumulated for the purposes of pension, vacation and other benefits. However, seniority for the purpose of job-bidding was neither by policy nor practice, credited to the returning employee. Although the court did not find the defendant's policy of providing temporary assignments for returning employees, specifically in the case of the plaintiff, retaliatory, the plaintiff was awarded back pay, reinstatement as a permanent employee credited with full seniority beginning with the date of her initial hire, and the recovery of attorney's fees.

The defendant sought and was granted an appeal. The case was heard on August 8, 1975 by the U.S. Court of Appeals, Sixth Circuit for Cincinnati. The defendant argued that its seemingly disparate dissemination of benefits with respect to maternity and nonmaternity disabilities was in keeping with the decision handed down in *Geduldig v. Aiello*. In that case the court allowed such "dual standards" provided there was a legitimate state interest at stake to justify the action. The appeals court however, turned to the EEOC's interpretation of Title VII, considering the Commission's guidelines to be controlling in such matters. In so doing, the court held that the protection provided by Title VII extended beyond the reach of the Equal Protection Clause of the Fourteenth Amendment of the Constitution. Saying this, the appeals court affirmed the decision handed down in the district court.

Full text of opinion

MORTON, District Judge: — This cause of action was brought pursuant to Title VII of the Civil Rights Act of 1964 (42 U.S.C. § 2000e et seq.) alleging sex discrimination in defendant's employment policies with respect to pregnancy. Plaintiff seeks back wages, lost benefits, attorney's fees and injunctive relief. Plaintiff further alleges that her employment was terminated because she complained about the allegedly discriminatory policies.

There is no dispute as to the jurisdiction of this court under Title VII of the Civil Rights Act of 1964.

Originally the cause was brought as a class action. However, the parties stipulated that the number of persons whom plaintiff may properly represent is not sufficiently numerous to permit maintenance of a class action under Rule 23, Federal Rules of Civil Procedure.

Simultaneously with filing of this action, plaintiff filed a motion for entry of a preliminary injunction requiring defendant to reinstate her as an employee and enjoining defendant from retaliatory measures. A hearing was held upon plaintiff's motion on July 10, 1974. At the close of the hearing, the court determined that a preliminary injunction would not be issued because plaintiff failed to establish that irreparable harm would be suffered by denial of the motion and it appeared that monetary damages could compensate plaintiff for any injury she might suffer.

The threshold question is whether or not defendant's employment policies, with respect to pregnancy, constitute unlawful sex discrimination.

The parties have stipulated as to the following statement describing defendant's policy of health insurance:

As a condition of employment, every employee of Nashville Gas Company is required to be covered under a group life, health and accident policy issued by Provident Life and Accident Insurance Company. The cost of such policy is borne half by the Company and half by the employees. In addition to other health and hospitalization benefits, said policy also provides for payment of 50% of the customary and reasonable fees incurred in connection with pregnancy. Such pregnancy benefits apply to female employees and dependent wives of male employees. Although the insurance plan terminates with respect to an employee at the time such employee's active employment ceases, the maternity benefits continue to apply for up to nine months after termination and if such benefits would have been payable had delivery occurred on the date such active employment ceases.

Plaintiff's theory is that defendant's group insurance program discriminates on the basis of sex because a reduced benefit is paid in the case of pregnancy when compared with hospitalizations for other causes. There is no doubt that the insurance program makes a distinction in the case of pregnancy as to the extent of benefits available. However, the pregnancy distinction applies to both male and female employee-beneficiaries of the plan. The insurance proceeds are paid on behalf of the employee, male or female, according to a single formula in all pregnancy cases. Thus, for a male employee whose wife is pregnant, the insurance benefit is the same as provided to a pregnant female employee such as plaintiff.

The parties further stipulated that pregnancy is a temporary disabling condition resulting from a normal bodily function. In this case the plaintiff had a normal pregnancy and childbirth. Also, the parties have agreed that defendant does not have a disability insurance plan for its employees. This is not a situation where a female employee receives a lesser benefit for her disability than those received by males. Defendant's insurance plan pays no benefit whatsoever for disabilities. The only benefit under defendant's insurance plan is for payment of medical expenses. The issue in this case is whether defendant's insurance program discriminates unlawfully between male and female employees in the payment of medical expenses.

No evidence has been introduced to show a failure on defendant's part to comply with the Equal Employment Opportunity Commission guidelines on fringe benefits. Title 29, Code of Federal Regulations, Section 1604.9(d) provides:

It shall be an unlawful employment practice for an employer to make available benefits for the wives and families of male employees where the same benefits are not made available for the husbands and families of female employees; or to make available benefits for the wives of male employees which are not available for female employees; or to make available benefits to the husbands of female employees which are not available for male employees. An example of such an unlawful employment practice is a situation in which wives of male employees receive maternity benefits while female employees receive no such benefits.

So far as the issue relating to the insurance program is concerned, the court finds no distinction in the application, operation, or effect of the insurance plan to support a finding of unlawful discrimination by reason of sex since all employees, male or female, receive the same benefit.

It has been and is now the policy of defendant to require pregnant employees to take maternity leave. Although defendant's "Employee Policy Manual," of September 27, 1971, presents availability of maternity leave in permissive terms, to wit:

In case of pregnancy, an employee, upon written request *may* be granted a leave of absence . . . (emphasis added)

actual practice demonstrates that a pregnant employee may not decline to accept maternity leave, and still retain employee affiliation with the defendant company. Once an employee is placed in maternity leave status, she may remain in the status for up to one year. There is no statement of policy concerning the status of an employee on maternity leave who is unable to return to work after one year. A fair inference is that such an employee would be terminated.

Once an employee is classified as being in a leave status, i.e., leave of absence or pregnancy leave, it is defendant's policy to offer such an employee temporary work, when available, until a permanent position is open. After an employee returns from leave status and acquires permanent employment, the defendant credits such person with seniority previously accumulated for the purposes of pension, vacation, and other employee benefits based on seniority. However, defendant does not credit an employee returning from leave status who is subsequently classified as a temporary or permanent employee with previously accumulated seniority for the purpose of bidding on job openings. The significance of this policy is illustrated in the present case where plaintiff returned from pregnancy leave as a temporary employee after more than four (4) years of continuous employment, next preceding maternity leave, and defendant failed to place her in one of several permanent job openings. All of these openings were filed by other employees credited with greater job-bidding seniority even though plaintiff had the earlier date of initial employment. It appears that seniority is the primary factor in the job-bidding process and failure to credit plaintiff with seniority for this purpose is the sole reason she failed to gain a permanent position with defendant following her return from maternity leave.

Defendant asserts that the job-bidding policies are the same for all employees, male or female, returning from a leave status.

The gravamen of defendant's contention is that only pregnant women are required to take leave. In all cases other than maternity the decision to take leave is entirely a voluntary matter with each employee.

It further appears that defendant maintains a policy of allowing leave in connection with non-work related illness or injury without loss of seniority or other indicia of good standing on the part of an employee where the non-work related disability does not concern pregnancy. It is only in the case of pregnancy that an employee is denied the opportunity to take "sick leave."

Defendant does not have a disability insurance plan for its employees, but does provide a specific number of sick leave days based on the employee's seniority. Employees, like plaintiff, who are placed on pregnancy leave are not paid for accumulated sick leave, but are paid for accumulated vacation time. Defendant's policy has been to allow employees who have been absent due to illness or non-work related disabilities to take "sick leave." Only in the case of pregnancy is an employee denied the right to take sick leave. It further appears that employees returning from long periods of absence due to non-job related injuries do not lose their seniority and in fact their seniority continues to accumulate while absent.

Defendant asserts that the classification of employees as pregnant employees and non-pregnant employees for application of the aforementioned policies does not constitute unlawful sex discrimination under Title VII. Defendant acknowledges that a number of court decisions under Title VII, and the position of the Equal Employment Opportunity Commission, indicate that policies affording different treatment for temporary disability due to pregnancy than for all other non-work related disabilities is discrimination based on sex. However, it is asserted that the recent United States Supreme Court decision in Geduldig v.

Aiello, 417 U.S. 484, 94 S.Ct. 2485, 41 L.Ed.2d 256 (1974), determined that disparity of treatment between pregnancy related disability and other disabilities does not constitute sex discrimination.

If defendant's reliance on the *Geduldig* decision were proper, then it would not be necessary to consider other cases in this area. For the reasons stated below, the court concludes that defendant's reliance on the *Geduldig* decision is not well founded.

In *Geduldig* the sole question presented was whether classifications under a disability insurance program established and administered under the laws of California violated the Equal Protection Clause of the Fourteenth Amendment. The asserted constitutional violation was based on the exclusion of disabilities in connection with normal pregnancies from coverage under the insurance program. The United States Supreme Court held that the exclusion of normal pregnancies from benefit coverage did not involve improper state action. The standard applied by the Court to test the constitutional question was one of "reasonableness." There was no question concerning the legitimacy of the state's action in establishing the disability insurance program to supplement the workman's compensation program. The analytic key to the *Geduldig* decision is found in the following language:

This Court has held that, consistently with the Equal Protection Clause, a State "may take one step at a time, addressing itself to the phase of the problem which seems most acute to the legislative mind. . . . The legislature may select one phase of one field and apply a remedy there, neglecting the others. . . ." . . . Particularly with respect to social welfare programs, *so long as the line drawn by the State is rationally supportable,* the courts will not interpose their judgment as to the appropriate stopping point. "[T]he Equal Protection Clause does not require that a State must choose between attacking every aspect of a problem or not attacking the problem at all." . . . . (417 U.S. 484, 495, 94 S.Ct. 2485, 2491, 41 L.Ed.2d 256, 263-264. [emphasis added])

In finding a rational basis for the exclusion of normal pregnancies under the California disability insurance program, the Court noted several factors relating to the fiscal soundness of the program which were found sufficient.

It should be noted that *Geduldig* did not involve an assertion of unlawful action under the Civil Rights Act of 1964. The plaintiff in *Geduldig* was not an employee nor prospective employee claiming unlawful discrimination by reason of the State's employment practices. The question of whether the California disability insurance program sufficiently affects interstate commerce so as to be subject to the Civil Rights Act of 1964 does not appear to have been litigated.

In discussing the rational basis of California's exclusion of pregnancy benefits, the Court referred to the cases of Reed v. Reed, 404 U.S. 71, 92 S.Ct. 251, 30 L.Ed.2d 225, and Frontiero v. Richardson, 411 U.S. 677, 93 S.Ct 1764, 36 L.Ed.2d 583. Both of these cases were brought under the Equal Protection Clause of the Fourteenth Amendment and in each case the Court found there was no rational basis for discrimination. In the *Reed* case the Court found a provision of the Idaho Probate Code giving preference to males in appointment of administrators to be violative of the Equal Protection Clause. Writing for the Court, the Chief Justice stated the test to be applied in Equal Protection type cases:

. . . [T]his Court has consistently recognized that the Fourteenth Amendment does not deny to States the power to treat different classes of persons in different ways. . . . The Equal Protection Clause of that amendment does, however, deny to States the power to legislate that different treatment be accorded to persons placed by a statute into different classes on the basis of criteria wholly unrelated to the objective of that statute. A classification "must be reasonable, not arbitrary, and must rest upon some ground of difference having a fair and substantial relation to the object of the legislation, so that all persons similarly circumstanced shall be treated alike." (404 U.S. 71, 75, 92 S.Ct. 251, 253, 30 L.Ed.2d 225, 229).

In the final analysis the Court concluded that the Idaho statute had no rationale sufficient to sustain the different classifications established for men and women.

In the *Frontiero* decision the Court again found there was no rational basis for the distinction drawn in the payment of benefits between male and female members of the military services.

The standard applicable to state action under the Equal Protection Clause of the Fourteenth Amendment is distinct from the lawful power of Congress to establish different standards for conduct affecting interstate commerce. Under the Commerce Clause the Congress has plenary power to regulate all aspects of interstate commerce. Gibbons v. Ogden, 9 Wheat. (22 U.S.) 1, 6 L.Ed. 23 (1824); United States v. Darby, 312 U.S. 100, 61 S.Ct. 451, 85 L.Ed. 609 (1941); Heart of Atlanta Motel v. United States, 379 U.S. 241, 85 S.Ct. 348, 13 L.Ed.2d 258 (1964); Maryland v. Wirtz, 392 U.S. 193, 88 S.Ct. 2017, 20 L.Ed.2d 1020 (1968). In effect Congress has established a standard for testing employment discrimination that goes beyond the standard of "reasonableness" traditionally applied to the States under the Equal Protection Clause of the Fourteenth Amendment.

To further illustrate the distinction between the two standards of permissible discrimination, it is helpful to consider the legislative history of Title VII. Title 42 U.S.C. Sec. 2000e et seq. presents the standard to be applied in cases of employment discrimination. In 1972 Congress amended Title VII by deleting a portion of 42 U.S.C. Sec. 2000e(c) which originally provided:

. . . but shall not include an agency of the United States, or an agency of a State or political subdivision of a State, except that such term shall include the United States Employment Service and the system of State and local employment services receiving Federal assistance . . .

The effect of the 1972 amendment was to broaden the scope of Title VII and extend the employment standard to the States.

The case of Maryland v. Wirtz, *supra,* demonstrates the power of Congress under the Commerce Clause to prescribe the standard against which conduct will be gauged if that conduct affects interstate commerce. In noting that States are susceptible to the congressionally prescribed standards, the Court stated:

But while the commerce power has limits, valid general regulations of commerce do not cease to be regulations of commerce because a State is involved. If a State is engaging in economic activities that are validly regulated by the Federal Government when engaged in by private persons, the State too may be forced to conform its activities to federal regulations. (392 U.S. 193, 196, 88 S.Ct. 2017, 2024, 20 L.Ed.2d 1020, 1031)

The congressional standard to be applied under the Civil Rights Act of 1964 is stated in 42 U.S.C. Sec. 2000e-2 for those cases alleging discriminatory employment practices. The only exception to the standard that could have relevance in the instant case is found in 42 U.S.C. Sec. 2000e-2(e)(1) which provides that a classification based on sex, etc., is permissible *if* there is:

. . . a bona fide occupational qualification reasonably necessary to the normal operation of that particular business or enterprise . . .

In light of the Maryland v. Wirtz decision, *supra,* it would appear that the proper standard to be applied in all employment discrimination cases properly brought under Title VII is the congressionally mandated standard outlined above.

All sex discrimination cases do not fall within the same category. As this discussion has illustrated, there are at least two classifications of sex discrimination cases: those arising under the Equal Protection Clause of the Fourteenth Amendment and those arising under Title VII of the Civil Rights Act of 1964. These two categories involve the application of different standards for the determination of whether distinctions based on sex are permissible. Under the Equal Protection Clause there need be only a "reasonable basis" for the legislative determination. However, under the Civil Rights Act of 1964, there must be an actual business necessity for employment policies that discriminate on the basis of sex. See Moody v. Albemarle Paper Co., 474 F.2d 134 (4th Cir. 1973); Diaz v. Pan American World Airways, Inc., 442 F.2d 385 (5th Cir. 1971); Williams v. American St. Gobain Corp., 447 F.2d 561 (10th Cir. 1971).

The *Geduldig* case was brought under the Equal Protection Clause and not under Title VII. Thus, the standard involved was one of legislative reasonableness. Since *Geduldig* was not an employment case, it would be improper to draw a negative inference as to the power of Congress to establish a different standard of permissible discrimination for employers admittedly affecting interstate commerce. For these reasons, defendant's contention that *Geduldig* controls in the instant case is rejected.

In the opinion of this court, defendant's employment practices are discriminatory in the following respects: (1) only pregnant women are required to take leave and thereby lose job-bidding seniority and no leave is required in other non-work related disabilities; and (2) only pregnant women are denied sick leave benefits while in all other cases of non-work related disability sick leave benefits are available. Dessenberg v. American Metal Founding Co., 8 FEP Cases, 291 (D.C.Ohio); Hutchinson v. Lake Oswego School District, 374 F.Supp. 1056 (D.C.1974); Gilbert v. General Electric Co., 375 F.Supp. 367 (D.C. 1974). Defendant has introduced no proof of any business necessity in support of these discriminatory policies. The court must therefore assume no justification exists.

Plaintiff further alleges that defendant's action in not holding her job open for her while she was on pregnancy leave constitutes discrimination based on sex. This allegation must be considered in light of certain business factors.

Plaintiff's principal duties prior to being placed on maternity leave involved the posting of merchandise accounts. It appears that defendant was considering prior to plaintiff's pregnancy, and has now initiated, the transfer of certain accounting functions to its computer processing department. Further, defendant has undertaken to discontinue its merchandise business. Both of these factors suggest a legitimate basis for the decision not to hold plaintiff's job open in the accounting department. The court discerns no discriminatory conduct by defendant with reference to this issue.

It is further asserted that defendant's action in requiring plaintiff to begin her pregnancy leave on December 29, 1972, was arbitrary and in violation of Title VII.

Although defendant's "Employee Policy Manual" suggests that pregnancy leave commence during the fourth month, actual practice shows that no set time is arbitrarily established to determine when leave shall be taken. Defendant's Vice President-Personnel has stated that several factors are weighed when reaching the decision to start pregnancy leave. These factors include: the opinion of the employee's doctor; the employee's duties; work area; and degree of public contact. Although the Vice President-Personnel was to be the final judge of when these factors should dictate the commencement of leave, there is no showing of abuse in reaching that decision.

Following employee holidays on Friday, December 22, and Monday, December 25, 1972, plaintiff failed to report for work on the next four consecutive work days. The proof shows that she was having a problem with water retention at that time and that she also had a common cold. After being placed on maternity leave on December 29, 1972, plaintiff gave birth to her child on January 23, 1973, some twenty-five days after maternity leave had commenced.

It is of paramount significance that defendant's policies as actually practiced do not fix an arbitrary month or date on which pregnancy leave must begin. The facts in each situation are considered on an individual basis. Given plaintiff's problem with water retention and the subsequent birth of her child on the 25th day of maternity leave, defendant's action does not appear to be arbitrary or irrational. See Cleveland Board of Ed. v. LaFleur, 414 U.S. 632, 94 S.Ct. 791, 39 L.Ed.2d 52 (1974).

A further issue in this cause is whether the termination of plaintiff's temporary employment on April 13, 1973, was in retaliation for her complaining about defendant's employment policies with respect to pregnancy.

Plaintiff returned to work with defendant as a temporary employee on March 14, 1973. It was defendant's policy to place women returning from maternity leave in available temporary positions until a permanent opening was awarded on the basis of job bidding. Plaintiff worked as a temporary employee until April 13, 1973, when the temporary project to which she was assigned was completed. Plaintiff continued to apply for permanent job positions but was frustrated in her efforts by those policies causing her to lose credit for accumulated seniority in job bidding. The court finds no evidence of retaliatory termination of plaintiff for assertion of her civil rights. However, it is clear that plaintiff's termination request was the result of her inability to retain permanent employment following forfeiture of her job-bidding seniority rights by defendant.

The court concludes that plaintiff is entitled to the following relief:

Recovery of sick leave benefits that should have been paid during her maternity leave. Plaintiff is also entitled to have sick leave benefits credited and accumulated from the time she returned from maternity leave on March 14, 1973.

Back wages from March 14, 1973, until the present. The back wages shall be computed on the rate of pay earned by plaintiff on December 29, 1972, plus any across the board increases which may have occurred since that time. However, back pay will be reduced by amounts paid for temporary work with defendant, unemployment compensation received from the State of Tennessee, and wages from other employment.

Reinstatement as a permanent employee as of the date that the first permanent position after March 14, 1973, was filled with another employee having less seniority than plaintiff. Plaintiff will be credited with full seniority from the date of her initial hiring by defendant.

Recovery of reasonable attorney's fees.

The court authorizes the defendant to submit affidavits concerning plaintiff's status upon reinstatement. If there has been a reduction in force by defendant which would have caused plaintiff's termination sometime after March 14, 1973, based on seniority computed from the date of her initial hiring, that fact may be shown to properly adjust the relief awarded plaintiff. Such affidavits should also reflect applicable "bumping" procedures, if any, to clarify whether or not plaintiff would have been entitled to a lesser position in defendant's company. Defendant may submit other data relating to the entitlement of plaintiff under the terms of this memorandum. However, defendant shall furnish copies of such affidavits to plaintiff's counsel and plaintiff shall have an opportunity to respond. The court will review such affidavits as are submitted relative to the determination of plaintiff's reinstatement and back wages, and if any material issue of fact is presented, a further hearing will be ordered on that matter. Defendant is allowed fifteen (15) days for the submission of affidavits and plaintiff shall have ten (10) days following defendant's submission to file counter-affidavits.

Counsel for plaintiff will submit an order consistent with the provisions of this memorandum.

The following is the text of the appellate decision 522 F.2d 850 (6th Cir. 1975)

ROBERT L. TAYLOR, District Judge:—After exhausting her remedies through the Equal Employment Opportunity Commission, this action was initiated by Nora Satty against the Nashville Gas Company for alleged sex discrimination in violation of Title VII of the Civil Rights Act of 1964, 42 U.S.C. § 2000e *et seq.* The District Court after hearing testimony from plaintiff denied her motion for a temporary injunction but thereafter on November 4, 1974 awarded reinstatement with seniority, back pay, including sick leave, and attorney fees. For the reasons set forth below, we affirm.

Undisputed, the facts are relatively simple. Plaintiff was initially hired by Nashville Gas as a junior clerk in the customer accounting department on March 24, 1969, and was later promoted to clerk on December 2, 1969. Having previously informed her employer in August 1972 of her pregnancy, she was placed on maternity leave on December 29, 1972, pursuant to the request of the vice-president in charge of personnel. Plaintiff's child was born twenty-five days later on January 23, 1973. Under Nashville Gas' policy, an employee can be granted pregnancy leave for a period of up to one year. Following the child's birth and after a six week checkup the employee is permitted to return to full-time status when a permanent position becomes available and when the opening is not bid on by a permanent employee. During the interim between the six week checkup and reemployment on a permanent basis, Nashville Gas attempts to provide the employee with temporary work. As a consequence of this policy, the employee who is placed on pregnancy leave, unlike the male employee who is absent due to a nonwork-related disability, loses her accumulated seniority for job-bidding purposes but otherwise retains her accrued vacation and pension seniority. Similarly, while the employee is permitted to apply her accumulated vacation time to her absence during pregnancy, sick leave may not be applied to a pregnancy-related absence. It is these latter two specific policies that are the object of plaintiff's attack.

On March 14, 1973, plaintiff returned to work as a temporary employee and was paid $130.80 per week, as opposed to $140.80 she earned prior to her leaving in December, 1972; however, this temporary employment ended on April 13, 1973 when her job was completed. Thereafter, in order to collect unemployment compensation insurance, plaintiff requested Nashville Gas to change her employment status from pregnancy leave to complete termination. It was stipulated by the parties that between December 29, 1972 and May 10, 1973, plaintiff applied for three full-time positions with Nashville Gas which became available; however, in each case a permanent employee with job seniority was awarded the position. Had plaintiff retained her job-bidding seniority, she would have been awarded the positions.

Against this background, the principal issue before the Court is whether Nashville Gas' pregnancy policy violates Title VII of the Civil Rights Act of 1964, 42 U.S.C. § 2000-5, as amended. In holding that defendant's policy is violative of the Civil Rights Act of 1964, we note that this question, as framed in the context of the impact of the Supreme Court's decision in *Geduldig v. Aiello*, 417 U.S. 484, 94 S.Ct. 2485, 41 L.Ed.2d 256 (1974), is one of first impression in this Circuit. The same issue has been addressed in four other circuits.

Central to the dispute here is the controlling impact of the Supreme Court's decision in *Aiello* and, more particularly, the weight this Court should attribute to footnote 20 of that opinion. If *Aiello* and footnote 20 are dispositive of the issue whether a distinction between pregnancy-related disabilities and other disabilities is sex based, then the threshold issue is easily resolved against plaintiff. If however, *Aiello* is not viewed as dispositive, then the Court must proceed to consider alternative constructions.

California, in establishing an employee supported disability insurance system for nonwork-related injuries, chose to exclude pregnancy-related disabilities from the scope of the program's operation. Four women who had experienced a period of pregnancy-related disability challenged their exclusion from the program's benefits, and a three-judge district court found such exclusion violated the Equal Protection Clause. However, Justice Stewart speaking for the majority, adopted the "rationally supportable" standard of justification, and held that the state's legitimate interest in seeking to protect the program's financial integrity and self-supporting character allowed it to address "itself to the phase of the problem which seems most acute to the legislative mind . . ." Thus, cast in terms of the administration of a social welfare program, under the Court's interpretation the line drawn by the California legislature was between preganacy-related disabilities and other disabilities, not between male and female employees. The Court peripherally amplified in footnote 20 its basis for concluding that disability and not sex was the line drawn by California legislature:

"The dissenting opinion to the contrary, this case is thus a far cry from cases like *Reed v. Reed,* 404 U.S. 71, 92 S.Ct. 251, 30 L.Ed.2d 225 (1971), and *Frontiero v. Richardson,* 411 U.S. 677, 93 S.Ct. 1764, 36 L.Ed.2d 583 (1973), involving discrimination based upon gender as such. The California insurance program does not exclude anyone from benefit eligibility because of gender but merely removes one physical condition—pregnancy—from the list of compensable disabilities. While it is true that only women can become pregnant, it does not follow that every legislative classification concerning pregnancy is a sex-based classification like those considered in *Reed, Supra,* and *Frontiero, supra.* Normal pregnancy is an objectively identifiable physical condition with unique characteristics. Absent a showing that distinctions involving pregnancy are mere pretexts designed to effect an invidious discrimination against the members of one sex or the other, *lawmakers are constitutionally free* to include or exclude pregnancy from the coverage of legislation such as this on any reasonable basis, just as with respect to any other physical condition." 417 U.S. at 496, n. 20, 94 S.Ct. at 2492 (emphasis added).

It is apparent from our reading of footnote 20 that the Court's observations are made in the particular and narrow confines of the state's power to draw flexible and pragmatic lines in the social welfare area. To conclude that the Court's footnote is dispositive of an action brought under Title VII would be to ignore the traditional doctrine that the precedential value of a decision should be limited to the four corners of the decisions' factual setting. The reasoning and policy behind this doctrine are readily appreciated when *Aiello* is compared with the facts in this case. Here, the question is whether the exclusion by a private employer of pregnancy-related disabilities from its sick leave and seniority program is a violation of a congressional statute, essentially, a dissimilar question from the issue before the *Aiello* Court—whether a legislative classification dividing disabilities into two classes for the purposes of a disability income protection program finds a rational basis. It is this very degree of dissimilarity that rejects a blind adherence to footnote 20. To import a different effect to footnote 20 would be to extend the impact of *Aiello* beyond its intended effect. It would appear harsh to read into footnote 20 that the Court expected, in passing on the propriety of a legislative classification under the Equal Protection Clause, to preclude all future discussion of statutory interpretation under a relatively new act such as the Civil Rights Act of 1964. Unless squarely faced with the Act, the Court has evidenced a reluctance to examine its parameters or the interpretive functions of the Equal Employment Opportunity Commission (E.E.O.C.). While mindful of the Court's language in footnote 20, caution dictates that we not make it a talisman for Title VII actions.

Turning from *Aiello* for guidance, it is logical that we should look to the agency charged with the administration of Title VII. In this regard, 29 C.F.R. § 1604.10(b) provides:

"(b) Disabilities caused or contributed to by pregnancy, miscarriage, abortion, childbirth, and recovery therefrom are, for all job-related purposes, temporary disabilities and should be treated as such under any health or temporary disability insurance or sick leave plan available in connection with employment. Written and unwritten employment policies and practices involving matters such as the commencement and duration of leave, the availability of extensions, and accrual of seniority and other benefits and privileges, reinstatement, and payment under any health or temporary disability insurance or sick leave plan, formal or informal, shall be applied to disability due to pregnancy or childbirth on the same terms and conditions as they are applied to other temporary disabilities."

We are urged in this case to reject the lessons of *Griggs v. Duke Power Co.*, 401 U.S. 424, 91 S.Ct. 849, 28 L.Ed.2d 158 (1971), and *Phillips v. Martin Marietta Corp.*, 400 U.S. 542, 545, 90 S.Ct. 496, 27 L.Ed.2d 613 (1971) (Marshall, J., concurring), which accord deference to the Commission's interpretation, under the authority of the Supreme Court's recent decision in *Espinoza v. Farah Manufacturing Co.*, 414 U.S. 86, 96, 94 S.Ct. 334, 38 L.Ed.2d 287 (1973). There, the Court, rejecting the Commission's regulation that discrimination on the basis of citizenship is tantamount to discrimination on the basis of national origin, noted that the agency had formerly held a different view, but, most importantly, the Court emphasized that "application of the guideline would be inconsistent with an obvious congressional intent . . ." Unlike the situation before the Court in *Espinoza*, we do not have before us any legislative history indicating that the E.E.O.C. interpretation conflicts with the congressional intent. We are not in a position to say that the agency position contravenes the letter or spirit of the Act. Thus, absent clear indicia in the form of legislative history that the agency interpretation is unreasonable or unnatural, we must defer to the Commission's construction of the statute as articulated under 29 C.F.R. § 1604.10(b).

We note that in holding that disparate treatment between pregnancy leave and other sick leave constitutes a violation of Title VII, we reaffirm this Court's former decision in *Farkas v. Southwestern City School District*, 506 F.2d 1400 (6th Cir. 1974), where the District Court was affirmed and the conclusion reached that exclusion of normal pregnancy from a sick leave program constituted sex discrimination under Title VII. We are not persuaded that that position is incorrect. Though the legislative history of Title VII contains no explicit reference to sex discrimination, we learn from its declaration of policy that its principal aim was to eliminate artificial barriers that fostered disparate treatment, absent a compelling and founded reason for such disparity.

Appellant contends that the test of the validity of an employment policy under Title VII is not different from the test of validity under the

Fourteenth Amendment. This argument, however, presupposes that the lawful scope of employment policies under the former Act is coextensive with the latter constitutional provision. We believe that the better approach permits Title VII under the Commerce Clause to extend beyond the reach of the Equal Protection Clause. *Heart of Atlanta Motel v. United States*, 379 U.S. 241, 85 S.Ct. 348, 13 L.Ed.2d 258 (1964); *Katzenbach v. McClung*, 379 U.S. 294, 85 S.Ct. 377, 13 L.Ed.2d 20. Otherwise, Title VII's effective reach would be limited by the decisions of the Supreme Court, a result effectively curtailing its implementation.

The District Court, finding that Nashville Gas' policy violated the provisions of 42 U.S.C. § 2000e-5, ordered that plaintiff recover sick leave benefits that should have been paid during her maternity leave; back wages from March 14, 1973, including any across the board increases, and reduced by temporary wages and unemployment insurance; reinstatement with full seniority and recovery of reasonable attorney fees.

Under the guidelines of *Meadows v. Ford Motor Company*, 510 F.2d 939 (1975), and *Head v. Timken Roller Bearing Company*, 486 F.2d 870 (6th Cir. 1973), we find the District Court's relief appropriate.

The judgment of the District Court is Affirmed.

EEOC v. Children's Hospital of Pittsburgh

[415 F. Supp. 1345 (W.D. Pa. 1976), 556 F.2d 222 (3rd Cir. 1977), *petition for cert. filed* _____ U.S. _____ (July 13, 1977)]

Denial of use of sick leave for pregnancy violates Title VII

Analysis of the issue

The EEOC filed proceedings against Children's Hospital of Pittsburgh on behalf of Mrs. Harriet Baum and all female employees of the hospital who experienced the denial of the use of accumulated sick leave for maternity purposes. The complaint which resulted in the EEOC's interest in the case was registered by Mrs. Baum. The situation began when Mrs. Baum first learned that she was pregnant and accordingly notified her supervisor of her wish to utilize her accumulated sick leave during the final stage of pregnancy, thus saving her maternity leave of absence for the period following child birth. Although she was granted maternity leave, the request to use sick leave was denied. The supervisor explained that the use of sick leave for pregnancy-related purposes was contrary to hospital policy. Left with no alternative, the plaintiff used her vacation time during the period leading up to child birth and maternity leave thereafter. She was scheduled to return to work on November 30. On November 23 she was notified by mail that due to economic necessity, her position had been eliminated. Mrs. Baum believed that her discharge was a retaliatory action taken against her because of her filing a complaint with the EEOC. In these proceedings the plaintiff asserts that the hospital's policy of not allowing female employees to use sick leave for pregnancy or child birth-related disabilities is, within the meaning of Title VII, discriminatory against women. The hospital, on the other hand, argued that its policy did not violate Title VII because the policy was not a part of wages or salary, was applied equitably to both male and female employees, and was emphatic in not allowing employees to schedule sick days ahead of time. The court, however, ruled for the plaintiff, saying that Mrs. Baum was forced to labor under conditions of temporary disability, and denying employees suffering such disabilities the use of their accumulated sick leave constituted discrimination on the basis of sex. The hospital was ordered to pay Mrs. Baum for the sick days that she was unlawfully denied the use of, plus interest on the amount of accrued salary. Because the hospital was successful in proving that Mrs. Baum was one of several employees whose positions were terminated due to a cut in funding experienced by the hospital, the discharge was not deemed retaliatory by the court.

In appealing the district court's decision the EEOC attempted to win a monetary award for all members of the affected class. Before the appeals case [556 F.2d (3rd Cir., 1977)] commenced, the Supreme Court handed down a decision in *General Electric Company v. Gilbert* saying that the exclusion of pregnancy-related disabilities from a disability plan does not violate Title VII. Although the Supreme Court's decision was controlling, the EEOC persisted in its appeal, which resulted in the individual plaintiff's loss of monetary relief. The full text of the appeals case follows the district court action.

Full text of opinion

GOURLEY, Senior District Judge: — This is a civil rights proceeding filed by the plaintiff, Equal Employment Opportunity Commission, against the defendant, Children's Hospital of Pittsburgh, in behalf of Harriet Baum and all other similarly situated female employees of the defendant hospital for alleged violations of the Civil Rights Act, more particularly, Sections 703(a) and 704(a) of Title VII of the Civil Rights Act of 1964, as amended, 42 U.S.C.A. § 2000e et seq. The court has held a full and complete trial in this proceeding and afforded counsel every opportunity to present any and all evidence, oral or documentary in nature, to support their respective positions.

The facts may be briefly stated. Harriet Baum, a female, was first employed by the defendant, Children's Hospital, as a growth and developmental specialist in its Developmental Clinic, on August 7, 1968. Throughout her employment with the Children's Hospital, Harriet Baum worked thirty hours per week and was granted vacation pay and sick pay in amounts equal to three quarters of those granted to full-time employees.

When Mrs. Baum learned of her pregnancy in January of 1973, she immediately notified her supervisor, Dr. Grace Gregg, of her condition and communicated her desire to return to work following a leave of absence. Mrs. Baum also sought and requested of defendant to have her unpaid leave of absence begin at the end of her accumulated sick days and vacation days. Suffice to say, Mrs. Baum was subsequently informed that her leave of absence was approved; however, her request to have her accumulated sick days used up prior to the beginning of her leave of absence was denied as being contrary to hospital policy. Thereafter, on May 10, 1973, Harriet Baum filed with the Equal Employment Opportunity Commission a charge against the defendant alleging discrimination through its denial to permit her to use the accumulated sick leave for a maternity related disability.

Mrs. Baum remained in the defendant's employ until July 20, 1973, just four days prior to the birth of her daughter on July 24, 1973. Since Mrs. Baum did not begin her maternity leave until August 21, 1973, at the conclusion of her vacation days, she was not scheduled to return to work until November 30, 1973. Accordingly, Mrs. Baum contacted the defendant in the early part of November, 1973, indicating that she was willing and ready to return to work at the conclusion of her maternity leave which was to have ended on November 30, 1973. However, on November 23, 1973, Mrs. Baum received a letter from defendant notifying her that due to economic cuts in the hospital's budget, her position as a growth and developmental specialist had been eliminated and that her services at the hospital were no longer required. This notice and action by the defendant prompted Mrs. Baum to file a second charge with the Equal Employment Opportunity Commission on November 26, 1973, alleging that her discharge was due to the previous charge filed against the defendant with the Equal Employment Opportunity Commission.

It is the plaintiff's contention that the defendant hospital's policy of prohibiting female employees to use their accumulated sick leave for pregnancy or child-birth related disabilities discriminated against women employees in violation of Title VII.

Defendant, on the other hand, asserts that this policy is not in violation of Title VII in that sick leave is not a part of wages or salary and that said "sick leave policy" is administered and applied upon the same terms and conditions to all employees, male or female, pregnant or not. More particularly, that no employee is permitted to schedule sick days prior to the actual date of illness and that sick days can only be applied when an employee is scheduled to work.

The court is satisfied after a full and complete trial and after considering the briefs and arguments of counsel that the defendant's sick leave policy which prohibited Harriet Baum from using her accumulated sick leave prior to commencing her leave of absence was discriminatory and in violation of Title VII. The principal aim of Title VII is to protect employees from any form of disparate treatment because of, inter alia, sex, absent a compelling and founded reason for such disparity. Civil Rights Act of 1964, as amended, § 701 et seq.; 42 U.S.C.A. § 2000e et seq.

The law with respect to rights of the pregnant employee is becoming most firm and definite and consistent with the teachings of *Griggs v. Duke Power Co.*, 401 U.S. 424, 91 S.Ct. 849, 28 L.Ed.2d 158 (1971), the court has accorded great deference to the Commission's guidelines as providing the proper interpretation of Title VII.

"Disabilities caused or contributed to by pregnancy, miscarriage, abortion, childbirth, and recovery therefrom are, for all job-related purposes, temporary disabilities and should be treated as such under any health or temporary disability insurance or sick leave plan available in connection with employment. Written and unwritten employment policies and practices involving matters such as the commencement and duration of leave, the availability of extensions, the accrual of seniority and other benefits and privileges, reinstatement, and payment under any health or temporary disability insurance or sick leave plan, formal or informal, shall be applied to disability due to pregnancy or childbirth on the same terms and conditions as they are applied to other temporary disabilities." Employment Policies Relating to Pregnancy and Childbirth, 29 C.F.R. § 1604.10(b) (1972).

The United States Court of Appeals for the Third Circuit, in *Liberty Mutual Insurance Company v. Wetzel*, 421 U.S. 987, 95 S.Ct. 1989, 44 L.Ed.2d 476 511 F.2d 199 (3rd Cir. 1975) (vacated and remanded on other grounds), affirmed the District Court's decision on the merits in which it was found that the insurance benefits and maternity leave regulations of the employer, Liberty Mutual, discriminated against women in violation of Title VII of the Civil Rights Act of 1964, 42 U.S.C.A., § 2000e et seq.

The employer, Liberty Mutual, had excluded maternity benefits from its income protection plan and the court viewed this type of practice as treating persons in a disparate manner. The court went on to state:

". . . We believe that pregnancy should be treated as any other temporary disability. Employers offer disability insurance plans to their employees to alleviate the economic burdens caused by the loss of income and the incurrence of medical expenses that arise from the inability to work.

A woman, disabled by pregnancy, has much in common with a person disabled by a temporary illness. They both suffer a loss of income because of absence from work; they both incur medical expenses; and the pregnant woman will probably have hospital expenses while the other person may have none, choosing to convalesce at home.

Thus pregnancy is no different than any other temporary disability under an income protection plan offered to help employees through the financially difficult times caused by illness."

In light of the expressions set forth in *Wetzel*, supra, the court is convinced that logic and justice require the conclusion that any sick leave policy which treats pregnant women differently than employees with other sicknesses or disabilities is sex discrimination in violation of Title VII, since pregnancy is only common to women. The mere fact that defendant applied its sick leave policy equally to male, female, pregnant, nonpregnant employees is of no consequence if in the administration of said policy a protected class of employees is affected in a disparate manner. *Griggs v. Duke Power Co.*, supra, *Wetzel*, supra. Pregnancy and childbirth, which is common only to women, for all practical intents and purposes becomes a temporary disability at some point in time and it is just not practical or realistic to treat said disability differently than any other sickness or disability. Moreover, the court in reviewing the record could find no basis in which to conclude that there was a legitimate nondiscriminatory reason for prohibiting female employees from using their accumulated sick leave during a pregnancy related disability.

The court is satisfied that in the instant proceeding Mrs. Baum was in fact laboring under a temporary disability after the birth of her child and that she was entitled to have her accumulated sick leave used up prior to the commencing of her maternity leave of absence. See also: *Zichy v. City of Philadelphia*, 9 E.P.D. ¶ 10211 (E.D.Pa. 1975), where the court held that the denial of sick leave to the employee disabled because of pregnancy or childbirth institutes a different treatment of that employee's needs than those of the employee otherwise disabled but without a rational basis for such distinction. Citing *Wetzel*, supra, the court held:

"While Wetzel dealt with an income protection plan, we believe the same reasoning applies readily to a sick leave plan. Such plans are instituted to alleviate the hardship which would otherwise befall an employee temporarily physically disabled from working. The employee disabled from pregnancy or childbirth has just as much need for such protection as the employee disabled because of strictly defined illness or injury. Denial of sick leave to the employee disabled because of pregnancy or childbirth thus constitutes different treatment of that employee's needs than those of the employee otherwise disabled, but without rational basis for such distinction.

Indeed, we would note that an employee stands to lose far more by not having use of a sick leave plan like that involved here than an income protection plan like that involved in Wetzel. Whereas the income protection plan preserves only a portion of the employee's pay, the absent employee under the city's sick leave plan here continues not only to receive his full salary, but also to accrue future sick leave as well as time for pension, vacation, promotional, and anniversary date purposes, and other fringe benefits. If the 'illness/non-illness' rationale cannot justify the difference in treatment involved in the income protection plan in Wetzel, even less can it justify the substantially greater difference in treatment which the sick leave plan here in issue involves."

The plaintiff also seeks relief for all other similarly situated female employees of defendant who were pregnant between July 10, 1971 and the present. However, the only evidence introduced by plaintiff to support this claim, consisted of a stipulation that the personnel records of those individuals listed contained a reference to either maternity or pregnancy as the reason for beginning their leave of absence or terminating their employment and a list of those individuals alleged to be in the same posture as Harriet Baum. This list contained the following information relative to their claim: Pertinent Date of Hire; Date of Termination or Commencement of Leave of Absence; Hourly Salary at Date of Termination or Commencement of Leave of Absence; Accumulated Unused Sick Days (the Day Represents 8 hours) at Date of Termination or Commencement of Leave of Absence; and Date Returned to Work.

For reasons which will not be discussed, the court is satisfied that the granting of defendant's Motion to Dismiss as to all claims against defendant other than those presented by Harriet Baum was proper.

Pregnancy, in and of itself, is not a disability. To require the defendant to pay the full amount of accumulated sick leave to each pregnant employee who terminated her employment or who went on a leave of absence without more would be most unjust. Sick leave benefits only accrue where the individual is laboring under some sickness or disability. Unquestionably, a pregnant woman, at some point in time, will suffer some temporary disability as a result of her pregnancy, thereby, entitling her to the right to have her sick leave benefits while she remains under that disability. However, the court is not permitted to speculate as to when this condition will occur or how long said disability will last. The case of every woman is different and, therefore, before a woman is entitled to have the benefit of the accumulated sick leave applied to a pregnancy related disability there must be some evidence as to when and how long the individual actually labored under said disability.

Very simply, the court is not sufficiently informed as to whether any of the individuals listed were in fact sick or disabled and if so, when and for how long. In view thereof, the court is of the considered opinion that the plaintiff has failed to establish that those employees listed were in fact similarly situated to Harriet Baum.

Finally, the court can find no merit to plaintiff's contention that Harriet Baum was discharged from her employment in retaliation for her filing charges for discrimination with the Equal Employment Opportunity Commission. The record reflects that Mrs. Baum's leave of absence was to have expired on November 30, 1973 and that on November 23,

1973, she received a phone call from defendant advising her that her position at the clinic had been eliminated because of a cut in monies which the hospital was to have received from the Allegheny County Mental Health/Mental Retardation Program to operate the Developmental Clinic. Even after a full and fair opportunity had been afforded to the plaintiff, the court is unpersuaded that Mrs. Baum's termination by defendant was in retaliation for her voicing opposition to the hospital's sick pay policies and the filing of a charge with the Equal Employment Opportunity Commission.

The court is satisfied that under all the facts and circumstances defendant's decision to terminate some of its personnel to accommodate for the cut in funding was done for a justifiable economic reason, and the court can find nothing in the record to support plaintiff's contention that defendant's reason for dismissing Mrs. Baum was pretextual. Although the record reflects that the defendant hospital did not experience as great a cut in funding as it had expected, this fact was not known to the defendant at the time the positions were eliminated in the Growth and Developmental Clinic. Defendant hospital terminated Mrs. Baum's position on the good faith and belief that their funding had been reduced and it was not until sometime subsequent to her termination that defendant was informed that part of their funding had been restored. Very simply, the court is convinced that after a most careful review of the record, that there is no basis upon which the court can conclude that the termination of Mrs. Baum was the result of retaliation on the part of the defendant. On the contrary, the record reflects that the sole basis for defendant's actions was founded on economic considerations.

Accordingly, the court can find no basis for the awarding of any damages or back pay since Mrs. Baum's termination was not the result of retaliation on the part of defendant.

In view thereof, Harriet Baum is entitled to receive payment for her accumulated sick days as computed below:

166 hours (accumulated sick days in hours for 1973)

$\times$

5.19 (rate of pay per hour in 1973) = \$861.87

Findings of fact and conclusions of law have not been separately stated but are included in the body of the foregoing opinion as specifically authorized by Rule 52(a) of the Federal Rules of Civil Procedure.

An appropriate order is entered.

AND NOW, this 30th day of June, 1976, judgment is hereby entered in favor of Harriet Baum only and against the defendant, Children's Hospital of Pittsburgh, for payment of accumulated sick days in the amount of \$861.87 with interest at the rate of 6% from the date she officially began her leave of absence.

IT IS FURTHER ORDERED AND DECREED that judgment is hereby entered in favor of the defendant, Children's Hospital of Pittsburgh, and against the plaintiff, Equal Employment Opportunity Commission, for any and all claims presented in behalf of those persons other than Mrs. Harriet Baum.

AND NOW, this 1st day of July, 1976, the court, through an apparent oversight, failed and neglected to refer in its order of June 30, 1976 to make any reference to plaintiff's request for injunctive relief.

IT IS FURTHER ORDERED AND DECREED that Children's Hospital, its officers, agents, employees, successors, assigns and all persons in active concert or participation with it, are hereby permanently enjoined from denying any female employee from using accumulated sick days for any pregnancy related or childbirth disability upon proof and application of same.

The following is the text of the appellate decision 556 F.2d 222 (3rd Cir. 1977)

Children's Hospital of Pittsburgh (the "Hospital") appeals from an order granting class injunction relief and money damages to an individual victim of alleged sex discrimination in the denial of sick leave for pregnancy-related disabilities. The Equal Employment Opportunity Commission (the "EEOC") appeals from the portion of that order denying monetary relief to the class. The suit by the EEOC charges that the Hospital's policy of prohibiting female employees to use their accumulated sick leave for pregnancy-related disabilities violates Title VII of the Civil Rights Act of 1964, as amended, 42 U.S.C. § 2000e et seq. The district court agreed. However, after the EEOC filed its initial appellate brief the Supreme Court decided *General Electric Company v. Gilbert*, 429 U.S. 125, 97 S.Ct. 401, 50 L.Ed.2d 343 (1976), holding that the exclusion of pregnancy-related disabilities from a disability plan does not violate Title VII. That decision is controlling. It requires the reversal of the district court's judgment granting class injunctive relief and money damages to the charging party, and the affirmance of the denial of monetary relief to the class.

After the decision in *Gilbert* and before the Hospital's brief was due, its attorney called the case to the EEOC's attention and urged that the appeal be disposed of by a mutual agreement which would dissolve the injunction and terminate all damage claims. The EEOC elected to go forward with the appeal, necessitating the expenditure of additional time and effort on the part of the Hospital's attorney. In a reply brief the EEOC attempts to distinguish *Gilbert;* a distinction we find unpersuasive. The Hospital urges that, in light of *Gilbert,* the EEOC's refusal to discontinue this appeal was vexatious, and accordingly seeks an award of attorney's fees for time and effort expended since the *Gilbert* decision was announced.

In *United States Steel Corporation v. United States*, 519 F.2d 359 (3d Cir. 1975), we held that attorney's fees could be awarded against the EEOC under § 706(k) of Title VII, at least in cases where a proceeding was maintained in bad faith. We cited with approval the holding of the Ninth Circuit in *Van Hoomissen v. Xerox Corp.*, 503 F.2d 1131 (9th Cir. 1974), approving such awards in cases of vexatious appeals. But although we have found the EEOC's effort to distinguish *Gilbert* to be unpersuasive, we cannot say that the effort was made vexatiously or in bad faith. Certainly there are factual differences between the benefit plan considered in *Gilbert* and that of the Hospital. In pointing out those differences the EEOC did no more than might be expected of a conscientious litigant charged with the duty of advancing the policies of Title VII. Thus we will deny the Hospital's fee application.

The judgment of the district court will be reversed insofar as it awards class injunctive relief and damages to the charging party, and affirmed insofar as it denies monetary relief to the class of female employees. Costs taxed in favor of Children's Hospital of Pittsburgh.

Mitchell v. Board of Trustees
[415 F. Supp. 512 (D.S.C. 1976)]

Failure to renew contract because of employee's pregnancy violates Title VII

Analysis of the issue

The plaintiff who instituted this action under Title VII and the Equal Protection Clause of the Fourteenth Amendment of the Constitution was a schoolteacher whose contract was not renewed due to fact that she was pregnant. The court found that the bona fide occupational qualification exception to Title VII did not apply; it being common knowledge that pregnant teachers are able to teach and often do teach for the major portion of the pregnancy. Accepting this as fact, the court could see nothing to support an assertion that excluding pregnant teachers was necessary for the normal operation of school. The court, ruling for the plaintiff, ordered the defendant to award the teacher with back pay and to pay the plaintiff's attorney's fees.

Full text of opinion

CHAPMAN, District Judge:—Plaintiff brought this action because defendants, when informed of plaintiff's pregnancy, failed to rehire or to renew plaintiff's teaching contract for the entirety of the 1972-73 school year, allegedly in violation of her rights secured by the Constitution of the United States and the Civil Rights Act of 1964, as amended.

The amended complaint in this case contains two causes of action which were the basis of two prior actions. Civil Action 72-1123 was an action by plaintiff alleging constitutional infringements cognizable under 42 U.S.C. § 1981 and § 1983. Relying largely on the en banc decision by the Fourth Circuit Court of Appeals in *Cohen v. Chesterfield County School Board*, 474 F.2d 395 (1973) this Court granted defendants' motion for summary judgment and plaintiff filed a notice of appeal on April 30, 1973. On May 30, 1973, plaintiff commenced Civil Action No. 73-634 alleging substantially the same facts but evoking the jurisdiction of the court pursuant to Title VII of the Civil Rights Act of 1964, specifically 42 U.S.C. § 2000e-5. By order filed October 31, 1973, this Court denied defendants' motion to dismiss Civil Action No. 73-634 finding that Civil Action 72-1123 was not res judicata. Subsequently, the Fourth Circuit ordered that the appeal of Civil Action 72-1123 be held in abeyance pending the Supreme Court's decision in the *Cohen* case, and this Court ordered that Civil Action 73-631 also be held in abeyance pending that decision. On August 2, 1974 the Fourth Circuit vacated and remanded this Court's decision in Civil Action 72-1123. In light of those developments, this Court, on January 24, 1975, approved and signed a consent order pursuant to which plaintiff filed her amended complaint, commencing the action now before the Court, which essentially joins

Civil Action 72-1123 and Civil Action 73-634 in one complaint. The consent order further provided that upon termination of a reopened discovery period, the case would be submitted to the Court upon the entire record, including but not limited to, depositions, interrogatories, stipulations and legal memoranda, for a decision on the merits.

The basic allegation of the amended complaint is that plaintiff was denied re-employment by the defendants solely because of her existing pregnancy. As stated previously, plaintiff alleges two separate theories of liability. The first cause of action alleges violations of her rights to "due process" and "equal protection" under the Fourteenth Amendment of the United States Constitution. The second cause of action alleges violations of her rights to be free from sexual discrimination as provided in Title VII of the Civil Rights Act of 1964, as amended, 42 U.S.C. § 2000e-2 and guidelines thereunder promulgated, principally found at 29 C.F.R. § 1604(a)-(f) and § 1604.10(a)-(b).

Initially plaintiff sought relief in the form of injunctive relief, back pay and reinstatement, and attorney's fees. Due to changes in her personal and professional life, plaintiff has informed the Court through her attorney that she abandons her claim for reinstatement and her position that defendants' subsequent job offer was not bona fide; and the only relief now sought in this case is as follows: (1) An Order of the Court declaring that the defendants violated plaintiff's rights in not renewing her contract; (2) An Order declaring the defendants liable for back pay to which she would have been entitled during the fall semester only, had she been permitted to teach until such time as a substitute was required; and (3) An Order directing the defendants to pay to the plaintiff court costs and attorney's fees.

Most of the factual allegations in the amended complaint are admitted in defendants' answer; however, liability, under any theory, is denied.

Since the provisions of the previously mentioned consent order have been complied with, there is no necessity for the taking of testimony and the case is ripe for decision. There is very little dispute as to the factual situation set forth in paragraphs 8, 9 and 10 of the amended complaint. The issue here involves mainly a question of law. After reviewing the entire record and studying the applicable law, the Court, pursuant to Rule 52 of the Federal Rules of Civil Procedure, makes the following:

1. Plaintiff holds a professional teaching certificate for the State of South Carolina and is certified in Spanish and other subjects. She was employed at Easley High School by defendants on May 4, 1971 for the school year 1971-72, and she served in that capacity teaching five classes in Spanish. Plaintiff performed with excellence as a teacher; and during February 1972, she signed the defendants' form letter of intent to be renewed for the next school year of 1972-73.

2. On April 4, 1972, plaintiff determined she was pregnant, and her personal physician anticipated delivery on or about November 6, 1972. Prior to the date for negotiating the contracts for school year 1972-73, plaintiff gave notice of her condition to the school administrators and engaged in conferences with her principal, making clear her perference to work as long as possible during the 1972-73 school year.

3. Christmas holidays were to be December 15, 1972 through January 1, 1973. The first semester was to end January 16, 1973 and the second semester was to commence January 17, 1973.

4. Barring any unforeseen difficulties, which in fact she did not experience in connection with delivery, plaintiff discussed with her principal the necessity of her being absent for approximately six weeks during the time that classes would be in session, her leave being anticipated to extend from approximately November 1, 1972 through January 1, 1973. The principal suggested that it might be possible for plaintiff to retain her teaching position with prearrangement for her maternity leave.

5. Plaintiff secured the consent of a Mrs. Carter, a person not certified for teaching Spanish, to act as a substitute during the period of plaintiff's absence with the aid of plaintiff's teaching materials and coaching. The principal agreed to this arrangement with the caveat that implementation of such an arrangement would be contingent on the approval by the school superintendent, Dr. Curtis A. Sidden. The superintendent did not approve the plan; and consequently, plaintiff was offered no teaching contract for the school year 1972-73.

6. Plaintiff urged the superintendent to reconsider his position. She stressed the importance of her teaching second year Spanish to those she had taught the first year course. The superintendent did not change his position. At a regular meeting of the defendant Board of Trustees, some of plaintiff's students appeared and presented petitions, signed by 114 of plaintiff's Spanish students, on her behalf. The defendant Board discussed the matter and affirmed the superintendent's decision not to renew plaintiff's contract.

7. The reason defendants did not renew plaintiff's contract for the school year 1972-73 was because they believed a predicted long period of absence from the classroom would cause administrative problems for the school and break the continuity of teaching for the students. This policy is not expressed in the Teacher's Manual given plaintiff prior to the incident in question or any other written form. However, it does appear that defendants' reasoning in the instant case is consistent with an unwritten policy followed by defendants. Defendant Sidden's testimony, wherein he refers to affidavits of various persons including school principals, reveals that applicants have been denied employment in the defendant school district because the applicant would not commit himself for the full academic year or it was anticipated the applicant would not be able to work the full contract year. For example, several female applicants were not rehired for the next school year because their husbands planned to graduate from Clemson University in December, and they may be moving from the area. Defendants' policy is also evidenced by defendants' refusal to consider a teaching position for a male applicant because he informed defendants he had applied for a civil service position and would take the position if and when he was accepted.

8. Defendants show no examples of denials of employment because of anticipated physical disabilities as in the instant case. However, the Court finds defendants' actions in this case were made in good faith with legitimate interests for the educational system and its students in mind.

In spite of defendants' good faith, defendants' action of non-renewal was directly attributable to plaintiff's then existing pregnancy.

9. Plaintiff has complied with all administrative procedures necessary to bring an action under Title VII. On or about August 24, 1972, plaintiff filed a complaint, charging employment discrimination against her because of sex, with the United States Equal Employment Opportunity Commission, which organization administers Title VII of the Civil Rights Act of 1962, as amended. After investigation, the director of the EEOC, Atlanta Regional Office, issued a document finding violations of 42 U.S.C. § 2000e relative to prohibitions against employment discrimination based on sex, as set forth in 29 C.F.R. § 1604.10(a) and (b). Defendants rejected the EEOC conciliation proposal, and plaintiff was advised she had the right to institute a civil action under Title VII. Having exhausted all administrative remedies, plaintiff thereafter commenced Civil Action No. 73-634 within the 90 day limitation.

1. The Board of Trustees of Pickens County School District "A" and its agents are "employers" within the appropriate section of Title VII of the Civil Rights Act of 1964, as amended, 42 U.S.C. § 2000e(b). Prior to March 24, 1972 educational institutions were specifically exempt from the provisions of Title VII. However, the EEOC Act of 1972 amended Title VII to withdraw those exemptions. See 42 U.S.C. § 2000e-1. In this case the decision denying employment to plaintiff took place after March 24, 1972; therefore, the provisions of Title VII apply to plaintiff, a school teacher in a public school. *LaFleur v. Cleveland Board of Education*, 465 F.2d 1184, 1186 (6th Cir. 1972), affirmed 414 U.S. 632, 94 S.Ct. 791, 39 L.Ed.2d 52 (1974).

2. 42 U.S.C. § 2000e-2 provides, in part, as follows:

"(a) It shall be an unlawful employment practice for an employer—
(1) to fail or refuse to hire or to discharge any individual, or otherwise to discriminate against any individual with respect to his compensation, terms, conditions, or privileges of employment, because of such individual's race, color, religion, sex, or national origin; or

(2) to limit, segregate, or classify his employees or applicants for employment in any way which would deprive or tend to deprive any individual of employment opportunities or otherwise adversely affect his status as an employee, because of such individual's race, color, religion, sex, or national origin."

The EEOC is the administrative body created by Title VII. It has issued guidelines and these administrative interpretations are entitled to "great deference" in applying the Act. See *Griggs v. Duke Power Co.*, 401 U.S. 424, 434, 91 S.Ct. 849, 855, 28 L.Ed.2d 158, 165 (1971). The pertinent guidelines in this case are as follows:

"29 CFR § 1604.10—Employment Policies Relating to Pregnancy and Childbirth.

(a) A written or unwritten employment policy or practice which excludes for employment applicants or employees because of pregnancy is a prima facie violation of Title VII.

(b) Disabilities caused or contributed to by pregnancy, miscarriage, abortion, childbirth and recovery therefrom are, for all job related purposes, temporary disabilities and should be treated as such under any health or sick leave plan available in connection with employment. Written and unwritten employment policies and practices involving matters such as the commencement and duration of leave, the availability of extensions, the accrual of seniority and other benefits and privileges; reinstatement, and payment under any health or temporary insurance or sick leave plan, formal or informal, shall be applied to disability due to pregnancy or childbirth on the same terms and conditions as they are applied to other temporary disabilities."

3. The Court concludes that defendants' actions violated the above mentioned provisions of Title VII of the Civil Rights Act of 1964, as amended, and the EEOC guidelines promulgated thereunder. This conclusion is based on the finding that plaintiff was denied employment or renewal of her employment solely because of her pregnancy.

4. As revealed in Findings of Fact No. 7, defendants' policy of not hiring applicants or rehiring teachers for the next year when it was foreseeable that they would be unable to complete the year, was not limited to females. However, the other denials mentioned in Findings of Fact No. 7 did not involve physical disabilities, but rather the inability of the person to commit himself to an entire school year because he or she anticipated a different job offer or a relocation from the area of employment. The fact defendants denied plaintiff employment because of her pregnancy is the key to this case because that condition is so much a part of womanhood. Most other physical conditions are shared by men and women alike, in which case plaintiff would be precluded from asserting discrimination based on sex. The Court recognizes that there are physical conditions unique to men, such as a malfunction of the prostate gland. If plaintiff were a male who was not rehired because of an anticipated prostate operation, discrimination based on sex might still be argued. Since individuals of both sexes can suffer physical conditions unique to one sex, this Court finds logic in the position that neither should be allowed to assert discrimination on the basis of sex. However, pregnancy is a physical condition that has received special treatment in the law as it has developed.

5. Defendants argue that their actions were not based upon plaintiff's sex, but upon their desire to prevent a known interruption in the teaching and learning processes. The Court is impressed with defendants' concerns; and, as stated previously, the Court finds that defendants did not intend to discriminate against the plaintiff because of her sex. However, the pertinent provisions of Title VII have been interpreted to proscribe acts that result in sexual discrimination, whether or not the employer acted in good faith. For example, *Gilbert v. General Electric Co.*, 519 F.2d 661 (4th Cir. 1975) involved a Title VII attack upon General Electric's employee disability benefits program which excluded pregnancy-related disabilities. The Fourth Circuit stated the purpose of Title VII as follows:

"The legislative purpose behind Title VII was to protect employees from any form of disparate treatment because of race, color, religion, sex or national origin or, as one commentator has stated it, 'to make employment decisions sex-blind, as well as colorblind'." (cite omitted) (519 F.2d at p. 663).

In affirming the lower court's decision that General Electric's plan was violative of Title VII, Judge Russell, citing *Griggs, supra*, states: "It is of no moment that an employer may not have deliberately intended sex-related discrimination; the statute looks to 'consequences', not intent." Since pregnancy is a disability possible only among women the "consequence" of General Electric's disability program was a less comprehensive program of employee compensation and benefits for women employees than for men employees. Similarly, defendants' actions in the instant case resulted in the denial of a teaching job to plaintiff solely because of pregnancy.

6. The one exception to the statutory command of nondiscrimination occurs in those certain instances ". . . where religion, sex, or national origin is a bona fide occupational qualification reasonably necessary to the normal operation of that particular business or enterprise . . ." 42 U.S.C. § 2000e-2(e). However, this exception should be interpreted narrowly. 29 C.F.R. § 1604.2(a) (1972) and see *Gilbert, supra,* footnote 22. The Court finds no support for the assertion that excluding pregnant women from teaching jobs is necessary to the normal operation of a school. It is common knowledge that pregnant teachers are able to teach and do teach in many instances for the greater portion of the period of the pregnancy.

7. Continuity of instruction as an objective of school officials is discussed at length in *LaFleur, supra. LaFleur* involved a successful attack on the mandatory School Board rules requiring pregnant school teachers to take maternity leave at specified times before expected delivery. The attack was based on constitutional grounds rather than Title VII, which did not apply to state agencies and educational institutions at that time; therefore, continuity is discussed in terms of the state's interest.

"It cannot be denied that continuity of instruction is a significant and legitimate educational goal. Regulations requiring pregnant teachers to provide early notice of their condition to school authorities undoubtedly facilitate administrative planning toward the important objective of continuity. But, as the Court of Appeals for the Second Circuit noted in *Green v. Waterford Board of Education,* 473 F.2d 629, 635:

> 'Where a pregnant teacher provides the Board with a date certain for commencement of leave . . . that value [continuity] is preserved; an arbitrary leave date set at the end of the fifth month is no more calculated to facilitate a planned and orderly transition between the teacher and a substitute than is a date fixed closer to confinement. Indeed, the latter . . . would afford the Board more, not less, time to procure a satisfactory long-term substitute.' (Footnote omitted.)"

LaFleur, supra, 414 U.S. at pages 641 and 642, 94 S.Ct. at page 797, 39 L.Ed.2d at page 61.

The Supreme Court in *LaFleur* makes the point several times that early advance notice helps the school administrators plan for changes and thus serves the goal of continuity. In the instant case plaintiff gave notice in early April 1972 that she would probably be unable to work the first semester beyond November 1, 1972. Defendants cannot complain about the notice given here. In addition plaintiff found a substitute and took other steps to insure that her classes would be able to continue with minimum confusion in her absence. The record clearly indicates that the plaintiff's proposal for her maternity leave would not create the many interruptions asserted by defendants.

8. Since plaintiff had not yet entered into a contract for the 1972-73 school year this case is distinguishable, as stressed by defendants, from

LaFleur and other cases where the inability to continue employment is made known after employment has begun. However, the statute and regulations quoted herein clearly state it is an "unlawful employment practice" under Title VII to practice sexual discrimination against applicants as well as existing employees. Additionally, plaintiff is not an "applicant" in the usual meaning of that term. She was working for defendants at the time their decision not to rehire her was made, and she had already proven herself to be an excellent teacher as defendants admit. Defendants would have this Court penalize plaintiff because she advised the defendants of her condition when she first learned of its existence, rather than waiting until it became obvious and until after she had the opportunity of signing a contract for 1972-73. If plaintiff had made her pregnancy known after signing the contract, it appears, from defendant Sidden's deposition, that plaintiff would have been allowed to continue with her work as long as she desired within reason, even though the Teacher's Manual calls for termination in a different manner.

9. Citing *Geduldig v. Aiello*, 417 U.S. 484, 94 S.Ct. 2485, 41 L.Ed.2d 256 (1974), defendants assert not every classification concerning pregnancy is a sex-biased classification; and absent a showing that distinctions involving pregnancy are mere pretexts designed to effect an invidious discrimination against the member of one sex or the other there can be no valid claim of sex discrimination. In *Aiello* the Supreme Court upheld a legislatively created social welfare program for private employees in which a differentiation between pregnancy related and other disabilities was made. *Aiello* dealt with a constitutional attack under the Equal Protection Clause of the Fourteenth Amendment and the Court applied the customary standards in testing legislation under the Equal Protection Clause. It is not necessary that this Court apply those same constitutional standards because the decision here is based on a Title VII violation. Defendants argue that the approach to actions under the Constitution and Title VII are not distinguishable, but the Fourth Circuit in *Gilbert, supra,* has held otherwise.

"In this case, on the contrary, the issue is not whether the exclusion of pregnancy benefits under a social welfare program is 'rationally supportable' or 'invidious' but whether Title VII, the Congressional statute, in language and intent, prohibits such exclusion. Accordingly, as the Court in *Wetzel v. Liberty Mutual Insurance Co.,* [3 Cir., 511 F.2d 199] supra, aptly observed, 'our case is one of statutory interpretation rather than one of constitutional analysis.' There is a well-recognized difference of approach in applying *constitutional* standards under the Equal Protection clause as in *Aiello* and in the statutory construction of the 'sex-blind' mandate of Title VII. To satisfy constitutional Equal Protection standards, a discrimination need only be 'rationally supportable' and that was the situation in *Aiello,* as well as in *Reed* [v. Reed, 404 U.S. 71, 92, S.Ct. 251, 30 L.Ed.2d 225] and *Frontiero* [v. Richardson, 411 U.S. 677, 93 S.Ct. 1764, 36 L.Ed.2d 583]. The test in those cases was legislative reasonableness. Title VII, however, authorizes no such 'rationality' test in determining the propriety of its application. It represents a flat and absolute prohibition against all sex discrimination in conditions of employment. It is not concerned with whether the discrimination is 'invidious' or not. It outlaws all sex discrimination in the conditions of employment." (Cite omitted). 519 F.2d p. 667.

10. The Court concludes the denial of employment to plaintiff was a violation of her rights under Title VII. This is the real question in this case. In keeping with the general policy in the Federal Courts to avoid

unnecessary constitutional questions, the Court makes no decision on the issue of a possible constitutional violation of plaintiff's rights.

11. Since plaintiff's rights under Title VII have been violated she is entitled to back pay for the fall semester of 1972 up until November 1, 1972, the date plaintiff and her physician predicted that a substitute would be necessary. In addition, the Court pursuant to 42 U.S.C. § 2000e-5(k), directs defendants to pay plaintiff's attorney's fee in the amount of One Thousand Two Hundred and No/100 ($1,200.00) Dollars.

AND IT IS SO ORDERED.

ON MOTIONS TO AMEND FINDINGS AND FOR RELIEF FROM ORDER

This matter is before the Court upon defendants' motions seeking amendments to and relief from this Court's Order filed January 22, 1976.

Rule 52(b) of the Federal Rules of Civil Procedure provides, in part, that "Upon motion of a party made not later than ten days after entry of judgment the court may amend its findings or make additional findings and may amend the judgment accordingly."

Defendants seek amendments in the form of (1) additions and deletions of certain words to the first sentence of Findings of Fact No. 7 and (2) additional findings of fact. After reviewing the record, considering the defendant's requests and the plaintiff's objections thereto, the Court feels that certain modifications are appropriate for the purposes of clarification and in keeping with this Court's desire that its Order convey a correct understanding of the factual issues determined by the Court. Therefore, *the first sentence only of Findings of Fact No. 7 is hereby amended* to read as follows:

"7. The reason defendants did not renew or offer to renew plaintiff's contract for the fall semester of school year 1972-73 or the entire school year 1972-73 was because they believed a predicted long period of absence from the classroom would break the continuity of teaching for the students."

In addition, *Findings of Fact No. 8 is hereby amended in its entirety* to read as follows:

"8. Defendants show no examples of denials of employment because of anticipated physical disabilities as in the instant case. However, the Court finds defendants' actions in this case were made in good faith with legitimate interests for the educational system and its students in mind. It was the wish of the defendants to return plaintiff to her teaching responsibilities as soon as such could be accomplished with minimal disruption of instructional continuity. A logical breaking point in the instructional process is between the first and second semesters. Two separate efforts were made to achieve this end. First, the deposition of plaintiff's principal, J. Milton Butler, taken October 27, 1972 in Civil Action No. 72-1123 reveals his attempts to hire a Spanish teacher for the first semester so that plaintiff could return to that position the second semester. Secondly, plaintiff was offered, in January 1972, a teaching job as a reading teacher beginning the second semester; however, plaintiff refused this offer. In spite of defendants' good faith, defendants' action of non-renewal was directly attributable to plaintiff's then existing pregnancy."

Defendants make the additional motion for relief from final judgment pursuant to Rule 60(b)(6):

"On motion and upon such terms as are just, the court may relieve a party or his legal representative from a final judgment, order, or proceeding for the following reasons: . . . (6) any other reason justifying relief from the operation of the judgment."

Defendants contend the relief sought is justified because this Court's Order is essentially bottomed on the June 27, 1975 Fourth Circuit Opinion in *Gilbert v. General Electric Co.*, 519 F.2d 661, which is on appeal. It is plaintiff's contention that there is a possibility the Supreme Court's decision would not be directly on point resulting in more confusion and more delay.

The Court feels that the Supreme Court decision may well decide controlling questions. *Gilbert* has been argued in the Supreme Court since defendants' motion and plaintiff's reply memorandum were filed; therefore, the decision will probably be forthcoming in the near future. In addition, it is significant that the relief to which plaintiff is entitled under this Court's Order is back pay for only two months. We are not dealing with a situation involving reinstatement, the delay of which would be burdensome and prejudicial to plaintiff. The Court concludes relief from the judgment is justified pending the Supreme Court's decision in Gilbert.

For the reasons stated above, defendants' motion to amend findings is granted with certain modifications; and defendants' motion for relief from judgment is granting pending the Supreme Court's decision in *Gilbert*.

AND IT IS SO ORDERED.

Sylvania Education Association v. Sylvania Board of Education

[_____ F. Supp. _____ (N.D. Ohio 1976)]

Local policy denying use of sick leave for maternity purposes is not sanctioned by state law

Analysis of the issue

The Sylvania Education Association, on behalf of Ms. Barbara Ziesmer and similarly situated female teachers, alleged that the Sylvania Board of Education's policies regarding maternity leave and sick leave violate the Fourteenth Amendment of the Constitution and 42 U.S.C. § 1983. Basically, the School Board's policy does not allow the use of sick leave for normal pregnancy. Accumulated sick leave may be used only in cases where the woman suffers complications resulting from an abnormal pregnancy. This policy runs contrary to an Ohio law which requires that normal pregnancy be included as an instance when sick leave may be used. The particulars of Ms. Ziesmer's case begin with her notifying the Superintendent of Schools in September of 1974 that she was pregnant, with January 18, 1975 being the estimated date of delivery. At the time of her giving notice, the plaintiff requested a leave of absence from December 20, 1974 to March 1, 1975, but in October altered her request to one asking for the use of accumulated sick leave to cover the period from January 2-24. Although the plaintiff furnished a statement from her physician attesting to the plaintiff's ability to work through the month of December, her request for sick leave was denied and she was forced to begin maternity leave; that is, leave without pay beginning December 21. Imposing the mandatory maternity leave of absence, must, according to School Board policy, take effect no later than 30 days prior to the estimated delivery date. This policy contrasts with the Board's policy regarding nonmaternity leave due to illness; a policy which allows the employee's accumulated sick leave to expire before the leave of absence commences. Furthermore, the imposition of any type of leave of absence, maternity or otherwise can only be accomplished, according to Ohio law, following an employee's request. Finding the School Board's policies to be in conflict with 42 U.S.C. § 1983, the court ordered the Sylvania Board of Education to refrain from implementing the policies and to award the plaintiffs with sufficient remedy to cover attorney's fees and related expenses.

Full text of opinion

DON J. YOUNG, District Judge:—This cause comes before the Court upon plaintiffs' motion for summary judgment. The issues presented are whether several policies of defendants regarding sick leave and maternity leave claimed by pregnant teachers violate 42 U.S.C. § 1983.

Jurisdiction of this action is alleged under 28 U.S.C. § 1343 and 28 U.S.C. § 1331.

Plaintiffs Barbara Ziesmer and the Sylvania Education Association, a labor organization representing teachers at schools under the direction of the defendants, allege that they have been denied Equal Protection and Due Process within the meaning of the Fourteenth Amendment and § 1983 by the enforcement of defendants' policies regarding maternity leave and sick leave. At issue are Board Policy 4151.1 and Board Policy 4152.3. Board Policy 4151.1 disallows the use of accumulated sick leave for normal pregnancy absent "undue complications." Board Policy 4152.3 requires that pregnant teachers take a maternity leave without pay to commence not less than thirty (30) days prior to the estimated date of delivery.

The parties have stipulated the following material facts: In September 1974 Plaintiff Ziesmer notified the Superintendent of Schools that she was pregnant and estimated her delivery date to be January 18, 1975. Initially she requested a leave of absence from December 20, 1974, to March 1, 1975. In October 1974 she requested that her accumulated sick leave be applied for the period January 2-24, 1975. Plaintiff Ziesmer submitted to the Board the statement of her physician, to the effect that plaintiff would be physically able to teach through December 1974. Plaintiff's request was denied and she was placed on maternity leave beginning December 21, 1974.

The first issue presented is whether plaintiffs' rights to Due Process and Equal Protection are violated by Board Policy 4151.1 which reads in pertinent part:

"All fulltime professional staff members regularly appointed by the Board of Education shall be granted sick leave without loss of pay for absence due to illness, injury, or exposure to contagious disease which could be communicated to other employees.
Illness shall include the undue complications of pregnancy not expected during a normal pregnancy." (Adopted 1961; amended April 30, 1973)

Plaintiffs contend that the Due Process Clause of the Fourteenth Amendment requires defendants to treat incapacitating discomfort from a normal pregnancy as it treats illnesses generally.

The Court agrees. If plaintiffs have a property or liberty interest entitling them to sick leave for normal illness during pregnancy, defendants' denial of sick leave violates Due Process. To raise a claim under the Civil Rights Act plaintiffs must point to a property or liberty interest created by state law or some independent source of entitlement. Board of Regents v. Roth, 408 U.S. 564, 577 (1972).

A property interest under state law exists here. Ohio Rev. Code § 3319.141 (Supp. 1975) provides in pertinent part:

"Each person who is employed by any board of education in this state shall be entitled to fifteen days sick leave with pay, for each year under contract. . . . Teachers and nonteaching school employees, upon approval of the responsible administrative officer of the school district, may use sick leave for absence due to personal illness, pregnancy, injury, exposure to contagious disease which could be communicated to others, and for absence due to illness, injury, or death in the employee's immediate family."

The Ohio Legislature has chosen to include normal pregnancy as an instance when sick leave may be used. The statute uses the terms "shall be entitled" to fifteen days of sick leave. A claim for sick leave is subject to administrative verification, but nothing in § 3319.4 vests authority in a school board to withdraw the sick leave granted by statute to permanently employed teachers. In contrast, the legislature clearly expressed in § 3319.141 its intention to vest discretion in school boards to limit the sick leave to substitute teachers.

"Each board of education may establish regulations for the entitlement, crediting, and use of sick leave by those substitute teachers employed by such board pursuant to section 3319.10 of the Ohio Rev. Code who are not otherwise entitled to sick leave pursuant to such section."

It appears that no Ohio courts have construed this particular section of the Ohio Revised Code, but a closely related section with nearly identical language has been construed to the effect that the mandatory grant of sick leave by the legislature cannot be rescinded by local units of government. Medley v. Civil Service Com'n of City of Portsmouth, 23 Ohio Misc. 311, 52 Ohio Op.2d 277, 261 N.F.2d 918, 920 (Scioto County 1970); Birkbeck v. Wadsworth, 17 Ohio Misc. 213 46 Ohio Op.2d 326, 245 N.E.2d 745, 749 (Medina County 1969). In these opinions two Ohio Courts of Common Pleas construed the sick leave provision of § 142.29 Ohio Rev. Code (now Ohio Rev. Code § 124.39). Sections 3319.141 and 143.29 were amended simultaneously to include pregnancy as a condition qualifying for the use of sick leave. 136 Ohio Laws. S.B. 174 (1973). The Court finds the Ohio authorities and the plain meaning of the statute § 3319.141 authoritative. Denial of sick leave for pregnancy, prior to the commencement of maternity leave, violates the Due Process requirements of § 1983.

The second issue is whether defendants' imposition of mandatory maternity leave without pay for a pregnant teacher, beginning thirty days prior to the estimated date of delivery violates Due Process. Board Policy 4152.3 provides in pertinent part:

"maternity leave shall begin or employment shall terminate not less than thirty (30) days prior to the estimated delivery date."

In contrast to this rule, defendants have a second rule for nonmaternity leaves of absence due to illness, one that provides that a staff member is automatically placed on leave of absence only when sick leave expires. Board Policy 4152.

The Court finds that Board Policy 4152.3 violates Due Process. Ohio Rev. Code § 3319.141 provides that employees may accumulate up to one hundred twenty work days of unused sick leave. Illness due to pregnancy has been designated as one purpose for which sick leave may be used. Board Policy 4152.3 is contrary to the plaintiff's rights under the statute to the extent that the Rule denies pregnant teachers the right to use accumulated sick leave when they are ill during the final thirty days of pregnancy.

Board Policy 4152.3 also conflicts with Ohio Rev. Code § 3319.13. The statute permits the board of education to grant a leave of absence upon a teacher's request. The statute does not authorize defendant to impose a mandatory leave of absence upon any teacher, pregnant or otherwise. If a pregnant teacher requests maternity leave of absence, the Board may grant the request. If a pregnant teacher does not request a maternity leave of absence, she may use accumulated sick leave for normal illness during pregnancy, just as she could use accumulated sick leave for any purpose designated by the statute, subject to the same factual verification.

The Court need not reach the issues of Equal Protection, because the Ohio statutes are affirmative grants of entitlement that defendants cannot alter by administrative rules.

Defendants raise several issues regarding jurisdiction and liability:

(1) that the Sylvania Board of Education is not a "person" within the meaning of § 1983;

(2) that plaintiff Sylvania Education Association lacks standing to sue;

(3) that the individual defendants enjoy a qualified immunity to damages; and

(4) that attorneys' fees may not be awarded in this action.

The Court of Appeals for the Sixth Circuit has held that a school board is not a "person" under § 1983. Memphis Am. Fed. of Teachers v. Bd. of Ed., 534 F.2d 699, 702 (6th Cir. 1976). Thus the Court must dismiss the defendant Board.

The Sylvania Education Association has a standing to sue since it has demonstrated actual injury to a member. Simon v. Eastern Kentucky Welfare Rights Organization, 44 LW 4724, 4728 (July 1, 1976); Memphis Am. Fed. of Teachers, supra, at 702.

The Supreme Court has held that in the context of school discipline a school board member is immune from liability for damages under § 1983 unless "He knows or reasonably should have known that the action he took within the sphere of his official responsibility would violate the constitutional rights of the [person] affected, or if he took the action with malicious intention to cause a deprivation of constitutional rights or other injury to the [person]." Wood v. Strickland, 420 U.S. 308, 322 (1975). The same rule of immunity applies to infringement of a pregnant teacher's liberty and property rights by a school board. Shirley v. Chagrin Falls Exempted Vil. Schs. Bd. of Ed., 521 F.2d 1329, 1332 (6th Cir. 1975). An action against individual board members seeking a monetary award is essentially a claim for damages, even though the relief sought may be styled back pay. Shirley, supra, at 1334. Absent a construction of Ohio Code § 3319.141 by Ohio courts clearly vesting in plaintiffs the right to use sick leave for pregnancy-related discomfort other than undue complications, this Court cannot find that defendant Board members should have known that Board Policies 4151.1 and 4152.3 violate § 1983 of the Civil Rights Act. No monetary award is appropriate in this action.

It is appropriate to award plaintiffs their attorneys' fees because they have vindicated important policies contained in a civil rights statute. Civil Rights Attorneys' Fees Awards Act of 1976, P.L. 94-559 (October 19, 1976), U.S. Code Cong. & Ad. News, 90 Stat. 2641 (1976). The Court is hopeful that the parties can agree as to the amount of attorneys' fees, but if they cannot, plaintiffs should file a motion for fees supported by an itemized affidavit.

Therefore, for the reasons stated herein, good cause appearing, it is

ORDERED that plaintiffs' motion for summary judgment be, and it hereby is, granted in part and denied in part; and it is

FURTHER ORDERED that the Sylvania Board of Education Policy 4152.3 violates 42 U.S.C. § 1983 insofar as that Policy imposes upon pregnant teachers a mandatory leave of absence without pay during any period of pregnancy, without allowing pregnant teachers to apply un-used sick leave to periods of normal illness during pregnancy as provided by Ohio Rev. Code § 3319.141; and it is

FURTHER ORDERED that the Sylvania Board of Education Policy 4151.1 violates 42 U.S.C. § 1983 insofar as the Policy denies pregnant teachers the right to use sick leave granted pursuant to Ohio Rev. Code § 3319.141 during normal pregnancy; and it is

FURTHER ORDERED that the defendant members of the Sylvania Board of Education, their officers, agents, servants, employees, and those persons in active concert with them should be, and hereby are, permanently enjoined from implementing Board Policy 4151.1 and Board Policy 4152.3 to the extent that those Policies deny pregnant teachers the right to use sick leave granted pursuant to Ohio Rev. Code § 3319.141 during normal pregnancy; and it is

FURTHER ORDERED that the plaintiffs are entitled to recover their costs herein expended, together with reasonable attorneys' fees and expenses, the amount thereof to be paid from the operating funds of the Sylvania Board of Education. The parties to agree upon the amount of attorneys' fees, and if they are unable to do so, upon application the Court will set the matter for hearing.

6 Women in the labor force

Women's employment by occupations and industries*

Employment by occupation

The large increase in employment of women in recent years has been accompanied by a changing occupational distribution. Although women are still concentrated in relatively few occupations, the degree of concentration has been decreasing. Significant numbers of women have been entering occupations in which few women have been previously employed.

The employment of women by occupation and the shifts in women's working patterns will be discussed in three different groupings of occupations. One is by type of work—a classification of occupations into white-collar, blue-collar, service, and farm work. A second grouping includes the nine major occupation groups. The third grouping covers the detailed occupational distribution of women.

Type of work

The employment distribution of women by type of work varies considerably from that of men. The distribution, therefore, is an important factor in understanding the faster growth in employment by women than by men. This is because employment in white-collar work, in which women are concentrated, has been increasing at a much faster rate than employment as a whole. Of the more than 33 million women 16 years of age and over employed in April 1974, more than three-fifths (62 percent) were employed in white-collar jobs. About one-fifth (21 percent) were employed in service work, less than one-sixth (16 percent) were in blue-collar occupations, and less than 2 percent were in farm jobs. The employment of men was distributed quite differently. About two-fifths of the men (41 percent) were in white-collar jobs, nearly half (46 percent) were in blue-collar occupations, only about 8 percent were in service jobs, and 5 percent were in farm work.

The proportion of all women workers who were in white-collar jobs increased from 54.9 percent in 1959 to 61.9 percent in April 1974. The proportion of women employed in each of the other types of work declined. In blue-collar work, the proportion dropped from 16.9 to 15.5 percent; in service work the decrease was from 23.5 to 21.3 percent, and the proportion in farm work dropped from 4.8 to 1.4 percent.

Major occupation groups

Data from the Current Population Survey provide information on the number of persons employed in nine broad occupation groups. More employed women 16 years of age and over (34.5 percent) were in clerical occupations in April 1974 than in any other major occupation group. The second largest group was service workers, with 21.3 percent of all women workers (3.9 percent were private household workers and 17.4 percent were other service workers). Professional workers were the

*Handbook on Women Workers, U.S. Department of Labor, Women's Bureau.

third largest group, accounting for 15.6 percent of women workers. More than 13 percent of women workers were operatives. The other groups in order of size were sales workers (6.8 percent), managers and administrators (5 percent), craft and kindred workers and farm workers (1.4 percent each), and nonfarm laborers (1 percent).

Women's employment has expanded in nearly all of the major occupation groups since 1959 (see table 36). The greatest growth has been in clerical occupations, in which employment increased from 6.3 million to nearly 11.5 million over the 15-year period. The fastest rate of growth among women workers was in the professional and technical occupation group where employment doubled from 2.6 to 5.2 million. Major increases were registered in the number of teachers, health personnel (nurses and health technicians), and social workers.

Although the number of women in operative jobs increased by about 1.1 million and the number of women in sales and in managerial jobs increased by about 600,000 each in the 1959–74 period, the proportion of all women employed in each of these occupation groups declined during the 15-year period. The number of women workers declined greatly in two groups—farm work and private household work. The number of farm workers declined by more than half and the number of private household workers by nearly one-third. Low earnings and the lack of benefits, as well as increasing opportunities for women in other lines of work, have been given reasons for the decline in the number of private household workers.

Occupational employment difference between women and men
The occupational distribution of women is quite different from that of men (see chart I). Whereas more than one-third of all women workers (34.5 percent) were employed in clerical occupations in April 1974, less than 7 percent of men held clerical jobs. Men were concentrated in craft or operative jobs. About 21 percent of the men workers but only 1.4 percent of women workers were in craft jobs. Over 18 percent of the men employed in April 1974 had operative jobs, compared with about 13 percent of all women workers.

Nearly 1 out of 7 men was in a managerial or administrative occupation, as compared with 1 out of 20 women. About 1 percent of all women held nonfarm laborer jobs; this compares with nearly 8 percent of men in this occupation group. Nearly 5 percent of men workers were employed in farm jobs, as compared with less than 2 percent of women workers.

Many more women (7.1 million) than men (4.3 million) had service jobs either inside or outside the home. About 3.9 percent of all women workers held jobs in private households and 17.4 percent held service jobs other than those in private households. The comparable proportions for men were 0.4 and 8.2 percent. A somewhat larger proportion of the women (6.8 percent) than of the men (6.1 percent) were sales workers, although the number of men sales workers exceeded that of women by nearly 40 percent (3.2 million versus 2.3 million).

Proportion of workers who are women
Another way of viewing the difference in the occupational distribution of women and men is by examining the varying proportions women

Table 36 —Major occupation groups of employed women, 1959, 1964, 1969, and April 1974

(Women 16 years of age and over)

Major occupation group	Number (in thousands)				Percent distribution			
	April 1974	1969	1964	1959	April 1974	1969	1964	1959
Total	33,265	29,084	23,831	21,164	100.0	100.0	100.0	100.0
Professional, technical workers	5,179	4,018	3,107	2,558	15.6	13.8	13.0	12.1
Managers, administrators	1,654	1,261	1,108	1,078	5.0	4.3	4.6	5.1
Sales workers	2,260	2,017	1,730	1,661	6.8	6.9	7.3	7.8
Clerical workers	11,463	9,975	7,436	6,322	34.5	34.3	31.2	29.9
Craft and kindred workers	476	339	250	213	1.4	1.2	1.0	1.0
Operatives	4,344	4,489	3,643	3,258	13.1	15.4	15.3	15.4
Nonfarm laborers	339	146	88	100	1.0	.5	.4	.5
Service workers	7,091	6,271	5,694	4,965	21.3	21.6	23.9	23.5
Private household	1,290	1,592	1,995	1,915	3.9	5.5	8.4	9.0
Other	5,800	4,679	3,699	3,050	17.4	16.1	15.5	14.4
Farm workers	460	569	778	1,009	1.4	2.0	3.3	4.8

Source: Manpower Report of the President, April 1974.

Chart I—Employment in different occupation groups varies by sex

Major occupation groups of employed women and men ~ April 1974

▨▨ Women ☐ Men

percent women		millions of workers	0	2	4	6	8	10	12	14	16
77.2	Clerical workers										
57.8	Service workers (except private household)										
41.6	Professional & technical										
31.4	Operatives										
41.7	Sales workers										
18.6	Managers & administrators										
98.5	Private household workers										
4.2	Craft & kindred workers										
15.0	Farm workers										

Source: U.S. Department of Labor, Bureau of Labor Statistics.

were of all workers in each of the major occupation groups. Women accounted for nearly all (98.5 percent) of the private household workers in April 1974 (see table 37). Women also held nearly three-fifths (58 percent) of service jobs other than in private households. Women predominated in one other occupation group—clerical workers—in which they held more than three-fourths (77 percent) of the jobs.

The proportion that women were of all professional and technical workers and of sales workers (42 percent each) exceeded the average for women in all occupations—39 percent. At the other end of the scale, women held a small share of all craft and kindred jobs (4 percent), nonfarm laborer jobs (8 percent), and farm jobs (15 percent) in April 1974. Women accounted for less than 32 percent of all operatives.

Table 37 also shows how women's proportion of all employed persons in each occupation group has changed. Women increased as a proportion of all employed workers from less than 33 percent in 1959 to 39 percent in April 1974. The proportion women were of all farm workers decreased, but women's proportion in all other occupation groups increased. In the professional and technical group, the proportion of women grew from 36 to 42 percent; in clerical occupations, from 68 to 77 percent; and among managers and administrators, from less than 16 to nearly 19 percent. The proportion of women increased from 53 percent to nearly 58 percent among service workers other than private household; nearly all private household workers were women in both 1959 and 1974. Among blue-collar occupations, the proportion of women increased from 3 to 8 percent of nonfarm laborers, from 2.5 to more than 4 percent of craft workers, and from 28 to 32 percent of operatives.

Table 37 ——Women as percent of all employed persons, by major occupation group, 1959 and April 1974

Major occupation group	April 1974	1959 Annual average
Total of all employed persons	39.0	32.7
Professional, technical workers	41.6	35.8
Managers, administrators	18.6	15.5
Sales workers	41.7	39.5
Clerical workers	77.2	67.9
Craft and kindred workers	4.2	2.5
Operatives	31.6	27.6
Nonfarm laborers	8.3	2.8
Service workers	62.5	64.5
Private household	98.5	98.3
Other	57.8	53.1
Farm workers	15.0	18.9

Source: U.S. Department of Labor, Bureau of Labor Statistics: Employment and Earnings, May 1974 and January 1960.

Detailed occupational distribution of women

The principal source of current data on the detailed occupations of employed persons are the statistics on the employment status of the population and its characteristics, compiled monthly by the Bureau of the Census for the Bureau of Labor Statistics from the Current Population Survey (CPS). Because of their relative sample sizes, very detailed occupational employment estimates are subject to a larger degree of sampling error than are major employment estimates. Occupational data are also affected to a greater extent by response bias. Primarily for these reasons, the statistics are presented on an annual basis, and smaller occupations are not shown separately.

Table 38 presents estimates of employment in selected detailed occupations in 1973 (annual average) for women and men separately. The total employment percentages of women in each occupation are shown.

Concentration of women in a small number of occupations
Although increasing numbers of women have become employed in traditionally male career fields in the last decade and a half, women are still concentrated in a relatively small number of occupations. For example, in 1973 more than two-fifths of all women workers were employed in 10 occupations—secretary, retail trade salesworker, bookkeeper, private household worker, elementary school teacher, waitress, typist, cashier, sewer and stitcher, and registered nurse. Each of these occupatons employed more than 800,000 women.

Table 38 — Employed persons in selected occupations, by sex, 1973 annual averages

Occupation	Women			Men	
	Number (in thousands)	Percent distribution	As percent of total employment	Number (in thousands)	Percent distribution
Total _____	32,446	100.0	38.4	51,963	100.0
WHITE-COLLAR WORKERS _____	19,681	60.7	48.7	20,704	39.8
Professional, technical workers _____	4,711	14.5	40.0	7,066	13.6
Accountants _____	162	.5	21.6	587	1.1
Computer specialists _____	56	.2	19.5	231	.4
Librarians, archivists, and curators	133	.4	82.1	(*)	(*)
Personnel and labor relations workers _____	104	.3	33.7	205	.4
Physicians _____	42	.1	12.2	302	.6
Registered nurses _____	805	2.5	97.8	(*)	(*)
Health technologists and technicians	236	.7	71.5	94	.2
Social workers _____	161	.5	60.8	104	.2
Teachers, college and university ___	133	.4	27.1	356	.7
Teachers (except college and univ.) _____	2,038	6.3	69.9	878	1.7
Elementary school teachers _____	1,094	3.4	84.5	200	.4
Kindergarten and prekindergarten teachers _____	185	.6	97.9	(*)	(*)
Secondary school teachers _____	565	1.7	49.5	577	1.1
Engineering and science technicians	87	.3	10.2	763	1.5
Writers, artists, and entertainers__	313	1.0	33.7	616	1.2
Managers, administrators _____	1,590	4.9	18.4	7,054	13.6
Bank officers and financial managers	99	.3	19.4	410	.8
Buyers and purchasing agents ____	95	.3	25.1	284	.5
Restaurant, cafeteria, and bar managers _____	160	.5	32.4	334	.6
Sales managers and department heads (retail trade) _____	84	.3	28.9	207	.4
School administrators _____	90	.3	29.0	220	.4
Sales workers _____	2,240	6.9	41.4	3,175	6.1
Hucksters and peddlers _____	169	.5	77.2	(*)	(*)
Insurance agents, brokers, and underwriters _____	61	.2	12.9	413	.8
Real estate agents and brokers ___	142	.4	36.4	248	.5
Sales clerks (retail trade) _____	1,561	4.8	69.0	701	1.3
Clerical workers _____	11,140	34.3	76.6	3,409	6.6
Bank tellers _____	293	.9	89.9	(*)	(*)
Billing clerks _____	137	.4	83.0	(*)	(*)
Bookkeepers _____	1,466	4.5	88.3	194	.4
Cashiers _____	909	2.8	86.7	138	.3
Counter clerks (except food) _____	266	.8	76.2	(*)	(*)
Estimators and investigators (n.e.c.) _____	164	.5	49.5	168	.3
File clerks _____	245	.8	86.3	(*)	(*)
Computer and peripheral equipment operators _____	87	.3	40.3	128	.2

Table 38 —Employed persons in selected occupations, by sex, 1973 annual averages—continued

Occupation	Women			Men	
	Number (in thousands)	Percent distribution	As percent of total employment	Number (in thousands)	Percent distribution
Keypunch operators	230	.7	90.9	(*)	(*)
Payroll and timekeeping clerks	143	.4	72.2	(*)	(*)
Postal clerks	81	.2	26.9	220	.4
Receptionists	431	1.3	96.9	(*)	(*)
Secretaries	3,037	9.4	99.1	(*)	(*)
Shipping and receiving clerks	66	.2	14.4	392	.8
Statistical clerks	204	.6	68.5	94	.2
Stock clerks and storekeepers	120	.4	25.3	354	.7
Teachers aides (except school monitors)	207	.6	90.4	(*)	(*)
Telephone operators	372	1.1	95.9	(*)	(*)
Typists	999	3.1	96.6	(*)	(*)
BLUE-COLLAR WORKERS	5,244	16.2	17.6	24,625	47.4
Craft and kindred workers	463	1.4	4.1	10,826	20.8
Blue collar supervisors	109	.3	7.5	1,351	2.6
Printing craft workers	68	.2	17.0	331	.6
Operatives	4,482	13.8	31.4	9,787	18.8
Assemblers	600	1.8	49.7	608	1.2
Checkers, examiners and inspectors (manufacturing)	377	1.2	49.5	385	.7
Clothing ironers and pressers	118	.4	77.1	(*)	(*)
Dressmakers and seamstresses (except factory)	131	.4	96.3	(*)	(*)
Laundry and dry cleaning operators (n.e.c.)	112	.3	63.3	(*)	(*)
Packers and wrappers (n.e.c.)	420	1.3	61.5	263	.5
Sewers and stitchers	891	2.7	95.5	(*)	(*)
Textile operatives	240	.7	56.9	182	.4
Bus drivers	97	.3	36.6	169	.3
Nonfarm laborers	299	.9	6.9	4,012	7.7
Stockhandlers	130	.4	17.3	622	1.2
SERVICE WORKERS	7,008	21.6	63.0	4,120	7.9
Private household workers	1,330	4.1	98.3	(*)	(*)
Child care workers	532	1.6	98.3	(*)	(*)
Private household cleaners and servants	631	1.9	98.3	(*)	(*)
Service workers (except private household)	5,678	17.5	58.1	4,097	7.9
Cleaning service workers	707	2.2	34.1	1,369	2.6
Building interior cleaners	358	1.1	54.2	302	.6
Lodging quarters cleaners	196	.6	96.6	(*)	(*)
Janitors and sextons	153	.5	12.6	1,061	2.0
Food service workers	2,370	7.3	69.7	1,032	2.0
Bartenders	65	.2	30.2	150	.3

Table 38 —Employed persons in selected occupations, by sex, 1973 annual averages—continued

Occupation	Women			Men	
	Number (in thousands)	Percent distribution	As percent of total employment	Number (in thousands)	Percent distribution
Cooks _____	555	1.7	59.8	373	.7
Dishwashers _____	74	.2	37.8	122	.2
Food counter and fountain workers _____	254	.8	80.9	(*)	(*)
Waiters, waitresses, and helpers_	1,082	3.3	82.9	222	.4
Health service workers _____	1,398	4.3	87.6	198	.4
Dental assistants _____	112	.3	98.2	(*)	(*)
Health aides and trainees (excluding nursing) _____	150	.5	82.4	(*)	(*)
Nursing aides, orderlies, and attendants _____	790	2.4	83.9	152	.3
Practical nurses _____	345	1.1	96.4	(*)	(*)
Personal service workers _____	1,140	3.5	73.9	403	.8
Child care workers _____	342	1.1	95.5	(*)	(*)
Hairdressers and cosmetologists_	458	1.4	91.8	(*)	(*)
FARM WORKERS _____	514	1.6	17.0	2,513	4.8
Farmers and farm managers _____	103	.3	6.2	1,561	3.0
Farm laborers and supervisors _____	411	1.3	30.2	952	1.8
Farm laborers (wage workers) ___	137	.4	15.1	770	1.5
Farm laborers (unpaid family workers) _____	270	.8	66.3	137	.3

*Number too small for reliable estimate.

Source: U.S. Department of Labor, Bureau of Labor Statistics. (Unpublished data.)

There were 57 occupations in which at least 100,000 women were employed. About three-fourths of all women workers were employed in these 57 occupations. Thirty of these occupations were white-collar, 14 were service, and the remaining 13 were blue-collar or farm. The number of occupations in which 100,000 or more women were employed increased to 57 in 1973 from 36 in 1960 and 29 in 1950.

An indication of the continued occupational concentration of women's employment can be seen by examining the percentage women make up of all employees in the 57 occupations. In 17 of the occupations, women accounted for 90 percent or more of all employees. In more than half of the occupations (31 of the 57), women made up 75 percent or more of all employees.

Male employment showed much less occupational concentration. The 10 largest occupations for men employed less than 20 percent of all male workers, and 52 percent of the men were employed in the 57 largest occupations. (As indicated previously, the comparable proportions for women were about 40 percent and 75 percent.)

Shifts to nontraditional jobs for women

Despite the continued concentration of women in a relatively small number of traditionally women's fields, the 1970 Decennial Census reveals that women workers entered predominantly male fields in large numbers during the 1960's. Data for 1973 from the Current Population Survey indicate that the movement of women into nontraditional jobs is continuing.

Perhaps the most dramatic shift that occurred between 1960 and 1970 was the large influx of women into the skilled trades. In 1970 almost half a million women (495,000) were working in the skilled occupations (craft and kindred worker group), up from 277,000 in 1960. The rate of increase (nearly 80 percent) was twice that for women in all occupations. It was 8 times the rate of increase for men in the skilled trades.

Employment increased in almost all the skilled trades—in construction, mechanic and repair, and supervisory blue-collar occupations. Most of the individual craft jobs listed in the 1960 and 1970 censuses showed rates of increase for women that exceeded the rate of growth for men; in some, the numerical increase for women was greater than that for men as well. For example, the employment of women carpenters increased by nearly 8,000 (from about 3,300 to about 11,000), compared with a growth of less than 6,000 among male carpenters. The female share of carpenter employment increased from 0.4 to 1.3 percent. Other skilled trades registering significant gains in employment of women were: electricians from 2,500 to 8,700 (0.7 to 1.8 percent); plumbers from about 1,000 to 4,000 (0.3 to 1.1 percent); auto mechanics from about 2,300 to about 11,000 (0.4 to 1.4 percent); painters from about 6,400 to 13,400 (1.9 to 4.1 percent); tool and die makers from about 1,100 to 4,200 (0.6 to 2.1 percent); and machinists from about 6,700 to about 11,800 (1.3 to 3.1 percent). In one skilled occupation, that of compositor and typesetter, the number of women increased from 15,500 to nearly 24,000, whereas the number of men employed in the occupation declined.

Women also made significant employment gains in some predominantly male professions. Employment of women lawyers grew from less than 5,000 to more than 12,000 between 1960 and 1970 and women nearly doubled their proportion of all employed lawyers (2.4 to 4.7 percent). Similar gains in employment were made in the medical professions. The number of women physicians increased from about 16,000 to nearly 26,000, and the proportion of doctors who were women rose from 7 to 9 percent. The number of women dentists increased from about 1,900 to more than 3,100 (from 2.3 to 3.4 percent of all dentists).

Enrollment data indicate that the number and percent of women in law and medicine can be expected to grow sharply. For example, the number of women enrolled in law schools in 1973 (16,760) was 3½ times the number in 1969 (4,715); the proportion women were of all law students increased from 7 to 16 percent. Similarly, the number of women enrolled in U.S. medical schools increased from 3,392 in the 1969–70 school year to 7,824 in the 1973–74 school year. The proportion women were of all medical school students increased from 9 to more than 15 percent in this 4-year period.

Women appeared to have made substantial inroads into some other predominantly male professional occupations. Women in engineering increased from about 7,000 to about 19,600 between 1960 and 1970, growing by more than 4½ times the rate for men. Employment of women accountants grew from 80,400 to 183,000, also more than quadrupling the growth rate for men.

Women also have made noticeable inroads into several traditionally male sales occupations. Employment of women insurance agents and brokers increased from about 35,300 to nearly 56,600 and from 9.6 to 12.4 percent of all employees in this occupational field. Similarly, women real estate sales agents increased in number from about 46,100 to 83,600 and women stock and bond sales agents from 2,100 to 8,900.

Among the managerial occupations, the number of women bank officers and financial managers grew rapidly (as branch banking expanded) from 2,100 to 54,500, and women's share of total employment more than doubled. The number of women sales managers (except retail trade) grew dramatically, increasing from less than 100 to 8,700.

Among clerical occupations, women had a large relative growth in the postal occupations. The number of women mail carriers increased from 4,200 to 19,600 and women's proportion of total employment rose from 2.2 to 7.8 percent. The number of postal clerks increased from 39,800 to 91,800 (this was a growth from 17.2 to 30.4 percent of all postal clerks).

Protective service occupations showed substantial increases in female employment during the 1960's. Women employed as guards tripled in number (from 4,900 to 16,300), whereas the number of men employed as guards grew by only one-fourth. The number of women police almost doubled—rising from 6,800 to 13,100.

Other occupations also showed considerable growth in the number and percentage of women workers. For example, the number of women bartenders doubled—from 19,300 in 1960 to 39,400 in 1970. Over the same period, the number of men employed as bartenders declined somewhat. The number of women bus drivers more than tripled during the 1960's, increasing from 18,300 to 66,100. In the same period, the number of male bus drivers increased by less than 5 percent (from 163,500 to 170,100).

It should be noted that during the period when women were entering predominantly male occupations in large numbers, men were also making significant inroads into occupations where women traditionally predominated. For example, the number of male librarians grew from 10,800 in 1960 to more than 22,000 in 1970. The rate of growth for men nearly doubled that for women in this occupation. Male elementary school teachers increased in number from less than 140,000 to more than 231,000 and their proportion grew from 14.2 to 16.4 percent of all elementary school teachers. Men working as typists more than doubled in number during the 1960's, increasing from 25,000 to 57,300. Employment of male telephone operators increased by about one-half (from 15,100 to 22,700); this was about 4 times the growth rate for women.

The increase in the number of women entering traditionally male occupations was undoubtedly affected by the affirmative action programs required of Federal contractors.

Professional and technical occupations
More than 4.7 million women—about 1 out of 7 employed women—were in professional and technical occupations in 1973. About 2 million more women were employed in professional occupations in 1973 than in 1960. The large increase in the number of women professional workers may be attributed to a variety of social and economic developments. The

school-age population expanded greatly, resulting in the employment of a rising number of women as teachers, other educational personnel, and librarians. The concern for the health of the American population, and especially of older persons, resulted in enlarged medical facilities and expanded health programs which provided increasing numbers of jobs for women as nurses, therapists, dietitians, pharmacists, clinical laboratory technologists and technicians, and other professional and technical health workers. The growth of business and industry and of government operations provided opportunities for many more women as accountants and computer specialists. The sharp growth in social welfare and recreation programs contributed to an increase in the number of women as professional, social, and recreation workers.

Teaching is by far the largest professional occupation for women. In 1973 the more than 2 million women noncollege teachers accounted for over 43 percent of the women employed in professional occupations. More than half (1.1 million) of the women teachers were employed in elementary teaching; 565,000 taught at the secondary level; 185,000 were prekindergarten and kindergarten teachers; and the remainder taught adult education or other specialized classes. The number of women in noncollege teaching in 1973 was about three-fifths more than the 1.3 million recorded as employed in the 1960 census. In 1973 women accounted for nearly 85 percent of the Nation's elementary school teachers but less than half of the secondary school teachers. About 133,000 women were employed as teachers in colleges and universities, nearly 3 times the 46,000 shown as employed in the field in the 1960 census. There has been an increase in the proportion of women among teachers at the college level from 22 percent in 1960 to 27 percent in 1973.

Another large group of professional women are employed as health workers. In 1973 they numbered 1.2 million and made up about one-fourth of all women professional workers. The largest occupation in this group is that of professional nurse. About 805,000 women were employed as registered nurses in 1973, about one-third more than the 603,000 shown by the 1960 census. Another large number of women— about 236,000—were employed in a group of occupations collectively called health technologists and technicians. The largest individual occupations in this group are clinical laboratory technician and technologist, radiologic technologist and technician, and dental hygienist. As discussed previously, the number of women employed as physicians and dentists has increased sharply in recent years, although women still account for only a small percentage of all persons in these professions.

Women also hold a variety of professional jobs outside of teaching and the health fields; however, they account for only about one-fifth of professional and technical workers in these fields. In 1973 about 162,000 women were employed as accountants; 161,000 as social workers; 133,000 as librarians, archivists, or curators; 104,000 as personnel and labor relations workers, 87,000 as engineering and science technicians; and 56,000 as computer specialists.

Managers and administrators

Nearly 1.6 million women were working as managers or administrators in 1973. This is a relatively small occupation group for women—only about 5 percent of all women workers. Women accounted for only about 18 percent of all workers in this occupation group.

About 1 out of 5 women workers employed in this major occupation group was a self-employed or unpaid family worker. Many were operating or helping to operate retail establishments such as food stores, eating and drinking places, and apparel and accessory stores.

Many of the salaried managers were also employed in retail trade, especially as restaurant, cafeteria, and bar managers. Others worked as buyers in stores, as officials and administrators for government agencies, and as school administrators. The employment of women as bank officials and financial managers has expanded rapidly in recent years.

Clerical occupations

More than 11 million women, over one-third of all women workers, were employed in clerical work—the largest occupation group employing women in 1973. Women accounted for more than three-fourths of all clerical workers. This has been one of the fastest growing occupation groups for women, increasing by about 68 percent during the 1960–73 period. The growth in the number of clerical workers resulted from increasing paperwork that accompanied the expansion of large and complex business and government organizations. The trend in retail stores toward transferring to clerical workers the functions that had previously been performed by sales persons also tended to increase employment needs for clerical workers. Increasing numbers of clerical workers were also employed to handle jobs created by rapidly expanding electronic data processing operations.

Another factor in the employment growth of women in clerical work is the rapid development of the "temporary help" industry. In this industry, employees are sent out on assignments by agencies set up for the purpose of filling temporary vacancies in clerical, industrial, or professional jobs. These workers are then employees of the agencies rather than of the firm for which they work. Generally speaking, their assignments are of short duration. It is estimated that about 70 percent of the temporary employees work in the clerical sector and most temporary clerical workers are women. No firm data on the number of workers employed by temporary help agencies are available, but it has been estimated that the number grew from about 40,000 workers in 1963 to perhaps 2 million individuals who worked as "temporary help" some time during the calendar year 1973.

More women are in secretarial work than in any other clerical occupation. More than 3 million women were employed as secretaries in 1973, and another 1.1 million were employed as typists or stenographers. Together, these three occupations accounted for about 3 out of 8 women clerical workers. The growth of business and industry and of government operations has brought a rising demand for workers in these occupations to handle correspondence, interoffice communication, and other forms of paperwork. The number of women workers in these occupations has increased by nearly 90 percent between 1960 and 1973.

Another large group of women clerical workers consists of bookkeepers. The number of bookkeepers nearly doubled between 1960 and

1973—from 774,000 to nearly 1.5 million. Cashiers are another large occupational field for women clerical workers. Employment in this occupation increased at an even faster rate than bookkeepers, growing from about 374,000 in 1960 to more than 900,000 in 1973. The rise in women's employment as bank tellers has been particularly rapid; the number more than tripled in the 1960–73 period—from 93,000 to 293,000. In 1973 nearly 9 out of 10 bank tellers were women, in contrast to 1960 when 7 out of 10 were women. About 450,000 women were employed as office machine operators; more than half of these were keypunch operators.

Other occupations in which significant numbers of women clerical workers were employed include receptionist (431,000); telephone operators (372,000); counter clerks, except food (266,000); file clerks (245,000); and statistical clerks (204,000). More than 200,000 women were employed as teachers' aides.

Service occupations

The second largest occupation group employing women in 1973 was service work, in which about 7 million women were employed — 52 percent more than in 1960. About 1.3 million of the women service workers were in private households. Most performed domestic tasks such as preparing and serving meals, making beds, cleaning and doing laundry, and caring for children. The number of women in private household work has decreased since 1960, as fewer women have been willing to accept jobs in this occupation group because of the relatively low pay and lack of benefits and because of opportunities in other occupational fields.

Women service workers other than in private households numbered nearly 5.7 million in 1973—92 percent more than in 1960. Employment in this occupation group rose as a result of the growing demand for hospital and other medical services; the increasing need for protective services in growing urban areas; and the more frequent use of restaurants, beauty parlors, and other services as income levels rose and as increasing numbers of housewives took jobs outside the home.

The largest group of women service workers—2.4 million—were employed in food service occupations in 1973. More than 1 million of these workers were waitresses, over half a million were cooks, and one-fourth of a million were food, counter, and fountain workers. Nearly 7 out of 10 of all food service workers were women.

More than 1.4 million women were employed in health service occupations in 1973. The largest occupations for women in this group were: nursing aide, orderly, and attendant (790,000); practical nurse (345,000); health aide and trainee (150,000); and dental assistant (112,000). The number of women employed in health service occupations—one of the faster growing groups for women workers—more than doubled in number since 1960.

About 1.1 million women were employed in personal service occupations. The largest occupation in this group was that of hairdresser and cosmetologist, with nearly 460,000 women employed in 1973. Women employed in cleaning service jobs made up another large group of service workers—about 700,000. Nearly 360,000 of these workers were classified as building interior cleaners and nearly 200,000 as lodging quarters cleaners (except private household).

Sales occupations

About 2.2 million women were employed in sales jobs in 1973—one-third more than 1960. Some two-thirds of all women sales workers were sales clerks in retail trade. Women retail sales persons increased only moderately in number between 1960 and 1973 (about 17 percent), despite a relatively large increase (46 percent) in employment in the retail trade industry. One reason for the slower growth in number of retail sales clerks is the trend in retail stores of transferring to clerical workers functions that had been performed previously by sales persons. Employment of women expanded significantly in two male-dominated sales occupations. The number of women employed as real estate agents and brokers increased from 46,000 in 1960 to 142,000 in 1973. The proportion women were in this occupation increased from less than 25 percent to more than 36 percent. The number of women employed as insurance agents and brokers increased from 35,000 to 61,000 and women's share of these jobs grew from less than 10 percent in 1960 to nearly 13 percent in 1973.

Blue-collar workers

About 4.5 million women were employed as operatives (sometimes called semiskilled workers) in 1973. They made up about 31 percent of all workers in this occupation group. Most of the women were employed in factories—assembling or inspecting goods, operating sewing and other machines, and working as packers or wrappers; or they operated equipment in laundries and dry cleaning plants.

The number of women in operative jobs increased by about 40 percent in the 1960–73 period. The largest occupations for women in the operative group were: sewer and stitcher (890,000); assembler (600,000); packer and wrapper (420,000); and checker, examiner, and inspector (manufacturing) (380,000). Nearly 100,000 women were employed as bus drivers in 1973—more than 5 times as many as in 1960.

Only about 463,000 women were employed in craft jobs in 1973—about 4.1 percent of all workers in this occupation group. As indicated previously, the number of women has been growing rapidly in this occupation group, almost doubling since 1960. About 300,000 women were employed as nonfarm laborers in 1973; they accounted for about 7 percent of all workers in this group.

Farm workers

Women farm workers—including farmers, farm managers and farm laborers and supervisors—numbered more than 500,000 in 1973. More than half of the women farm workers (270,000) were unpaid family workers; that is, wives or daughters of farm owners or tenants. The number of women employed as farm workers decreased by about 46 percent in the 1960–73 period, as the number of farms declined and the average size of farms increased.

Female labor force participation: why projections have been too low [*]

Introduction

From 1950 to 1975, the sex composition of the civilian labor force in the American economy underwent a sharp transformation. During 1950, women age 16 and over represented only 29 percent of the Nation's civilian labor force; however, by 1975, women's share of the civilian labor force had risen to approximately 40 percent[1]—a percentage point increase almost as large as that of the preceding 60 years.[2]

This study describes the growth of the female civilian labor force in the Nation from 1950 to 1975 and examines the role of female population growth and changing civilian labor force participation rates of women in producing the rise in the female labor force. We will also analyze the upward shift in the civilian labor force participation rate from a flow perspective to determine the role of various factors that have produced the rise in the civilian labor force participation rate of women during the 1960–62 period to the 1970–72 period in the American economy.[3] We will do this by disaggregating the rate into two key components—the proportion of women who actively participate in the civilian labor force during some period within the year and the mean number of weeks spent by these participants in the civilian labor force during the year. This analysis indicates that 34 percent of the total gain in the female civilian labor force participation rate during the period under study was accounted for by a rise in the mean number of weeks spent by female participants in the civilian labor force. The findings of this review are examined in terms of their implications for projecting employment requirements, particularly replacement demand in those occupations in which women workers are predominant.[4]

Growth of the female civilian labor force, 1950–75

Table 1 contains information on the size of the civilian labor force, both in total and for women, during the 1950–75 period. The data are annual averages based upon the Current Population Survey of employment and unemployment. During this period, the civilian labor force rose by 30.4 million persons to 92.6 million—a gain of 48.9 percent. The growth rate has accelerated in recent years, rising from 11.9 percent during 1950–60 to 18.8 percent during the 1960's to an estimated decennial growth rate of 24.0 percent from 1970 to 1975.

The female civilian labor force experienced a dramatic increase between 1950 and 1975, rising from 18.4 million to 37.0 million, representing a 101.2- percent gain. Because the growth rate of the female civilian labor force was more than twice that of the civilian labor force, the

*Monthly Labor Review, U.S. Department of Labor, Bureau of Labor Statistics, Andrew M. Sum, July 1977.

Table 1 —The civilian labor force of the United States, by sex, 1950, 1960, 1970, and 1975

[Numbers in thousands]

Year	Civilian labor force, total	Civilian labor force, female	Female civilian labor force as a percent of total civilian labor force
1950......	62,208	18,389	29.6
1960......	69,628	23,240	33.4
1970......	82,715	31,520	38.1
1975......	92,613	36,998	39.9

	Changes				Changes in female civilian labor force as a percent of total changes in civilian labor force
	Number	Percent	Number	Percent	
1950–75 ...	30,405	48.9	18,609	101.2	61.2
1950–60 ...	7,420	11.9	4,851	26.4	65.4
1960–70 ...	13,087	18.8	8,280	35.6	63.3
1970–75 ...	9,898	12.0	5,478	17.4	55.3

Source: U.S. Department of Labor, *Employment and Training Report of the President: 1976* (Washington, 1976), table A–1, pp. 211–12.

female share of the civilian labor force exhibited a continuous rise during this period, increasing from 29.6 percent in 1950 to 39.9 percent in 1975. From 1950 to 1975, women made up more than three-fifths of all the net additions to the civilian labor force.

The growth rate of the female civilian labor force was also not uniform throughout this period. During 1950–60, the female civilian labor force expanded by 26.4 percent; however, from 1960 to 1970, the growth rate accelerated to 35.6 percent. In 1970–75, the expansion approximated a decennial growth rate of 35.0 percent, which is essentially the same as that of the decade of the 1960's. The female growth rate relative to that of the total civilian labor force has, however, slowed down in recent years. As a result, the female share of the total civilian labor force, although still increasing, is doing so at a decreasing rate.

Rising population or rising participation rates?
An increase in the size of the civilian labor force of a particular sex or age group can occur as the result of either population growth or a rise in the civilian labor force participation rate. The civilian labor force is simply the product of population and the civilian labor force participation rate, which itself is the ratio of the civilian labor force age 16 and over to the civilian noninstitutional population of the same age. The relationship can be presented algebraically in the following manner, Let,

L = The size of the civilian labor force age 16 and over
P = The size of the civilian noninstitutional population age 16 and over
Then, L/P = The civilian labor force participation rate

And, $L = P \cdot L/P$

The data in table 2 provide information on the role of both population increases and rising civilian labor force participation rates in producing the sharp expansion of the female civilian labor force that occurred during the 1950–75 period. From 1950 to 1975, the female civilian noninstitutional population age 16 and over increased from 54.3 million to 79.9 million, or 47.2 percent. Yet, during the same period, the female

Table 2 — The female civilian noninstitutional population, civilian labor force, and civilian labor force participation rates, 1950, 1960, 1970, and 1975

[Numbers in thousands]

Year	Female civilian noninstitutional population[1]	Female civilian labor force	Female civilian labor force participation rate (in percent)
1950......	54,270	18,389	33.9
1960......	61,583	23,240	37.7
1970......	72,734	31,520	43.3
1975......	79,865	36,998	46.3

	Changes				Percent change in female civilian labor force participation rate
	Number	Percent	Number	Percent	
1950–75 ...	25,595	47.2	18,609	101.2	+ 12.4

[1]The civilian noninstitutional population was derived by subtracting the number of women in the Armed Forces from the total female noninstitutional population. All data are for persons age 16 and over.

Source: U.S. Department of Labor, *Employment and Training Report of the President: 1976* (Washington, 1976), table A–1, pp. 211–12.

civilian labor force of these ages rose by more than 100 percent. Thus, a major portion of the overall growth of the female civilian labor force was attributable to rising labor force participation rates of women.

From 1950 to 1975, the participation rate increased from 33.9 to 46.3 percent. The significance of this rise can be seen more clearly by comparing the actual 1975 female civilian labor force with the hypothetical 1975 civilian labor force that would have been produced if participation rates of women had remained at their 1950 levels. In the absence of any change in the participation rate, the 1975 female civilian labor force would have stood at a level of only 27.1 million, or 9.9 million below that of the actual 1975 civilian labor force of 37.0 million. Thus, more than half of the overall increase in the female civilian labor force that occurred between 1950 and 1975 was the result of rising civilian labor force participation rates.

BLS labor force projections

The Bureau of Labor Statistics has been projecting labor force growth for the Nation during the past 15 years. These projections have fallen short of the actual size of the labor force as estimated by the CPS household surveys—by 0.2 percent in 1965, 1.7 percent in 1970, and 2.2 percent in 1975. In each period, all of the shortfall resulted from an underestimation of the growth of the female labor force; the projected male labor force always exceeded the CPS estimate. (See table 3.)

The magnitude of the gap between the projected and the actual female labor force also increased—from 219,000 or 0.8 percent of the projected level in 1965 to 3.2 million or 9.3 percent of the projected level by 1975. The underestimate of the female civilian labor force resulted entirely from an underestimation of the labor force participation rate of women rather than from underestimates of the number of women in the population. The remainder of this study analyzes several of the factors producing this rise in the female labor force participation rate and concentrates on the change in the civilian labor force participation rate of women that took place during the 1960–62 to 1970–72 period. A central point is that we can get a better grip on women's attachment to the labor force and its implications for replacement demand if we view if from a

Table 3 — Comparisons of BLS projected labor force figures with actual labor force estimates for the U.S.: 1965, 1970, and 1975

[Numbers in thousands]

Year and labor force group	Projected labor force	CPS estimated labor force	Projected less actual	Column 3 divided by column 1 (in percent)
1965				
Total	78,198	78,358	−160	−0.2
Men	51,764	51,705	+59	+.1
Women	26,434	26,653	−219	−.8
1970				
Total	85,999	87,432	−1,433	−1.7
Men	55,844	55,235	+609	+1.1
Women	30,155	32,197	−2,042	−6.8
1975				
Total	92,792	94,793	−2,001	−2.2
Men	58,876	57,706	+1,170	+2.0
Women	33,916	37,087	−3,171	−9.3

NOTE: Before 1975, data apply to persons age 14 and over; 1975 data apply to persons age 16 and over.

Source: U.S. Department of Labor, *Manpower Report of the President: 1963* (Washington, 1963) table D–8, p. 179; U.S. Department of Labor, *Manpower Report of the President: 1965* (Washington, 1965), table E–3, p. 249; U.S. Department of Labor, *Manpower Report of the President: 1971* (Washington, 1971), table E–2, p. 291; U.S. Department of Labor, *Employment and Training Report of the President: 1976* (Washington, 1976), table A–2, p. 213.

flow perspective, focusing both on the participation rate at a single point in time and the duration of time spent by female participants in the civilian labor force during a given year.

Stocks versus flows

The civilian labor force is generally thought of as a stock of persons measured at a point in time. For example, the female civilian labor force age 16 and over is estimated on a monthly basis by the Bureau of Labor Statistics based on the CPS household survey data. For a given month, it is simply the sum of the employed and unemployed women estimated by the CPS. When this stock of persons is divided by the estimate of the female civilian noninstitutional population age 16 and over, the result is the civilian labor force participation rate of women age 16 and over for the month. The monthly participation rate is thus the ratio of two stocks measured at one time.

Let L/P = The civilian labor force participation rate at a single point in time

Where L = The estimate of the size of the civilian labor force which itself is the sum of the estimated number of employed and unemployed persons

And P = The estimated size of the civilian noninstitutional population age 16 and over

Suppose, P = 100   Employed = 45

Unemployed = 5

L = 50

Then, L/P = 50/100 = 50.0 percent

In the above example, the civilian labor force for the month was estimated at 50 persons, and the civilian noninstitutional population was estimated at 100 persons. The civilian labor force participation rate for this month is thus the ratio of the two stocks, or 50/100, which is equal to 50.0 percent. The annual average civilian labor force participation rate is derived by taking the ratio of the mean civilian labor force for the 12 months to the mean civilian noninstitutional population.

To understand the forces producing changes in civilian labor force participation rates, it is necessary to examine the flows producing the rates. This requires a disaggregation of the civilian labor force participation rate into its two key components—the proportion of the civilian noninstitutional population that actively participates in the labor force during some time period within the year and the mean number of weeks spent in the civilian labor force by those who participated during the year. A rise in the civilian labor force participation rate of women can thus be produced if either the proportion of women in the civilian population who actively participate in the labor force increases, or if the mean number of weeks spent by each participant in the labor force during the year increases, or both.

The following examples illustrate this point. The civilian labor force participation rate can be reformulated in the following manner:

$$\frac{L}{P} = \frac{N}{P} (X) \frac{\bar{L}}{52} \quad \text{or} \quad \frac{N (X) \bar{L}}{P (X) 52}$$

Where $N =$ The number of women who participated in the civilian labor force at some point during the year, including those women who looked for work but could not find a job during the year

$\bar{L} =$ The mean number of weeks spent by the above participants (N) in the civilian labor force during the year

$N (X) \bar{L} =$ The total number of weeks spent in the civilian labor force by women age 16 and over during the year

$P(X) 52 =$ The maximum number of weeks that the female civilian noninstitutional population age 16 and over could have spent in the civilian labor force.

The ratio of $[N (X) \bar{L}]$ to $[P (X) 52]$ simply represents the proportion of total weeks during the year that were spent by women of working age in the civilian labor force, or the civilian labor force participation rate. The key point of this exercise focusing on the flow analysis of participation rates is that a given annual average civilian labor force participation rate can be produced by a variety of factors. For example, the 50-percent civilian labor force participation rate cited above could have been generated in any one of the following three ways:

Case I: $N = 50$
            $\bar{L} = 52$
            $\frac{L}{P} = \frac{50}{100} (X) \frac{52}{52} = 50.0$ percent

Case II: $N = 75$
            $\bar{L} = 34.7$
            $\frac{L}{P} = \frac{75}{100} (X) \frac{34.7}{52} = \frac{2600}{5200} = 50.0$ percent

Case III: $N = 100$
$\overline{L} = 26$
$$\frac{L}{P} = \frac{100}{100}(X)\frac{26}{52} = \frac{2600}{5200} = 50.0 \text{ percent}$$

In case I, the civilian labor force participation rate of 50.0 percent was produced by one-half of the female civilian population, each of whom participated in the civilian labor force for all 52 weeks during the year. In case II, a 50.0-percent participation rate was generated by having three-fourths of the female civilian population active in the labor force during the year for an average of 34.7 weeks. In case III, the 50.0-percent rate was the result of active participation in the civilian labor force by every woman age 16 and over in the civilian noninstitutional population, each of whom remained in the labor force for 26 weeks (or who remained in the labor force for varying number of weeks whose mean, however, was 26 weeks).

The remainder of this review applies this type of an analysis to actual data, examining the forces producing the rise in the civilian labor force participation rate of women of working age during the 1960–62 period to the 1970–72 period. The findings will be analyzed in terms of their significance for projecting replacement demands for occupations in future years, particularly those occupations in which women are preponderant. Separation rates for an occupation are calculated on the basis of the age-sex characteristics of the workers. For men, the separation rate is based simply upon deaths and retirements; however, for women, the separation rate is also based upon other forms of labor force withdrawal, such as leaving to marry or rear children. Changes in labor force withdrawal rates of women will, thus, not only affect the participation rate of women, but also affect replacement demand for those occupations in which women are employed.

Sorting out the factors
Data on the female civilian labor force participation rate during the 1960–62 and 1970–72 periods are presented in table 4. The overall female unemployment rate was quite similar during the two periods (a mean annual rate of 6.4 percent during the former period and 6.5 per-

Table 4 —Civilian labor force participation rates of women age 16 and over, 1960 to 1972

[Number in thousands]

Year	Female civilian non-institutional population age 16 and over	Female civilian labor force	Civilian labor force participation rate (in percent)
1960......	61,583	23,240	37.7
1961......	62,485	23,806	38.1
1962......	63,322	24,014	37.9
1960–62 ...	62,463	23,687	37.9
1970......	72,734	31,520	43.3
1971......	74,043	32,091	43.3
1972......	75,868	33,277	43.9
1970–72 ...	74,215	32,296	43.5

Source: U.S. Department of Labor, *Employment and Training Report of the President: 1976* (Washington, 1976), table A–1, p. 212.

cent during the latter period). Thus, the participation rates for both periods should not be affected by differences in labor market conditions, which have been shown to influence labor force participation behavior of women.[5]

The mean annual participation rate of women age 16 and over during the 1960–62 period was 37.9 percent; during the 1970–72 period, it was 43.5 percent. Thus, from 1960–62 to 1970–72, the civilian labor force participation of women increased 5.6 percentage points. The sources of this increase need to be examined in detail. This involves calculating changes in (N) and (N/P), the proportion of the female population participation in the civilian labor force during the year and changes in $(\bar{L})$ and $(\bar{L}/52)$, the mean number of weeks female participants spent in the labor force during the year.

The following tabulation shows the percent distribution of employed women by weeks worked during the 1960–62, 1965–67, and 1970–72 periods:[6]

Year	50–52 Weeks	27–49 Weeks	1–26 Weeks
1960	46.9	21.2	31.8
1961	46.6	21.4	32.0
1962	46.4	22.2	31.4
1960–62	46.6	21.6	31.7
1965	48.0	20.5	31.6
1966	48.8	20.3	30.9
1967	52.0	19.2	28.7
1965–67	49.6	20.0	30.4
1970	50.7	20.3	28.9
1971	52.8	19.4	27.7
1972	52.8	19.1	28.0
1970–72	52.1	19.6	28.2
Change from 1960–62 to 1970–72	+5.5	−2.0	−3.5

The findings (based upon the Work Experience Surveys conducted in March of the following year) reveal that the proportion of women working 50–52 weeks during the year has been rising steadily in recent years. During the 1960–62 period, only 46.6 percent of employed women worked 50–52 weeks. The proportion of year-round workers increased to 49.6 percent during the 1965–67 period and to 52.1 percent during the 1970–72 period. Thus, the proportion of year-round female workers increased by 5.5 percentage points from 1960–62 to 1970–72. This rise was accompanied by a decline in the shares of women working 27 to 49 weeks (–2.0 percentage points) and particularly those working 1 to 26 weeks during the year (–3.5 percentage points). The evidence contained in the preceding tabulation thus provides support for the hypothesis that the rising participation rate of women resulted in part from an increase in the mean number of weeks spent by female participants in the civilian labor force during the year.

Proportion of women participating.   Information on the number of women age 16 and over with some work experience in each year during 1960–62 and 1970–72 is presented in table 5. During 1960–62, the mean yearly number of females age 14 and over with work experience was 30.8 million. Excluding girls 14 and 15 reduces the number to 30.0 million or 48.1 percent of the female civilian noninstitutional population age 16 and over. For the 1970–72 period, the WES survey has estimated that 39.2 million women of those ages had some work experience during the year, or 52.8 percent of the female noninstitutional civilian population age 16 and over during these years. The findings contained in table 5 thus indicate a rise in the proportion of the female population age 16 and over with work experience of 4.7 percentage points form 1960–62 to 1970–72.

These proportions, together with information on the number of women who looked for work during the year but could not find a job, enable calculation of N and N/P. These estimates are also presented in table 5.

During the 1960–62 period, the mean annual number of females age 14 and over who looked for work but could not find a job was 1.0 million. When estimates of the number of unemployed 14 to 15-year-old women during the year are excluded, the total falls to 990,000. For the 1970–72 period, the mean yearly number of women age 16 and over who looked for work but could not find a job has been estimated at slightly more than 1.2 million, an increase of 241,000 over the mean annual number during the 1960–62 period.

Columns 1 and 2 of table 5 can now be combined to provide estimates of both N and N/P. Column 3 provides the results of the calculations. Column 1 presents the estimates of the number of women age 16 and over with work experience during each year, and column 2 provides

Table 5 —Number of women who participated in the civilian labor force at some point during the year, 1960–62 and 1970–72

[Numbers in thousands]

Year	Women with work experience during year	Women unemployed with no work experience during year	Women who participated in civilian labor force during year	Number of women in civilian labor force as percent of female civilian noninstitutional population (16 +)
1960	29,885	976	30,861	50.1
1961	29,589	904	30,493	48.8
1962	30,561	1,091	31,652	50.0
1960–62. .	30,012	990	31,002	49.6
1970	38,704	1,049	39,753	54.7
1971	39,014	1,330	40,344	54.5
1972	39,918	1,315	41,233	54.3
1970–72. .	39,212	1,231	40,443	54.5

	Changes						
	Number	Percent	Number	Percent	Number	Percent	Percent
1960–62 to 1970–72. .	+9,200	30.7	+241	24.3	+9,441	30.5	+4.9

NOTE: All data were adjusted to refer to women age 16 and over.

Source: U.S. Department of Labor, *Manpower Report of the President: 1975* (Washington, 1975), tables B–14, B–15, and B–18, pp. 272–73, 276; and U.S. Department of Labor, *Manpower Report of the President: 1971* (Washington, 1971), table B–17, p. 254.

the estimates of the number of women age 16 and over who looked for work but could not find a job during each year. Column 3 simply represents the sum of columns 1 and 2. This sum represents the total number of women age 16 and over who participated in the civilian labor force at some time during each year.

During the 1960–62 period, the mean number of women who participated in the civilian labor force during the year was 31.0 million, or 49.6 percent of the female civilian noninstitutional population age 16 and over. For the 1970–72 period, the mean number of women who participated in the civilian labor force at some time during the year was 40.4 million, or 54.5 percent of the female civilian noninstitutional population age 16 and over. Thus, from 1960–62 to 1970–72, (N/P) rose from 49.6 percent to 54.5 percent.

Mean number of weeks. The findings in table 5 can now be used to calculate $\bar{L}/52$ and $\bar{L}$, the mean number of weeks spent in the civilian labor force by female participants during the year. Our previous equation for the civilian labor force participation rate was

$$\frac{L}{P} = \frac{N}{P} \ (X) \ \frac{\bar{L}}{52}$$

Given L/P and N/P, we can solve for $\bar{L}/52$ and $\bar{L}$:

$$\frac{\bar{L}}{52} = \frac{L}{P} \cdot \frac{P}{N}$$

$$\bar{L} = \frac{L}{P} \cdot \frac{P}{N} \cdot 52$$

Table 6 contains the results of the calculations for both $\bar{L}/52$ and $\bar{L}$. For the 1960–62 period, $\bar{L}/52$ had a mean value of 76.4 percent, yielding

Table 6 —Components of the civilian labor force participation rate of women age 16 and over in the United States, 1960–62 and 1970–72

Year	Civilian labor force participation rate of women (annual average) ($\frac{L}{P}$)	Number of women in civilian labor force during year as a percent of female population ($\frac{N}{P}$)	Ratio of mean number of weeks in civilian labor force to total weeks in year (in percent) ($\frac{\bar{L}}{52}$)	Mean number of weeks in civilian labor force ($\bar{L}$)
1960 ...	37.7	50.1	75.2	39.1
1961 ...	38.1	48.8	78.1	40.6
1962 ...	37.9	50.0	75.8	39.4
1960–62 .	37.9	49.6	76.4	39.7
1970 ...	43.3	54.7	79.2	41.2
1971 ...	43.3	54.5	79.4	41.3
1972 ...	43.9	54.3	80.8	42.0
1970–72 .	43.5	54.5	79.8	41.5

NOTE: All data refer to women age 16 and over.

an $\bar{L}$ value of 39.7 weeks. For the 1970–72 period, $\bar{L}/52$ had a mean value of 79.8 percent, yielding a mean $\bar{L}$ of 41.5 weeks. Thus, from 1960–62 to 1970–72, the mean duration of participation by women in the labor force rose from 39.7 weeks to 41.5 weeks, an increase of 1.8 weeks. The overall rise in the civilian labor force participation rate of women age 16 and over from 37.9 to 43.5 percent during 1960–62 to the 1970–72 period was produced by a combination of a rise in the proportion of the female population, age 16 and over that participated in the labor force (N/P rose from 49.6 to 54.5 percent) and a rise in the mean number of weeks spent by participants in the civilian labor force during the year ($\bar{L}$ rose from 39.7 weeks to 41.5 weeks).

To judge more clearly the contribution of the increase in $\bar{L}$, the mean number of weeks, to the overall rise in the female civilian labor force participation rate during the 1960–62 to 1970–72 periods, a hypothetical civilian labor force participation rate of women for the 1970–72 period was calculated. If $\bar{L}$ had not increased during this 10-year period, the mean civilian labor force participation rate of women during the 1970–72 period would have only been 41.6 percent rather than the actual 43.5 percent estimated rate from the CPS survey. Thus, one could conclude that of the overall 5.6 percentage-point rise in the female civilian labor force participation rate 1.9 percent, or 34 percent of the total gain, was attributable to an increase in the mean number of weeks spent by female participants in the civilian labor force during the year.

Implications for occupational projections

The finding that a substantial fraction of the rise in the female civilian labor force participation rate has been accounted for by an increase in the mean number of weeks spent in the civilian labor force by participants has a number of implications for projections of occupational employment requirements. As noted earlier, projections of replacement demand for an occupation are based upon estimates of separation rates. The female separation rate includes an estimate of temporary withdrawals from the labor force for childbearing and other family-related reasons. The findings of an increase in $\bar{L}$ (mean number of weeks) for female participants suggest that the temporary withdrawal rate is being reduced in magnitude over time. Replacement demand projections that rely upon separation rates which are based upon temporary withdrawal rates of previous years may thus overstate replacement requirements for occupations in which women are a primary source of employees. What is not known, however, is whether the temporary withdrawal rates are being reduced uniformly across all occupations or whether only the higher level occupations (professional, technical, and managerial) are characterized by lower temporary withdrawal rates. If such interoccupational differences do exist (as one might well anticipate given the variations in earnings), then replacement demand estimates may be exaggerated only for a select number of occupations, for which the relative size of the overestimate could, however, be rather substantial.[7]

If the rise in $\bar{L}$ has been anticipated by projections of the female labor force participation rate for 1980 and beyond, then one need not revise the estimates of the future size of the female civilian labor force.[8] If $\bar{L}$ increases, however, have not been anticipated, then the participation rate for women may be projected at too low a level. This result would, other things being equal, lead to an increase in the expected rate of unemployment. Any increase in $\bar{L}$ beyond that built into the labor force projection will reduce replacement demand, increase the size of the female civilian labor force, and require an increase in net new jobs to prevent a rise in unemployment.

FOOTNOTES

[1]The civilian labor force data cited in the text are annual averages from the CPS Household Survey of Employment and Unemployment. See U.S. Department of Labor, *Employment and Training Report of the President: 1976* (Washington, D.C., 1976), table A–1, pp. 211–12.

[2]The labor force data for 1890 to 1950 are based upon the findings of the decennial censuses for those years, which are based upon labor force participation behavior of persons age 14 and over during the month of the census, rather than annual averages. See *Employment and Training Report of the President: 1976*, table BB–2, p. 380.

[3]It is *not* the intent of this study to analyze in detail the diverse set of social, cultural, and economic forces which are believed to have influenced the increasing tendency of women to enter and remain in the labor force. A review of the factors influencing the rising labor force participation of women can be found in the following text: Juanita Kreps and Robert Clark, *Sex, Age, and Work: The Changing Composition of the Labor Force*, (Baltimore, Johns Hopkins University Press, 1975).

[4]Occupational projections conducted by the State Employment Security Agencies throughout the Nation yield estimates of annual net demand for an occupation, which represents expected job openings during the year due to growth and replacement. Replacement demand estimates are based upon expected separation rates for each occupation, including projections of temporary labor force withdrawals of women for childbearing and other reasons. To the extent that women remain in the labor force for longer periods of time, replacement demand will be reduced.

[5]For an empirical analysis of the sensitivity of labor force participation rates of various age-sex groups to employment conditions, see George Perry, "Labor Force Structure, Potential Output, and Productivity," *Brookings Papers on Economic Activity* (volume 3, 1971), pp. 533–65.

   The findings of the CPS surveys on discouraged workers which have been conducted since 1967 have revealed that women constitute more than two-thirds of the total number of discouraged workers. From 1967 to 1975, the mean proportion of females has been 67.8 percent, ranging from 65.4 percent in 1970 to 69.7 percent in 1967. See *Employment and Training Report of the President: 1976*, table A–12, p. 230.

[6]Number of weeks worked includes paid vacations and paid sick leave. Full-time workers (35 hours or more per week) and part-time workers were combined in deriving the distribution of employed persons by weeks of work. Beginning with 1967, data refer to females age 16 and over; the other data refer to females age 14 and over. See U.S. Department of Labor, *Manpower Report of the President: 1975* (Washington, D.C., 1975), table B–14, p. 272.

[7]A recent analysis of the occupational mobility of workers in the United States conducted by Dixie Sommers and Alan Eck provides some empirical support for this view. The authors discovered for the 1965–70 period that separation rates of women employed in professional, technical, and managerial positions based upon the findings of the 1970 Census were below those obtained by methods applying age-specific separation rates based upon working life tables to females working in those occupations. Both the absolute and the relative sizes of the estimated gaps between the Census and working-life table separation rates were greater for women employed in professional, technical, and managerial occupations than for female workers in clerical, sales, operatives, laborers, and service occupations. See Dixie Sommers and Alan Eck, "Occupational mobility in the American labor force," *Monthly Labor Review*, January 1977, pp. 3–19.

[8]The Bureau of Labor Statistics has recently revised its projections of the size of the U.S. civilian labor force for the period 1980 to 1990. The revised results have included an upward adjustment in the projected size of the female civilian labor force, given recent gains in the female labor force participation rate exceeding those built into previous projections. The civilian labor force participation rate of women is projected to continue to rise during the 1975–90 period although at a decreasing rate. See Howard N. Fullerton, Jr., and Paul O. Flaim, "New labor force projections to 1990," *Monthly Labor Review*, December 1976, pp. 3–13.

The changing economic role of women[*]

Introduction

Clear indications that women workers account for significantly larger proportions of the unemployed during the present recession than they did in earlier downturns have underscored the change in the economic role assumed by women in the last decade or more. The same phenomenon raises important issues concerning the situation of women workers in a slackening labor market, where those facing layoffs may become the subject of conflicting pressures between seniority systems and traditional attitudes, on the one hand, and equal employment obligations, on the other.

The proclamation of 1975 as International Women's Year by the United Nation's General Assembly—an observance which was underscored by the issuance of Executive Order 11832 by President Ford on January 9, 1975—has focused world-wide attention on the labor market characteristics of working women. This review explores American women's rapidly changing work profiles, focusing, in turn, on current trends in laborforce activity, on demographic and social transitions affecting women's work lives, and on some of the special problems now affecting women workers in the United States. In the first section, the rapid rises in women's labor force participation rates over the past 25 years are explored in terms of certain key variables. Of major importance among these is the substantial rise in the proportion of 25- to 34-year-old women who have chosen to seek employment in spite of the presence of preschool- or school-age children in the home. Among other important factors have been the greatly reduced impact of marriage itself upon the labor force activity of women and rising levels of educational attainment, which have encouraged many women to enter an expanding range of jobs.

Generally rising levels of labor force attachment, however, have not diminished the importance of several problems, each of which is linked to sex and/or race discrimination in the workplace or in society at large. First, the large wage differential between male and female workers has persisted over the last two decades, although earnings for both sexes have continued to rise in absolute terms. Second, this rise in absolute

[*]Manpower Report of the President, 1975.

earnings has benefited only a minority of women in the labor force, since nearly two-thirds of all full-time, year-round female workers earned less than $7,000 in 1972. Third, women remain overwhelmingly concentrated in a relatively small number of lower paying occupations. Fourth, while about 1 out of every 8 families is headed by a woman, the 1974 unemployment rate for female family heads averaged about 7.0 percent. Finally, the high levels of labor force attachment among black married women aged 25 and over reflect in considerable degree their continuing obligation to supply a substantial proportion of family income in order to help compensate for the generally low wages of their husbands.

The review's second section turns to an examination of the recent demographic and social changes which have encouraged and reinforced women's labor force attachment. Especially important among these has been the steep drop in average family size since the late 1960's, accompanied by increasingly widespread acceptance of childless marriages. Rising divorce and separation rates, as well as later marriage and expectations of greater longevity at midlife, have also been contributing factors. Yet these changes in lifestyle and family size may be no more than symptomatic of deeper changes in social attitudes and expectations both among and toward women. Career commitment and occupational aspirations are on the rise among younger women, and many older women employees indicate that they would continue to work even if they could live comfortably without their earnings. Moreover, within the last few years, these attitudinal transformations have been reflected in the push for legislation and policy directed toward eliminating employment discrimination and enhancing equal job opportunity.

The third section reviews some of the special problems of women workers, beginning with an examination of the poverty and economic insecurity experienced by female-headed families. The difficulties associated with intermittent labor force participation and the scheduling of home and market work are also scrutinized in this section. The study closes with a brief review of some questions for the future, whose resolution would remove many of women's remaining employment problems during the last quarter of the 20th century.

Women's labor market experience

Labor force participation

The proportion of women of working age in the labor market, which was 33.9 percent in 1950, rose by one-third to 44.7 percent in 1973. This rapid rise in women's labor force participation rates during the past quarter century has had a marked effect on the size and composition of the work force, on the growth in national product, and on the lifestyles of both men and women. Among the many factors promoting or discouraging labor force entry, several—including marital status, presence and age of children, educational level, husband's income, race, general economic conditions, and potential earnings—can play a determining role in the decision of a woman to seek paid work.

The age factor.   Although the effects of age on women's labor force activity resemble those prevailing 25 years ago, important changes have occurred in participation rates at all ages (see chart 6). During the 1950's and early 1960's, the proportion of older women in the work force rose dramatically (partly because many women who had worked during World War II were eager to seek employment again, once their children had entered or completed school). From 38 percent in 1950, the participation rate for women 45 to 54 years of age rose to 51 percent in 1964, while the rate for women 55 to 64 rose from 27 percent to 40 percent (see table 1). The mid-1960's then saw an upsurge in participation by younger women, as the 20- to 24-year-old group increased its participation rate from 50 percent in 1964 to 61 percent in 1973, and the 25- to 34-year age group from 37 percent to 50 percent during the same period. Both the earlier rise in participation by older women and the later rise by younger women were accompanied by a steady growth in particitpation by the intermediate 35- to 44-year age group during the two and a half decades.

Increases in labor force participation rates are expected to continue for all but the youngest and oldest groups, but a remarkable shift has already occurred. While age still has the same relative effect on participation rates as it did in 1950, the growth in participation rates for all women has been so rapid that the proportion of women aged 25 to 34 who are in the work force today has reached the rate of the most active age groups of 1950. And mothers with school-age children are just as likely to work today as were unmarried young women of the 1950's.

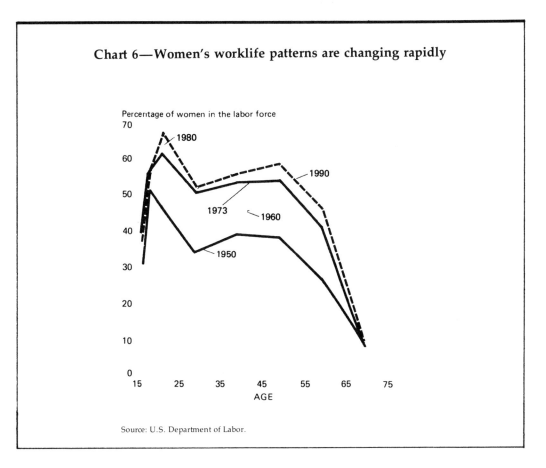

Chart 6—Women's worklife patterns are changing rapidly

Percentage of women in the labor force

Source: U.S. Department of Labor.

Table 1 —Labor force participation rates of women, by age group, selected years 1950 to 1973 and projected 1980 and 1990

Age	1950	1960	1970	1973	1980	1990
Total	33. 9	37. 8	43. 4	44. 7	45. 6	46. 5
16 and 17 years	30. 1	29. 1	34. 9	39. 1	36. 1	37. 4
18 and 19 years	51. 3	51. 1	53. 7	56. 9	55. 0	56. 3
20 to 24 years	46. 1	46. 2	57. 8	61. 1	63. 6	36. 4
25 to 34 years	34. 0	36. 0	45. 0	50. 1	50. 4	51. 6
35 to 44 years	39. 1	43. 5	51. 1	53. 3	53. 5	55. 4
45 to 54 years	38. 0	49. 8	54. 4	53. 7	56. 6	58. 3
55 to 64 years	27. 0	37. 2	43. 0	41. 1	45. 1	46. 1
65 years and over	9. 7	10. 8	9. 7	8. 9	9. 1	8. 8

Marital status and children. Women who have never married have much higher rates of labor force activity than do women who have (see table 2). Still, the participation rates of married women have risen sharply since 1950, when they were 14 percentage points below the rate for widowed, divorced, or separated women and nearly 27 percentage points below that for single women. While just over half of the single women were in the work force, the same was true of less than 1 out of every 4 married women with husbands present. By 1974, however, 43 percent of married women with husbands present were in the labor force, compared with 57 percent of single and 41 percent of widowed, separated, or divorced women. Thus, while marriage still reduces the labor market activity of women, its impact has been greatly lessened. Participation rates for married women are expected to continue to rise, as marital status becomes a less significant factor in determining work force activity.

Married women, however, still have significantly different participation rates when they have preschool-age children (chart 7). In March 1974, married women without children under 18 years of age had a participation rate of 43.0 percent, and married women with only school-age children had a participation rate of about 51 percent. By

Table 2 —Labor force participation rates[1] of women, by marital status, selected years, 1950 to 1974

Year	Never married	Married, husband present	Widowed, divorced, or separated
1950	50. 5	23. 8	37. 8
1955	46. 4	27. 7	39. 6
1960	44. 1	30. 5	40. 0
1965	40. 5	34. 7	38. 9
1970	53. 0	40. 8	39. 1
1973	55. 8	42. 2	39. 6
1974	57. 2	43. 0	40. 9

[1] Percent of noninstitutional population in the labor force.

Chart 7—The presence of preschool children remains important in reducing labor force participation among married women

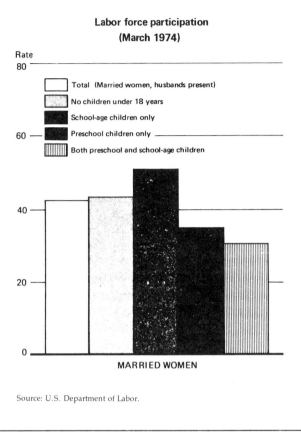

Labor force participation
(March 1974)

Rate

80

☐ Total (Married women, husbands present)
▨ No children under 18 years
■ School-age children only
■ Preschool children only
▥ Both preschool and school-age children

60

40

20

0

MARRIED WOMEN

Source: U.S. Department of Labor.

contrast, the rate for married women with preschool-age children was 36 percent, while that for women with both preschool- and school-age children was 33 percent.

Although the presence of preschool-age children therefore remains a significant factor in reducing the participation rates of married women, it is important to note a considerable growth in work force participation of this group. In fact, married women with preschool-age children are now in the work force as often as were married women who either had no children under 18 or who had only school-age children in 1950. This development is certain to have important consequences in terms of the cumulative labor force experience and employment continuity of working wives.

The presence of greater numbers of children in the same age group tends to reduce the participation rate of married women, but the age of the children statistically swamps the effect of greater numbers. For example, 59 percent of the married women aged 30 to 34 with three or more children aged 12 to 17 worked in 1970. But when only one child under 3 years of age was present, the participation rate was 32 percent.

However, just as the impact of household duties on women's market work has lessened, so too the constraints imposed by having young children seem to be less severe than in earlier years (or, conversely, the financial and psychological constraints of not working may have become more crucial). Whereas 1950 participation rates for 25- to 34-year-old women were about one-fourth lower than the rates for women aged 20 to 24, by 1974 the participation rate of the 25-to-34 group was less than a fifth below that of the younger women. If this trend continues, traditional female worklife patterns will gradually be replaced by something closer to the patterns of their male coworkers.

Educational attainment and husbands' earnings   Another important factor in female participation rates is the level of education attained. Work force activity rises with educational attainment in a consistent pattern, except for the slightly lower rates for women with 1 to 3 years of college, whose earnings differ only moderately from those of high school graduates. The association of earnings with educational attainment provides a partial explanation of this positive correlation; earnings rise with increased educational attainment, the higher wages providing an added incentive to many women to undertake paid work, even when it is combined with household obligations. In 1952, the average level of educational attainment for working women in the United States was 12.0 years, rising to 12.2 years in 1962 and 12.4 years in 1972—a steady growth that has attracted some women into a widening range of jobs.

It should be noted, however, that higher earnings provide only a portion of the explanation for higher labor force participation rates among college-educated women. Other causal elements may include, for example, the fact that commitment to a particular vocation is likely to be more intense among women who have been willing to pursue supplementary years of education. Exposure in college to an emphasis on lifetime careers may well be another factor of considerable importance in influencing decisions to work.

Although improved educational levels and earning have been accompanied by higher work force rates for women, higher earnings by husbands have been associated with lower participation rates by their wives. While this still appears to be true to some extent, two important changes have occurred in the last 20 years. First, there has been a continuing upward shift in participation rates by wives with husbands at all income levels, reflecting women's improved earnings and employment opportunities as well as the continuing pressure of family budgetary needs. The positive effect of increases in women's own earnings has more than offset the negative impact of higher earnings of husbands, resulting in increases in both family income and the participation rate of wives over time.

Second, the inverse relationship between husbands' earnings and wives' participation rates has become less consistent. While 1951 participation rates of wives were highest for those whose husbands earned less than $3,000 (in 1973 dollars), wives whose husbands' earnings were in the $5,000–to–$6,999 bracket (in 1973 dollars) were the most likely to be in the labor market by 1960; by 1973, the highest participation rates had shifted to wives with husbands earning between $7,000 and $9,999 (in 1973 dollars). The increased earnings and employment opportunities available to wives with higher levels of educational attainment thus may be changing the earlier inverse relationship between husbands' earnings and wives' participation rates.

Racial factors.   It is important to consider the effect of race, along with age, education, and husbands' earnings, on female labor force participation rates. Except among those who are single or aged 16 to 24 years, the proportion of black women of working age who are in the labor market is significantly higher than that of white women, irrespective of the other factors considered. At each age level, except in the 16- to 24-year-old groups, black women had higher participation rates in 1973, as shown below:

Labor force participation rates of women, 1973

Age	Black	White
16 to 17 years	24. 3	41. 7
18 to 19 years	45. 1	58. 9
20 to 24 years	57. 5	61. 6
25 to 34 years	61. 0	48. 5
35 to 44 years	60. 7	52. 2
45 to 54 years	56. 4	53. 4
55 to 64 years	44. 7	40. 8

Source: *Handbook of Labor Statistics*, 1974, table 4, pp. 38–39.

The lower participation rates for younger black women appear to be slightly more related to such factors as school attendance and job-search difficulties than to home maintenance responsibilities. In a 1973 survey of young women aged 16 to 24 who were not in the labor force, 44.1 percent of the whites, but only 36.7 percent of the blacks, gave home responsibilities as the reason for nonparticipation. In contrast, 46.0 percent of the black women in the sample listed school responsibilities, while only 42.8 percent of the white ones gave this reason.

Except for single women, who are primarily in the 16- to 24-year age group and have lower participation rates, and women who head families, black women have higher rates of labor market activity than white ones of comparable marital status. For example, among married women, blacks display higher participation rates than whites, regardless of husbands' earnings. Indeed, 54 percent of black married women with husbands present were in the labor force in 1973, in contrast to 41 percent of white women of similar marital status; and 44 percent of black women who were widowed, divorced, or separated were working or seeking work, in contrast to 39 percent of their white counterparts. The presence of children, especially young children, is also less of a constraint to black married women than it is to white ones, While 54 percent of black women with children under 6 years of age were labor force members in 1973, this was true of only 31 percent of white women with preschool-age children.

Education, particularly college education, raises participation rates more for black than for white women. However, while black women (including those whose husbands earn $10,000 or more per year) have traditionally shown a much greater attachment to the labor force than white women, the recent rise in white women's participation rates has been much faster, as the following tabulation shows:

Labor force participation rates of women

Selected years	Black	White
1950	46. 9	32. 6
1955	46. 1	34. 5
1960	48. 2	36. 5
1965	48. 6	38. 1
1970	49. 5	42. 6
1973	49. 1	44. 1
1974	49. 1	45. 2

Source: U.S. Department of Labor, Bureau of Labor Statistics.

Consequently, the longstanding difference between participation rates of black and white women is narrowing, as the general rise in these rates continues.

Occupations and pay

Differences in the occupational distribution of men and women workers remain substantial, both among industry groups and between white- and blue-collar categories. For example, women account for 49 percent of white-collar workers, but only 17 percent of those in blue-collar jobs; similarly, in the service sector, 63 percent of jobholders are women. These differences require further breakdown, however, since significant variations occur within occupational groups. For example, approximately equal proportions of women and men are professional or technical workers, but women are heavily concentrated in the lower paying teaching and nursing fields, while more men are found in such higher paying professions as law, medicine, and engineering.

The service sector remains the most important employer of women, as shown in chart 8. Nearly one-fourth of all women workers are em-

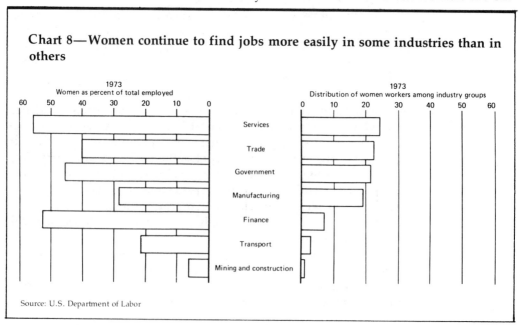

Chart 8—Women continue to find jobs more easily in some industries than in others

Source: U.S. Department of Labor

ployed in the industry, where they make up over one-half of all employees.

Within the service industry category, nearly two-thirds of the workers in education, and three-fourths of those in medical-health and personal services (including work performed in hotels and private homes), are female. The predominance of women in these areas has been attributed to the similarity of the work to the activities traditionally carried out by women in the home. Teaching children and young adults, nursing the sick, and preparing food are seen as extensions of what women do as homemakers. In addition, the availability of part-time or shift work in this sector is attractive to women who have young children.

The growing number of services available in recent years has provided more and more jobs in the types of work that were familiar to women. Conversely, the rapid growth in the American economy during that period was made possible because the fastest growing sector had access to a large supply of women workers who were able to perform a wide range of services. Tradition notwithstanding, women are also heavily represented in government, retail trade, and manufacturing. Indeed, in 1973, these three groups, along with the service category, accounted for nearly 90 percent of female employment.

Women workers have also entered other industrial sectors in significant numbers, however. Women's share of employment in finance, for example, now exceeds half of all jobs; and in transportation, women have more than one-fifth of the total employment.

These apparent gains are tempered, however, by the continued poor representation of women in senior positions within each industry category. There has been a significant decline within the service sector in the proportion of women in professional and technical positions over the last quarter century, offsetting the increase in the numbers of professional and technical women in the trade and manufacturing groups.

Still, some penetration of the industrial sectors traditionally closed to women is occurring. Associated with this is an increase in the proportion of women seeking the necessary training required to undertake new career opportunities. However, much greater progress is needed in this regard if an oversupply of women in the traditional areas of employment is to be avoided in the future, and if women are to attain the level of responsibility within the labor force that their proportional representation in the labor market warrants.

Certain issues—the scheduling of work, the level of unemployment suffered, and wages earned—are of particular importance in this context:

—*Full-Time and Part-Time Work:* About 7 out of 10 women workers have full-time jobs at some time during the year, but only about 4 out of 10 maintain full-time jobs throughout the year. Students, women with family responsibilities, and women over 65 years of age often prefer part-time employment, which is most frequently available in the service and trade industry categories.

—*Unemployment:* Teenage black women suffer the highest unemployment rates of any group classified by age, race, or sex. About 1 out of every 3 young minority women was unemployed in 1974. White women of all ages and minority women aged 20 and over suffered less joblessness than black female teenagers —but, for all classifications, the unemployment rates for women are

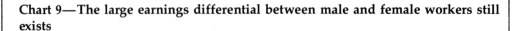

Chart 9—The large earnings differential between male and female workers still exists

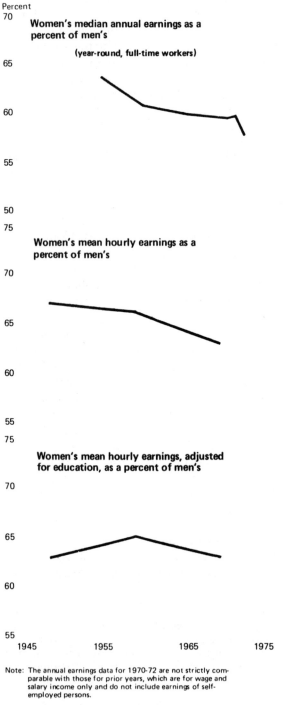

Percent

Women's median annual earnings as a percent of men's

(year-round, full-time workers)

Women's mean hourly earnings as a percent of men's

Women's mean hourly earnings, adjusted for education, as a percent of men's

1945   1955   1965   1975

Note: The annual earnings data for 1970-72 are not strictly comparable with those for prior years, which are for wage and salary income only and do not include earnings of self-employed persons.

Source: U.S. Department of Labor and Council of Economic Advisers.

significantly higher than those for men (often because of the difficulties experienced by many women in finding re-entry jobs after a period of absence from the labor force). Recent job market trends show a worsening of female unemployment as the labor market continues to slacken, particularly as layoffs first affect those with the least seniority. Recently hired workers, including many women and minority group members, have become the early casualties of the economic downturn. In some cases, such layoffs have highlighted the potential legal conflict between affirmative action plans and seniority rules within individual firms, but litigation on this issue is still in process.

—Earnings: Nearly two-thirds of all full-time, year-round female workers earned less than $7,000 in 1972. In the same year, over three-fourths of full-time, year-round male workers earned over $7,000. Moreover, the large earnings differential between male and female workers has persisted over the past two decades, even when adjusted for hours of work and level of education (see chart 9).

Furthermore, a classification of occupations by earnings reveals a marked similarity to a classification of jobs by sex. In fact, overall average earnings in private industry were $4.06 per hour in March 1974, but average rates in occupations with high proportions of women were often nearer to $3 than to $4. By contrast, the areas of extensive unionization and the lowest female participation, construction (where only 6 percent of the workers were women) and mining (with 8 percent women), had average earnings of $6.75 and $4.99, respectively.

Women are not only concentrated in the lower paying industries but they are also found in relatively large numbers in non-unionized business enterprises and in the lower paying occupational groups, including clerical workers and service workers. In addition, even when both sexes are well represented in an occupational group, women's earnings are substantially lower than those of men (see table 3).

Various studies have found the overall discrepancy between male and female earnings to be around 40 percent. Some researchers have argued that they could explain nearly all of this sex differential by controlling for such factors as part-time employment and differences in job

Table 3 —Median incomes of full-time women workers by occupation, 1972.

Major occupation group	Median income	Percent of men's income
Professional and technical workers__	$8,796	68
Nonfarm managers and administrators_____	7,306	53
Clerical workers_____	6,039	63
Sales workers_____	4,575	40
Operatives, including transportation_	5,021	58
Service workers (except private household)_____	4,606	59
Private household_____	2,365	(1)
Nonfarm laborers_____	4,755	63

[1] Percent not shown where median income of men is based on fewer than 75,000 individuals.

Source: Revised tables for the "Fact Sheet on the Earnings Gap" (Washington: U.S. Department of Labor. Women's Bureau, March 1974).

responsibilities, education, and length of service. Most of these studies, however, find that large differentials remain; in addition, case studies have found earnings differences even for the same job assignment and with great similarity in performance. One case study indicated that variations in such factors as education and experience explained only half of the difference between men and women in job level assignments.

Although recent action to strengthen equal pay laws may eventually overcome discrimination in earnings for the same job assignments, it will be much more difficult to remove discrimination in the making of job assignments. However, recent evidence suggests that pressures for change may be building. While the average annual discrepancy between the mean incomes of men and women working full time, year round remained substantially unchanged over the 1969–73 period, reports of occupational discrimination doubled.

To a considerable degree, female occupational distribution results from a culmination of influences that start in childhood. Role differentiation in early life later affects educational and occupational choices, hours and location of work, and other factors which relegate women to lower level positions in the lower paying industries. Altering this occupational distribution requires not only the legal prohibition of discrimination but also some fundamental changes in attitudes within the home, the school, and the workplace.

Demographic and social change

Changes in lifestyle and life expectancy
Traditionally, childbearing has brought with it not merely a temporary absence from paid employment but a complete withdrawal from the work force for a period of years (the time being extended by the birth of each successive child). Of crucial importance to the woman worker's career development is the fact that this withdrawal generally occurs during those years in which job advancement would be most rapid. Thus, women lose the opportunity to establish their careers or to gain seniority or experience prior to withdrawal. The longer the absence, the less meaningful is previous work in providing credentials for reentry.

The greater the number of children, the more profoundly marked are these effects. It is of major significance, therefore, that recent years have brought a drastic decline in average family size. From 1965 to 1973, the average number of children per husband-wife family with children dropped from 2.44 to 2.18. This decline is not just a postponement of births; the average total number of births expected by women (aged 18 to 24) during their lifetime was 3.2 in 1965, but only 2.3 by 1972. The Nation's birth rate in 1974 was down to 14.8 per thousand of population—lower even than the level reached in the depression of the 1930's. Whereas wives 18 to 24 in 1950 most often expected to have four or more children, in 1972 the commonly expected number was two.

Acceptance of childless marriages is also increasingly widespread. Indeed, as women find paid employment more appealing, the trend toward smaller family size is accentuated. Public concern over the implications of unlimited population growth, along with the greater availability and sophistication of contraceptive devices which enable the spacing and timing of births to conform more nearly to the mother's work preferences, should continue to reduce the average length of time women are out of the work force in the years ahead.

Along with these changes in fertility, other significant family-related factors are encouraging female labor force participation. For example, divorced or separated women with children have had consistently higher participation rates than married women with children, as shown below. Hence, some of the recent increases in female labor force participation must be attributed to rises in the divorce rate.

Participation rates of women by presence of husband and presence and age of children, 1973

	Married, husband present	Widowed, divorced, or separated
Children under 18 years old_____	41. 7	59. 7
Children 6 to 17 years old_____	50. 1	68. 3
Children 3 to 5 years old_____	38. 3	54. 8
Children under 3 years old_____	29. 4	38. 5

Source: U.S. Department of Labor, Special Labor Force Report, No. 164, table F, p. 19.

In addition to work-inducing changes in family lifestyles, there has been a dramatic rise in female life expectancy during the past half century. The life expectancy of a girl born in 1971 was 74.8 year, nearly 7½ years longer than that of a boy born in the same year. (In 1920, the gap was only 1 year.) The improvement in women's chances for survival after childbirth is illustrated by the increase in life expectancy at age 20. While it rose 2.5 years for white and 4.2 years for black men between 1940 and 1970, it increased 5.7 and 9.5 years for white and black women, respectively, over the same period. A longer lifespan affords an increase as well in the potential worklife of women. In effect, employment for older women has come to fill years that women in earlier eras did not have, since many did not survive far beyond the childbearing age.

Changes in attitudes and expectations

Mature women are now in the labor force far more frequently than they expected to be in their earlier years. A longitudinal study of young women aged 14 to 24 in 1968 over the 1968–70 period indicated that about two-fifths of those surveyed altered their plans for age 35. And, overwhelmingly, they moved in the direction of labor force entry:

Proportion of women (14 to 24) planning to work at age 35

Race	1968	1970
Black_____	47	59
White_____	27	42

Source: "Years for Decision," vol. 3 (Columbus: The Ohio State University, Center for Human Resource Research, December 1973), p. 15.

Moreover, these revisions in plans are consistent with those currently exhibited by women in the 35- to 44-year age group, whose present participation rates are 61 percent and 51 percent for black and white women, respectively.

The study attributes women's plans for increased work to their reduced childbearing expectations and their own changing concept of the role of women. Since the young women who were attending school during the period of the survey exhibited the greatest change in plans concerning work, educational influences seem to have played a significant role in forming family and work goals.

Occupational aspirations of this same group of women are even more indicative of an increasing commitment to market careers. About three-fourths of the white and two-thirds of the black women indicated preferences for white-collar occupations, with fully half of the white-collar aspirants looking forward to work in professional, technical, or managerial jobs. These goals appear overly optimistic when compared with the performance of women in the 30- to 44-year age group who were surveyed in a similar longitudinal study. In 1967, only 23 percent of the white and less than 14 percent of the black women who were then 35 to 39 years of age and were employed as wage and salary workers were in professional or managerial positions. Even with increasing educational attainment and greater job market opportunities for women, it is doubtful, therefore, that the aspirations of the younger women will be achieved. However, their stated goals indicate that women not only expect to enter the work force in increasing numbers, but are also aiming at higher level positions than women workers are currently achieving.

Some of the strongest evidence of the commitment of women to market work has emerged from the survey of women aged 30 to 44. Among the women in this age group, 60 percent of the white and 67 percent of the black workers reported that they would continue to work even if they could live comfortably without their earnings. The survey's findings are reinforced by the fact that the same women displayed considerable attachment to their current jobs; 40 percent of the white and 25 percent of the black respondents indicated that they would not change jobs even for a considerable wage increase. While this may reflect the women's perceptions of the limited jobs available to them, the results nevertheless illustrate the extent to which women have made permanent job commitments. And although most women are found in the lower paying, lower status jobs, they nevertheless express a surprising degree of satisfaction in the jobs held. Over two-thirds of white women and nearly three-fifths of black women reported that they liked their jobs "very much." Whether younger women entering the work force with higher levels of education and aspirations will be similarly content with lower level jobs is uncertain, however.

A married woman's perception of her husband's attitude toward her working is also an important determinant of her labor market decision. White women who reported their husbands' attitudes as favorable were in the labor force nearly four times as long, according to the 1967 survey, as those who reported unfavorable attitudes. For black women, the work period was over 1½ times as long. It is not clear whether husbands' attitudes are becoming more supportive of female work force participation, but it is clear that wives' commitment to work is becoming more and more like that of their spouses.

One recent study of job satisfaction reports that no significant sex-related difference in overall job satisfaction was found in national surveys conducted during the 1962–73 period. Furthermore, even though women were found to be more concerned with the social and psychological aspects of their jobs, men and women were equally dissatisfied with intellectually undemanding jobs. Finally, just as men work for a living, women, too, work for much more than "pin money." Two out of five working women are economically independent, and in many poorer families, women provided the bulk of the family income.

Educational changes

In the past, the relatively small proportion of women continuing through college and graduate training was predictable, given the existence of social mores that downgraded feminine education and the lack of suitable job opportunities for educated women. Perception of this lower likely return on investment in human capital discouraged investments in higher education by women and thereby helped to create a chain of factors which maintained the stereotyped occupational distribution of women workers. Enlarged career opportunities and changing attitudes show that this chain may be weakening, however. In recent years, about 70 percent of the girls aged 14 to 17 years expected post-secondary education, while only 29 percent of those aged 20 to 24 and 26 percent of those aged 25 to 29 actually had one or more years of such education. Again, the aspirations of today's 14- to 17-year-olds may be unrealistically high. But they demonstrate an attitude that brings a new perspective to women's future work force participation.

More women than men workers have completed high school, but only three-fourths as many women as men have gone on to college. Furthermore, in 1971, while women earned 42 percent of all bachelor's degrees and 40 percent of all master's degrees, they gained only 14 percent of the doctorates. But, while graduate enrollments are currently falling (for a total decline of 9 percent 1969), the proportion of women in graduate school is rising. By 1974, the distribution of the female work force in the United States by educational attainment was approaching that of the male, with more women continuing past high school, as shown below:

Educational attainment of the labor force, 1974

Level of education	Percent distribution	
	Women	Men
Total	100. 0	100. 0
College: 4 or more years	12. 8	16. 4
1 to 3 years	15. 2	14. 9
High school: 4 years	44. 2	36. 0
1 to 3 years	18. 1	18. 0
Elementary: 8 years or less	9. 7	14. 7

Source: B. J. McEaddy, "Educational Attainment of Workers, March 1974," *Monthly Labor Review*, February 1975, p. 66.

Despite these trends in the education of women, many educational traditions reinforce the stereotyping of male-female job roles. In vocational and technical secondary school courses, for example, girls are concentrated in business and commercial courses (which are 79 percent female) and in health courses (95 percent female), while boys form a vast majority (98 percent) of those taking technical, industrial, and trade subjects.

One of the most significant changes in recent years has been the narrowing of the gap between the educational attainment of white and black women. In just two decades, the median number of school years completed by black women rose from 8.1 in 1952 to 12.3 in 1974, cutting the difference in educational attainment levels of white and black women from 4.0 years to 0.2 year.

Apart from helping to raise worker participation rates, rising levels of educational attainment may bring about social benefits resulting from a reallocation of many women's time, as one researcher predicts:

. . . when the average woman has more schooling and higher income than today, she will indeed spend a greater proportion of her lifetime in the labor force. Although she will probably spend less of her increasingly valuable time in most home production activities, she is likely to spend even more of it with her children.

Legislative and policy changes

Women's greatly expanded role in the labor market has been accompanied by changes in legislation and policy that have broadened equal opportunity in the labor market. The legal framework created by recent legislation and executive action consequently plays a major role in the resolution of many issues which continue to hamper women's work force activity.

Action to end discrimination.   Most of the legislation has been directed toward ending discrimination resulting from employer behavior. The Equal Pay Act of 1963 was an early step toward equalizing earnings for men and women workers. Enforced by the Department of Labor's Wage and Hour Division, this act requires employers to compensate men and women in the same establishment equally (in terms of both wages and fringe benefits) for work of equivalent skill, effort, and responsibility performed under similar working conditions. A landmark Federal court decision later asserted that jobs of men and women need only be "substantially equal," rather than identical, in order to merit equal pay under the act. Successive amendments have extended the act's application to executive, administrative, and professional employees and, more recently, to most Federal, State, and local government employees.

Under title VII of the Civil Rights Act of 1964, employers are prohibited from discrimination in hiring, firing, promotion, job assignment, compensation, training, or other ". . . terms, conditions, or privileges of employment." Enforcement of these provisions is the task of the Equal Employment Opportunity Commission (EEOC). Title VII has become a major instrument in assuring equal status for men and women in the work force, since equal pay legislation by itself could not insure equal opportunity. Government action during the past decade has been directed at strengthening the enforcement agencies and attempting to speed up the process of eliminating race and sex bias.

EEOC has issued guidelines on discrimination because of sex under title VII. The guidelines, which were last revised April 5, 1972, would bar hiring based on stereotyped characterization of the sexes, classification or labeling of "men's jobs" and "women's jobs," or advertising under male or female headings. They specify that the bona fide occupational qualification exemption should be interpreted narrowly and that State laws that prohibit or limit the employment of women—in certain occupations, or in jobs that require lifting or carrying weights in excess of prescribed limits, during certain hours of the night, for more than a specified number of hours per day or per week, or for certain periods before and after childbirth—conflict with and are preempted by title VII. Accordingly, these "protective" State labor laws cannot be used as a reason for refusing to employ women.

One move to accelerate compliance did not come until 1971. At that time, the Department of Labor's Office of Federal Contract Compliance (OFCC), pursuant ot Executive Order 11246, as amended by Executive Order 11375, issued Revised Order No. 4 (41 CFR Part 60–2), which required the affirmative action programs of Government supply and service contractors and subcontractors with 50 or more employees and a contract of $50,000 or more to include an analysis of areas within which the contractor is deficient in providing equal opportunity for women employees. It also required goals and timetables to correct the deficiencies and thus achieve prompt and full utilization of women at all levels and in all segments of the employer's work force where deficiencies exist. The OFCC has also issued sex discrimination guidelines. The affirmative action concept requires that an employer seeking to do business with the Federal Government do more than refrain from discriminatory practices, going beyond the maintenance of policies of passive nondiscrimination by taking positive steps toward the elimination of employment barriers to women. Sanctions include contract cancellation, termination, or suspension and possible court action. Similar restrictions on Federal support have been included in other Government legislation, such as the Public Health Services Act and the Higher Education Act.

Further scope for enforcement was achieved by the Equal Employment Opportunity Act of 1972, which amended title VII of the Civil Rights Act of 1964 to permit court action by the EEOC. The EEOC was authorized to bring suit in an appropriate Federal district court if conciliation efforts were not successful (the single exception being that only the Attorney General can bring suit against State and local governments). Recent court cases have furthered implementation of the legislative objectives. For example, in January 1973, the American Telephone and Telegraph Company agreed to pay $15 million in back wages to 15,000 employees (80 percent of whom were women) in a consent decree under title VII and Executive Order 11246. It also provided for significant increases in employment opportunities for women. In addition, back pay and comprehensive relief to remedy discrimination and provide affirmative action for women in the steel industry are reflected in an April 1974 consent decree.

In 1967, Executive Order 11478 reaffirmed the longstanding policy of equal opportunity in Federal employment on the basis of merit and fitness and without discrimination because of race, color, religion, sex, or national origin. Accordingly, departments and agencies are required to establish a Federal Women's Program, whose purpose is to enhance employment and advancement opportunities for women.

Equal rights amendment.   Action has also been taken in areas other than employer discrimination, especially in the form of legislation guaranteeing equal access to credit. The most general law guaranteeing equal opportunity still awaits ratification, however. The Equal Rights Amendment (ERA) to the U.S. Constitution could have a significant impact in such areas as taxation and property rights. Although passed by the U.S. House in 1971 and by the U.S. Senate in 1972, the ERA has yet to be approved by the required number of States. If it is ratified, it will guarantee equality of all rights under the law between men and women, effectively canceling almost all legislative provisions that accord differential treatment to men and women on the basis of sex.

As construed by the Citizens' Advisory Council on the Status of Women, the ERA would require that, whenever a law confers a benefit, a privilege, or an obligation of citizenship, it will be extended to both sexes equally, but whenever such a law denies opportunities to either sex, it will be declared unconstitutional.

Examples of the kinds of legislation that would be affected by this amendment include protective labor laws, domestic relations laws, and criminal laws. In the area of protective labor legislation, laws which insure genuinely safe and healthful working conditions would be extended to both sexes, but restrictive work laws limiting hours of work, night work, or employment in particular occupations or under certain conditions for women only would be invalidated. In all cases, an individual's ability to perform the job would be the sole criterion for employment. If obligatory military service were revived, women would be subject to the draft along with men, but they would not be required to fill jobs for which they were not suited (a rule equally applicable to male inductees).

Marital and family relations laws would also be affected by the proposed amendment. Special restrictions on the property rights of married women would no longer be allowed; married women could engage in business as freely as men; and the inheritance rights of widows and widowers would be the same. In cases of divorce, alimony would be awarded to either spouse solely on the basis of need; child support, based on means, could also be derived from either spouse; and custody of children would be determined on the basis of their best interest.

Finally, some changes would be forthcoming in criminal laws. State laws providing longer or shorter prison sentences for women than for men for the same offenses would no longer be valid. However, laws governing sexual offenses, such as rape or prostitution, would remain unchanged.

Although the effects of the amendment would eventually be far reaching, according to the Citizens' Advisory Council, equality under ERA would not mean that men and women were regarded as identical under the law. Laws that apply to only one sex because of reproductive differences (such as most maternity benefits) or that relate to the right of privacy (separate washrooms) would not be affected.

Unique problems of women workers

Sex stereotyping of jobs

Despite the greatly increased labor force participation of women since 1950 and their changing work profiles, women are far from achieving equality in terms of occupational status. As noted earlier, the earnings differential between men and women has remained substantial over the last two decades, and women are still concentrated in the lower paid, traditionally female occupations and industries.

A major goal of the Department of Labor is to increase employment opportunities for women, especially by encouraging the advancement of women workers to more skilled and responsible jobs in the economy. As a means of improving the skill and compensation levels of women's jobs, the Department is seeking to encourage the movement of women into nontraditional occupations and to expand their occupational choices.

Barriers to the entrance of women into skilled craft jobs or into certain professional occupations are often based on outmoded concepts of the degree of physical strength required or on outmoded ideas about women's worklife expectancy and, by implication, the value of providing educational and training opportunities to women. In order to facilitate the entry of women into nontraditional jobs, the Department has funded a number of demonstration and outreach programs in recent years. For example, the Minority Women Employment Program in Atlanta, Ga., has been successful in placing black women in professional and managerial occupations where they have not heretofore been employed. Originally operated by the Southern Regional Council, the program has been duplicated in Houston, Tex., under the Recruitment and Training Program, Inc., and is being extended to five other cities in fiscal 1975.

Below the professional level, skilled trades and apprentice-type jobs have been projected for the 1970's as an area of rapid employment increase. This area is also one in which women are greatly underrepresented, although Federal Executive orders and the regulations calling for equal employment opportunity and affirmative action to eliminate sex discrimination have opened many doors formerly closed to women. Data from the 1973 Current Population Survey show 561,000 women employed as craft workers (about 4 percent of the total), compared with 277,140 in 1960 and 494,871 in 1970. Another positive trend is reflected in vocational school enrollment data for 1972. In that year, 33,006 women enrolled in technical programs, up from 22,890 in 1966–67. The increase was even greater among women enrolled in trade and industrial training courses, rising from 155,808 in 1966–67 to 279,680 in 1972.

The Department's Manpower Administration and Women's Bureau are cooperating in two major projects to encourage the entrance of women into these kinds of skilled occupations. They are the Apprenticeship Outreach Program for Women and the project to facilitate nontraditional job placements through the Work Incentive Program. In connection with both of these projects, the Women's Bureau is sponsoring conferences around the country to urge employers and unions to provide more opportunities for women in these areas and to encourage women to seek this kind of training and employment.

Apprenticeship outreach program for women. In 1964, the Apprenticeship Outreach Program (AOP) was established through a Taconic Foundation grant. Three years later, the Department funded the first AOP's directed primarily toward recruiting minority men for apprenticeship. Then, in April 1974, it initiated a pilot project in which three AOP's are attempting to place women in apprenticeable and nontraditional occupations.

After the inception of this project, the Manpower Administration added language to new AOP contracts stating that the contractor will make an effort to place women in such occupations. The Manpower Administration also funds AOP's designed specifically to place women.

Nontraditional occupations for women in WIN. The Manpower Administration and the Women's Bureau have developed a training package to facilitate the opening of nontraditional occupations to women in the Work Incentive (WIN II) Program. The objectives are to enable WIN project staff to develop a broader perspective of nonstereotyped training and employment opportunities available to WIN participants; to counter sex-role stereotyping more effectively among participants and employers; and to initiate job development strategies for increasing placement of WIN participants in nontraditional jobs.

Other projects financed or assisted by the Department of Labor to encourage nontraditional jobs for women include apprenticeship programs in San Francisco, Denver, and Madison, Wisc., as well as job placement efforts in Chattanooga and Memphis, Tenn.

Poverty and female-headed families

Half the women who head families are divorced or separated, and growing rates of divorce and separation make the existence of female-headed families an increasingly common phenomenon. However, the responsibility for supporting a family is a difficult one for a woman, who often faces severe obstacles in her job search.

Dependent children require support, but make full-time market activity a special problem in the one-parent family. Among female-headed families, 37 percent of the women heads are widowed, 13 percent are unmarried, and the remaining one-half are divorced or separated. The presence of young children is a critical factor in determining labor force participation, particularly among women heads aged 25 to 44, nearly half of whom have three or more children. High child-care costs and low earnings potential reduce the feasibility of paid employment and in many cases make it uneconomical. Indeed, 61 percent of female heads of poor families do not even seek outside employment—some through discouragement and others through a reluctance to surrender child-care responsibilities to others. Moreover, divorced and separated women are often ill-equipped for market occupations other than those requiring a minimum of education and skill.

Long-term unemployment. A reflection of these problems is the fact that, of the 4.2 million women heads of families who worked or looked for work during 1973, 17.1 percent experienced some unemployment.

About one-fourth of these women did not work during the year; for over another fourth who did work, their unemployment totaled over 6 months in one or more spells of jobseeking.

It is essential to note that two-thirds of all female heads of families have less than a high school education. Nearly three-fourths of women family heads who are employed work in clerical, operative, and service occupations, with more than half of the female heads of poor families in low-paying operative and service positions. Private household employment and part-time occupations predominate, but earnings and benefits in these areas remain exceptionally low. Median earnings for year-round, full-time household employment in 1971 were $1,926, with few paid vacations or sick leave and almost no protection via unemployment benefits or workers' compensation.

As a result of obstacles such as these, poverty is widespread among female-headed families. While a large number of families were able to move out of poverty in the decade of the 1960's, the proportion of poor families with a female head rose from less than 1 in 4 to more than 1 in 3 over the decade. In 1972 the median income was $4,469 for female-headed families with children under 18 years of age and $3,351 for those with preschool-age children. The poverty threshold for a four-person nonfarm family headed by a woman in 1972 was $4,254. While fewer than 1 out of every 10 male-headed families had income below the poverty threshold in 1972, more than 5 out of every 10 female-headed families fell in that category.

Alimony, child support, welfare, and social security provide a large source of income for female-headed families. But the preponderance of poverty among women in this group indicates that these payments represent only a partial solution to their multiple problems.

Denial of credit.   Apart from the difficulty of gaining adequately paid employment, female heads of families face other obstacles to gaining economic independence. Traditionally, for example, women have experienced difficulty in achieving the financial security needed to obtain credit (particularly mortgage credit). Women who are single, divorced, separated, or widowed may be refused credit simply because of marital status. When a woman is divorced, separated, or widowed, she may be denied credit on the grounds that she has no established credit record, even when she applies to the same companies where she has held accounts with her husband. Similar problems also arise in such areas as automobile and medical insurance. Although recently passed Federal and State laws have lowered some of the barriers preventing equal access to credit, discriminatory practices continue.

Black female family heads.   Within the category of female heads of families, black and other minority women constitute an even more economically disadvantaged group. Nearly one-third of all families headed by women are black, and 1 out of every 3 black families is headed by a woman compared to 1 out of 10 white families. The 1972 median earnings of black female family heads was $3,370, only three-fourths that of white female heads and $884 below the poverty threshold for a four-person nonfarm family headed by a woman. Larger numbers of children, lower levels of education, concentration in low-skill low-paying jobs, and high rates of unemployment combine to produce poverty for black families dependent on women.

Intermittent labor force participation

For the majority of women, high school is the only time that formal career planning takes place. Generally, such plans have been geared to preparing women for a short period of employment in anticipation of an extended or even permanent withdrawal from the labor market—but, with a growing proportion of women continuing to work or reentering the work force after childbearing, the disadvantages of such shortrun planning have become clear. Reentry into the jobs held before withdrawal is often unsatisfactory, even impossible, since many of the earlier positions no longer exist. Yet little attention has been given to the need for retraining for new occupations.

Widening occupational choice.   Women's need for a wider range of occupational choice remains acute. It is not surprising, therefore, that continuing education programs have been highly successful during the past two decades, in part because they were aimed at meeting the critical needs of women to develop the skills required for reentering the work force on a permanent basis. The desirability of such retraining is illustrated by the fact that in the longitudinal survey of women aged 30 to 44, more women retrogressed in their careers than progressed.

Since most women complete high school, there is an obvious need for college-level course offerings that allow older women some flexibility in entrance requirements and class schedules. Restrictions set by the woman's location and her domestic responsibilities have been mitigated somewhat by the growth of community colleges, but there is a need for consideration of additional steps aimed specifically at easing the labor force reentry problems of women.

Reentry into the work force might be eased by programs designed to employ women on a part-time basis as a prelude to full-time work. The object of such programs would be to enable women to recover skills during a period of readjustment to full-time labor market activity. The extent and nature of part-time jobs could be negotiated according to the amount of retraining required. When the period of absence from work has been relatively short, problems of retraining may be secondary to lack of promotional opportunities. Childbearing may necessitate an absence of only a few weeks or months. Yet restrictions on leave and the frequency with which promotions are based on continuous work experience make it difficult for a woman to pick up her career where she left off. Childbearing still leads to resignation in many cases and resignation necessitates a reentry, compounded by all the problems of an initial job search and acclimatization.

Maternity leave.   A variety of maternity leave provisions exists in the United States; in the majority of cases, however, coverage is quite limited and the availability of maternity leave is growing only very slowly, even though EEOC guidelines are encouraging provision of these rights. Still, a 1973 University of Michigan survey showed that, over the preceding 3 years, the availability of full reemployment rights increased by 14 percent and the availability of leave with pay by 12 percent.

The notion that fathers might care for infants is beginning to spread within the United States. Several schools and public agencies have provisions for parental leave without pay for periods of 30 days to 4 years. However, most union labor agreements provide fathers with no more than 1 to 3 days of paid leave when children are born.

Since more and more women now intend to continue their careers after giving birth, the possible loss of job security or consideration for promotion because of short absences on maternity leave is becoming an important issue in many private firms and public sector institutions. More than 90 percent of today's women expect to have one, two, or three children. These family-size expectations need to be taken into account, but can no longer be viewed automatically as the cause of long interruptions in the worklives of American women.

Mobility problems. In addition to the intermittency associated with childbirth and early childrearing, women workers also face a special constraint imposed by mobility factors. The relocations required by the demands of a husband's job can interrupt a woman's career, greatly reducing her possibilities of progress and even of maintaining employment. Migration of husbands causes considerable interruption in the employment of wives, according to recent studies. Wives' jobs, on the other hand, appear to be little hindrance to husbands' job change and movement, since the rates of interstate moving for married men with wives employed in 1965 and 1970 were only slightly below those for married men with wives not employed in either year.

In every age category, the proportion of wives working in both 1965 and 1970 was much lower when relocation had occurred. Thus, the geographic mobility of the household tends to disrupt the worklife of the married woman. On the other hand, a married woman suffers from a lack of geographic mobility in her own job. While husbands appear relatively unhampered by marital ties in their ability to migrate, wives appear to have the opposite problem.

Minimizing the undesired mobility or immobility faced by working wives involves some compromise arrangements within businesses and within families. While no agreement among members of a dual-career family can achieve the mobility that could be available to each member operating independently, considerable flexibility can still be attained.

Unemployment compensation. Related to the issue of labor force participation by working wives is the question of the fairness of unemployment compensation laws. In the past several years, substantial improvements have been made in eliminating statutory discrimination against women unemployment insurance claimants. Three areas in particular have registered important advances, although complete equality is still unrealized.

A major area of improvement involves disqualification from benefits solely because of pregnancy. In January 1973, 37 State unemployment insurance laws contained this provision, and, of these, only 3 permitted rebuttal. The others flatly denied benefits for a certain number of weeks before and after childbirth, required subsequent earnings to requalify for entitlement, or delayed entitlement for a period after ability to work had been reestablished—action comparable to that taken in the case of a "voluntary quit without good cause." Nevertheless, the number of States denying benefits because of pregnancy alone has been steadily declining to 31 by July 1973 and to 24 by October 1974.

Leaving work because of marital or family obligations—moving with the spouse to another area, for example—constitutes another reason for disqualification from benefits in several States. Such terminations usually raise the issue of availability and willingness to work after the job separation. At one time, 23 States denied benefits for this reason, and 7 restricted application of the provision to women. In about half of these 23 States, subsequent employment or earnings were required to requalify for benefits. At the present time, only 13 States disqualify claimants on this basis, and, in all cases, the provision is applied equally to men and women. Nevertheless, since women are more likely than men to follow their spouses to a new job location, in practice such provisions still disqualify women more often than men.

Finally, in the 11 States that offer dependents' allowances as part of their regular unemployment benefits, statutory provisions are no longer more restrictive for women claimants than they are for men. Nevertheless, because such allowances are usually limited to the individual who provides at least 50 percent of the total family support and the laws generally exclude parents from dependent status, the proportion of women claimants is much lower than that of men claimants.

Dual careers

Nearly two-thirds of all women who work have childrearing responsibilities in addition to their jobs. The presumption that women have the major responsibility for child care and household maintenance, whether or not they work, means that women with family responsibilities who enter the labor force usually undertake a new role in addition to their many other tasks.

Arranging child care. When a wife takes on paid employment, her husband's contribution to the work of the household tends to remain unchanged. A study by the Organization for Economic Co-operation and Development found that total workloads for married women increased by an average of 13 hours per week, while the total workload of their husbands actually dropped by an average of 1½ hours per week. But regardless of the amount of additional work the married woman entering the job market is willing to undertake, there is no way that she can provide full-time child-care services. In households where both parents work, the necessity of having someone else assume a major responsibility for the care of young children raises important questions regarding the availability of child-care facilities.

In the Ohio State University National Longitudinal Survey of women aged 30 to 44, a mid-1967 survey of the types and costs of child-care arrangements found that about 7 out of 10 children were cared for in their own or in relatives' homes and almost 1 out of 4 in other private homes, usually in pooled neighborhood arrangements. Relatives were the most frequent source of child care, while group care in day-care centers, nursery schools, and the like accounted for fewer than 1 out of 10 children, as shown below:

Child-care arrangements of employed women aged 30–44 using child care, 1967

Type of arrangement	Percent distribution [1]	
	White	Black
Total	100	100
In home:		
By relative	24	31
By nonrelative	25	11
In other private home:		
By relative	18	28
By nonrelative	24	19
In group center	8	12

[1] Detail may not add to totals because of rounding.

Source: Computed from *Dual Careers*, vol. 1, table 4:13, p. 123.

On the other hand, a 1971 survey of child-care arrangements of working mothers in New York City found that up to 18 percent of all child care was undertaken by such group facilities. Comprehensive national figures are still unavailable, however, and it is not clear whether the increasing use of child-care arrangements is tending more toward group care than private arrangements.

The question of who should bear the cost of providing day care for children remains unanswered. From the parents' point of view, the higher the child-care costs, the fewer the job opportunities that are economically viable to the family. Although in many cases such costs do not pose severe limitations (in the National Longitudinal Survey about half the relatives provided the child-care services free of charge), the cost of care provided in the home of a nonrelative or in a group facility is significant. More than half the women using these arrangements paid between $2 and $4 a day in 1967. Even more costly was the care provided in the child's own home by a nonrelative; here nearly two-thirds of the women paid $4 or more per day for the service.

Such institutional developments as the industry-subsidized creches of Japan and the governmentally provided "école maternelle" system for 3- to 6-year-olds in Belgium and France remain rare in the United States. Nevertheless, the number of American preschool children with mothers in the work force has risen dramatically, from about 4 million in 1960 to more than 6 million in 1973. Although licensed day-care facilities more than doubled their estimated capacity between 1965 and 1973, the space available could at most accommodate only 1 out of every 6 preschool children of mothers in the work force at the end of this period.

Scheduling market work. Women's responsibility for household services often precludes full-time employment. Notwithstanding remarkable advances in household technology, cleaning, laundry, and food preparation are still time-consuming tasks that impede women's attempts to handle full-time employment. The fact that 1 out of every 4 women workers had part-time jobs in 1973, while another 1 out of every 4 worked only part year, reflects the problem many women have in taking on a full time job in addition to household duties. (It also reflects the difficulties many experience in obtaining full-time jobs even when they would prefer such employment.)

Some believe that variations in work schedules can provide a partial solution to this dilemma. The traditional approach has been for the woman to take a part-time job that allowed her to continue providing the domestic services needed by the family. However, part-time employment that fully utilizes the capabilities of women is quite scarce. The consequent loss suffered by both women and the society has been described by the Department's Women's Bureau:

> . . . many women who have skills in demand in the labor market are unable to find part-time jobs which would permit them to make a contribution to family income or to the economy as well as to handle home responsibilities, including the care of school-age children.

Reallocation of domestic responsibilities between husband and wife and a rescheduling of working hours in industry to allow for these shifts in responsibility might well improve human resource allocation. Some movement in the latter direction is beginning to occur in the United States, but recent developments in rescheduling working hours have placed major emphasis on compressing the workweek to 4 days. In the course of these changes, both management and labor organizations have expressed concern that such compression of work schedules could be particularly hard on married women with families—yet surveys of married women workers reveal that they prefer the 3-day weekends these timetables allow. At present, however, less than 1 percent of all workers in the United States are on a 4-day workweek.

Rather than compressing the workweek for all, European experiments have stressed "flexitime," an arrangement that permits workers to set their own arrival and departure hours within a prescribed band of time in the morning and afternoon. The workday can vary in length as well as starting and finishing times, as long as workers complete the total number of hours required in a given period, usually a month. The most extensive application of flexitime has occurred in Switzerland, where an estimated 15 to 20 percent of all industrial firms are using it. One of the main advantages for workers lies in the fact that flexitime enables a variety of personal and family matters to be undertaken that were previously difficult to arrange in the context of a rigid work schedule. Still, legal and contractual provisions for overtime pay after 8 hours a day or after a 40-hour week might well hamper the introduction of flexible schedules into the United States. In addition, it is difficult to apply such a scheme to service workers and blue-collar workers in production jobs, which require certain hours of performance or a high degree of worker coordination. Nonstandard, part-time arrangements have usually offered few of the job options or fringe benefits, even on a pro rata basis, that full-time occupations provide. Along with these problems, women face a number of statutory provisions that explicitly or implicitly exclude them from any form of unemployment insurance.

Changes in standard work practices will not be achieved without experimentation; nevertheless, the opportunities such changes could offer husbands and wives to arrange compatible careers could be crucial to women's market work.

Government and women workers: three key areas*

Numerous government operations relate to women and work. The three included here—the U.S. Employment Service, the Equal Employment Opportunity Commission, and occupational licensing—were selected either because they relate significantly to the employment and training of women, or because a significant body of sponsored research relates to them.

The U.S. Employment Service (USES)

The Federal-State employment system is a vital part of employment and training programs. Moreover, sponsored research has recently turned considerable attention to employment services.

Established in 1933, the Federal-State employment system contains 50 autonomous agencies (the State Employment Services), a network of over 2,400 offices and 40,000 employees who register job applicants, offer some counseling and testing service, develop jobs, and refer applicants to jobs. It is the primary source of referrals to employment and training programs and vocational education programs. Unemployment insurance and employable welfare recipients are required to register with the Employment Service. Special services are also offered to older workers, youth, the handicapped, the disadvantaged. The Service develops occupational and labor market information, maintains a program on occupational research which prepares materials such as the *Dictionary of Occupational Titles*, occupational classification systems and techniques, occupational brochures, and methodology for job structuring.

USES and women

About 2.5 million women were referred to jobs by State Employment Service offices in fiscal year 1975, and almost 1.3 million women were placed in nonagricultural jobs in that year, amounting to 40 percent of the total in both cases. About 412,000 women received some job counseling and 440,000 were tested during the year. The average starting wage for women placed by the ES was $2.60 an hour.

The USES requires reports from its State affiliates on the number of women registered, the number placed, and the wages paid. It does not record the occupations of placements by sex, so it cannot be determined from USES data what kinds of jobs women were placed in, relative to men.

ES staff cannot accept employer orders that violate laws on pay, hours of work, race. It cannot accept orders that designate men or women in hiring except as a bona fide job requirement. ES staff has been informed that affirmative action is ES policy. No method exists, however, for determining to what extent affirmative action is applied and to what extent referrals are sex neutral. Records are not kept by sex on

*Women and Work, U.S. Department of Labor, Employment and Training Administration, R&D Monograph 46.

occupation, employer, or firm of placement, so the data required for affirmative action evaluations are lacking.

ES has reportedly made progress in getting women into the apprenticeship trades. State agencies have also been instructed to prepare information for clients on licensed day-care centers and guides to the selection of child-care facilities.

To stimulate interest in the special needs of women, the USES has asked State affiliates to submit plans for improving service to women applicants.

In 1973, the Secretary of Labor, after meeting with seven national women's organizations, set up a group to make recommendations on improving women's status in the Manpower Administration (now the Employment and Training Administration) and in job and training programs. On March 14, 1974, the first in a series of directives was sent out to all State employment agencies on "Improving ES Services to Women Job Seekers." The agencies were asked to submit materials they had found useful in improving services to women.

Washington Opportunities for Women (WOW), on a Manpower Administration grant, has provided volunteers for an information and referral service for women at the local ES office. Other cities (Atlanta, Richmond, Baltimore, Boston, Providence, and Montpelier) have been funded to do similar work in ES offices. Several States have adopted the experimental techniques on a permanent basis.

As for ES staff, in states with a strong civil service merit system, women have better opportunities for promotion within ES than in other States. Women generally have more training and experience in supervisory jobs than men who work at the same level in USES. In 1975 there were only 5 women at grade 13; 4 at grade 14, and none at grade 15.

ES has apparently not done much to promote part-time jobs, which would be of special benefit to women and older people. It has not been regarded as a high or an appealing priority.

At one time ES had a separate professional placement service. In view of the oversupply of professional women in the market, it has been suggested that the ES return to the former setup. Even professional women apparently find it more difficult than men to locate jobs, so they are in greater need of a specialized placement service.

Although directives on women from USES have had some reported impact, there appears to be no followup procedure or means of determining to what extent directives are followed.

ES offices now usually have a special representative for veterans and one for minorities. A similar representative for women is clearly in order, one who would be acquainted with the special needs of women and who would serve as an advocate in enforcing the law on sex discrimination.

According to USES staff interviewed, the most significant change that has taken place in the Employment Service with respect to women has been the revision of the *Dictionary of Occupational Titles*. This revision has desexed the titles and raised the skill codes in some traditionally female occupations. The desexing of titles in particular has, in the opinion of staff, had a significant effect on the way people in the ES think and what they talk about. It has, in effect, raised the level of consciousness of ES staff because the DOT is so basic to their work.

Revisions include changes in over 3,000 titles: From salesman to sales agent, sales associate, sales representative, etc.; from foreman to supervisor; from draftsman to drafter; from repairman to repairer; patrolman to police officer; serviceman to servicer; assemblyman to assembler; seamstress to sewer; bellman to bellhop; airplane stewardess to airplane flight attendant.

Most changes occurred, proportionately, in the service and structural work code groups. Fewest were made in the professional/ managerial codes, as shown in table 11.

Who uses USES?
Users in middle-size cities.   A study of job search, recruitment, and the USES described labor exchange activities in cities of 100,000 to 250,000 population. The Employment Service, the study found, was consulted by about 25 percent of all employers and 28 percent of all jobfinders in these cities during the last 6 months of 1974. At one time or another, about half of all employers and jobfinders had consulted with the ES about employment needs. Most recruitment and job search, however, were carried on by informal methods such as direct application and contact with friends or relatives.

Of formal methods, newspaper ads were used most often and placed people most often in jobs, followed by the ES. But all formal methods combined (including private agencies, unions, and other agencies) placed only about one-third of workers in their jobs, and the ES placed only about 1 worker in 18 (see table 12).

The ES was used mainly by large employers. Small and marginal employers seldom listed vacancies. Because of their size, however, the 25 percent of employers who used the ES represented 36 percent of all vacancies. Those who listed with the ES were likely to list most of their vacancies with the exception of those in professional, technical, and managerial occupations.

Employers listed a disproportionately small percent of their clerical and sales order with ES, but a disproportionately high percent of people

Table 11 —Title changes in DOT code groups

Code group	Occupational group	Number of titles		Percent of titles desexed
		Total	Desexed	
1	Professional/ managerial	2,550	160	6.3
2	Clerical and sales	1,493	275	18.4
3	Service	988	265	26.8
4	Farming, fishery, forestry, and related	764	102	13.3
5	Processing	4,644	833	17.9
6	Machine trades	3,369	535	15.8
7	Benchwork	4,579	469	10.2
8	Structural work	1,621	413	25.4
9	Miscellaneous	1,793	340	18.9

Table 12 —Use and success of job search methods in medium-size cities (100,000–200,000 population), July–December 1974

Search method used	Percent of jobfinders		Percent of users succeeding
	Using	Hired	
All methods	100.0[1]	100.0[2]	
Employment Service	27.6	5.6	20.3
Private agency	14.5	5.6	38.6
Employer direct	82.1	29.8	36.3
Looked at want ads	62.5	—	
(Answered ads)	47.5	16.6	34.9
Labor unions	6.2	1.4	22.5
Friends/relatives	65.0	30.7	47.2
Business associates	33.1	3.3	9.9
Community organizaton ...	1.6	0.4	21.9
School placement	10.9	3.0	27.5
Professional journal	6.4		
(Answered)	(2.5)		

[1]Sum of items exceeds 100.0 percent because most jobfinders used more than one method.

[2]Includes about 300 respondents who did not answer the "how found job" question and who are, therefore, exluded from the distribution by search method.

with clerical and sales skills used ES in their job search. This may reflect an employer desire to avoid hiring minority clerical women.

Only 20 percent of applicants were counseled by ES, 15 percent were tested, and 6 percent were provided, or referred to, other services. This heavy emphasis on placement represented a departure from the late 1960's when the ES emphasized employability development.

People with some high school were placed almost twice as often as those with less than a ninth-grade education. This was not because of employer response but because ES referred to jobs only 15 percent of those without high school, compared to 45 percent of those with at least a ninth-grade education.

Employers were most concerned about the suitability of referrals received from ES. They hired only about one referral in three.

The mean hourly wage of women placed on jobs by ES was $2.96, and of men, $4.12. For both sexes, these rates were slightly higher than those of all employees who found jobs by other means.

It was also noted that overall, 35 percent of all people and 50 percent of all women applying to the ES did not obtain jobs between the time they applied and the date of the study (an average of 7 months).

Although the report clearly has implications for women job seekers, very little specific information on women applicants to ES was included.

ES competitors in the job search. A comprehensive review of job-seeking methods used by American workers in 1972 showed that, in the country as a whole (vs. the medium-sized cities covered in the study just discussed), the ES plays an even smaller role in jobseeking and jobfinding:

Two out of three jobseekers applied directly to employers without suggestions or referrals by anyone. The next four methods used most frequently, but by much smaller proportions of workers, were: Asking friends about jobs where they work; answering local newspaper ads; asking friends about jobs at places other than where they work; and checking with the State employment service.

Thirty-five percent of the workers obtained jobs through direct application to employers, and 12 percent each by asking friends about jobs where they work and by answering local newspaper ads. About equal proportions (5 to 6 percent) of the jobseekers obtained their jobs through the State employment service and through private employment agencies.

Of all persons who applied directly to employers for work, about half found their job that way —about double the percentage for the methods with the next two highest rates.

The four methods most commonly used and the method by which the largest proportion of workers obtained jobs were the same for men and for women, and with minor exceptions, for most other characteristics by which jobfinders were grouped.

Greater proportions of blacks than whites asked friends and relatives about jobs where they worked, took Civil Service tests, checked with State employment service, and contacted local assistance organizations. Smaller proportions applied directly to employers or answered local newspaper ads, methods which have relatively high effectiveness rates. Blacks should be encouraged to use these two methods to a greater extent, now that government and industry programs are in force to eliminate discriminatory hiring practices. Continued high dependence on friends and relatives for job leads will limit the range of job opportunities for blacks.

Greater proportions of blacks than whites who contacted the State employment service and local organizations found jobs through these methods. Smaller proportions of blacks than whites who applied directly to employers, answered local newspaper ads, and checked with private employment agencies and school placement offices obtained jobs through these methods.

Before finding a job, the average jobseeker used four methods. The number tended to rise with the length of search and to vary widely by occupation and demographic characteristics. Men used more methods than women. Many persons who did not find a job within relatively few weeks subsequently tried additional methods, which suggests that use of as many methods as possible early in the search could improve the chances of finding a job.

Of the 5.4 million jobseekers who were employed just before beginning their job search, nearly half started to look for a new job while still on the old one. Of those who did not look while still working, 2 out of 5 began their search within 1 or 2 days after leaving their old job. Among persons who waited more than 2 days, 2 out of 5 waited because they wanted to take some time off. It took about as long to find a job for persons who started to look for work after leaving their job as for those who started their search while still employed. Some joblessness could be decreased, if not prevented, if employers could notify employees well in advance of a layoff and permit them to take off a few hours a week, with pay, to look for another job.

A majority of jobhunters found jobs within 4 weeks, including time spent looking while still employed. Relatively fewer men than women found jobs within 4 weeks. Duration of job search was generally about the same regardless of the method by which the job was found. In a given economic climate, finding a job quickly depends more on many other factors, such as wage expectations, geographic location, experience and skills, motivation, and financial resources, than on methods used.

Jobseekers searched for work comparatively few hours a week and looked relatively close to home. About two-thirds of the jobseekers spent 5 hours or less per week on their job search, and nearly 3 out of 4 traveled no farther than 25 miles from home to look for work. Intensity or hours of job search a week apparently had no effect on the duration of the search.

One out of three jobseekers turned down an offer. Three out of 10 who declined offers did so because of low pay, and an equal proportion because the location, hours, or other working conditions were unsatisfactory. A greater proportion of whites than blacks refused job offers.

Nearly 45 percent of jobseekers were women. Somewhat over one-half of the female jobseekers were married. Thirty-seven percent of the men and 15 percent of the women traveled more than 25 miles to look for work. Among both men and women, much larger proportions of jobseekers who obtained jobs as professional workers or as managers traveled over 100 miles from home to look for work. Among men, about one-third of the professionals and one-fourth of the managers went over 100 miles to look for work; among women, about 18 percent of jobseekers in these two occupations traveled that distance. One-third of the men and one-half of the women found jobs within 5 miles of home. While 66.5 percent of males seeking jobs as managers and administrators applied directly to employers, only 52.4 percent of their female counterparts did.

Want ads: unfair competition.   To make the ES more effective in its services to minorities and women, attention needs to be given to existing forms of discrimination in newspaper want ads, the leading formal source of job placement. Employers who wish to discriminate may simply avoid ES services and fill their openings through sex-designated newspaper ads, despite the illegality of that practice.

Want ads in newspapers in Salt Lake City and San Francisco, and in 19 other newspapers, were found to present a distorted picture of local job markets because of ad duplications. Ads were highly successful in matching applicants to job openings for a rather small but important group of employers, mainly large firms in selected industries of the two cities.

Weaknesses in the want ads are: inadequate information about job titles advertised, less than scrupulous concern with identifying and separating advertising for job openings from ads for other types of earning opportunities, haphazard organization of want ad columns and ad script, and disregard for established, legislated public policy as it regards discriminatory advertising practices.

The study found that want ads discriminate against women, that newspapers permit employers to make sex designations in their ads. Such practices are illegal, but newspapers claimed they did not want to take on the role of law enforcer in the case of sex designations, though all the papers enforced the law against race designations.

In June 1973, the U.S. Supreme Court ruled on the case of *Pittsburgh Press v. Pittsburgh Commission on Human Relations* and upheld a Pittsburgh ordinance banning sex designations in newspaper want ad headings. The decision placed both the help wanted ads and their arrangement in the realm of commercial speech and thereby subject to government regulation.

The Supreme Court ruling against sex-designated want ad headings came about because the National Organization of Women compiled massive evidence of violations and took legal action. In San Francisco, one women's organization picketed the San Francisco *Chronical-Examiner* in protest of discriminatory language in its want ads. The mere existence of the Civil Rights Act, passed in 1964, did not ensure that law enforcement agencies would focus on ending discriminatory practices.

The report concluded, however, that the only want ad user constituency "demonstrating sustained interest, group coherency, articulation, and power are the private employment agencies." Other constituencies, or government regulation and enforcement, the report suggested, are needed to overcome want ad bias, distortion, and misleading listings.

The shifting ES clientele

"A faded blue shirt collar nestles next to a starched white one on a bare table. This eye-catching photograph decorates the cover of a glossy brochure designed to persuade Wisconsin employers that the State's public employment offices, long considered strictly a source of blue-collar laborers, can help locate more highly skilled white-collar employees, too."

Far from using the no-fee services of ES's $600-million-a-year placement services to fill higher paying jobs, "most companies are busy dodging a slackly enforced, 5-year-old Federal regulation" designed to force Federal contractors to list such openings with the ES.

The agency says its goal is to increase professional listings, which are now only 7 percent of the total. "Yet such goals have repeatedly eluded the agency, which was created in 1933 to help the unemployed find jobs. It has been trying for 5 years to woo employers turned off by its late-1960's stress on helping poor and minority workers. In this effort, is has been hampered by the fact that most unemployment compensation claimants and able-bodied welfare recipients must register with USES."

A 1971 executive order known as the "mandatory listings" rule requires that Federal Government contractors list all vacancies paying up to $18,000 a year (as of 1976) with the ES. "The Labor Department estimates only 'between one-third and one-half' of all employers are complying with the rule; it can't be more specific since it isn't even sure how many Federal contractors the rule affects."

Why isn't the law obeyed? "For one thing the mandatory job-listing rule is easily evaded. Responsibility for enforcing it rests with Federal 'contract compliance' officials preoccupied with policing regulations banning employment discrimination on the basis of race or sex. Moreover, officials in the Employment Service's field offices are reluctant to snap at the corporate hands that toss them even a few job openings.

"Also, many employers secretly fear that seeking USES referrals will expose them to more pressure to hire females and minority groups members." Security Pacific National Bank in Los Angeles, however, reports a "tremendous" increase in its job listings with USES since local officials began enforcing the mandatory listing rule in 1973. The bank reports it is pleased with ES and has hired six entry level managers through the service.

A "Job Service Improvement Program," which is being introduced into 30 State employment offices in 1976, is appointing "account executives" to personalize services to companies. Employer advisory committees are also being created to get ES staff mingling with company personnel officers.

The efforts of ES to serve the disadvantaged, and perhaps women also, may actually be declining, despite demands for increased service to these groups.

A report on the impact of CETA found "signs that the Employment Service may be returning to its role of serving the job-ready while CETA serves the disadvantaged. This would negate the 10-year effort to make the Employment Service more responsive to the needs of the disadvantaged.

"A two-tier manpower system may emerge: One for the disadvantaged and another for the better-qualified workers." The extent to which the Employment Service effectively serves women jobseekers was not discussed.

Conclusions

The USES has been attempting to improve its service to women, who are, of course, but one group of the claimants for its services. The review of ES services to women and the research on the role and image of the ES in the job market suggest that there is still room for improvement. Additional steps that might be taken are:

1. Legislative examination of the advisability of requiring employers to list job openings with the ES.
2. Examination of the discrepancy between the clerical jobs listed by employers and number of clerical applicants to ES, with a view to improving ES services to clerical workers.
3. Including a women's representative on the staff of all large ES offices.
4. Followup on directives pertaining to women.
5. Inclusion of sex breakdown on placement occupations and industries.
6. Review of ES staff hiring and promotion practices.
7. More work with employers on job development for women.
8. Greater attention to developing rewarding part-time jobs.
9. Review of the need for a separate professional placement service, in view of high unemployment among women professionals.

The Equal Employment Opportunity Commission (EEOC)

The EEOC operates under title VII of the Civil Rights Act of 1964, as amended in 1972. Title VII prohibits discrimination because of sex, race, color, religion, or national origin, in all employment practices, including hiring, firing, layoffs, promotion, wages, training, disciplinary action, and other terms, privileges, conditions, or benefits of employment. Title VII covers private employers of 15 or more persons, employment agencies both public and private, labor unions with 15 or more members, joint labor-management apprenticeship committees, educational instructions both public and private, and State and local governments.

The EEOC enforces title VII except in behalf of Federal employees (handled by the U.S. Civil Service Commission), employees of State and local governments (handled by the Department of Justice), and employees of Federal contractors (handled by the Department of Labor.)

When the EEOC receives a charge alleging job discrimination, filed by an individual or a group on behalf of an individual, it investigates the charge. If the facts indicate discrimination, EEOC conciliates and tries to persuade the employer voluntarily to stop the discriminatory practice but, if conciliation fails, it files suit in Federal court. Individuals may, if they choose, initiate their own private suits.

In 1967, EEOC received 1,880 sex discrimination charges from women and 123 from men. By 1974, this had risen to 15,617 for women and 3,047 for men, representing 37 percent of all charges. More than a third of the total charges received were resolved by conciliation or litigation.

In the early days almost all charges of sex discrimination came from blue-collar women. Professionals were reluctant to file charges out of fear of retaliation or trouble. Since 1972, when EEOC received jurisdiction over educational institutions, it now gets many white collar cases. Of all charges in higher education, 95 percent were sex based and came mainly from women.

Even the Ph.D. requirement for employment in some jobs is being challenged: Companies have reanalyzed some jobs for engineers and have found that a third or a quarter of the work being done by engineers does not require any engineering degree at all. Less qualified people can be hired to do the nonengineering work, and jobs can be opened to women who are less likely than men to be trained engineers. In some cases, companies have found they needed good salespeople rather than engineers.

Considerable attention has been given to selection standards as they apply to minorities (tests, job requirements, interviews, etc.), but little attention has been given to the consequences for women.

Unintentional systemic discrimination is a matter of some concern and applicability to women. This kind of discrimination is a consequence of the fact that most of the hiring for better quality jobs is done by word of mouth, through "in-house" social networks, with the result that white males tend to be perpetuated in these better jobs. In this respect, the Griggs decision of the Supreme Court is very important. In that decision, discrimination was defined as "effect," rather than "intent," and the burden of proof was put on the employer to prove nondiscrimination.

No analysis is available of the substance of charges received by EEOC, but it is reported informally that most of the charges received from the private sector in 1974 had to do with discriminatory pay and compensation, and the second most common charge had to do with terms of employment. In compensation cases, charges may be filed under both the Equal Pay Act and the Civil Rights Act. The Equal Pay Act, administered by the Department of Labor, has a large administrative staff, and it can process charges faster than EEOC, despite a large backlog of cases. It is often able to convince employers to go along without court action. At EEOC equal pay charges go into a very large backlog. EEOC is also concerned with fringe benefits as well as hourly pay, and with sex segregated departments within firms. EEOC will investigate complaints alleging such segregation and may call for a reassignment of jobs. At Corning Glass, it was found, for example, that women and men in certain occupations did exactly the same work but only men could work nights and night work paid more.

Lifting restrictions on jobs now has to be based on personal ability rather than on sex. EEOC has not found "protective laws" an issue, since in practice most of these laws have been used to exclude women from many preferred jobs.

In its National Programs Division, EEOC tries to speed up the settlement of cases in an industry where many complaints have been received. By handling them all at once, it tries to settle with the industry rather than with individual firms. An example is the communications industry, where an EEOC case against American Telephone and Telegraph culminated in a court decision. In the steel industry, settlement was effected by a consent decree. Priorities are based on the number of charges received. Five major national corporations were on the priorities list in 1975.

EEOC has issued guidelines on maternity leaves which classify childbirth as a physical disability. A case on forced maternity leaves was first won by schoolteachers who were required to take leave after the fifth month of pregnancy. The Supreme Court decided that the teachers could not be forced to leave before childbirth. The issue of whether pregnancy should be treated as a temporary disability, however, has not yet gone to the Supreme Court. The Communications Workers of America have challenged the General Electric Company to follow the guidelines on disability, and GE has challenged the EEOC guidelines in court.

Treating childbirth as a disability means that women get disability insurance during the period of disability, however long it continues. Estimates of the cost of such insurance range from $4.4 million to $12.8 million (in Wisconsin alone), depending on coverage and benefit level. This might increase insurance costs by 9 percent, a not insignificant sum.

In 1972 EEOC was given powers for litigation. Until then, it could only investigate and refer cases to the Department of Justice for litigation. The Commission is understaffed and the backlog of cases is very large. Many groups pursue their own cases in court because EEOC is so slow.

Before EEOC had litigation powers, employers tended not to take the guidelines seriously; now, according to staff, they are taken much more seriously. Guidelines have often been challenged, but they have been consistently upheld in the courts. Cases can take 3 years and back compensation can be awarded from 2 years before charges were filed. Class action suits can cost employers a great deal of money in back pay to employees. Employers, therefore, are often interested in settling. Change in employer practices is likely to be greatest between the time charges are filed and the time EEOC investigates, a process that may take several years.

In reviewing the operations of EEOC, one is struck by the scope and significance of its operations, and by the real and potential impact of its activities on the employment of women. At the same time, one is struck by the dearth of research, data, and analysis relating to its activities, a consequence, no doubt, of the general work overload on its staff.

Clearly efforts should be made to improve the quantity and quality of information available. Similar efforts are also needed with respect to discriminatory practices of government employers (Federal from the U.S. Civil Service Commission and State and local from the Department of Justice) and of Federal contractors (from the U.S. Civil Service Commission and State and local from the Department of Justice) and of Federal contractors (from the Department of Labor).

These matters are obviously fundamental to the solution of the problems of inequality in the employment of women. Only one study among the rich variety of manpower research efforts has dealt with the impact of antidiscrimination laws per se on the employment of women. This study found that the laws had had little or no impact on the aggregate demand for women workers in Oregon by 1970, and that employers by 1972 had little or no knowledge of the laws. The study is dated and limited in scope but it points up the need for more research on impact and on a wide variety of other subjects.

Nor has the vast body of data that is reported to the EEOC been much used. Establishments must report their employment in each occupational group (for example, professional and technical workers) by sex and ethnic origin on Form EEO-1 each year if they employ 100 or more persons. Smaller subsidiary branch establishments must also report if the entire firm employs 100 or more. The major study of black employment in the South utilized these data for the seven cities it covered. They are a fertile source of information for local groups that are concerned with employment opportunities for women.

For example, EEO-1 data for 1972—8 years after enactment of the Civil Rights Act—add a new dimension to the finding of extensive sex segregation in employment. In the 2,795 San Francisco establishments which filed the EEO-1 report for 1972, 62 percent of all the women employees were in establishments where they accounted for at least half the work force. Indeed, 59 of the firms had a work force that was 90 percent or more female. At the other extreme, 57 firms employed no women. Similarly, in Atlanta, only 40 of the 1,736 reporting establishments could get along without any women on the payroll, but 60 percent of the women worked in establishments where they were in the majority. And the hundreds of establishments in Atlanta's 10 leading industries employed a total of only 48 Negro women in professional and technical jobs, although 1 of every 14 workers on their payrolls was a black woman. But in both San Francisco and Atlanta, as well as in Chicago, Houston, and Pittsburgh, half or more of the establishments had *no* black women on the payroll. These figures make it clear that the employment patterns of the past are only grudgingly responsive to present efforts to change them. The data could well serve attempts to step up the pace of progress for women.

Occupational licensing

Licensing is another function of law and government that has a significant effect on work and occupations. Unfortunately, little attention has been given to the effects of licensing laws and practices on women per se.

Licensing gives people who qualify for specific, licensed occupations the right to practice that occupation and, conversely, denies the right to practice of those who do not qualify. Frequently, licensing boards are, in effect, controlled by the occupational association being licensed. Such control enables the association to set entry qualifications and limit access to the occupation. Pressures for licensing come from the practitioners of occupations, not from the public. The sponsoring group usually drafts the needed legislation and has it introduced by a friendly legislator. Letter writing and pressure campaigns are then mounted to persuade legislators to include the occupation under the licensing laws. Conflict of interest results when the control of licensing is then put in the hands of the group being regulated.

In 1967 the Manpower Administration funded the Educational Testing Service (ETS) to study the feasibility of a national inquiry into the impact of licensing on skilled nonprofessional workers. ETS found serious problems in the examination procedures and in the geographic immobility licensing imposes on workers, often restricting movement even within a single State.

The Manpower Administration then commissioned two followup studies: One by ETS of selected skilled occupations in several States and cities; another by Michigan State University to devise procedures for collecting national data on licensed occupations. The report on these two projects was largely a result of the ETS study.

The growth of licensing, the study found, has been "a haphazard, uncoordinated, and chaotic process." Licensing and certification are often confused. Licensing gives a legal right, conferred by some agency of government, to an individual to practice an occupation. Certification or registration rarely provides a legal right. In the two basic patterns of certification (nongovernmental means of granting recognition), (1) the professional association handles certification (as with dietitians and occupational therapists); or (2) an ostensibly independent agency is created by one or more professional groups. An example of such an agency is the Board of Registry of Medical Technologists which is under the control of the American Society of Clinical Pathologists who hire the technologists.

Licensing often has profound, unanticipated consequences, as in education, where the curriculum that prepared people for licensing is inevitably controlled by licensing standards, which are in some cases ridiculously outmoded. Educational credentials are frequently a requirement for licensing. Courts may decide, however, that demonstrated competence on the job may be substituted for formal training. Both educational requirements and tests used by licensing boards have come under question. Often neither actually reflects what is required in the performance of an occupation, but are imposed by boards in order to limit the number of people in the occupation, upgrade the status and rewards of the occupation, and control the types of people who enter (especially minorities and women).

EEOC guidelines state that "the use of any test which adversely affects hiring, promotion, transfer, or any other employment or membership opportunity of classes protected by title VII constitutes discrimination unless (a) the test has been validated and evidences a high degree of utility as hereinafter described and (b) the person giving or acting upon the results of the particular test can demonstrate that alternative suitable hiring, transfer, or promotion procedures are available for his use." Instances of higher rejection rates of women than of men would indicate possible discrimination. A differential rejection rate based on a test "must be relevant to performance on the jobs in question."

Moroever, in the Duke Power Company case, the U.S. Supreme Court ruled that educational qualifications and tests as a condition for promotion to higher level jobs discriminated against blacks and was therefore illegal. The Court decided the tests must be job-related and properly used. "History is filled with examples of men and women who rendered highly effective performance without the usual badges of accomplishment in terms of certificates, diplomas, or degrees," And again, the Court said, "Diplomas and tests are useful servants, but Congress has mandated the commonsense proposition that they are not to become masters of reality."

In another important court decision, the U.S. District Court for the Southern District of New York found that the examinations used by the Board of Examiners in New York City had the "de facto effect of discriminating significantly and substantially against Negro and Puerto Rican applicants." White candidates who took the exam received passing grades at almost one and a half times the rate of the other group, and on at least one important administrative exam, they passed at twice the rate of the other group.

The study concludes that there is an urgent need for more information about all aspects of licensing, as well as a need to disseminate information about licensing requirements to workers, counselors, and curriculum specialists.

The need is also apparent for an examination of the effects of licensing practices on women, and the extent to which requirements (educational credentials, testing, interviews, etc.) handicap women in qualifying for licenses. It also needs to be determined how many women sit on licensing boards, and what the licensing status of "women's occupations" is. The same inquiry should be made into certification procedures. Dissemination of information to women and the counselors of women on these practices will also help women gain access to these licensed and certified occupations, which are often desirable and rewarding.

7

An education
and training
profile of the
contemporary
women's work
force

Education, training and employment of women*

Introduction

The work status of a woman is greatly affected by her educational attainment. The more education she has received, the greater the likelihood she will be engaged in paid employment. Unemployment rates for women generally decline with increasing amounts of formal education. Moreover, with more education, when a woman is employed, it is likely she will earn more. To a great extent, the amount and type of education or training a woman has also determines the type of job she can obtain.

The amount of education that women receive has been growing steadily. Current and projected school enrollment data indicate that the educational attainment of women workers will continue its long-term rise during the 1970's and 1980's.

Education of women in the population and labor force

In March 1974, 25.5 million women workers, or more than 72 percent of those 16 years of age or over in the labor force, had completed at least 4 years of high school. About 39 percent of these high school graduates had completed 1 year of college or more, and about 18 percent were college graduates. At the lower end of the educational scale, nearly 10 percent of the women workers had 8 or fewer years of schooling and nearly 18 percent had completed only 1 to 3 years of high school (see chart R).

Women 16 years of age or over in the labor force had more schooling, on the average, than did women who were not in the labor force. The median school years completed was 12.5 for women labor force members, compared with 12.0 for women who were not in the labor force. The difference was much more marked for women who were college graduates: more than twice as high a proportion of women in the labor force (13 percent) as women not in the labor force (6 percent) were college graduates. A much higher proportion of women who were not in the labor force had 8 or fewer years of schooling (25.5 percent) than did labor force members (9.7 percent) (see table 78).

Rise in educational attainment

The educational attainment of women workers has been rising steadily. In October 1952, only about half (51 percent) of the women workers 18 to 64 years of age had completed at least 4 years of high school. In March 1973 nearly three-fourths of all women workers were high school graduates. The proportion of women with some college education increased from about one-sixth of all women workers in October 1952 to more than one-fourth in March 1973. Perhaps an even more dramatic change occurred in the proportion of women workers with 8 years of schooling or less. More than 30 percent of all women in the labor force in

*Handbook on Women Workers, U.S. Department of Labor, Women's Bureau.

Chart R—More than 7 out of 10 women workers are at least high school graduates

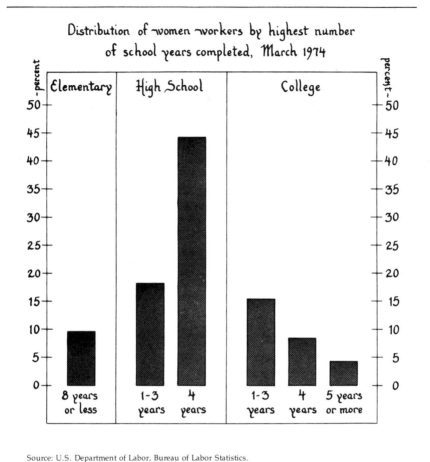

Distribution of women workers by highest number of school years completed, March 1974

Elementary	High School		College		
8 years or less	1-3 years	4 years	1-3 years	4 years	5 years or more

Source: U.S. Department of Labor, Bureau of Labor Statistics.

October 1952 had completed 8 or fewer years of school. By March 1973 the proportion had declined to less than 10 percent (see table 79).

Projections made by the Bureau of Labor Statistics indicate that the rise in the educational attainment of women workers is expected to continue. The percentage of women who will complete at least 4 years of high school is projected to increase to nearly 78 percent by 1985. The projected educational attainment of women workers at the lower end of the educational ladder is particularly significant. The proportion of women with 8 or fewer years of formal schooling is expected to continue to decline rapidly, so that by 1985 the percentage will be about half of that in 1973. In contrast, the proportion of women workers with 4 or more years of college is expected to increase to about one-sixth of all women workers, as compared with less than one-eighth in March 1973.

Table 78 —Distribution of persons in the labor force and not in the labor force, by number of school years completed, March 1974[1]

(Persons 16 years of age and over)

Number of school years completed	Women		Men	
	In labor force	Not in labor force	In labor force	Not in labor force
Total (number in thousands) __	35,321	42,791	54,312	15,392
Percent _____	100.0	100.0	100.0	100.0
No years _____	.2	1.4	.4	2.7
Elementary:				
1 to 4 years _____	.9	3.6	1.9	7.1
5 to 7 years _____	3.4	8.4	5.0	11.5
8 years _____	5.2	12.1	7.4	16.8
High School:				
1 to 3 years _____	18.1	22.9	18.0	26.7
4 years _____	44.2	34.6	36.0	17.5
College:				
1 to 3 years _____	15.2	10.9	14.9	12.0
4 years _____	8.6	4.5	9.1	3.6
5 years or more _____	4.2	1.5	7.3	2.2
Median school years completed ___	12.5	12.0	12.5	10.3

[1] Preliminary data.

Source: U.S. Department of Labor, Bureau of Labor Statistics: Special Labor Force Report No. 175.

Educational attainment of women workers by selected characteristics
Age.   Younger workers—both women and men—have more education than older workers. Of the women workers in the 20- to 34-year-age group in March 1973, for example, more than 85 percent were high school graduates. In contrast, only about 66 percent of women workers 35 years of age or older had completed high school. the proportion of women workers who had 1 year or more of college education was also much greater in the younger group. Nearly 37 percent of the 20- to 34-year-old women workers had completed at least 1 year of college compared with less than 22 percent of women 35 years of age or older (see table 80).

Race.   Minority race women workers in 1973 had less education, on the average, than did white women workers. The median school years completed by white women workers was 12.5 years, as compared with 12.1 years for minority race women. Almost three-fifths of minority race women, compared with almost three-fourths of white women workers, were high school graduates. About one-fifth of minority race women workers had completed at least 1 year of college, as compared with more than one-fourth of white women workers. A much higher percentage of minority race women than of white women were concentrated at the lower end of the educational ladder. About 17 percent of the minority race women workers had completed 8 or fewer years of schooling, as compared with less than 10 percent of white women workers.

Table 79 — Historical comparisons of women in the civilian labor force, by years of school completed, selected years 1940 to 1973[1]

| Year [2] | Total, 18 to 64 years (in thousands) | Percent distribution by years of school completed | | | | | | | Median school years completed |
| | | Total | Elementary | | High School | | College | | |
			Less than 5 years [3]	5 to 8 years	1 to 3 years	4 years	1 to 3 years	4 years or more	
1940 [4]	13,150	100.0	6.4	30.9	18.7	28.6	8.8	6.6	11.0
1952	18,310	100.0	5.2	25.0	18.4	34.7	9.0	7.7	12.0
1957	19,548	100.0	3.9	21.9	19.1	37.3	9.3	8.4	12.1
1959	20,431	100.0	3.3	20.6	19.2	39.0	9.8	8.2	12.2
1962	21,996	100.0	2.8	17.8	18.8	39.7	11.2	9.7	12.3
1964	23,327	100.0	2.1	17.1	18.9	41.8	10.7	9.5	12.3
1965	23,845	100.0	2.0	15.8	18.9	42.9	10.5	9.9	12.3
1966	24,571	100.0	1.7	15.0	18.5	43.9	11.0	9.9	12.3
1967	25,674	100.0	1.9	14.0	18.5	43.8	11.9	9.9	12.4
1968	26,859	100.0	1.6	13.3	17.7	44.5	12.3	10.6	12.4
1969	27,783	100.0	1.6	12.1	17.4	45.9	12.5	10.5	12.4
1970	28,950	100.0	1.4	11.3	17.0	46.3	13.3	10.7	12.4
1971	29,429	100.0	1.3	10.7	16.4	46.2	14.0	11.4	12.5
1972	30,566	100.0	1.2	9.6	16.4	47.1	13.9	11.8	12.5
1973	31,530	100.0	1.2	8.7	15.5	47.6	14.6	12.5	12.5

[1] Data for 1940–59 include only persons reporting educational attainment.

[2] Figures for each year refer to March of that year, with the exception of 1940 and 1952. For these years, data refer to April and October, respectively.

[3] Includes persons reporting no school years completed.

[4] 1940 Census of Population figures revised for comparability with labor force estimates from the Current Population Survey for 1952–59.

Note.—In other tables in this chapter, population and labor force comprise all persons 16 years old and over in the civilian noninstitutional population and labor force rather than those 18 to 64. Because of rounding, sums of individual items may not equal totals.

Source: U.S. Department of Labor, Bureau of Labor Statistics: Special Labor Force Report No. 161.

Comparison with prior years shows a significant closing of the gap between the educational attainment of white and minority race women workers (see chart S). Between 1962 and 1973 the median number of school years completed by minority race women workers rose from 10.5 to 12.1. For white women, the comparable figures were 12.3 to 12.5 years. In 1962 less than 38 percent of minority race women workers were high school graduates; in 1973 nearly 59 percent had completed at least 4

Table 80 — Distribution of women workers by educational attainment and age, March 1973

(Women 16 years of age and over)

| Age | Total | | Less than 4 years of high school | High school graduates | | | |
	Number (in thousands)	Percent		Total	4 years of high school	1 to 3 years of college	4 years or more of college
16 years and over ____	33,905	100.0	29.1	70.9	45.1	13.8	12.0
16 to 19 years _____	3,423	100.0	55.3	44.7	37.9	6.8	.1
20 to 34 years _____	12,561	100.0	14.9	85.1	48.4	19.8	16.9
35 years and over __	17,921	100.0	34.0	66.0	44.3	11.0	10.7

Source: U.S. Department of Labor, Bureau of Labor Statistics: Special Labor Force Report No. 161.

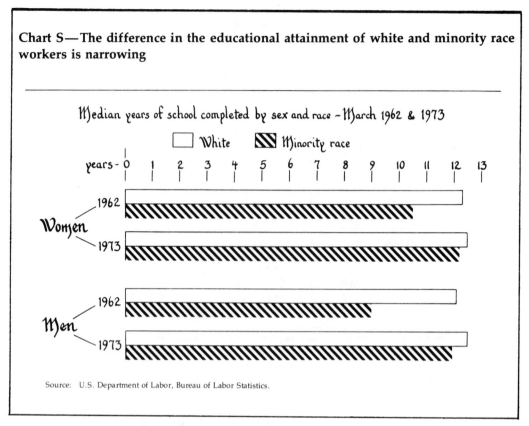

Chart S—The difference in the educational attainment of white and minority race workers is narrowing

Median years of school completed by sex and race – March 1962 & 1973

☐ White   ▨ Minority race

years - 0 1 2 3 4 5 6 7 8 9 10 11 12 13

Women
1962
1973

Men
1962
1973

Source: U.S. Department of Labor, Bureau of Labor Statistics.

years of high school. For white women, the comparable proportions were 63 and 73 percent. The largest change has been at the lowest educational level. In 1962 nearly 37 percent of minority race women workers had completed 8 or fewer years of formal schooling; by 1973 the proportion had declined to about 17 percent.

Comparison of educational attainment of women and men
A higher proportion of women workers (72 percent) than of men workers (67 percent) had completed high school in March 1974. However, a higher proportion of men workers (31 percent) than of women workers (28 percent) had had some college education. A smaller proportion of women workers than of men workers were in the lowest educational groups. Less than 10 percent of women workers but nearly 15 percent of men workers had completed 8 years of schooling or less (see table 78).

Between men and women workers, the gap in average (mean) years of schooling completed has been narrowing since 1940 and has now almost disappeared. In 1940 the mean years completed by women workers 18 to 64 years of age was 9.8 years—1.2 years above that for men workers. By 1973 the corresponding means were 12.1 among women workers and 12.0 among men workers.

Educational attainment and labor force participation
Whether a woman is in the labor force or not is affected greatly by the amount of schooling she has had. As mentioned earlier, the more education a woman has received, the greater the likelihood that she will be

engaged in paid employment. A high school diploma is a prerequisite for many jobs today, and education beyond high school is being required for an increasing number of jobs. Women with college degrees are more likely than other women to be in the labor force because they are motivated to seek employment outside the home by the higher earnings available to them and because of their desire to use the skills they have acquired through higher education.

In March 1974 nearly 70 percent of women 16 years of age or older who had completed 5 years of college or more and 61 percent of those with 4 years of college were in the labor force. About half of the women who were high school graduates (but who had not gone to college) were in the labor force. For women high school dropouts, the proportion was about two-fifths, and for those with 8 years of schooling only, it was about one-fourth.

The relationship between educational attainment and labor force participation is also evident when women are distributed by marital status. The highest labor force participation rates were for women with 4 years of college or more, and the lowest rates were for those with 8 or fewer years of schooling—whether the women were single, married (husband present), widowed, divorced, or separated. Even when the data on women were distributed by marital status and age, the pattern of greater labor force participation among women with higher educational attainment generally held true. The median school years completed by women who were in the labor force was higher than that for women who were not in the labor force; this was true for women who were single, married (husband present), widowed, divorced, or separated.

Educational attainment and occupational distribution of women workers

The amount of education a woman has received greatly affects the type of job she can obtain (see table 81 and chart T). In March 1973, for example, nearly three-fourths of the employed women who were college graduates were in professional and technical occupations. On the other hand, four-fifths who had fewer than 8 years of schooling were operatives or service workers either inside or outside the home.

Among women who had attended college, there was a significant difference in occupational distribution according to the number of years of schooling completed. For example, about 83 percent of the women with 5 years or more of college were in professional and technical occupations and another 8 percent were managers or administrators. For those with 4 years of college, 69 percent were in professional and technical occupations and 6 percent were managers or administrators. In contrast, only 25 percent of the women who had completed only 1 to 3 years of college were in professional and technical or managerial occupations.

Among women who had completed high school but had not gone on to college, 47 percent were in clerical positions and nearly 12 percent were in professional and technical or managerial occupations. On the other hand, a much smaller proportion (21 percent) of the women who dropped out of school before completing high school were clerical workers; they were mainly operatives (24 percent) or service workers outside the home (27 percent).

Table 81 —Occupational distribution of employed women, by years of school completed, March 1973

(Women 16 years of age and over)

Major occupation group	Total	Elementary		High school		College		
		Less than 8 years	8 years	1 to 3 years	4 years	1 to 3 years	4 years	5 years or more
Number (in thousands) __	31,924	1,511	1,807	5,685	14,492	4,485	2,668	1,277
Percent _____	100.0	100.0	100.0	100.0	100.0	100.0	100.0	100.0
Professional, technical workers _____	15.1	1.0	2.3	2.0	6.3	18.7	69.1	82.7
Manager, administrators (except farm) _	5.0	3.0	3.4	3.0	5.3	6.6	6.2	7.9
Sales workers ____	6.8	2.2	6.5	8.4	7.6	7.3	3.2	.7
Clerical workers _	34.1	5.4	9.7	20.8	47.0	48.0	15.5	5.5
Craft and kindred workers _____	1.3	2.1	1.9	1.8	1.4	.9	.4	.2
Operatives (except transport)_	13.2	32.7	31.4	23.1	11.5	3.3	1.3	.6
Transport equipment operatives _____	.5	—	.8	.7	.6	.4	.1	—
Laborers (except farm) ____	.9	2.6	1.3	1.4	.8	.4	.1	—
Private household workers ___	4.3	18.7	9.3	9.9	1.9	1.3	.5	.5
Service workers (except private household) ____	17.5	28.4	29.5	27.0	16.6	12.7	3.5	1.4
Farm workers ___	1.3	3.9	3.9	1.9	1.0	.4	.1	.5

Source: U.S. Department of Labor, Bureau of Labor Statistics: Special Labor Force Report No. 161.

The relationship between the amount of education received by women and the occupation held is perhaps more clearly illustrated by examining the distribution of women employed in each occupation group by educational attainment. Of the 4.8 million women employed in professional and technical occupations in March 1973, nearly 78 percent had attended college and 60 percent had at least a bachelor's degree. Of the 10.9 million clerical workers, about 24 percent had attended college and an additional 63 percent were high school graduates (with no college attendance). Only about 11 percent of the clerical workers were school dropouts and only about 2 percent had not attended high school. Women in private household work had the least amount of schooling of women in any other occupation group. About one-third of these women had 8 or fewer years of schooling and more than two-fifths had 1 to 3 years of high school.

The effect of the level of education on the kinds of jobs women are able to obtain can be demonstrated further by comparing the occupational distribution in October 1973 of 1973 high school graduates not enrolled in college with 1972–73 school dropouts (see table 82). Whereas

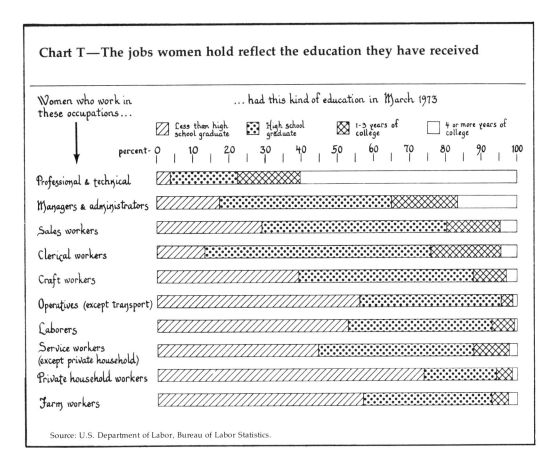

Chart T—The jobs women hold reflect the education they have received

Women who work in these occupations... ... had this kind of education in March 1973

☑ Less than high school graduate   ▨ High school graduate   ⊠ 1-3 years of college   ☐ 4 or more years of college

percent- 0 | 10 | 20 | 30 | 40 | 50 | 60 | 70 | 80 | 90 | 100

Professional & technical
Managers & administrators
Sales workers
Clerical workers
Craft workers
Operatives (except transport)
Laborers
Service workers (except private household)
Private household workers
Farm workers

Source: U.S. Department of Labor, Bureau of Labor Statistics.

Table 82 —Major occupation group of employed 1973 women high school graduates not enrolled in college and of 1972–73 school dropouts, October 1973

Major occupation group	1973 high school graduates	1972–73 school dropouts
All occupation groups:		
Number (in thousands)	560	182
Percent	100.0	100.0
Professional, technical workers	2.9	.6
Managers, administrators (except farm)	.4	—
Sales workers	10.2	3.9
Clerical workers	47.8	18.9
Craft and kindred workers	.7	.6
Operatives (except transport)	13.1	24.4
Transport equipment operatives	—	—
Laborers (except farm)	1.6	2.8
Private household workers	3.2	11.1
Service workers (except private household)	19.9	37.2
Farmers and farm managers	—	—
Farm laborers and supervisors	.4	.6

Source: U.S. Department of Labor, Bureau of Labor Statistics: Special Labor Force Report No. 170.

about 48 percent of the women high school graduates were employed in clerical jobs, less than 19 percent of the employed women who had dropped out of school held clerical jobs. Similarly, more than 10 percent of the women high school graduates, compared with less than 4 percent of women school dropouts, were employed in sales jobs. About 48 percent of the school dropouts were in service jobs (both in and outside private households), whereas only about 23 percent of high school graduates were employed in service jobs. About 24 percent of women school dropouts but only 13 percent of high school graduates were employed in operative jobs.

Educational attainment and unemployment

In general, there is an inverse relationship between the amount of education women workers have and the percentage who are unemployed; that is, the less education, the higher the unemployment rate. For example, in March 1973 women who had completed 8 years of schooling had an unemployment rate of 6.3 percent; women with 4 years of high school, 5.3 percent; those with 1 to 3 years of college, 4.3 percent; and women college graduates, 2.7 percent. Also, as has been indicated, women workers with more schooling generally have higher earnings (see chart U).

However, women with 1 to 3 years of high school had the highest unemployment rate (9.7 percent)—even higher than that for women with less than 5 years of schooling (8.0 percent). This paradox is ex-

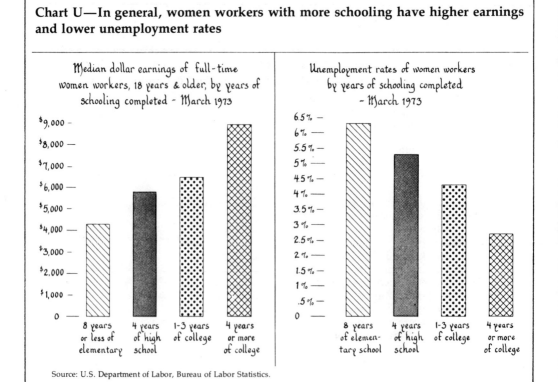

Chart U—In general, women workers with more schooling have higher earnings and lower unemployment rates

Median dollar earnings of full-time women workers, 18 years & older, by years of schooling completed - March 1973

Unemployment rates of women workers by years of schooling completed - March 1973

Source: U.S. Department of Labor, Bureau of Labor Statistics.

plained in large part by the differing age composition of workers in these two groups. About one-third of the workers with 1 to 3 years of high school are 16 to 24 years old, while workers with 5 years of school or less are predominantly 25 years of age or older. The unemployment rates of the younger persons are several times higher than for persons 25 years of age and over, regardless of the number of years of schooling. This is due, in part, to the fact that older workers are more likely to have developed occupational skills and to have acquired job seniority.

Table 83 shows the unemployment rates of women workers 18 years of age and over for March 1968 through March 1973 for all women workers and for white and minority race women separately for the group with the lowest unemployment rate—college graduates—and the group with the highest rate—school dropouts. For school dropouts, the unemployment rates for minority race women in March 1972 and 1973 were about double those for white women. But for college graduates, there was little difference in the unemployment rates for white and minority race women.

The effect of limited educational attainment on unemployment is demonstrated by a comparison of unemployment rates in October 1973 of the 1973 high school graduates (not enrolled in college) and the 1972–73 school dropouts. The unemployment rate for all women high school graduates not in college was 15.2 percent; for single women high school graduates, it was 14.8 percent. The comparable rates for school dropouts were 18.0 percent for all women and 20.0 for single women. The differences in unemployment rates between high school graduates and school dropouts were much greater among men than among women. For 1973 male school graduates who had not enrolled in college, the unemployment rate was 9.4 percent in October 1973; for male 1972–73 school dropouts, the unemployment rate was 24 percent.

Educational attainment and hours of work
Women with a limited amount of formal education are more likely to be employed part time than are highly educated women. Many of the occupational opportunities open to women with little schooling are in

---

Table 83 —Unemployment rates of women workers, by educational attainment and race, March 1968 to March 1973

(Women 18 years of age and over)

Education and race	1968	1969	1970	1971	1972	1973
High school, 1 to 3 years						
All women	6.6	6.2	7.4	9.8	9.2	8.0
White	5.8	5.5	6.7	8.8	7.7	6.8
Minority races [1]	10.3	9.2	10.3	14.3	15.5	13.3
College, 4 years or more						
All women	1.6	1.1	2.0	2.8	3.1	2.7
White	1.7	1.2	2.1	2.6	3.1	2.6
Minority races [1]	.6	.7	1.5	5.3	3.0	2.8

[1] The term minority races denotes Negro, American Indian, Japanese, Chinese, Filipino, Korean and persons of all other races except white. Negroes constituted 89 percent of persons other than white in the United States in 1970.

Source: U.S. Department of Labor, Bureau of Labor Statistics: Special Labor Force Report No. 161.

private households, other service work, and retail sales work. Many of these jobs are part time. Among women employed in nonagricultural industries in March 1973, the likelihood of working part time was generally diminished with each higher level of educational attainment (see table 84). For example, nearly 47 percent of school dropouts were working part time, whereas less than 29 percent of high school graduates were working part time.

Educational attainment and earnings
Women with more years of schooling generally have significantly higher earnings than women with less education. Median dollar earnings of year-round full-time women workers who were college graduates, for example, were more than twice as high as for women who had 8 or fewer years of schooling. As can be seen in table 85, the median earnings generally rise with the increase in educational attainment, even when women workers were distributed by occupation group.

School enrollments

The rise in the educational attainment of women reflects the increase in the enrollment of women in high school and college. In October 1973 nearly 28 million females 5 to 34 years of age were attending school. From 1964 to 1971, the number of women enrolled in school increased from less than 17 million to nearly 29 million. Between 1971 and 1973, the number declined by about a million. The recent decrease in school enrollment resulted primarily from a drop in the number of elementary

Table 84 —Distribution of women employed in nonagricultural industries, by full- and part-time status and educational attainment, March 1973

(Women 18 years of age and over)

| Years of school completed | Number (in thousands) | Percent distribution | | |
		Total	Full time 35 hours or more a week	Part time 1 to 34 hours a week
Total_____	31,414	100.0	67.2	32.8
Elementary school:				
Less than 8 years [1] _____	1,447	100.0	64.9	35.1
8 years _____	1,731	100.0	63.7	36.3
High school:				
1 to 3 years _____	5,558	100.0	53.2	46.8
4 years _____	14,305	100.0	71.1	28.9
College:				
1 to 3 years _____	4,445	100.0	65.6	34.4
4 years or more _____	3,928	100.0	77.1	22.9

[1] Includes women reporting no school years completed.

Source: U.S. Department of Labor, Bureau of Labor Statistics: Special Labor Force Report No. 161.

Table 85 — Median dollar earnings of year-round, full-time women workers, by educational attainment, March 1973

(Women 18 years of age and over)

Occupation	Total	Elementary, 8 years or less	High school		College	
			1 to 3 years	4 years	1 to 3 years	4 years or more
Total_____	$5,970	$4,303	$5,037	$5,769	$6,465	$8,925
White-collar workers _____	6,664	5,102	5,692	6,071	6,649	8,997
Professional and technical workers _____	8,725	5,500	6,306	7,819	8,146	9,232
Managers and administrators (except farm) _	7,063	6,000	5,781	6,581	7,906	10,350
Clerical and sales workers_	5,899	4,871	5,611	5,876	6,097	6,934
Blue-collar workers _____	5,070	4,486	5,105	5,386	5,469	5,853
Service workers _____	3,308	3,758	4,039	4,551	5,429	6,278
Farmers and farm laborers__	2,861	3,350	2,667	1,250	750	5,750

WOMEN'S MEDIAN EARNINGS AS PERCENT OF MEN'S

Occupation	Total	Elementary, 8 years or less	1 to 3 years	4 years	1 to 3 years	4 years or more
Total_____	58.5	56.8	56.3	57.3	59.0	60.9
White-collar workers _____	54.9	58.0	56.8	56.6	55.8	59.8
Professional and technical workers _____	66.1	62.5	58.1	65.4	68.9	63.9
Managers and administrators (except farm) _	54.3	62.4	56.0	55.1	59.2	59.9
Clerical and sales workers_	57.7	59.8	58.5	59.8	58.2	53.9
Blue-collar workers _____	54.0	55.4	56.3	54.0	54.4	54.2
Service workers _____	55.2	60.2	58.1	52.1	56.9	58.4
Farmers and farm laborers__	54.9	81.7	56.6	20.3	9.8	65.7

Source: U.S. Department of Labor, Bureau of Labor Statistics: Special Labor Force Report No. 161.

school students. This reflects a decrease in recent years in the number of persons of kindergarten and elementary school age as the children born in the mid-1960's replace on the school rolls those born in the high fertility period in the 1950's. The number of births in the United States began to decline in the early 1960's and elementary school enrollment decreased after 1970 as those children reached school age.

Enrollments by age

Nearly all elementary school-age girls 7 to 13 years (99 percent) were enrolled in school in 1973. More than 97 percent of teenage girls 14 and 15 were also attending school. As young women pass age 16 (the compulsory school attendance age in many States), the proportion who remain in school drops—it decreased to 87 percent among 16- and 17-year-olds in 1973. With graduation from high school, the proportion of young women attending school dropped to about 38 percent for those 18 and 19 and to 26 percent for those 20 and 21.

Relatively fewer females 5 to 34 years of age than males of the same age group were attending school in 1973 (see table 86). There was little difference in the proportion of males and females age 5 to 17 who were enrolled in school. But among those 18 years of age and over, there was

Table 86 —Enrollment status of the population[1] 3 to 34 years old, by age, race, and sex, October 1973

(Numbers in thousands)

	Females						Males	
	All		White		Black			
	Enrolled in school		Enrolled in school		Enrolled in school		Enrolled in school	
Age	Number	Percent of population	Number	Percent of population	Number	Percent of population	Number	Percent of population
3 and 4 years	816	23.8	657	22.9	142	28.5	876	24.5
5 and 6 years	3,066	92.9	2,584	93.2	421	90.9	3,162	92.2
7 to 9 years	5,426	99.3	4,556	99.3	799	99.2	5,610	99.0
10 to 13 years	7,979	99.2	6,762	99.3	1,104	98.9	8,274	99.2
14 and 15 years	3,973	97.1	3,376	97.1	543	96.5	4,145	97.9
16 and 17 years	3,536	87.2	3,011	87.3	475	86.4	3,700	89.4
18 and 19 years	1,500	38.2	1,297	38.7	173	32.8	1,783	47.9
20 and 21 years	987	26.3	881	27.4	81	17.3	1,157	34.4
22 to 24 years	553	10.2	465	9.9	75	11.1	961	19.1
25 to 29 years	431	5.4	375	5.4	48	5.5	878	11.8
30 to 34 years	238	3.6	206	3.6	28	3.8	342	5.6

[1] Civilian noninstitutional population.

Source: U.S. Department of Commerce, Bureau of the Census: School Enrollment in the United States: October 1973 (Advance report), Current Population Reports, P–20, No. 261, March 1974.

a significant difference in the proportion enrolled. In October 1973 nearly 48 percent of the males 18 and 19 years of age were enrolled in school, compared with 38 percent of the females. Similarly, among those 20 and 21, more than 34 percent of the men were attending school, as compared with 26 percent of the women. Among those 22 to 34, the proportion of men attending school—nearly 12 percent—was almost double that of women.

A higher percentage of white females than of black females 5 to 34 years of age were enrolled in school in October 1973. The enrollment rate for white and black females was about the same for those aged 5 through 17. But for those aged 18 and 19, nearly 39 percent of white women, compared with less than 33 percent of black women, were enrolled in school. The biggest difference was in the age group 20 and 21 years; 27 percent of the white women and 17 percent of the black women were enrolled in school in October 1973. This would indicate that black females are still somewhat less likely than white females to continue in school past the compulsory attendance age. High school dropout rates (that is, the proportion of the age group not enrolled in school and not high school graduates) were higher for black women than for white. Of those 18 and 19 years old, about 23 percent of the black women, compared with 13 percent of the white women, were not enrolled in school nor were they high school graduates.

Enrollments by type of school

Of the 28.5 million girls and women age 3 to 34 who were enrolled in the fall of 1973, about 17.5 million (61 percent) were in elementary school or kindergarten and nursery school; 7.5 million (26 percent) were in high school (grades 9–12); and 3.5 million (12 percent) were in college. There were almost as many female students as male students at the elementary and secondary school levels. But there were about one-third more men than women at the college level. About 8 percent of the females enrolled in high school were attending private schools; nearly 23 percent of college women were enrolled in private colleges.

Secondary School. The number of young persons (both women and men) who enrolled in and graduated from high school rose steadily during the 1960's and the early 1970's. The increase, in part, resulted from the growth of the number of young persons in the population. It also resulted from the rising percentages of young people who remained in high school until graduation. The decline in the school dropout rate undoubtedly reflects the awareness of young people and their parents of the necessity of securing a high school diploma in order to qualify for most jobs.

From 1964 to 1973 the number of young women enrolled in high school (grades 9–12) increased from less than 6.4 million to more than 7.5 million, or 18 percent. The number of young women who graduated from high school increased by nearly one-third over this period—from 1,167,000 in the 1963–64 school year to 1,522,000 in the 1972–73 school year. Projections by the Office of Education indicate that the number of high school graduates will begin to decline after the 1976–77 school year as the number of young people in the 17- and 18-year-age group begins to decrease, reflecting the continuous decline in the number of births since 1960.

The percentage that high school graduates were of 18-year-olds in the population increased substantially from the school years 1961–62 to 1965–66; for women, it rose from 72 percent to nearly 78 percent; and for men, from 67 percent to 74 percent. From school year 1965–66 to 1972–73, the percentage did not change greatly (see table 87). Large numbers of young women and men still leave school before earning their high school diploma. About 784,000 young persons 16 years of age or older dropped out of high school between October 1972 and October 1973; of these, 342,000 were women. About 1 out of 3 of the women dropouts had been married. In addition to those 16 years and over, about 126,000 persons 14 and 15 years of age dropped out of school.

Higher education. *High school graduates entering college.* —Nearly 3.1 million persons graduated from high school in 1973. About 47 percent of them were enrolled in college the following October. The proportion of women going on to college in the fall following graduation from high school was down to 43 percent in 1973 from a high of 50 percent in 1971 (see table 88). The proportion of men going on to college in the fall following high school graduation also declined—to 50 percent in 1973 from the peak of 63 percent in 1968, when young men had the added incentive to go to college to postpone military service. Factors contributing to the decline in college enrollment in the early 1970's may be the increase in tuition and related costs and the greater difficulty young college graduates have had in finding suitable jobs in recent years.

Because many young women and men delay entering college after graduating from high school, the percentage of high school graduates that eventually go on to college is greater than that shown previously

Table 87 —Number of high school graduates and percent they are of persons 18 years old, by sex, 1962–73

(Numbers in thousands)

School year	High school graduates — Number		Number of 18-year-olds[1]			Percent graduates are of 18-year-olds	
	Women	Men	Year	Women	Men	Women	Men
1961–62	984	941	1962	1,368	1,404	71.9	67.0
1962–63	991	959	1963	1,419	1,456	69.8	65.9
1963–64	1,167	1,123	1964	1,643	1,692	71.0	66.4
1964–65	1,351	1,314	1965	1,774	1,829	76.2	71.8
1965–66	1,346	1,326	1966	1,736	1,790	77.5	74.1
1966–67	1,348	1,332	1967	1,746	1,800	77.2	74.0
1967–68	1,360	1,341	1968	1,786	1,840	76.1	72.9
1968–69	1,427	1,402	1969	1,841	1,898	77.5	73.9
1969–70	1,463	1,433	1970	1,882	1,944	77.7	73.7
1970–71	1,487	1,456	1971	1,924	1,992	77.3	73.1
1971–72	1,520	1,495	1972	1,971	2,042	77.1	73.2
1972–73[2]	1,552	1,524	1973[2]	2,010	2,080	77.2	73.3

[1] Age 18 as of October 1 of the year.

[2] Estimated.

Source: U.S. Department of Health, Education, and Welfare, Office of Education: "Projections of Educational Statistics, 1982–83," OE–74–11105.

and in table 88. For example, about 10 percent of the 16- to 24-year-old persons enrolled in college in October 1972 had not been in school the previous October—295,000 women and 384,000 men. About half of them were freshmen. Apparently many of the late entrants had worked, traveled, or served in the military between graduating from high school and entering college. About one-third of the women and men students in this group were married.

There are some data which indicate that some women delay enrolling in college for several years after graduating from high school. For

Table 88 —Proportion of high school graduates enrolled in college in October of the year of graduation, by sex, 1962–73

(Percent)

Year of graduation	All persons	Women	Men
1962	49	43	55
1963	45	39	52
1964	48	41	57
1965	51	45	57
1966	50	43	59
1967	52	47	58
1968	55	49	63
1969	54	47	60
1970	52	49	55
1971	53	50	58
1972	49	46	53
1973	47	43	50

Source: U.S. Department of Labor, Bureau of Labor Statistics: Special Labor Force Reports Nos. 155 and 168, and Summary Special Labor Force Report, April 1974.

example, in a nationwide study, Jewish high school students in the 10th, 11th, and 12th grades were interviewed about their college and career plans. Eight years later these same young persons were contacted (by mail) and questioned about their educational experience. It was found that 5, 6, or 7 years after graduating from high school 6.9 percent of the young women were college freshmen and another 4.8 percent were college sophomores.

College enrollments. Women attended college in increasing numbers during the 1960's and early 1970's. However, still in 1973 about one-third more men than women were in college (see table 89). Women were more likely to have attended college at the freshman or sophomore level than at the upper college level. About 47 percent of freshmen were women, compared with 42 percent of juniors and seniors and 36 percent of graduate students (see table 90).

There were about 3.5 million women under 35 years of age enrolled in college in October 1973. The number of women in college in October 1973 was nearly double that in 1964. The number of men attending college (4.7 million) was about three-fifths more than in 1964. Women accounted for nearly 43 percent of college students under 35 years of age in 1973, compared with 38 percent in 1964.

Of the 3.5 million women under 35 years of age who attended college in October 1978, 88.7 percent were white, 9.3 percent were black, and 2 percent were members of other races. The number of black women in college in October 1973 (326,000) was nearly 3 times the number in October 1964.

The Office of Education provides information on enrollments in higher education by type of institution. Opening fall enrollment in 1973 showed about 2.9 million women in 4-year institutions of higher education. The number of women in 4-year institutions more than doubled in the decade 1963 to 1973. Nearly all the women (more than 98 percent) in

---

Table 89 —College enrollment of the population[1] 14 to 34 years old, by race and sex, October 1964 to October 1973

(Numbers in thousands)

Year	All races			White			Black		
	Total	Female	Male	Total	Female	Male	Total	Female	Male
1973_____	8,179	3,502	4,677	7,324	3,105	4,218	684	326	358
1972_____	8,313	3,460	4,853	7,458	3,061	4,397	727	343	384
1971_____	8,087	3,236	4,850	7,273	2,867	4,407	680	317	363
1970_____	7,413	3,013	4,401	6,759	2,693	4,066	522	269	253
1969_____	7,435	2,987	4,448	6,827	2,681	4,146	492	256	236
1968_____	6,801	2,677	4,124	6,255	2,412	3,843	434	213	221
1967_____	6,401	2,560	3,841	5,905	2,345	3,560	370	171	199
1966_____	6,085	2,337	3,749	5,708	2,172	3,536	282	128	154
1965_____	5,675	2,172	3,503	5,317	1,991	3,326	274	148	126
1964_____	4,643	1,755	2,888	4,337	1,617	2,720	234	114	120

[1] Civilian noninstitutional population.

Source: U.S. Department of Commerce, Bureau of the Census: "School Enrollment in the United States: October 1973" (Advance report), Current Population Reports, Series P–20, No. 261, March 1974.

Table 90 —College enrollment of persons 14 to 34 years old,[1] by type of college and year of enrollment, October 1973

(Numbers in thousands)

College and year of enrollment	Total	Female	Male
ALL COLLEGES [2]			
Total [2]	8,179	3,502	4,677
First year	2,282	1,077	1,205
Second year	1,807	787	1,020
Third year	1,476	625	851
Fourth year	1,230	515	715
Fifth year or higher	1,384	498	886
2-YEAR COLLEGES			
Total	1,798	785	1,013
First year	929	452	477
Second year	743	285	458
Third year	126	48	78
4-YEAR INSTITUTIONS			
Total	6,160	2,610	3,551
First year	1,226	557	669
Second year	1,018	479	539
Third year	1,302	561	742
Fourth year	1,230	515	715
Fifth year or higher	1,384	498	886

[1] Civilian noninstitutional population.

[2] Includes enrollment not reported by type of college.

Source: U.S. Department of Commerce, Bureau of the Census: "School Enrollment in the United States: October 1973" (Advance report), Current Population Reports, P–20, No. 261, March 1974.

4-year institutions were taking courses creditable towards a bachelor's or higher degree.

About 32 percent of women college students were enrolled in 2-year institutions of higher education in the fall of 1973. The number of women in 2-year institutions in the fall of 1973 (1,365,019) was more than 4 times the enrollment in such schools in 1963. Nearly one-third of the women attending 2-year colleges were in occupational or general studies programs not chiefly creditable towards a bachelor's degree but which prepared them for technical, semiprofessional, craft, or clerical positions. The proportion of women in 2-year colleges who were in nondegree programs increased from about 21 percent in 1962 to more than 32 percent in 1972.

The growth in attendance in 2-year colleges can be attributed in part, to the increasing enrollment pressures in the last decade on all institutions of higher education. But there have been other factors which have influenced the faster growth in 2-year institutions. Two-year community colleges bring higher education within financial and commuting reach of many students who might not otherwise be able to attend college. Furthermore, 2-year colleges serve students who seek courses beyond the high school level which will prepare them for immediate employment. These colleges frequently offer educational facilities to adults who wish to improve or refresh their skills or expand their general education. Some States, by various means, are deliberately channeling students into public 2-year institutions because the expenditures per student are considerably less in community colleges than in large State universities or public 4-year colleges.

About 38 percent of all students enrolled in institutions of higher education in the fall of 1973 were attending school only part time. Among students attending part time, there was considerable difference between the proportion of those in 2-year institutions and those in 4-year institutions. Nearly 56 percent of students at 2-year institutions were part time, compared with about 30 percent of those at 4-year colleges. Similarly, a much higher percentage of students in nondegree programs were attending school part time as compared with students in degree credit programs.

About 78 percent of all college students were attending public-supported colleges in the fall of 1973. Nearly 95 percent of students in 2-year institutions were attending public colleges, whereas about 70 percent in 4-year institutions were in such schools.

There were about 943,000 graduate students attending college in the United States in the fall of 1972; 372,000, or 39 percent of them were women. Of all women attending 4-year colleges, about 13 percent were graduate students.

Women earning degrees

In the 1972–73 school year, women earned nearly 529,300 bachelor's or higher level degrees from U.S. colleges and universities. About 415,000 of these degrees (78 percent) were bachelor's; 104,400 (20 percent), master's; 4,200 (0.8 percent), first professional; and 5,700 (1.1 percent), doctor's, except first professional. The number of degrees earned by women increased greatly in the 1962–63 to 1972–73 decade. The number of bachelor's degrees earned in 1972–73 was nearly 2.5 times that in 1962–63, and the number of master's degrees earned by women was more than 3 times as great in 1972–73 as in 1962–63.

Fields of study in which women earned degrees
Although women earn degrees in a broad and varied range of subjects, most of the degrees received by women are concentrated in a very limited number of fields of study. The field of education alone accounted for 36 percent of the bachelor's degrees earned by women in the 1970–71 school year and for 54 percent of the master's degrees.

Degrees below bachelor's level.   Of the associate degrees and other awards granted in 1970–71, about 154,000 were in occupational curriculums at the technical or semiprofessional level. Women received about 70,000, or 46 percent, of these degrees or awards. Most of the degrees or awards made to women were in the health or medical fields (for example, registered nurse, practical nurse, dental hygienist, dental assistant); business and commerce (secretarial technology and market-ing); and data processing and public service fields.

Bachelor's degrees.   More than 132,000 women received bachelor's degrees in education in the 1970–71 school year (see table 91). The number of women receiving bachelor's degrees in education has in-creased from about 87,000 in the 1965–66 school year and from about 70,000 in the 1961–62 school year. However, as a percentage of all bachelor's degrees conferred on women, those earned in the field of education decreased from more than 45 percent in 1961–62 and from 39 percent in 1965–66 to 36 percent in the 1970–71 school year. Women received about three-fourths of all bachelor's degrees in education awarded in 1970–71. Most of the bachelor's degrees earned by women (nearly 83,000) were in elementary education.

The second largest number of bachelor's degrees conferred on women was in the social sciences—mainly in sociology and history. The number of bachelor's degrees obtained by women in this field increased

Table 91 —Earned bachelor's degrees conferred on women, by selected fields of study, 1961–62, 1965–66, and 1970–71

| Field of study | 1970–71 | | | 1965–66 | 1961–62 [1] |
	Number	Percent distri-bution	As percent of all bachelor's degrees conferred	Number	Number
All fields _____	367,687	100.0	43.5	221,052	154,009
Agriculture and natural resources _____	539	.1	4.2	160	95
Architecture and environ-mental design _____	667	.2	12.0	102	55
Biological sciences _____	10,571	2.9	29.3	7,535	4,779
Business and management ____	10,803	2.9	9.3	5,263	3,903
Communications _____	3,813	1.0	35.3	1,221	826
Computer and information sciences _____	324	.1	13.6	1	--
Education _____	132,236	36.0	74.4	86,694	70,101
Engineering _____	403	.1	.8	166	131
Fine and applied arts _____	18,169	4.9	59.7	10,746	7,566
Foreign languages _____	15,285	4.2	74.8	10,747	5,188
Health professions _____	19,680	5.4	77.2	11,693	8,871
Letters _____	44,782	12.2	61.0	28,740	17,481
Library sciences _____	932	.3	92.0	589	338
Mathematics and statistics ____	9,494	2.6	38.1	6,651	4,239
Physical sciences _____	3,014	.8	14.0	2,307	2,123
Psychology _____	17,037	4.6	44.7	6,842	3,780
Public affairs and services ____	4,566	1.2	49.1	1,218	443
Social sciences _____	57,918	15.8	37.0	31,512	17,323
Others [2] _____	17,454	4.7	53.7	8,865	6,764

[1] Not comparable with data for later years. Prior to 1965–66, bachelor's degrees were de-fined as those which required 4 but less than 5 years of college education. In 1966 bachelor's degrees were redefined to include those requiring 4 or 5 years of college.

[2] Includes home economics, military sciences, theology, interdisciplinary studies, and area studies.

Source: U.S. Department of Health, Education, and Welfare, National Center for Educational Statistics.

sharply in recent years from about 17,000 in 1961–62 and about 32,000 in 1965–66 to nearly 58,000 in 1970–71. Social science accounted for nearly 16 percent of all bachelor's degrees conferred on women in 1970 compared with 11 percent of all bachelor's degrees conferred on women in 1970 compared with 11 percent in 1961–62 and 14 percent in 1965–66. In 1970–71 nearly 45,000 women received bachelor's degrees in letters (principally English), nearly 20,000 in nursing and other health professions, 18,000 in fine and applied arts, 17,000 in psychology, 15,000 in foreign languages, nearly 11,000 each in business management and biological sciences, and more than 9,000 in mathematics and statistics. A particularly rapid growth in the number of bachelor's degrees received by women between 1961–62 and 1970–71 was in some of the smaller fields in which women majored. The number receiving degrees in communications increased from about 800 to about 3,800, and the number in public affairs and services grew from 443 to nearly 4,600.

Master's degrees.   Master's degrees earned by women in 1970–71 were even more concentrated in the field of education than were bachelor's degrees—56 percent compared with 36 percent (see table 92). Women who have majored in another field of study at the undergraduate level often obtain their master's degree in education in order to qualify for teaching jobs in secondary schools.

   Other than education, the largest proportion of master's degrees conferred on women was in letters, primarily English and speech (7.9 percent), library sciences (6.1 percent), social sciences (5.1 percent), and public affairs and services (4.4 percent). Women received about 40 percent of all master's degrees. By field, they received 81 percent of those in library sciences, 65 percent of those in foreign languages, 58 percent of those in letters, and 56 percent of those in education. In contrast, women received less than 4 percent of all master's degrees awarded in business and management, 13 percent of those in the physical sciences, 28 percent of those in social sciences, and 29 percent in mathematics and statistics.

Doctor's degrees (except first professional).   Compared with bachelor's or master's degrees, a smaller percentage of doctor's degrees awarded to women in 1970–71 was in education. Of all doctor's degrees earned by women, less than 30 percent were in education (see table 93). About 13 percent were in the biological sciences, 12 percent in letters, 11 percent in the social sciences, 9 percent in psychology, and nearly 7 percent in foreign languages. Although women earned only 14 percent of all doctor's degrees conferred in 1970–71, their share in some fields was considerably larger—38 percent in foreign languages, 24 percent in psychology, 24 percent in letters, 22 percent in fine and applied arts, and 21 percent in education. On the other hand, women accounted for less than 1 percent of all doctor's degrees awarded in engineering, 3 percent of those in business and management, 3 percent of those in agriculture and natural resources, and 6 percent of those in physical sciences.

First professional degrees.   In the 1970–71 school year, more than 2,400 women received first professional degrees (see table 94). This was more than double the number in 1965–66 and more than 3 times the

Table 92 —Earned master's degrees conferred on women, by selected fields of study, 1961–62, 1965–66, and 1970–71

| Field of study | 1970–71 | | | 1965–66 | 1961–62 [1] |
	Number	Percent distribution	As percent of all master's degrees conferred	Number	Number
All fields _____	92,896	100.0	40.1	47,485	28,704
Agriculture and natural resources _____	144	.2	5.9	82	41
Architecture and environmental design _____	243	.3	14.1	41	15
Biological sciences _____	1,943	2.1	33.8	1,148	660
Business and management ____	1,045	1.1	3.9	336	180
Communications _____	642	.7	34.6	128	54
Computer and information sciences _____	164	.2	10.3	15	--
Education _____	50,020	53.8	56.2	24,198	15,952
Engineering _____	185	.2	1.1	76	40
Fine and applied arts _____	3,165	3.4	47.4	2,259	1,293
Foreign languages _____	3,126	3.4	65.4	1,957	768
Health professions _____	3,272	3.5	55.4	1,249	667
Letters _____	7,328	7.9	57.5	4,182	2,100
Library sciences _____	5,713	6.1	81.3	2,914	1,707
Mathematics and statistics ____	1,524	1.6	29.3	1,000	501
Physical sciences _____	853	.9	13.4	515	370
Psychology _____	1,651	1.8	37.2	798	563
Public affairs and services ____	4,099	4.4	48.8	2,331	1,435
Social sciences _____	4,710	5.1	28.5	2,761	1,497
Others [2] _____	3,069	3.3	39.1	1,495	861

[1] Not comparable with data for later years. Certain degrees such as master of library science and master of social work were classified as first professional in 1961–62 but were reclassified as master's degrees in 1966.

[2] Includes home economics, military sciences, theology, interdisciplinary studies and area studies.

Source: U.S. Department of Health, Education, and Welfare, National Center for Educational Statistics.

number in 1961–62. Despite this increase, women earned only 6.3 percent of all first professional degrees awarded in 1970–71. More than half of the first professional degrees earned by women were in law. The number of women receiving law degrees increased from 273 in 1961–62 and 470 in 1965–66 to 1,240 in 1970–71. Nevertheless, women received only about 7 percent of the law degrees awarded in 1970–71. Most of the other first professional degrees conferred other than law were in medicine. About 9 percent of all degrees in medicine awarded in 1970–71 went to women.

Enrollment data of the last few years would indicate that the number of women receiving degrees in law and medicine can be expected to increase greatly. Enrollment of women in law schools increased dramatically from 1,883 (3.8 percent of total enrollment) in 1963, and 3,704 (5.9 percent of total enrollment) in 1968, to 16,760 (15.8 percent of total enrollment) in 1973. The first-year enrollment of women in law schools increased from 3,542 in the fall of 1970 to 7,464 in the fall of 1973.

Table 93 —Earned doctor's degrees[1] conferred on women, by selected fields of study, 1961–62, 1965–66, and 1970–71

| Field of study | 1970–71 | | | 1965–66 | Number |
	Number	Percent distribution	As percent of all doctor's degrees conferred	Number	1961–62 [1]
All fields	4,579	100.0	14.3	2,116	1,245
Agriculture and natural resources	31	.7	2.9	9	3
Architecture and environmental design	3	.1	8.3	1	--
Biological sciences	595	13.0	16.3	305	159
Business and management	23	.5	2.8	17	5
Communications	19	.4	13.1	3	--
Computer and information sciences	3	.1	2.3	--	--
Education	1,355	29.6	21.2	596	359
Engineering	23	.5	.6	9	4
Fine and applied arts	138	3.0	22.2	80	54
Foreign languages	297	6.5	38.0	123	65
Health professions	77	1.7	16.5	26	9
Letters	567	12.4	23.5	225	119
Library sciences	11	.2	28.2	5	3
Mathematics and statistics	93	2.0	7.8	57	24
Physical sciences	246	5.4	5.6	131	87
Psychology	427	9.3	24.0	217	149
Public affairs and services	43	.9	24.2	32	16
Social sciences	507	11.1	13.9	211	128
Others [2]	121	2.6	17.4	69	61

[1] Except first professional.

[2] Includes home economics, military sciences, theology, interdisciplinary studies, and area studies.

Women were 10 percent of first-year students in fall 1970 and 20 percent in fall 1973.

Enrollment of women in medical schools also increased greatly. For example, there were 2,786 women first-year students in U.S. medical schools, and they represented 19.7 percent of all first-year students in the 1973–74 school year. In contrast, in the 1969–70 school year, there were only 948 women first-year students in U.S. medical schools, and they accounted for only 9.1 percent of all first-year students. The 7,824 women enrolled in medical schools at every level in the 1973–74 school year represented 15.4 percent of total enrollment. This compares with a female enrollment of 3,392 in the 1969–70 school year (9 percent of total enrollment), and female enrollment of 2,244 in the 1963–64 school year (7 percent of total enrollment).

Women returning to school

One of every 50 women and men age 35 and over were attending school in October 1972 in order to earn a degree or to train for an occupation (see table 95). Many were studying to keep up with new developments in their chosen field or to obtain the credentials necessary to enter a

Table 94 — Earned first professional degrees conferred on women, by selected field of study, 1961–62, 1965–66, and 1970–71

| Field of study | 1970–71 | | | 1965–66 | 1961–62 [1] |
	Number	Percent distribution	As percent of all first professional degrees conferred	Number	Number
All fields _____	2,402	100.0	6.3	1,142	771
Medicine [2] _____	809	33.7	9.1	503	389
Dentistry [3] _____	42	1.7	1.1	33	17
Other health professions [4] __	127	5.3	5.1	62	31
Law [5] _____	1,240	51.6	7.1	470	273
Theology and others [6] _____	184	7.7	3.4	74	61

[1] First professional degrees include professional degrees requiring 5 years or more of higher education. In 1966 they were redefined to include only professional degrees requiring 6 years or more of higher education. Master of library science and master of social work, included as first professional degrees from 1961 to 1965, were reclassified as master's degrees in 1966.

[2] M.D. degrees only.

[3] D.D.S. or D.M.D. degrees.

[4] Includes degrees in chiropody or podiatry, optometry, osteopathy, and veterinary medicine.

[5] LL.B. or J.D. degrees.

[6] In 1971 theological professions made up 94 percent of this category.

Source: U.S. Department of Health, Education, and Welfare, National Center for Educational Statistics.

different line of work. Some were housewives taking college courses to obtain undergraduate or graduate degrees before reentering the labor market. Others were workers seeking high school diplomas or college degrees in response to rising employer requirements for hiring and promotion.

College attendance. About 788,000 adults 35 years of age and over were in college either as undergraduate or as graduate students in October 1972. Over half of these adults (53 percent) were women (in contrast, among college students under age 35, only 42 percent were women). About 12 percent of the college students 35 or over were persons of minority races; about the same proportion as among college students under 35.

Table 95 — Type of school attended by persons 35 years old and over, by sex and race, October 1972

| Sex and race | Total | | Elementary and high school | College | | Trade or vocational school |
	Number (in thousands)	Percent		Full time	Part time	
Both sexes ____	1,458	100.0	6.9	9.1	45.0	39.1
Women _____	748	100.0	7.4	7.4	48.8	36.5
Men _____	710	100.0	6.3	10.8	41.0	41.8
White _____	1,289	100.0	5.0	8.4	45.7	40.9
Minority races ____	169	100.0	20.7	14.2	39.6	25.4

The overwhelming majority of women age 35 and over who were attending college in October 1972 were going to school part time. Nearly 3 out of 4 of these part-time women students were working or seeking work—a proportion much higher than for women in the same age group who were not in school. Nearly 7 out of 10 of all women college students age 35 and over were married, and nearly all of these women were in school part time. Even though they had home responsibilities, the great majority of these married women students were in the labor force in October 1972.

Elementary and secondary school attendance.   About 100,000 persons age 35 and over were in elementary or high school in October 1972. Slightly more than half were women. Some of these persons may have needed educational credentials in order to get a job or to advance in their present job. Others may have had personal reasons for returning to school—perhaps to communicate better with their children or to satisfy a long-delayed ambition to finish school.

These adults were enrolled in basic education classes at the elementary school level or in general education classes which prepare for the high school equivalency examination. As many were age 45 and over as were 35 to 39 years old. Six out of 10 of all women students enrolled in elementary or high school classes were working or seeking work.

Trade or vocational school attendance.   About 39 percent (570,000) of all persons age 35 and over who were attending school in October 1972 were in trade or vocational schools. Women and men were enrolled in these schools in about equal numbers. More than half of the women were in the labor force. These schools may or may not require a high school diploma for entrance and they vary greatly in the kind of training offered and in hours of instruction. Such schools provide instruction in a wide range of skills, including secretarial training, bookkeeping, practical nursing, cosmetology, barbering, auto mechanics, electronics, and truck driving.

Adults in trade or vocational schools tended to be older than those in regular schools: about 45 percent of those in such schools were age 45 or over; about 34 percent of those in regular schools were in this age group. Older workers may be more interested in going to trade or vocational schools to learn a specific skill rather than investing several years to obtain more generalized training in college.

Women in trade or vocational schools were less likely to be working or seeking work while attending school than were women in college. This partly because women who enter trade or vocational school may have had fewer years of schooling than women who enter or return to college, and labor force rates tend to be directly related to years of schooling.

8 Future prospects for women workers

Outlook for women workers[*]

Overview

A number of factors will significantly affect the outlook for women workers in the next decade. Changes in general economic conditions are extremely important factors in determining the immediate job prospects for women as well as men. This chapter, however, deals primarily with long-term factors which affect both the supply and the demand for women workers.

In terms of supply, there are expected to be many more women participating in the labor force—8 million more in 1985 than in 1972. Another factor is that the age composition of women workers will be changing. The Bureau of Labor Statistics (BLS) projections of labor force growth for the 1972–85 period indicate that the major increase in the female labor force is expected to occur among women 20 to 34 years of age. The number of women workers under 20 is expected to decline during this period.

Women in the labor force in 1985 will have had more years of schooling. In 1972 less than 70 percent of the women workers had completed at least 4 years of high school. By 1985 the proportion is expected to be nearly 78 percent. The outlook for the supply of women workers at opposite extremes of the educational ladder is particularly significant. Between March 1972 and 1985, the number of women workers with 8 years or less of education is projected to decline by about 3.6 percent a year on the average, while the number of women college graduates rises on the average of 4.7 percent a year.

In terms of overall demand for workers by occupation, most long-term trends in the employment by occupation groups are expected to continue during the period until 1985. White-collar jobs in which most women are currently employed will increase as a proportion of total employment from 47.8 percent to 52.9 percent in the 1972–85 period. Service workers, other than in private households, another large area of employment for women workers, will also show a significant rise. Each of the blue-collar occupation groups is expected to grow but will decline as a proportion of total employment. The number of farm workers is expected to decline by nearly 50 percent and private household workers by about 30 percent.

The large increase in the supply of women college graduates in the labor force will coincide with an expected slowdown in the growth in demand for elementary and secondary school teachers, occupations in which a large proportion of college women have been employed in the past. The absorption of increasing numbers of college-educated women into the labor force might, therefore, require a movement of these women into traditionally male-dominated professional, technical, and managerial occupations, and/or into occupations which are not now generally filled by college graduates.

---

[*]Handbook for Women Workers, U.S. Department of Labor, Women's Bureau.

Projections of the labor force

The total labor force in the United States is projected to increase by 13 million between 1972 and 1980—from about 89 to about 102 million. Between 1980 and 1985, a further increase of almost 6 million is expected to bring the labor force to just under 108 million (see table 99 and chart V).

The labor force projections reveal a major shift in the distribution of the entire labor force by age. The postwar "baby boom" which swelled the ranks of teenage workers during the late 1960's will manifest itself in the ranks of workers 20 to 35 years of age between 1972 and 1985. This shift can be illustrated by the ratio of workers (both sexes) between 20 and 34 years of age to those between 35 and 54. In 1960 the ratio was .72; by 1972, it had risen to .96; by 1980, it is expected to rise to 1.20; and by 1985, it should decline moderately to 1.13.

The labor force is expected to grow at a faster rate in the middle and late 1970's than in the 1980–85 period. Between 1972 and 1980, the labor force is expected to increase at an average annual rate of 1.7 percent; between 1980 and 1985, it is expected to grow by about 1.1 percent a year. The two periods will also show a difference in the age composition of the labor force. Over three-fourths of the projected 1972–80 labor force growth is expected to occur among the group 20 to 34 years old. This group will grow from 36.5 percent of the labor force in 1972 to 41.5 percent by 1980. In absolute numbers, the group will rise by nearly 10 million, and half of the increase in this age group will be women. The age groups 35 to 54 and 55 and over will also grow, though more moderately. By contrast, the number of teenage workers (16 to 19)—whose massive growth between 1960 and 1972 helped to create problems of jobs for youth—will actually decline in the 1972–80 period.

The relative labor force growth of men and women will change significantly. During the 1960–72 period, women made up 60 percent of the net increase in the labor force. Between 1972 and 1980, they are projected to account for only 46 percent of the net growth. The BLS projections indicate that the proportion of women workers in the labor force is expected to continue to rise, but at a much more moderate pace than during the 1960–72 period. In that period, the proportion of women increased from 32.3 to 37.4 percent. By the end of 1974 the proportion had risen to 39.1 percent. Little change is projected in the 1980–85 period. The BLS attributes the anticipated slowdown to (1) the increase in the woman population to 1980 being concentrated in the 25- to 34-year-old group, which has a lower labor force participation rate than the groups (under 25 and 35 to 54), which grew most rapidly in the 1960's, and (2) the assumed halt in the decline of women's fertility rates, which implies that increased labor force participation attributable to declining fertility will not be as evident over the coming years.

Between 1980 and 1985, not only will the labor force as a whole grow at a slower rate than in the 1972–80 period, but growth patterns will change. The "baby boom" group, which will cause those 20 to 34 years old to lead labor force growth in the 1972–80 period, will shift into the 35 to 54 age group during 1980–85. Nearly three-fourths of the projected growth in the labor force during the 1980–85 period is expected to occur in this group—some 4.3 million of the net gain of 5.9 million workers. By contrast, the size of the teenage labor force is pro-

Table 99 — Total labor force, by age and sex, annual average 1960, 1972, and projected to 1980 and 1985

Sex and age	Number (in thousands)				Percent distribution			
	1960	1972	1980	1985	1960	1972	1980	1985
BOTH SEXES								
Total, 16 years and over	72,142	88,991	101,809	107,716	100.0	100.0	100.0	100.0
16 to 19 years	5,246	8,367	8,337	7,165	7.3	9.4	8.2	6.7
20 to 34 years	22,749	32,463	42,223	44,758	31.5	36.5	41.5	41.6
35 to 54 years	31,562	33,689	35,165	39,463	43.7	37.9	34.5	36.6
55 years and over	12,585	14,472	16,084	16,330	17.4	16.3	15.8	15.2
Median age in years	39.8	37.2	35.2	35.8	—	—	—	—
MEN								
Total, 16 years and over	48,870	55,671	62,590	66,017	67.7	62.6	61.5	61.3
16 to 19 years	3,184	4,791	4,668	3,962	4.4	5.4	4.6	3.7
20 to 34 years	16,019	20,601	26,375	27,896	22.2	23.1	25.9	25.9
35 to 54 years	20,974	21,116	21,759	24,361	29.1	23.7	21.4	22.6
55 years and over	8,692	9,163	9,788	9,798	12.0	10.3	9.6	9.1
WOMEN								
Total, 16 years and over	23,272	33,320	39,219	41,699	32.3	37.4	38.5	38.7
16 to 19 years	2,062	3,576	3,669	3,203	2.8	4.0	3.6	3.0
20 to 34 years	6,730	11,862	15,848	16,862	9.3	13.3	15.6	15.7
35 to 54 years	10,588	12,573	13,406	15,102	14.7	14.1	13.2	14.0
55 years and over	3,893	5,309	6,296	6,532	5.4	6.0	6.2	6.1

Source: For 1960 and 1972, U.S. Department of Labor, 1973 Manpower Report of the President, Table A–2; for 1980 and 1985, "The U.S. Labor Force: Projections to 1990," Monthly Labor Review, July 1973.

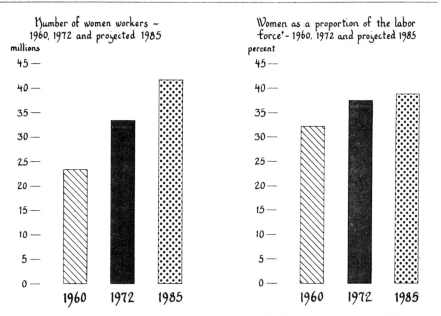

Chart V —The number of women workers and their proportion of the labor force will continue to grow

Number of women workers –
1960, 1972 and projected 1985
millions

Women as a proportion of the labor force† – 1960, 1972 and projected 1985
percent

1960   1972   1985

1960   1972   1985

Source: U.S. Department of Labor, Bureau of Labor Statistics.

† Total labor force including Armed Forces.

jected to fall steadily by about 240,000 a year, reaching 7.2 million in 1985. The young adult labor force (20 to 34) is expected to increase by only 500,000 a year in contrast to 1.2 million a year during the 1972–80 period. Finally, the number of older workers is expected to rise very slowly during this period. This is because the steady increase in the size of the older population will be counterbalanced by the expected continuation of the decline in the labor force participation rate of older persons. Women will account for about 42 percent of the net growth in the labor force in the 1980–85 period, compared with about 46 percent in the 1972–80 period.

Projected education of workers

The educational attainment of the labor force is expected to rise significantly (see chart W). In March 1972, two-thirds of the people 16 years old and over in the civilian labor force had completed at least 4 years of high school, and nearly 1 worker in 7 had completed at least 4 years of college. According to the latest projection, over 3 out of 4 persons in the civilian labor force will be high school graduates by 1985. At that time nearly 1 worker in 5 will have completed 4 years of college or more.

When fewer women were in the labor force, their educational attainment was, on the average, considerably higher than that of men. However, as more women have entered the labor force, the educational distribution of women workers has become more similar to that of working men, since more women with only average amounts of schooling

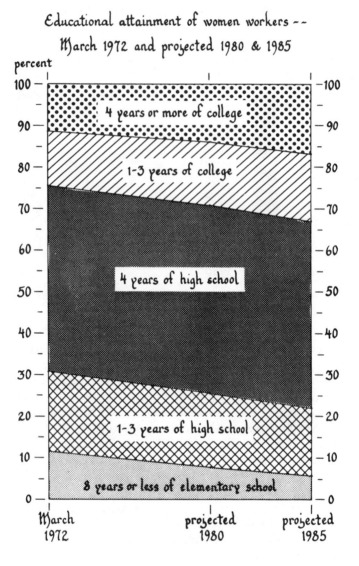

Chart IV —Women workers in the future will have more education

Educational attainment of women workers --
March 1972 and projected 1980 & 1985

percent

4 years or more of college

1-3 years of college

4 years of high school

1-3 years of high school

8 years or less of elementary school

March
1972

projected
1980

projected
1985

Source: U.S. Department of Labor, Bureau of Labor Statistics.

have been drawn into the labor force. For example, in March 1962 almost three-fifths of women workers had completed 4 years of high school or more compared with roughly half of working men. By March 1972 almost seven-tenths of women workers had that much schooling compared with well over three-fifths of male workers. This covergence is expected to continue; between March 1972 and 1985, the proportion of high school graduates among working men is projected to increase until it almost matches the proportion of women graduates—76.5 percent compared with 77.8 percent.

The supply of workers at opposite ends of the educational ladder will have very different growth patterns. The proportion of workers (both sexes) with 8 years or less of formal schooling is projected to decline rapidly by about 3.6 percent a year and from about 1 worker in 7 in March 1972 to about 1 in 13 by 1985. Numerically, they would drop from about 12.8 million in 1972 down to 7.9 million in 1985. In contrast, the number of workers with 4 years of college or more is projected to increase from 11.6 million in 1972 to 20.3 million in 1985 (about 4.2 percent a year) and will account for nearly 1 in 5 workers in the 1985 labor force.

Even though the average educational attainment of women and men is becoming more similar, there are still expected to be differences, especially at both ends of the educational spectrum. The proportion of male workers in both the highest and lowest educational levels will be greater than the corresponding proportion for female workers. The proportion of all male workers who will have 4 or more years of college in 1985 is expected to be higher than that for female workers—20.8 percent versus 16.7 percent. However, a greater proportion of men than women will have 8 or fewer years of school—8.6 versus 5.8 percent.

The supply of college graduates in the Nation's labor force is projected to increase at over 2.5 times the rate of increase of the labor force as a whole. This rapid buildup, it should be noted, is not a new phenomenon. A similar disparity between the growing supply of the college-educated and the growth of the labor force as a whole has been characteristic of the entire postwar period. Nevertheless, the expected continuation of this disparity suggests either the need for continued rapid expansion in the kinds of careers for which highly educated workers are qualified or the entry of many college-educated workers into occupations which did not formerly attract many college graduates. There may be special concern for women college graduates whose numbers are projected to grow by about 4.7 percent a year, on the average, to 1985, compared with 4.0 percent for male college graduates. The problem is made more difficult by the slowing down in the rate of increase in demand for elementary and secondary school teachers—occupations which employ a large proportion of college-educated women.

Projected employment by industry

Projection of employment by major industry sectors made by BLS indicates continuation of employment shifts taking place for most of the postwar period. Changes tend to be in degree rather than direction, with a few notable exceptions.

Between 1972 and 1985, total employment (by job count) is expected to rise by about 22 million. Employment growth is expected to average about 2.2 million a year through 1980 and about 1.2 million a year between 1980 and 1985. When industries are classified as either goods-producing or service-producing, one can see that the Nation's economy is becoming increasingly service oriented. Service-producing industries (communication and utilities; trade; finance, insurance, and real estate;

transportation; other services; and government) will account for 71 percent of projected employment in 1985. The proportion in 1972 was 68 percent; in 1960, 61 percent; and in 1955, 57 percent. Higher proportions of women are employed in these types of industries than in goods-producing. Looking at the situation in another way, it is rather significant to observe that by 1985, less than 3 out of 10 jobs will be in goods-producing industries (manufacturing, construction, mining, and agriculture), where a smaller proportion of women are employed (see table 100).

Among goods-producing industries, employment in agriculture is expected to continue its long-term decline, dropping below 2 million in 1985. Even though the growth in manufacturing employment is projected at about 1.5 percent a year, because of the size of the sector, employment in 1985 is projected to be more than 4 million greater than in 1972. Employment in construction is expected to grow by about 800,000, and in mining it is expected to stabilize after several years of steady decline, primarily because of the resurgence of coal as an energy source.

Among the service-producing industries, government employment is expected to increase by over 5 million in the 1972–85 period. Despite this substantial growth, the rate of increase in government employment is projected to slow down. This is due primarily to the reduction in the growth of employment in public education, where about half of all State

Table 100 —Total employment,[1] by major sector, 1972 and projected to 1980 and 1985

(Numbers in thousands)

Sector	Actual 1972	Projected 1980	Projected 1985
All sectors	85,597	101,576	107,609
Government	13,290	16,610	18,800
Private	72,307	84,966	88,809
Agriculture	3,450	2,300	1,900
Nonagriculture	68,857	82,666	86,909
Mining	645	655	632
Construction	4,352	4,908	5,184
Manufacturing	19,281	22,923	23,499
Durable	11,091	13,629	14,154
Nondurable	8,190	9,294	9,345
Transportation, communication, and public utilities	4,726	5,321	5,368
Transportation	2,842	3,250	3,266
Communication	1,150	1,300	1,312
Public utilities	724	771	790
Trade	18,432	21,695	22,381
Wholesale trade	4,235	4,946	5,123
Retail trade	14,197	16,749	17,258
Finance, insurance, and real estate	4,303	5,349	5,932
Other services [2]	17,815	21,815	23,913

[1] Employment is on a jobs concept and includes wage and salary workers, the self-employed, and unpaid family workers. Persons holding more than one job are counted in each job held.

[2] Includes paid household employment.

Source: U.S. Department of Labor, Bureau of Labor Statistics: Monthly Labor Review, December 1973.

and local government jobs are found. Nearly all the growth in government employment will be at the State and local levels. Federal employment is projected to increase at a relatively slow rate over the 1972–85 period. The largest expansion in employment among industry divisions will be in the other services sector, where employment is expected to grow by 7 million during the 1972–85 period. By 1985 this sector will have over 22 percent of total employment. Especially fast growth will occur in the business, professional, and medical services industries.

Retail trade employment is expected to increase by about 3 million during the 1972–85 period, but there will be substantially slower growth in this sector between 1980 and 1985 than during the 1970's. Retail trade has been a job source for many, particularly for women seeking only part-time employment. As this sector slows somewhat more than the economy in the 1980's, job entrants may have to seek part-time jobs or employment in other sectors of the economy, or they may not be in the labor force at all if they are interested only in part-time work.

Projected change in employment by type of work

Most long-term trends in the employment of white-collar, blue-collar, service, and farm workers are expected to continue during the next decade, but some important changes will occur in the mix of occupations within these broad categories, according to BLS projections of the U.S. economy to 1985. Technological changes will cause employment to increase in some occupations and to decrease in others. The spread of the computer will continue to be a notable example of this. Also, differences in industrial growth will boost some occupations (for example, those in the health field), while others will grow more slowly than in the recent past (the educational field), and still others will continue to decline relatively (mining jobs).

Total occupational employment is expected to increase by nearly one-fourth between 1972 and 1985, rising from almost 82 million to more than 101 million. White-collar jobs, in which most women are employed, will rise by nearly 15 million (37 percent) in the 1972–85 period and will increase as a proportion of total employment from less than 48 percent to nearly 53 percent. Blue-collar employment will increase by more than 4 million (15 percent) during the period, but the rate of increase will be less than that for total employment. The service worker group, other than private household, in which women outnumber men, is projected to increase at a faster rate than total employment. However, private household workers are expected to decline by about 23 percent over the period, and farm workers, by about 48 percent (see tables 101 and 102).

Occupational growth and replacement needs

Occupational employment opportunities depend upon two principal factors. One is growth in size of the occupation. The other is the necessity of replacing workers who retire or die or leave the labor force for other reasons. Over the 1972–85 period, about twice as many openings will result from replacements as from growth. Over 61 million openings will occur due to occupational growth and replacement needs during 1972–85, an average of about 4.7 million jobs annually. Of these, re-

Table 101 —Employment by major occupation group, 1960, and 1972, and projected 1980 and 1985

(Numbers in thousands)

Occupation group	1960 [1]	1972	1980	1985
Total	65,778	81,703	95,800	101,500
White-collar workers	28,351	39,092	49,400	53,700
Professional, technical workers	7,236	11,459	15,000	17,000
Managers, administrators	7,367	8,032	10,100	10,500
Sales workers	4,210	5,354	6,300	6,500
Clerical workers	9,538	14,247	17,900	19,700
Blue-collar workers	23,877	28,576	31,700	32,800
Craft and kindred workers	8,748	10,810	12,200	13,000
Operatives [2]	11,380	13,549	15,000	15,300
Nonfarm laborers	3,749	4,217	4,500	4,500
Service workers	8,354	10,966	12,700	13,400
Private household workers	1,965	1,437	1,300	1,100
Other service workers	6,387	9,529	11,400	12,300
Farm workers	5,196	3,069	2,000	1,600

[1] Data for 1960 were adjusted to reflect the occupational classification in the 1970 census to make it comparable to the 1972 and projected 1980 and 1985 data.

[2] Includes the 1970 census classification "operatives except transport and transport equipment operatives."

Source: U.S. Department of Labor, Bureau of Labor Statistics: Monthly Labor Review, December, 1973.

placement needs will account for 2 out of 3 job openings (see table 103). Replacement needs will be the most significant source of job openings in each of the major occupation areas—white-collar, blue-collar, service, and farm. However, in individual occupations expected to increase rapidly, growth requirements are likely to exceed those for replacement. On the other hand, replacement needs are likely to exceed the average in those occupations that (a) employ many young women who may leave the labor force to assume family responsibilties, and (b) have a large proportion of older workers who have relatively few years of working life remaining.

Projected employment by occupation group
The projections of employment presented later and on chart X are based on requirements by occupation for persons regardless of sex. It is difficult to project the relative outlook for women compared with men in the same fields. Some clues are available that might indicate the degree of future penetration by women into fields previously dominated by men. These include recent trends in the proportion of new entrants into individual fields, and data on enrollment of women in education and training programs (for example, enrollments in medical and law schools and in apprenticeship programs for craft work). However, it is difficult to assess the effectiveness of antidiscrimination laws and government policy (including affirmative action programs) in opening up or increas-

Table 102 — Percent distribution of employment by major occupation group, 1960 and 1972, and projected to 1980 and 1985

Occupation group	1960 [1]	1972	1980	1985
Total	100.0	100.0	100.0	100.0
White-collar workers	43.1	47.8	51.5	52.9
Professional, technical workers	11.0	14.0	15.7	16.8
Managers, administrators	11.2	9.8	10.5	10.3
Sales workers	6.4	6.6	6.6	6.4
Clerical workers	14.5	17.4	18.7	19.4
Blue-collar workers	36.3	35.0	33.1	32.3
Craft and kindred workers	13.3	13.2	12.8	12.8
Operatives [2]	17.3	16.6	15.6	15.1
Nonfarm laborers	5.7	5.2	4.7	4.4
Service workers	12.7	13.4	13.3	13.2
Private household workers	3.0	1.8	1.3	1.1
Other service workers	9.7	11.6	12.0	12.9
Farm workers	7.9	3.8	2.1	1.6

[1] Data for 1960 were adjusted to reflect the occupational classification in the 1970 census to make it comparable to the 1972 and projected 1980 and 1985 data.

[2] Includes the 1970 census classification "operatives except transport and transport equipment operatives."

Source: U.S. Department of Labor, Bureau of Labor Statistics: Monthly Labor Review, December 1973.

ing women's participation in some fields. Moreover, the changing pattern of labor force participation of women (especially the growing percentage of mothers of small children who continue to work) is resulting in less interruption of women's work careers.

These factors will affect the attitudes of some employers with respect to selecting or promoting women for responsible positions. They might also affect the attitude of women themselves regarding their decision to enter or remain in the labor force, the kinds of jobs they aspire to, and the amount of investment in education and training they are willing to make.

Professional and technical workers. This occupation group in which 41.6 percent of the workers were women in April 1974 will continue to be the fastest growing major occupation group; employment is projected to increase from about 11.5 million workers in 1972 to about 17 million in 1985. This is about 1.5 times the annual rate of employment increase projected for all occupations combined. Despite this, the projected 1972–85 growth is slower than it was between 1960 and 1972. A major reason for this is the expected slowdown in the growth of jobs for secondary and elementary school teachers and engineers (which together accounted for more than one-fourth of all professional workers in 1972). The growth in the number of teaching positions, which greatly affects employment opportunities for women college graduates, will slow down as the increase in the number of pupils slows. The rate of increase

Table 103 —Job openings[1] by major occupation group, 1972–85

(Numbers in thousands)

Occupation group	Total	Growth	Replacement
Total ---------------------------	61,200	19,800	41,400
White-collar workers ------------------	38,800	14,600	24,200
Professional, technical workers ------	12,000	5,600	6,400
Managers, administrators ----------	5,900	2,400	3,500
Sales workers ---------------------	3,800	1,100	2,700
Clerical workers -------------------	17,000	5,400	11,600
Blue-collar workers ------------------	13,800	4,200	9,600
Craft and kindred workers ----------	5,300	2,200	3,100
Operatives[2] ---------------------	7,200	1,800	5,500
Nonfarm laborers ------------------	1,300	200	1,000
Service workers ---------------------	8,500	2,400	6,000
Private household workers ----------	700	−400	1,100
Other service workers --------------	7,800	2,800	4,900
Farm workers ---------------------	50	−1,400	1,400

[1] Resulting from occupational growth and replacement of workers who leave the labor force.

[2] Includes 1970 census classification "operatives except transport and transport equipment operatives."

Note.—Details may not add to totals because of rounding.

Source: U.S. Department of Labor, Bureau of Labor Statistics: Monthly Labor Review, December 1973.

in engineering jobs, which was rapid in the 1960's largely as a result of expanded space exploration and increased research and development, will be reduced because these activities are not expected to have a comparable effect through the mid-1980's. A small but growing number of women are employed as engineers.

Growth in demand for goods and services, resulting from population growth and rising business and personal incomes, will continue to be a major reason underlying job growth among these highly trained workers. As the population continues to concentrate in metropolitan areas, requirements are expected to increase for professional and technical workers in environmental protection, urban renewal, and mass transportation. Requirements for professional workers also should increase because of continuing growth of research in the natural and social sciences, although the rate of growth in these activities as a whole is likely to slow from the very rapid pace of the 1960's. Demand for professional workers to develop and use computer resources also is expected to grow rapidly in the 1972–85 period.

Managers and administrators. Employment in this occupational group is expected to reach 10.5 million in 1985, up from 8 million in 1972. This is a much higher annual rate of growth than occurred in the 1960–72 period. Changes in business size and organization have caused the number of salaried managers to go up, while numbers of self-employed

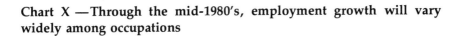

Chart X —Through the mid-1980's, employment growth will vary widely among occupations

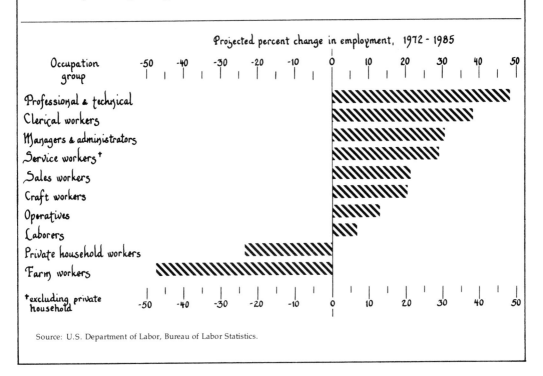

Projected percent change in employment, 1972 - 1985

Occupation group		

Professional & technical
Clerical workers
Managers & administrators
Service workers†
Sales workers
Craft workers
Operatives
Laborers
Private household workers
Farm workers

†excluding private household

Source: U.S. Department of Labor, Bureau of Labor Statistics.

managers have declined. Demand for the salaried is expected to continue to grow rapidly as industry and government increasingly depend upon them. Technology will also contribute to their employment growth. For example, an increasing number of technically trained managers will be needed to administer research and development programs and to make decisions on the installation and use of automated machinery an automatic data processing systems. By contrast, the number of self-employed managers (proprietors) is projected to continue to decline as the trend toward larger firms continues. The expansion of quick-service grocery stores, self-service laundries and drycleaners, and hamburger and frozen custard drive-ins, however, is expected to slow the rate of decline. Women have been increasing as a proportion of all managerial workers. In April 1974, 18.6 percent of the workers in this occupation group were women; in 1959 women made up 15.5 percent of managerial employment.

Clerical workers. Employment in clerical jobs is expected to grow faster than total employment, rising to about 19.7 million in 1985 from about 14.2 million in 1972. This is an important field for employment opportunites for women. More than 77 percent of clerical workers in April 1974 were women. Among the major occupation groups, only employment of professional workers is expected to grow faster. Nevertheless, the projected clerical rate of growth is slower than that during the 1960–72 period.

Clerical workers, the largest major occupation group in 1972, will be greatly affected by developments in computers, office equipment, and communication devices—all of which are expected to retard the growth of employment for some clerical occupations and increase it for others. For example, the use of computers and bookkeeping machines to handle routine, repetitive work is expected to reduce the utilization of clerks in filing, payroll computation, inventory control, and customer billing. On the other hand, the number of clerical workers needed to prepare material for the computer is projected to increase greatly. Other types of clerical workers, however, are unlikely to be affected significantly by technology. For example, secretaries, typists, receptionists, and others whose tasks involve contact with the public should not be greatly affected. Increased use of secretaries, typists, and receptionists in industries that employ large numbers of them (such as miscellaneous business services and legal services) is projected to account for a growth of 2.5 million workers during the 1972–85 period, a large proportion of whom will be women. This would represent about half the total growth in the clerical occupation group over this period.

Sales workers. The anticipated expansion of trade is expected to increase the need for sales workers, while changing techniques in merchandising are expected to hold down some of the increase. Employment is projected to rise about 1 million—from 5.4 million in 1972 to 6.5 million in 1985, but the rate of increase is slower than that expected in total employment. As a result, sales workers' share of total employment is projected to decrease slightly. The projected 1972–85 rate of growth, slower than that experienced by this group over the 1960–72 period, is caused by the projected slower growth of trade, which employs over two-thirds of all sales workers. As stores remain open longer and expand in suburban areas, an increase in demand is expected for retail sales workers, who account for about half of all workers in the group. Most retail sales clerks, especially those who work part time, are women. However, changes in merchandising techniques, such as increased use of self-service, checkout counters, and vending machines, will retard the increase. In April 1974, nearly 42 percent of all sales workers were women.

Service workers. The growing population, expanding business activity, increasing leisure time, and rising levels of disposable personal income are the major factors underlying increased needs for service workers. These occupations encompass a wide variety of jobs and skills. They include such diverse jobs as FBI agents, police officers, beauty operators, and janitors. Employment of service workers is projected to rise from 11 million in 1972 to over 13 million in 1985, a somewhat slower rate of growth than that projected for total employment. However, employment of private household workers is projected to decline from 1.4 million to 1.1 million. If private household workers were excluded from the calculations, service workers would show a faster rate of growth (29.1 percent) than total employment. More than 98 percent of private household workers and nearly 58 percent of other service workers in April 1974 were women.

Craft workers.   Employment in the highly skilled blue-collar occupations is expected to rise from just under 11 million in 1972 to 13.0 million in 1985, a slower rate of growth than over the 1960–72 period. The rising demand for these workers is expected to stem from the growth in the two major industry groups that employ large numbers of craft workers—manufacturing and construction. Construction activity has a major effect on the number of craft workers because 1 out 2 workers in this industry is in this group. Expected requirements for construction craft workers are projected to account for about one-third of the total growth. Because of its much larger size, manufacturing—in which about 1 out of 5 workers is a craft worker—employs about an equal number of craft workers as does construction. Only slightly over 4 percent of workers in this occupation group in April 1974 were women, but the number and proportion of women in craft jobs have been expanding.

Operatives.   More blue-collar workers are in this group than in any other. Employment of operatives is projected to rise from 13.5 million in 1972 to over 15 million in 1985, a much slower rate of increase than that for total employment. Through the projected period, sophisticated technological advances are expected to slow employment growth greatly for operatives. Three out of 5 semiskilled workers in 1972 were employed as operatives in manufacturing. Large numbers were assemblers or inspectors, and many worked as operators of material-moving equipment such as powered forklift trucks. Among the operatives employed outside factories, drivers of trucks, buses, and taxicabs made up the largest group. Nearly 32 percent of all operatives in April 1974 were women; in 1959 the proportion was less than 28 percent.

Nonfarm laborers.   Employment requirements for laborers are expected to increase slowly between 1972 and 1985, despite the employment rise anticipated in manufacturing and construction—the two industries which employ two-fifths of laborers. This reflects a change from the 1960–72 period when employment of laborers increased nearly 1 percent a year. Increases in demand for laborers, as employment in construction and manufacturing rise, are expected to be offset roughly by rising output per worker resulting from the continuing substitution of machinery for manual labor. For example, power-driven equipment such as forklift trucks, derricks, cranes, hoists, and conveyor belts will take over more of the handling of materials in factories, at freight terminals, and in warehouses. Other power-driven machines will do excavating, ditch digging, and similar work. About 8 percent of nonfarm laborers in April 1974 were women.

Farm workers.   These workers, who make up nearly 90 percent of all workers in agriculture, are expected to decline nearly a half (3.1 million in 1972 to 1.6 million in 1985); this represents a somewhat faster rate of decline than in the 1960–72 period. Consequently, farm workers' share of total employment also is expected to fall between 1972–85 from 3.8 to 1.6 percent. Declining needs for these workers continue to be related to rising productivity on farms. Improved machinery, fertilizers, seeds, and feed will permit farmers to increase output with fewer employees. For example, improved mechanical harvesters for vegetables and fruits will decrease the need for seasonal or other hired labor. Developments in packing, inspection, and sorting systems for fruits, vegetables, and other farm products also will reduce employment requirements. About 15 percent of all farm workers in April 1974 were women.

Implications for trained personnel

In the past two decades, the rise in the educational level of the labor force was paralleled by rising educational requirements of jobs. This was reflected in a more rapid growth of the major occupation groups with the highest educational attainment. The major apparent gaps were a shortage of college graduates trained to work in engineering, scientific, teaching, and medical professions during the late 1950's to the mid-1960's. In looking to the future, the question arises as to whether the increasing educational attainment of women workers will continue to be matched by an increase in jobs which are available to them and which require their educational qualifications. The projected supply-demand picture for college graduates points up some concerns. United States colleges and universities—principal suppliers of the country's most trained personnel—are expected to continue turning out record numbers of graduates through the mid-1980's. The Office of Education has projected that a total of 20.1 million degrees, including first professional, will be awarded over the 1972–85 period.

Degree	Projected number of awards from 1972–85 (in millions)	Percent increase, 1972–85
Total	20.1	46
Bachelor's	14.6	44
Master's	4.0	41
Doctor's	.6	66
First professional	.9	85

Not all degree recipients, however, can be considered part of the effective new supply of college-educated workers. Most master's and doctor's degree recipients are employed before receiving their advanced degrees and are already considered part of the existing supply of college-educated workers. Other degree recipients, especially at the bachelor's level, delay entry into the labor force to continue their education, enter the Armed Forces, or become full-time housewives.

Relying on past patterns of entry into the labor force, the BLS estimated that 13.2 million persons will enter the civilian labor force between 1972 and 1985 upon receiving their degrees—11.2 million with bachelor's, 1.2 million master's, approximately 20,000 doctor's, and 750,000 with first professional degrees (see table 104).

In addition, the supply of new graduates will be augmented by more than 2.0 million persons with college-level training who will come into the labor force between 1972 and 1985. These expected additions will consist of over 900,000 immigrants as well as delayed entrants and reentrants into the labor force—primarily women who delayed seeking

Table 104 —Projected supply of college graduates, 1972–85

(Numbers in thousands)

Source of entrants	1972–85	1972–80	1980–85
Total _____	15,250	8,850	6,400
New college graduates _____	13,170	7,540	5,630
Bachelor's degree _____	11,200	6,405	4,795
Master's degree _____	1,220	700	520
Doctor's degree _____	20	10	10
First professional degree _____	750	425	325
Military separations _____	1,150	750	400
Others _____	910	560	350

Source: U.S. Department of Labor, Bureau of Labor Statistics: Monthly Labor Review, December 1973.

a job or who were working in earlier years but withdrew from the labor force—and nearly 1.2 million persons (mainly men) entering the civilian labor force after separation from the military. The new supply of college-educated personnel expected to enter the labor force from 1972–85 will total about 15.3 million.

Job opportunities for college-educated workers will stem generally from three sources: growth in employment of occupations currently requiring a college degree for entry; the need to replace workers in such occupations who die, retire, or leave the labor force for other reasons; and the trend toward hiring college graduates for jobs once performed by workers with less educational attainment.

An analysis of growth, replacement, and rising entry requirements indicates that 14.5 million new college graduates will be needed between 1972 and 1985—7.7 million to take care of occupational growth and rising entry requirements, and 6.8 million for replacements. The following tabulation shows proportions for selected periods:

	1972–85	1972–80	1980–85
		(In millions)	
Total	14.5	8.8	5.7
Growth	7.7	5.0	2.7
Replacements	6.8	3.8	3.0

Thus, the available supply of college graduates would be about 800,000 above projected job requirements over the 1972–85 period. The situation in which potential supply is greater than prospective requirements is projected to be much more acute in the 1980–85 period than in 1972–80. The prospective "gap" is small, roughly 100,000 for the 1972–80 period, but is 700,000 for the 1980–85 period, or about 140,000 a year, more than 10 percent of the projected supply. The supply-demand situation may be of special concern to women since the supply of women college graduates will be growing at a faster rate than that of male graduates.

Despite the apparent surplus of college graduates for the 1980–85 period, which is generated by statistics based on past patterns, it is unlikely that there will be large-scale unemployment among college graduates. Rather, it is likely that college graduates will obtain jobs generally filled by individuals with less than 4 years of college. In the past, graduates have reacted to changes in the job situation by taking the best available job, and there is no reason to assume that this will not be the case in the future. Moreover, employers have traditionally preferred to hire persons with the highest educational qualifications available, especially for white-collar jobs, even when the educational attainment of the individual hired is above that really needed to perform the job. Thus, in competing for employment, college graduates are expected to continue to have an advantage over those with less education. Problems for college graduates will more likely be underemployment and job dissatisfaction, resulting in increasing occupational mobility rather than unemployment.

College-educated women will need to enter male-dominated fields in greater numbers to make maximum use of their training. Evidence of this movement to professional occupations in which women constituted only a small proportion of total employment has already been mentioned—in such fields as medicine, dentistry, law, and engineering. Another indication of movement of college-educated women to male-dominated fields comes from the survey of hiring plans of large business and industrial firms. The 1974 Endicott report, the annual survey of policy and practice in the employment of college and university graduates in business and industry, covering a total of 196 well-known companies, revealed the hiring of growing numbers of women. The report states:

Separate tabulation in these surveys of the number of college women employed by responding companies makes it possible to report some interesting trends. For example, in 1963, or ten years ago, the number of women graduates employed by the responding companies was 7% of the number of bachelor's level college men who were hired. In 1968, or five years ago, the corresponding figure was 11%. In 1973, the total of 1,998 college women employed was 18% of the number of men hired. If, in 1974, the reporting companies are able to hire the number of women and the number of men shown in this report, the women will represent 24% of the number of men to be employed. To some, these percentages may appear to be small, but a clear upward trend is indicated.

The availability of more college-trained women and men is expected to have an adverse effect on many of the less educated. It is likely to mean that, in the future, workers with less than a college education, particularly women, will have less chance of advancing to professional positions, as many could do in the past, particularly in professions such as accounting. They will also have less opportunity for promotion to higher level positions in sales, managerial, and some clerical and service occupations. This is essentially a problem of credentials. If the required educational qualifications for a job rise more rapidly than the actual education required to perform the job, the availability of more college-educated workers will limit advancement of workers with fewer years of schooling. Such situations are very likely to occur in sales.

College graduates, however, will not be in a more favorable position in all occupations. In the crafts, workers in greatest demand will be those who have vocational training rather than a college education; as in the past, persons with college degrees will make little inroad in the crafts. Similarly, employers seeking operatives and laborers will be reluctant to hire college graduates except for some part-time or temporary jobs because of the obvious potential for job dissatisfaction. Moreover, in another broad occupational area closely related to professional work—paraprofessional and technical work—college graduates are likely to face stiffer competition. Community and junior colleges and other postsecondary schools have proven they can train women and men for many occupations in this category through 2-year programs or less, and the number of students completing these career educational programs is expected to increase even more rapidly than college graduates.

Another condition which may arise is that young people in high school will become aware of the plight of new college graduates who are not able to enter the field of their choice, and thereby change their aspiration for a college education. Because current society esteems a college degree and recognizes the benefit of a college education to aspects of life other than work, such changed aspirations are not anticipated in great numbers. The complexity of the problem suggests the need for growing emphasis on vocational guidance to provide young people with the background needed to make a satisfactory choice for education and career.

In summary, the outlook is for a continued increase in the number of women in the labor force in the decade ahead. An especially rapid growth is anticipated in the number of women workers in the 20- to 34-year-old group. The employment outlook appears favorable for industries employing large numbers of women; for example, service-producing industries such as health services, retail trade, government, finance, and insurance. Most long-term trends in the employment by occupation groups are expected to continue. White-collar jobs in which most women are currently employed will increase as a proportion of total employment. Service workers, other than private household, another large area of employment for women workers, will also show a significant rise. The number of women in the labor force who are college graduates will rise significantly. This will coincide with an expected slowdown in the growth in some traditional occupations for women college graduates (especially elementary and secondary school teachers). The absorption of college-educated women in the labor force might therefore require a movement of these women in large numbers into traditionally male-dominated occupations and point to the need for more realistic career planning by women.

Employment outlook in individual fields

Women's opportunities for rewarding employment will be directly related not only to their level of skill and experience but also to the labor market demands in the decade ahead. The Occupational Outlook Handbook prepared by the Bureau of Labor Statistics provides an assessment of the employment outlook in a great many individual occupations. It also provides information on the nature of work, training requirements, earnings, working conditions, and places of employment in individual fields. The following section provides a brief statement on employment trends and prospects for individual fields from the 1974–75 edition of the Occupational Outlook Handbook. It also provides information on estimated employment in the occupation and average annual openings. The percentage that women make up of total employment in the occupation is listed. These projections may help women make more realistic plans for careers in which openings will be available, in which they can more fully utilize their skills, and in which they can earn better wages. In order to become competitive for the more challenging jobs with advancement possibilities, women and girls should plan to train for nontraditional as well as traditional occupations.

The occupations are grouped by related jobs into clusters. These groupings enable the reader interested in a broad field to locate easily the employment prospects for a number of related specific occupations. For example, persons interested in health careers can find information on about 16 occupations in this field having different educational and training requirements.

Employment outlook in individual fields

Occupation	Percent women [1]	Estimated employment 1972 [2]	Projected employment 1985	Average annual openings [3]	Employment trends and prospects
EDUCATION AND RELATED OCCUPATIONS					
Teaching Occupations					
College and university teachers	27	525,000	630,000	24,000	Entrants may face keen competition through the mid-1980's. New doctor's and master's degree holders, the main source of supply, are expected to more than meet the expanding demand for college and university teachers.
Kindergarten and elementary school teachers	86	1,274,000	1,590,000	105,000	Competition is expected through the mid-1980's. If patterns of entry and reentry continue, the number of persons qualified to teach in elementary schools will exceed the number of openings.
Secondary school teachers	49	1,023,000	1,045,000	40,000	If past trends of entry continue through the mid-1980's, the supply will greatly exceed anticipated requirements. Keen competition for prospective teachers, although a recent survey found teacher shortages in mathematics, industrial arts, special education, and some vocational-technical subjects.
Library Occupations					
Librarians	83	120,000	162,000	11,200	Favorable overall opportunities, but some librarians may have to compete for jobs of their choice. Best employment prospects in public and special libraries.
Library technical assistants	(*)	25,000	(*)	(*)	Good employment prospects particularly for graduates of academic programs. Especially favorable opportunities in large public and college and university libraries.

Employment outlook in individual fields—continued

Occupation	Percent women [1]	Estimated employment 1972 [2]	Projected employment 1985	Average annual openings [3]	Employment trends and prospects
HEALTH OCCUPATIONS					
Dental Occupations					
Dental Assistants	98	115,000	155,000	13,000	Excellent employment prospects for dental assistants, especially for graduates of approved training programs.
Dental Hygienists	96	17,000	50,000	4,800	Demand is likely to continue to outstrip supply. Very good opportunities for both full- and part-time workers.
Dental laboratory technicians	(⁴)	32,000	43,000	2,000	Very good employment prospects for experienced technicians. Very favorable opportunities for recent graduates of approved training programs.
Dentists	3	105,000	140,000	5,300	Favorable employment opportunities through the mid-1980's. Newly added teaching facilities in dental schools should allow the supply to approach needs by 1985.
Medical Practitioner Occupations					
Chiropractors	9	16,000	19,500	1,000	Favorable opportunities. Population growth and inclusion of chiropractic services in many insurance programs are expected to result in a moderate increase in demand.
Optometrists	(⁴)	18,700	23,300	900	Favorable employment outlook for this moderately growing occupation. Most openings will result from deaths and retirements.
Physicians and osteopathic physicians	12	330,000	485,000	19,000	Very good employment opportunities for physicians.
Veterinarians	5	26,000	37,000	1,400	Favorable employment outlook. Supply is expected to increase more rapidly than in the past, however, because of increased capacity of veterinary schools.

Medical Technician, Technologist, and Assistant Occupations

		More than			Employment outlook
Medical assistants	(*)	200,000	320,000	25,000	Excellent employment opportunities due to the very rapid growth in the number of physicians, the principal employers. Graduates of 2-year college programs will be especially in demand.
Medical laboratory workers	(*)	165,000	210,000	13,000	Moderate employment expansion as a result of wide use of laboratory services by physicians.
Radiologic technologists	70	55,000	87,000	6,500	Favorable outlook for both full- and part-time workers due to expansion in the use of X-ray equipment and the growing demand for medical services in general.
Nursing Occupations					
Licensed practical nurses	97	425,000	835,000	70,000	Very good opportunities as health facilities continue to expand and as practical nurses are increasingly utilized to lighten the load of registered nurses.
Nursing aides, orderlies, and attendants	84	900,000	1,360,000	100,000	Very rapid employment rise. Most openings will occur from the need to replace workers who die or retire.
Registered nurses	98	748,000	1,050,000	75,000	Favorable employment prospects especially for nurses with graduate training seeking positions as teachers and administrators.
Other Health Occupations					
Dietitians	92	33,000	44,000	3,100	Rapid employment growth to meet the needs for management in the nutrition and food fields in hospitals and extended care facilities, schools, industrial plants, and commercial eating places.

See footnotes at end of table.

Employment outlook in individual fields—continued

Occupation	Percent women [1]	Estimated employment 1972 [2]	Projected employment 1985	Average annual openings [3]	Employment trends and prospects
Pharmacists	14	131,000	163,000	7,700	Very good outlook due to moderate employment growth and openings from deaths and retirements. Many openings are expected in pharmacies in new communities and through the more extensive use in hospitals and clinics.
SOCIAL SERVICE OCCUPATIONS					
School counselors	(*)	43,000	59,000	2,900	Favorable employment opportunities in the long run due mainly to the Federal Government's Career Education Program. A decline in school enrollments until the late 1970's will moderate immediate growth.
Home economists	(*)	120,000	140,000	9,200	Despite an anticipated slow growth in employment, many job openings will be available due to deaths and retirements. Those wishing to teach in high schools may face competition but those with graduate degrees should find good employment prospects in college and university teaching.
Psychologists	40	57,000	90,000	4,300	Good job outlook for clinical and counseling psychologists. Those wishing to teach or do research in large colleges and universities may face some competition.
Recreation workers	46	55,000	90,000	5,500	Excellent employment opportunities for young people with a bachelor's degree in recreation. There will be many opportunities for part-time work.
Social workers	61	185,000	275,000	17,500	Excellent employment opportunities for those with graduate degrees. Favorable outlook through the 1970's for those with bachelor's degrees, although competition may increase in the 1980's.

SOCIAL SCIENCE OCCUPATIONS

Economists	19	36,000	46,000	1,500	Economists with master's and doctor's degrees may find keen competition for better jobs in colleges and universities and private industry. Basic research will offer the best opportunities for those with a bachelor's degree.
Historians	(¹)	24,000	30,000	1,500	Experienced Ph. D.'s are expected to face keen competition for college teaching. New Ph. D. recipients and those with lesser degrees are likely to face very keen competition. High school teaching positions may be available for those meeting certification requirements.
Sociologists	35	15,000	23,000	1,200	Employment opportunities for Ph. D.'s are expected to be favorable though they may face some competition for choice academic jobs. Those with master's degrees are likely to face some competition for academic positions, but jobs in government and private industry will be available.

SCIENTIFIC AND TECHNICAL OCCUPATIONS

Life scientists	12	180,000	235,000	9,200	New graduates may face severe competition since the number of graduates is expected to grow more rapidly than employment opportunities. However, those with advanced degrees, especially the Ph. D., will experience the least competition. Medical scientists should find the best opportunities due to the emphasis on research of cancer, heart, and other diseases. Those with only an undergraduate degree may be limited to research assistant or technician jobs.

See footnotes at end of table.

Employment outlook in individual fields—continued

Occupation	Percent women [1]	Estimated employment 1972 [2]	Projected employment 1985	Average annual openings [3]	Employment trends and prospects
Statisticians	43	23,000	32,000	1,700	Favorable employment prospects for persons who can combine training in statistics with knowledge of a field where it can be applied, such as economics.
Chemists	12	134,000	184,000	6,800	Favorable employment opportunities. Demand for industrial products, further research on urgent pollution and fuel shortage problems, and the need for health-related research will contribute to the need for additional chemists.
Drafters	8	327,000	485,000	17,900	Skilled drafters, especially those with post-high school training, are expected to have favorable employment opportunities.
Engineering and science technicians	6	707,000	1,050,000	39,600	Favorable employment opportunities, especially for graduates of postsecondary training programs. Rapid growth will result from industrial expansion and increasing opportunities in the fields of atomic energy, environmental control, and urban development.
OFFICE OCCUPATIONS *Clerical Occupations*					
Bookkeeping workers	88	1,584,000	1,900,000	118,000	Limited employment growth because of increasing automation of recordkeeping. Most job openings will result from deaths and retirements.
Cashiers	87	998,000	1,360,000	96,000	Rapid growth in employment. Best prospects for persons with typing and bookkeeping skills. Favorable opportunities for part-time work.
File clerks	86	272,000	318,000	22,800	Increased demand for adequate recordkeeping should result in many job openings. Limited growth due to the increasing use of computers to store and retrieve data.

Occupation					Outlook
Office machine operators	74	195,000	230,000	13,700	Despite expected growth in the volume of office work, employment growth should be slow due to the expansion of automated recordkeeping.
Receptionists	97	436,000	650,000	55,100	Very rapid employment growth due to the expansion of businesses employing receptionists. Because this work is of a personal nature, prospects should not be affected by office automation.
Stenographers and secretaries	97	3,074,000	4,950,000	411,000	The increasing use of dictating machines will limit opportunities for office stenographers. Excellent prospects for secretaries and shorthand reporters.
Stock clerks	25	511,000	750,000	34,800	Very rapid employment growth as manufacturing firms, wholesale establishments, and retail stores continue to expand. Some competition for jobs can be expected because many young people seek this work as a first job.
Typists	97	1,021,000	1,400,000	115,700	Rapid employment growth with good opportunities for competent typists, especially those familiar with automatic typewriters.
Computer and Related Occupations Computer operating personnel	(*)	480,000	531,000	27,000	Rapid rise in employment of console and auxiliary equipment operators as the number of computer installations increases. Declining demand for keypunch operators because of improved methods of data entry.

See footnotes at end of table.

Employment outlook in individual fields—continued

Occupation	Percent women [1]	Estimated employment 1972 [2]	Projected employment 1985	Average annual openings [3]	Employment trends and prospects
Programers	22	186,000	290,000	13,000	Rapid employment growth as computers are used increasingly in business and government operations. Best opportunities for persons qualified in both programing and systems analysis.
Systems analysts	14	103,000	185,000	8,300	Very rapid employment growth as requirements for data processing systems expand because of increased use of computers.
Banking Occupations Bank clerks	(*)	473,000	665,000	43,200	Rapid employment growth as new and existing banks expand their services. Best prospects for data processing workers.
Bank officers	18	219,000	308,000	13,600	Rapid employment gains as the number of banks increases and the services they offer expand.
Bank tellers	90	248,000	350,000	25,000	Rapid employment growth as banks expand their services. Favorable opportunities for part-time work during peak business hours.
Insurance Occupations Claim adjusters	(*)	128,000	152,000	5,800	Moderate employment increase due to expanding insurance sales and resulting claims. Declining opportunities for adjusters who specialize in automobile claims as more States adopt no-fault insurance plans; very good prospects for other types of adjusters.
Underwriters	(*)	61,000	71,000	2,500	Many opportunities as the demand for insurance protection increases. Best prospects for those with college training.

Occupation					Statement of prospects
Administrative and Related Occupations					
Accountants	22	714,000	935,000	41,900	Good opportunities. Because of the growing complexity of business accounting requirements, those with college degrees will be in greater demand than those without degrees.
Lawyers	6	303,000	380,000	16,500	Moderate employment rise due to the growth of legal action in such areas as consumer protection and the environment and the greater use of attorneys by low- and middle-income groups. Prospects for establishing a new practice probably will be best in small towns and **growing suburban areas**; most salaried positions will become available in urban areas. Keen competition for salaried positions.
Personnel workers	34	240,000	(')	(')	Excellent opportunities. Particularly good job prospects for persons trained in psychological testing and in handling work-related problems. Limited chances to enter field from clerical or subprofessional jobs.
Public relations workers	29	87,000	(')	(')	Moderate employment increase due to growth in importance of public relations.
SERVICE OCCUPATIONS					
Cleaning and Related Occupations					
Building custodians	13	1,885,000	2,430,000	136,000	Moderate employment growth due to construction of apartment houses, motels, and other buildings that use custodial services. Maintenance needs of condominiums also will contribute to employment growth.

See footnotes at end of table.

Employment outlook in individual fields—continued

Occupation	Percent women[1]	Estimated employment 1972[2]	Projected employment 1985	Average annual openings[3]	Employment trends and prospects
Hotel housekeepers and assistants	([4])	17,000	24,000	1,700	Rapid employment growth as the number of hotels increases. The best opportunities will be in new hotels and luxury motels.
Food Service Occupations Bartenders	30	200,000	235,000	8,800	Moderate employment increase as new restaurants, bars, and hotels open.
Cooks and chefs	60	866,000	1,000,000	52,000	Moderate growth in employment. Most starting jobs will be in small restaurants and other eating places where food preparation is fairly simple.
Waiters and waitresses	88	1,124,000	1,300,000	86,000	Moderate employment increase due to the construction of new hotels and restaurants. Most openings, however, will stem from high turnover.
Personal Service Occupations Cosmetologists	92	500,000	670,000	51,000	Very good job opportunities for experienced workers and newcomers. Good prospects also for those seeking part-time work.
Private Household Service Occupations Private household workers	98	1,437,000	1,000,000	51,000	Despite the expected employment decline, job opportunities will be very good. Many openings will result as persons discouraged by low wages seek employment in other fields.
Protective and Related Service Occupations Guards	5	250,000	320,000	19,300	Moderate employment growth due to the mounting incidence of crime and the increasing numbers of plants, offices, and stores requiring protection.

Occupation					
Police officers	3	370,000	490,000	14,300	Increased demand for protective services should create very good employment opportunities; specialized training will become increasingly important.
Other Service Occupations Telephone operators	96	230,000	232,000	16,000	Although direct dialing and other automatic devices will restrict growth, there will be thousands of openings each year as operators retire, die, or leave the labor force for other reasons.
SALES OCCUPATIONS Insurance agents and brokers	13	385,000	450,000	16,000	Moderate employment growth. Despite an expected increase in sales volume, selling is expected to remain keenly competitive.
Manufacturers' sales workers	9	423,000	545,000	20,000	Greater business competition should stimulate employment of manufacturers' sales workers. Most favorable opportunities for those trained to sell technical products.
Real estate sales workers and brokers	36	349,000	435,000	25,000	Moderate employment increase to result from the growing demand for home purchases and rentals. Mature workers, including those transferring from other kinds of sales work, are likely to find many job opportunities.
Retail trade sales workers	70	2,778,000	3,330,000	190,000	Good employment opportunities for full- and part-time workers as income levels rise and stores continue to remain open longer.

See footnotes at end of table.

Employment outlook in individual fields—continued

Occupation	Percent women [1]	Estimated employment 1972 [2]	Projected employment 1985	Average annual openings [3]	Employment trends and prospects
Securities sales workers	9	220,000	290,000	11,900	Moderate employment growth as funds available for investment increase. Many openings will also result from deaths and retirements. Transfers of sales workers who have left their jobs because they were unable to establish a successful clientele should also create many additional opportunities.
Wholesale trade sales workers	6	688,000	860,000	31,000	Moderate employment growth resulting from expansion of wholesalers' customer services, the duties of sales workers and business in general.
CONSTRUCTION OCCUPATIONS Carpenters	1	1,000,000	1,200,000	37,000	Moderate employment growth from increased construction and greater demand for carpenters in the maintenance departments of factories, stores, and large apartment and government buildings.
Electricians (construction)	2	240,000	325,000	11,100	Rapid employment increase as construction expands and more electric outlets, switches, and wiring are needed for appliances, air-conditioning systems, electronic data processing equipment, and electrical control devices.
Painters and paperhangers	4	420,000	460,000	14,700	While most openings will be for painters, several hundred jobs for paperhangers are expected to become available yearly.
Plumbers and pipefitters	1	400,000	500,000	16,300	Moderate employment increase due to rising construction activity and growth of industries which use extensive pipework in their processing activities, such as chemical and petroleum refining. Also, the trends toward more bathrooms per home and more central air-conditioning will result in increased demand for these workers.

OCCUPATIONS IN TRANSPORTATION ACTIVITIES

Air Transportation Occupations

Occupation				Prospects
Flight attendants	95	39,000	76,000	8,000	Very rapid employment increase as aircraft become larger and increase in number. Many additional openings will occur as attendants transfer to other occupations. Continued fuel shortages may adversely affect employment growth.
Traffic agents and clerks	(*)	59,000	110,000	7,000	Very rapid employment increase because of the anticipated growth of passenger and cargo traffic.
Driving Occupations					
Local transit busdrivers	(*)	68,000	71,500	1,600	Slow employment rise as bus service is improved and expanded in urban areas.
Local truckdrivers	(*)	1,600,000	1,800,000	46,000	Moderate employment increase because of growth in the volume of freight.
Taxi drivers	12	92,000	85,000	1,600	Slow decline in employment because of the increased use of private and rented cars and buses and subways. There will, however, be many openings each year from deaths and retirements. Transfer to other occupations will create additional openings.

INDUSTRIAL PRODUCTION AND RELATED OCCUPATIONS

Occupation				Prospects
All-round machinists	3	320,000	400,000	13,100	Moderate employment growth due to rising demand for machined goods such as automobiles, household appliances, and industrial products.
Bookbinders and related workers	65	32,000	38,000	550	Moderate employment increase

See footnotes at end of table.

Employment outlook in individual fields—continued

Occupation	Percent women[1]	Estimated employment 1972[2]	Projected employment 1985	Average annual openings[3]	Employment trends and prospects
Composing room occupations	15	170,000	166,000	4,300	Slowly declining employment due to more efficient type-setting equipment. A few thousand openings are expected yearly to replace workers who retire or die.
Assemblers	50	1,017,000	1,100,000	40,500	Slow employment growth, but thousands of openings will occur each year from deaths and retirements in this large field.
Welders and flamecutters	6	554,000	770,000	27,200	Rapid employment increase due to growth of metalworking industries and wider use of welding.

[1] Based on 1973 CPS data in occupations for which reliable data were available; otherwise based on 1970 Decennial Census data.

[2] Many of the employment estimates included in the Occupational Outlook Handbook are based on CPS data. Estimates for other occupations are based on other sources. The BLS and other Government agencies collect data on selected categories of occupational employment directly from employers. Many professional associations compile statistics on occupational employment from licensing statistics or from their own membership records. The U.S. Civil Service Commission compiles data on occupational employment in the Federal Government. Sources of employment data other than that derived from the CPS are provided in BLS Bulletin 1738, Occupational Employment Statistics, 1960-70.

[3] Openings due to growth, retirements, and other separations from the labor force. Does not include transfers out of the occupations.

[4] Estimate not available.

Source: Occupational Outlook Handbook in Brief, 1974-75 Edition, and Occupational Outlook Quarterly, Summer 1974.

Appendix

Appendix A

Title VII of The Civil Rights Act of 1964

TITLE VII—EQUAL EMPLOYMENT OPPORTUNITY

DEFINITIONS

SEC. 701. For the purposes of this title—

(a) The term "person" includes one or more individuals, governments, governmental agencies, political subdivisions labor unions, partnerships, associations, corporations, legal representatives, mutual companies, joint-stock companies, trusts, unincorporated organizations, trustees, trustees in bankruptcy, or receivers. Public Law 92–261

(b) The term "employer" means a person engaged in an industry affecting commerce who has fifteen or more employees for each working day in each of twenty or more calendar weeks in the current or preceding calendar year, and any agent of such a person, but such term does not include (1) the United States, a corporation wholly owned by the Government of the United States, an Indian tribe, or any department or agency of the District of Columbia subject by statute to procedures of the competitive service (as defined in section 2102 of title 5 of the United States Code), or (2) a bona fide private membership club (other than a labor organization) which is exempt from taxation under section 501(c) of the Internal Revenue Code of 1954, except that during the first year after the date of enactment of the Equal Employment Opportunity Act of 1972, persons having fewer than twenty-five employees (and their agents) shall not be considered employers. Public Law 92–261

(c) The term "employment agency" means any person regularly undertaking with or without compensation to procure employees for an employer or to procure for employees opportunities to work for an employer and includes an agent of such a person. Public Law 92–261

(d) The term "labor organization" means a labor organization engaged in an industry affecting commerce, and any agent of such an organization, and includes any organization of any kind, any agency, or employee representation committee, group, association, or plan so engaged in which employees participate and which exists for the purpose, in whole or in part, of dealing with employers concerning grievances, labor disputes, wages, rates of pay, hours, or other items or conditions of employment, and any conference, general committee, joint or system board, or joint council so engaged which is subordinate to a national or international labor organization.

(e) A labor organization shall be deemed to be engaged in an industry affecting commerce if (1) it maintains or operates a hiring hall or hiring office which procures employees for an employer or procures for employees opportunities to work for an employer, or (2) the number of its members (or, where it is a labor organization composed of other labor organizations or their representatives, if the aggregate number of the members of such other labor organization) is (A) twenty-five or more during the first year after the date of enactment of the Equal Employment Opportunity Act of 1972, or (B) fifteen or more thereafter, and such labor organization—

Public Law
92–261

(1) is the certified representative of employees under the provisions of the National Labor Relations Act, as amended, or the Railway Labor Act, as amended;

(2) although not certified, is a national or international labor organization or a local labor organization recognized or acting as the representative of employees of an employer or employers engaged in an industry affecting commerce; or

(3) has chartered a local labor organization or subsidiary body which is representing or actively seeking to represent employees of employers within the meaning of paragraph (1) or (2); or

(4) has been chartered by a labor organization representing or actively seeking to represent employees within the meaning of paragraph (1) or (2) as the local or subordinate body through which such employees may enjoy membership or become affiliated with such labor organization; or

(5) is a conference, general committee, joint or system board, or joint council subordinate to a national or international labor organization, which includes a labor organization engaged in an industry affecting commerce within the meaning of any of the preceding paragraphs of this subsection.

(f) The term "employee" means an individual employed by an employer, except that the term "employee" shall not include any person elected to public office in any State or political subdivision of any State by the qualified voters thereof, or any person chosen by such officer to be on such officer's personal staff, or an appointee on the policy making level or an immediate adviser with respect to the exercise of the constitutional or legal powers of the office. The exemption set forth in the preceding sentence shall not include employees subject to the civil service laws of a State government, governmental agency or political subdivision.

Public Law
92–261

(g) The term "commerce" means trade, traffic, commerce, transportation, transmission or communication among the several States; or between a State and any place outside thereof; or within the District of Columbia, or a possession of the United States; or between points in the same State but through a point outside thereof.

(h) The term "industry affecting commerce" means any activity, business, or industry in commerce or in which a labor dispute would hinder or obstruct commerce or the free flow of commerce and includes any activity or industry "affecting commerce" within the meaning of the Labor-Management Reporting and Disclosure Act of 1959, and further includes any governmental industry, business, or activity.

Public Law 92–261

(i) The term "State" includes a State of the United States, the District of Columbia, Puerto Rico, the Virgin Islands, American Samoa, Guam, Wake Island, the Canal Zone, and Outer Continental Shelf lands defined in the Outer Continental Shelf Lands Act.

(j) The term "religion" includes all aspects of religious observance and practice, as well as belief, unless an employer demonstrates that he is unable to reasonably accommodate to an employee's or prospective employee's religious observance or practice without undue hardship on the conduct of the employer's business.

Public Law 92–261

EXEMPTION

SEC. 702. This title shall not apply to an employer with respect to the employment of aliens outside any State, or to a religious corporation, association, educational institution, or society with respect to the employment of individuals of a particular religion to perform work connected with the carrying on by such corporation, association, educational institution, or society of its activities.

Public Law 92–261

DISCRIMINATION BECAUSE OF RACE, COLOR, RELIGION, SEX, OR NATIONAL ORIGIN

SEC. 703. (a) It shall be an unlawful employment practice for an employer—

(1) to fail or refuse to hire or to discharge any individual, or otherwise to discriminate against any individual with respect to his compensation, terms, conditions, or privileges of employment, because of such individual's race, color, religion, sex, or national origin; or

(2) to limit, segregate, or classify his employees or applicants for employment in any way which would deprive or tend to deprive any individual of employment opportunities or otherwise adversely affect his status as an employee, because of such individual's race, color, religion, sex, or national origin.

Public Law 92–261

(b) It shall be an unlawful employment practice for an employment agency to fail or refuse to refer for employment, or otherwise discriminate against, any individual because of his race, color, religion, sex, or national origin, or to classify or refer for employment any individual on the basis of his race, color, religion, sex, or national origin.

(c) It shall be an unlawful employment practice for a labor organization—

(1) to exclude or to expel from its membership or applicants for membership, or otherwise to discriminate against, any individual because of his race, color, religion, sex, or national origin;

(2) to limit, segregate, or classify its membership, or to classify or fail or refuse to refer for employment any individual, in any way which would deprive or tend to deprive any individual of employment opportunities, or would limit such employment opportunities or otherwise adversely affect his status as an employee or as an applicant for employment, because of such individual's race, color, religion, sex, or national origin; or

(3) to cause or attempt to cause an employer to discriminate against an individual in violation of this section.

(d) It shall be an unlawful employment practice for any employer, labor organization, or joint labor-management committee controlling apprenticeship or other training or retraining, including on-the-job training programs to discriminate against any individual because of his race, color, religion, sex, or national origin in admission to, or employment in, any program established to provide apprenticeship or other training.

(e) Notwithstanding any other provision of this title, (1) it shall not be an unlawful employment practice for an employer to hire and employ employees, for an employment agency to classify, or refer for employment any individual, for a labor organization to classify its membership or to classify or refer for employment any individual, or for an employer, labor organization, or joint labor-management committee controlling apprenticeship or other training or retraining programs to admit or employ any individual in any such program, on the basis of his religion, sex, or national origin in those certain instances where religion, sex, or national origin is a bona fide occupational qualification reasonably necessary to the normal operation of that particular business or enterprice. and (2) it shall not be an unlawful employment practice for a school, college, university, or other educational institution or institution of learning to hire and employ employees of a particular religion if such school, college, university, or other educational institution or institution of learning is, in whole or in substantial part, owned, supported, controlled, or managed by a particular religion or by a particular religious corporation, association, or society, or if the curriculum of such school, college, university, or other educational institution or institution of learning is directed toward the propagation of a particular religion.

(f) As used in this title, the phrase "unlawful employment practice" shall not be deemed to include any action or measure taken by an employer, labor organization, joint labor-management committee, or employment agency with respect to an individual who is a member of the Communist Party of the United States or of any other organization required to register as a Communist-action or Communist-front organization by final order of the Subversive Activities Control Board pursuant to the Subversive Activities Control Act of 1950.

(g) Notwithstanding any other provision of this title, it shall not be an unlawful employment practice for an employer to fail or refuse to hire and employ any individual for any position, for an employer to discharge any individual from any position, or for an employment agency to fail or refuse to refer any individual for employment in any position, or for a labor organization to fail or refuse to refer any individual for employment in any position, if—

(1) the occupancy of such position, or access to the premises in or upon which any part of the duties of such position is performed or is to be performed, is subject to any requirement imposed in the interest of the national security of the United States under any security program in effect pursuant to or administered under any statute of the United States or any Executive order of the President; and

(2) such individual has not fulfilled or has ceased to fulfill that requirement.

(h) Notwithstanding any other provision of this title, it shall not be an unlawful employment practice for an employer to apply different standards of compensation, or different terms, conditions, or privileges of employment pursuant to a bona fide seniority or merit system, or a system which measures earnings by quantity or quality of production or to employees who work in different locations, provided that such differences are not the result of an intention to discriminate because of race, color, religion, sex, or national origin, nor shall it be an unlawful employment practice for an employer to give and to act upon the results of any professionally developed ability test provided that such test, its administration or action upon the results is not designed, intended or used to discriminate because of race, color, religion, sex or national origin. It shall not be an unlawful employment practice under this title for any employer to differentiate upon the basis of sex in determining the amount of the wages or compensation paid or to be paid to employees of such employer if such differentiation is authorized by the provisions of section 6(d) of the Fair Labor Standards Act of 1938, as amended (29 U.S.C. 206(d)).

(i) Nothing contained in this title shall apply to any business or enterprise on or near an Indian reservation with respect to any publicly announced employment practice of such business or enterprise under which a preferential treatment is given to any individual because he is an Indian living on or near a reservation.

Public Law
92-261

(j) Nothing contained in this title shall be interpreted to require any employer, employment agency, labor organization, or joint labor-management committee subject to this title to grant preferential treatment to any individual or to any group because of the race, color, religion, sex, or national origin of such individual or group on account of an imbalance which may exist with respect to the total number or percentage of persons of any race, color, religion, sex, or national origin employed by any employer, referred or classified for employment by any employment agency or labor organization, admitted to membership or classified by any labor organization, or admitted to, or employed in, any apprenticeship or other training program, in comparison with the total number or percentage of persons of such race, color, religion, sex, or national origin in any community, State, section, or other area, or in the available work force in any community, State, section, or other area.

OTHER UNLAWFUL EMPLOYMENT PRACTICES

Sec. 704. (a) It shall be an unlawful employment practice for an employer to discriminate against any of his employees or applicants for employment, for an employment agency, or joint labor-management committee controlling apprenticeship or other training or retraining, including on-the-job training programs, to discriminate against any individual, or for a labor organization to discriminate against any member thereof or applicant for membership, because he has opposed any practice made an unlawful employment practice by this title, or because he has made a charge, testified, assisted, or participated in any manner in an investigation, proceeding, or hearing under this title.

Public Law 92–261

(b) It shall be an unlawful employment practice for an employer, labor organization, employment agency, or joint labor-management committee controlling apprenticeship or other training or retraining including on-the-job training programs, to print or publish or cause to be printed or published any notice or advertisement relating to employment by such an employer or membership in or any classification or referral for employment by such a labor organization, or relating to any classification or referral for employment by such an employment agency, or relating to admission to, or employment in, any program established to provide apprenticeship or other training by such a joint labor-management committee indicating any preference, limitation, specification, or discrimination, based on race, color, religion, sex, or national original, except that such a notice or advertisement may indicate a preference, limitation, specification, or discrimination based on religion, sex, or national origin when religion, sex, or national origin is a bona fide occupational qualification for employment.

Public Law 92–261

EQUAL EMPLOYMENT OPPORTUNITY COMMISSION

Sec. 705. (a) There is hereby created a Commission to be known as the Equal Employment Opportunity Commission, which shall be composed of five members, not more than three of whom shall be members of the same political party. Members of the Commission shall be appointed by the President by and with the advice and consent of the Senate for a term of five years. Any individual chosen to fill a vacancy shall be appointed only for the unexpired term of the member whom he shall succeed, and all members of the Commission shall continue to serve until their successors are appointed and qualified, except that no such member of the Commission shall continue to serve (1) for more than sixty days when the Congress is in session unless a nomination to fill such vacancy shall have been submitted to the Senate, or (2) after the adjournment sine die of the session of the Senate in which such nomination was submitted. The President shall designate one member to serve as Chairman of the Commission, and one member to serve as Vice Chairman. The Chairman shall be responsible on behalf of the Commission for the administrative operations of the Commission, and, except as provided in subsection (b), shall appoint, in accordance with the provisions of title 5, United States Code, governing appointments in the competitive service, such officers, agents, attorneys, hearing examiners, and employees as he deems necessary to assist it in the performance of its functions and to fix their compensation in accordance with the provisions of chapter 51 and subchapter III of chapter 53 of title 5, United States Code, relating to classification and General Schedule pay rates: *Provided*, That assignment, removal, and compensation of hearing examiners shall be in accordance with sections 3105, 3344, 5362, and 7521 of title 5, United States Code.

Public Law
92–261

(b) (1) There shall be a General Counsel of the Commission appointed by the President, by and with the advice and consent of the Senate, for a term of four years. The General Counsel shall have responsibility for the conduct of litigation as provided in sections 706 and 707 of this title. The General Counsel shall have such other duties as the Commission may prescribe or as may be provided by law and shall concur with the Chairman of the Commission on the appointment and supervision of regional attorneys. The General Counsel of the Commission on the effective date of this Act shall continue in such position and perform the functions specified in this subsection until a successor is appointed and qualified.

(2) Attorneys appointed under this section may, at the direction of the Commission, appear for and represent the Commission in any case in court, provided that the Attorney General shall conduct all litigation to which the Commission is a party in the Supreme Court pursuant to this title.

(c) A vacancy in the Commission shall not impair the right of the remaining members to exercise all the powers of the Commission and three members thereof shall constitute a quorum.

(d) The Commission shall have an official seal which shall be judicially noticed.

(e) The Commission shall at the close of each fiscal year report to the Congress and to the President concerning the action it has taken; the names, salaries, and duties of all individuals in its employ and the moneys it has disbursed; and shall make such further reports on the cause of and means of eliminating discrimination and such recommendations for further legislation as may appear desirable.

(f) The principal office of the Commission shall be in or near the District of Columbia, but it may meet or exercise any or all its powers at any other place. The Commission may establish such regional or State offices as it deems necessary to accomplish the purpose of this title.

(g) The Commission shall have power—

(1) to cooperate with, and, with their consent, utilize regional, State, local, and other agencies, both public and private, and individuals;

(2) to pay to witnesses whose depositions are taken or who are summoned before the Commission or any of its agents the same witness and mileage fees as are paid to witnesses in the courts of the United States;

(3) to furnish to persons subject to this title such technical assistance as they may request to further their compliance with this title or an order issued thereunder;

(4) upon the request of (i) any employer, whose employees or some of them, or (ii) any labor organization, whose members or some of them, refuse or threaten to refuse to cooperate in effectuating the provisions of this title, to assist in such effectuation by conciliation or such other remedial action as is provided by this title;

(5) to make such technical studies as are appropriate to effectuate the purposes and policies of this title and to make the results of such studies available to the public;

(6) to intervene in a civil action brought under section 706 by an aggrieved party against a respondent other than a government, governmental agency or political subdivision.

Public Law 92-261

(h) The Commission shall, in any of its educational or promotional activities, cooperate with other departments and agencies in the performance of such educational and promotional activities.

(i) All officers, agents, attorneys, and employees of the Commission shall be subject to the provisions of section 9 of the Act of August 2, 1939, as amended (the Hatch Act), notwithstanding any exemption contained in such section.

PREVENTION OF UNLAWFUL EMPLOYMENT PRACTICES

SEC. 706. (a) The Commission is empowered, as hereinafter provided, to prevent any person from engaging in any unlawful employment practice as set forth in section 703 or 704 of this title.

(b) Whenever a charge is filed by or on behalf of a person claiming to be aggrieved, or by a member of the Commission, alleging that an employer, employment agency, labor organization, or joint labor-management committee controlling apprenticeship or other training or retraining, including on-the-job training programs, has engaged in an unlawful employment practice, the Commission shall serve a notice of the charge (including the date, place and circumstances of the alleged unlawful employment practice) on such employer, employment agency, labor organization, or joint labor-management committee (hereinafter referred to as the "respondent") within ten days, and shall make an investigation thereof. Charges shall be in writing under oath or affirmation and shall contain such information and be in such form as the Commission requires. Charges shall not be made public by the Commission. If the Commission determines after such investigation that there is not reasonable cause to believe that the charge is true, it shall dismiss the charge and promptly notify the person claiming to be aggrieved and the respondent of its action. In determining whether reasonable cause exists, the Commission shall accord substantial weight to final findings and orders made by State or local authorities in proceedings commenced under State or local law pursuant to the requirements of subsections (c) and (d). If the Commission determines after such investigation that there is reasonable cause to believe that the charge is true, the Commission shall endeavor to eliminate any such alleged unlawful employment practice by informal methods of conference, conciliation, and persuasion. Nothing said or done during and as a part of such informal endeavors may be made public by the Commission, its officers or employees, or used as evidence in a subsequent proceeding without the written consent of the persons concerned. Any person who makes public information in violation of this subsection shall be fined not more than $1,000 or imprisoned for not more than one year, or both. The Commission shall make its determination on reasonable cause as promptly as possible and, so far as practicable, not later than one hundred and twenty days from the filing of the charge or, where applicable under subsection (c) or (d), from the date upon which the Commission is authorized to take action with respect to the charge.

Public Law
92–261

(c) In the case of an alleged unlawful employment practice occurring in a State, or political subdivision of a State, which has a State or local law prohibiting the unlawful employment practice alleged and establishing or authorizing a State or local authority to grant or seek relief from such practice or to institute criminal proceedings with respect thereto upon receiving notice thereof, no charge may be filed under subsection (a) by the person aggrieved before the expiration of sixty days after proceedings have been commenced under the State or local law, unless such proceedings have been earlier terminated, provided that such sixty-day period shall be extended to one hundred and twenty days during the first year after the effective date of such State or local law. If any requirement for the commencement of such proceedings is imposed by a State or local authority other than a requirement of the filing of a written and signed

Public Law
92–261

statement of the facts upon which the proceeding is based, the proceeding shall be deemed to have been commenced for the purposes of this subsection at the time such statement is sent by registered mail to the appropriate State or local authority.

(d) In the case of any charge filed by a member of the Commission alleging an unlawful employment practice occurring in a State or political subdivision of a State which has a State or local law prohibiting the practice alleged and establishing or authorizing a State or local authority to grant or seek relief from such practice or to institute criminal proceedings with respect thereto upon receiving notice thereof, the Commission shall, before taking any action with respect to such charge, notify the appropriate State or local officials and, upon request, afford them a reasonable time, but not less than sixty days (provided that such sixty-day period shall be extended to one hundred and twenty days during the first year after the effective day of such State or local law), unless a shorter period is requested, to act under such State or local law to remedy the practice alleged.

(e) A charge under this section shall be filed within one hundred and eighty days after the alleged unlawful employment practice occurred and notice of the charge (including the date, place and circumstances of the alleged unlawful employment practice) shall be served upon the person against whom such charge is made within ten days thereafter, except that in a case of an unlawful employment practice with respect to which the person aggrieved has initially instituted proceedings with a State or local agency whith authority to grant or seek relief from such practice or to institute criminal proceedings with respect thereto upon receiving notice thereof, such charge shall be filed by or on behalf of the person aggrieved within three hundred days after the alleged unlawful employment practice occurred, or within thirty-days after receiving notice that the State or local agency has terminated the proceedings under the State or local law, whichever is earlier, and a copy of such charge shall be filed by the Commission with the State or local agency.

(f) (1) If within thirty days after a charge is filed with the Commission or within thirty days after expiration of any period of reference under subsection (c) or (d), the Commission has been unable to secure from the respondent a conciliation agreement acceptable to the Commission, the Commission may bring a civil action against any respondent not a government, governmental agency, or political subdivision named in the charge. In the case of a respondent which is a government, governmental agency, or political subdivision, if the Commission has been unable to secure from the respondent a conciliation agreement acceptable to the Commission, the Commission shall take no further action and shall refer the case to the Attorney General who may bring a civil action against such respondent in the appropriate United States district court. The person or persons aggrieved shall have the right to intervene in a civil action brought by the Commission or the Attorney General in a case involving a government, governmental agency, or political subdivision. If a charge filed with the Commission pursuant to subsection (b) is dismissed by the Commission, or if within one hundred and eighty days from the filing of such charge or the expiration of any period of reference under subsection (c) or (d), whichever is later, the Commission has not filed a civil action under this section or the Attorney General has not filed a civil action in a case involving a government, governmental agency, or political subdivision, shall so notify the person aggrieved and conciliation agreement to which the person aggrieved is a party, the Commission, or the Attorney General in a case involving a government, governmental agency, or political subdivision, shall so notify the person aggrieved and within ninety days after the giving of such notice a civil action may be brought against the respondent named in the charge (A) by the person claiming to be aggrieved or (B) if such charge was filed by a member of the Commission, by any person whom the charge alleges was aggrieved by the alleged unlawful employment practice. Upon application by the complainant and in such circumstances as the court may deem just, the court may appoint an attorney for such complainant and may authorize the commencement of the action without the payment of fees, costs, or security. Upon timely application, the court may, in its discretion, permit the Commission, or the Attorney General in a case involving a government, governmental agency, or political subdivision, to intervene in such civil action upon certification that the case is of general public importance. Upon request, the court may, in its discretion, stay further proceedings for not more than sixty days pending the termination of State or local proceedings described in subsection (c) or (d) of this section or further efforts of the Commission to obtain voluntary compliance.

Public Law
92–261

(2) Whenever a charge is filed with the Commission and the Commission concludes on the basis of a preliminary investigation that prompt judicial action is necessary to carry out the purposes of this Act, the Commission, or the Attorney General in a case involving a government, governmental agency, or political subdivision, may bring an action for appropriate temporary or preliminary relief pending final disposition of such charge. Any temporary restraining order or other order granting preliminary or temporary relief shall be issued in accordance with rule 65 of the Federal Rules of Civil Procedure. It shall be the duty of a court having jurisdiction over proceedings under this section to assign cases for hearing at the earliest practicable date and to cause such cases to be in every way expedited.

(3) Each United States district court and each United States court of a place subject to the jurisdiction of the United States shall have jurisdiction of actions brought under this title. Such an action may be brought in any

judicial district in the State in which the unlawful employment practice is alleged to have been committed, in the judicial district in which the employment records relevant to such practice are maintained and administered, or in the judicial district in which the aggrieved person would have worked but for the alleged unlawful employment practice, but if the respondent is not found within any such district, such an action may be brought within the judicial district in which the respondent has his principal office. For purposes of sections 1404 and 1406 of title 28 of the United States Code, the judicial district in which the respondent has his principal office shall in all cases be considered a district in which the action might have been brought.

(4) It shall be the duty of the chief judge of the district (or in his absence, the acting chief judge) in which the case is pending immediately to designate a judge in such district to hear and determine the case. In the event that no judge in the district is available to hear and determine the case, the chief judge of the district, or the acting chief judge, as the case may be, shall certify this fact to the chief judge of the circuit (or in his absence, the acting chief judge) who shall then designate a district or circuit judge of the circuit to hear and determine the case.

Public Law 92–261

(5) It shall be the duty of the judge designated pursuant to this subsection to assign the case for hearing at the earliest practicable date and to cause the case to be in every way expedited. If such judge has not scheduled the case for trial within one hundred and twenty days after issue has been joined, that judge may appoint a master pursuant to rule 53 of the Federal Rules of Civil Procedure.

(g) If the court finds that the respondent has intentionally engaged in or is intentionally engaging in an unlawful employment practice charged in the complaint, the court may enjoin the respondent from engaging in such unlawful employment practice, and order such affirmative action as may be appropriate, which may include, but is not limited to, reinstatement or hiring of employees, with or without back pay (payable by the employer, employment agency, or labor organization, as the case may be, responsible for the unlawful employment practice), or any other equitable relief as the court deems appropriate. Back pay liability shall not accrue from a date more than two years prior to the filing of a charge with the Commission. Interim earnings or amounts earnable with reasonable diligence by the person or persons discriminated against shall operate to reduce the back pay otherwise allowable. No order of the court shall require the admission or reinstatement of an individual as a member of a union, or the hiring, reinstatement, or promotion of an individual as an employee, or the payment to him of any back pay, if such individual was refused admission, suspended, or expelled, or was refused employment or advancement or was suspended or discharged for any reason other than discrimination on account of race, color, religion, sex, or national origin or in violation of section 704(a).

(h) The provisions of the Act entitled "An Act to amend the Judicial Code and to define and limit the jurisdiction of courts sitting in equity, and for other purposes," approved March 23, 1932 (29 U.S.C. 101–115), shall not apply with respect to civil actions brought under this section.

(i) In any case in which an employer, employment agency, or labor organization fails to comply with an order of a court issued in a civil action brought under this section, the Commission may commence proceedings to compel compliance with such order.

(j) Any civil action brought under this section and any proceedings brought under subsection (i) shall be subject to appeal as provided in sections 1291 and 1292, title 28, United States Code.

(k) In any action or proceeding under this title the court, in its discretion, may allow the prevailing party, other than the Commission or the United States, a reasonable attorney's fee as part of the costs, and the Commission and the United States shall be liable for costs the same as a private person.

SEC. 707. (a) Whenever the Attorney General has reasonable cause to believe that any person or group of persons is engaged in a pattern or practice of resistance to the full enjoyment of any of the rights secured by this title, and that the pattern or practice is of such a nature and is intended to deny the full exercise of the rights herein described, the Attorney General may bring a civil action in the appropriate district court of the United States by filing with it a complaint (1) signed by him (or in his absence the Acting Attorney General), (2) setting forth facts pertaining to such pattern or practice, and (3) requesting such relief, including an application for a permanent or temporary injunction, restraining order or other order against the person or persons responsible for such pattern or practice, as he deems necessary to insure the full enjoyment of the rights herein described.

(b) The district courts of the United States shall have and shall exercise jurisdiction of proceedings instituted pursuant to this section, and in any such proceeding the Attorney General may file with the clerk of such court a request that court of three judges be convened to hear and determine the case. Such request by the Attorney General shall be accompanied by a certificate that, in his opinion, the case is of general public importance. A copy of the certificate and request for a three-judge court shall be immediately furnished by such clerk to the chief judge of the circuit (or in his absence, the presiding circuit judge of the circuit) in which the case is pending. Upon receipt of such request it shall be the duty of the chief judge of the circuit or the presiding circuit judge, as the case may be, to designate immediately three judges in such circuit, of whom at least one shall be a circuit judge and another of whom shall be a district judge of the court in which the proceeding was instituted, to hear and determine such case, and it shall be the duty of the judges so designated to assign the case for hearing at the earliest practicable date, to participate in the hearing and determination thereof, and to cause the case to be in every way expedited. An appeal from the final judgment of such court will lie to the Supreme Court.

In the event the Attorney General fails to file such a request in any such proceeding, it shall be the duty of the chief judge of the district (or in his absence, the acting chief judge) in which the case is pending immediately to designate a judge in such district to hear and determine the case. In the event that no judge in the district is available to hear and determine the case, the chief judge of the district, or the acting chief judge, as the case may be, shall certify this fact to the chief judge of the circuit (or in his absence, the acting chief judge) who shall then designate a district or circuit judge of the circuit to hear and determine the case.

It shall be the duty of the judge designated pursuant to this section to assign the case for hearing at the earliest practicable date and to cause the case to be in every way expedited.

(c) Effective two years after the date of enactment of the Equal Employment Opportunity Act of 1972, the functions of the Attorney General under this section shall be transferred to the Commission, together with such personnel, property, records, and unexpended balances of appropriations, allocations, and other funds employed, used, held, available, or to be made available in connection with such functions unless the President submits, and neither House of Congress vetoes, a reorganization plan pursuant to chapter 9 of title 5, United States Code, inconsistent with the provisions of this subsection. The Commission shall carry out such functions in accordance with subsections (d) and (e) of this section. Public Law 92-261

(d) Upon the transfer of functions provided for in subsection (c) of this section, in all suits commenced pursuant to this section prior to the date of such transfer, proceedings shall continue without abatement, all court orders and decrees shall remain in effect, and the Commission shall be substituted as a party for the United States of America, the Attorney General, or the Acting Attorney General as appropriate. Public Law 92-261

(e) Subsequent to the date of enactment of the Equal Employment Opportunity Act of 1972, the Commission shall have authority to investigate and act on a charge of a pattern or practice of discrimination, whether filed by or on behalf of a person claiming to be aggrieved or by a member of the Commission. All such actions shall be conducted in accordance with the procedures set forth in section 706 of this Act. Public Law 92-261

Sec. 708. Nothing in this title shall be deemed to exempt or relieve any person from any liability, duty, penalty, or punishment provided by any present or future law of any State or political subdivision of a State, other than any such law which purports to require or permit the doing of any act which would be an unlawful employment practice under this title.

INVESTIGATIONS, INSPECTIONS, RECORDS, STATE AGENCIES

Sec. 709. (a) In connection with any investigation of a charge filed under section 706, the Commission or its designated representative shall at all reasonable times have access to, for the purposes of examination, and the right to copy any evidence of any person being investigated or proceeded against that relates to unlawful employment practices covered by this title and is relevant to the charge under investigation.

Public Law
92–261

(b) The Commission may cooperate with State and local agencies charged with the administration of State fair employment practices laws and, with the consent of such agencies, may, for the purpose of carrying out its functions and duties under this title and within the limitation of funds appropriated specifically for such purpose, engage in and contribute to the cost of research and other projects of mutual interest undertaken by such agencies, and utilize the services of such agencies and their employees, and, notwithstanding any other provision of law, pay by advance or reimbursement such agencies and their employees for services rendered to assist the Commission in carrying out this title. In furtherance of such cooperative efforts, the Commission may enter into written agreements with such State or local agencies and such agreements may include provisions under which the Commission shall refrain from processing a charge in any cases or class of cases specified in such agreements or under which the Commission shall relieve any person or class of persons in such State or locality from requirements imposed under this section. The Commission shall rescind any such agreement whenever it determines that the agreement no longer serves the interest of effective enforcement of this title.

(c) Every employer, employment agency, and labor organization subject to this title shall (1) make and keep such records relevant to the determinations of whether unlawful employment practices have been or are being committed, (2) preserve such records for such periods, and (3) make such reports therefrom as the Commission shall prescribe by regulation or order, after public hearing, as reasonable, necessary, or appropriate for the enforcement of this title or the regulations or orders thereunder. The Commission shall, by regulation, require each employer, labor organization, and joint labor-management committee subject to this title which controls an apprenticeship or other training program to maintain such records as are reasonably necessary to carry out the purposes of this title, including, but not limited to, a list of applicants who wish to participate in such program, including the chronological order in which applications were received, and to furnish to the Commission upon request, a detailed description of the manner in which persons are selected to participate in the apprenticeship or other training program. Any employer, employment agency, labor organization, or joint labor-management committee which believes that the application to it of any regulation or order issued under this section would result in undue hardship may apply to the Commission for an exemption from the application of such regulation or order, and, if such application for an exemption is denied, bring a civil action in the United States district court for the district where such records are kept. If the Commission or the court, as the case may be, finds that the application of the regulation or order to the employer, employment agency, or labor organization in question would impose an undue hardship, the Commission or the court, as the case may be, may grant appropriate relief. If any person required to comply with the provisions of this subsection fails or refuses to do so, the United States district court for the district in which such person is found, resides, or transacts business, shall, upon application of the Commission, or the Attorney General in a case involving a government, governmental agency or political subdivision, have jurisdiction to issue to such person an order requiring him to comply.

(d) In prescribing requirements pursuant to subsection (c) of this section, the Commission shall consult with other interested State and Federal agencies and shall endeavor to coordinate its requirements with those adopted by such agencies. The Commission shall furnish upon request and without cost to any State or local agency charged with the administration of a fair employment practice law information obtained pursuant to subsection (c) of this section from any employer, employment agency, labor organization, or joint labor-management committee subject to the jurisdiction of such agency. Such information shall be furnished on condition that it not be made public by the recipient agency prior to the institution of a proceeding under State or local law involving such information. If this condition is violated by a recipient agency, the Commission may decline to honor subsequent requests pursuant to this subsection.

(e) It shall be unlawful for any officer or employee of the Commission to make public in any manner whatever any information obtained by the Commission pursuant to its authority under this section prior to the institution of any proceeding under this title involving such information. Any officer or employee of the Commission who shall make public in any manner whatever any information in violation of this subsection shall be guilty of a misdemeanor and upon conviction thereof, shall be fined not more than $1,000, or imprisoned not more than one year.

INVESTIGATORY POWERS

Public Law
92-261

SEC. 710. For the purpose of all hearings and investigations conducted by the Commission or its duly authorized agents or agencies, section 11 of the National Labor Relations Act (49 Stat. 455; 29 U.S.C. 161) shall apply.

NOTICES TO BE POSTED

SEC. 711. (a) Every employer, employment agency, and labor organization, as the case may be, shall post and keep posted in conspicuous places upon its premises where notices to employees, applicants for employment, and members are customarily posted a notice to be prepared or approved by the Commission setting forth excerpts from, or summaries of, the pertinent provisions of this title and information pertinent to the filing of a complaint.

(b) A willful violation of this section shall be punishable by a fine of not more than $100 for each separate offense.

VETERANS' PREFERENCE

SEC. 712. Nothing contained in this title shall be construed to repeal or modify any Federal, State, territorial, or local law creating special rights or preference for veterans.

RULES AND REGULATIONS

SEC. 713. (a) The Commission shall have authority from time to time to issue, amend, or rescind suitable procedural regulations to carry out the provisions of this title. Regulations issued under this section shall be in conformity with the standards and limitations of the Administrative Procedure Act.

(b) In any action or proceeding based on any alleged unlawful employment practice, no person shall be subject to any liability or punishment for or on account of (1) the commission by such person of an unlawful employment practice if he pleads and proves that the act or omission complained of was in good faith, in conformity with, and in reliance on any written interpretation or opinion of the Commission, or (2) the failure of such person to publish and file any information required by any provision of this title if he pleads and proves that he failed to publish and file such information in good faith, in conformity with the instructions of the Commission issued under this title regarding the filing of such information. Such a defense, if established, shall be a bar to the action or proceeding, notwithstanding that (A) after such act or omission, such interpretation or opinion is modified or rescinded or is determined by judicial authority to be invalid or of no legal effect, or (B) after publishing or filing the description and annual reports, such publication or filing is determined by judicial authority not to be in conformity with the requirements of this title.

FORCIBLY RESISTING THE COMMISSION OR ITS REPRESENTATIVES

SEC. 714. The provisions of section 111 and 1114, title 18, United States Code, shall apply to officers, agents, and employees of the Commission in the performance of their official duties. Notwithstanding the provisions of sections 111 and 1114 of title 18, United States Code, whoever in violation of the provisions of section 1114 of such title kills a person while engaged in or on account of the performance of his official functions under this Act shall be punished by imprisonment for any term of years or for life.

Public Law 92–261

EQUAL EMPLOYMENT OPPORTUNITY COORDINATING COUNCIL

SEC. 715. There shall be established an Equal Employment Opportunity Coordinating Council (hereinafter referred to in this section as the Council) composed of the Secretary of Labor, the Chairman of the Equal Employment Opportunity Commission, the Attorney General, the Chairman of the United States Civil Service Commission, and the Chairman of the United States Civil Rights Commission, or their respective delegates. The Council shall have the responsibility for developing and implementing agreements, policies and practices designed to maximize effort, promote efficiency, and eliminate conflict, competition, duplication and inconsistency among the operations, functions and jurisdictions of the various departments, agencies and branches of the Federal Government responsible for the implementation and enforcement of equal employment opportunity legislation, orders, and policies. On or before July 1 of each year, the Council shall transmit to the President and to the Congress a report of its activities, together with such recommendations for legislative or administrative changes as it concludes are desirable to further promote the purposes of this section.

Public Law 92–261

EFFECTIVE DATE

SEC. 716. (a) This title shall become effective one year after the date of its enactment.

(b) Notwithstanding subsection (a), sections of this title other than sections 703, 704, 706, and 707 shall become effective immediately.

(c) The President shall, as soon as feasible after the enactment of this title, convene one or more conferences for the purpose of enabling the leaders of groups whose members will be affected by this title to become familiar with the rights afforded and obligations imposed by its provisions, and for the purpose of making plans which will result in the fair and effective administration of this title when all of its provisions become effective. The President shall invite the participation in such conference or conferences of (1) the members of the President's Committee on Equal Employment Opportunity, (2) the members of the Commission on Civil Rights, (3) representatives of State and local agencies engaged in furthering equal employment opportunity, (4) representatives of private agencies engaged in furthering equal employment opportunity, and (5) representatives of employers, labor organizations, and employment agencies who will be subject to this title.

NONDISCRIMINATION IN FEDERAL GOVERNMENT
EMPLOYMENT

SEC. 717. (a) All personnel actions affecting employees or applicants for employment (except with regard to aliens employed outside the limits of the United States) in miliary departments as defined in section 102 of title 5, United States Code, in executive agencies (other than the General Accounting Office) as defined in section 105 of title 5, United States Code (including employees and applicants for employment who are paid from nonappropriated funds), in the United States Postal Service and the Postal Rate Commission, in those units of the Government of the District of Columbia having positions in the competitive service, and in those units of the legislative and judicial branches of the Federal Government having positions in the competitive service, and in the Library of Congress shall be made free from any discrimination based on race, color, religion, sex, or national origin.

Public Law
92-261

(b) Except as otherwise provided in this subsection, the Civil Service Commission shall have authority to enforce the provisions of subsection (a) through appropriate remedies, including reinstatement or hiring of employees with or without back pay, as will effectuate the policies of this section, and shall issue such rules, regulations, orders and instructions as it deems necessary and appropriate to carry out its responsibilities under this section. The Civil Service Commission shall—

(1) be responsible for the annual review and approval of a national and regional equal employment opportunity plan which each department and agency and each appropriate unit referred to in subsection (a) of this section shall submit in order to maintain an affirmative program of equal employment opportunity for all such employees and applicants for employment;

(2) be responsible for the review and evaluation of the operation of all agency equal employment opportunity programs, periodically obtaining and publishing (on at least a semiannual basis) progress reports from each such department, agency, or unit; and

(3) consult with and solicit the recommendations of interested individuals, groups, and organizations relating to equal employment opportunity.

The head of each such department, agency, or unit shall comply with such rules, regulations, orders, and instructions which shall include a provision that an employee or applicant for employment shall be notified of any final action taken on any complaint of discrimination filed by him thereunder. The plan submitted by each department, agency, and unit shall include, but not be limited to—

(1) provision for the establishment of training and education programs designed to provide a maximum opportunity for employees to advance so as to perform at their highest potential; and

(2) a description of the qualifications in terms of training and experience relating to equal employment opportunity for the principal and operating officials of each such department, agency, or unit responsible for carrying out the equal employment opportunity program and of the allocation of personnel and resources proposed by such department, agency, or unit to carry out its equal employment opportunity program.

With respect to employment in the Library of Congress, authorities granted in this subsection to the Civil Service Commission shall be exercised by the Librarian of Congress.

(c) Within thirty days of receipt of notice of final action taken by a department, agency, or unit referred to in subsection 717(a), or by the Civil Service Commission upon an appeal from a decision or order of such department, agency, or unit on a complaint of discrimination based on race, color, religion, sex or national origin, brought pursuant to subsection (a) of this section, Executive Order 11478 or any succeeding Executive orders, or after one hundred and eighty days from the filing of the initial charge with the department, agency, or unit or with the Civil Service Commission on appeal from a decision or order of such department, agency, or unit until such time as final action may be taken by a department, agency, or unit, an employee or applicant for employment, if aggrieved by the final disposition of his complaint, or by the failure to take final action on his complaint, may file a civil action as provided in section 706, in which civil action the head of the department, agency, or unit, as appropriate, shall be the defendant.

(d) The provisions of section 706 (f) through (k), as applicable, shall govern civil actions brought hereunder.

(e) Nothing contained in this Act shall relieve any Government agency or official of its or his primary responsibility to assure nondiscrimination in employment as required by the Constitution and statutes or of its or his responsibilities under Executive Order 11478 relating to equal employment opportunity in the Federal Government.

SPECIAL PROVISION WITH RESPECT TO DENIAL, TERMINATION, AND SUSPENSION OF GOVERNMENT CONTRACTS

SEC. 718. No Government contract, or portion thereof, with any employer, shall be denied, withheld, terminated, or suspended, by any agency or officer of the United States under any equal employment opportunity law or

Public Law 92–261

order, where such employer has an affirmative action plan which has previously been accepted by the Government for the same facility within the past twelve months without first according such employer full hearing and adjudication under the provisions of title 5, United States Code, section 554, and the following pertinent sections: *Provided*, That if such employer has deviated substantially from such previously agreed to affirmative action plan, this section shall not apply: *Provided further*, That for the purposes of this section an affirmative action plan shall be deemed to have been accepted by the Government at the time the appropriate compliance agency has accepted such plan unless within forty-five days thereafter the Office of Federal Contract Compliance has disapproved such plan.

Appendix B

Fair Labor Standards Act, as amended
(Includes Equal Pay Act of 1963)

Fair Labor Standards Act of 1938, as amended[1]

(29 U.S.C. 201, et seq.)

(Revised text[1] showing in bold face type new or amended language provided by the Fair Labor Standards Amendments of 1961, as enacted May 5, 1961 (P.L. 87-30, 75 Stat. 65), and showing in italics new or amended language provided by the Fair Labor Standards Amendments of 1966, as enacted September 23, 1966 (P.L. 89-601, 80 Stat. 830), and showing in **bold face italics** the new and amended language provided by the Education Amendments of 1972, as enacted June 23, 1972 (P.L. 92-318, 86 Stat. 235 at 375), and the new or amended language provided by the Fair Labor Standards Amendments of 1974, as enacted April 8, 1974 (P.L. 93-259, 88 Stat. 55). In cases where annual changes are to be made in provisions, as in the case of the gradual phase-out of exemptions, the changes are shown in bold face italics immediately following the provision to which they apply and are enclosed in brackets.)

[1]52 Stat. 1060, as amended by the Act of August 9, 1939 (53 Stat. 1266); by section 404 of Reorganization Plan No. II of 1939 (53 Stat. 1436); by sections 3(c)–3(f) of the Act of June 26, 1940 (54 Stat. 615); by the Act of October 29, 1941 (55 Stat. 756); by Reorganization Plan No. 2 of 1946 (60 Stat. 1095); by the Portal-to-Portal Act of 1947 (61 Stat. 84); by the Act of July 20, 1949 (63 Stat. 446); by the Fair Labor Standards Amendments of 1949 (63 Stat. 910); by Reorganization Plan No. 6 of 1950 (64 Stat. 1263); by the Fair Labor Standards Amendments of 1955 (69 Stat. 711); by the American Samoa Labor Standards Amendments of 1956 (70 Stat. 1118); by the Act of August 30, 1957 (71 Stat. 514); by the Act of August 25, 1958 (72 Stat. 844); by section 22 of the Act of August 28, 1958 (72 Stat. 948); by the Act of July 12, 1960 (74 Stat. 417); by the Fair Labor Standards Amendments of 1961 (75 Stat. 65); by the Equal Pay Act of 1963 (77 Stat. 56); by the Fair Labor Standards Amendments of 1966 (80 Stat. 830); by section 8 of the Department of Transportation Act (80 Stat. 931); by the Act of September 11, 1967, amending Title 5 of the U.S.C. (81 Stat. 222); by section 906 of the Education Amendments of 1972 (86 Stat. 235); and by the Fair Labor Standards Amendments of 1974 (P.L. 93–259, 88 Stat. 55), which became effective on May 1, 1974.

The original text of the Fair Labor Standards Act of 1938 as set forth in 52 Stat. 1060 has been revised in this publication to reflect the changes effected by the amendments listed in this footnote, which may be found in official text at the cited pages of the Statutes at Large. Added or amended language as enacted by the Fair Labor Standards Amendments of 1961 is shown in bold face type. Added or amended language as enacted by the Fair Labor Standards Amendments of 1966 is shown in italics. Added or amended language as enacted by the Education Amendments of 1972 and by the Fair Labor Standards Amendments of 1974 is shown in bold face italics. The footnotes in this revision show where prior changes have been made and refer to the specific amendments relied upon so that a comparison may be made with the official text.

This revised text has been prepared in the Office of the Solicitor, U.S. Department of Labor.

An act

To provide for the establishment of fair labor standards in employments in and affecting interstate commerce, and for other purposes.

Be it enacted by the Senate and House of Representatives of the United States of America in Congress assembled, That this Act may be cited as the "Fair Labor Standards Act of 1938."

Finding and Declaration of Policy
SEC. 2.

(a) The Congress hereby finds that the existence, in industries engaged in commerce or in the production of goods for commerce, of labor conditions detrimental to the maintenance of the minimum standard of living necessary for health, efficiency, and general well-being of workers (1) causes commerce and the channels and instrumentalities of commerce to be used to spread and perpetuate such labor conditions among the workers of the several States; (2) burdens commerce and the free flow of goods in commerce; (3) constitutes an unfair method of competition in commerce; (4) leads to labor disputes burdening and obstructing commerce and the free flow of goods in commerce; and (5) interferes with the orderly and fair marketing of goods in commerce. *The Congress further finds that the employment of persons in domestic service in households affects commerce.*

(b) It is hereby declared to be the policy of this Act, through the exercise by Congress of its power to regulate commerce among the several States and with foreign nations, to correct and as rapidly as practicable to eliminate the conditions above referred to in such industries without substantially curtailing employment or earning power.[2]

Definitions
SEC. 3. As used in this Act—

(a) "Person" means an individual, partnership, association, corporation, business trust, legal representative, or any organized group of persons.

(b) "Commerce" means trade, commerce, transportation, transmission, or communication among the several States or between any State and any place outside thereof.[3]

(c) "State" means any State of the United States or the District of Columbia or any Territory or possession of the United States.

(d) "Employer" includes any person acting directly or indirectly in the interest of an employer in relation to an employee *and includes a public agency,*[4] *but does not include* any labor organization (other than when acting as an employer) or anyone acting in the capacity of officer or agent of such labor organization.

[2]As amended by section 2 of the Fair Labor Standards Amendments of 1949.
[3]As amended by section 3(a) of the Fair Labor Standards Amendments of 1949.
[4]Public agencies were specifically excluded from the Act's coverage until the Fair Labor Standards Amendments of 1966, when Congress extended coverage to "employees of a State or a political subdivision thereof, employed (1) in a hospital, institution, or school referred to in the last sentence of subsection (r) of this section, or (2) in the operation of a railway or carrier referred to in such sentence * * *."

(e) *(1) Except as provided in paragraphs (2) and (3), the term* "employee" *means* any individual employed by an employer.

(2) *In the case of an individual employed by a public agency, such term means—*

(A) any individual employed by the Government of the United States—

(i) as a civilian in the military departments (as defined in section 102 of title 5, United States Code),

(ii) in any executive agency (as defined in section 105 of such title).

(iii) in any unit of the legislative or judicial branch of the Government which has positions in the competitive service,

(iv) in a nonappropriated fund instrumentality under the jurisdiction of the Armed Forces, or

(v) in the Library of Congress;

(B) any individual employed by the United States Postal Service or the Postal Rate Commission; and

(C) any individual employed by a State, political subdivision of a State, or an interstate governmental agency, other than such an individual—

(i) who is not subject to the civil service laws of the State, political subdivision, or agency which employs him; and

(ii) who—

(I) holds a public elective office of that State, political subdivision, or agency,

(II) is selected by the holder of such an office to be a member of his personal staff,

(III) is appointed by such an officeholder to serve on a policymaking level, or

(IV) who is an immediate adviser to such an officeholder with respect to the constitutional or legal powers of his office.

(3) *For purposes of subsection (u), such term does not include any individual employed by an employer engaged in agriculture if such individual is the parent, spouse, child, or other member of the employer's immediate family.*[5]

(f) "Agriculture" includes farming in all its branches and among other things includes the cultivation and tillage of the soil, dairying, the production, cultivation, growing, and harvesting of any agricultural or horticultural commodities (including commodities defined as agricultural commodities in section 15(g) of the Agricultural Marketing Act, as amended), the raising of livestock, bees, fur-bearing animals, or poultry, and any practices (including any forestry or lumbering operations) performed by a farmer or on a farm as an incident to or in conjunction with such farming operations, including preparation.

---

[5]Similar language was added to the Act by the Fair Labor Standards Amendments of 1966. Those amendments also excluded from the definition of employee "any individual who is employed by an employer engaged in agriculture if such individual (A) is employed as a hand harvest laborer and is paid on a piece rate basis in an operation which has been, and is customarily and generally recognized as having been, paid on a piece rate basis in the region of employment, (B) commutes daily from his permanent residence to the farm on which he is so employed, and (C) has been employed in agriculture less than thirteen weeks during the preceding calendar year." These individuals are now included.

for market, delivery to storage or to market or to carriers for transportation to market.

(g) "Employ" includes to suffer or permit to work.

(h) "Industry" means a trade, business, industry, *or other activity, or branch or group thereof,* in which individuals are gainfully employed.

(i) "Goods" means goods (including ships and marine equipment), wares, products, commodities, merchandise, or articles or subjects of commerce of any character, or any part or ingredient thereof, but does not include goods after their delivery into the actual physical possession of the ultimate consumer thereof other than a producer, manufacturer, or processor thereof.

(j) "Produced" means produced, manufactured, mined, handled, or in any other manner worked on in any State; and for the purposes of this Act an employee shall be deemed to have been engaged in the production of goods if such employee was employed in producing, manufacturing, mining, handling, transporting, or in any other manner working on such goods, or in any closely related process or occupation directly essential to the production thereof, in any State.[6]

(k) "Sale" or "sell" includes any sale, exchange, contract to sell, consignment for sale, shipment for sale, or other disposition.

(l) "Oppressive child labor" means a condition of employment under which (1) any employee under the age of sixteen years is employed by an employer (other than a parent or a person standing in place of a parent employing his own child or a child in his custody under the age of sixteen years in an occupation other than manufacturing or mining or an occupation found by the Secretary of Labor to be particularly hazardous for the employment of children between the ages of sixteen and eighteen years or detrimental to their health or well-being) in any occupation,[7] or (2) any employee between the ages of sixteen and eighteen years is employed by an employer in any occupation which the Secretary of Labor[8] shall find and by order declare to be particularly hazardous for the employment of children between such ages or detrimental to their health or well-being; but oppressive child labor shall not be deemed to exist by virtue of the employment in any occupation of any person with respect to whom the employer shall have on file an unexpired certificate issued and held pursuant to regulations of the Secretary of Labor[9] certifying that such person is above the oppressive child labor age. The Secretary of Labor[10] shall provide by regulation or by order that the employment of employees between the ages of fourteen and sixteen years in occupations other than manufacturing and mining shall not be deemed to constitute oppressive child labor if and to the extent that the Secretary of Labor[11] determines that such employment is confined to periods

[6]As amended by section 3(b) of the Fair Labor Standards Amendments of 1949.
[7]As amended by section 3(c) of the Fair Labor Standards Amendments of 1949.
[8]Reorganization Plan No. 2 of 1946 provided that the functions of the Children's Bureau and of the Chief of the Children's Bureau under the Act as originally enacted be transferred to the Secretary of Labor.
[9]Ibid.
[10]Ibid.
[11]Ibid.

which will not interfere with their schooling and to conditions which will not interfere with their health and well-being.

(m)"Wage" paid to any employee includes the reasonable cost, as determined by the Secretary of Labor,[12] to the employer of furnishing such employee with board, lodging, or other facilities, if such board, lodging, or other facilities are customarily furnished by such employer to his employees: *Provided,* **That the cost of board, lodging, or other facilities shall not be included as a part of the wage paid to any employee to the extent it is excluded therefrom under the terms of a bona fide collective-bargaining agreement applicable to the particular employee:** *Provided further,* **That the Secretary is authorized to determine the fair value of such board, lodging, or other facilities for defined classes of employees and in defined areas, based on average cost to the employer or to groups of employers similarly situated, or average value to groups of employees, or other appropriate measures of fair value. Such evaluations, where applicable and pertinent, shall be used in lieu of actual measure of cost in determining the wage paid to any employee.** *In determining the wage of a tipped employee, the amount paid such employee by his employer shall be deemed to be increased on account of tips by an amount determined by the employer, but not by an amount in excess of 50 per centum of the applicable minimum wage rate, except that* **the amount of the increase on account of tips determined by the employer may not exceed the value of tips actually received by the employee. The previous sentence shall not apply with respect to any tipped employee unless (1) such employee has been informed by the employer of the provisions of this subsection, and (2) all tips received by such employee have been retained by the employee, except that this subsection shall not be construed to prohibit the pooling of tips among employees who customarily and regularly receive tips.**

(n) "Resale" shall not include the sale of goods to be used in residential or farm building construction, repair, or maintenance: *Provided,* That the sale is recognized as a bona fide retail sale in the industry.[13]

(o) Hours worked. —In determining for the purposes of sections 6 and 7 the hours for which an employee is employed, there shall be excluded any time spent in changing clothes or washing at the beginning or end of each workday which was excluded from measured working time during the week involved by the express terms of or by custom or practice under a bona fide collective-bargaining agreement applicable to the particular employee.[14]

(p) **"American vessel" includes any vessel which is documented or numbered under the laws of the United States.**

(q) **"Secretary" means the Secretary of Labor.**

(r) **"Enterprise" means the related activities performed (either through unified operation or common control) by any person or persons for a common business purpose, and includes all such activities whether performed in one or more establishments or by one or more corporate or other organizational units including departments of an**

---

[12]As amended by Reorganization Plan No. 5 of 1950, set out under section 4(a).

[13] [14]Section 3(d) of the Fair Labor Standards Amendments of 1949. (The original language of section 3(n) was restored by the Fair Labor Standards Amendments of 1966.)

establishment operated through leasing arrangements, but shall not include the related activities performed for such enterprise by an independent contractor: *Provided,* That, within the meaning of this subsection, a retail or service establishment which is under independent ownership shall not be deemed to be so operated or controlled as to be other than a separate and distinct enterprise by reason of any arrangement, which includes, but is not necessarily limited to, an agreement, (1) that it will sell, or sell only, certain goods specified by a particular manufacturer, distributor, or advertiser, or (2) that it will join with other such establishments in the same industry for the purpose of collective purchasing, or (3) that it will have the exclusive right to sell the goods or use the brand name of a manufacturer, distributor, or advertiser within a specified area, or by reason of the fact that it occupies premises leased to it by a person who also leases premises to other retail or service establishments. *For purposes of this subsection, the activities performed by any person or persons—*

(1) *in connection with the operation of a hospital, an institution primarily engaged in the care of the sick, the aged, the mentally ill or defective who reside on the premises of such institution, a school for mentally or physically handicapped or gifted children,* **a preschool,**[15] *elementary or secondary school, or an institution of higher education (regardless of whether or not such hospital, institution, or school is public or private or operated for profit or not for profit, or*

(2) *in connection with the operation of a street, suburban or interurban electric railway, or local trolley or motorbus carrier, if the rates and services of such railway or carrier are subject to regulation by a State or local agency (regardless of whether or not such railway or carrier is public or private or operated for profit or not for profit).* **or**

(3) **in connection with the activities of a public agency,**
shall be deemed to be activities performed for a business purpose.

(s) *"Enterprise engaged in commerce or in the production of goods for commerce" means an enterprise which has employees engaged in commerce or in the production of goods for commerce,* **or employees handling, selling, or otherwise working on goods or materials** *that have been moved in or produced for commerce by any person, and which—*

(1) *during the period February 1, 1967, through January 31, 1969, is an enterprise whose annual gross volume of sales made or business done is not less than $500,000 (exclusive of excise taxes at the retail level which are sepa-*

---

[15]"A preschool" was added by the Education Amendments of 1972.

[16]Prior to the Fair Labor Standards Amendments of 1966, the dollar volume test for enterprise coverage (except in the case of an enterprise engaged in construction or reconstruction or one which was a gasoline service establishment) was $1,000,000. The dollar volume test was $350,000 for a construction or reconstruction enterprise, and $250,000 for a gasoline service establishment. In addition, enterprises with one or more retail or service establishments, in order to be covered, had to purchase or receive "goods for resale that move or have moved across State lines (not in deliveries from the reselling establishment) which amount in total annual volume to $250,000 or more." Finally, under the 1961 Amendments, enterprises (except those engaged in construction or reconstruction, or in the business of operating a street, suburban or interurban electric railway, or local trolley or motorbus carrier, or gasoline service establishments) were covered only with respect to those establishments "which ha[d] employees engaged in commerce or in the production of goods for commerce."

rately stated)[16] *or is a gasoline service establishment whose annual gross volume of sales is not less than $250,000 (exclusive of excise taxes at the retail level which are separately stated), and beginning February 1, 1969, is an enterprise whose annual gross volume of sales made or business done is not less than $250,000 (exclusive of excise taxes at the retail level which are separately stated);*

(2) *is engaged in laundering, cleaning, or repairing clothing or fabrics;*[17]

(3) *is engaged in the business of construction or reconstruction, or both;*[18]

(4) *is engaged in the operation of a hospital, an institution primarily engaged in the care of the sick, the aged, the mentally ill or defective who reside on the premises of such institution, a school for mentally or physically handicapped or gifted children,* **a preschool,**[15] *elementary or secondary school or an institution of higher education (regardless of whether or not such hospital, institution, or school is public or private or operated for profit or not for profit;*[19] *or*

(5) *is an activity of a public agency.*

Any establishment which has as its only regular employees the owner thereof or the parent, spouse, child, or other member of the immediate family of such owner shall not be considered to be an enterprise engaged in commerce or in the production of goods for commerce or a part of such an enterprise, and the sales of such establishment shall not be included for the purpose of determining the annual gross volume of sales of any enterprise for the purpose of this subsection. **The employees of an enterprise which is a public agency shall for purposes of this subsection be deemed to be employees engaged in commerce, or in the production of goods for commerce, or employees handling, selling, or otherwise working on goods or materials that have been moved in or produced for commerce.**

(t) *"Tipped employee" means any employee engaged in an occupation in which he customarily and regularly receives more than $20 a month in tips.*

(u) *"Man-day" means any day during which an employee performs any agricultural labor for not less than one hour.*

(v) *"Elementary school" means a day or residential school which provides elementary education, as determined under State law.*

(w) *"Secondary school" means a day or residential school which provides secondary education, as determined under State law.*

---

[17]Prior to the Fair Labor Standards Amendments of 1966, the Act's minimum wage and overtime requirements did not generally apply to employees of laundry or dry cleaning establishments, even if such establishments were part of a covered enterprise, because of the language in section 13(a)(3) (since repealed) which exempted "any employee employed by an establishment engaged in laundering, cleaning or repairing clothing or fabrics, more than 50 per centum of which establishment's annual dollar volume of sales of such services is made within the State in which the establishment is located: Provided, that 75 per centum of such establishment's annual dollar volume of sales of such services is made to customers who are not engaged in a mining, manufacturing, transportation, or communication business."

[18]See footnote 16.

[19]Prior to the Fair Labor Standards Amendments of 1966, the Act's minimum wage and overtime requirements did not apply to most of the establishments listed in this subsection, because section 13(a)(2)(iii), as it then read, exempted employees of a hospital, or an institution which is primarily engaged in the care of sick, the aged, the mentally ill or defective, residing on the premises of such institution, or a school for physically or mentally handicapped or gifted children. Public schools were also exempt by virtue of the Act's definition of the word "employer," which, prior to 1966, excluded States and their political subdivisions.

(x) *"Public agency" means the Government of the United States; the government of a State or political subdivision thereof; any agency of the United States (including the United States Postal Service and Postal Rate Commission), a State, or a political subdivision of a State; or any interstate governmental agency.*

Administration[20]

SEC. 4.

(a) There is hereby created in the Department of Labor a Wage and Hour Division which shall be under the direction of an Administrator, to be known as the Administrator of the Wage and Hour Division (in this Act referred to as the "Administrator"). The Administrator shall be appointed by the President, by and with the advice and consent of the Senate, and shall receive compensation at the rate of $36,000[21] a year.

Excerpts From Reorganization Plan No. 6 of 1950, 64 Stat. 1263.
"Except as otherwise provided [with respect to hearing examiners], there are hereby transferred to the Secretary of Labor all functions of all other officers of the Department of Labor and all functions of all agencies and employees of such Department***. The Secretary of Labor may from time to time make such provisions as he shall deem appropriate authorizing the performance by any other officer, or by any agency or employee, of the Department of Labor of any function of the Secretary, including any function transferred to the Secretary by the provisions of this reorganization plan."

(b) The Secretary of Labor[22] may, subject to the civil service laws, appoint such employees as he deems necessary to carry out his functions and duties under this Act and shall fix their compensation in accordance with the Classification Act of 1949[23] as amended. The Secretary[24] may establish and utilize such regional, local, or other agencies, and utilize such voluntary and uncompensated services, as may from time to time be needed. Attorneys appointed under this section may appear for and represent the Secretary[25] in any litigation, but all such litigation shall be subject to the direction and control of the Attorney General. In the appointment, selection, classification, and promotion of officers and employees of the Secretary,[26] no political test or qualification shall be permitted or given consideration, but all such appointments and promotions shall be given and made on the basis of merit and efficiency.

(c) The principal office of the Secretary[27] shall be in the District of Columbia, but he or his duly authorized representative may exercise any or all of his powers in any place.

[20]Heading revised to reflect changes made by Reorganization Plan No. 6 of 1950.
[21]Executive Order 11811 of October 7, 1974.
[22]As amended by section 404 of Reorganization Plan No. II of 1939 (53 Stat. 1436) and by Reorganization Plan No. 6 of 1950 (64 Stat. 1263).
[23]As amended by section 1106 of the Act of October 28, 1949 (63 Stat. 972).
[24]See footnote 22.
[25]Ibid.
[26]Ibid.
[27]As amended by Reorganization Plan No. 6 of 1950.

(d) *(1)* The Secretary[28] shall submit annually in January a report to the Congress covering his activities for the preceding year and including such information, data, and recommendations for further legislation in connection with the matters covered by this Act as he may find advisable. Such report shall contain an evaluation and appraisal by the Secretary of the minimum wages *and overtime coverage* established by this Act, together with his recommendations to the Congress. In making such evaluation and appraisal, the Secretary shall take into consideration any changes which may have occurred in the cost of living and in productivity and the level of wages in manufacturing, the ability of employers to absorb wage increases, and such other factors as he may deem pertinent.[29] *Such report shall also include a summary of the special certificates issued under section 14(b).*

(2) The Secretary shall conduct studies on the justification or lack thereof for each of the special exemptions set forth in section 13 of this Act, and the extent to which such exemptions apply to employees of establishments described in subsection (g) of such section and the economic efforts of the application of such exemptions to such employees. The Secretary shall submit a report of his findings and recommendations to the Congress with respect to the studies conducted under this paragraph not later than January 1, 1976.

(3) The Secretary shall conduct a continuing study on means to prevent curtailment of employment opportunities for manpwoer groups which have had historically high incidences of unemployment (such as disadvantaged minorities, youth, elderly, and such other groups as the Secretary may designate). The first report of the results of such study shall be transmitted to the Congress not later than one year after the effective date of the Fair Labor Standards Amendments of 1974. Subsequent reports on such study shall be transmitted to the Congress at two-year intervals after such effective date. Each such report shall include suggestions respecting the Secretary's authority under section 14 of this Act.

(e) Whenever the Secretary has reason to believe that in any industry under this Act the competition of foreign producers in United States markets or in markets abroad, or both, has resulted, or is likely to result, in increased unemployment in the United States, he shall undertake an investigation to gain full information with respect to the matter. If he determines such increased unemployment has in fact resulted, or is in fact likely to result, from such competition, he shall make a full and complete report of his findings and determinations to the President and to the Congress: *Provided,* That he may also include in such report information on the increased employment resulting from additional exports in any industry under this Act as he may determine to be pertinent to such report.

(f) The Secretary is authorized to enter into an agreement with the Librarian of Congress with respect to individuals employed in the Library of Congress to provide for the carrying out of the Secretary's functions under this Act with respect to such individuals. Not-

---

[28]Ibid.
[29]Section 2 of the Fair Labor Standards Amendments of 1955.

withstanding any other provision of this Act, or any other law, the Civil Service Commission is authorized to administer the provisions of this Act with respect to any individual employed by the United States (other than an individual employed in the Library of Congress, United States Postal Service, Postal Rate Commission, or the Tennessee Valley Authority). Nothing in this subsection shall be construed to affect the right of an employee to bring an action for unpaid minimum wages, or unpaid overtime compensation, and liquidated damages under section 16(b) of this Act.

Special industry committees for Puerto Rico and the Virgin Islands
SEC. 5.[30]

(a) The Secretary of Labor[31] shall as soon as practicable appoint a special industry committee to recommend the minimum rate or rates of wages to be paid under section 6 to employees in Puerto Rico or the Virgin Islands, or in Puerto Rico and the Virgin Islands, engaged in commerce or in the production of goods for commerce **or employed in any enterprise engaged in commerce or in the production of goods for commerce,** or the Secretary[32] may appoint separate industry committees to recommend the minimum rate or rates of wages to be paid under section 6 to employees therein engaged in commerce or in the production of goods for commerce **or employed in any enterprise engaged in commerce or in the production of goods for commerce** in particular industries. An industry committee appointed under this subsection shall be composed of residents of such island or islands where the employees with respect to whom such committee was appointed are employed and residents of the United States outside of Puerto Rico and the Virgin Islands. In determining the minimum rate or rates of wages to be paid, and in determining classifications, such industry committees[33] shall be subject to the provisions of section 8.

(b) An industry committee shall be appointed by the Secretary[34] without regard to any other provisions of law regarding the appointment and compensation of employees of the United States. It shall include a number of disinterested persons representing the public, one of whom the Secretary[35] shall designate as chairman, a like number of persons representing employees in the industry, and a like number representing employers in the industry. In the appointment of the persons representing each group, the Secretary[36] shall give due regard to the geographical regions in which the industry is carried on.

(c) Two-thirds of the members of an industry committee shall constitute a quorum, and the decision of the committee shall require a vote of

[30]Section 5 as amended by section 3(c) of the Act of June 26, 1940 (54 Stat. 615); by section 5 of the Fair Labor Standards Amendments of 1949; by section 4 of the Fair Labor Standards Amendments of 1961; by section 5 of the Fair Labor Standards Amendments of 1974; and as further amended as noted. Paragraphs (b), (c), and (d) (except for the substitution of "Secretary" for "Administrator") read as in the original Act.
[31]See footnote 27.
[32]Ibid.
[33]As amended by section 5(a) of the Fair Labor Standards Amendments of 1955.
[34]See footnote 27.
[35]Ibid.
[36]Ibid.

not less than a majority of all its members. Members of an industry committee shall receive as compensation for their services a reasonable per diem, which the Secretary[37] shall by rules and regulations prescribe, for each day actually spent in the work of the committee, and shall in addition be reimbursed for their necessary traveling and other expenses. The Secretary[38] shall furnish the committee with adequate legal, stenographic, clerical, and other assistance, and shall by rules and regulations prescribe the procedure to be followed by the committee.

(d) The Secretary[39] shall submit to an industry committee from time to time such data as he may have available on the matters referred to it, and shall cause to be brought before it in connection with such matters any witnesses whom he deems material. An industry committee may summon other witnesses or call upon the Secretary[40] to furnish additional information to aid it in deliberations.

(e) *The provisions of this section, section 6(c), and section 8 shall not apply with respect to the minimum wage rate of any employee employed in Puerto Rico or the Virgin Islands (1) by the United States or by the government of the Virgin Islands, (2) by an establishment which is a hotel, motel, or restaurant, or (3) by any other retail or service establishment which employs such employee primarily in connection with the preparation or offering of food or beverages for human consumption, either on the premises, or by such services as catering, banquet, box lunch, or curb or counter service, to the public, to employees, or to members or guests of members of clubs. The minimum wage rate of such an employee shall be determined under this Act in the same manner as the minimum wage rate for employees employed in a State of the United States is determined under this Act. As used in the preceding sentence, the term "State" does not include a territory or possession of the United States.*

Minimum wages

SEC. 6.

(a) Every employer shall pay to each of his employees who **in any workweek** is engaged in commerce or in the production of goods for commerce, *or is employed in an enterprise engaged in commerce or in the production of goods for commerce, wages at the following rates:*

(1) *not less than $2 an hour during the period ending December 31, 1974,[41] not less than $2.10 an hour during the year beginning January 1, 1975, and not less than $2.30 an hour after December 31, 1975, except as otherwise provided in this section;*

(2)[42] if such employee is a home worker in Puerto Rico or the Virgin Islands, not less than the minimum piece rate prescribed by regulation or order; or, if no such minimum piece rate is in effect, any piece

---

[37]Ibid.
[38]Ibid.
[39]Ibid.
[40]Ibid.
[41]$2.00 rate became effective May 1, 1974. Section 29(a) of the Fair Labor Standards Amendments of 1974.
[42]Paragraph number changed from (5) to (2) by section 6(b) of the Fair Labor Standards Amendments of 1949.

rate adopted by such employer which shall yield, to the proportion or class of employees prescribed by regulation or order, not less than the applicable minimum hourly wage rate. Such minimum piece rates or employer piece rates shall be commensurate with, and shall be paid in lieu of, the minimum hourly wage rate applicable under the provisions of this section. The Secretary of Labor,[43] or his authorized representative, shall have power to make such regulations or orders as are necessary or appropriate to carry out any of the provisions of this paragraph, including the power without limiting the generality of the foregoing, to define any operation or occupation which is performed by such home work employees in Puerto Rico or the Virgin Islands; to establish minimum piece rates for any operation or occupation so defined; to prescribe the method and procedure for ascertaining and promulgating minimum piece rates; to prescribe standards for employer piece rates, including the proportion or class of employees who shall receive not less than the minimum hourly wage rate; to define the term "home worker"; and to prescribe the conditions under which employers, agents, contractors, and subcontractors shall cause goods to be produced by home workers;[44]

(3) if such employee is employed in American Samoa, in lieu of the rate or rates provided by this subsection or subsection (b), not less than the applicable rate established by the Secretary of Labor in accordance with recommendations of a special industry committee or committees which he shall appoint in the same manner and pursuant to the same provisions as are applicable to the special industry committees provided for Puerto Rico and the Virgin Islands by this Act as amended from time to time. Each such committee shall have the same powers and duties and shall apply the same standards with respect to the application of the provisions of this Act to employees employed in American Samoa as pertain to special industry committees established under section 5 with respect to employees employed in Puerto Rico or the Virgin Islands. The minimum wage rate thus established shall not exceed the rate prescribed in paragraph (1) of this subsection;[45]

(4) *if such employee is employed as a seaman on an American vessel, not less than the rate which will provide to the employee, for the period covered by the wage payment, wages equal to compensation at the hourly rate prescribed by paragraph (1) of this subsection for all hours during such period when he was actually on duty (including periods aboard ship when the employee was on watch or was, at the direction of a superior officer, performing work or standing by, but not including off-duty periods which are provided pursuant to the employment agreement); or*

(5) *if such employee is employed in agriculture, not less than—*
   (A) *$1.60 an hour during the period ending December 31, 1974,*[46]

---

[43]See footnote 27.

[44]Section 3(f) of the Act of June 26, 1940 (54 Stat. 616).

[45]Section 2 of the American Samoa Labor Standards Amendments of 1956, as amended by section 5 of the Fair Labor Standards Amendments of 1961.

[46]The $1.60 rate provided in section 6(a)(5) and the $1.90 rate provided in section 6(b) of this Act both became effective May 1, 1974, as a result of the Fair Labor Standards Amendments of 1974.

(B) *$1.80 an hour during the year beginning January 1, 1975,*

(C) *$2 an hour during the year beginning January 1, 1976,*

(D) *$2.20 an hour during the year beginning January 1, 1977, and*

(E) *$2.30 an hour after December 31, 1977.*

(b) *Every employer shall pay to each of his employees (other than an employee to whom subsection (a)(5) applies) who in any workweek is engaged in commerce or in the production of goods for commerce, or is employed in an enterprise engaged in commerce or in the production of goods for commerce, and who in such workweek is brought within the purview of this section by the amendments made to this Act by the Fair Labor Standards Amendments of 1966,* **title IX of the Education Amendments of 1972, or the Fair Labor Standards Amendments of 1974,** *wages at the following rates:*

(1) *not less than $1.90 an hour during the period ending December 31, 1974,* [47]

(2) *not less than $2.00 an hour during the year beginning January 1, 1975,*

(3) *Not less than $2.20 an hour during the year beginning January 1, 1976, and*

(4) *not less than $2.30 an hour after December 31, 1976.*

(c) **(1) The rate or rates provided by subsections (a) and (b) of this section shall be superseded in the case of any employee in Puerto Rico or the Virgin Islands only for so long as and insofar as such employee is covered by a wage order heretofore or hereafter issued by the Secretary pursuant to the recommendations of a special industry committee appointed pursuant to section 5.**

(2) [48] *Except as provided in paragraphs (4) and (5), in the case of any employee who is covered by such a wage order on the date of enactment of the Fair Labor Standards Amendments of 1974 and to whom the rate or rates prescribed by subsection (a) or (b) would otherwise apply, the wage rate applicable to such employee shall be increased as follows:*

(A) *Effective on the effective date of the Fair Labor Standards Amendments of 1974,* [49] *the wage order rate applicable to such employee on the day before such date shall—*

(i) *if such rate is under $1.40 an hour, be increased by $0.12 an hour, and*

(ii) *if such rate is $1.40 or more an hour, be increased by $0.15 an hour.*

(B) *Effective on the first day of the second and each subsequent year after such date, the highest wage order rate applicable to such employees on the date before such first day shall—*

(i) *if such rate is under $1.40 an hour, be increased by $0.12 an hour, and*

(ii) *if such rate is $1.40 or more an hour, be increased by $0.15 an hour.*

---

[47]Ibid.

[48]The Fair Labor Standards Amendments of 1974 deleted from subsection (c) of section 6 prior paragraphs (2), (3), and (4) and inserted in lieu thereof new paragraphs (2), (3), (4), (5), and (6) printed in bold face italics.

[49]May 1, 1974.

In the case of any employee employed in agriculture who is covered by a wage order issued by the Secretary pursuant to the recommendations of a special industry committee appointed pursuant to section 5, to whom the rate or rates prescribed by subsection (a)(5) would otherwise apply, and whose hourly wage is increased above the wage rate prescribed by such wage order by a subsidy (or income supplement) paid, in whole or in part, by the government of Puerto Rico, the increases prescribed by this paragraph shall be applied to the sum of the wage rate in effect under such wage order and the amount by which the employee's hourly wage rate is increased by the subsidy (or income supplement) above the wage rate in effect under such wage order.

(3) In the case of any employee employed in Puerto Rico or the Virgin Islands to whom this section is made applicable by the amendments made to this Act by the Fair Labor Standards Amendments of 1974, the Secretary shall, as soon as practicable after the date of enactment of the Fair Labor Standards Amendments of 1974, appoint a special industry committee in accordance with section 5 to recommend the highest minimum wage rate or rates, which shall be not less than 60 per centum of the otherwise applicable minimum wage rate in effect under subsection (b) or $1.00 an hour, whichever is greater, to be applicable to such employee in lieu of the rate or rates prescribed by subsection (b). The rate recommended by the special industry committee shall (A) be effective with respect to such employee upon the effective date of the wage order issued pursuant to such recommendation, but not before sixty days after the effective date of the Fair Labor Standards Amendments of 1974, and (B) except in the case of employees of the government of Puerto Rico or any political subdivision thereof, be increased in accordance with paragraph (2)(B).

(4) (A) Notwithstanding paragraph (2)(A) or (3), the wage rate of any employee in Puerto Rico or the Virgin Islands which is subject to paragraph (2)(A) or (3) of this subsection shall, on the effective date of the wage increase under paragraph (2)(A) or of the wage rate recommended under paragraph (3), as the case may be, be not less than 60 per centum of the otherwise applicable rate under subsection (a) or (b) or $1.00, whichever is higher.

(B) Notwithstanding paragraph (2)(B), the wage rate of any employee in Puerto Rico or the Virgin Islands which is subject to paragraph (2)(B), shall, on and after the effective date of the first wage increase under paragraph (2)(B), be not less than 60 per centum of the otherwise applicable rate under subsection (a) or (b) or $1.00, whichever is higher.

(5) If the wage rate of an employee is to be increased under this subsection to a wage rate which equals or is greater than the wage rate under subsection (a) or (b) which, but for paragraph (1) of this subsection, would be applicable to such employee, this subsection shall be inapplicable to such employee and the applicable rate under such subsection shall apply to such employee.

(6) Each minimum wage rate prescribed by or under paragraph (2) or (3) shall be in effect unless such minimum wage rate has been superseded by a wage order (issued by the Secretary pursuant to the recommendation of a special industry committee convened under section 8) fixing a higher minimum wage rate.

(d)[50](1) No employer having employees subject to any provisions of this section shall discriminate, with any establishment in which such employees are employed, between employees on the basis of sex by paying wages to employees in such establishment at a rate less than the rate at which he pays wages to employees of the opposite sex in such establishment for equal work on jobs the performance of which requires equal skill, effort, and responsibility, and which are performed under similar working conditions, except where such payment is made pursuant to (i) a seniority system; (ii) a merit system; (iii) a system which measures earnings by quantity or quality of production; or (iv) a differential based on any other factor other than sex: *Provided*, That an employer who is paying a wage rate differential in violation of this subsection shall not, in order to comply with the provisions of this subsection, reduce the wage rate of any employee.

(2) No labor organization, or its agents, representing employees of an employer having employees subject to any provisions of this section shall cause or attempt to cause such an employer to discriminate against an employee in violation of paragraph (1) of this subsection.

(3) For purposes of administration and enforcement, any amounts owing to any employee which have been withheld in violation of this subsection shall be deemed to be unpaid minimum wages or unpaid overtime compensation under this Act.

(4) As used in this subsection, the term "labor organization" means any organization of any kind, or any agency or employee representation committee or plan, in which employees participate and which exists for the purpose, in whole or in part, of dealing with employers concerning grievances, labor disputes, wages, rates of pay, hours of employment, or conditions of work.

(e) *(1) Notwithstanding the provisions of section 13 of this Act (except subsections (a)(1) and (f) thereof), every employer providing any contract services (other than linen supply services) under a contract with the United States or any subcontract thereunder shall pay to each of his employees whose rate of pay is not governed by the Service Contract Act of 1965 (41 U.S.C. 351– 357) or to whom subsection (a)(1) of this section is not applicable, wages at rates not less than the rates provided for in subsection (b) of this section.*

(2) Notwithstanding the provisions of section 13 of this Act (except subsections (a)(1) and (f) thereof) and the provisions of the Service Contract Act of 1965, every employer in an establishment providing linen supply services to the United States under a contract with the United States or any subcontract thereunder shall pay to each of his employees in such establishment wages at rates not less than those prescribed in subsection (b), except that if more than 50 per centum of the gross annual dollar volume of sales made or business done by such establishment is derived from providing such linen supply services under any such contracts or subcontracts, such employer shall pay to each of his employees in such establishment wages at rates not less than those prescribed in subsection (a)(1) of this section.

(f) Any employee—

---

[50]Subsection (d) added by Equal Pay Act of 1963, 77 Stat. 56 (effective on and after June 11, 1964 except for employees covered by collective bargaining agreements in certain cases).

(1) *who in any workweek is employed in domestic service in a household shall be paid wages at a rate not less than the wage rate in effect under section 6(b) unless such employee's compensation for such service would not because of section 209(g) of the Social Security Act constitute wages for the purposes of title II of such Act, or*

(2) *who in any workweek—*

    (A) is employed in domestic service in one or more households, and

    (B) is so employed for more than 8 hours in the aggregate,

shall be paid wages for such employment in such workweek at a rate not less than the wage rate in effect under section 6(b).

Maximum hours

SEC. 7.[51]*

(a) **(1)** Except as otherwise provided in this section, no employer shall employ any of his employees who **in any workweek** is engaged in commerce or in the production of goods for commerce, *or is employed in an enterprise engaged in commerce or in the production of goods for commerce,* for a workweek longer than forty hours unless such employee receives compensation for his employment in excess of the hours above specified at a rate not less than one and one-half times the regular rate at which he is employed.

(2) *No employer shall employ any of his employees who in any workweek is engaged in commerce or in the production of goods for commerce, or is employed in an enterprise engaged in commerce or in the production of goods for commerce, and who in such workweek is brought within the purview of this subsection by the amendments made to this Act by the Fair Labor Standards Amendments of 1966—*

    (A) for a workweek longer than forty-four hours during the first year from the effective date of the Fair Labor Standards Amendments of 1966,

    (B) for a workweek longer than forty-two hours during the second year from such date, or

    (C) for a workweek longer than forty hours after the expiration of the second year from such date,

unless such employee receives compensation for his employment in excess of the hours above specified at a rate not less than one and one-half times the regular rate at which he is employed.

(b) No employer shall be deemed to have violated subsection (a) by employing any employee for a workweek in excess of that specified in such subsection without paying the compensation for overtime employment prescribed therein if such employee is so employed—

*(1) in pursuance of an agreement, made as a result of collective bargaining by representatives of employees certified as bona fide by the National Labor Relations Board, which provides that no employee shall be employed more than one thousand and forty hours during any period of twenty-six consecutive weeks, or

---

[51]Section 7 as amended by section 7 of the Fair Labor Standards Amendments of 1949, and as further amended as noted. Single asterisk (*) indicates provision amended by the 1949 Act; double asterisk (**) indicates provision added by the 1949 Act. Bold face type indicates amendment made by the Fair Labor Standards Amendments of 1961. Italic type indicates amendments made by the Fair Labor Standards Amendments of 1966. Bold face italic type indicates amendment made by the Fair Labor Standards Amendments of 1974.

*(2) in pursuance of an agreement, made as a result of collective bargaining by representatives of employees certified as bona fide by the National Labor Relations Board which provides that during a specified period of fifty-two consecutive weeks the employee shall be employed not more than two thousand two hundred and forty hours and shall be guaranteed not less than one thousand eight hundred and forty hours (or not less than forty-six weeks at the normal number of hours worked per week, but not less than thirty hours per week) and not more than two thousand and eighty hours of employment for which he shall receive compensation for all hours guaranteed or worked at rates not less than those applicable under the agreement to the work performed and for all hours in excess of the guaranty which are also **in excess of the maximum workweek applicable to such employee under subsection (a)** or two thousand and eighty in such period at rates not less than one and one-half times the regular rate at which he is employed: or

(3)[52]*by an independently owned and controlled local enterprise (including an enterprise with more than one bulk storage establishment) engaged in the wholesale or bulk distribution of petroleum products if—*

(A) the annual gross volume of sales of such enterprise is less than $1,000,000 exclusive of excise taxes,

(B) more than 75 per centum of such enterprise's annual dollar volume of sales is made within the State in which such enterprise is located, and

(C) not more than 25 per centum of the annual dollar volume of sales of such enterprise is to customers who are engaged in the bulk distribution of such products for resale,

and such employee receives compensation for employment in excess of forty hours in any workweek at a rate not less than one.and one-half times the minimum wage rate applicable to him under section 6,

and if such employee receives compensation for employment in excess of twelve hours in any workday, or for employment in excess of fifty-six hours in any workweek, as the case may be, at a rate not less than one and one-half times the regular rate at which he is employed.

(c) *For a period or periods of not more than* **seven** *workweeks in the aggregate in any calendar year, or* **ten** *workweeks in the aggregate in the case of an employer who does not qualify for the exemption in subsection (d) of this section, any employer may employ any employee for a workweek in excess of that specified in subsection (a) without paying the compensation for overtime employment prescribed in such subsection if such employee (1) is employed by such employer in an industry found by the Secretary to be of a seasonal nature, and (2) receives compensation for employment by such employer in excess of ten hours in any workday, or for employment by such employer in excess of* **forty-eight** *hours in any workweek, as the case may be, at a rate not less than one and one-half times the regular rate at which he is employed.*

---

[52]Section 212 of the Fair Labor Standards Amendments of 1966 substituted this provision for the complete exemption from overtime contained in former section 13(b)(10) enacted in the 1961 amendments. Former clause (3) of section 7(b) as enacted in the 1938 Act was replaced by new section 7(c) as enacted by section 204(c) of the Fair Labor Standards Amendments of 1966.

[Effective January 1, 1975, sections 7(c) and 7(d) are each amended—
(1) by striking out "seven workweeks" and inserting in lieu thereof "five workweeks", and
(2) by striking out "ten workweeks" and inserting in lieu thereof "seven workweeks". Effective January 1, 1976, section 7(c) and 7(d) are each amended—
(1) by striking out "five workweeks" and inserting in lieu thereof "three workweeks", and
(2) by striking out "seven workweeks" and inserting in lieu thereof "five workweeks".

Effective December 31, 1976, sections 7(c) and 7(d) are repealed.]

*(d) For a period or periods of not more than **seven** workweeks in the aggregate in any calendar year, or **ten** workweeks in the aggregate in the case of an employer who does not qualify for the exemption in subsection (c) of this section, any employer may employ any employee for a workweek in excess of that specified in subsection (a) without paying the compensation for overtime employment prescribed in such subsection, if such employee—*

(1) is employed by such employer in an enterprise which is in an industry found by the Secretary—

(A) to be characterized by marked annually recurring seasonal peaks of operation at the places of first marketing or first processing of agricultural or horticultural commodities from farms if such industry is engaged in the handling, packaging, preparing, storing, first processing, or canning of any perishable agricultural or horticultural commodities in their raw or natural state, or

(B) to be of a seasonal nature and engaged in the handling, packing, storing, preparing, first processing, or canning of any perishable agricultural or horticultural commodities in their raw or natural state, and

(2) receives compensation for employment by such employer in excess of ten hours in any workday, or for employment in excess of forty-eight hours in any workweek, as the case may be, at a rate not less than one and one-half times the regular rate at which he is employed.

[Note: For changes effective January 1, 1975, January 1, 1976, and December 31, 1976, see notation following section 7(c).]

**(e) As used in this section the "regular rate" at which an employee is employed shall be deemed to include all remuneration for employment paid to, or on behalf of, the employee, but shall not be deemed to include—

**(1) sums paid as gifts; payments in the nature of gifts made at Christmas time or on other special occasions, as a reward for service, the amounts of which are not measured by or dependent on hours worked, production, or efficiency;

**(2) payments made for occasional periods when no work is performed due to vacation, holiday, illness, failure of the employer to provide sufficient work, or other similar cause; reasonable payments for traveling expenses, or other expenses, incurred by an employee in the furtherance of his employer's interests and properly reimbursable by the employer; and other similar payments to an employee which are not made as compensation for his hours of employment;

**(3) sums paid in recognition of services performed during a given period if either, (a) both the fact that payment is to be made and the amount of the payment are determined at the sole discretion of the employer at or near the end of the period and not pursuant to any prior contract, agreement, or promise causing the employee to expect such payments regularly; or (b) the payments are made pursuant to a bona fide profit-sharing plan or trust or bona fide thrift or savings plan, meeting the requirements of the Secretary of Labor[53] set forth in appropriate regulation which he shall issue, having due regard among other relevant factors, to the extent to which the amounts paid to the employee are determined without regard to hours of work, production, or efficiency; or (c) the payments are talent fees (as such talent fees are defined and delimited by regulations of the Secretary[54]) paid to performers, including announcers, on radio and television programs;

**(4) contributions irrevocably made by an employer to a trustee or third person pursuant to a bona fide plan for providing old-age, retirement, life, accident, or health insurance or similar benefits for employees;

(5) extra compensation provided by a premium rate paid for certain hours worked by the employee in any day or workweek because such hours are hours worked in excess of eight in a day or **in excess of the maximum workweek applicable to such employee under subsection (a) or in excess of the employee's normal working hours or regular working hours, as the case may be;

*(6) extra compensation provided by a premium rate paid for work by the employee on Saturdays, Sundays, holidays, or regular days of rest, or on the sixth or seventh day of the workweek, where such premium rate is not less than one and one-half times the rate established in good faith for like work performed in nonovertime hours on other days;[55] or

*(7) extra compensation provided by a premium rate paid to the employee, in pursuance of an applicable employment contract or collective-bargaining agreement, for work outside of the hours established in good faith by the contract or agreement as the basic, normal, or regular workday (not exceeding eight hours) or workweek (not exceeding **the maximum workweek applicable to such employee under subsection (a)**), where such premium rate is not less than one and one-half times the rate established in good faith by the contract or agreement for like work performed during such workday or workweek.[56]

(f) No employer shall be deemed to have violated subsection (a) by employing any employee for a workweek in excess of **the maximum workweek applicable to such employee under subsection (a) if such employee is employed pursuant to a bona fide individual contract, or pursuant to an agreement made as a result of collective bargaining by representatives of employees, if the

---

[53]See footnote 27.
[54]Ibid.
[55]Paragraphs (6) and (7) together with section 7(g) continue in effect provisions of section 1 of the Act of July 20, 1949 (63 Stat. 446), which Act was repealed as of the effective date of the Fair Labor Standards Amendments of 1949.
[56]Ibid.

duties of such employee necessitate irregular hours of work, and the contract or agreement (1) specifies a regular rate of pay of not less than the minimum hourly rate provided in **subsection (a) or (b) of section 6 (whichever may be applicable)** and compensation at not less than one and one-half times such rate for all hours worked in excess of **such maximum** workweek, and (2) provides a weekly guaranty of pay for not more than sixty hours based on the rates so specified.

(g) No employer shall be deemed to have violated subsection (a) by employing any employee for a workweek in excess of **the maximum workweek applicable to such employee under such subsection if, pursuant to an agreement or understanding arrived at between the employer and the employee before performance of the work, the amount paid to the employee for the number of hours worked by him in such workweek in excess of **the maximum workweek applicable to such employee under such subsection—**

(1) in the case of an employee employed at piece rates, is computed at piece rates not less than one and one-half times the bona fide piece rates applicable to the same work when performed during nonovertime hours; or

(2) in the case of an employee performing two or more kinds of work for which different hourly or piece rates have been established, is computed at rates not less than one and one-half times such bona fide rates applicable to the same work when performed during nonovertime hours; or

(3) is computed at a rate not less than one and one-half times the rate established by such agreement or understanding as the basic rate to be used in computing overtime compensation thereunder: *Provided,* That the rate so established shall be authorized by regulation by the Secretary of Labor[57] as being substantially equivalent to the average hourly earnings of the employee, exclusive of overtime premiums, in the particular work over a representative period of time;

and if (i) the employee's average hourly earnings for the workweek exclusive of payments described in paragraphs (1) through (7) of subsection (e) are not less than the minimum hourly rate required by applicable law, and (ii) extra overtime compensation is properly computed and paid on other forms of additional pay required to be included in computing the regular rate.

*(h) Extra compensation paid as described in paragraphs (5), (6), and (7) of subsection (e) shall be creditable toward overtime compensation payable pursuant to this section.[58]

(i) **No employer shall be deemed to have violated subsection (a) by employing any employee of a retail or service establishment for a workweek in excess of the applicable workweek specified therein, if (1) the regular rate of pay of such employee is in excess of one and one-half times the minimum hourly rate applicable to him under section 6, and (2) more than half his compensation for a representative period (not less than one month) represents commissions on**

[57]See footnote 27.

[58]Amendment provided by section 7 of the Fair Labor Standards Amendments of 1949. See also footnote 54.

goods or services. *In determining the proportion of compensation representing commissions, all earnings resulting from the application of a bona fide commission rate shall be deemed commissions on goods or services without regard to whether the computed commissions exceed the draw or guarantee.*

(j) *No employer engaged in the operation of a hospital **or an establishment which is an institution primarily engaged in the care of the sick, the aged, or the mentally ill or defective who reside on the premises** shall be deemed to have violated subsection (a) if, pursuant to an agreement or understanding arrived at between the employer and employee before performance of the work, a work period of fourteen consecutive days is accepted in lieu of the workweek of seven consecutive days for purposes of overtime computation and if, for his employment in excess of eight hours in any workday and in excess of eighty hours in such fourteen-day period, the employee receives compensation at a rate not less than one and one-half times the regular rate at which he is employed.*

[*Effective January 1, 1975, section 7 is amended by adding at the end thereof the following new subsection:*

(k)[59] *No public agency shall be deemed to have violated subsection (a) with respect to the employment of any employee in fire protection activities or any employee in law enforcement activities (including security personnel in correctional institutions) if—*

(1) *in a work period of 28 consecutive days the employee receives for tours of duty which in the aggregate exceed 240 hours; or*

(2) *in the case of such an employee to whom a work period of at least 7 but less than 28 days applies, in his work period the employee receives for tours of duty which in the aggregate exceed a number of hours which bears the same ratio to the number of consecutive days in his work period as 240 hours bears to 28 days,*

compensation at a rate not less than one and one-half times the regular rate at which he is employed.

Effective January 1, 1976, section 7(k) is amended by striking out "240 hours" each place it occurs and inserting in lieu thereof "232 hours".

Effective January 1, 1977, such section is amended by striking out "232 hours" each place it occurs and inserting in lieu thereof "216 hours".

Effective January 1, 1978, such section is amended—

    (i) by striking out "exceed 216 hours" in paragraph (1) and inserting in lieu thereof "exceed the lesser of (A) 216 hours, or (B) the average number of hours (as determined by the Secretary pursuant to section 6(c)(3) of the Fair Labor Standards Amendments of 1974) in tours of duty of employees engaged in such activities in work periods of 28 consecutive days in calendar year 1975"; and

    (ii) by striking out "as 216 hours bears to 28 days" in paragraph (2) and inserting in lieu thereof "as 216 hours (or if lower, the number of hours referred to in clause (B) of paragraph (1)) bears to 28 days".]

---

[59]Effective January 1, 1975, the complete overtime exemption provided by section 6(c)(2)(A) of the Fair Labor Standards Amendments of 1974 will be replaced by the more limited exemption in section 7(k). The complete exemption remains applicable only to public agencies employing less than 5 employees in fire protection or law enforcement activities. See section 13(b)(20), *infra.*

(1) No employer shall employ any employee in domestic service in one or more households for a workweek longer than forty hours unless such employee receives compensation for such employment in accordance with subsection (a).

(m) For a period or periods of not more than fourteen workweeks in the aggregate in any calendar year, any employer may employ any employee for a workweek in excess of that specified in subsection (a) without paying the compensation for overtime employment prescribed in such subsection, if such employee—

(1) is employed by such employer—

(A) to provide services (including stripping and grading) necessary and incidental to the sale at auction of green leaf tobacco of type 11, 12, 13, 14, 21, 22, 23, 24, 31, 35, 36, or 37 (as such types are defined by the Secretary of Agriculture), or in auction sale, buying, handling, stemming, redrying, packing, and storing of such tobacco,

(B) in auction sale, buying, handling, sorting, grading, packing, or storing green leaf tobacco of type 32 (as such type is defined by the Secretary of Agriculture), or

(C) in auction sale, buying, handling, stripping, sorting, grading, sizing, packing, or stemming prior to packing, of perishable cigar leaf tobacco of type 41, 42, 43, 44, 45, 46, 51, 52, 53, 54, 55, 61, or 62 (as such types are defined by the Secretary of Agriculture); and

(2) receives for—

(A) such employment by such employer which is in excess of ten hours in any workday, and

(B) such employment by such employer which is in excess of forty-eight hours in any workweek,

compensation at a rate not less than one and one-half times the regular rate at which he is employed.

An employer who receives an exemption under this subsection shall not be eligible for any other exemption under this section.

(n) In the case of an employee of an employer engaged in the business of operating a street, suburban or interurban electric railway, or local trolley or motorbus carrier (regardless of whether or not such railway or carrier is public or private or operated for profit or not for profit), in determining the hours of employment of such an employee to which the rate prescribed by subsection (a) applies there shall be excluded the hours such employee was employed in charter activities by such employer if (1) the employee's employment in such activities was pursuant to an agreement or understanding with his employer arrived at before engaging in such employment, and (2) if employment in such activities is not part of such employee's regular employment.

Wage orders in Puerto Rico and the Virgin Islands
Sec. 8.[60]

(a) The policy of this Act with respect to industries **or enterprises** in

[60]Section 8 as amended by section 8 of the Fair Labor Standards Amendments of 1949; by section 7 of the Fair Labor Standards Amendments of 1961; by section 5(d) of the Fair Labor Standards Amendments of 1974; and as further amended as noted. Paragraphs (b), (c), (d), (e), and (f) as amended by the 1949 Act read substantially the same as paragraphs (b) and (c) (except for the parenthetical reference to the minimum wage rate provided in section 6(a), (d), (f), and (g) in the original Act).

Puerto Rico and the Virgin Islands engaged in commerce or in the production of goods for commerce is to reach as rapidly as is economically feasible without substantially curtailing employment the objective of *the minimum wage rate which would apply in each such industry under paragraph (1) or (5) of section 6(a) but for section 6(c).* The Secretary of Labor[61] shall from time to time convene an industry committee or committees, appointed pursuant to section 5, and any such industry committee shall from time to time recommend the minimum rate or rates of wages to be paid under section 6 by employers in Puerto Rico or the Virgin Islands, or in Puerto Rico and the Virgin Islands, engaged in commerce or in the production of goods for commerce **or in any enterprise engaged in commerce or in the production of goods for commerce** in any such industry or classification therein. Minimum rates of wages established in accordance with this section which are not equal to *the otherwise applicable minimum wage rate in effect under paragraph (1) or (5) of section 6(a)* shall be reviewed by such a Committee once during each biennial period, beginning with the biennial period commencing July 1, 1958, except that the Secretary,[62] in his discretion, may order an additional review during any such biennial period.[63]

(b) Upon the convening of any such industry committee, the Secretary[64] shall refer to it the question of the minimum wage rate or rates to be fixed for such industry. The industry committee shall investigate conditions in the industry and the committee, or any authorized subcommittee thereof, shall after due notice hear such witnesses and receive such evidence as may be necessary or apppropriate to enable the committee to perform its duties and functions under this Act.[65] The committee shall recommend to the Secretary[66] the highest minimum wage rates for the industry which it determines, having due regard to economic and competitive conditions, will not substantially curtail employment in the industry, and will not give any industry in Puerto Rico or in the Virgin Islands a competitive advantage over any industry in the United States outside of Puerto Rico and the Virgin Islands; *except that the committee shall recommend to the Secretary the minimum wage rate prescribed in section 6(a) or 6(b), which would be applicable but for section 6(c), unless there is substantial documentary evidence, including pertinent unabridged profit and loss statements and balance sheets for a representative period of years or in the case of employees of public agencies other appropriate information, in the record which establishes that the industry, or a predominant portion thereof, is unable to pay that wage.*

(c) The industry committee shall recommend such reasonable classifications within any industry as it determines to be necessary for the purpose of fixing for each classification within such industry the highest minimum wage rate (not in excess of that *in effect under*

[61]See footnote 27.
[62]Act of August 25, 1958 (72 Stat. 844).
[63]As amended by Act of August 25, 1958 (72 Stat. 844).
[64]See footnote 27.
[65]As amended by section 5(b) of the Fair Labor Standards Amendments of 1955.
[66]See footnote 27.

paragraph (1) or (5) of section 6(a) (as the case may be)) which (1) will not substantially curtail employment in such classification and (2) will not give a competitive advantage to any group in the industry, and shall recommend for each classification in the industry the highest minimum wage rate which the committee determines will not substantially curtail employment in such classification. In determining whether such classifications should be made in any industry, in making such classifications, and in determining the minimum wage rates for such classifications, no classifications shall be made, and no minimum wage rate shall be fixed, solely on a regional basis, but the industry committee[67] shall consider among other relevant factors the following:

(1) competitive conditions as affected by transportation, living, and production costs;

(2) the wages established for work of like or comparable character by collective labor agreements negotiated between employers and employees by representatives of their own choosing; and

(3) the wages paid for work of like or comparable character by employers who voluntarily maintain minimum wage standards in the industry.

No classification shall be made under this section on the basis of age or sex.

(d) The industry committee shall file with the Secretary a report containing its findings of fact and recommendations with respect to the matters referred to it. Upon the filing of such report, the Secretary shall publish such recommendations in the Federal Register and shall provide by order that the recommendations contained in such report shall take effect upon the expiration of 15 days after the date of such publication.[68]

(e) Orders issued under this section shall define the industries and classifications therein to which they are to apply, and shall contain such terms and conditions as the Secretary[69] finds necessary to carry out the purposes of such orders, to prevent the circumvention or evasion thereof, and to safeguard the minimum wage rates established therein.[70]

(f) Due notice of any hearing provided for in this section shall be given by publication in the Federal Register and by such other means as the Secretary[71] deems reasonably calculated to give general notice to interested persons.

Attendance of witnesses
SEC. 9.

For the purpose of any hearing or investigation provided for in this Act, the provisions of sections 9 and 10 (relating to the attendance of

---

[67]As amended by sections 5(c) and 5(d) of the Fair Labor Standards Amendments of 1955 (eliminating review by the Secretary of Labor of the recommendations of the industry committee).

[68]Ibid.

[69]See footnote 27.

[70]As amended by section 5(e) of the Fair Labor Standards Amendments of 1955.

[71]See footnote 27.

witnesses and the production of books, papers and documents) of the Federal Trade Commission Act of September 16, 1914, as amended (U.S.C., 1934 edition, title 15, secs. 49 and 50), are hereby made applicable to the jurisdiction, powers, and duties of the Secretary of Labor[72] and the industry committees.

Court review

Sec. 10.[73]

(a) Any person aggrieved by an order of the Secretary issued under section 8 may obtain a review of such order in the United States Court of Appeals for any circuit wherein such person resides or has his principal place of business, or in the United States Court of Appeals for the District of Columbia, by filing in such court, within 60 days after the entry of such order a written petition praying that the order of the Secretary be modified or set aside in whole or in part. A copy of such petition shall forthwith be transmitted by the clerk of the court to the Secretary, and thereupon the Secretary shall file in the court the record of the industry committee upon which the order complained of was entered, as provided in section 2112 of title 28, United States Code. Upon the filing of such petition such court shall have exclusive jurisdiction to affirm, modify *(including provision for the payment of an appropriate minimum wage rate)*, or set aside such order in whole or in part, so far as it is applicable to the petitioner.[74] The review by the court shall be limited to questions of law, and findings of fact by such industry committee when supported by substantial evidence shall be conclusive. No objection to the order of the Secretary shall be considered by the court unless such objection shall have been urged before such industry committee or unless there were reasonable grounds for failure so to do. If application is made to the court for leave to adduce additional evidence, and it is shown to the satisfaction of the court that such additional evidence may materially affect the result of the proceeding and that there were reasonable grounds for failure to adduce such evidence in the proceedings before such industry committee, the court may order such additional evidence to be taken before an industry committee and to be adduced upon the hearing in such manner and upon such terms and conditions as to the court may seem proper. Such industry committee may modify the initial findings by reason of the additional evidence so taken, and shall file with the court such modified or new findings which if supported by substantial evidence shall be conclusive, and shall also file its recommendation, if any, for the modification or setting aside of the original order. The judgment and decree of the court shall be final, subject to review by the Supreme Court of the United States upon certiorari or certification as provided in section 1254 of title 28 of the United States Code.

[72]Ibid.
[73]Section 10(a) as amended by section 5(f) of the Fair Labor Standards Amendments of 1955, and as further amended as noted.
[74]Section 22 of the Act of August 28, 1958 (72 Stat. 948).

(b) The commencement of proceedings under subsection (a) shall not, unless specifically ordered by the court, operate as a stay of the Secretary's[75] order. The court shall not grant any stay of the order unless the person complaining of such order shall file in court an undertaking with a surety or sureties satisfactory to the court for the payment to the employees affected by the order, in the event such order is affirmed, of the amount by which the compensation such employees are entitled to receive under the order exceeds the compensation they actually receive while such stay is in effect.

Investigations, inspections, records, and homework regulations
SEC. 11.

(a) The Secretary of Labor[76] or his designated representatives may investigate and gather data regarding the wages, hours, and other conditions and practices of employment in any industry subject to this Act, and may enter and inspect such places and such records (and make such transcriptions thereof), question such employees, and investigate such facts, conditions, practices, or matters as he may deem necessary or appropriate to determine whether any person has violated any provision of this Act, or which may aid in the enforcement of the provisions of this Act. Except as provided in section 12 and in subsection (b) of this section, the Secretary[77] shall utilize the bureaus and divisions of the Department of Labor for all the investigations and inspections necessary under this section. Except as provided in section 12, the Secretary[78] shall bring all actions under section 17 to restrain violations of this Act.

(b) With the consent and cooperation of State agencies charged with the administration of State labor laws, the Secretary of Labor[79] may, for the purpose of carrying out his functions and duties under this Act, utilize the services of State and local agencies and their employees and, notwithstanding any other provision of law, may reimburse such State and local agencies and their employees for services rendered for such purposes.

(c) Every employer subject to any provision of this Act or of any order issued under this Act shall make, keep, and preserve such records of the persons employed by him and of the wages, hours, and other conditions and practices of employment maintained by him, and shall preserve such records for such periods of time, and shall make such reports therefrom to the Secretary[80] as he shall prescribe by regulation or order as necessary or appropriate for the enforcement of the provisions of this Act or the regulations or orders thereunder.

(d) The Secretary is authorized to make such regulations and orders regulating, restricting, or prohibiting industrial homework as are necessary or appropriate to prevent the circumvention or evasion of and to safeguard the minimum wage rate prescribed in this Act, and

[75]See footnote 27.
[76]Ibid.
[77]Ibid.
[78]Ibid.
[79]See footnotes 8 and 27.
[80]See footnote 27.

all existing regulations or orders of the Administrator relating to industrial homework are hereby continued in full force and effect.[81]

Child labor provisions
SEC. 12.

(a) No producer, manufacturer, or dealer shall ship or deliver for shipment in commerce any goods produced in an establishment situated in the United States in or about which within thirty days prior to the removal of such goods therefrom any oppressive child labor has been employed: *Provided,* That any such shipment or delivery for shipment of such goods by a purchaser who acquired them in good faith in reliance on written assurance from the producer, manufacturer, or dealer that the goods were produced in compliance with the requirements of this section, and who acquired such goods for value without notice of any such violation, shall not be deemed prohibited by this subsection: *And provided further,* That a prosecution and conviction of a defendant for the shipment or delivery for shipment of any goods under the conditions herein prohibited shall be a bar to any further prosecution against the same defendant for shipments or deliveries for shipment of any such goods before the beginning of said prosecution.[82]

(b) The Secretary of Labor,[83] or any of his authorized representatives, shall make all investigations and inspections under section 11(a) with respect to the employment of minors, and, subject to the direction and control of the Attorney General, shall bring all actions under section 17 to enjoin any act or practice which is unlawful by reason of the existence of oppressive child labor, and shall administer all other provisions of this Act relating to oppressive child labor.

(c) No employer shall employ any oppressive child labor in commerce or in the production of goods for commerce **or in any enterprise engaged in commerce or in the production of goods for commerce.**[84]

(d) *In order to carry out the objectives of this section, the Secretary may by regulation require employers to obtain from any employee proof of age.*

Exemptions
SEC. 13.[85]

(a) **The provisions of sections 6** *(except section 6(d) in the case of paragraph (1) of this subsection)*[86] **and 7 shall not apply with respect to—**

(1) **any employee employed in a bona fide executive, administrative, or professional capacity** *(including any employee employed in the capacity of*

---

[81]Section 9 of the Fair Labor Standards Amendments of 1949, as amended by Reorganization Plan No. 6 of 1950.

[82]As amended by section 10(a) of the Fair Labor Standards Amendments of 1949.

[83]See footnotes 8 and 27.

[84]Section 10(b) of the Fair Labor Standards Amendments of 1949 as amended by section 8 of the Fair Labor Standards Amendments of 1961.

[85]Section 13 as amended by section 11 of the Fair Labor Standards Amendments of 1949; by Reorganization Plan No. 6 of 1950; and as further amended by the Fair Labor Standards Amendments of 1961, 1966, and 1974.

[86]As amended by the Education Amendments of 1972, 86 Stat. 235 at 375, effective July 1, 1972.

academic administrative personnel or teacher in elementary or secondary schools), or in the capacity of outside salesman (as such terms are defined and delimited from time to time by regulations of the Secretary, subject to the provisions of the Administrative Procedure Act, except that an employee of a retail or service establishment shall not be excluded from the definition of employee employed in a bona fide executive or administrative capacity because of the number of hours in his workweek which he devotes to activities not directly or closely related to the performance of executive or administrative activities, if less than 40 per centum of his hours worked in the workweek are devoted to such activities); or

(2) *any employee employed by any retail or service establishment (except an establishment or employee engaged in laundering, cleaning, or repairing clothing or fabrics or an establishment engaged in the operation of a hospital, institution, or school described in section 3(s) (4)), if more than 50 per centum of such establishment's annual dollar volume of sales of goods or services is made within the State in which the establishment is located, and such establishment is not in an enterprise described in section 3(s) or such establishment has an annual dollar volume of sales which is less than $250,000 (exclusive of excise taxes at the retail level which are separately stated).* A "retail or service establishment" shall mean an establishment 75 per centum of whose annual dollar volume of sales of goods or services (or of both) is not for resale and is recognized as retail sales or services in the particular industry; or

[*Effective January 1, 1975, section 13(a)(2) (relating to employees of retail and service establishments) is amended by striking out "$250,000" and inserting in lieu thereof "$225,000".*

Effective January 1, 1976, such section is amended by striking out "$225,000" and inserting in lieu thereof "$200,000".

Effective January 1, 1977, such section is amended by striking out "or such establishment has an annual dollar volume of sales which is less than $200,000 (exclusive of excise taxes at the retail level which are separately stated)"][87]

(3) *any employee employed by an establishment which is an amusement or recreational establishment, if (A) it does not operate for more than seven months in any calendar year, or (B) during the preceding calendar year, its average receipts for any six months of such year were not more than 33 1/3 per centum of its average receipts for the other six months of such year; or*

(4) any employee employed by an establishment which qualifies as an exempt retail establishment under clause (2) of this subsection and is recognized as a retail establishment in the particular industry notwithstanding that such establishment makes or processes at the retail establishment the goods that it sells: *Provided,* That more than 85 per centum of such establishment's annual dollar volume of sales of goods so made or processed is made within the State in which the establishment is located; or

(5) any employee employed in the catching, taking, propagating, harvesting, cultivating, or farming of any kind of fish, shellfish, crustacea, sponges, seaweeds, or other aquatic forms of animal and

---

[87]See section 13(g), which makes additional limitations on the applicability of the section 13(a)(2) and section 13(a)(6) exemptions to certain large businesses.

vegetable life, or in the first processing, canning or packing such marine products at sea as an incident to, or in conjunction with, such fishing operations, including the going to and returning from work and loading and unloading when performed by any such employee; or

(6) *any employee employed in agriculture (A) if such employee is employed by an employer who did not, during any calendar quarter during the preceding calendar year, use more than five hundred man-days of agricultural labor, (B) if such employee is the parent, spouse, child, or other member of his employer's immediate family, (C) if such employee (i) is employed as a hand harvest laborer and is paid on a piece rate basis in an operation which has been, and is customarily and generally recognized as having been, paid on a piece rate basis in the region of employment, (ii) commutes daily from his permanent residence to the farm on which he is so employed, and (iii) has been employed in agriculture less than thirteen weeks during the preceding calendar year, (D) if such employee (other than an employee described in clause (C) of this subsection) (i) is sixteen years of age or under and is employed as a hand harvest laborer, is paid on a piece rate basis in an operation which has been, and is customarily and generally recognized as having been, paid on a piece rate basis in the region of employment, (ii) is employed on the same farm as his parent or person standing in the place of his parent, and (iii) is paid at the same piece rate as employees over age sixteen are paid on the same farm, or (E) if such employee is principally engaged in the range production of livestock;*[88] or*

(7) **any employee to the extent that such employee is exempted by regulations, order,** *or certificate* **of the Secretary issued under section 14; or**

(8)[89] **any employee employed in connection with the publication of any weekly, semi-weekly, or daily newspaper with a circulation of less than four thousand the major part of which circulation is within the county where published or counties contiguous thereto; or**

(9) * * * *(Repealed)*
[*Note: Section 13(a)(9) (relating to motion picture theater employees) was repealed by Section 23 of the Fair Labor Standards Amendments of 1974. The 1974 amendments created an exemption for such employees from the overtime provisions only in section 13(b)(27).*]

(10) **any switchboard operator employed by an independently owned public telephone company which has not more than seven hundred and fifty stations; or**

(11) * * * *(Repealed)*
[*Note: Section 13(a)(11) (relating to telegraph agency employees) was repealed by Section 10 of the Fair Labor Standards Amendments of 1974. The 1974 amendments created an exemption from the overtime provisions only in section 13(b)(23).*]

(12) **any employee employed as a seaman on a vessel other than an American vessel; or**

[88]Prior to the Fair Labor Standards Amendments of 1966, the section 13(a)(6) exemption was applicable to all agricultural employees. For additional changes made by the Fair Labor Standards Amendments of 1974, see footnote 87.

[89]As amended by the Fair Labor Standards Amendments of 1966 (which deleted the words "printed and" which formerly preceded the word "published").

(13) * * * *(Repealed)*

[*Note: Section 13(a)(13) (relating to small logging crews) was repealed by Section 23 of the Fair Labor Standards Amendments of 1974. The 1974 amendments created an exemption for such employees from the overtime provisions only in Section 13(b)(28).*]

(14) * * * *(Repealed)*

[*Note: Section 13(a)(14) (relating to employees employed in growing and harvesting of shade grown tobacco) was repealed by Section 9 of the Fair Labor Standards Amendments of 1974. The 1974 amendments created an exemption for certain tobacco producing employees from the overtime provisions only in section 13(b)(22).*]

(15) *any employee employed on a casual basis in domestic service employment to provide babysitting services or any employee employed in domestic service employment to provide companionship services for individuals who (because of age or infirmity) are unable to care for themselves (as such terms are defined and delimited by regulations of the Secretary).*

(b) The provisions of section 7 shall not apply with respect to—

(1) any employee with respect to whom the Secretary of Transportation[90] has power to establish qualifications and maximum hours of service pursuant to the provisions of section 204 of the Motor Carrier Act, 1935; or

(2) any employee of an employer *engaged in the operation of a common carrier by rail and* subject to the provisions of part I of the Interstate Commerce Act; or

(3) any employee of a carrier by air subject to the provisions of title II of the Railway Labor Act; or

(4) any employee *who is* employed in the canning, processing, marketing, freezing, curing, storing, packing for shipment, or distributing of any kind of fish, shellfish, or other aquatic forms of animal or vegetable life, or any byproduct thereof, *and who receives compensation for employment in excess of forty-eight hours in any workweek at a rate not less than one and one-half times the regular rate at which he is employed;* or

[*Effective one year after the effective date of the Fair Labor Standards Amendments of 1974, section 13(b)(4) is amended by striking out "forty-eight hours" and inserting in lieu thereof "forty-four hours".*

Effective two years after such date, section 13(b)(4) is repealed.]

(5) any individual employed as an outside buyer of poultry, eggs, cream, or milk, in their raw or natural state; or

(6) any employee employed as a seaman; or

(7) *any driver, operator, or conductor employed by an employer engaged in the business of operating a street, suburban or interurban electric railway, or local trolley or motorbus carrier (regardless of whether or not such railway or carrier is public or private or operated for profit or not for profit), if such employee receives compensation for employment in excess of forty-eight hours in any workweek at a rate not less than one and one-half times the regular rate at which he is employed;*[91] or

[90]As amended by the Department of Transportation Act, 80 Stat. 931, which substituted "Secretary of Transportation" for "Interstate Commerce Commission".

[91]Prior to the Fair Labor Standards Amendments of 1966, employees of local transit companies were exempt from both the Act's minimum wage and overtime requirements.

[Effective one year after the effective date of the Fair Labor Standards Amendments of 1974, such section is amended by striking out "forty-eight hours" and inserting in lieu thereof "forty-four hours".

Effective two years after such date, such section is repealed.]

(8) (A) [92] *any employee (other than an employee of a hotel or motel who performs maid or custodial services) who is employed by an establishment which is a hotel, motel, or restaurant [93] and who receives compensation for employment in excess of forty-eight hours in any workweek at a rate not less than one and one-half times the regular rate at which he is employed; or*

(B) *any employee of a hotel or motel who performs maid or custodial services and who receives compensation for employment in excess of forty-eight hours in any workweek at a rate not less than one and one-half times the regular rate at which he is employed; or*

[Effective one year after the effective date of the Fair Labor Standards Amendments of 1974, subparagraphs (A) and (B) of section 13(b)(8) are each amended by striking out "forty-eight hours" and inserting in lieu thereof "forty-six hours".

Effective two years after such date, subparagraph (B) of section 13(b)(8) is amended by striking out "forty-six hours" and inserting in lieu thereof "forty-four hours".

Effective three years after such date, subparagraph (B) of section 13(b)(8) is repealed and such section is amended by striking out "(A)".]

(9) any employee employed as an announcer, news editor, or chief engineer by a radio or television station the major studio of which is located (A) in a city or town of one hundred thousand population or less, according to the latest available decennial census figures as compiled by the Bureau of the Census, except where such city or town is part of a standard metropolitan statistical area, as defined and designated by the Bureau of the Budget, which has a total population in excess of one hundred thousand, or (B) in a city or town of twenty-five thousand population or less, which is part of such an area but is at least 40 airline miles from the principal city in such area; or

(10) (A) *any salesman, partsman, or mechanic primarily engaged in selling or servicing automobiles, trucks, or farm implements, if he is employed by a nonmanufacturing establishment primarily engaged in the business of selling such vehicles or implements to ultimate purchasers; or*

(B) *any salesman primarily engaged in selling trailers, boats, or aircraft, if he is employed by a nonmanufacturing establishment primarily engaged in the business of selling trailers, boats, or aircraft to ultimate purchasers; [94] or*

[92]The portion of section 13(b)(8) pertaining to "an institution (other than a hospital) primarily engaged in the care of the sick, the aged or the mentally ill or defective" was deleted by the 1974 Amendments as provision was made for such establishments in section 7(j).

[93]Prior to the Fair Labor Standards Amendments of 1966, all hotel, motel and restaurant employees were exempt from both the Act's minimum wage and overtime requirements.

[94]Boats were added by the Fair Labor Standards Amendments of 1974. Prior to these Amendments, the overtime exemption in subsection (B) also applied to partsmen and mechanics. An earlier minimum wage exemption for any employee of a retail or service establishment which is primarily engaged in the business of selling automobiles, trucks or farm implements was repealed by the Fair Labor Standards Amendments of 1966.

(11) **any employee employed as a driver or driver's helper making local deliveries, who is compensated for such employment on the basis of trip rates, or other delivery payment plan, if the Secretary shall find that such plan has the general purpose and effect of reducing hours worked by such employees to, or below, the maximum workweek applicable to them under section 7(a)**; *or*

(12) *any employee employed in agriculture or in connection with the operation or maintenance of ditches, canals, reservoirs, or waterways, not owned or operated for profit, or operated on a sharecrop basis, and which are used exclusively for supply and storing of water for agriculture purposes;*[95] *or*

(13) *any employee with respect to his employment in agriculture by a farmer, notwithstanding other employment of such employee in connection with livestock auction operations in which such farmer is engaged as an adjunct to the raising of livestock, either on his own account or in conjunction with other farmers, if such employee (A) is primarily employed during his workweek in agriculture by such farmer, and (B) is paid for his employment in connection with such livestock auction operations at a wage rate not less than that prescribed by section 6(a)(1);*[96] *or*

(14) *any employee employed within the area of production (as defined by the Secretary) by an establishment commonly recognized as a country elevator, including such an establishment which sells products and services used in the operation of a farm, if no more than five employees are employed in the establishment in such operations;*[97] *or*

(15) *any employee engaged in the processing of maple sap into sugar (other than refined sugar) or syrup;*[98] *or*

(16) *any employee engaged (A) in the transportation and preparation for transportation of fruits or vegetables, whether or not performed by the farmer, from the farm to a place of first processing or first marketing within the same State, or (B) in transportation, whether or not performed by the farmer, between the farm and any point within the same State of persons employed or to be employed in the harvesting of fruits or vegetables;*[99] *or*

(17) *any driver employed by an employer engaged in the business of operating taxicabs;*[100] *or*

(18) *any employee of a retail or service establishment who is employed primarily in connection with the preparation or offering of food or beverages for human consumption, either on the premises, or by such services as catering, banquet, box lunch, or curb or counter service, to the public, to employees, or to members or guests of members of clubs* **and who receives compensation for employment in excess of forty-eight hours in any workweek at a rate not less than one and one-half times the regular rate at which he is employed;**[101] *or*

---

[95] A minimum wage exemption for these employees was repealed by the Fair Labor Standards Amendments of 1966.

[96] Ibid.

[97] Ibid.

[98] The exemption applicable to the ginning of cotton and the processing of sugar beets and sugar cane was deleted from section 13(b)(15) by the Fair Labor Standards Amendments of 1974 and provision was made for such employees in sections 13(b)(25) and 13(b)(26).

[99] See footnote 95.

[100] Ibid.

[101] Ibid.

[*Effective one year after the effective date of the Fair Labor Standards Amendments of 1974, such section is amended by striking out "forty-eight hours" and inserting in lieu thereof "forty-four hours".*

Effective two years after such date, such section is repealed.]

(19) *any employee of a bowling establishment if such employee receives compensation for employment in excess of forty-eight hours in any workweek at a rate not less than one and one-half times the regular rate at which he is employed; or*

[*Effective one year after the effective date of the Fair Labor Standards Amendments of 1974, section 13(b)(19) (relating to employees of bowling establishments) is amended by striking out "forty-eight hours" and inserting in lieu thereof "forty-four hours".*

Effective two years after such date, such section is repealed.]

(20) *any employee of a public agency who is employed in fire protection or law enforcement activities (including security personnel in correctional institutions); or*

[*(A) Effective January 1, 1975, section 13(b)(20) is amended to read as follows:*

"(20) any employee of a public agency who in any workweek is employed in fire protection activities or any employee of a public agency who in any workweek is employed in law enforcement activities (including security personnel in correctional institutions), if the public agency employs during the workweek less than 5 employees in fire protection or law enforcement activities, as the case may be;[102] or"

(B) *The Secretary of Labor shall in the calendar year beginning January 1, 1976, conduct (A) a study of the average number of hours in tours of duty in work periods in the preceding calendar year of employees (other than employees exempt from section 7 of the Fair Labor Standards Act of 1938 by section 13(b)(20) of such Act) of public agencies who are employed in fire protection activities, and (B) a study of the average number of hours in tours of duty in work periods in the preceding calendar year of employees (other than employees exempt from section 7 of the Fair Labor Standards Act of 1938 by section 13(b)(20) of such Act) of public agencies who are employed in law enforcement activities (including security personnel in correctional institutions). The Secretary shall publish the results of each such study in the Federal Register.*]

(21) *any employee who is employed in domestic service in a household and who resides in such household; or*

(22) *any agricultural employee employed in the growing and harvesting of shade-grown tobacco who is engaged in the processing (including, but not limited to, drying, curing, fermenting, bulking, rebulking, sorting, grading, aging, and baling) of such tobacco, prior to the stemming process, for use as cigar wrapper tobacco;[103] or*

(23) *any employee or proprietor in a retail or service establishment which qualifies as an exempt retail or service establishment under*

---

[102]A partial overtime exemption for public agencies having more than 5 such employees is provided by section 7(k) of the Act.

[103]A minimum wage exemption for these employees was repealed by the Fair Labor Standards Amendments of 1974.

paragraph (2) of subsection (a) with respect to whom the provisions of sections 6 and 7 would not otherwise apply, who is engaged in handling telegraphic messages for the public under an agency or contract arrangement with a telegraph company where the telegraph message revenue of such agency does not exceed $500 a month, and who receives compensation for employment in excess of forty-eight hours in any workweek at a rate not less than one and one-half times the regular rate at which he is employed; [104] *or*

[Effective one year after the effective date of the Fair Labor Standards Amendments of 1974, section 13(b)(23) is amended by striking out "forty-eight hours" and inserting in lieu thereof "forty-four hours".

Effective two years after such date, section 13(b)(23) is repealed.]

(24) any employee who is employed with his spouse by a non-profit educational institution to serve as the parents of children—

(A) who are orphans or one of whose natural parents is deceased, and [105]

(B) who are enrolled in such institution and reside in residential facilities of the institution,

while such children are in residence at such institution, if such employee and his spouse reside in such facilities, receive, without cost, board and lodging from such institution, and are together compensated, on a cash basis, at an annual rate of not less than $10,000; or

(25) any employee who is engaged in ginning of cotton for market in any place of employment located in a county where cotton is grown in commercial quantities and who receives compensation for employment in excess of—

(A) seventy-two hours in any workweek for not more than six workweeks in a year,

(B) sixty-four hours in any workweek for not more than four workweeks in that year,

(C) fifty-four hours in any workweek for not more than two workweeks in that year, and

(D) forty-eight hours in any other workweek in that year,

at a rate not less than one and one-half times the regular rate at which he is employed; [106] *or*

[Effective January 1, 1975, section 13(b)(25) is amended—

(A) by striking out "seventy-two" and inserting in lieu thereof "sixty-six";

(B) by striking out "sixty-four" and inserting in lieu thereof "sixty";

(C) by striking out "fifty-four" and inserting in lieu thereof "fifty";

(D) by striking out "and" at the end of subparagraph (C); and

(E) by striking out "forty-eight hours in any other workweek in that year," and inserting in lieu thereof the following: "forty-six hours in any workweek for not more than two workweeks in that year, and

"(E) forty-four hours in any other workweek in that year,".

Effective January 1, 1976, section 13(b)(25) is amended—

---

[104] Ibid.

[105] The word "and" is substituted for the word "or" pursuant to 120 Cong. Rec. H2297 (March 28, 1974; statement of Congressman Dent).

[106] A minimum wage exemption for these employees was repealed by the Fair Labor Standards Amendments of 1966.

(A) by striking out "sixty-six" in subparagraph (A) and inserting in lieu thereof "sixty";

(B) by striking out "sixty" in subparagraph (B) and inserting in lieu thereof "fifty-six";

(C) by striking out "fifty" and inserting in lieu thereof "forty-eight";

(D) by striking out "forty-six" and inserting in lieu thereof "forty-four"; and

(E) by striking out "forty-four" in subparagraph (E) and inserting in lieu thereof "forty".]

(26) any employee who is engaged in the processing of sugar beets, sugar beet molasses, or sugarcane into sugar (other than refined sugar) or syrup and who receives compensation for employment in excess of—

(A) seventy-two hours in any workweek for not more than six workweeks in a year,

(B) sixty-four hours in any workweek for not more than four workweeks in that year,

(C) fifty-four hours in any workweek for not more than two workweeks in that year, and

(D) forty-eight hours in any other workweek in that year,

at a rate not less than one and one-half times the regular rate at which he is employed; or

[Effective January 1, 1975, section 13(b)(26) is amended—

(A) by striking out "seventy-two" and inserting in lieu thereof "sixty-six";

(B) by striking out "sixty-four" and inserting in lieu thereof "sixty";

(C) by striking out "fifty-four" and inserting in lieu thereof "fifty";

(D) by striking out "and" at the end of subparagraph (C); and

(E) by striking out "forty-eight hours in any other workweek in that year," and inserting in lieu thereof the following: "forty-six hours in any workweek for not more than two workweeks in that year, and

"(E) forty-four hours in any other workweek in that year,".

Effective January 1, 1976, section 13(b)(26) is amended—

(A) by striking out "sixty-six" in subparagraph (A) and inserting in lieu thereof "sixty";

(B) by striking out "sixty" in subparagraph (B) and inserting in lieu thereof "fifty-six";

(C) by striking out "fifty" in subparagraph (C) and inserting in lieu thereof "forty-eight";

(D) by striking out "forty-six" in subparagraph (D) and inserting in lieu thereof "forty-four"; and

(E) by striking out "forty-four" in subparagraph (E) and inserting in lieu thereof "forty".]

(27) any employee employed by an establishment which is a motion picture theater;[107] or

(28) any employee employed in planting or tending trees, cruising, surveying, or felling timber, or in preparing or transporting logs or other forestry products to the mill, processing plant, railroad, or other transportation terminal, if the number of employees employed

---

[107]A minimum wage exemption for these employees was repealed by the Fair Labor Standards Amendments of 1974.

by his employer in such forestry or lumbering operations does not exceed eight.[108]

(c) (1) *Except as provided in paragraph (2), the provisions of section 12 relating to child labor shall not apply to any employee employed in agriculture outside of school hours for the school district where such employee is living while he is so employed, if such employee—*

(A) is less than twelve years of age and (i) is employed by his parent, or by a person standing in the place of his parent, on a farm owned or operated by such parent or person, or (ii) is employed, with the consent of his parent or person standing in the place of his parent, on a farm, none of the employees of which are (because of section 13(a)(6)(A)) required to be paid at the wage rate prescribed by section 6(a)(5),

(B) is twelve years or thirteen years of age and (i) such employment is with the consent of his parent or person standing in the place of his parent, or (ii) his parent or such person is employed on the same farm as such employee, or

(C) is fourteen years of age or older.

(2) *The provisions of section 12 relating to child labor shall apply to an employee below the age of sixteen employed in agriculture in an occupation that the Secretary of Labor finds and declares to be particularly hazardous for the employment of children below the age of sixteen, except where such employee is employed by his parent or by a person standing in the place of his parent on a farm owned or operated by such parent or person.*

(3) *The provisions of section 12 relating to child labor shall not apply to any child employed as an actor or performer in motion pictures or theatrical productions, or in radio or television productions.*

(d) The provisions of sections 6, 7, and 12 shall not apply with respect to any employee engaged in the delivery of newspapers to the consumer **or to any homeworker engaged in the making of wreaths composed principally of natural holly, pine, cedar, or other evergreens (including the harvesting of the evergreens or other forest products used in making such wreaths).**

(e) The provisions of section 7 shall not apply with respect to employees for whom the Secretary of Labor is authorized to establish minimum wage rates as provided in section 6(a)(3), except with respect to employees for whom such rates are in effect; and with respect to such employees the Secretary may make rules and regulations providing reasonable limitations and allowing reasonable variations, tolerances, and exemptions to and from any or all of the provisions of section 7 if he shall find, after a public hearing on the matter, and taking into account the factors set forth in section 6(a)(3), that economic conditions warrant such action.[109]

(f) The provisions of sections 6, 7, 11, and 12 shall not apply with respect to any employee whose services during the workweek are performed in a workplace within a foreign country or within territory under the jurisdiction of the United States other than the following: a State of the United States; the District of Columbia; Puerto Rico; the Virgin Islands; outer Continental Shelf lands defined in the Outer Continental Shelf Lands Act (ch. 345, 67 Stat. 462); American Samoa;

[108]Ibid.

[109]Section 3 of the American Samoa Labor Standards Amendments of 1956.

Guam; Wake Island; *Eniwetok Atoll; Kwajalein Atoll; Johnston Island;* and the Canal Zone.[110]

(g) *The exemption from section 6 provided by paragraphs (2) and (6) of subsection (a) of this section shall not apply with respect to any employee employed by an establishment (1) which controls, is controlled by, or is under common control with, another establishment the activities of which are not related for a common business purpose to, but materially support the activities of the establishment employing such employee; and (2) whose annual gross volume of sales made or business done, when combined with the annual gross volume of sales made or business done by each establishment which controls, is controlled by, or is under common control with, the establishment employing such employee, exceeds $10,000,000 (exclusive of excise taxes at the retail level which are separately stated), except that the exemption from section 6 provided by paragraph (2) of subsection (a) of this section shall apply with respect to any establishment described in this subsection which has an annual dollar volume of sales which would permit it to qualify for the exemption provided in paragraph (2) of subsection (a) if it were in an enterprise described in section 3(s).*

(h) *The provisions of section 7 shall not apply for a period or periods of not more than fourteen workweeks in the aggregate in any calendar year to any employee who—*

(1) *is employed by such employer—*

(A) *exclusively to provide services necessary and incidental to the ginning of cotton in an establishment primarily engaged in the ginning of cotton;*

(B) *exclusively to provide services necessary and incidental to the receiving, handling, and storing of raw cotton and the compressing of raw cotton when performed at a cotton warehouse or compress-warehouse facility, other than one operated in conjunction with a cotton mill, primarily engaged in storing and compressing;*

(C) *exclusively to provide services necessary and incidental to the receiving, handling, storing, and processing of cottonseed in an establishment primarily engaged in the receiving, handling, storing, and processing of cottonseed; or*

(D) *exclusively to provide services necessary and incidental to the processing of sugar cane or sugar beets in an establishment primarily engaged in the processing of sugar cane or sugar beets; and*

(2) *receives for—*

(A) *such employment by such employer which is in excess of ten hours in any workday, and*

(B) *such employment by such employer which is in excess of forty-eight hours in any workweek,*
compensation at a rate not less than one and one-half times the regular rate at which he is employed.

Any employer who receives an exemption under this subsection shall not be eligible for any other exemption under this section or section 7.

---

[110]Section 1(1) of the Act of August 30, 1957 (71 Stat. 514), as amended by section 21(b) of the Act of July 12, 1960 (74 Stat. 417), and by section 213 of the Fair Labor Standards Amendments of 1966.

Learners, apprentices, students, and handicapped workers
Sec. 14.[111]

(a) *The Secretary, to the extent necessary in order to prevent curtailment of opportunities for employment, shall by regulations or by orders provide for the employment of learners, of apprentices, and of messengers employed primarily in delivering letters and messages, under special certificates issued pursuant to regulations of the Secretary, at such wages lower than the minimum wage applicable under section 6 and subject to such limitations as to time, number, proportion, and length of service as the Secretary shall prescribe.*

(b)(1)(A) *The Secretary, to the extent necessary in order to prevent curtailment of opportunities for employment, shall by special certificate issued under a regulation or order provide, in accordance with subparagraph (B), for the employment, at a wage rate not less than 85 per centum of the otherwise applicable wage rate in effect under section 6 or not less than $1.60 an hour, whichever is the higher (or in the case of employment in Puerto Rico or the Virgin Islands not described in section 5(e), at a wage rate not less than 85 per centum of the otherwise applicable wage rate in effect under section 6(c)), of full-time students (regardless of age but in compliance with applicable child labor laws) in retail or service establishments.*

(B) *Except as provided in paragraph (4)(B), during any month in which full-time students are to be employed in any retail or service establishment under certificates issued under this subsection the proportion of student hours of employment to the total hours of employment of all employees in such establishment may not exceed—*

(i) *in the case of a retail or service establishment whose employees (other than employees engaged in commerce or in the production of goods for commerce) were covered by this Act before the effective date of the Fair Labor Standards Amendments of 1974—*

(I) *the proportion of student hours of employment to the total hours of employment of all employees in such establishment for the corresponding month of the immediately preceding twelve-month period,*

(II) *the maximum proportion for any corresponding month of student hours of employment to the total hours of employment of all employees in such establishment applicable to the issuance of certificates under this section at any time before the effective date of the Fair Labor Standards Amendments of 1974 for the employment of students by such employer, or*

(III) *a proportion equal to one-tenth of the total hours of employment of all employees in such establishment,*
whichever is greater;

(ii) *in the case of retail or service establishment whose employees (other than employees engaged in commerce or in the production of goods for commerce) are covered for the first time on or after the effective date of the Fair Labor Standards Amendments of 1974—*

(I) *the proportion of hours of employment of students in such establishment to the total hours of employment of all employees in such establishment for the corresponding month of the twelve-month period immediately prior to the effective date of such Amendments,*

---

[111]As amended by Section 24 of the Fair Labor Standards Amendments of 1974.

(II) the proportion of student hours of employment to the total hours of employment of all employees in such establishment for the corresponding month of the immediately preceding twelve-month period, or

(III) a proportion equal to one-tenth of the total hours of employment of all employees in such establishment,
whichever is greater; or

(iii) in the case of a retail or service establishment for which records of student hours worked are not available, the proportion of student hours of employment to the total hours of employment of all employees based on the practice during the immediately preceding twelve-month period in (I) similar establishments of the same employer in the same general metropolitan area in which such establishment is located, (II) similar establishments of the same or nearby communities if such establishment is not in a metropolitan area, or (III) other establishments of the same general character operating in the community or the nearest comparable community.

For purpose of clauses (i), (ii), and (iii) of this subparagraph, the term "student hours of employment" means hours during which students are employed in a retail or service establishment under certificates issued under this subsection.

(2) The Secretary, to the extent necessary in order to prevent curtailment of opportunities for employment, shall by special certificate issued under a regulation or order provide for the employment, at a wage rate not less than 85 per centum of the wage rate in effect under section 6(a)(5) or not less than $1.30 an hour, whichever is the higher (or in the case of employment in Puerto Rico or the Virgin Islands not described in section 5(e), at a wage rate not less than 85 per centum of the wage rate in effect under section 6(c)), of full-time students (regardless of age but in compliance with applicable child labor laws) in any occupation in agriculture.

(3) The Secretary, to the extent necessary in order to prevent curtailment of opportunities for employment, shall by special certificate issued under a regulation or order provide for the employment by an institution of higher education, at a wage rate not less than 85 per centum of the otherwise applicable wage rate in effect under section 6 or not less than $1.60 an hour, whichever is the higher (or in the case of employment in Puerto Rico or the Virgin Islands not described in section 5(e), at a wage rate not less than 85 per centum of the wage rate in effect under section 6(c)), of full-time students (regardless of age but in compliance with applicable child labor laws) who are enrolled in such institution. The Secretary shall by regulation prescribe standards and requirements to insure that this paragraph will not create a substantial probability of reducing the full-time employment opportunities of persons other than those to whom the minimum wage rate authorized by this paragraph is applicable.

(4) (A) A special certificate issued under paragraph (1), (2), or (3) shall provide that the student or students for whom it is issued shall, except during vacation periods, be employed on a part-time basis and not in excess of twenty hours in any workweek.

(B) If the issuance of a special certificate under paragraph (1) or (2) for an employer will cause the number of students employed by such

employer under special certificates issued under this subsection to ex-
ceed four, the Secretary may not issue such a special certificate for the
employment of a student by such employer unless the Secretary finds
employment of such student will not create a substantial probability of
reducing the full-time employment opportunities of persons other than
those employed under special certificates issued under this subsection. If
the issuance of a special certificate under paragraph (1) or (2) for an
employer will not cause the number of students employed by such em-
ployer under special certificates issued under this subsection to exceed
four—

    (i) the Secretary may issue a special certificate under paragraph (1)
or (2) for the employment of a student by such employer if such employer
certifies to the Secretary that the employment of such student will not
reduce the full-time employment opportunities of persons other than
those employed under special certificates issued under this subsection,
and

    (ii) in the case of an employer which is a retail or service establish-
ment, subparagraph (B) of paragraph (1) shall not apply with respect to
the issuance of special certificates for such employer under such para-
graph.

    The requirement of this subparagraph shall not apply in the case of the
issuance of special certificates under paragraph (3) for the employment of
full-time students by institutions of higher education; except that if the
Secretary determines that an institution of higher education is employing
students under certificates issued under paragraph (3) but in violation of
the requirements of that paragraph or of regulations issued thereunder,
the requirements of this subparagraph shall apply with respect to the
issuance of special certificates under paragraph (3) for the employment of
students by such institution.

    (C) No special certificate may be issued under this subsection unless
the employer for whom the certificate is to be issued provides evidence
satisfactory to the Secretary of the student status of the employees to be
employed under such special certificate.

(c) (1) Except as otherwise provided in paragraphs (2) and (3) of this subsec-
tion, the Secretary of Labor, to the extent necessary in order to prevent
curtailment of opportunities for employment, shall by regulation or order
provide for the employment under special certificates of individuals (includ-
ing individuals employed in agriculture) whose earning or productive capac-
ity is impaired by age or physical or mental deficiency or injury, at wages
which are lower than the minimum wage applicable under section 6 of this
Act but not less than 50 per centum of such wage and which are commensu-
rate with those paid nonhandicapped workers in industry in the vicinity for
essentially the same type, quality, and quantity of work.

(2) The Secretary, pursuant to such regulations as he shall prescribe and upon
certification of the State agency administering or supervising the adminis-
tration of vocational rehabilitation services, may issue special certificates for
the employment of—

    (A) handicapped workers engaged in work which is incidental to training or
evaluation programs, and

    (B) multihandicapped individuals and other individuals whose earning capac-
ity is so severely impaired that they are unable to engage in competitive employ-

ment, at wages which are less than those required by this subsection and which are related to the worker's productivity.

(3) *(A) The Secretary may by regulation or order provide for the employment of handicapped clients in work activities centers under special certificates at wages which are less than the minimums applicable under section 6 of this Act or prescribed by paragraph (1) of this subsection and which constitute equitable compensation for such clients in work activities centers.*

(B) For purposes of this section, the term "work activities centers" shall mean centers planned and designed exclusively to provide therapeutic activities for handicapped clients whose physical or mental impairment is so severe as to make their productive capacity inconsequential.

(d) The Secretary may by regulation or order provide that sections 6 and 7 shall not apply with respect to the employment by any elementary or secondary school of its students if such employment constitutes, as determined under regulations prescribed by the Secretary, an integral part of the regular education program provided by such school and such employment is in accordance with applicable child labor laws.

Prohibited acts

SEC. 15.

(a) After the expiration of one hundred and twenty days from the date of enactment of this Act, it shall be unlawful for any person—

(1) to transport, offer for transportation, ship, deliver, or sell in commerce, or to ship, deliver, or sell with knowledge that shipment or delivery or sale thereof in commerce is intended, any goods in the production of which any employee was employed in violation of section 6 or section 7, or in violation of any regulation or order of the Secretary of Labor[112] issued under section 14; except that no provision of this Act shall impose any liability upon any common carrier for the transportation in commerce in the regular course of its business of any goods not produced by such common carrier, and no provision of this Act shall excuse any common carrier from its obligation to accept any goods for transportation; and except that any such transportation, offer, shipment, delivery, or sale of such goods by a purchaser who acquired them in good faith in reliance on written assurance from the producer that the goods were produced in compliance with the requirements of the Act, and who acquired such goods for value without notice of any such violation, shall not be deemed unlawful;[113]

(2) to violate any of the provisions of section 6 or section 7, or any of the provisions of any regulation or order of the Secretary[114] issued under section 14;

(3) to discharge or in any other manner discriminate against any employee because such employee has filed any complaint or instituted or caused to be instituted any proceeding under or related to this Act, or has testified or is about to testify in any such proceeding, or has served or is about to serve on an industry committee;

[112]See footnote 27.
[113]As amended by section 13(a) of the Fair Labor Standards Amendments of 1949.
[114]See footnote 27.

(4) to violate any of the provisions of section 12;

(5) to violate any of the provisions of section 11(c) or any regulation or order made or continued in effect under the provisions of section 11(d), or to make any statement, report, or record filed or kept pursuant to the provisions of such section or of any regulation or order thereunder, knowing such statement, report, or record to be false in a material respect.[115]

(b) For the purposes of subsection (a)(1) proof that any employee was employed in any place of employment where goods shipped or sold in commerce were produced, within ninety days prior to the removal of the goods from such place of employment, shall be prima facie evidence that such employee was engaged in the production of such goods.

Penalties[116]
SEC. 16.

(a) Any person who willfully violates any of the provisions of section 15 shall upon conviction thereof be subject to a fine of not more than $10,000, or to imprisonment for not more than six months, or both. No person shall be imprisoned under this subsection except for an offense committed after the conviction of such person for a prior offense under this subsection.

(b) Any employer who violates the provisions of section 6 or section 7 of this Act shall be liable to the employee or employees affected in the amount of their unpaid minimum wages, or their unpaid overtime compensation, as the case may be, and in an additional equal amount as liquidated damages. Action[117] to recover such liability may be maintained *against any employer (including a public agency)* in any *Federal or State* court of competent jurisdiction by any one or more employees for and in behalf of himself or themselves and other employees similarly situated. No employee shall be a party plaintiff to any such action unless he gives his consent in writing to become such a party and such consent is filed in the court in which such action is brought.[118] The court in such action shall, in addition to any judgment awarded to the plaintiff or plaintiffs, allow a reasonable attorney's fee to be paid by the defendant, and costs of the action. **The right provided by this subsection to bring an action by or on behalf of any employee, and the right of any employee to become a party plaintiff to any such action, shall terminate upon the filing of a complaint by the Secretary of Labor in an action under section 17 in which restraint is sought of any further delay in the payment of unpaid minimum wages, or the amount of unpaid overtime compensation, as the case may be, owing to such employee under section 6 or section 7 of this Act by an employer liable therefor under the provisions of this subsection.**[119]

---

[115]As amended by section 13(b) of the Fair Labor Standards Amendments of 1949.
[116]The Portal-to-Portal Act of 1947 relieves employers from certain liabilities and punishments under this Act in circumstances specified in that Act.
[117]Periods of limitation for such actions are established by sections 6–8 inclusive of the Portal-to-Portal Act of 1947.
[118]Amendment provided by section 5(a) of the Portal-to-Portal Act of 1947.
[119]As amended by section 12 of the Fair Labor Standards Amendments of 1961.

(c) The Secretary[120] is authorized to supervise the payment of the unpaid minimum wages or the unpaid overtime compensation owing to any employee or employees under section 6 or 7 of this Act, and the agreement of any employee to accept such payment shall upon payment in full constitute a waiver by such employee of any right he may have under subsection (b) of this section to such unpaid minimum wages or unpaid overtime compensation and an additional equal amount as liquidated damages. The Secretary may bring an action in any court of competent jurisdiction to recover the amount of *the unpaid minimum wages or overtime compensation and an equal amount as liquidated damages.*[121] *The right provided by subsection (b) to bring an action by or on behalf of any employee and of any employee to become a party plaintiff to any such action shall terminate upon the filing of a complaint by the Secretary in an action under this subsection in which a recovery is sought of unpaid minimum wages or unpaid overtime compensation under sections 6 and 7 or liquidated or other damages provided by this subsection owing to such employee by an employer liable under the provisions of subsection (b), unless such action is dismissed without prejudice on motion of the Secretary.*

Any sums thus recovered by the Secretary on behalf of an employee pursuant to this subsection shall be held in a special deposit account and shall be paid, on order of the Secretary, directly to the employee or employees affected. Any such sums not paid to an employee because of inability to do so within a period of three years shall be covered into the Treasury of the United States as miscellaneous receipts. In determining when an action is commenced by the Secretary under this subsection for the purposes of the *statutes*[122] of limitations provided in section 6(a) of the Portal-to-Portal Act of 1947, it shall be considered to be commenced in the case of any individual claimant on the date when the complaint is filed if he is specifically named as a party plaintiff in the complaint, or if his name did not so appear, on the subsequent date on which his name is added as a party plaintiff in such action.[123]

(d) In any action or proceeding commenced prior to, on, or after the date of enactment of this subsection, no employer shall be subject to any liability or punishment under this Act or the Portal-to-Portal Act of 1947 on account of his failure to comply with any provision or provisions of such Acts (1) with respect to work heretofore or hereafter performed in a workplace to which the exemption in section 13(f) is applicable, (2) with respect to work performed in Guam, the Canal Zone or Wake Island before the effective date of this amendment of subsection (d), or (3) with respect to work performed in a possession named in section 6(a)(3) at any time prior to the establishment by the

[120]See footnote 27.

[121]The provision for liquidated damages was added by the Fair Labor Standards Amendments of 1974. These Amendments also deleted the prior requirements that section 16(c) suits be brought only on the written request of the employee and if the case did not involve any issue of law which has not been finally settled by the courts.

[122]Amended by section 601 of the Fair Labor Standards Amendments of 1966.

[123]Section 14 of the Fair Labor Standards Amendments of 1949, as amended by Reorganization Plan No. 6 of 1950 and the Fair Labor Standards Amendments of 1966.

Secretary, as provided therein, of a minimum wage rate applicable to such work.[124]

(e) *Any person who violates the provisions of section 12, relating to child labor, or any regulation issued under that section, shall be subject to a civil penalty of not to exceed $1,000 for each such violation. In determining the amount of such penalty, the appropriateness of such penalty to the size of the business of the person charged and the gravity of the violation shall be considered. The amount of such penalty, when finally determined, may be—*

(1) *deducted from any sums owing by the United States to the person charged;*

(2) *recovered in a civil action brought by the Secretary in any court of competent jurisdiction, in which litigation the Secretary shall be represented by the Solicitor of Labor; or*

(3) *ordered by the court, in an action brought for a violation of section 15(a)(4), to be paid to the Secretary.*

Any administrative determination by the Secretary of the amount of such penalty shall be final, unless within fifteen days after receipt of notice thereof by certified mail the person charged with the violation takes exception to the determination that the violations for which the penalty is imposed occurred, in which event final determination of the penalty shall be made in an administrative proceeding after opportunity for hearing in accordance with section 554 of title 5, United States Code, and regulations to be promulgated by the Secretary. Sums collected as penalties pursuant to this section shall be applied toward reimbursement of the costs of determining the violations and assessing and collecting such penalties, in accordance with the provision of section 2 of an Act entitled "An Act to authorize the Department of Labor to make special statistical studies upon payment of the cost thereof, and for other purposes" (29 U.S.C. 9a).

Injunction proceedings
SEC. 17.

The district courts, together with the United States District Court for the District of the Canal Zone, the District Court of the Virgin Islands, and the District Court of Guam shall have jurisdiction, for cause shown, to restrain violations of section 15, including in the case of violations of section 15(a)(2) the restraint of any withholding of payment of minimum wages or overtime compensation found by the court to be due to employees under this Act (except sums which employees are barred from recovering, at the time of the commencement of the action to restrain the violations, by virtue of the provisions of section 6 of the Portal-to-Portal Act of 1947).[125]

Relation to other laws
SEC. 18.

(a) No provision of this Act or of any order thereunder shall excuse noncompliance with any Federal or State law or municipal ordinance

---

[124]Section 4 of the American Samoa Labor Standards Amendments of 1956, as amended by section 1(2) of the Act of August 30, 1957 (71 Stat. 514), effective November 27, 1957.
[125]See footnote 119.

establishing a minimum wage higher than the minimum wage established under this Act or a maximum workweek lower than the maximum workweek established under this Act, and no provision of this Act relating to the employment of child labor shall justify noncompliance with any Federal or State law or municipal ordinance establishing a higher standard than the standard established under this Act. No provision of this Act shall justify any employer in reducing a wage paid by him which is in excess of the applicable minimum wage under this Act, or justify any employer in increasing hours of employment maintained by him which are shorter than the maximum hours applicable under this Act.

(b) *Notwithstanding any other provision of this Act (other than section 13(f)) or any other law—*

(1) *any Federal employee in the Canal Zone engaged in employment of the kind described in section 5102(c)(7) of title 5, United States Code, or* [126]

(2) *any employee employed in a nonappropriated fund instrumentality under the jurisdiction of the Armed Forces,* [127]

shall have his basic compensation fixed or adjusted at a wage rate which is not less than the appropriate wage rate provided for in section 6(a)(1) of this Act (except that the wage rate provided for in section 6(b) shall apply to any employee who performed services during the workweek in a work place within the Canal Zone), and shall have his overtime compensation set at an hourly rate not less than the overtime rate provided for in section 7(a)(1) of this Act.

Separability of provisions
SEC. 19.

If any provision of this Act or the application of such provision to any person or circumstances is held invalid, the remainder of the Act and the application of such provision to other persons or circumstances shall not be affected thereby.

Approved, June 25, 1938. [128]

[126]Paragraph (1), as amended by Public Law 90–83, 81 Stat. 222, omits reference to other employees covered under paragraph (1) of this subsection as enacted in the Fair Labor Standards Amendments of 1966, section 306, whose compensation requirements under such Amendments are now incorporated in 5 U.S.C. 5341 and 5 U.S.C. 5544.

[127]Paragraph (2) was formerly paragraph (3) of subsection (b) as enacted in the Fair Labor Standards Amendments of 1966, section 306. It was renumbered in the amendment by Public Law 90–83, 81 Stat. 222, which omitted the former paragraph (2) referring to employees described in 10 U.S.C. 7474 because of repeal of the latter provision by Public Law 89–554, 80 Stat. 663.

[128]The Fair Labor Standards Amendments of 1949 were approved October 26, 1949; the Fair Labor Standards Amendments of 1955 were approved August 12, 1955; the American Samoa Labor Standards Amendments were approved August 8, 1956; the Fair Labor Standards Amendments of 1961 were approved May 5, 1961; the Fair Labor Standards Amendments of 1966 were approved September 23, 1966; the Fair Labor Standards Amendments of 1974 were approved April 8, 1974.

Additional provisions of Fair Labor Standards Amendments of 1974

(88 Stat. 55) [Public Law 93-259] [93rd Congress] [2d Session]

An act

To amend the Fair Labor Standards Act of 1938 to increase the minimum wage rate under that Act, to expand the coverage of the Act, and for other purposes.

Be it enacted by the Senate and House of Representatives of the United States of America in Congress assembled, That this Act may be cited as the "Fair Labor Standards Amendments of 1974".

[Sections 2 through 6(d)(1) and sections 7 through 27, inclusive, of the Fair Labor Standards Amendments of 1974 amend the Fair Labor Standards Act of 1938, and are incorporated in their proper place in the Act. Section 6(d)(2)(A) and (B) amends the Portal-to-Portal Act of 1947 and is set forth below.]

Federal and state employees
SEC. 6. * * *
(2) (A) Section 6 of the Portal-to-Portal Pay Act of 1947 is amended by striking out the period at the end of paragraph (c) and by inserting in lieu thereof a semicolon and by adding after such paragraph the following:

"(d) with respect to any cause of action brought under section 16(b) of the Fair Labor Standards Act of 1938 against a State or a political subdivision of a State in a district court of the United States on or before April 18, 1973, the running of the statutory periods of limitation shall be deemed suspended during the period beginning with the commencement of any such action and ending one hundred and eighty days after the effective date of the Fair Labor Standards Amendments of 1974, except that such suspension shall not be applicable if in such action judgment has been entered for the defendant on the grounds other than State immunity from Federal jurisdiction."

Effective date
SEC. 29 (a) Except as otherwise specifically provided, the amendments made by this Act shall take effect on May 1, 1974.
(b) Notwithstanding subsection (a), on and after the date of the enactment of this Act the Secretary of Labor is authorized to prescribe

necessary rules, regulations, and orders with regard to the amend-
ments made by this Act.
Approved April 8, 1974.

Additional provisions of Fair Labor Standards Amendments of 1966
(80 Stat. 830) [Public Law 89-601] [89th Congress] [2d Session]

An act

To amend the Fair Labor Standards Act of 1938 to extend its protection to additional employees, to raise the minimum wage, and for other purposes.

Be it enacted by the Senate and House of Representatives of the United States of America in Congress assembled, That this Act may be cited as the "Fair Labor Standards Amendments of 1966".

[Sections 101 to 501, inclusive, and section 601(a) of the Fair Labor Standards Amendments of 1966 amend the Fair Labor Standards Act of 1938, and are incorporated in their proper place in the act.]

Statute of limitations
SEC. 601. * * *
(b) *Section 6(a) of the Portal-to-Portal Act of 1947 (Public Law 49, Eightieth Congress) is amended by inserting before the semicolon at the end thereof the following: ", except that a cause of action arising out of a willful violation may be commenced within three years after the cause of action accrued".*

Effective date
SEC. 602. *Except as otherwise provided in this Act, the amendments made by this Act shall take effect on February 1, 1967. On and after the date of the enactment of this Act the Secretary is authorized to promulgate necessary rules, regulations, or orders with regard to the amendments made by this Act.*

Study of excessive overtime
SEC. 603. *The Secretary of Labor is hereby instructed to commence immediately a complete study of present practices dealing with overtime payments for work in excess of forty hours per week and the extent to which such overtime work impedes the creation of new job opportunities in American industry. The Secretary is further instructed to report to the Congress by July 1, 1967, the findings of such survey with appropriate recommendations.*

SEC. 604. *The Secretary of Labor, in cooperation with the Secretary of Defense and the Secretary of State, shall (1) undertake a study with respect to (A) wage rates payable to Federal employees in the Canal Zone engaged in employment of the kind described in paragraph (7) of section 202 of the Classification Act of 1949 (5 U.S.C. 1082(7)) and (B) the requirements of an effective and economical operation of the Panama Canal, and (2) report to the Congress not later than July 1, 1968, the results of his study together with such recommendations as he may deem appropriate.*

Study of wages paid handicapped clients in sheltered workshops

SEC. 605. *The Secretary of Labor is hereby instructed to commence immediately a complete study of wage payments to handicapped clients of sheltered workshops and of the feasibility of raising existing wage standards in such workshops. The Secretary is further instructed to report to the Congress by July 1, 1967, the findings of such study with appropriate recommendations.*

Prevention of discrimination because of age

SEC. 606. *The Secretary of Labor is hereby directed to submit to the Congress not later than January 1, 1967, his specific legislative recommendations for implementing the conclusions and recommendations contained in his report on age discrimination in employment made pursuant to section 715 of Public Law 88-352. Such legislative recommendations shall include, without limitation, provisions specifying appropriate enforcement procedures, a particular administering agency, and the standards, coverage, and exemptions, if any, to be included in the proposed enactment.*

Approved September 23, 1966.

Additional provisions of Fair Labor Standards Amendments of 1961
(75 Stat. 65) [Public Law 87-30] [87th Congress] [1st Session]

An act

To amend the Fair Labor Standards Act of 1938, as amended, to provide coverage for employees of large enterprises engaged in retail trade or service and of other employers engaged in commerce or in the production of goods for commerce, to increase the minimum wage under the Act to $1.25 an hour, and for other purposes.

Be it enacted by the Senate and House of Representatives of the United States of America in Congress assembled, That this Act may be cited as the "Fair Labor Standards Amendments of 1961".

[Sections 2 to 12, inclusive, of the Fair Labor Standards Amendments of 1961 amend the Fair Labor Standards Act of 1938, and are incorporated in their proper place in the Act.]

Effective date

SEC. 14. The amendments made by this Act shall take effect upon the expiration of one hundred and twenty days after the date of its enactment, except as otherwise provided in such amendments and except that the authority to promulgate necessary rules, regulations, or orders with regard to amendments made by this Act, under the Fair Labor Standards Act of 1938 and amendments thereto, including amendments made by this Act, may be exercised by the Secretary on and after the date of enactment of this Act.

Approved May 5, 1961.

Additional provisions of Fair Labor Standards Amendments of 1949
(63 Stat. 917) [Public Law 393—81st Congress]
[Chapter 736—1st Session]

An act

To provide for the amendment of the Fair Labor Standards Act of 1938, and for other purposes.

Be it enacted by the Senate and House of Representatives of the United States of America in Congress assembled, That this Act may be cited as the "Fair Labor Standards Amendments of 1949".

[Section 2 to 15, inclusive, of the Fair Labor Standards Amendments of 1949 amend the Fair Labor Standards Act of 1938, and are incorporated in their proper place in the Act.]

Miscellaneous and effective date

SEC. 16.

(a) The amendments made by this Act shall take effect upon the expiration of ninety days from the date of its enactment; except that the amendment made by section 4 shall take effect on the date of its enactment.

(b) Except as provided in section 3(o) and in the last sentence of section 16(c) of the Fair Labor Standards Act of 1938, as amended, no amendment made by this Act shall be construed as amending, modifying, or repealing any provision of the Portal-to-Portal Act of 1947.

(c) Any order, regulation, or interpretation of the Administrator of the Wage and Hour Division or of the Secretary of Labor, and any agreement entered into by the Administrator or the Secretary, in effect under the provisions of the Fair Labor Standards Act of 1938, as amended, on the effective date of this Act, shall remain in effect as an order, regulation, interpretation, or agreement of the Administrator or the Secretary, as the case may be, pursuant to this Act, except to the extent that any such order, regulation, interpretation, or agreement may be inconsistent with the provisions of this Act, or may from time to time be amended, modified, or rescinded by the Administrator or the Secretary, as the case may be, in accordance with the provisions of this Act.[1]

(d) No amendment made by this Act shall affect any penalty or liability with respect to any act or omission occurring prior to the effective date of this Act; but, after the expiration of two years from such effective date, no action shall be instituted under section 16(b) of the Fair Labor Standards Act of 1938, as amended, with respect to any liability accruing thereunder for any act or omission occurring prior to the effective date of this Act.

(e) No employer shall be subject to any liability or punishment under the Fair Labor Standards Act of 1938, as amended (in any action or proceeding commenced prior to or on or after the effective date of this Act), on account of the failure of said employer to pay an employee compensation for any period of overtime work performed prior to July 20, 1949, if the compensation paid prior to July 20, 1949 for such work was at least equal to the compensation which would have been payable for such work had section 7(d)(6) and (7) and section 7(g) of the Fair Labor Standards Act of 1938, as amended, been in effect at the time of such payment.

(f) Public Law 177, Eighty-first Congress, approved July 20, 1949, is hereby repealed as of the effective date of this Act.[2]

Approved, October 26, 1949.

---

[1]Effective May 24, 1950, all functions of Administrator were transferred to the Secretary of Labor by Reorganization Plan No. 6 of 1950, 64 Stat. 1263. See text set out under section 4(a) of the Fair Labor Standards Act.

[2]The provisions of the repealed statute are now contained in substance in sections 7(e)(5), (6), (7), and (h) of the Fair Labor Standards Act, as amended.

Pertinent provisions affecting the Fair Labor Standards Act from the Portal-To-Portal Act of 1947

(61 Stat. 84) [Public Law 49—80th Congress]
[Chapter 52—1st Session] [H.R. 2157]

An act

To relieve employers from certain liabilities and punishments under the Fair Labor Standards Act of 1938, as amended, the Walsh-Healey Act, and the Bacon-Davis Act, and for other purposes.

Be it enacted by the Senate and House of Representatives of the United States of America in Congress assembled,

Part I

Findings and policy
SECTION 1.

(a) The Congress hereby finds that the Fair Labor Standards Act of 1938, as amended, has been interpreted judicially in disregard of long-established customs, practices, and contracts between employers and employees, thereby creating wholly unexpected liabilities, immense in amount and retroactive in operation, upon employers with the results that, if said Act as so interpreted or claims arising under such interpretations were permitted to stand, (1) the payment of such liabilities would bring about financial ruin of many employers and seriously impair the capital resources of many others, thereby resulting in the reduction of industrial operations, halting of expansion and development, curtailing employment, and the earning power of employees; (2) the credit of many employers would be seriously impaired; (3) there would be created both an extended and continuous uncertainty on the part of industry, both employer and employee, as to the financial condition of productive establishments and a gross inequality of competitive conditions between employers and between industries; (4) employees would receive windfall payments, including liquidated damages, of sums for activities performed by them without any expectation of reward beyond that included in their agreed rates of pay; (5) there would occur the promotion of increasing demands for payment to employees for engaging in activities no compensation for which had been contemplated by either the employer or employee at the time they were engaged in; (6) voluntary collective bargaining would be interfered with and industrial disputes between employees and employers and between employees and employees would be created; (7) the courts of the country would be burdened with excessive and needless litigation and champertous practices would be encouraged; (8) the Public Treasury would be deprived of large sums of revenues and public finances would be seriously deranged by claims against the Public Treasury for refunds of taxes already paid; (9) the cost to the Government of goods and services heretofore and hereafter purchased by its various departments and agencies would be unreasonably increased and the Public Treasury would be seriously affected by consequent increased cost of war contracts; and (10) serious and adverse effects upon the revenues of Federal, State, and local governments would occur.

The Congress further finds that all of the foregoing constitutes a substantial burden on commerce and a substantial obstruction to the free flow of goods in commerce.

The Congress, therefore, further finds and declares that it is in the national public interest and for the general welfare, essential to national defense, and necessary to aid, protect, and foster commerce, that this Act be enacted.

The Congress further finds that the varying and extended periods of time for which, under the laws of the several States, potential retroactive liability may be imposed upon employers, have given and will give rise to great difficulties in the sound and orderly conduct of business and industry.

The Congress further finds and declares that all of the results which have arisen or may arise under the Fair Labor Standards Act of 1938, as amended, as aforesaid, may (except as to liability for liquidated damages) arise with respect to the Walsh-Healey and Bacon-Davis Acts and that it is therefore, in the national public interest and for the general welfare, essential to national defense, and necessary to aid, protect, and foster commerce, that this Act shall apply to the Walsh-Healey Act and the Bacon-Davis Act.

(b) It is hereby declared to be the policy of the Congress in order to meet the existing emergency and to correct existing evils (1) to relieve and protect interstate commerce from practices which burden and obstruct it; (2) to protect the right of collective bargaining; and (3) to define and limit the jurisdiction of the courts.

* * * * *

Part III

Future claims

SEC. 4. RELIEF FROM CERTAIN FUTURE CLAIMS UNDER THE FAIR LABOR STANDARDS ACT OF 1938, AS AMENDED, THE WALSH-HEALEY ACT, AND THE BACON-DAVIS ACT.—

(a) Except as provided in subsection (b), no employer shall be subject to any liability or punishment under the Fair Labor Standards Act of 1938, as amended, the Walsh-Healey Act, or the Bacon-Davis Act, on account of the failure of such employer to pay an employee minimum wages, or to pay an employee overtime compensation, for or on account of any of the following activities of such employee engaged in on or after the date of the enactment of this Act—

(1) walking, riding, or traveling to and from the actual place of performance of the principal activity or activities which such employee is
employed to perform, and

(2) activities which are preliminary to or postliminary to said principal
activity or activities,

which occur either prior to the time on any particular workday at which
such employee commences, or subsequent to the time on any particular
workday at which he ceases, such principal activity or activities.

(b) Notwithstanding the provisions of subsection (a) which relieve an
employer from liability and punishment with respect to an activity,
the employer, shall not be so relieved if such activity is compensable
by either—

(1) an express provision of a written or nonwritten contract in effect, at
the time of such activity, between such employee, his agent, or
collective-bargaining representative and his employer; or

(2) a custom or practice in effect, at the time of such activity, at the
establishment or other place where such employee is employed,
covering such activity, not inconsistent with a written or nonwritten
contract, in effect at the time of such activity, between such employee, his agent, or collective-bargaining representative and his
employer.

(c) For the purposes of subsection (b), an activity shall be considered as
compensable under such contract provision or such custom or practice only when it is engaged in during the portion of the day with
respect to which it is so made compensable.

(d) In the application of the minimum wage and overtime compensation
provisions of the Fair Labor Standards Act of 1938, as amended, of
the Walsh-Healey Act, or of the Bacon-Davis Act, in determining the
time for which an employer employs an employee with respect to
walking, riding, traveling or other preliminary or postliminary activities described in subsection (a) of this section, there shall be
counted all that time, but only that time, during which the employee
engages in any such activity which is compensable within the meaning of subsections (b) and (c) of this section.

Part IV

Miscellaneous

SEC. 6. STATUTE OF LIMITATIONS.—Any action commenced on
or after the date of the enactment of this Act to enforce any cause of
action for unpaid minimum wages, unpaid overtime compensation, or
liquidated damages, under the Fair Labor Standards Act of 1938, as
amended, the Walsh-Healey Act, or the Bacon-Davis Act—

(a) if the cause of action accrues on or after the date of enactment of this
Act—may be commenced within two years after the cause of action
accrued, and every such action shall be forever barred unless commenced within two years after the cause of action accrued, *except that
a cause of action arising out of a willful violation may be commenced within
three years after the cause of action accrued;*[1]

* * * * *

[1]As amended by section 601 of the Fair Labor Standards Amendments of 1966, 80 Stat. 830.

(d) with respect to any cause of action brought under section 16(b) of the Fair Labor Standards Act of 1938 against a State or a political subdivision of a State in a district court of the United States on or before April 18, 1973, the running of the statutory periods of limitation shall be deemed suspended during the period beginning with the commencement of any such action and ending one hundred and eighty days after the effective date of the Fair Labor Standards Amendments of 1974, except that such suspension shall not be applicable if in such action judgment has been entered for the defendant on the grounds other than State immunity from Federal jurisdiction.[2]

SEC. 7. DETERMINATION OF COMMENCEMENT OF FUTURE ACTIONS. — In determining when an action is commenced for the purposes of section 6, an action commenced on or after the date of the enactment of this Act under the Fair Labor Standards Act of 1938, as amended, the Walsh-Healey Act, or the Bacon-Davis Act, shall be considered to be commenced on the date when the complaint is filed; except that in the case of a collective or class action instituted under the Fair Labor Standards Act of 1938, as amended, or the Bacon-Davis Act, it shall be considered to be commenced in the case of any individual claimant—

(a) on the date when the complaint is filed, if he is specifically named as a party plaintiff in the complaint and his written consent to become a party plaintiff is filed on such date in the court in which the action is brought; or

(b) if such written consent was not so filed or if his name did not so appear—on the subsequent date on which such written consent is filed in the court in which the action was commenced.

* * * * *

SEC. 10. RELIANCE IN FUTURE ON ADMINISTRATIVE RULINGS, ETC. —

(a) In any action or proceeding based on any act or omission on or after the date of the enactment of this Act, no employer shall be subject to any liability or punishment for or on account of the failure of the employer to pay minimum wages or overtime compensation under the Fair Labor Standards Act of 1938, as amended, the Walsh-Healey Act, or the Bacon-Davis Act, if he pleads and proves that the act or omission complained of was in good faith in conformity with and in reliance on any written administrative regulation, order, ruling, approval, or interpretation, of the agency of the United States specified in subsection (b) of this section, or any administrative practice or enforcement policy of such agency with respect to the class of employers to which he belonged. Such a defense, if established, shall be a bar to the action or proceeding, notwithstanding that after such act or omission, such administrative regulation, order, ruling, approval, interpretation, practice, or enforcement policy is modified or rescinded or is determined by judicial authority to be invalid or of no legal effect.

[2]Added by the Fair Labor Standards Amendments of 1974, 88 Stat. 55.

(b) The agency referred to in subsection (a) shall be—
   (1) in the case of the Fair Labor Standards Act of 1938, as amended—
      the Secretary of Labor[3];

* * * * *

SEC. 11. LIQUIDATED DAMAGES.—In any action commenced prior to or on or after the date of the enactment of this Act to recover unpaid minimum wages, unpaid overtime compensation, or liquidated damages, under the Fair Labor Standards Act of 1938, as amended, if the employer shows to the satisfaction of the court that the act or omission giving rise to such action was in good faith and that he had reasonable grounds for believing that his act or omission was not a violation of the Fair Labor Standards Act of 1938, as amended, the court may, in its sound discretion, award no liquidated damages or award any amount thereof not to exceed the amount specified in section 16 of such Act.

* * * * *

SEC. 13. DEFINITIONS.—
(a) When the terms "employer", "employee", and "wage" are used in this Act in relation to the Fair Labor Standards Act of 1938, as amended, they shall have the same meaning as when used in such Act of 1938.

* * * * *

(e) As used in section 6 the term "State" means any State of the United States or the District of Columbia or any Territory or possession of the United States.

SEC. 14. SEPARABILITY.—If any provision of this Act or the application of such provision to any person or circumstance is held invalid, the remainder of this Act and the application of such provision to other persons or circumstances shall not be affected thereby.

SEC. 15. SHORT TITLE.—This Act may be cited as the "Portal-to-Portal Act of 1947".
Approved May 14, 1947.

[3]As amended by Reorganization Plan No. 6 of 1950, 64 Stat. 1263.

Additional provisions of Equal Pay Act of 1963

(77 Stat. 56) [Public Law 88-38] [88th Congress, S. 1409] [June 10, 1963]

An act

To prohibit discrimination on account of sex in the payment of wages by employers engaged in commerce or in the production of goods for commerce.

Be it enacted by the Senate and House of Representatives of the United States of America in Congress assembled, That this Act may be cited as the "Equal Pay Act of 1963".

Declaration of purpose
SEC. 2.
(a) The Congress hereby finds that the existence in industries engaged in commerce or in the production of goods for commerce of wage differentials based on sex—
 (1) depresses wages and living standards for employees necessary for their health and efficiency;
 (2) prevents the maximum utilization of the available labor resources;
 (3) tends to cause labor disputes, thereby burdening, affecting, and obstructing commerce;
 (4) burdens commerce and the free flow of goods in commerce; and
 (5) constitutes an unfair method of competition.
(b) It is hereby declared to be the policy of this Act, through exercise by Congress of its power to regulate commerce among the several States and with foreign nations, to correct the conditions above referred to in such industries.

[Section 3 of the Equal Pay Act of 1963 amends section 6 of the Fair Labor Standards Act by adding a new subsection (d). The amendment is incorporated in the revised text of the Act.]

Effective date
SEC. 4. The amendments made by this Act shall take effect upon the expiration of one year from the date of its enactment: *Provided,* That in the case of employees covered by a bona fide collective bargaining agreement in effect at least thirty days prior to the date of enactment of this Act, entered into by a labor organization (as defined in section 6(d)(4) of the Fair Labor Standards Act of 1938, as amended), the amendments made by this Act shall take effect upon the termination of such collective bargaining agreement or upon the expiration of two years from the date of enactment of this Act, whichever shall first occur.

Approved June 10, 1963, 12:00 m.

Appendix C

Executive Order 11246 as amended by Executive Order 11375

Under and by virtue of the authority vested in me as President of the United States, it is ordered as follows:

PART I—NONDISCRIMINATION IN GOVERNMENT EMPLOYMENT [1]

PART II—NONDISCRIMINATION IN EMPLOYMENT BY GOVERNMENT CONTRACTORS AND SUBCONTRACTORS

Subpart A—Duties of the Secretary of Labor

SEC. 201. The Secretary of Labor shall be responsible for the administration of parts II and III of this order and shall adopt such rules and regulations and issue such orders as he deems necessary and appropriate to achieve the purposes thereof.

Subpart B—Contractors' Agreements

SEC. 202. Except in contracts exempted in accordance with section 204 of this order, all Government contracting agencies shall include in every Government contract hereafter entered into the following provisions:

During the performance of this contract, the contractor agrees as follows:

(1) The contractor will not discriminate against any employee or applicant for employment because of race, color, religion, sex, or national origin. The contractor will take affirmative action to ensure that applicants are employed, and that employees are treated during employment, without regard to their race, color, religion, sex, or national origin. Such action shall include, but not be limited to the following: employment, upgrading, demotion, or transfer; recruitment or recruitment advertising; layoff or termination; rates of pay or other forms of compensation; and selection for training, including apprenticeship. The contractor agrees to post in conspicuous places, available to employees and applicants for employment, notices to be provided by the contracting officer setting forth the provisions of this nondiscrimination clause.[2]

(2) The contractor will, in all solicitations or advertisements for employees placed by or on behalf of the contractor, state that all qualified applicants will receive consideration for employment without regard to race, color, religion, sex, or national origin.[3]

(3) The contractor will send to each labor union or representative of workers with which he has a collective bargaining agreement or other contract or understanding, a notice, to be provided by the agency contracting officer, advising the labor union or workers' representative of the contractor's commitments under section 202 of Executive Order No. 11246 of September 24, 1965, and shall post copies of the notice in conspicuous places available to employees and applicants for employment.

(4) The contractor will comply with all provisions of Executive Order No. 11246 of September 24, 1965, and of the rules, regulations, and relevant orders of the Secretary of Labor.

---

[1] Secs. 101 through 105 of pt. I of Executive Order 11246 dealing with discrimination in Federal employment were superseded by Executive Order 11478. Executive Order 11478, which is concerned exclusively with Government employment, expanded considerably the obligation of the Government itself to undertake equal employment opportunity within its own organization. Executive Order 11478 was signed by President Richard Nixon on Aug. 8, 1969.
[2] Sec. 202, paragraphs (1) and (2) and sec. 203, subsec. (d) were amended by Executive Order 11375 to encompass sex discrimination. Executive Order 11375 was signed by President Lyndon B. Johnson on Sept. 24, 1965.
[3] Ibid.

(5) The contractor will furnish all information and reports required by Executive Order No. 11246 of September 24, 1965, and by the rules, regulations, and orders of the Secretary of Labor, or pursuant thereto, and will permit access to his books, records, and accounts by the contracting agency and the Secretary of Labor for purposes of investigation to ascertain compliance with such rules, regulations, and orders.

(6) In the event of the contractor's noncompliance with the nondiscrimination clauses of this contract or with any of such rules, regulations, or orders, this contract may be cancelled, terminated, or suspended in whole or in part and the contractor may be declared ineligible for further Government contracts in accordance with procedures authorized in Executive Order No. 11246 of September 24, 1965, and such other sanctions may be imposed and remedies involved as provided in Executive Order No. 11246 of September 24, 1965, or by rule, regulation, or order of the Secretary of Labor, or as otherwise provided by law.

(7) The contractor will include the provisions of paragraphs (1) through (7) in every subcontract or purchase order unless exempted by rules, regulations, or orders of the Secretary of Labor issued pursuant to section 204 of Executive Order No. 11246 of September 24, 1965, so that such provisions will be binding upon each subcontractor or vendor. The contractor will take such action with respect to any subcontract or purchase order as the contracting agency may direct as a means of enforcing such provisions including sanctions for noncompliance: *Provided, however,* That in the event the contractor becomes involved in, or threatened with, litigation with a subcontractor or vendor as a result of such direction by the contracting agency, the contractor may request the United States to enter into such litigation to protect the interests of the United States.

SEC. 203. (a) Each contractor having a contract containing the provisions prescribed in section 202 shall file, and shall cause each of his subcontractors to file, compliance reports with the contracting agency or the Secretary of Labor as may be directed. Compliance reports shall be filed within such times and shall contain such information as to the practices, policies, programs, and employment policies, programs, and employment statistics of the contractor and each subcontractor, and shall be in such form, as the Secretary of Labor may prescribe.

(b) Bidders or prospective contractors or subcontractors may be required to state whether they have participated in any previous contract subject to the provisions of this order, or any preceding similar executive order, and in that event to submit, on behalf of themselves and their proposed subcontractors, compliance reports prior to or as an initial part of their bid or negotiation of a contract.

(c) Whenever the contractor or subcontractor has a collective bargaining agreement or other contract or understanding with a labor union or an agency referring workers or providing or supervising apprenticeship or training for such workers, the compliance report shall include such information as to such labor union's or agency's practices and policies affecting compliance as the Secretary of Labor may prescribe: *Provided,* That to the extent such information is within the exclusive possession of a labor union or an agency referring workers or providing or supervising apprenticeship or training and such labor union or agency shall refuse to furnish such information to the contractor, the contractor shall so certify to the contracting agency as part of its compliance report and shall set forth what efforts he has made to obtain such information.

(d) The contracting agency or the Secretary of Labor may direct that any bidder or prospective contractor or subcontractor shall submit, as part of his compliance report, a statement in writing, signed by an authorized officer or agent on behalf of any labor union or agency referring workers or providing or supervising apprenticeship or other training, with which the bidder or prospective contractor deals, with supporting information, to the effect that the signer's practices and policies do not discriminate on the grounds of race, color, religion, sex, or national origin, and that the signer either will affirmatively cooperate in the implementation of the policy and provisions of this order or that it consents and agrees that recruitment, employment, and the terms and conditions of employment under the proposed contract shall be in accordance with the purposes and provisions of the order. In the event that the union, or the agency, shall refuse to execute such a statement, the compliance report shall so certify and set forth what efforts have been made to secure such a statement and such additional factual material as the contracting agency or the Secretary of Labor may require.[4]

SEC. 204. The Secretary of Labor may, when he deems that special circumstances in the national interest so require, exempt a contracting agency from the requirement of including any or all of the provisions of section 202 of this order in any specific contract, subcontract, or purchase order. The Secretary of Labor may, by rule or regulation, also exempt certain classes of contracts, subcontracts, or purchase orders: (1) whenever work is to be or has been performed outside the United States and no recruitment of workers within the limits of the United States is involved; (2) for standard commercial supplies or raw materials; (3) involving less than specified amounts of money or specified numbers of workers; or (4) to the extent that they involve subcontracts below a specified tier. The Secretary of Labor may also provide, by rule, regulation, or order, for the exemption of facilities of a contractor which are in all respects separate and distinct from activities of the contractor related to the performance of the contract: *Provided,* That such an exemption will not interfere with or impede the effectuation of the purposes of this order: *And provided further,* That in the absence of such an exemption all facilities shall be covered by the provisions of this order.

Subpart C — Powers and Duties of the Secretary of Labor and the Contracting Agencies

SEC. 205. Each contracting agency shall be primarily responsible for obtaining compliance with the rules, regulations, and orders of the Secretary of Labor with respect to contracts entered into by such agency or its contractors. All contracting agencies shall comply with the rules of the Secretary of Labor in discharging their primary responsibility for securing compliance with the provisions of contracts and otherwise with the terms of this order and of the rules, regulations, and orders of the Secretary of Labor issued pursuant to this order. They are directed to cooperate with the Secretary of Labor and to furnish the Secretary of Labor such information and assistance as he may require in the performance of his functions under this order. They are further directed to appoint or designate, from among the agency's personnel, compliance officers. It shall be the duty of such officers to seek compliance with the objectives of this order by conference, conciliation, mediation, or persuasion.

SEC. 206. (a) The Secretary of Labor may investigate the employment practices of any Government contractor or subcontractor, or initiate such investigation by the appropriate contracting agency, to determine whether or not the contractual provisions specified in section 202 of this order have been violated. Such investigation shall be conducted in accordance with the procedures established by the Secretary of Labor and the investigating agency shall report to the Secretary of Labor any action taken or recommended.

(b) The Secretary of Labor may receive and investigate or cause to be investigated complaints by employees or prospective employees of a Government contractor or subcontractor which allege discrimination contrary to the contractual provisions specified in section 202 of this order. If this investigation is conducted for the Secretary of Labor by a contracting agency, that agency shall report to the Secretary what action has been taken or is recommended with regard to such complaints.

SEC. 207. The Secretary of Labor shall use his best efforts, directly and through contracting agencies, other interested Federal, State, and local agencies, contractors, and all other available instrumentalities to cause any

---

[4] Ibid.

labor union engaged in work under Government contracts or any agency referring workers or providing or supervising apprenticeship or training for or in the course of such work to cooperate in the implementation of the purposes of this order. The Secretary of Labor shall, in appropriate cases, notify the Equal Employment Opportunity Commission, the Department of Justice, or other appropriate Federal agencies whenever it has reason to believe that the practices of any such labor organization or agency violate Titles VI or VII of the Civil Rights Act of 1964 or other provision of Federal law.

SEC. 208. (a) The Secretary of Labor, or any agency, officer, or employee in the executive branch of the Government designated by rule, regulation, or order of the Secretary, may hold such hearings, public or private, as the Secretary may deem advisable for compliance, enforcement, or educational purposes.

(b) The Secretary of Labor may hold, or cause to be held, hearings in accordance with subsection (a) of this section prior to imposing, ordering, or recommending the imposition of penalties and sanctions under this order. No order for debarment of any contractor from further Government contracts under section 209(a)(6) shall be made without affording the contractor an opportunity for a hearing.

Subpart D—Sanctions and Penalties

SEC. 209. (a) In accordance with such rules, regulations, or orders as the Secretary of Labor may issue or adopt, the Secretary or the appropriate contracting agency may:

(1) Publish, or cause to be published, the names of contractors or unions which it has concluded have complied or have failed to comply with the provisions of this order or of the rules, regulations, and orders of the Secretary of Labor.

(2) Recommend to the Department of Justice that, in cases in which there is substantial or material violation or the threat of substantial or material violation of the contractual provisions set forth in section 202 of this order, appropriate proceedings be brought to enforce those provisions, including the enjoining, within the limitations of applicable law, of organizations, individuals, or groups who prevent directly or indirectly, or seek to prevent directly or indirectly, compliance with the provisions of this order.

(3) Recommend to the Equal Employment Opportunity Commission or the Department of Justice that appropriate proceedings be instituted under Title VII of the Civil Rights Act of 1964.

(4) Recommend to the Department of Justice that criminal proceedings be brought for the furnishing of false information to any contracting agency or to the Secretary of Labor as the case may be.

(5) Cancel, terminate, suspend, or cause to be cancelled, terminated, or suspended any contract, or any portion or portions thereof, for failure of the contractor or subcontractor to comply with the nondiscrimination provisions of the contract. Contracts may be cancelled, terminated, or suspended absolutely or continuance of contracts may be conditioned upon a program for future compliance approved by the contracting agency.

(6) Provide that any contracting agency shall refrain from entering into further contracts, or extensions or other modifications of existing contracts, with any noncomplying contractor, until such contractor has satisfied the Secretary of Labor that such contractor has established and will carry out personnel and employment policies in compliance with the provisions of this order.

(b) Under rules and regulations prescribed by the Secretary of Labor, each contracting agency shall make reasonable efforts within a reasonable time limitation to secure compliance with the contract provisions of this order by methods of conference, conciliation, mediation, and persuasion before proceedings shall be instituted under subsection (a)(2) of this section, or before a contract shall be cancelled or terminated in whole or part under subsection (a)(5) of this section for failure of a contractor or subcontractor to comply with the contract provisions of this order.

SEC. 210. Any contracting agency taking any action authorized by this subpart, whether on its own motion, or as directed by the Secretary of Labor, or under the rules and regulations of the Secretary, shall promptly notify the Secretary of such action. Whenever the Secretary of Labor makes a determination under this section, he shall promptly notify the appropriate contracting agency of the action recommended. The agency shall take such action and shall report the results thereof to the Secretary of Labor within such time as the Secretary shall specify.

SEC. 211. If the Secretary shall so direct, contracting agencies shall not enter into contracts with any bidder or prospective contractor unless the bidder or prospective contractor has satisfactorily complied with the provisions of this order or submits a program for compliance acceptable to the Secretary of Labor or, if the Secretary so authorizes, to the contracting agency.

SEC. 212. Whenever a contracting agency cancels or terminates a contract, or whenever a contractor has been debarred from further Government contracts, under section 209(a)(6) because of noncompliance with the contract provisions with regard to nondiscrimination, the Secretary of Labor, or the contracting agency involved, shall promptly notify the Comptroller General of the United States. Any such debarment may be rescinded by the Secretary of Labor or by the contracting agency which imposed the sanction.

Subpart E—Certificates of Merit

SEC. 213. The Secretary of Labor may provide for issuance of a U.S. Government certificate of merit to employers or labor unions, or other agencies which are or may hereafter be engaged in work under Government contracts, if the Secretary is satisfied that the personnel and employment practices of the employer, or that the personnel, training, apprenticeship, membership, grievance and representation, upgrading, and other practices and policies of the labor union or other agency conform to the purposes and provisions of this order.

SEC. 214. Any certificate of merit may at any time be suspended or revoked by the Secretary of Labor if the holder thereof, in the judgment of the Secretary, has failed to comply with the provisions of this order.

SEC. 215. The Secretary of Labor may provide for the exemption of any employer, labor union, or other agency from any reporting requirements imposed under or pursuant to this order if such employer, labor union, or other agency has been awarded a certificate of merit which has not been suspended or revoked.

PART III—NONDISCRIMINATION PROVISIONS IN FEDERALLY ASSISTED CONSTRUCTION CONTRACTS

SEC. 301. Each executive department and agency which administers a program involving Federal financial assistance shall require as a condition for the approval of any grant, contract, loan, insurance, or guarantee thereunder, which may involve a construction contract, that the applicant for Federal assistance undertake and agree to incorporate, or cause to be incorporated, into all construction contracts paid for in whole or in part with funds obtained from the Federal Government or borrowed on the credit of the Federal Government pursuant to such grant, contract, loan, insurance, or guarantee, or undertaken pursuant to any Federal program involving such grant, contract, loan, insurance, or guarantee, the provisions prescribed for Government contracts by section 202 of this order or such modification thereof, preserving in substance the contractor's obligations thereunder, as may be approved by the Secretary of Labor, together with such additional provisions as the Secretary deems appropriate to establish and protect the interest of the United States in the enforcement of those obligations. Each such applicant shall also undertake and agree: (1) to assist and cooperate actively with the administering department or agency and the Secretary of Labor in obtaining the compliance of contractors and subcontractors with those contract provisions and with the rules, regulations, and relevant orders of the Secretary; (2) to obtain and to furnish to the administering department or agency and to the Secretary of Labor such information as they may require for the supervision of such compliance; (3) to carry out sanctions and penalties for violation of such obligations imposed upon contractors and subcontractors by the Secretary of Labor or the administering department or agency pursuant to part II, subpart D, of this order; and (4) to refrain from entering into any contract subject to this order, or extension or other modification of such a contract with a contractor debarred from Government contracts under part II, subpart D, of this order.

SEC. 302. (a) "Construction contract" as used in this order means any contract for the construction, rehabilitation, alteration, conversion, extension, or repair of buildings, highways, or other improvements to real property.

(b) The provisions of part II of this order shall apply to such construction contracts, and for purposes of such application, the administering department or agency shall be considered the contracting agency referred to therein.

(c) The term "applicant" as used in this order means an applicant for Federal assistance or, as determined by agency regulation, other program participant, with respect to whom an application for any grant, contract, loan, insurance, or guarantee is not finally acted upon prior to the effective date of this part, and it includes such an applicant after he becomes a recipient of such Federal assistance.

SEC. 303 (a) Each administering department and agency shall be responsible for obtaining the compliance of such applicants with their undertakings under this order. Each administering department and agency is directed to cooperate with the Secretary of Labor, and to furnish the Secretary such information and assistance as he may require in the performance of his functions under this order.

(b) In the event an applicant fails and refuses to comply with his undertakings, the administering department or agency may take any or all of the following actions: (1) cancel, terminate, or suspend in whole or in part the agreement, contract, or other arrangement with such applicant with respect to which the failure and refusal occurred; (2) refrain from extending any further assistance to the applicant under the program with respect to which the failure or refusal occurred until satisfactory assurance of future compliance has been received from such applicant; and (3) refer the case to the Department of Justice for appropriate legal proceedings.

(c) Any action with respect to an applicant pursuant to subsection (b) shall be taken in conformity with section 602 of the Civil Rights Act of 1964 (and the regulations of the administering department or agency issued thereunder), to the extent applicable. In no case shall action be taken with respect to an applicant pursuant to clause (1) or (2) of subsection (b) without notice and opportunity for hearing before the administering department or agency.

SEC. 304. Any executive department or agency which imposes by rule, regulation, or order requirements of nondiscrimination in employment, other than requirements imposed pursuant to this order, may delegate to the Secretary of Labor by agreement such responsibilities with respect to compliance standards, reports, and procedures as would tend to bring the administration of such requirements into conformity with the administration of requirements imposed under this order: *Provided*, That actions to effect compliance by recipients of Federal financial assistance with requirements imposed pursuant to Title VI of the Civil Rights Act of 1964 shall be taken in conformity with the procedures and limitations prescribed in section 602 thereof and the regulations of the administering department or agency issued thereunder.

PART IV — MISCELLANEOUS

SEC. 401. The Secretary of Labor may delegate to any officer, agency, or employee in the executive branch of the Government, any function or duty of the Secretary under parts II and III of this order, except authority to promulgate rules and regulations of a general nature.

SEC. 402. The Secretary of Labor shall provide administrative support for the execution of the program known as the "Plans of Progress."

SEC. 403. (a) Executive Orders Nos. 10590 (Jan. 18, 1955), 10722 (Aug. 5, 1957), 10925 (Mar. 6, 1961), 11114 (June 22, 1963), and 11162 (July 28, 1964), are hereby superseded and the President's Committee on Equal Employment Opportunity established by Executive Order No. 10925 is hereby abolished. All records and property in the custody of the committee shall be transferred to the Civil Service Commission and the Secretary of Labor, as appropriate.

(b) Nothing in this order shall be deemed to relieve any person of any obligation assumed or imposed under or pursuant to any executive order superseded by this order. All rules, regulations, orders, instructions, designations, and other directives issued by the President's Committee on Equal Employment Opportunity and those issued by the heads of various departments or agencies under or pursuant to any of the executive orders superseded by this order, shall, to the extent that they are not inconsistent with this order, remain in full force and effect unless and until revoked or superseded by appropriate authority. References in such directives to provisions of the superseded orders shall be deemed to be references to the comparable provisions of this order.

SEC. 404. The General Services Administration shall take appropriate action to revise the standard Government contract forms to accord with the provisions of this order and of the rules and regulations of the Secretary of Labor.

SEC. 405. This order shall become effective 30 days after the date of this order.

LYNDON B. JOHNSON

THE WHITE HOUSE
September 24, 1965

Index

Willingham v. Macon Telegraph Publishing Company, 193-200
Zichy et al. v. City of Philadelphia, 266-275, 292-293
Causey v. Ford Motor Company, 167
Certification, 374
Child care, 360-361, 364
Children's Hospital of Pittsburgh, 289-291, 294
Citizens' Advisory Council on the Status of Women, 66, 354
Civil Rights Act of 1964
    Title VI, 110
    See also Title VII
Civil Rights Commission, 97
Civil Service Commission, U.S., 12, 97
Classified ads. *See* Advertisements
Clerical occupations
    distribution of women, 312, 313, 315, 321, 323-324
    education and, 357, 383, 386, 420
    employment projections, 415-416
    job search and, 383
Cleveland Board of Education. *See* LaFleur v. Cleveland Board of Education
Cohen v. Chesterfield County School Board, 72
Colgate-Palmolive Company, 216, 218
Commission rates, 94
Communications Workers of America, 36, 372
Communications Workers of America v. American Telephone and Telegraph Co., Long Lines Department, 74
Compensation. *See* Benefit plans; Wages
Congress, U.S.
    maternity discrimination amendment, 33-35
Connor, James C., 203-208, 212-214
Constitution, U.S.
    Equal Rights Amendment, 354
Corne v. Bausch and Lomb, Inc., 153, 156
Corning Glass, 371
Corning Glass Works v. Brennan, 6
Craft and kindred occupations
    distribution of women, 313, 315, 320
    education and, 421
    employment projections, 417
    sex stereotyping, 355
Cramer v. Virginia Commonwealth University, 61
Credit, 357
Current Population Survey, 326, 328, 329

D

Davies Medical Center. *See* Voyles v. Davies Medical Center
Death benefits, 91
Degrees
    associate, 395-396

bachelor's, 396-397, 418
doctoral, 397, 399, 418
fields of study, 395
master's, 397, 398, 418
professional, 397-399, 400, 418
See also Education
Demographic changes
    family size, 348
    life expectancy, 349
Demotions, 133
Diaz v. Pan American World Airways, 198, 229
Dictionary of Occupational Titles, 364-365
Disability insurance, 258, 260-261
    maternity benefits, 31, 37-45, 65, 67-75, 92, 242-265, 269-274, 372
Dismissals
    guidelines, 106-107, 133, 134
    homosexuals, 76-77
    maternity and, 31, 36, 65, 67, 69, 71, 107, 158-164
    sexual harassment, 141-157
    transsexuals, 169-170
    See also Layoffs
Dodge v. Giant Food, Inc., 146, 199
Dress codes. *See* Grooming codes
Dual careers, 359, 360-362
Duke Power Company. *See* Griggs v. Duke Power Co.
DuShane Emergency Fund, 72

E

Earnings
    education and, 342, 378, 386, 388, 389
    labor force participation and, 342-343
    male-female differential, 346, 347-348
    median income, 357, 358
    See also Minimum wage laws; Wages
Education
    age and, 380, 399-401
    apprenticeship, 60, 356, 364
    college, 395-401, 418-421
    continuing, 358, 399-401
    earnings and, 342, 378, 386, 388, 389
    hours and, 387-388
    increase, 378-379, 380
    job supply and, 418-421
    labor force participation and, 342, 343, 350, 351-352, 355, 357, 382-383
    level of, 378, 380, 404, 407-409
    licensing requirements, 374
    male-female differential, 382, 391-392, 393
    occupational distribution and, 383-386
    promotion requirement, 375
    race and, 343, 352, 358, 380-382, 387, 390, 393, 400
    school enrollment, 388-394, 398-399, 400-401

training programs, 103-104, 129, 131, 132, 355-356
  two-year programs, 421
  unemployment and, 386-387
  vocational, 401, 421
Educational Testing Service (ETS), 374
Education Amendments of 1972, 68-69
EEOC v. Children's Hospital of Pittsburgh, 289-296
EEOC v. Local 638, 60, 62
Employee Retirement Income Security Act of 1974 (P.L. 93-406), 12-15
Employment agencies, 7, 11, 83, 136, 369
  governmental, 363-370
Employment and Training Administration. *See* Manpower Administration
Employment applications. *See* Recruiting
Equal Employment Advisory Council (EEAC)
  reverse discrimination brief, 51-63
Equal Employment Opportunity Act of 1972, 80, 110, 353
Equal Employment Opportunity Commission (EEOC)
  benefit plan guidelines, 232, 240
  charge filing, 220-223
  employee selection guidelines, 7, 97, 98
  enforcement, 7, 24, 25, 74, 75, 83, 91, 111, 112, 352, 370-373
  grooming code position, 89, 193, 197
  hours guidelines, 8
  layoff requirements, 104, 105-106
  litigation powers, 289-296, 353, 371, 372
  maternity benefits brief, 73
  maternity guidelines, 8, 31, 67, 74, 88, 92, 247-248, 263-264, 266, 271-272, 273-274, 278, 287, 300-301
  promotion requirements, 100, 101
  protective laws, 7-8, 31, 32, 33
  sex discrimination guidelines, 7-8, 24, 31, 218-219, 253-254, 352-353
  structure, 6
  supervisory performance rating guidelines, 99
  testing regulations, 96, 97, 374-375
  weight-lifting guidelines, 7-8, 29, 372
  See also Affirmative action programs
Equal Employment Opportunity Coordinating Council (EEOCC)
  employee selection guidelines, 97, 98
Equal employment opportunity laws
  history, 26
  legal issues, 27-28
  See also Equal Employment Opportunity Act of 1972
Equal Employment Opportunity Statements, 114-117, 136
Equal Pay Act of 1963, 4-5, 22, 110, 131
  coverage, 5, 93
  differentials allowed, 5, 93, 95, 224, 229-232, 236, 248
  enforcement, 5-6, 83, 352, 371

  equal work standards, 95-96
  extra task rulings, 5-6
  substantially equal test, 6
  working conditions rule, 6
Equal pay laws, 16, 21-23
Equal Rights Amendment (ERA), 354
Espinoza v. Farah Manufacturing Co., 287
Executive Order 11246, 8-9, 54-55, 85-86, 110, 137
  advertising guidelines, 82-83
  benefit plan guidelines, 91-92
  coverage, 9, 55
  enforcement, 9, 55-56, 111, 353
  maternity guidelines, 9, 68
  text as amended, 515-521
  See also Affirmative action programs; Office of Federal Contract Compliance Programs
Executive Order 11375. *See* Executive Order 11246
Executive Order 11478, 353

F

Facilities. *See* Separate facilities
Fagan v. National Cash Register Co., 199, 200
Fair employment practices laws (FEP)
  administration of, 23
  age discrimination, 25-26
  enforcement, 7, 24, 25, 26
  maternity, 69-71
  pay discrimination, 22
  sex discrimination, 24-25
Fair Labor Standards Act (FLSA)
  coverage, 3-4, 20
  enforcement, 4
  exemptions, 4
  minimum wage, 2-4, 16
  1974 amendments, 3-4, 20, 26
  overtime pay, 2, 3-4, 21, 94
  text as amended, 459-515
  See also Equal Pay Act of 1963
Farkas v. South Western City School District, 74, 287
Farm workers
  distribution of women, 312, 313, 315, 325
  employment projections, 411, 417-418
  minimum wage, 16, 20-21
  overtime pay, 21
Federal contracts
  advertising guidelines, 82-83
  affirmative action requirements, 53-63, 111, 124, 135, 137-138, 353
  construction, 9, 10, 36
  handicapped hiring requirements, 11-12
  job listing requirements, 369
  liabilities, 10, 12, 353
  sex discrimination requirements, 8-10
  subcontractors, 55, 137-138
  See also Affirmative action programs; Executive Order 11246
Federal wage and hour law. *See* Fair Labor

power Administration; Office of Federal Contract Compliance Programs; Wage and Hour Division

Laborers. *See* Farm workers; Nonfarm laborers

Labor force
age composition, 404, 405, 407-409
demand, 409-436
educational level, 404, 407, 418-421
growth, 326-327
intermittent participation, 358-360
mobility, 359, 360
projections, 328-329, 335-336, 355, 379, 404-436
reentry, 358-360
replacement needs, 411-412
supply, 404-407
See also Occupational distribution; Participation rates

Labor-Management Services Administration, 15

Labor organizations
antidiscrimination compliance, 5, 7, 11, 60, 133
dress codes and, 190-192
layoff agreements, 104-105
maternity benefits, 35-41, 372
parental leave, 359
pension plans, 12, 225
training programs, 60, 104
weight-lifting requirements, 216-218, 220, 221

LaFleur v. Cleveland Board of Education, 72, 162, 302-303

Lau v. Nichols, 255

Layoffs, 104-106, 131, 132, 216

Leave. *See* Maternity; Parental leave; Sick leave; Vacation leave

Liberty Mutual Insurance Co. *See* Wetzel v. Liberty Mutual Insurance Co.

Licensing, 373-375

Lie detector tests, 86

M

Macon Telegraph Publishing Company, 193

Managers and administrators
distribution of women, 313, 321, 322-323
education and, 383
employment projections, 414-415
job search and, 368

Manhart v. City of Los Angeles, 224-241

Manpower Administration, 355-356, 364, 374

Marital status
head of household, 343, 356-358
labor force and, 340-342, 343, 349
maternity and, 158-164

Maryland v. Wirtz, 281-282

Maternity
disability benefits, 31, 37-45, 48, 65, 67-69, 71-75, 92, 242-265, 269-274, 372
discrimination amendment, 29, 31, 33-48
employment restriction, 64-65, 67-70, 72, 73, 92, 93, 107, 297-305
federal guidelines, 8, 9, 31, 66-69, 74, 92-93
leave, 65, 67, 68-72, 74, 92-93, 268-269, 276, 278-279, 282, 283, 285-288, 289, 290, 306-310, 358-359, 372
marital status, 158-164
preemployment inquiry, 71, 84
reinstatement, 31, 65, 67, 69, 70, 71, 72, 93, 107, 279, 283-288, 289, 290-291, 293-294, 359
sick leave, 37, 266-276, 279, 282, 284, 285, 289-296, 306-310
state regulations, 29, 31, 64-66, 69-72, 302-310
teacher contract renewal, 297-305
unemployment compensation, 66, 359-360

Maximum hours laws, 28, 30

McDonnell Douglas Corp. v. Green, 208-209

Meal periods, 31-32

Merit systems, 5, 7, 93

Miller v. Bank of America, 153, 155-157

Minimum wage laws
coverage, 16-17, 18, 20-21, 27
federal, 2-4, 16, 19, 93, 95
history, 17-19
rates, 16
statutory rate, 16, 19-20
types, 16, 19-20
wage boards, 16, 17, 19, 20
See also Fair Labor Standards Act; Overtime pay laws

Minorities
age factors, 343, 345, 349, 350
discrimination, 373, 375
earnings, 357
education, 343, 352, 358, 380-382, 387, 390, 393, 400
head of household, 343, 357-358
job satisfaction, 350
job search methods, 367-368
marital status factors, 343
participation rates, 343-344, 349
placement programs, 355, 367
test discrimination, 178, 182-183
unemployment, 345, 358, 387

Minority Women Employment Program, 355

Mitchell v. Board of Trustees, 297-305

N

NAACP v. Allen, 59

Nangle, John F., 184

Nashville Gas Co. *See* Satty v. Nashville Gas Co.

National Association of Manufacturers (NAM)
  maternity discrimination testimony, 43-48
National Education Association, 72
National Labor Relations Act, 110, 133, 173
National War Labor Board, 22
Newspapers. *See* Advertisements
Nightwork limitations, 28
Nonfarm laborers
  distribution of women, 313, 315, 325
  education and, 388, 421
  employment projections, 417
  hours, 388
Nonsupervisory employees, 17

O

Oatis v. Crown Zellerbach Corp., 222
Occupational distribution
  changes, 319-321
  concentration, 316, 319
  education and, 383-386
  fields of interest, 421-436
  groups, 312-313, 314, 321-325, 344, 412-418
  industry, 409-411
  male-female differential, 313, 314
  proportional, 313, 314-316, 317-319
  type of work, 312, 411
Occupational limitations, 29
Occupational Outlook Handbook, 421-422
Office of Employee Benefits Security, 15
Office of Federal Contract Compliance Programs (OFCCP), 9-10, 55, 135
  enforcement, 9, 111, 112, 135, 353
  sex discrimination guidelines, 9, 67, 99, 353
  utilization analysis requirement, 118-119, 124
  See also Affirmative action programs
Operatives
  distribution of women, 313, 315, 325
  education and, 357, 383, 386, 421
  employment projections, 417
Ostapowicz v. Johnson Bronze Co., 58-59
Overtime pay laws, 8, 21, 22, 27
  See also Fair Labor Standards Act
Ozark Airlines. *See* Boyd v. Ozark Airlines

P

Parental leave, 359
Parham v. Southwestern Bell Telephone Company, 211
Participation rates, 327-329
  age factor, 338-340, 343, 349-350, 405
  calculation of, 331-335
  children and, 340-341, 342, 343, 348, 356
  education and, 342, 343, 351-352, 382-383
  flow approach, 330-331
  husband's earnings and, 343-343

implications, 335-336
  marital status factor, 340, 343, 349, 358-360
  racial factors, 343-344
  separation rate, 331, 335
  stock approach, 329-330
Part-time work. *See* Hours
Patterson v. American Tobacco Co., 59
Peck, John W., 178
Pension Benefit Guaranty Corporation, 14, 15
Pension plans
  contributions to, 224-241
  federal regulations, 9, 12-15, 91
Pension Reform Act. *See* Employee Retirement Income Security Act of 1974
Phillips v. Martin Marietta Corp., 145, 197, 198
Pittsburgh Press Co. v. Pittsburgh Commission on Human Relations, 25, 368
Pond v. Braniff Airways, Incorporated, 210
Popson, S. J., 159-160
Potlatch Forests, Inc. v. Hayes et al., 8
Poverty, 357
Powell, Sharon M. (Michael D.), 176
Powell v. Read's Inc., 176-177
Pregnancy. *See* Maternity
Premium pay laws. *See* Overtime pay laws
Private household workers
  distribution of women, 312, 313, 315, 324
  education and, 357, 384, 388
  employment projections, 411, 416
  hours, 388
  minimum wage, 3, 16, 20
Production measure system, 5, 93
Professional and technical occupations
  distribution of women, 312-313, 315, 320, 321-322
  education and, 383, 384, 420, 421
  employment projections, 413-414
  job search, 368
  sex discrimination charges, 371
  sex stereotyping, 355
Profit-sharing plans, 91
Promotions
  affirmative action compliance, 129, 130
  automatic, 100-101
  company discretion, 101
  employee request, 101-102
  job posting, 99-100, 101
  lie detector tests, 86
  qualifications, 375
  seniority, 102
  testing, 99
Protective laws. *See* Women's labor laws
Public Service Electric and Gas Co. *See* Tomkins v. Public Service Electric and Gas Co.
Purdue Mechanical Ability Test, 98

Q

Quotas. *See* Reverse discrimination

92, 235-236, 238-241, 242-265, 280-281
equal pay ruling, 5, 6
good faith defense, 234
job requirements ruling, 179-181, 281-282
maternity leave ruling, 302, 372
minimum wage ruling, 17
money judgement ruling, 167
promotion qualifications ruling, 375
race discrimination ruling, 8, 371
reverse discrimination case, 50-51
sex plus ruling, 196-197
Sweets, Martin, 161
Sylvania Education Association v. Sylvania Board of Education, 306-310

T

Taft Broadcasting Co. *See* Barker v. Taft Broadcasting Co.
Termination. *See* Dismissals
Testing, 96-97
    employee selection, 96-99, 178, 182-183
    licensing, 374-375
    performance appraisal, 99
    promotion, 375
    validation, 97-99, 182
T.I.M.E.D.C. v. U.S., 57
Tipler v. E. I. duPont deNemours and Co., 164
Tips, 3
Title VII, 24
    affirmative action requirements, 10, 56, 57, 58, 60-61, 92, 110, 111
    disability benefits, 242-265, 276-288
    bona fide occupational qualifications, 7, 352
    coverage, 6, 370
    employment testing, 178, 182-183
    enforcement, 6, 7-8, 111-112, 352-353, 370
    failure to hire, 201-215
    fringe benefits, 15
    grooming codes, 89, 190-200
    historical trends, 26
    homosexual rights, 76-77
    impact of, 27-33
    layoffs, 105
    marital status, 158-164
    maternity discrimination amendment, 33-48
    maternity leave, 297-305
    name change, 165-168
    pension plans, 224-241
    physical job requirements, 178-189
    recruiting compliance, 80, 81, 83, 85, 88, 89, 91, 96, 99, 136
    seniority systems, 102, 105, 216, 218, 219
    sexual harassment, 75-76, 141-157
    sick leave, 266-275, 276, 279, 282, 284, 285, 289-296
    text of, 438-458

training programs, 103
transsexual rights, 169-177
weight-lifting requirements, 216, 218-220
See also Affirmative action programs; Equal Employment Opportunity Commission
Tomkins, Adrienne, 150
Tomkins v. Public Service Electric and Gas Co., 150-154
Training programs, 103-104, 129, 131, 132, 355-356
Transfers, 102-103, 129, 130
Transsexuals, 169-177
Treasury, U.S. Department of. *See* Internal Revenue Service

U

Unemployment, 345, 347
    age and, 387
    education and, 378, 386-387
    head of household, 356-357, 358
    race and, 345, 358
Unemployment compensation, 66, 359-360
Unions. *See* Labor organizations
United States v. Lathers, Local 46, 111
United States v. N.L. Industries, Inc., 187
United Steelworkers Union, 60
University of California, 50-51
U.S. Employment Service (USES)
    professional listings, 369-370
    use, 365-368
    women's services, 363-365, 370

V

Vacation leave, 92, 94
    maternity and, 93, 285, 289, 290
Vietnam Era Veterans Readjustment Assistance Act of 1974, 110-111
Voyles v. Davies Medical Center, 169-170, 176-177

W

Wage and Hour Division, 45, 232, 236, 240, 249, 352
Wage boards, 16, 17, 20
Wages
    affirmative action compliance, 131
    back, 4, 5, 6, 62-63, 112, 131, 159, 201, 214-215, 216, 284, 304, 353
    differentials allowed, 5, 7
    equal pay compliance, 5, 6, 95-96
    overtime, 2-4, 8, 21, 22, 27, 94
    transfer and, 103
    See also Minimum wage laws; Overtime pay laws
Want ads. *See* Advertisements
Washington Opportunities for Women (WOW), 364
Weber v. Kaiser Aluminum and Chemical